Lecture Notes in Computer Scien

T0238513

Commenced Publication in 1973
Founding and Former Series Editors:
Gerhard Goos, Juris Hartmanis, and Jan van Leeuwen

Viktória Zsók   Zoltán Horváth
Rinus Plasmeijer (Eds.)

Central European Functional Programming School

4th Summer School, CEFP 2011
Budapest, Hungary, June 14-24, 2011
Revised Selected Papers

 Springer

Volume Editors

Viktória Zsók
Eötvös Loránd University, Faculty of Informatics
Department of Programming Languages and Compilers
Pázmány Péter Sétány 1/C, 1117 Budapest, Hungary
E-mail: zsv@inf.elte.hu

Zoltán Horváth
Eötvös Loránd University, Faculty of Informatics
Department of Programming Languages and Compilers
Pázmány Péter Sétány 1/C, 1117 Budapest, Hungary
E-mail: hz@inf.elte.hu

Rinus Plasmeijer
Radboud University, Computer and Information Sciences Institute
Heyendaalseweg 135, 6525 AJ Nijmegen, The Netherlands
E-mail: rinus@cs.ru.nl

ISSN 0302-9743
ISBN 978-3-642-32095-8
DOI 10.1007/978-3-642-32096-5

e-ISSN 1611-3349
e-ISBN 978-3-642-32096-5

Springer Heidelberg Dordrecht London New York

Library of Congress Control Number: 2012942467

CR Subject Classification (1998): D.1.1, D.1.3, D.2, D.3.2

LNCS Sublibrary: SL 1 – Theoretical Computer Science and General Issues

Typesetting: Camera-ready by author, data conversion by Scientific Publishing Services, Chennai, India

Printed on acid-free paper

Springer is part of Springer Science+Business Media (www.springer.com)

Preface

This volume presents the revised lecture notes of selected talks given at the fourth Central European Functional Programming School, CEFP 2011, held during June 14–24, in Budapest (Hungary) at Eötvös Loránd University, Faculty of Informatics.

The summer school was organized in the spirit of the advanced programming schools. CEFP involves an ever-growing number of students, researchers, and teachers from across Europe, providing opportunities especially for students from Central, and Eastern European countries.

The intensive program offered a creative, inspiring environment for presentations and exchange of ideas on new specific programming topics. The lectures covered a wide range of distributed and multicore functional programming subjects.

We are very grateful to the lecturers and researchers for the time and effort they devoted to their talks and lecture notes. The lecture notes were each carefully checked by reviewers selected from experts on functional programming. The papers were revised by the lecturers based on the reviews. This revision process guaranteed that only high-quality papers were accepted for the volume.

The last two papers in the volume are selected papers of the PhD Workshop organized for the participants of the summer school.

We would like to express our gratitude for the work of all the members of the Program Committee and the Organizing Committee.

The website for the summer school can be found at: http://plc.inf.elte.hu/cefp/.

March 2012   Viktória Zsók
                                                                Zoltán Horváth
                                                                Rinus Plasmeijer

Organization

CEFP 2011 was organized by Eötvös Loránd University, Budapest, Hungary, and Pannonia Tourist Service, Budapest, Hungary.

Sponsoring Institutions

The summer school was supported by the:

- Erasmus Intensive Programme (IP) Project No. ERA-IP2010/11 10/0242-E/4006
- CEEPUS program via the CEEPUS CII-HU-19 Network
- Ericsson Hungary
- Morgan Stanley Hungary

The scientific editorial process of the summer school proceedings was supported by the European Union and co-financed by the European Social Fund (Grant Agreement no. TAMOP 4.2.1/B-09/1/KMR-2010-0003).

Table of Contents

A Programming Tutor for Haskell

Johan Jeuring[1,2], Alex Gerdes[1], and Bastiaan Heeren[1]

[1] School of Computer Science, Open Universiteit Nederland,
P.O. Box 2960, 6401 DL Heerlen, The Netherlands
{jje,age,bhr}@ou.nl
[2] Department of Information and Computing Sciences, Universiteit Utrecht

Abstract. In these lectures we will introduce an interactive system that supports writing simple functional programs. Using this system, students learning functional programming:

- develop their programs incrementally,
- receive feedback about whether or not they are on the right track,
- can ask for a hint when they are stuck,
- see how a complete program is stepwise constructed,
- get suggestions about how to refactor their program.

The system itself is implemented as a functional program, and uses fundamental concepts such as rewriting, parsing, strategies, program transformations and higher-order combinators such as the fold. We will introduce these concepts, and show how they are used in the implementation of the interactive functional programming tutor.

1 Introduction

How do you write a functional program? How can I learn it? Our answer to these questions depends on who is asking. If it is a first-year bachelor computer science student who just finished an introductory object-oriented programming course, we would start with explaining the basic ideas of functional programming, and set many small functional programming exercises for the student to solve. If it is a starting computer science Ph.D. student with a basic knowledge of functional programming, we would take a serious piece of software developed in a functional programming language, analyse it, discuss the advanced concepts used in the implementation, and set a task in which the software is extended or changed. These answers are based on our (and others) experience as teachers: there is no final answer (yet) to the question how programming is learned best, and what makes programming hard [Fincher and Petre, 2004]. We borrow from research that studies how complex cognitive skills are learned, in which the importance of providing worked-out examples [Merriënboer and Paas, 1990], giving hints, and giving immediate feedback on actions of students [Hattie and Timperley, 2007] is emphasised.

These lecture notes address the question 'How do you write a functional program' with the audience of advanced graduate students or starting Ph.D. students in mind. The serious piece of software addresses the same question: 'How

V. Zsók, Z. Horváth, and R. Plasmeijer (Eds.): CEFP 2011, LNCS 7241, pp. 1–45, 2012.
© Springer-Verlag Berlin Heidelberg 2012

do you write a functional program?', but now with a first-year bachelor student computer science in mind. We will introduce an intelligent functional programming tutoring system for Haskell [Peyton Jones et al., 2003], using which a student can:

- develop a program incrementally,
- receive feedback about whether or not she is on the right track,
- ask for a hint when she is stuck,
- can see how a complete program is stepwise constructed,
- get suggestions about how to refactor her program.

As far as we are aware, this is the first intelligent tutoring system for Haskell.

The implementation of the intelligent functional programming tutor uses many advanced functional programming concepts. To support incremental development of programs and refactoring, the tutor uses rewrite and refinement rules. To give feedback about whether or not a student is on the right track the tutor uses strategies to describe the various solutions, and parsing to follow the student's behaviour. To give hints to a student that is stuck, the system uses several analysis functions on strategies, viewing a strategy as a context-free grammar. These notes will introduce all of these concepts.

These notes are organised as follows. Section 2 introduces our intelligent functional programming tutor by means of some example interactions. Section 3 gives the architecture of the software for the tutor. Section 4 discusses rewrite and refinement rules and shows how they are used in the tutor. Section 5 introduces strategies for solving functional programming problems. Section 6 introduces our strategy language. Section 7 shows how we use techniques from parsing to follow student behaviour, and to give hints to a student that is stuck. Section 8 discusses related and future work, and concludes.

2   A Programming Tutor for Haskell

This section introduces our intelligent functional programming tutoring system by means of some interactions of a hypothetical student with the tutor. The functional programming tutor is an example of an intelligent tutoring system for the domain of functional programming. An intelligent tutoring system is an environment that sets tasks for a student, and offers support to the student when solving these tasks, by means of hints, corrections, and worked-out solutions [VanLehn, 2006]. So the intelligent functional programming tutor sets small functional programming tasks, and gives feedback in interactions with the student.

2.1   Reverse

Elisa just started a course on functional programming, and has attended lectures on how to write simple functional programs on lists. Her teacher has set a couple

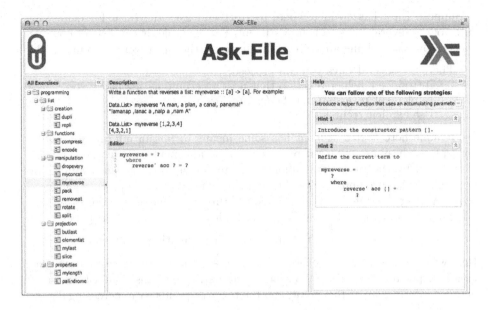

Fig. 1. The web-based functional programming tutor

of exercises from H-99: Ninety-nine Haskell Problems[1], in particular problem 5: reverse a list.

We now show a couple of possible scenarios in which Elisa interacts with the tutor to solve this problem. A screenshot of the tutor is shown in Figure 1. At the start of a tutoring session the tutor gives a problem description: Write a function that reverses a list. For example:

> *Data.List*⟩ *reverse* "A man, a plan, a canal, panama!"
> "!amanap ,lanac a ,nalp a ,nam A"
> *Data.List*⟩ *reverse* [1, 2, 3, 4]
> [4, 3, 2, 1]

and displays the name of the function to be defined:

> *reverse* = ⊥

The task of a student is to refine the incomplete parts, denoted by ⊥, of the program. The symbol ⊥ is used as a placeholder for a hole in a program that needs to be refined to a complete program. A student can use such holes to defer the refinement of parts of the program. After each refinement, a student can ask the tutor whether or not the refinement is bringing him or her closer to a correct solution, or, if the student doesn't know how to proceed, ask the tutor for a hint. Besides holes, a student can also introduce new declarations, function bindings, alternatives, and refine patterns.

---

[1] http://www.haskell.org/haskellwiki/99_Haskell_exercises

Suppose Elisa has no idea where to start and asks the tutor for help. The tutor offers several ways to help a student. For example, it can list all possible ways to proceed solving an exercise. In this case, the tutor would respond with:

> There are several ways you can proceed:
> − Introduce a helper function that uses an accumulating parameter.
> − Implement reverse using the *foldl* function.
> − Use explicit recursion.

We assume here that a student has some means to obtain information about concepts such as accumulated parameters that are mentioned in the feedback texts given by the tutor. This information might be obtained via lectures, an assistant, or lecture notes, or might even be included in the tutor at some later stage. Among the different possibilities, the tutor can make a choice, so if Elisa doesn't want to choose, but just wants a single hint to proceed, she gets:

> Introduce a helper function that uses an accumulating parameter.

Here we assume that the teacher has set up the tutor to prefer the solution that uses a helper function with an accumulating parameter. Elisa can ask for more detailed information at this point, and the tutor responds with increasing detail:

> Define function reverse in terms of a function reverse', which takes an extra parameter in which the reversed list is accumulated.

with the final bottom-out hint:

> Define:
>
> $reverse = reverse' \perp$
>   **where** $reverse' \ acc = \perp$

At this point, Elisa can refine the function at multiple positions. In this exercise we do not impose an order on the sequence of refinements. However, the tutor offers a teacher the possibility to enforce a particular order of refinements. Suppose that Elisa chooses to implement *reverse'* by pattern matching on the second argument, which is a list, starting with the empty list case:

> $reverse = reverse' \ [\,]$
>   **where**
> $reverse' \ acc \ [\,] = \perp$

Note that this step consists of two smaller steps: the argument to *reverse'* has been instantiated to $[\,]$, and the definition of *reverse'* got an extra argument. She continues with:

> $reverse = reverse' \ [\,]$
>   **where**
> $reverse' \ acc \ [\,] = [\,]$

The tutor responds with:

> Incorrect $[\,]$ in the right hand side of reverse' on line 3

Correcting the error, Elisa enters:

$$reverse = reverse' \; [\,]$$
$$\textbf{where}$$
$$reverse' \; acc \; [\,] = acc$$

which is accepted by the tutor. If Elisa now asks for a hint, the tutor responds with:

Define the non-empty list case of reverse'

She continues with

$$reverse = reverse' \; [\,]$$
$$\textbf{where}$$
$$reverse' \; acc \; [\,] \qquad = acc$$
$$reverse' \; acc \; (x:xs) = \bot$$

which is accepted, and then

$$reverse = reverse' \; [\,]$$
$$\textbf{where}$$
$$reverse' \; acc \; [\,] \qquad = acc$$
$$reverse' \; acc \; (x:xs) = reverse' \; (y:acc) \; \bot$$

which gives:

Error: undefined variable y

This is an error message generated by the compiler for the programming language. Elisa continues with:

$$reverse = reverse' \; [\,]$$
$$\textbf{where}$$
$$reverse' \; acc \; [\,] \qquad = acc$$
$$reverse' \; acc \; (x:xs) = reverse' \; (x:acc) \; xs$$

Done! You have correctly solved the exercise.

The third model solution described at an abstract level in the hint at the start of the exercise is the naive, quadratic time solution for *reverse*, implemented by means of an explicit recursive definition:

$$reverse \; [\,] \qquad = [\,]$$
$$reverse \; (x:xs) = reverse \; xs \; +\!\!+ \; [x]$$

If a student implements this version of *reverse*, the tutor can tell the student that this is a correct definition of *reverse*, but that it is a quadratic time algorithm, and that a linear-time algorithm is preferable.

2.2   Integers within a Range

The next example we show is problem 22 from the Haskell 99 questions: Create a list containing all integers within a given range. For example:

> *Data.List⟩ range* 4 9
> $[4,5,6,7,8,9]$

The Haskell 99 questions mentions six solutions to this problem; here is one:

> *range x y* = *unfoldr* $(\lambda i \rightarrow$ **if** i == *succ y* **then** *Nothing* **else** *Just* $(i, succ\ i))$ *x*

This solution uses the *unfoldr* function defined by:

> *unfoldr*   :: $(b \rightarrow Maybe\ (a, b)) \rightarrow b \rightarrow [a]$
> *unfoldr f b* = **case** *f b* **of**
>   *Just* $(a, new\_b) \rightarrow a :$ *unfoldr f new_b*
>   *Nothing* $\rightarrow []$

Our system prefers the solution using *unfoldr*. If a student asks for a worked-out solution, the system would respond with the derivation given in Figure 2.

These interactions show that our tutor can

- give hints about which step to take next, in various levels of detail,
- list all possible ways in which to proceed,
- point out that an error, such as a parse error, a dependency error (such as using an unbound variable), or a type error has been made, and where the error appears to be,
- show a complete worked-out example.

3   The Architecture of the Tutor

Our tutor can be accessed via a browser[2]. On the main page, a student selects an exercise to work on (such as *reverse*). The tutor provides a starting point ($\perp$), and the student can then start refining the $\perp$ step-wise to a complete program that implements reverse. While developing the program, a student can check that (s)he is still on a path to a correct solution, ask for a single hint or all possible choices on how to proceed at a particular stage, or ask for a worked-out solution.

The feedback that we offer, such as giving a hint, is derived from a *strategy*. Strategies have a central role in our approach. We use strategies to capture the procedure of how to solve an exercise. A strategy describes which basic steps have to be taken, and how these steps are combined to arrive at a solution. In case of a functional programming exercise, the strategy outlines how to incrementally construct a program. We have developed an embedded domain-specific language for defining such strategies. Our strategy language is described in detail in Section 6.

---

[2] http://ideas.cs.uu.nl/ProgTutor/

$range = \bot$

$\Rightarrow$ { Introduce parameters }

$range\ x\ y = \bot$

$\Rightarrow$ { Use *unfoldr* }

$range\ x\ y = unfoldr\ \bot\ \bot$

$\Rightarrow$ { Start at x }

$range\ x\ y = unfoldr\ \bot\ x$

$\Rightarrow$ { Introduce a lambda-abstraction }

$range\ x\ y = unfoldr\ (\lambda i \rightarrow \bot)\ x$

$\Rightarrow$ { Introduce an **if-then-else** to specify a stop criterion }

$range\ x\ y = unfoldr\ (\lambda i \rightarrow \textbf{if}\ \bot\ \textbf{then}\ \bot\ \textbf{else}\ \bot)\ x$

$\Rightarrow$ { Introduce the stop criterion }

$range\ x\ y = unfoldr\ (\lambda i \rightarrow \textbf{if}\ i == succ\ y\ \textbf{then}\ \bot\ \textbf{else}\ \bot)\ x$

$\Rightarrow$ { Return *Nothing* for the stop criterion }

$range\ x\ y = unfoldr\ (\lambda i \rightarrow \textbf{if}\ i == succ\ y\ \textbf{then}\ Nothing\ \textbf{else}\ \bot)\ x$

$\Rightarrow$ { Give the output value and the value for the next iteration }

$range\ x\ y = unfoldr\ (\lambda i \rightarrow \textbf{if}\ i == succ\ y\ \textbf{then}\ Nothing\ \textbf{else}\ Just\ (i, succ\ i))\ x$

Fig. 2. Derivation of the definition of *range*

The feedback functionality, which is based on strategies, is provided to external environments as a web-service. Each time a student clicks a button such as Check or Hint, our programming environment (the front-end) sends a service request [Gerdes et al., 2008] to our functional programming domain reasoner (the back-end). The domain reasoner is stateless: all information the domain reasoner needs is included in the service request. For example, a request to check a program sends the strategy for solving the exercise (the strategy for *reverse*), and the previous and new expression of the student to the *diagnose* feedback-service. The following table describes the most relevant feedback services:

allfirsts. The *allfirsts* service returns all next steps that are allowed by a strategy.

onefirst. The *onefirst* service returns a single possible next step that follows a strategy. The functional programming domain reasoner offers the possibility to specify an order on steps, to select a single step among multiple possible steps.

derivation. The *derivation* service returns a worked-out solution of an exercise starting with the current program.

finished. The *finished* service checks whether or not the program is accepted as a final answer.

stepsremaining. The *stepsremaining* service returns the number of steps that remain to be done according to the strategy. This is achieved by calculating the length of the derivation returned by the *derivation* service.

diagnose. The *diagnose* service diagnoses a program submitted by a student.

The diagnose feedback-service (and all our other feedback-services) uses the Helium compiler for Haskell to calculate feedback. The Helium compiler has been developed to give better feedback to students on the level of syntax and types [Heeren et al., 2003]. We reuse Helium's error messages when a student makes a syntax-mistake, or develops a wrongly typed program. If a student submits a syntax- and type-correct program, we analyse the submitted program using the *diagnose*-service.

The diagnose-service takes the strategy, the previous program, and the current program as arguments. It determines if the current program can be derived from the previous program using any of the rules that are allowed by the strategy. The diagnose service is flexible in the sense that a student may use different names for locally defined entities, and different syntactic constructs for the same expression (**let** versus **where**, and many other equivalences). The diagnose-service calculates a normal form of both the expected and the submitted programs, and checks that the submitted program appears in the set of expected programs. If the submitted program appears in the set of expected programs, the tutor accepts the step, and responds positively. If it doesn't, the tutor checks if the program can be recognised by any of the known wrong approaches (typical erroneous solutions that we have encountered in student solutions), and if it can reports this to student. Finally, if the student program cannot be recognised the student is asked to try again[3].

4   Rewriting and Refining

As the examples in the Section 2 show, a student develops a program by making small, incremental, changes to a previous version of the program. Other common scenarios in teaching programming are to give a student an incomplete program, and ask him to complete the program, or to give a student a program, and ask him to change the program at a particular point. In such assignments, a student *refines* or *rewrites* a program. Rewriting preserves the semantics of a program; refining possibly makes a program more precise. This section discusses how students can refine and rewrite functional programs.

We offer a number of refinement rules to students. Section 2 already gives some examples:

$$\bot \Rightarrow \lambda \bot \rightarrow \bot \qquad \text{Introduce lambda abstraction}$$
$$\bot \Rightarrow \textbf{if } \bot \textbf{ then } \bot \textbf{ else } \bot \qquad \text{Introduce \textbf{if-then-else}}$$
$$\bot \Rightarrow v \qquad \text{Introduce variable } v$$

A hole represents a value, and such values may have different types. For example, a hole may represent an expression, as in all of the above examples, or a declaration, as in

$$\bot \Rightarrow f \bot = \bot \qquad \text{Introduce function binding}$$

---

[3] In Section 8 on future work we explain how we intend to relax this restriction in the future.

A refinement rule replaces a hole with a value of its type, which possibly contains holes again. Internally, such a value is represented by a value of the datatype representing the abstract syntax of a type. For example, the abstract syntax for expressions would typically contain the following constructors:

```
data Expr = Lambda Pattern Expr
          | If Expr Expr Expr
          | App Expr Expr
          | Var String
          | Hole
```

and more. A refinement rule takes the same number of arguments as its abstract syntax constructor. So the refinement rule introducing an **if-then-else** expression takes three expression arguments. The arguments may be holes or terms containing holes. As another example, the refinement rule that introduces a lambda abstraction takes a pattern, and an expression (the body of the lambda expression) as arguments. As a final example, the refinement rule that introduces a variable takes the name of that variable (such as v in Figure 3) as an argument, and returns an expression that does not contain a hole anymore. Note that the variable introduced might be bound or unbound; refinement rules are unaware of the binding structure of the language. The refinement rules are kept simple and basically encapsulate a constructor.

A refinement rule refines a program on the level of the context-free syntax, and not on the level of tokens, so, for example, we don't have a rule that says $the \perp \Rightarrow$ **then**.

Holes are the central concept in our refinement rules. Where can they appear? Refinement rules refine:

- expressions, such as the $\perp$ in $\lambda i \rightarrow \perp$,
- declarations (the second $\perp$ in *reverse* = *reverse'* $\perp$ **where** $\perp$),
- function bindings ($f\ [\ ] = 0 \Rightarrow f\ [\ ] = 0;\ f\perp = \perp$),
- alternatives (**case** xs **of** $[\ ] \rightarrow 0 \Rightarrow$ **case** xs **of** $[\ ] \rightarrow 0;\ \perp \rightarrow \perp$),
- patterns (**case** xs **of** $\perp \rightarrow \perp \Rightarrow$ **case** xs **of** $[\ ] \rightarrow \perp$).

We do not introduce refinement rules for other syntactic categories such as modules or classes, because these concepts hardly show up in our beginners' programs. Of course, this might change when the range of applications of the tutor is extended.

How do we come up with a set of refinement rules? A simple solution would be to take the context-free description of Haskell, and turn all productions into refinement rules. However, this general approach leads to all kinds of unnecessary and undesirable rules. For example, deriving a literal integer 4 using the context-free grammar for Haskell takes many steps, but a student would only see $\perp \Rightarrow 4$. Our leading argument is that a refinement rule should be useful to a student, in the sense that it changes the way a program looks. Furthermore, the set of refinement rules should completely cover the programming language constructs we want the students to use, so that any program can be constructed using refinement rules. Complete coverage of a set of rewrite rules is verified by checking that for every

Declarations
$$patBind: \quad \bot \Rightarrow \bot = \bot$$
$$funBinds: \quad \bot \Rightarrow \bot$$
$$\bot$$

Function bindings
$$funBind: \quad \bot \Rightarrow f\bot = \bot$$

Expressions
$$var: \quad \bot \Rightarrow v$$
$$lit: \quad \bot \Rightarrow l$$
$$app: \quad \bot \Rightarrow \bot \bot$$
$$lambda: \quad \bot \Rightarrow \lambda\bot \to \bot$$
$$case_-: \quad \bot \Rightarrow \textbf{case } \bot \textbf{ of } \bot$$

Alternatives
$$alt: \quad \bot \Rightarrow \bot \to \bot$$

Patterns
$$pVar: \quad \bot \Rightarrow v$$
$$pWildcard: \quad \bot \Rightarrow \_$$

Fig. 3. Some refinement rules for functional programming in Haskell

datatype containing holes in the abstract syntax of programs (datatypes for expressions, declarations, function bindings, alternatives, and patterns, in our case), there exist refinement rules from a hole to any other constructor of the datatype. These refinement rules should be as 'small' as possible, in the sense that if we would further split such a rule, we cannot represent the corresponding program anymore, since we cannot build an abstract syntax tree for a program that is halfway completing an abstract-syntax tree construction. For example, the **if-then-else** expression cannot be split into an **if-then** and an **else** part in Haskell. Preferably, the refinement rules are derived from looking at interactions of students in an editor, but lacking a tutor, we use our experience as programmers and teachers as a first approximation of the set of desirable refinement rules. We list some refinement rules that are often used in Figure 3.

Some refinement steps are performed silently, and are combined with one or more other refinement steps in a hint. For example, introducing an application in a Haskell program amounts to typing a space. We expect that few beginning students will view an application introduction as a step on its own, but instead always supply either a function or an argument name. Our domain reasoner offers the possibility to annotate a rule that is performed silently, by declaring it as a *minor* rule. We use these minor rules to increase the step size, and avoid showing steps like $\bot \Rightarrow \bot \bot$. If application is declared to be a minor rule, a user can refine a hole to an application of a particular function, such as *unfoldr*, to one or more as yet unknown arguments. Minor rules are not only used for increasing the step size, to avoid showing steps that make no sense to students, but also to perform administrative tasks, such as modifying an environment that we maintain next to the program.

At the moment, our tutor mainly supports the incremental construction of a program by means of refinement. However, it can also be used to rewrite a program, preserving its semantics, but changing some other aspects. For example, we might want to ask a student to change her program from using an explicit recursive definition of *reverse* to a definition using *foldl*, as in

$$reverse = reverse' \, [\,]$$
$$\textbf{where}$$
$$\quad reverse' \; acc \, [\,] \qquad = acc$$
$$\quad reverse' \; acc \, (x:xs) = reverse' \; (x:acc) \; xs$$
$\Rightarrow$ { Definition of *flip* }
$$reverse = reverse' \, [\,]$$
$$\textbf{where}$$
$$\quad reverse' \; acc \, [\,] \qquad = acc$$
$$\quad reverse' \; acc \, (x:xs) = reverse' \; (flip \; (:) \; acc \; x) \; xs$$
$\Rightarrow$ { Definition of *foldl* }
$$reverse = reverse' \, [\,]$$
$$\textbf{where}$$
$$\quad reverse' \; acc = foldl \; (flip \; (:)) \; acc$$
$\Rightarrow$ { Inline and β-reduce }
$$reverse = foldl \; (flip \; (:)) \; [\,]$$

To support such an exercise, each of our rewrite rules works both ways: we can remove *flip* (:) by applying the definition of *flip*, or we can introduce it as in the above derivation.

In the code for the tutor[4], rules are specified in the file `Domain/FP/Rules.hs`. The rules are specified as functions taking terms, which may contain holes, as arguments. The rule *introCase* looks as follows:

$$case\_ :: Expr \rightarrow [Alt] \rightarrow Rule \; Expr$$
$$case\_ \; e =$$
$$\quad toRefinement \; \texttt{"Introduce case"} \; \texttt{"case"} \circ Case \; e$$

where *Case* is a constructor of the datatype *Expr*, and *toRefinement* turns a description (`"Introduce case"`), an identifier (”case”), and a value of some type into a *Rule* of that type. The precise definitions of the *Rule*, *Expr* and *Alt* datatypes are not important for these notes.

5   Strategies in Functional Programming

The basic steps for constructing a solution for a programming task are program refinement rules introduced in the previous section. These rules typically replace an unknown part, a hole, by some term. A program refinement rule can introduce one or more new unknown parts. We are finished with an exercise as soon as

---

[4] See `http://ideas.cs.uu.nl/trac/wiki/Download`

all unknown parts have been completed. How do we guide a student in making progress to a complete solution?

Whatever aspect of intelligence you attempt to model in a computer program, the same needs arise over and over again [Bundy, 1983]:

- The need to have knowledge about the domain.
- The need to reason with that knowledge.
- The need for knowledge about how to direct or guide that reasoning.

Our tutor is built for the domain of functional programming. It supports reasoning about functional programs by means of refinement and rewrite rules. The knowledge about how to guide this reasoning is often captured by a so-called procedure or procedural skill. A procedure describes how basic steps may be combined to solve a particular problem. A procedure is often called a *strategy* (or meta-level reasoning, meta-level inference [Bundy, 1983], procedural nets [Brown and Burton, 1978], plans, tactics, etc.), and we have chosen to use this term.

A strategy for a functional program describes how a student should construct a functional program for a particular problem. Some well-known approaches to constructing correct programs are:

- specify a problem by means of pre- and post-conditions, and then calculate a program from the specification, or provide an implementation and prove that the implementation satisfies the specification [Hoare, 1969, Dijkstra, 1975],
- refine a specification by means of refinement rules until an executable program is obtained [Back, 1987, Morgan, 1990],
- specify a problem by means of a simple but possibly very inefficient program, and transform it to an efficient program using semantics-preserving transformation rules [Bird, 1987, Meertens, 1986].

If we would use one of the first two approaches in a programming tutor that can give hints to students on how to proceed, we would have to automatically construct correctness proofs, a problem that is known to be hard. The last approach has been studied extensively, and several program transformation systems have been developed. However, our main goal is to refine instead of transform programs, since this better reflects the activities of beginning programmers. To support program refinement in a tutor, we limit the solutions that are accepted by the tutor.

Our tutor supports the incremental construction, in a top-down fashion, of *model solutions*. It recognises incomplete versions of these solutions, together with all kinds of syntactical variants. We support the refinement of programs, but instead of showing that a program ensures a post-condition, we assume a program to be correct if we can determine it to be equal to a model solution.

This section introduces strategies, and shows how we formulate strategies for functional programming.

5.1   Strategies for Procedural Skills

A procedure often consists of multiple steps. For example, developing a function for *reverse* requires developing the complete program, which in the case of an explicit recursive definition consists of a case distinction between the empty list and the non-empty list, and a recursive call in the non-empty list case, amongst others. A procedure may also contain a choice between different (sequences of) steps. For example, we can choose to either use *foldl*, or an explicit recursive definition for *reverse*. Sometimes, the order in which the steps are performed is not relevant, as long as they are performed at some point.

We have developed a strategy language for describing procedures as rewrite strategies [Heeren et al., 2008]. Our strategy language is domain independent, and has been used to describe strategies for exercises in mathematics, logic, biology, and programming. The basic elements of the strategy language are rewrite rules or refinement rules. We use rewrite rules for exercises in mathematics, logic, and biology. Refinement rules are rewrite rules that may contain holes, and are used in the programming domain. The strategy language supports combining strategies by means of *strategy combinators*. For example, if *s* and *t* are strategies, then so are:

s <|> *t*	choice: do either *s* or *t*
s <*> *t*	sequence: do *s* before *t*
s <%> *t*	interleave: steps from *s* and *t* are performed in some order

Furthermore, we have a strategy *fail*, which always fails (the unit of choice), and a strategy *succeed*, which always succeeds (the unit of sequence). Section 6 gives a complete description of our strategy language and combinators. The contents of this section is not necessary for understanding the contents of Section 6, and readers interested in the strategy language only can skip this section.

5.2   Strategies for Functional Programs

For any programming problem, there are many solutions. Some of these solutions are syntactical variants of each other, but other solutions implement different ideas to solve a problem. We specify a strategy for solving a functional programming problem by means of model solutions for that problem. We can automatically *derive* a strategy from a model solution. A model solution is compiled into a programming strategy by inspecting its abstract syntax tree (AST), and matching the refinement rules with the AST. This is a standard tree matching algorithm, which yields a strategy that can later be adapted by a teacher for his own purposes. The strategies for the various model solutions are then combined into a single strategy using the choice combinator. So, for the *reverse* exercise from Section 2 we would get a single strategy combining the three strategies for the model solutions. For example, here is a strategy that is compiled from the definition of *reverse* in terms of *foldl*:

```
    patBind
<*> pVar "reverse"
```

```
<*> app <*> var "foldl"
      <*> (  (paren <*> app <*> var "flip"
                            <*> infixApp <*> con "(:)"
              )
         <%> con "[]"
         )
```

There are several things to note about this strategy. The ordering of the rules by means of the sequence combinator <*> indicates that this strategy for defining *reverse* recognises the top-down construction of *reverse*. Since we use the inter-leave combinator <%> to separate the arguments to *foldl*, a student can develop the arguments to *foldl* in any order. This strategy uses three rules we did not introduce in the previous section, namely *infixApp*, which introduces an infix application, *con*, which introduces a constructor of a datatype, and *paren*. The rule *paren* ensures that the first argument of *foldl* is in between parentheses. The hole introduced by this rule is filled by means of the strategy that introduces *flip* (:). The rule *paren* is minor, so when we give a hint for this part of the program, we don't just introduce parentheses, but also the function *flip* (and the invisible application operator, which is also introduced by a minor rule). Since rules correspond to abstract syntax tree constructors, this shows that our ab-stract syntax also contains constructors that represent parts of the program that correspond to concrete syntax, such as parentheses. This way we can also guide a student in the concrete syntax of a program. However, we might also leave concrete syntax guidance to the parsing and type-checking phase of Helium.

If the above strategy would be the complete strategy for defining *reverse*, then a student would only be allowed to construct exactly this definition. This would almost always be too restrictive. Therefore, we would typically use a strategy that combines a set of model solutions. However, our approach necessarily limits the solutions accepted by the tutor: a solution that uses an approach funda-mentally different from the specified model solutions will not be recognised by the tutor. Depending on the model solutions provided, this might be a severe restriction. However, in experiments with lab exercises in a first-year functional programming course [Gerdes et al., 2010], we found that our tutor recognises almost 90% of the correct student programs by means of a limited set of model solutions. The remaining 10% of correct solutions were solutions 'with a smell': correct, but using constructs we would never use in a model solution. We expect that restricting the possible solutions to programming problems is feasible for beginning programmers. It is rather uncommon that a beginning programmer develops a new model solution for a beginners' problem.

We discuss how to recognise as many variants of a solution as possible in the next two subsections. Subsection 5.3 describes strategies for Haskell's prelude, and Subsection 5.4 discusses a canonical form of Haskell programs.

5.3   Strategies for Haskell's Prelude

To recognise as many syntactic variants as possible of (a part of) a solution to a programming problem, we describe a strategy for functional programming at a high abstraction level. For example, we define special strategies *foldlS* and *flipS* for recognising occurrences of *foldl* and *flip* in programs. The strategy *flipS* not only recognises *flip* itself, but also its definition, which can be considered an inlined and β-reduced version of *flip*. The strategy *flipS* takes a strategy as argument, which recognises the argument of *flip*.

$$flipS\ fS\ =\ app <*> var\ \texttt{"flip"} <*> fS$$
$$<|> lambda <*> pVar\ x <*> pVar\ y$$
$$<*> app <*> fS <*> (var\ y <\%> var\ x)$$

The variable names *x* and *y*, used in the lambda-abstraction, are fresh and do not appear free in *fS*, in order to avoid variable capturing. The *flipS* (*con* "(:)") strategy recognises both *flip* (:) itself, and the β-reduced, infix constructor, form λ*xs* *x* → *x* : *xs*. The *flipS* strategy is used in a strategy *reverseS* for a model solution for *reverse* as follows:

$$reverseS = foldlS\ (paren <*> flipS\ consS)\ nilS$$
where
$$consS = infixApp <*> con\ \texttt{"(:)"}$$
$$nilS\ \ = con\ \texttt{"[]"}$$

It is important to specify model solutions for exercises using abstractions available in Haskell's prelude like *foldl*, *foldr*, *flip*, etc, if applicable. In the *reverseS* example we have for example used both *foldlS* and *flipS*. If a student would use these abstractions in a solution, where a model solution wouldn't, then the student's program wouldn't be accepted. A large part of the Haskell prelude is available in our strategy language. For any function in the prelude, a student may either use the function name itself in her program, such as for example (∘), or its implementation, such as λ*f* *g* *x* → *f* (*g* *x*). The strategies for functions in the prelude also contain some conversions between abstractions, such as

$$foldl\ op\ e\ \texttt{==}\ foldr\ (flip\ op)\ e \circ reverse$$

So, if a function that is specified by means of a *foldl* is implemented by means of a *foldr* together with *reverse*, this is also accepted. Of course, students can introduce their own abstractions.

A strategy cannot capture all variations of a program that a student can introduce. For example, the fact that a student uses different names for variables is hard, if not impossible, to express in a strategy. However, we do want to give a student the possibility to use her own variable names. We use *normalisation* to handle such kinds of variations. If a student introduces her own *foldr*, possibly using a different name, normalisation will successfully compare this against a model solution using the prelude's *foldr*.

5.4   A Canonical Form for Haskell Programs

The diagnose service checks whether or not a student submissions follows a strategy. To verify that a program submitted by a student follows a strategy, we apply all rules allowed by the strategy to the previous submission of the student (which is also passed to the diagnose service), normalise the programs thus obtained, and compare each of these programs against the normalised submitted student program. Using normalisation, which returns a canonical form of a program, we want to recognise as many syntactical variants of Haskell programs as possible. For example, sometimes a student doesn't explicitly specify all arguments to a function, and for that purpose we use η-reduction when analysing a student program:

$$\lambda x \to f\,x \Rightarrow f$$

Normalisation uses various program transformations to reach a canonical form of a Haskell program. We use amongst others inlining, α-renaming, β- and η-reduction, and desugaring program transformations. Our normalisation procedure starts with α-renaming, which gives all bound variables a fresh name. Then it desugars the program, restricting the syntax to a (core) subset of the full abstract syntax. The next step inlines local definitions, which makes some β-reductions possible. Finally, normalisation performs β- and η-reductions in applicative order (leftmost-innermost) and normalises a program to β-normal form.

In the remainder of this section we show some of the program transformations and discuss the limitations of our normalisation.

Desugaring. Desugaring removes syntactic sugar from a program. Syntactic sugar is usually introduced to conveniently write some kind of programs, such as writing $\lambda x\,y \to \ldots$ for $\lambda x \to \lambda y \to \ldots$ Syntactic sugar does not change the semantics of a program. However, if we want to compare a student program syntactically against (possibly partially complete) model solutions we want to ignore syntactic sugar. Desugaring consists of several program transformations such as removing superfluous parentheses, rewriting a **where** expression to a **let** expression, moving the arguments of a function binding to a lambda abstraction (e.g., $f\,x = y \Rightarrow f = \lambda x \to y$), and rewriting infix operators to (prefix) functions. The following derivation shows how a somewhat contrived example is desugared:

$reverse = foldl\,f\,[\,]$ **where** $f\,x\,y = y : x$
$\Rightarrow$ { **where** to **let** }
$reverse = $ **let** $f\,x\,y = y : x$ **in** $foldl\,f\,[\,]$
$\Rightarrow$ { Infix operators to (prefix) functions }
$reverse = $ **let** $f\,x\,y = (:)\,y\,x$ **in** $foldl\,f\,[\,]$
$\Rightarrow$ { Function bindings to lambda abstractions }
$reverse = $ **let** $f = \lambda x \to y \to (:)\,y\,x$ **in** $foldl\,f\,[\,]$

In the following paragraph on inlining we will see how the declaration of f is inlined in the $foldl$-expression.

Inlining. Inlining replaces a call to a user-defined function by its body. We perform inlining to make β-reduction possible. For example,

$reverse = $ **let** $f = \lambda x \to \lambda y \to (:)\,y\,x$ **in** $foldl\,f\,[\,]$

$\Rightarrow$ { Inline }
   $reverse = foldl\ (\lambda x \to \lambda y \to (:)\ y\ x)\ [\,]$

Constant arguments. An argument is constant if it is passed unchanged to *all* recursive function calls. Compilers often optimise such constant arguments away, to save space and increase speed. Consider the following naive implementation of the higher-order function *foldr*:

$foldr\ op\ b\ [\,] \qquad = b$
$foldr\ op\ b\ (x:xs) = x\ 'op'\ foldr\ op\ b\ xs$

This implementation has two constant arguments: *op* and *b*. A better implementation is:

$foldr\ op\ b = f$
  where $f\ [\,] \qquad = b$
       $f\ (x:xs) = x\ 'op'\ f\ xs$

The above definition is the standard definition for *foldr* from the Haskell prelude. Our goal with this transformation is not to optimise programs, but instead to increase the number of possibilities to apply β-reduction. Note that we do not inline recursive functions. Recursive functions are rewritten in terms of *fix*, which does not get β-reduced. However, the constant arguments of a recursive function *can* be β-reduced. The optimisation of a recursive function with constant arguments, such as the naive *foldr* function, separates the recursive (f in the example) from the non-recursive part of a function. Therefore, only after optimising constant arguments away does it help to inline the function. The optimised version of *foldr* will be inlined, but the recursive help function f will not be inlined.

Lambda calculus reductions. At the heart of our normalisation are program transformations based on the λ-calculus.

We use α-conversion to rename bound variables. To check that a program is syntactically equivalent to a model solution, we α-convert both the submitted student program as well as the model solution. α-conversion ensures that all variable names are unique. This simplifies the implementation of other program transformation steps, such as β-reduction, due to the fact that substitutions become capture avoiding.

η-reduction reduces a program to its η-short form, trying to remove as many lambda abstractions as possible. η-reduction replaces $\lambda x \to f\ x$ by f if x does not appear free in f.

Finally, we apply β-reduction. β-reduction takes the application of a lambda abstraction to an argument, and substitutes the argument for the lambda-abstracted variable: $(\lambda x \to expr)\ y \Rightarrow_\beta expr[x := y]$. The substitution $[x := y]$ replaces all free occurrences of the variable x by the expression y. For example, using β-reduction we get:

$(\lambda f\ x\ y \to f\ y\ x)\ (:) \Rightarrow \lambda x\ y \to (:)\ y\ x$

Although we don't expect a student to write a program containing a β-redex, this happens in practice.

Discussion. Correctness of a normalisation procedure depends on several aspects [Filinski and Korsholm Rohde, 2004]. A normalisation procedure is

- *sound* if the output term, if any, is β-equivalent to the input term,
- *standardising* if equivalent terms are mapped to the same result,
- *complete* if normalisation is defined for all terms that have normal forms.

We claim that our normalisation procedure is sound and complete but not standardising, but we have yet to prove this. The main reason for our normalisation procedure to be non-standardising is that we do not inline and β-reduce recursive functions. For example, while the terms *take* 3 $[1\,..]$ and $[1,2,3]$ are equivalent, the first will not be reduced by normalisation. Therefore, these terms have different normalisation results. We do not incorporate β-reduction of recursive function because this might lead to non-terminating normalisations.

We could extend our normalisation procedure with several other transformations, such as permuting function arguments, or swapping components of pairs, but haven't done so yet.

Normalisation by evaluation (NBE) [Berger et al., 1998] is an alternative approach to normalisation. NBE evaluates a λ-term to its (denotational) semantics and then reifies the semantics to a λ-term in β-normal and η-long form. The difference with our, more traditional, approach to normalisation is that NBE appeals to the semantics (by evaluation) of a term to obtain a normal form. The main goal of NBE is to efficiently normalise a term. We are not so much interested in efficiency, but it may well be that NBE improves standardisation of normalisation.

5.5   Relating Strategies to Locations in Programs

A program is constructed incrementally, in a top-down fashion. When starting the construction of a program there is usually a single hole. During the development, refinement rules introduce and refine many holes. For example, the *app* refinement rule introduces two new holes: one for an expression that is of a function type, and one for an expression that is the argument of that function. When used in a strategy for developing a particular program, a refinement rule always targets a particular location in the program. For example, the refinement rule that introduces the base argument expression in an *foldl* application cannot be applied to an arbitrary expression hole, but should be applied at exactly the location where the argument is needed in the program. In the next example this is the second expression hole (counted from left to right):

foldl (*flip* $\bot$) $\bot$ $\Rightarrow$ *foldl* (*flip* $\bot$) *some_argument*

To target a particular location in a program, every refinement rule is extended with information about the location of the hole it refines. A rewrite rule, on the other hand, may be applicable to more than one location in the AST.

When defining a strategy for developing a functional program, we need to relate the holes that appear in the refinement rules to the strategies that are used to refine these holes. For example, the holes introduced by the *app* refinement rule need to be connected to rules that refine them. Recall that our refinement rules just encapsulate a constructor of an abstract syntax datatype in a rule. For instance, the *app* rule encapsulates the *App* constructor from the *Expr* datatype in an expression refinement rule:

$$app :: Expr \rightarrow Expr \rightarrow Rule\ Expr$$
$$app\ f\ x = toRefinement\ \texttt{"Introduce application"}\ \texttt{"app"}\ (App\ f\ x)$$

The *app* refinement rule applies *App* to two expression holes. These holes should be connected to the rules that are going to refine them. The first might for example be a *var :: String → Expr* refinement rule that introduces a prelude function, as in *var* "length". The hole expression and the *var* rule have to be connected. We achieve this connection by giving a hole an *identifier* and specialising a rule only to be applicable to a hole with that particular identifier. We extend the *Hole* constructors of the various abstract syntax datatypes with an identifier field. For example, the *Hole* constructor of the *Expr* data type is extended as follows:

type *HoleID = Int*
data *Expr   = Hole HoleID | ...*

When combining refinement rules in a strategy, we do not only specify the refinement rule, but also the identifier of the hole it is going to refine. We define a datatype that combines a term containing one or more holes and a strategy that refines the holes in that term:

data *Refinement a = Ref {term :: a, strat :: Strategy a}*

Here is an example value of this datatype for a strategy that introduces the application of the prelude function *length* to the empty list $[\,]$:

$$Ref\ (App\ (Hole\ 1)\ (Hole\ 2))\ (var_1\ \texttt{"length"} <\%> con_2\ \texttt{"[]"})$$

The refinement rule is annotated with the identifier of the hole it should refine. So, the refinement rule var_1 is only applicable to a hole with identifier 1. The actual numbering of holes takes place in a state monad:

type *RefinementS a = State Int (Refinement a)*

After evaluating the state monad, every hole has a unique number. We define a function *bindRefinement* to bind a rule to a hole:

$$bindRefinement :: Rule\ a \rightarrow RefinementS\ a$$

This function takes a rule and returns, in the state monad, a term together with the strategy consisting of the argument rule. The *bindRefinement* function ensures that the refinement rule is applied to the right hole. We use generic programming techniques to locate a particular hole in an AST, but we omit the details.

Since strategy combinators combine rules, the combinators have to be aware of the relations between refinement rules and holes, and adapt them appropriately whenever rules are combined. For example, when combining two programming strategies by means of the choice combinator, both substrategies should refine the *same* hole. Since the concepts of refinement rules and holes are special for the programming domain, and do not appear in most of the other domains we have studied, we define lifted versions of the combinators introduced in Subsection 5.1 that deal with the relations between refinement rules and holes. For example, the lifted version of the choice combinator uses a 'plain' choice combinator to combine the substrategies, and updates the relation between holes and substrategies. A refinement rule is only applicable when the holes it refines are present in the AST. For instance, in the strategy for the application of the *length* function to the empty list, the *app* refinement rule is applied *before* the *var* "length" rule. We use the sequence combinator to enforce the order in which the refinements have to take place. When sequencing two programming substrategies, we ensure that the first substrategy refines to a term that can be refined by the second substrategy.

Relating holes and refinement rules using holes with identifiers has some consequences for the implementation of our functional programming domain reasoner. For the other domains we have developed, the domain reasoners operate on the term that has been submitted by the student. In the functional programming domain reasoner, however, we get an AST with holes without identifiers when we parse a student submission, due to the fact that the concrete syntax does not contain hole identifiers. Since we need holes with identifiers as specified in the strategy, we use information about the steps that a student has taken so far. We use the strategy and these steps to reconstruct the AST with the correct hole identifiers, which we can compare against the program of the student. Reconstructing the AST is easy because information about previous steps is maintained and communicated back and forth between the front- and back-end.

6 A Strategy Language

In the previous section we introduced strategies and strategy combinators informally. This section defines the semantics of these combinators, and the laws they satisfy. Our strategy language is very similar to the language for specifying context-free grammars (CFGs), and we will describe the equivalent concepts when applicable. This strategy language has been used extensively in domain reasoners for various mathematical domains [Heeren et al., 2008, Heeren and Jeuring, 2008, 2009, 2010, 2011].

We use a collection of standard combinators to combine strategies, resulting in more complex strategy descriptions. The semantics of the combinators is given in terms of the *language* of a strategy. The language of a strategy is a set of sentences, where each sentence is a sequence of refinement or rewrite rules. We use $a, b, c, ...$ to denote symbols, and x, y, z for sentences (sequences of such symbols). As usual, we write ϵ for the empty sequence, and xy (or ax) for concatenation. Function $\mathcal{L}$ generates the language of a strategy, by interpreting it as a context-free grammar.

6.1   Rules

The basic components of our strategy language, the alphabet, are the rewrite and refinement rules. The language of a strategy consisting of a single rule is just that rule:

$$\mathcal{L}\ (r)\ =\ \{r\}$$

6.2   Choice

The choice combinator $<\!|\!>$ allows solving a problem in two different ways. In CFGs, choice is introduced by having multiple production rules for a non-terminal symbol, which can be combined by means of the $|$-symbol, which explains our notation. The language generated by choice is the union of the languages of the arguments:

$$\mathcal{L}\ (s <\!|\!> t)\ =\ \mathcal{L}\ (s) \cup \mathcal{L}\ (t)$$

The *fail* combinator is a strategy that always fails. Its set of sentences is empty:

$$\mathcal{L}\ (\textit{fail})\ =\ \emptyset$$

It is a unit element of $<\!|\!>$:

$$\textit{fail} <\!|\!> s\ =\ s$$
$$s <\!|\!> \textit{fail}\ =\ s$$

6.3   Sequence

Often, a program is developed in a particular order: when developing the application of a function to an argument, we usually first develop the function, and only then the argument. So if fS is a strategy for developing f, and eS is a strategy for developing e, to develop $f\ e$, we first perform fS and then eS. Thus the development of this program follows a particular order. The *sequence* combinator, denoted by $<\!*\!>$, applies its second argument strategy after its first, thus allowing programs that require multiple refinement steps to be applied in some order. The right-hand side of a production rule in a CFG consists of a sequence of symbols. The sentences in the language of sequence are concatenations of sentences from the languages of the component strategies:

$$\mathcal{L}\ (s <\!*\!> t)\ =\ \{xy\ |\ x \in \mathcal{L}\ (s), y \in \mathcal{L}\ (t)\}$$

The *succeed* combinator is a strategy that always succeeds. Its set of sentences contains just the empty sentence:

$$\mathcal{L}\ (\textit{succeed})\ =\ \{\epsilon\}$$

The *fail* combinator is a zero element of <∗>, and *succeed* is a unit element:

$$
\begin{aligned}
fail <\!\ast\!> s &= fail \\
s <\!\ast\!> fail &= fail
\end{aligned}
$$

$$
\begin{aligned}
succeed <\!\ast\!> s &= s \\
s <\!\ast\!> succeed &= s
\end{aligned}
$$

6.4   Interleave

In a **case**-expression like

```
case xs of
  []    → ⊥
  x : xs → ⊥
```

a student may refine any of the two right-hand sides, in any order. She may even interleave the refinement of the two right-hand sides. To support this behaviour, we introduce the *interleave* combinator, denoted by <%>. This combinator expresses that the steps of its argument strategies have to be applied, but that the steps can be interleaved. For example, the result of interleaving a strategy *abc* that recognises the sequence of three symbols *a*, *b*, and *c*, with the strategy *de* that recognises the sequence of two symbols *d* and *e* (that is, *abc* <%> *de*) results in the following set:

$$
\{abcde, abdce, abdec, adbce, adbec, adebc, dabce, dabec, daebc, deabc\}
$$

Interleaving sentences. To define the semantics of interleave, we first define an interleave operator on sentences. The interleaving of two sentences (x <%> y) can be defined conveniently in terms of left-interleave (denoted by x %> y, and also known as the left-merge operator [Bergstra and Klop, 1985]), which expresses that the first symbol should be taken from the left-hand side operand. The algebra of communicating processes field traditionally defines interleave in terms of left-interleave (and "communication interleave") to obtain a sound and complete axiomatisation [Fokkink, 2000].

$$
\begin{aligned}
\epsilon <\%> x &= \{x\} \\
x <\%> \epsilon &= \{x\} \\
x <\%> y &= x \,\%\!> y \cup y \,\%\!> x \quad (x \neq \epsilon \wedge y \neq \epsilon)
\end{aligned}
$$

$$
\begin{aligned}
\epsilon \,\%\!> y &= \emptyset \\
ax \,\%\!> y &= \{az \mid z \in x <\%> y\}
\end{aligned}
$$

The set *abc* %> *de* (where *abc* and *de* are now sentences) only contains the six sentences that start with symbol *a*. It is worth noting that the number of interleavings for two sentences of lengths n and m equals $\frac{(n+m)!}{n!m!}$. This number grows quickly with longer sentences. An alternative definition of interleaving two sequences, presented by Hoare in his influential book on CSP [Hoare, 1985], is by means of three laws:

$$\epsilon \in (y <\!\%\!> z) \Leftrightarrow y = z = \epsilon$$
$$x \in (y <\!\%\!> z) \Leftrightarrow x \in (z <\!\%\!> y)$$
$$ax \in (y <\!\%\!> z) \Leftrightarrow (\exists y' : y = ay' \wedge x \in (y' <\!\%\!> z))$$
$$\vee \ (\exists z' : z = az' \wedge x \in (y <\!\%\!> z'))$$

Interleaving sets. The operations for interleaving sentences can be lifted to work on sets of sentences by considering all combinations of elements from the two sets. Let X, Y, and Z be sets of sentences. The lifted operators are defined as follows:

$$X <\!\%\!> Y = \bigcup \{x <\!\%\!> y \mid x \in X, y \in Y\}$$
$$X \%\!> Y = \bigcup \{x \%\!> y \mid x \in X, y \in Y\}$$

For instance, $\{a, ab\} <\!\%\!> \{c, cd\}$ yields a set containing 14 elements:

$$\{abc, abcd, ac, acb, acbd, acd, acdb, ca, cab, cabd, cad, cadb, cda, cdab\}$$

From these definitions, it follows that the lifted operator for interleaving is commutative, associative, and has $\{\epsilon\}$ as identity element. The left-interleave operator is not commutative nor associative, but has the interesting property that $(X \%\!> Y) \%\!> Z$ is equal to $X \%\!> (Y <\!\%\!> Z)$.

Atomicity. Interleaving assumes that there exist atomic steps, and we introduce a construct to introduce atomic blocks within sentences. In such a block, no interleaving should occur with other sentences. We write $\langle x \rangle$ to make sequence x atomic: if x is a singleton, the angle brackets may be dropped. Atomicity obeys some simple laws:

$$\langle \epsilon \rangle = \epsilon \qquad \text{(the empty sequence is atomic)}$$
$$\langle a \rangle = a \qquad \text{(all primitive symbols are atomic)}$$
$$\langle x \langle y \rangle z \rangle = \langle xyz \rangle \qquad \text{(nesting of atomic blocks has no effect)}$$

In particular, it follows that $\langle \langle x \rangle \rangle = \langle x \rangle$. Atomic blocks nicely work together with the definitions given for the interleaving operators, including the lifted operators: sentences now consist of a sequence of atomic blocks, where each block itself is a non-empty sequence of symbols. For instance, $a \langle bc \rangle <\!\%\!> \langle de \rangle f$ will return:

$$\{abcdef, adebcf, adefbc, deabcf, deafbc, defabc\}$$

In the end, when no more interleaving takes place, the blocks have no longer any meaning, and can be discarded.

The interleaving operators. The semantics of the interleaving operators is defined in terms of the lifted operators:

$$\mathcal{L}(\langle s \rangle) = \{\langle x \rangle \mid x \in \mathcal{L}(s)\}$$
$$\mathcal{L}(s <\!\%\!> t) = \mathcal{L}(s) <\!\%\!> \mathcal{L}(t)$$
$$\mathcal{L}(s \%\!> t) = \mathcal{L}(s) \%\!> \mathcal{L}(t)$$

The interleave combinator satisfies several laws: it is commutative and associative, and has *succeed* as identity element:

$$
\begin{aligned}
s <\!\%\!> t &= t <\!\%\!> s \\
s <\!\%\!> (t <\!\%\!> u) &= (s <\!\%\!> t) <\!\%\!> u \\
s <\!\%\!> succeed &= s
\end{aligned}
$$

Because interleaving distributes over choice

$$
s <\!\%\!> (t <\!|\!> u) \;=\; (s <\!\%\!> t) <\!|\!> (s <\!\%\!> u)
$$

we have a second semi-ring. Also left-interleave distributes over choice. The operator that makes a strategy atomic is idempotent, and distributes over choice $\langle s <\!|\!> t \rangle = \langle s \rangle <\!|\!> \langle t \rangle$. Many more properties can be found in the literature on ACP [Bergstra and Klop, 1985].

6.5   Label

When developing a program, a student may ask for a hint at any time. Of course, the tutor should take the actions of the student until he asks for a hint into account. We mark positions in the strategy with a *label*, which allows us to describe feedback. The *label* combinator takes a string (or a value of another type that is used for labelling purposes) and a strategy as arguments, and offers the possibility to attach a text to the argument strategy.

$$
\mathcal{L} \; (label \; \ell \; s) \;=\; \{ \text{ENTER}_\ell \; x \; \text{EXIT}_\ell \mid x \in \mathcal{L} \; (s) \}
$$

This interpretation introduces the special rules ENTER and EXIT (parameterised by some label ℓ) that show up in sentences. These rules are minor rules that are only used for tracing positions in strategies. Except for tracing, the label combinator is semantically the identity function.

6.6   Recursion

One aspect we haven't discussed yet is recursion. Recursion is used for example to specify that a user replaces *all* occurrences of a particular expression in a program by another expression. Recursion is specified by means of the fixed-point operator *fix*, which takes as argument a function that maps a strategy to a new strategy. The language of *fix* is defined by:

$$
\mathcal{L} \; (fix \, f) \;=\; \mathcal{L} \; (f \; (fix \, f))
$$

The *fix* operator is mainly used in traversals over the abstract syntax tree. It is the responsibility of the user to specify meaningful fixed-points. In our recogniser for the strategy language we specify a cutoff for the fixed-point operator.

6.7   Overview

We list the components of our strategy language introduced in the previous subsection in the following definition.

A strategy is an element of the language of the following grammar:

$$
\begin{array}{lll}
s ::= & r & \\
 | & s <|> s \quad | \quad \textit{fail} & \\
 | & s <*> s \quad | \quad \textit{succeed} & \\
 | & \textit{label } \ell \, s & \\
 | & \textit{fix } f & \\
 | & \langle s \rangle \quad | \quad s <\%> s \quad | \quad s \%> s &
\end{array}
$$

where r is a rewrite rule or a refinement rule, ℓ is a label, and f is a function that takes a strategy as argument, and returns a strategy.

The language of a strategy is defined by:

$$
\begin{array}{lll}
\mathcal{L}\,(r) & = & \{r\} \\
\mathcal{L}\,(s <|> t) & = & \mathcal{L}\,(s) \cup \mathcal{L}\,(t) \\
\mathcal{L}\,(\textit{fail}) & = & \varnothing \\
\mathcal{L}\,(s <*> t) & = & \{xy \mid x \in \mathcal{L}\,(s), y \in \mathcal{L}\,(t)\} \\
\mathcal{L}\,(\textit{succeed}) & = & \{\epsilon\} \\
\mathcal{L}\,(\textit{label } \ell \, s) & = & \{\text{ENTER}_\ell \, x \, \text{EXIT}_\ell \mid x \in \mathcal{L}\,(s)\} \\
\mathcal{L}\,(\textit{fix } f) & = & \mathcal{L}\,(f\,(\textit{fix } f)) \\
\mathcal{L}\,(\langle s \rangle) & = & \{\langle x \rangle \mid x \in \mathcal{L}\,(s)\} \\
\mathcal{L}\,(s_1 <\%> s_2) & = & \mathcal{L}\,(s_1) <\%> \mathcal{L}\,(s_2) \\
\mathcal{L}\,(s_1 \%> s_2) & = & \mathcal{L}\,(s_1) \%> \mathcal{L}\,(s_2)
\end{array}
$$

This definition can be used to tell whether a sequence of rules follows a strategy or not: the sequence of rules should be a sentence in the language generated by the strategy, or a prefix of a sentence, since we solve exercises incrementally. Not all sequences make sense, however. An exercise gives us an initial term (say t_0), and we are only interested in sequences of rules that can be applied successively to this term. Suppose that we have terms (denoted by t_i) and rules (denoted by r_i), and let t_{i+1} be the result of applying rule r_i to term t_i by means of function *apply*. Function *apply* takes a refinement or a rewrite rule and a term, tries to unify the term with the left-hand side of the rule, and, if it succeeds, applies the substitution obtained from unification to the right-hand side of the rule to obtain the rewritten or refined rule. A possible derivation that starts with t_0 can be depicted in the following way:

$$
t_0 \xrightarrow{r_0} t_1 \xrightarrow{r_1} t_2 \xrightarrow{r_2} t_3 \xrightarrow{r_3} \ldots
$$

To be precise, applying a rule to a term can yield multiple results, but most domain rules, such as the refinement rules for functional programs in Figure 3, return at most one term. Running a strategy with an initial term returns a set of terms, and is specified by:

$$run\ s\ t_0 = \{t_{n+1} \mid r_0 .. r_n \in \mathcal{L}\ (s), \forall_{i \in 0...n} : t_{i+1} \in apply\ r_i\ t_i\}$$

Recognising a strategy amounts to tracing the steps that a student takes, but how does a tutor get the sequence of rules? In a tutor that offers free input, such as our functional programming tutor, students submit intermediate terms. Therefore, the tutor first has to determine which of the known rules has been applied, or even which combination of rules has been used. Discovering which (sequence of) rule(s) has been used is obviously an important part of a tutor, and it influences the quality of the generated feedback. It is, however, not the topic of these notes, more information can be found in Gerdes et al. [2012]. An alternative to free input is to let students select a rule, which is then applied automatically to the current term. In this setup, it is no longer a problem to detect which rule has been used.

6.8   Applications of Strategies in Other Domains

Using our strategy language we can specify strategies for an arbitrary domain in which procedures are expressed in terms of rewriting and refinement rules. In this subsection we introduce two examples not related to the domain of functional programming in which we use our strategy language. The first example shows a general pattern that occurs in many different domains, the second example describes a procedure for calculating with fractions.

Example 1. Repetition, zero or more occurrences of something, is a well-known recursion pattern. We can define this pattern using our fixed point recursion combinator:

$$many\ s = fix\ (\lambda x \rightarrow succeed <\!|\!> (s <\!\ast\!> x))$$

The strategy that applies transformation rule r zero or more times would thus be:

$$
\begin{aligned}
&many\ r \\
&= succeed <\!|\!> (r <\!\ast\!> many\ r) \\
&= succeed <\!|\!> (r <\!\ast\!> (succeed <\!|\!> (r <\!\ast\!> many\ r))) \\
&= \dots
\end{aligned}
$$

Example 2. Consider the problem of adding two fractions, for example, $\frac{2}{5}$ and $\frac{2}{3}$: if the result is an improper fraction (the numerator is larger than or equal to the denominator), then it should be converted to a mixed number. Figure 4 displays four rewrite rules on fractions. The three rules at the right (B1 to B3) are buggy rules that capture common mistakes. A possible strategy to solve this type of exercise is the following:

  − *Step 1.* Find the least common denominator (LCD) of the fractions: let this be n

Rules

ADD:
$$\frac{a}{c} + \frac{b}{c} = \frac{a+b}{c}$$

MUL:
$$\frac{a}{b} \times \frac{c}{d} = \frac{a \times c}{b \times d}$$

RENAME:
$$\frac{b}{c} = \frac{a \times b}{a \times c}$$

SIMPL:
$$\frac{a+b}{b} = 1 + \frac{a}{b}$$

Buggy rules

B1:
$$\frac{a}{b} + \frac{c}{d} \neq \frac{a+c}{b+d}$$

B2:
$$a \times \frac{b}{c} \neq \frac{a \times b}{a \times c}$$

B3:
$$a + \frac{b}{c} \neq \frac{a+b}{c}$$

Fig. 4. Rules and buggy rules for fractions

- *Step 2.* Rename the fractions such that n is the denominator
- *Step 3.* Add the fractions by adding the numerators
- *Step 4.* Simplify the fraction if it is improper

We use the strategy combinators to turn this informal strategy description into a strategy specification:

$$addFractions = label\ \ell_0 \quad (\quad label\ \ell_1\ \text{LCD}$$
$$\texttt{<*>}\ label\ \ell_2\ (repeat\ (somewhere\ \text{RENAME}))$$
$$\texttt{<*>}\ label\ \ell_3\ \text{ADD}$$
$$\texttt{<*>}\ label\ \ell_4\ (try\ \text{SIMPL})$$
$$)$$

The strategy contains the labels ℓ_0 to ℓ_4, and uses the transformation rules given in Figure 4. The transformation LCD is somewhat different: it is a minor rule that does not change the term, but calculates the least common denominator and stores this in an environment. The rule RENAME for renaming a fraction uses the computed lcd to determine the value of a in its right-hand side.

The definition of *addFractions* uses the strategy combinators *repeat*, *try*, and *somewhere*. In an earlier paper [Heeren et al., 2008], we discussed how these combinators, and many others, can be defined conveniently in terms of the strategy language. The combinator *repeat* is a variant of the *many* combinator: it applies its argument strategy exhaustively. The check that the strategy can no longer be applied is a minor rule. The *try* combinator takes a strategy as argument, and tries to apply it. If the strategy cannot be applied, it succeeds.

The combinator *somewhere* changes the focus in an abstract syntax tree by means of one or more minor navigation rules, before it applies its argument strategy. The navigation rules are inspired by the operations on the zipper data structure [Huet, 1997]. These rules, usually called DOWN (go to the left-most child), RIGHT, LEFT, and UP, are used to navigate to a point of focus. Until now we have used holes to denote locations in terms, instead of a zipper. Using navigation rules and the zipper in the functional programming domain is less convenient. Whereas the strategy for adding fractions given above applies to any fraction, so that we do not know up front where our rules will be applied, our functional programming strategies describe the construction of a particular functional program, and recognise the construction of alternative versions. A strategy for a functional program describes exactly where all substrategies should be applied. For example, for the strategy for *reverse*, only the second argument to *foldl* should be refined to the empty list [ ]. This refinement is not applied bottom-up or somewhere: it is exactly applied at the location of the second argument of *foldl*. We could have specified this location by means of navigation rules, in which case we would have obtained a strategy for *reverse* consisting of amongst others:

$$
\begin{array}{ll}
\ldots & \textit{foldlS} \\
& <\!\!*\!\!> \text{ Down} \\
& <\!\!*\!\!> (\textit{flipS consS}) \\
& <\!\!*\!\!> \text{ Right} \\
& <\!\!*\!\!> \textit{nilS} \\
& <\!\!*\!\!> \text{ Up}
\end{array}
$$

and similarly for all other strategies. Since this information can be inferred automatically, as explained in Section 5, we use holes to denote locations in the functional programming domain.

6.9   Restrictions

To use strategies for tracking student behaviour and give feedback, we impose some restrictions on the form of strategies. These restrictions are similar to some of the restrictions imposed by parsing algorithms on context-free grammars.

Left-recursion. A context-free grammar is left-recursive if it contains a nonterminal that can be rewritten in one or more steps using the productions of the grammar to a sequence of symbols that starts with the same nonterminal. The same definition applies to strategies. For example, the following strategy is left-recursive:

$$\textit{leftRecursive} = \textit{fix } (\lambda x \rightarrow x <\!\!*\!\!> \text{ADD})$$

The left-recursion is obvious in this strategy, since x is in the leftmost position in the body of the abstraction. Left-recursion is not always this easy to spot. Strategies with leading minor rules may or may not be left-recursive. Strictly speaking, these strategies are not left-recursive because the strategy grammar does not differentiate between minor and major rules. However, in our semantics these strategies sometimes display left-recursive behaviour. For example, if we use a minor rule that increases a counter in the environment, which is an action that always succeeds, the strategy is left-recursive. On the other hand, in *leftRecursive'*:

$$\textit{leftRecursive'} = \textit{fix } (\lambda x \rightarrow \text{DOWN} <\!\!*\!\!> x <\!\!*\!\!> \text{ADD})$$

the minor rule DOWN is applied repeatedly until we reach the leaf of an expression tree, and stop. This strategy is not left-recursive. However, this is caused by a property of DOWN that is not shared by all other minor rules.

We use top-down recursive parsing to track student behaviour and give feedback, because we want to support the top-down, incremental construction of derivations (programs, but also derivations for other exercises). However, top-down recursive parsing using a left-recursive context-free grammar is difficult. A grammar expressed in parser combinators [Hutton, 1992] is not allowed to be left-recursive. Similarly, for a strategy to be used in our domain reasoner, it should not be left-recursive. In particular, trying to determine the next possible symbol(s) of a left-recursive strategy will loop. This problem would probably disappear if we would use a bottom-up parsing algorithm, but that would lead to other restrictions, which sometimes are harder to spot and repair (compare determining whether or not a grammar is LR(1) with determining whether or not a grammar is left-recursive). Left-recursion can sometimes be solved by using so-called chain combinators [Fokker, 1995].

Left-recursive strategies are not the only source of non-terminating strategy calculations. The fact that our strategy language has a fixed-point combinator (and hence recursion) implies that we are vulnerable to non-termination. The implementation of our strategy language has been augmented with a 'time-out' that stops the execution of a strategy when a threshold is reached, and reports an error message.

Left-factoring. Left-factoring is a grammar transformation that is useful when two productions for the same nonterminal start with the same sequence of terminal and/or nonterminal symbols. This transformation factors out the common part, called left-factor, of such productions. In a strategy, the equivalent transformation factors out common sequences of rewrite rules from substrategies separated by the choice combinator.

At the moment, a strategy that contains left-factors may lead to problems. Consider the following, somewhat contrived, strategy:

$$leftFactor \;=\; label\; \ell_1 \;(\text{ADD} <\!\!*\!\!> \text{SIMPL})$$
$$<\!|>\; label\; \ell_2 \;(\text{ADD} <\!\!*\!\!> \text{RENAME})$$

The two sub-strategies labelled ℓ_1 and ℓ_2 have a left-factor: the rewrite rule ADD. After the application of ADD, we have to decide which sub-strategy to follow. Either we follow sub-strategy ℓ_1, or we follow sub-strategy ℓ_2. Committing to a choice after recognising that ADD has been applied is unfortunate, since it will force the student to follow the same sub-strategy. For example, if ℓ_1 is chosen after a student applies ADD, and a student subsequently performs the RENAME step, we erroneously report that that step does not follow the strategy. Left-factoring a strategy is essential to not commit early to a particular sub-strategy. The example strategy is left-factored as follows:

$$leftFactor' \;=\; \text{ADD} <\!\!*\!\!> (\text{SIMPL} <\!|> \text{RENAME})$$

It is clear how to left-factor (major) rewrite rules, but how should we deal with labels, or minor rules in general? Pushing labels inside the choice combinator,

$$leftFactor'' = \text{ADD} <\!*\!> (label\ \ell_1\ \text{SIMPL} <\!|\!> label\ \ell_2\ \text{RENAME})$$

or making a choice between the two labels breaks the relation between the label and the strategy. Labels are used to mark positions in a strategy, and have corresponding feedback text, which very likely becomes inaccurate if labels are moved automatically.

At the moment we require strategies to be left-factored, so that we can decide which production to take based on the next input symbol, as in LL(1) grammars. However, this is very undesirable, since it makes it hard if not impossible to generate functional programming strategies from model solutions. We intend to use parallel top-down recursive parsing techniques to solve this problem. If we encounter a left-factor, i.e., the *firsts* set contains duplicates, we fork the parser into two or more parsers, depending on the number of duplicates, that run in parallel. Whenever a parsing branch fails, it is discarded. We have started implementing this approach, and the first results indicate that it is indeed possible to solve this problem [Gerdes et al., 2012].

7   Design of a Strategy Recogniser

The function *run*, defined in the previous section, specifies how to run a strategy. For this, it enumerates all sentences in the language of a strategy, and then applies the rules in such a sentence in sequence, starting with some initial term. Enumerating all sentences does not result in an efficient implementation because the number of sentences quickly becomes too large, making this approach infeasible in practice. Often, the language of a strategy is an infinite set. In our domain reasoners we take a different, more efficient approach to recognise student steps against a strategy definition. In this section we discuss the design of such a strategy recogniser.

Instead of designing our own recogniser, we could reuse existing parsing libraries and tools. There are many excellent parser generators and various parser combinator libraries around [Hutton, 1992, Swierstra and Duponcheel, 1996], and these are often highly optimised and efficient in both their time and space behaviour. However, the problem we are facing is quite different from other parsing applications. To start with, efficiency is not a key concern as long as we do not have to enumerate all sentences. Because we are recognising applications of rewrite or refinement rules applied by a student, the length of the input is very limited. Our experience until now is that speed poses no serious constraints on the design of the library. A second difference is that we are not building an abstract syntax tree.

The following issues are important for a strategy recogniser, but are not (sufficiently) addressed in traditional parsing libraries:

1. We are only interested in sequences of transformation rules that can be applied successively to some initial term, and this is hard to express in most

libraries. Parsing approaches that start by analysing the grammar for constructing a parsing table will not work in our setting because they cannot take the current term into account.

2. The ability to diagnose errors in the input highly influences the quality of the feedback services. It is not enough to detect that the input is incorrect, but we also want to know at which point the input deviates from the strategy, and what is expected at this point. Some of the more advanced parser tools have error correcting facilities, which helps diagnosing an error to some extent.

3. Exercises are solved incrementally, and therefore we do not only have to recognise full sentences, but also prefixes. We cannot use backtracking and look-ahead because we want to recognise strategies at each intermediate step. If we would use backtracking, we might give a hint that does not lead to a solution, which is very undesirable in learning environments.

4. Labels help to describe the structure of a strategy in the same way as nonterminals do in a grammar. For a good diagnosis it is vital that a recogniser knows at each intermediate step where it is in the strategy.

5. Current parsing libraries do not offer parser combinators for interleaving parsers, except for a (rather involved) extension implemented by Doaitse Swierstra on top of his parser combinator library [Swierstra, 2009].

6. A strategy should be serialisable, for instance because we want to communicate with other on-line tools and environments.

In earlier attempts to design a recogniser library for strategies, we tried to reuse an existing error-correcting parser combinator library [Swierstra and Duponcheel, 1996], but failed because (some) of the reasons listed above.

7.1 Representing Grammars

Because strategies are grammars, we start by exploring a suitable representation for grammars. The datatype for grammars is based on the alternatives of the strategy language discussed in Section 6, except that there is no constructor for labels.

```
data Grammar a = Symbol a
               | Succeed
               | Fail
               | Grammar a   :|:   Grammar a
               | Grammar a   :*:   Grammar a
               | Grammar a   :%:  Grammar a
               | Grammar a   :%>: Grammar a
               | Atomic (Grammar a)
               | Rec Int (Grammar a)   -- recursion point
               | Var Int               -- bound by corresponding Rec
```

The type variable a in this definition is an abstraction for the type of symbols: for strategies, the symbols are rules, but also ENTER and EXIT steps that are associated with a label. For now we will postpone the discussion on labels in grammars.

Another design choice is how to represent recursive grammars, for which we use the constructors *Rec* and *Var*. A *Rec* binds all the *Vars* in its scope that have the same integer. We assume that all our grammars are closed, i.e., there are no free occurrences of variables. This datatype makes it easy to manipulate and analyse grammars. Alternative representations for recursion are higher-order fixed point functions, or nameless terms using De Bruijn indices.

We use constructors such as $:*:$ and $:|:$ for sequence and choice, respectively, instead of the combinators $<*>$ and $<|>$ introduced earlier. Haskell infix constructors have to start with a colon, but the real motivation is that we use $<*>$ and $<|>$ as *smart constructors* later.

Example 3. The repetition combinator *many*, which we defined in Example 1, can be encoded with the *Grammar* datatype in the following way:

> *many* :: *Grammar a* → *Grammar a*
> *many s* = *Rec* 0 (*Succeed* :|: (*s* :*: *Var* 0))

Later we will see that the smart constructors are more convenient for writing such a combinator.

7.2   Empty and Firsts

We use the functions *empty* and *firsts* to recognise sentences. The function *empty* tests whether the empty sentence is part of the language: *empty* $(s) = \epsilon \in \mathcal{L}(s)$. The direct translation of this specification of *empty* to a functional program, using the definition of language $\mathcal{L}$, gives a very inefficient program. Instead, we derive the following recursive function from this characterisation, by performing case analysis on strategies:

> *empty* :: *Grammar a* → *Bool*
> *empty* (*Symbol a*) = *False*
> *empty Succeed*   = *True*
> *empty Fail*   = *False*
> *empty* (*s* :|: *t*)   = *empty s* ∨ *empty t*
> *empty* (*s* :*: *t*)   = *empty s* ∧ *empty t*
> *empty* (*s* :%: *t*)   = *empty s* ∧ *empty t*
> *empty* (*s* :%>: *t*) = *False*
> *empty* (*Atomic s*) = *empty s*
> *empty* (*Rec i s*)   = *empty s*
> *empty* (*Var i*)   = *False*

The left-interleave operator expresses that the first symbol is taken from its left-hand side operand. Hence, such a strategy cannot yield the empty sentence. The definition for the pattern *Rec i s* may come as a surprise: it calls *empty* recursively on *s* without changing the *Vars* that are bound by this *Rec*. We define *empty* (*Var i*) to be *False*. Note that there is no need to inspect recursive occurrences to determine the empty property for a strategy.

Given some strategy s, the function *firsts* returns every symbol that can start a sentence for s, paired with a strategy that represents the remainder of that sentence. This is made more precise in the following property (where a represents a symbol, and x a sequence of symbols):

$$\forall a, x : ax \in \mathcal{L}\ (s) \Leftrightarrow \exists s' : (a, s') \in \textit{firsts}\ (s) \wedge x \in \mathcal{L}\ (s')$$

As for the function *empty*, the direct translation of this specification into a functional program is infeasible. We again derive an efficient implementation for *firsts* by performing a case analysis on strategies.

Defining *firsts* for the two interleaving cases is somewhat challenging: this is exactly where we must deal with interleaving and atomicity. More specifically, we cannot easily determine the firsts for strategy $s\ \%{>}\ t$ based on the firsts for s and t (i.e., in a compositional way) since that would require more information about the atomic blocks in s and t. For a strategy $s\ \%{>}\ t$, we split s into an atomic part and a remainder, say *Atomic* $s'\ \langle\!*\!\rangle\ s''$. After s' without the empty sentence, we can continue with $s''\ \langle\%{>}\ t$. This approach is summarised by the following property, where the use of symbol a takes care of the non-empty condition:

$$((\langle a \mathrel{\langle\!*\!\rangle} s\rangle \mathrel{\langle\!*\!\rangle} t)\ \%{>}\ u = \langle a \mathrel{\langle\!*\!\rangle} s\rangle \mathrel{\langle\!*\!\rangle} (t \mathrel{\langle\%{>}} u)$$

The function *split* transforms a strategy into triples of the form (a, x, y), which should be interpreted as $\langle a \mathrel{\langle\!*\!\rangle} x\rangle \mathrel{\langle\!*\!\rangle} y$. We define *split* for each case of the *Grammar* datatype.

```
split :: Grammar a → [(a, Grammar a, Grammar a)]
split (Symbol a)  = [(a, Succeed, Succeed)]
split Succeed     = []
split Fail        = []
split (s :|: t)   = split s ++ split t
split (s :*: t)   = [(a, x, y :*: t) | (a, x, y) ← split s] ++
                      if empty s then split t else []
split (s :%: t)   = split (s :%>: t) ++ split (t :%>: s)
split (s :%>: t)  = [(a, x, y :%: t) | (a, x, y) ← split s]
split (Atomic s)  = [(a, x :*: y, Succeed) | (a, x, y) ← split s]
split (Rec i s)   = split (replaceVar i (Rec i s) s)
split (Var i)     = error "unbound Var"
```

For a sequence $s :*: t$, we determine which symbols can appear first for s, and we change the results to reflect that t is part of the remaining grammar. Furthermore, if s can be empty, then we also have to look at the *firsts* for t. For choices, we simply combine the results for both operands. If the grammar is a single symbol, then this symbol appears first, and the remaining parts are *Succeed* (we are done). To find the *firsts* for *Rec i s*, we have to look inside the body s. All occurrences of this recursion point are replaced by the grammar itself before we call *split* again. The replacement is performed by a helper-function: *replaceVar i s t* replaces all free occurrences of *Var i* in t by s. Hence, if we encounter a *Var*, it is unbound, which we do not allow. Recall that we assume our grammars to be closed.

We briefly discuss the definitions for the constructs related to interleaving, and argue why they are correct:

- *Case (Atomic s)*.   Because atomicity distributes over choice, we can consider the elements of *split s* (the recursive call) one by one. The transformation

$$\langle\langle a <\!\!*\!\!> x\rangle <\!\!*\!\!> y\rangle \;=\; \langle a <\!\!*\!\!> (x <\!\!*\!\!> y)\rangle <\!\!*\!\!> succeed$$

  is proven by first removing the inner atomic block, and basic properties of sequence.
- *Case (s₁ :%: s₂)*.   Expressing this strategy in terms of left-interleave is justified by the definition of $\mathcal{L}$ $(s_1 <\!\%\!> s_2)$. For function *split*, we only have to consider the non-empty sentences.
- *Case (s₁ :%>: s₂)*.   Left-interleave can be distributed over the alternatives. Furthermore, $(\langle a <\!\!*\!\!> x\rangle <\!\!*\!\!> y) \%\!> t = \langle a <\!\!*\!\!> x\rangle <\!\!*\!\!> (y <\!\%\!> t)$ follows from the definition of left-interleave on sentences (with atomic blocks).

With the function *split*, we can now define the function *firsts*, which is needed for most of our feedback services:

$$firsts :: Grammar\ a \rightarrow [\,(a, Grammar\ a)\,]$$
$$firsts\ s = [\,(a, x \;\text{:*:}\; y) \mid (a, x, y) \leftarrow split\ s\,]$$

In Section 6.9 we discussed restrictions that are imposed on strategies. It should now be clear from the definition of *firsts* why left-recursion is problematic. For example, consider the *many* combinator. A strategy writer has to use this combinator with great care to avoid constructing a left-recursive grammar: if grammar *s* accepts the empty sentence, then running the grammar *many s* can result in non-termination. The problem with left recursion can be partially circumvented by restricting the number of recursion points (*Recs* and *Vars*) that are unfolded in the definition of *split* (*Rec i s*).

7.3   Dealing with Labels

The *Grammar* datatype lacks an alternative for labels. Nevertheless, we can use label information to trace where we are in the strategy by inserting ENTER and EXIT steps for each labelled substrategy. These labels enable us to attach specialised feedback messages to certain locations in the strategy.

The sentences of the language generated for a strategy contain rules, ENTER steps, and EXIT steps, for which we introduce the following datatype:

data *Step l a = Enter l | Step (Rule a) | Exit l*

The type argument *l* represents the type of information associated with each label. For our strategies we assume that this information is only a string. The type *Rule* is parameterised by the type of values on which the rule can be applied. With the *Step* datatype, we can now specify a type for strategies:

```
type LabelInfo  = String
data Strategy a = S { unS :: Grammar (Step LabelInfo a) }
```

The *Strategy* datatype wraps a grammar, where the symbols of this grammar are steps. The following function helps to construct a strategy out of a single step:

```
fromStep :: Step LabelInfo a → Strategy a
fromStep = S ∘ Symbol
```

The (un)wrapping of strategies quickly becomes cumbersome when defining functions over strategies. We therefore introduce a type class for type constructors that can be converted into a *Strategy*:

```
class IsStrategy f where
   toStrategy :: f a → Strategy a
instance IsStrategy Rule where
   toStrategy = fromStep ∘ Step
instance IsStrategy Strategy where
   toStrategy = id
```

In addition to the *Strategy* datatype, we define the *LabeledStrategy* type for strategies that have a label. A labelled strategy can be turned into a (normal) strategy by surrounding its strategy with *Enter* and *Exit* steps.

```
data LabeledStrategy a = Label { labelInfo :: LabelInfo, unlabel :: Strategy a }
instance IsStrategy LabeledStrategy where
   toStrategy (Label a s) = fromStep (Enter a) <*> s <*> fromStep (Exit a)
```

In the next section we present smart constructors for strategies, including the strategy combinator <*> for sequences used twice in the instance declaration for *LabeledStrategy*.

7.4   Smart Constructors

A smart constructor is a function that in addition to constructing a value performs some checks, simplifications, or conversions. We use smart constructors for simplifying grammars. We introduce a smart constructor for every alternative of the strategy language given in Section 6.7. Definitions for *succeed* and *fail* are straightforward, and are given for consistency:

```
succeed, fail :: Strategy a
succeed = S Succeed
fail    = S Fail
```

The general approach is that we use the *IsStrategy* type class to automatically turn the subcomponents of a combinator into a strategy. As a result, we do not need a strategy constructor for rules, because *Rule* was made an instance of the

IsStrategy type class. It is the context that will turn the rule into a strategy, if required. This approach is illustrated by the definition of the *label* constructor, which is overloaded in its second argument:

$$label :: IsStrategy\ f \Rightarrow LabelInfo \to f\ a \to LabeledStrategy\ a$$
$$label\ s = Label\ s \circ toStrategy$$

All other constructors return a value of type *Strategy*, and overload their strategy arguments. We define helper-functions for lifting unary and binary constructors (*lift1* and *lift2*, respectively). These lift functions turn a function that works on the *Grammar* datatype into an overloaded function that returns a strategy.

```
-- Lift a unary/binary function on grammars to one on strategies
lift1 op = S     ∘ op ∘ unS ∘ toStrategy
lift2 op = lift1 ∘ op ∘ unS ∘ toStrategy
```

For choices, we remove occurrences of *Fail*, and we associate the alternatives to the right.

```
(<|>) :: (IsStrategy f, IsStrategy g) ⇒ f a → g a → Strategy a
(<|>) = lift2 op
  where
    op :: Grammar a → Grammar a → Grammar a
    op Fail    t    = t
    op s       Fail = s
    op (s :|: t) u  = s 'op' (t 'op' u)
    op s       t    = s :|: t
```

The smart constructor <∗> for sequences removes the unit element *Succeed*, and propagates the absorbing element *Fail*.

```
(<∗>) :: (IsStrategy f, IsStrategy g) ⇒ f a → g a → Strategy a
(<∗>) = lift2 op
  where
    op :: Grammar a → Grammar a → Grammar a
    op Succeed t       = t
    op s       Succeed = s
    op Fail    _       = Fail
    op _       Fail    = Fail
    op (s :∗: t) u     = s 'op' (t 'op' u)
    op s       t       = s :∗: t
```

The binary combinators for interleaving, <%> and %>, are defined in a similar fashion. The smart constructor *atomic*, which was denoted by ⟨·⟩ in Section 6, takes only one argument. It is defined in the following way:

$$atomic :: IsStrategy\ f \Rightarrow f\ a \to Strategy\ a$$
$$atomic = lift1\ op$$

where

$$op :: Grammar\ a \rightarrow Grammar\ a$$
$$op\ (Symbol\ a) = Symbol\ a$$
$$op\ Succeed\quad = Succeed$$
$$op\ Fail\quad\quad = Fail$$
$$op\ (Atomic\ s) = op\ s$$
$$op\ (s :\!\!\mid: t)\quad\ = op\ s :\!\!\mid: op\ t$$
$$op\ s\quad\quad\ \ = Atomic\ s$$

This definition is based on several properties of atomicity, such as idempotence and distributivity over choice.

The last combinator we present is for recursion. Internally we use numbered *Recs* and *Vars* in our *Grammar* datatype, but for the strategy writer it is much more convenient to write the recursion as a fixed-point, without worrying about the numbering. For this reason we do not define direct counterparts for the *Rec* and *Var* constructors, but only the higher-order function *fix*. This combinator is defined as follows:

$$fix :: (Strategy\ a \rightarrow Strategy\ a) \rightarrow Strategy\ a$$
$$fix\ f = lift1\ (Rec\ i)\ (make\ i)$$
where
$$make = f \circ S \circ Var$$
$$is\quad = usedNumbers\ (unS\ (make\ 0))$$
$$i\quad\ = \textbf{if}\ null\ is\ \textbf{then}\ 0\ \textbf{else}\ maximum\ is + 1$$

The trick is that function f is applied twice. First, we pass f a strategy with the grammar *Var* 0, and we inspect which numbers are used (variable *is* of type $[Int]$). Based on this information, we can now determine the next number to use (variable i). We apply f for the second time using grammar *Var* i, and bind these *Vars* to the top-level *Rec*. Note that this approach does not work for fixed-point functions that inspect their argument.

Example 4. We return to Example 3, and define the repetition combinator *many* with the smart constructors. Observe that *many*'s argument is also overloaded because of the smart constructors.

$$many :: IsStrategy\ f \Rightarrow f\ a \rightarrow Strategy\ a$$
$$many\ s = fix\ \$\ \lambda x \rightarrow succeed <\!|\!> (s <\!\!*\!\!> x)$$

7.5   Running a Strategy

So far, nothing specific about recognising strategies has been discussed. A strategy is a grammar over rewrite rules and *Enter* and *Exit* steps for labels. We first define a type class with the method *apply*: this function was already used in the *run* method defined in Section 6.7. It returns a list of results. Given that rules can be applied, we also give an instance declaration for the *Step* datatype,

where the *Enter* and *Exit* steps simply return a singleton list with the current
term, i.e., they do not have an effect.

class *Apply f* **where**
  apply :: *f a* → *a* → [*a*]
instance *Apply Rule*   -- implementation provided in framework
instance *Apply* (*Step l*) **where**
  apply (*Step r*) = *apply r*
  apply _   = *return*

We can now give an implementation for running grammars with symbols in the
Apply type class (see Section 6.7 for *run*'s specification). The implementation is
based on the functions *empty* and *firsts*.

$$run :: Apply\ f \Rightarrow Grammar\ (f\ a) \rightarrow a \rightarrow [a]$$
$$run\ s\ a = [a\ |\ empty\ s] \mathbin{+\!\!+} [c\ |\ (f,t) \leftarrow firsts\ s, b \leftarrow apply\ f\ a, c \leftarrow run\ t\ b]$$

The list of results returned by *run* consists of two parts: the first part tests
whether *empty s* holds, and if so, it yields the singleton list containing the term
a. The second part takes care of the non-empty alternatives. Let *f* be one of the
symbols that can appear first in strategy *s*. We are only interested in *f* if it can
be applied to the current term *a*, yielding a new term *b*. We run the remainder
of the strategy (that is, *t*) on this new term.

Now that we have defined the function *run* we can also make *Strategy* and
LabeledStrategy instances of class *Apply*:

instance *Apply Strategy* **where**
  apply = *run* ∘ *unS*
instance *Apply LabeledStrategy* **where**
  apply = *apply* ∘ *toStrategy*

The function *run* can produce an infinite list. In most cases, however, we are
only interested in a single result (and rely on lazy evaluation). The part that
considers the empty sentence is put at the front to return sentences with few
rewrite rules early. Nonetheless, the definition returns results in a depth-first
manner. We define a variant of *run* which exposes breadth-first behaviour:

$$runBF :: Apply\ f \Rightarrow Grammar\ (f\ a) \rightarrow a \rightarrow [[a]]$$
$$runBF\ s\ a = [a\ |\ empty\ s] : merge\ [runBF\ t\ b\ |\ (f,t) \leftarrow firsts\ s, b \leftarrow apply\ f\ a]$$
  where *merge* = *map concat* ∘ *transpose*

The function *runBF* produces a list of lists: results are grouped by the number
of rewrite steps that have been applied, thus making explicit the breadth-first
nature of the function. The helper-function *merge* merges the results of the recursive calls: by transposing the list of results, we combine results with the same
number of steps.

7.6   Tracing a Strategy

The *run* functions defined in the previous section do nothing with the labels. However, if we want to recognise (intermediate) terms submitted by a student, and report an informative feedback message if the answer is incorrect, then labels become important. Fortunately, it is rather straightforward to extend *run*'s definition, and to keep a trace of the steps that have been applied:

$$runTrace :: Apply\ f \Rightarrow Grammar\ (f\ a) \rightarrow a \rightarrow [(a, [f\ a])]$$
$$runTrace\ s\ a =$$
$$[(a, [\ ])\ |\ empty\ s]\ +\!\!+$$
$$[(c, (f : fs))\ |\ (f, t) \leftarrow firsts\ s, b \leftarrow apply\ f\ a, (c, fs) \leftarrow runTrace\ t\ b]$$

In case of a strategy, we can thus obtain the list of *Enter* and *Exit* steps seen so far. We illustrate this by means of an example.

Example 5. We return to the strategy for adding two fractions (*addFractions*, defined in 6.8). Suppose that we run this strategy on the term $\frac{2}{5} + \frac{2}{3}$. This would give us the following derivation:

$$\frac{2}{5} + \frac{2}{3} = \frac{6}{15} + \frac{2}{3} = \frac{6}{15} + \frac{10}{15} = \frac{16}{15} = 1\frac{1}{15}$$

The final answer, $1\frac{1}{15}$, is indeed what we would expect. In fact, this result is returned twice because the strategy does not specify which of the fractions should be renamed first, and as a result we get two different derivations. It is much more informative to step through such a derivation and see the intermediate steps.

```
[  Enter ℓ₀,      Enter ℓ₁,       Step LCD,   Exit ℓ₁,      Enter ℓ₂
,  Step down₍₀₎,  Step RENAME,    Step up,    Step down₍₁₎, Step RENAME
,  Step up,       Step not,       Exit ℓ₂,    Enter ℓ₃,     Step ADD
,  Exit ℓ₃,       Enter ℓ₄,       Step SIMPL, Exit ℓ₄,      Exit ℓ₀
]
```

The list has twenty steps, but only four correspond to actual steps from the derivation: the rules of those steps are underlined. The other rules are administrative: the navigation rules *up* and *down* are introduced by the *somewhere* combinator, whereas *not* comes from the use of *repeat*. Also observe that each *Enter* step has a matching *Exit* step. In principle, a label can be visited multiple times by a strategy.

The example clearly shows that we determine at each point in the derivation where we are in the strategy by enumerating the *Enter* steps without their corresponding *Exit* step. Based on this information we can fine-tune the feedback messages that are reported when a student submits an incorrect answer, or when she asks for a hint on how to continue. For reporting textual messages, we use feedback scripts, which is explained in the next section.

7.7   Feedback Scripts

All textual messages are declared in so-called *feedback scripts*. These scripts are external text files containing appropriate responses for various situations. Depending on the diagnosis that was made (e.g., a common mistake was recognised, or the submitted term is correct and complies with the specified strategy), a feedback message is selected from the script and reported back to the student. One of the criteria on which this selection can be based is the current location in the strategy, i.e., one of the labels in the strategy. Other selection criteria are the name of the rule that was recognised (possibly a buggy rule), or the submitted term being correct or not.

For the functional programming tutor, we give three levels of hints, which can be categorised as follows [Vanlehn et al., 2005]:

- *general:* a general, high-level statement about the next step to take;
- *specific:* a more detailed explanation of the next step in words;
- *bottom-out:* the exact next step to carry out, possibly accompanied with some literal code.

The level of the message is another available selection criterion in the feedback scripts. All textual messages are assigned to one of these three levels.

Having only static texts in the feedback scripts (that is, texts that appear verbatim in the script) severely restricts the expressiveness of the messages that can be reported. We allow a variety of attributes in the textual messages of a script, and these attributes are replaced by dynamic content depending on the situation at hand. In this way, messages can for instance contain snippets of code from the original student program, or report on the number of steps remaining. Feedback scripts contain some more constructs to facilitate the writing of feedback messages, such as local string definitions and an import mechanism. These topics are work in progress, and lie outside the scope of these lecture notes.

An important advantage of external feedback scripts is that they can be changed easily, without recompiling the tutoring software. This approach also allows us to add feedback scripts that support new (programming) exercises. A final benefit is that the support of multiple languages (as opposed to only English) comes quite natural, since each supported language can have its own feedback script.

8   Conclusions, Related and Future Work

We have discussed the design and implementation of a tutoring system for functional programming. The distinguishing characteristics of our tutoring system are:

- it supports the incremental development of programs: students can submit incomplete programs and receive feedback and/or hints.
- it calculates feedback automatically based on model solutions to exercises. A teacher does not have to author feedback.

– correctness is based on provable equivalence to a model solution, based on normal forms of functional programs.

The tutoring system targets students at the starting academic, or possibly end high-school, level.

8.1 Related Work

If ever the computer science education research field [Fincher and Petre, 2004] finds an answer to the question of what makes programming hard, and how programming environments can support learning how to program, it is likely to depend on the age, interests, major subject, motivation, and background knowledge of a student. Programming environments for novices come in many variants, and for many programming languages or paradigms [Guzdial, 2004]. Programming environments like Scratch and Alice target younger students than we do, and emphasise the importance of constructing software with a strong visual component, with which students can develop software to which they can relate. We target beginning computer science students, who expect to work with real-life programming languages instead of 'toy' programming languages.

The Lisp tutor [Anderson et al., 1986] is an intelligent tutoring system that supports the incremental construction of Lisp programs. At any point in the development a student can only take a single next step, which makes the interaction style of the tutor a bit restrictive. Furthermore, adding new material to the tutor is still quite some work. Using our approach based on strategies, the interaction style becomes flexible, and adding exercises becomes relatively easy. Soloway [1985] describes programming plans for constructing Lisp programs. These plans are instances of the higher-order function *foldr* and its companions. Our work structures the strategies described by Soloway.

In tutoring systems for Prolog, a number of strategies for Prolog programming have been developed [Hong, 2004]. Hong also uses the *reverse* example to exemplify his approach to Prolog tutoring. Strategies are matched against complete student solutions, and feedback is given after solving the exercise. We expect that these strategies can be translated to our strategy language, and can be reused for a programming language like Haskell.

Our work resembles the top-down Pascal editors developed in the Genie project [Miller et al., 1994]. These series of editors provide structure editing support, so that student don't have to remember the particular syntax of a programming language. In our case students do have to write programs using the syntax of Haskell, but the intermediate steps are comparable. The Genie editors did not offer strategical support.

Our functional programming tutoring system grew out of a program assessment tool, which automatically assesses student programs based on model solutions [Gerdes et al., 2010] and program transformations to rewrite programs to normal form. Similar transformations have been developed for C++-like languages [Xu and Chee, 2003].

8.2   Future Work

The functional programming tutor grew out of our work on assessing functional programs, and on providing feedback, mainly in learning environments for mathematics. The version presented at this school is the first public release of our tutor. We still need to work on several aspects.

First of all, we want to use the tutor in several courses, to receive feedback from students and teachers. We will start with obtaining feedback about usability and appreciation. For example, do the refinement rules we offer correspond to the refinement rules applied by students? At a later stage, we want to study the learning effect of our tutor together with researchers from the domain of learning sciences.

The restriction that a student cannot proceed if an intermediate solution does not follow a model solution is rather severe. This disallows, for example, a bottom-up approach to developing a program, where first a component is developed, without specifying how the component is used in the final solution. We want to investigate if we can specify properties for a program, which are used to check that a student solution is not provably wrong. We can then let a student go on developing a program as long as the properties specified cannot be falsified. Once a student connects the developed components to the main program, strategy checking kicks in again to see if the program is equivalent to a model solution. This approach is orthogonal to our current approach: using our tutor we can ensure that a student solution is equivalent to a model solution, and hence correct. However, if a student does not implement a model solution, we don't know if the student is wrong. On the other hand, using property checking we can prove that a student solution is wrong, but the absence of property violations does not necessarily imply that the student program is correct. We would achieve a mixed approach if we determine the propagation of post-conditions to components in our rewrite rules, and verify that the composition of the rewrite rules performed by the student results in a proof that a specified post-condition holds for a given program. However, we would need to manually support a prover to construct the proof in many cases, which might not be desirable for beginning programmers.

Teachers prefer different solutions, and sometimes want students to use particular constructs when solving a programming exercise ('use *foldr* to implement a function to ...'). It is important to offer teachers the possibility to adapt the tutor. We see two ways in which teachers can adapt the tutor. First, additional equalities satisfied by a particular component of a model solution can be specified separately, and can then be used in the normal form calculation. Second, a teacher can annotate a model solution with 'switches' to enforce or switch off particular ways to solve a problem, or to change the order in which subproblems have to be solved. For example, a teacher may want to enforce usage of *foldr* instead of its explicit recursive alternative. Or a teacher may allow the interleaved development of the **then** and **else** branches of an **if-then-else** expression. We want to add these facilities to our tutoring system.

Developing a function is an important part of functional programming. But so are testing a function, describing its properties, abstracting from recurring patterns, etc. [Felleisen et al., 2002]. We want to investigate how much of the program design process can be usefully integrated in an intelligent tutoring system for functional programming.

Our approach is not bound to functional programming: we could use the same approach to develop tutoring systems for other programming languages or paradigms. We think that our programming tutor is *language generic*, and we want to investigate the possibilities for automatically generating large parts of a programming tutor, based on a (probably annotated) grammatical description.

Acknowledgements. Peter van de Werken contributed to a first version of the programming tutor described in these notes. An anonymous reviewer suggested many improvements to these notes.

References

Anderson, J.R., Conrad, F.G., Corbett, A.T.: Skill acquisition and the LISP tutor. Cognitive Science 13, 467–505 (1986)

Back, R.-J.: A calculus of refinements for program derivations. In: Reports on Computer Science and Mathematics 54. Åbo Akademi (1987)

Berger, U., Eberl, M., Schwichtenberg, H.: Normalization by Evaluation. In: Möller, B., Tucker, J.V. (eds.) Prospects for Hardware Foundations. LNCS, vol. 1546, pp. 117–137. Springer, Heidelberg (1998)

Bergstra, J.A., Klop, J.W.: Algebra of communicating processes with abstraction. Theoretical Computer Science 37, 77–121 (1985)

Bird, R.S.: An introduction to the theory of lists. In: Broy, M. (ed.) Logic of Programming and Calculi of Discrete Design. NATO ASI Series, vol. F36, pp. 5–42. Springer (1987)

Brown, J.S., Burton, R.R.: Diagnostic models for procedural bugs in basic mathematical skills. Cognitive Science 2, 155–192 (1978)

Bundy, A.: The Computer Modelling of Mathematical Reasoning. Academic Press (1983)

Dijkstra, E.W.: Guarded commands, nondeterminacy and formal derivation of programs. Commun. ACM 18, 453–457 (1975)

Felleisen, M., Findler, R.B., Flatt, M., Krishnamurthi, S.: How to design programs: an introduction to programming and computing. MIT Press, Cambridge (2002)

Filinski, A., Rohde, H.K.: A Denotational Account of Untyped Normalization by Evaluation. In: Walukiewicz, I. (ed.) FOSSACS 2004. LNCS, vol. 2987, pp. 167–181. Springer, Heidelberg (2004)

Fincher, S., Petre, M. (eds.): Computer Science Education Research. RoutledgeFalmer (2004)

Fokker, J.: Functional Parsers. In: Jeuring, J., Meijer, E. (eds.) AFP 1995. LNCS, vol. 925, pp. 1–23. Springer, Heidelberg (1995)

Fokkink, W.: Introduction to Process Algebra. Springer (2000) ISBN 354066579X

Gerdes, A., Heeren, B., Jeuring, J., Stuurman, S.: Feedback services for exercise assistants. In: Remenyi, D. (ed.) ECEL 2007: Proceedings of the 7th European Conference on e-Learning, pp. 402–410. Academic Publishing Limited (2008); Also available as Technical report Utrecht University UU-CS-2008-018

Gerdes, A., Jeuring, J., Heeren, B.: Using strategies for assessment of programming exercises. In: Lewandowski, G., Wolfman, S.A., Cortina, T.J., Walker, E.L. (eds.) SIGCSE, pp. 441–445. ACM (2010)

Gerdes, A., Jeuring, J., Heeren, B.: Teachers and students in charge — using annotated model solutions in a functional programming tutor. Technical report, Utrecht University, Department of Computer Science (to appear, 2012)

Guzdial, M.: Programming environments for novices. In: Fincher, S., Petre, M. (eds.) Computer Science Education Research. RoutledgeFalmer (2004)

Hattie, J., Timperley, H.: The power of feedback. Review of Educational Research 77(1), 81–112 (2007)

Heeren, B., Jeuring, J.: Recognizing strategies. In: Middeldorp, A. (ed.) WRS 2008: Reduction Strategies in Rewriting and Programming, 8th International Workshop (2008)

Heeren, B., Jeuring, J.: Canonical Forms in Interactive Exercise Assistants. In: Carette, J., Dixon, L., Coen, C.S., Watt, S.M. (eds.) Calculemus/MKM 2009. LNCS (LNAI), vol. 5625, pp. 325–340. Springer, Heidelberg (2009)

Heeren, B., Jeuring, J.: Adapting Mathematical Domain Reasoners. In: Autexier, S., Calmet, J., Delahaye, D., Ion, P.D.F., Rideau, L., Rioboo, R., Sexton, A.P. (eds.) AISC/Calculemus/MKM 2010. LNCS (LNAI), vol. 6167, pp. 315–330. Springer, Heidelberg (2010)

Heeren, B., Jeuring, J.: Interleaving Strategies. In: Davenport, J.H., Farmer, W.M., Urban, J., Rabe, F. (eds.) Calculemus/MKM 2011. LNCS (LNAI), vol. 6824, pp. 196–211. Springer, Heidelberg (2011)

Heeren, B., Leijen, D., van IJzendoorn, A.: Helium, for learning Haskell. In: Haskell 2003: Proceedings of the 2003 ACM SIGPLAN Workshop on Haskell, pp. 62–71. ACM (2003)

Heeren, B., Jeuring, J., van Leeuwen, A., Gerdes, A.: Specifying Strategies for Exercises. In: Autexier, S., Campbell, J., Rubio, J., Sorge, V., Suzuki, M., Wiedijk, F. (eds.) AISC/Calculemus/MKM 2008. LNCS (LNAI), vol. 5144, pp. 430–445. Springer, Heidelberg (2008)

Hoare, C.A.R.: An axiomatic basis for computer programming. Commun. ACM 12, 576–580 (1969)

Hoare, C.A.R.: Communicating sequential processes. Prentice-Hall, Inc. (1985) ISBN 0-13-153271-5

Hong, J.: Guided programming and automated error analysis in an intelligent Prolog tutor. International Journal on Human-Computer Studies 61(4), 505–534 (2004)

Huet, G.: Functional Pearl: The Zipper. Journal of Functional Programming 7(5), 549–554 (1997)

Hutton, G.: Higher-order Functions for Parsing. Journal of Functional Programming 2(3), 323–343 (1992)

Meertens, L.: Algorithmics — towards programming as a mathematical activity. In: Proceedings of the CWI Symposium on Mathematics and Computer Science. CWI Monographs, vol. 1, pp. 289–334. North-Holland (1986)

van Merriënboer, J.J.G., Paas, F.G.W.C.: Automation and schema acquisition in learning elementary computer programming: Implications for the design of practice. Computers in Human Behavior 6, 273–289 (1990)

Miller, P., Pane, J., Meter, G., Vorthmann, S.: Evolution of Novice Programming Environments: The Structure Editors of Carnegie Mellon University. Interactive Learning Environments 4(2), 140–158 (1994)

Morgan, C.: Programming from specifications. Prentice-Hall, Inc. (1990)

Jones, S.P., et al.: Haskell 98, Language and Libraries. The Revised Report. Cambridge University Press (2003); A special issue of the Journal of Functional Programming, http://www.haskell.org/

Soloway, E.: From problems to programs via plans: the content and structure of knowledge for introductory LISP programming. Journal of Educational Computing Research 1(2), 157–172 (1985)

Doaitse Swierstra, S., Duponcheel, L.: Deterministic, Error-correcting Combinator Parsers. In: Launchbury, J., Meijer, E., Sheard, T. (eds.) AFP 1996. LNCS, vol. 1129, pp. 184–207. Springer, Heidelberg (1996)

Doaitse Swierstra, S.: Combinator Parsing: A Short Tutorial. In: Bove, A., Barbosa, L.S., Pardo, A., Pinto, J.S. (eds.) Language Engineering and Rigorous Software Development. LNCS, vol. 5520, pp. 252–300. Springer, Heidelberg (2009)

VanLehn, K.: The behavior of tutoring systems. International Journal on Artificial Intelligence in Education 16(3), 227–265 (2006)

Vanlehn, K., Lynch, C., Schulze, K., Shapiro, J.A., Shelby, R., Taylor, L., Treacy, D., Weinstein, A., Wintersgill, M.: The andes physics tutoring system: Lessons learned. International Journal on Artificial Intelligence in Education 15, 147–204 (2005)

Xu, S., Chee, Y.S.: Transformation-based diagnosis of student programs for programming tutoring systems. IEEE Transactions on Software Engineering 29(4), 360–384 (2003)

Defining Multi-user Web Applications with iTasks

Rinus Plasmeijer, Peter Achten, Bas Lijnse, and Steffen Michels

Institute for Computing and Information Sciences
Radboud University Nijmegen, P.O. Box 9010, 6500 GL Nijmegen, The Netherlands
{rinus,p.achten,b.lijnse}@cs.ru.nl, s.michels@science.ru.nl

Abstract. In these lecture notes we explain how multi-user web applications can be developed in a programming style that favors *tasks* as main building block for the construction of such systems. A task is work that has to be performed by human-beings and computers working together on the internet. This concept has been implemented in the iTask framework as a monadic combinator library that is embedded in the pure and lazy functional programming language Clean. These lecture notes consist of many examples and exercises, and also discusses the foundation of both the iTask system and task-oriented programming.

1 Introduction

In these CEFP lecture notes we explain how multi-user web applications can be defined in the iTask system [16]. An iTask program is focussed on the notion of tasks: work that has to be performed by human-beings and computers working together on the internet. One describes the tasks people collaborating with each other using the internet have to do, and the resulting iTask application creates, coordinates and monitors the work accordingly.

Workflow Management Systems (WFMS) are also software systems intended to coordinate work (examples are Business Process Manager, COSA Workflow, FLOWer, i-Flow 6.0, Staffware, Websphere MQ Workflow, BPEL, and YAWL). The iTask system, however, is *not* a WFMS application, but a toolbox which can also be used to create WFMS applications. It distinguishes itself from traditional WFMSs in many ways:

- The iTask system is a monadic [22] combinator library in the pure and lazy functional programming language Clean. The constructed WFMS application is embedded in Clean where the combinators are used to define how tasks are composed. Tasks are defined by higher-order functions which are pure and self contained.
- Most WFMSs take a workflow description specified in a workflow description language (WDL) and generate a partial workflow application that still requires substantial coding effort. An iTask specification on the other hand denotes a full-fledged, web-based, multi-user workflow application. It strongly supports the view that a WDL should be considered as a complete specification language rather than a partial description language.

V. Zsók, Z. Horváth, and R. Plasmeijer (Eds.): CEFP 2011, LNCS 7241, pp. 46–92, 2012.

- Despite the fact that an iTask specification denotes a complete workflow application, the workflow engineer is not confronted with boilerplate programming (data storage and retrieval, GUI rendering, form interaction, and so on) because this is all dealt with using generic programming techniques under the hood.
- The structure of an iTask workflow evolves dynamically, depending on user-input and results of subtasks.
- In addition to the host language features, the iTask system adds first-class tasks (workflow units that create and accept other workflow units) and recursion to the modelling repertoire of workflow engineers.
- In contrast with the large catalogue of common workflow patterns [1], iTask workflows are captured by means of a small number of core combinator functions.

The original iTask system [16] focussed on the concept of a typed task: a unit of work, which, when it finishes, delivers the result of the task, a value of type Task T. The result can be passed, in a monadic way, to the next task. Several papers on applying and improving the iTasks system have appeared since then.

- The iTask system has been used to describe complex workflows such as the Search and Rescue activities as undertaken by the Dutch coast guard [12].
- Client side evaluation of tasks [10,18] has been made possible by compiling Clean code to Javascript [5] making use of a SAPL interpreter [9]. SAPL, Simple Application Programming Language, is a core intermediate language that uses only (higher-order) functions. It comes with an interpreter that has competitive performance when compared with other functional language interpreters such as Hugs, Helium, GHCi, and Amanda.
- Workflows being executed can be changed while the work is going on [17].
- Tasks can become web applications including GUI elements like buttons, dialogues, windows and menus [15].
- The semantics of iTask combinators has been formally described [11,17].

One may conclude that the iTask system is growing into a huge and complex system. Still, even more functionality is needed. For instance, when a task is delegated, someone might want to monitor its progress. In the old system the delegator gets this information and she also obtains the power to change the properties of the delegated task, such as its priority, or, she can move the task to the desk of someone else. This is often useful, but is not always what is wanted. Perhaps one would like to inform other people involved as well. One also would like to define what kind of information is shown to a particular person and define what a manager can do with the tasks she is viewing. In the new iTask system, one can define such management tasks as well [19]. The view on and handling of tasks is not hard-wired in the system, but can defined as desired, just as any other task.

Adding all these extensions to the iTask system could easily have lead to a huge system. This leads to high maintenance costs and hampers formal reasoning. We therefore, once again, redesigned and re-implemented the iTask system (version 3). We managed to build the iTask system on only a very few core functions.

An important class of basic tasks in the iTask system are the editors. Editors are tasks demanding input from end-users. The iTask system offers many different flavors of editors (see Section 2, Section 4, and Section 5), which all have in common that the type of the task is used to render the demanded interactive view. All different editors are constructed with only *one* Swiss-Army-Knife core editor function (see Section 10).

Tasks are compositional. The iTask system offers several convenient combinators for combining task. However, the iTask system is based on only *two* core combinators (see Section 10). There is one combinator, a monadic `bind` (see Section 3), to express that two tasks have to be executed sequentially. With the `parallel` combinator (see Section 8 and Section 9) one can create a set of parallel tasks which can be dynamically extended. New in the iTask system is that tasks may share information, which can be used to communicate the state of affairs between tasks while the tasks are being performed.

With these few core functions, the simplicity of the iTask system can be retained and the maintainability can be improved. On top of these core functions we have defined a library with useful editors and combinators to facilitate the creation of workflows in a declarative, understandable style.

In this paper we introduce the new iTask system by giving several examples and exercises. Section by section we introduce more functionality. In Section 2 we start with the unit of user-interaction, the editor tasks. In Section 3 we show how results of tasks can be passed to one another by means of sequential composition and recursion, thus creating more complex applications. In Section 4 we extend tasks with actions, which moves the generated applications more towards GUI applications that deploy menus. In Section 5 we make applications aware of their context and each other by introducing shared data. In Section 6 we show how editor tasks can be enhanced with a model-view abstraction, thereby customizing the user-experience with these tasks. In Section 7 we take the step to distributed systems, and show how users can be assigned to tasks. Related to task distribution is parallel execution. We first show how to deal with parallel execution of fixed numbers of tasks in Section 8, and extend it with a dynamic number of tasks in Section 9. This concludes the part in which the iTask system is discussed from an external point of view. In Section 10 we proceed from an internal point of view and explain how all of the discussed elements can be defined in terms of an extremely small core of basic combinators and concepts. Finally, we discuss related work in Section 11 and conclude in Section 12.

Finally, here are a number of organizational remarks about the remainder of these lecture notes.

- Although iTask system is heavily making use of generic programming techniques, one does not need these skills here. We do assume that you have some experience with functional programming, preferably in Clean or Haskell, and that you are comfortable in working with recursive (higher-order) functions, algebraic data types and record types, and lists.

- For readability, all type signatures in these lecture notes omit strictness annotations (!) and uniqueness attribute variables (u: and .).
- Library types and function signatures are displayed as **code fragments** and are displayed in a frame. Example **code fragments** are numbered.
- All examples that are shown in these lecture notes are present in the iTask distribution under the directory *Examples / CEFP2011*. For each section n, a subdirectory with similar name has been created that contains a module Section$n$.dcl and Section$n$.icl. Each such module defines a function flows$n$ that exports the example workflows in these lecture notes. The main module CEFP.icl of the CEFP.prj project imports all section modules and their example workflows and integrates them in a single workflow application.
- These lecture notes have been written to encourage you to experiment with the system. For this reason, there are many small exercises to demonstrate parts of the system. However, it is still possible to comprehend the system when deciding to skip the exercises. The iTask system can be downloaded from http://wiki.clean.cs.ru.nl/ITasks.

2 Generic Editors

The iTask system is a *generic* toolkit. The simplest function that illustrates this is the task that displays information to the user (see module InteractionTasks.dcl):

```
viewInformation :: d [LocalViewOn m] m → Task m | descr d & iTask m
```

The parameters of type d and m are not polymorphic, but they are constrained. The type class descr is used to generate simple string information to users (in most cases, we use a **String** value). The iTask system pivots upon the generic type class iTask: it contains the entire generic machinery to serialize, deserialize, render, update, and store values of *arbitrary first order type*. The second argument of viewInformation can be used to define an alternative *view*, and can be used to influence *how* the value is presented to the end user. It does not concern us right now, the standard view is fine, and we will therefore keep the alternative view empty ([]) for the time being. The third argument is the value to be rendered.

Let us start with the ubiquitous *"Hello world"* example:

Example 1. *Hello world in iTask*

```
module Section2                                                      1
                                                                     2
import iTasks                                                        3
                                                                     4
Start :: *World → *World                                            5
Start world  = startEngine myTask World                             6
                                                                     7
myTask = viewInformation "Press Ok to terminate" [] "Hello world!"  8
```

Fig. 1. A screenshot of Example 1: *"Hello World."*

The code shown in Example 1 is complete and generates a working iTask web server application after compilation (see Figure 1). In the module one has to import the iTask library (line 3) and define a Start rule (lines 5-6) that starts the task to do, which is myTask in this case (line 8).

To run this example separately, the code has to be stored in a file with the same name as the module, Section2.icl in this case. When you compile it, you need to make a project first (settings are stored in Section2.prj), and select the iTask environment in the IDE. After compilation and linking, an executable application is generated, called Section2.exe. When this application is started, it will include a web server. Visit http://localhost/ with your browser and you will see what has been generated. For more detailed information, look at directions included in the iTask-CEFP distribution.

The iTask system always starts with the execution of *one* specific task, but this one can be a very complicated one. In Section 7 we show how several tasks can be started interactively and how tasks can be handled by multiple users. In the CEFP distribution we used this method to collect and test all examples given in this lecture notes in one iTask application. See also Section 1.

Exercise 1. *More basic types*
Alter the String value "Hello world!" of Example 1 to the Int value 42. Recompile and launch the application. What is changed? Do the same for the other basic types Bool, Real, and Char.

Note: do not forget to terminate the previously running instance, or you are likely to encounter the following linker-error message:

```
Linker error: could not create '....exe'
```

In that case, close the instance and then bring the application up-to-date.   ∎

The key advantage of the generic foundation is that an instance of the generic functions can be generated automatically for any value of any first order type. The only thing required of you, the programmer, is that you need to ask the compiler to derive these instances using the **derive class** keywords.

Example 2. *Custom types*

We add `Person` and `Gender` as custom types to Example 1 and request the availability of their generic instances at line 8:

```
:: Person = { firstName   :: String                    1
            , surName     :: String                     2
            , dateOfBirth :: Date                       3
            , gender      :: Gender                     4
            }                                           5
:: Gender = Male | Female                               6
                                                        7
derive class iTask Person, Gender                       8
```

Alter the `String` value `"Hello world!"` of Example 1 to an arbitrary `Person` value, say yourself. If we recompile and run this new application, we obtain a new view of this value.

Moving your mouse over the little icons attached to each form field informs you about their status. A *blue* icon means that the field has not been filled in yet. If you point on it, it tells you what kind of value is expected. A *red* icon indicates that you typed in something unexpected. A *green* icon indicates that the value typed in is of expected type. It is mandatory to fill in all fields because undefined values can not be displayed. If you want an optional field, you can use the type `Maybe`, which is defined as: `:: Maybe a = Just a | Nothing`. The value `Nothing` can be used to indicate that no value has been defined yet.

Although `Date` is not a basic Clean type, you do not have to request the generation of instances of the generic functions for values of this type. The iTask system uses *specialization* for this purpose: with specialization, you can overrule the generic instance for a type that would normally be generated, and instead define your preferred instance.

Exercise 2. *Specialized types*

The iTask system has specialized the iTask class functions for quite a few types. Some of them can be found in the `SystemTypes.dcl` module. Change, in a similar way as in Example 2, the displayed value to a value of type `Currency`, `Time`, `Note`, `Choice`, and `MultipleChoice` respectively, and observe the changes in the resulting application. (Note that in `SystemTypes.dcl` a number of functions are defined to easily create `Choice` and `MultipleChoice` values.) ∎

The `viewInformation` function displays information to the user. In order to obtain information from the user, iTask provides a number of functions. Before discussing all of them, we start with two dual functions of `viewInformation`:

```
updateInformation  :: d [LocalViewOn m] m → Task m | descr d & iTask m
enterInformation   :: d [LocalViewOn m]   → Task m | descr d & iTask m
```

Although the signature of updateInformation is identical to that of viewInformation, its behavior is radically different: in addition to showing its third parameter to the user, it allows her to *update* the value and change it to a new value of the same type (see also Figure 2). The *update* functions expect an initial value

Fig. 2. Entering or updating a value of type Person

that the user can work on. Sometimes it makes more sense not to provide an initial value, and instead expect the user just to *enter* one. When the function enterInformation is used, a blanc form to be filled in is offered to the user. The only difference is that an initial value is missing. Because of this, the type of the value you want to obtain from the user, must be clear from the context, or otherwise your program won't compile. In such cases you probably get a compile time error such as:

Overloading error [*location*]: internal overloading of "*f*" could not be solved

In general, it is sufficient to add a type signature to the (local) function definition.

Exercise 3. *Updating values*
Replace viewInformation in Example 1 with updateInformation and replace once more the third parameter with suitable values of the basic types of Exercise 1, the custom types of Example 2, and the specialized types of Exercise 2.

Exercise 4. *Entering values*
Same as Exercise 3, but replace updateInformation with enterInformation. Instead of offering a value of the requested type, add the desired type signature of myTask.

Exercise 5. *Entering list values*
Same as Exercise 4. Use enterInformation, and change the desired type signature of myTask in lists. Test the application with [Int], [Bool], [Note], [Person]. ∎

Besides updateInformation, iTask offers four functions (update(Multiple)Choice and enter(Multiple)Choice) to choose values, without further editing. Before delving into their types, we first discuss a simplified version of enterChoice and enterMultipleChoice:

```
enterChoice         :: d [LocalViewOn o] [o] → Task o  | descr d & iTask o
enterMultipleChoice :: d [LocalViewOn o] [o] → Task [o] | descr d & iTask o
```

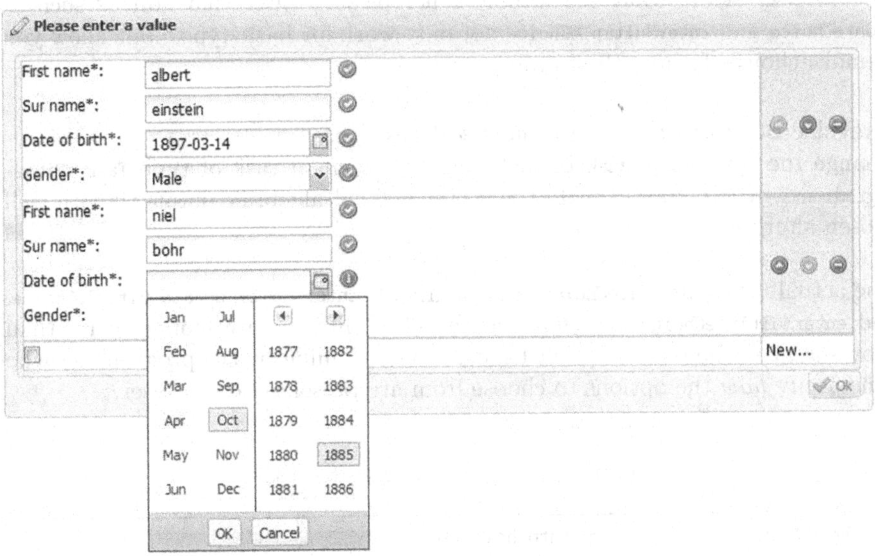

Fig. 3. A screenshot of Exercise 5: *Entering A List of Persons*

Here, [o] in the argument list is a list to choose from. The editor enterChoice returns the chosen item, while enterMultipleChoice returns a list of chosen items. An example of their use is:

Example 3. *Choice and Multiple Choice*

```
chooseNumber :: Task Int
chooseNumber = enterChoice "Choose a number" [] [0..10]

pizzaWith :: Task [String]
pizzaWith = enterMultipleChoice "What do you like on your pizza ?" []
                            ["Cheese","Tomato","Ansjofish","Salami"]
```

The function chooseNumber lets the user select a number. The function pizzaWith

Fig. 4. A screenshot of Example 3: *View on MultipleChoice*

lets the user select what she wants on her pizza. Notice that editors such as updateChoice and enterMultipleChoice not only work for basic types, but allow you to make choices for any (first order) type.

Exercise 6. *Choose from user defined types*
Change the function pizzaWith such that it returns a task of type Task [Pizza-Ingredient], where PizzaIngredient is a user defined algebraic datatype with well chosen alternatives. ∎

The actual types of updateChoice, and its friends enterChoice, updateMultipleChoice, and enterMultipleChoice as defined in the iTask library, are more general than shown above. The reason is that they allow fine tuning by the programmer who can specify *how* the options to choose from are presented to the user.

Table 1. Customizing editor tasks

```
:: ChoiceType            = AutoChoiceView
                         | ChooseFromRadioButtons
                         | ChooseFromComboBox
                         | ChooseFromTable
                         | ChooseFromTree
:: MultiChoiceType       = AutoMultiChoiceView
                         | ChooseFromCheckBoxes
:: ChoiceView choiceType o = ∃v: ChoiceContext v                    & iTask v
                           | ∃v: ChoiceView (choiceType, (o → v)) & iTask v

updateChoice         :: d [ChoiceView ChoiceType o]      (c o) o  → Task o
                     | descr d & iTask o & iTask (c o) & OptionContainer c
enterChoice          :: d [ChoiceView ChoiceType o]      (c o)    → Task o
                     | descr d & iTask o & iTask (c o) & OptionContainer c
updateMultipleChoice :: d [ChoiceView MultiChoiceType o] (c o) [o] → Task [o]
                     | descr d & iTask o & iTask (c o) & OptionContainer c
enterMultipleChoice  :: d [ChoiceView MultiChoiceType o] (c o)    → Task [o]
                     | descr d & iTask o & iTask (c o) & OptionContainer c
```

The function signatures in Table 1 clearly demonstrate that overloading is used intensively to make the functions more general. It allows the programmer not only to make a choice from a list [o] as is the case in the simplified version, but from other container types c of kind * → * to hold values of type o as well (c o). Furthermore, one can influence the *view* on this type, i.e. how the options to choose from are presented to the end user. This is indicated by the second parameter of the choice functions. By default, when the view is just an empty list, some suitable representation is chosen (AutoChoiceView). For example, if one offers a short list to chooseNumber it may offer the choice via radio buttons, in other cases it may use a pull-down menu.

When desired, one can influence the representation, indicated by ChoiceView ChoiceType o. Choices can be offered via radio buttons (ChooseFromRadioButtons), a pull-down menu (ChooseFromComboBox), a table (ChooseFromTable) or a tree (Choose-FromTree) to choose from, or one can present checkboxes (ChooseFromCheckBoxes, multiple choice only). The overloading mechanism enables adding other representations later on if needed.

To give an example of an application, look at chooseNumber2.

Example 4. *Choosing from a tree*

```
chooseNumber2 :: Task Int
chooseNumber2 = enterChoice "Choose a number"
                   [ChoiceView (ChooseFromTree, (<+++) "choose ")] [0..10]
```

It presents the choices in a tree structure, with each option i labeled as "choose i".

Exercise 7. *Google maps*
Make the following further changes to Example 1: add the line **import** GoogleMaps, and alter the type of myTask to Task GoogleMap. What is changed in the resulting application? Click on the picture and see what happens.   ∎

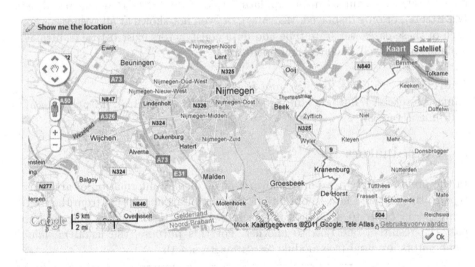

Fig. 5. A screenshot of Exercise 7: *A Google Map*

When creating an editor for a value, you do not always want to allow the end-user to have access to the entire value. In iTask, a couple of types have been specialized for this purpose (see module SystemTypes.dcl).

Table 2. Creating partial access to values

```
:: VisualizationHint a = VHEditable a | VHDisplay a | VHHidden a
:: Editable      a =   Editable a
:: Display       a =   Display  a
:: Hidden        a =   Hidden   a

fromVisualizationHint :: (VisualizationHint a) → a
toVisualizationHint   :: a → VisualizationHint a

fromEditable          :: (Editable a) → a
toEditable            :: a → Editable a

fromDisplay           :: (Display a) → a
toDisplay             :: a → Display a

fromHidden            :: (Hidden a) → a
toHidden              :: a → Hidden a
```

In Table 2, the type VisualizationHint and its data constructors are introduced that are useful when manipulating (parts of) values that can be edited (VHEditable), or only displayed (VHDisplay), or even not shown at all (VHHidden). For each of these cases, separate type and data constructors exist (Editable, Display, and Hidden), as well as conversion functions.

Exercise 8. *Editable, Display, and Hidden values*
Same as Exercise 4, but now edit values of type (Editable Person), (Display Person), and (Hidden Person).   ◼

3   Combinators

In the previous section we have shown how to display information of arbitrary type to the user and how to obtain information of arbitrary type from the user. However, in order to do something useful with this information, you need to pass the result of one task to another. For this purpose, the usual *monadic* combinators are used (see module CoreCombinators.dcl):

```
(>>=) infixl 1 :: (Task a) (a → Task b) → Task b | iTask a & iTask b
return       :: a                       → Task a | iTask a

(>>|) infixl 1 :: (Task a)    (Task b) → Task b | iTask a & iTask b
```

The (t >>= λx → tf x) task is a composite task that first executes task t. When t has finished it returns a value that is bound to variable x of some type a. If tf :: a → Task b, then (tf x) computes a new task of type (Task b). This new task is then executed. Its return value, of type b, is also the return value of the composite task. The (t >>| u) task is a composite task that first executes task t and then task u, while ignoring the result of task t. Hence, >>| is a derived combinator which can be expressed in terms of the bind operator >>=. The (return x) task is a basic task that immediately terminates with value x. You use it typically as the last task in a composition of tasks to return the correct value.

As an example, we create a slightly more interesting hello world example that combines enterInformation and viewInformation to first ask the user her name, and then welcome her:

Example 5. *Hello world in iTask*

```
hello :: Task String                                                         1
hello                                                                        2
   =            enterInformation "Please enter your name" []                 3
       >>= λname → viewInformation ("Hello " +++ name +++ "!") [] name       4
```

The hello task first executes the enterInformation task on line 3. Because it is clear from the context that a String value is required (+++ :: String String → String), we know that the entered value name is of type String. The task then executes viewInformation and greets the user with the entered name.

Exercise 9. *Sequence*
Write a workflow that asks the user to first enter her first name, then her surname, then her date of birth (a value of predefined type Date), and her gender (the custom type Gender). The workflow must return the result as a Person value. Person and Gender were defined in Example 2.   ■

iTask is *embedded* in Clean. This implies that you can use normal choice (if and case expressions) and recursion to create composite tasks. As a simple example, we define a workflow that allows the user to enter positive numbers, whose sum is returned as soon as the user enters a non-positive number.

Example 6. *Choice and recursion in iTask*

```
numbers :: Task Int                                                          1
numbers = viewInformation "number entered:" [] (numbers' 0)                  2
where                                                                        3
    numbers' :: Int → Task Int                                               4
    numbers' sum                                                             5
       =            enterInformation "Please enter a positive number" []     6
           >>= λn → if (n > 0) (numbers' (sum + n)) (return sum)             7
```

Here, numbers' is a recursive task. Its integer argument accumulates the sum of the entered positive numbers. In line 6, the user is asked to enter a positive number. With if it is decided whether to continue recursively (in case the entered number is positive), or whether to terminate the recursive task and return the accumulated sum.

Exercise 10. *Persons recursively*
Write a workflow in which the user can enter a number of `Person` values. The
result of this workflow must be of type [`Person`].

Exercise 11. *Persons as a list*
Write a workflow in which the user can enter a [`Person`] value. Compare this to
Exercise 10.   ∎

In iTask, tasks are *first-class citizens*, i.e. tasks can be arguments as well as
results of task functions. This is extremely useful to capture common workflow
patterns. We start with a simple example:

Example 7. *A simple first-class task function*

```
view :: (Task a) → Task a | iTask a                                          1
view t                                                                       2
    =            t                                                           3
    >>= λresult → viewInformation "The result is:" [] result                 4
```

(`view t`) is a function that takes an arbitrary task `t` of type `Task a` as argument
which is executed first (line 3). Whenever `t` terminates, its `result` value of type
`a` is displayed to the user (line 4).

For completeness, we show two alternative ways to define the same function
below. The first, `view2`, uses η-conversion to eliminate the need to write down
the intermediate result. The second, `view3`, uses the standard `flip` function to
move the task argument to the back, and thus apply η-conversion one more time
and obtain a point-free version of `view`. Because in Clean the arity of functions
is explicit in their type, `view3` has a different function type than `view2` and `view`.

```
view2 :: (Task a) → Task a | iTask a
view2 t = t >>= viewInformation "The result is:" []
```

```
view3 :: ((Task a) → Task a) | iTask a
view3 = flip (>>=) (viewInformation "The result is:" [])
```

Here is an example of first-class tasks as a *result*.

Example 8. *Working with first-class task results*

```
personList :: Task [Person]                                                  1
personList                                                                   2
    =              enterInformation "Please fill in the form" []             3
    >>= λp → enterChoice "One more ? " []                                    4
              [("Yes",Hidden (personList >>= λps → return [p:ps]))           5
              ,("No", Hidden              (return [p]  ))                     6
              ]                                                              7
    >>= λ(_,Hidden continuation) → continuation                             8
```

In Example 8, the user enters a `Person` value on line 3, the value of which is
bound to variable `p` (line 4), and then decides whether she wants to add more

persons (line 5) or whether she is done (line 6). The choices not only contain the possible answers (the strings "Yes" and "No"), but also the *task* that should be *continued* with as a Hidden value. In case the answer is "Yes", then more persons ps are entered, and p and ps are returned (line 5). In case the answer is "No", then only p is returned (line 6).

Another, more classical approach would be to leave out the continuation in the enterChoice editor as probably is chosen in Exercise 10. In that case one needs to make a case distinction to find out whether "Yes" or "No" has been chosen. For every possible choice a case alternative has to be defined with the proper task to do next. The advantage of the continuation style approach shown in Example 8 is that the choice and the task to do when the choice is made are combined. If a case distinction is used these two are separated which can more easily lead to a programming error.

The iTask system defines many first-class task combinator functions. You can find quite a number of them in module CommonCombinators.

Table 3. Some predefined first-class task combinator functions

(>>^)	infixl 1 ::	(Task a) (Task b)	→ Task a	| iTask a & iTask b
(>>?)	infixl 1 ::	(Task (Maybe a))		
		(a → Task (Maybe b))	→ Task (Maybe b)	| iTask a & iTask b
(<!)	infixl 6 ::	(Task a) (a → Bool)	→ Task a	| iTask a
(-||-)	infixr 3 ::	(Task a) (Task a)	→ Task a	| iTask a
(||-)	infixr 3 ::	(Task a) (Task b)	→ Task b	| iTask a & iTask b
(-||)	infixl 3 ::	(Task a) (Task b)	→ Task a	| iTask a & iTask b

Exercise 12. *Gathering behavior from types*
It is instructive to guess the likely behavior of the combinators from Table 3. Try this yourself. You can check your answers below. ∎

- (t >>^ u) first executes t and then u, and yields the result of t.
- (t >>? tf) first executes t. Only if that task returns a (Just x) value, then the second task (tf x) is computed, executed, and its result returned.
- (t <! p) executes t at least once. Each time predicate p yields false, t is executed again, and its new result is tested. The composite task terminates as soon as p yields true.
- (t -\|\|- u) executes both t and u and terminates as soon as either task finishes and returns that result.
- (t \|\|- u) and (u -\|\| t) are similar and return the result of task u as soon as it terminates.

One can imagine many more useful combinators. In Section 10, we explain that such combinators like the ones displayed in Table 3, are actually derived combinators. As iTask programmer, you can define your own combinators to capture often occurring working patterns. Here is an example of a custom combinator that repeats a task as long as the current user is not satisfied with its result:

Example 9. *A first-class task pattern*

```
repeatUntilApproved :: (Task a) → Task a | iTask a                      1
repeatUntilApproved t                                                   2
    =    t                                                              3
    >>= λv → enterChoice "Approve result: " [About v]                   4
            [("Yes",Hidden (return v))                                  5
            ,("No", Hidden (repeatUntilApproved t))                     6
            ]                                                           7
    >>= λ(_,Hidden c) → c                                              8
```

The same continuation technique is used as in Example 8. A new aspect in this example is the [About v] option that has been added to enterChoice. With this option, you can display any additional type that is a generic iTask class instance. Here it is used to display the return value of t.

Exercise 13.   *While pattern*
Write a workflow pattern while that has the following signature:

```
while :: (a → Bool) (a → Task a) a → Task a | iTask a
```

with the following meaning: (while c t a) repeats a task t as long as the predicate c is valid for the initial value a and subsequent values produced by applying t. Test this workflow pattern with:

```
positive :: Task Int
positive = while ((≥) 0) (updateInformation "Please enter a positive number" []) 0
```

∎

4   Enriching Tasks with GUI

Editors, created with enterInformation and updateInformation, are tasks that create an interface to the end user to enter or update a value of first order type. In this section we extend these tasks with *actions*. An action is a value of type Action (defined in module SystemTypes).

Table 4. Actions

```
:: Action      = Action ActionName | ActionFinish   | ActionClose
               | ActionOk          | ActionContinue | ActionHelp
               | ActionCancel      | ActionNew       | ActionAbout
               | ActionYes         | ActionOpen      | ActionFind
               | ActionNo          | ActionSave      | ActionDelete
               | ActionNext        | ActionSaveAs    | ActionEdit
               | ActionPrevious    | ActionQuit
:: ActionName :== String
```

Except for the very first, all data constructors in Table 4 have a default appearance in iTask. With (Action *name*), an action with name *name* is created. By default, an action is rendered as a button. However, if *name* is shaped as "$m/s_1/\ldots/s_n/c$" ($n \geq 0$), then m is rendered as a menu, the s_i are rendered as hierarchical sub menus, and c as the final menu command. Actions with identical prefixes are mapped to identical menu structures. Actions are most useful in combination with the following *multi-bind* combinator (see module CommonCombinators.dcl.

Table 5. The multi-bind combinator

```
(>?*) infixl 1 :: (Task a) [(Action,TaskContinuation a b)] → Task b | iTask a
                                                                    & iTask b

:: TaskContinuation a b = Always                                  (Task b)
                        | IfValid                (a  →         Task b)
                        | Sometimes ((InformationState a) → Maybe (Task b))
:: InformationState a   = { modelValue :: a
                          , localValid :: Bool
                          }
```

The composition (t >?* [(a_1,c_1)...(a_n,c_n)]) ($n \geq 0$) performs task t. If t is an editor task (one of the enter- and update- combinators introduced in Section 2), then its current value x is inspected by >?* using the continuation criteria c_i. If c_i = Always t', then action a_i is always enabled and can be selected by the user, in which case task t' is continued with. If c_i = IfValid ft, then action a_i is only enabled if x is valid. Selecting a_i causes continuation of the task computed by (ft x). Finally, if c_i = Sometimes ft, then the select state of action a_i is determined by ft. The function is given value x as well as a boolean v telling whether x is valid in the record value st = {modelValue = x, localValid = v}. If (ft st) yields Nothing, then action a_i is not enabled; if it yields Just t', then t' is the task that is continued with if the user selects action a_i. If t is not an editor task, then its return value x is inspected exactly once.

Example 10. *Using multi-bind to add actions*

```
absolute :: Task Int                                                          1
absolute = enterInformation "Enter a number" []                               2
        >?* [(Action "Always",    Always   (return 42))                       3
            ,(Action "If valid",  IfValid  (λx → return (abs x)))             4
            ,(Action "Sometimes", Sometimes (onlyIf  (λx → x ≥ 0) return))    5
            ]                                                                  6
                                                                              7
onlyIf :: (a → Bool) (a → Task b) (InformationState a) → Maybe (Task b)       8
onlyIf pred taskf  s                                                          9
| s.localValid && pred s.modelValue = Just (taskf s.modelValue)              10
| otherwise = Nothing                                                        11
```

This task enhances the `enterInformation` task on line 2 with three actions:

1. The action labeled "`Always`" is continuously available to the user. Selecting it causes `absolute` to return value 42.
2. The action labeled "`If valid`" is only available if the user has edited a legal `Int` value. Initially, the editor is empty, and hence this task is disabled. Whenever a number is entered, the action becomes enabled. If selected, it returns the absolute entered value.
3. The action labeled "`Sometimes`" is enabled only if the user has entered a positive number, which is also the return value of the action that is chosen. The function `onlyIf` is a handy utility function which checks whether a valid value has been typed in obeying a given predicate.

Fig. 6. A screenshot of Example 10: *Conditional Selectable Action Buttons*

As another example, consider this variation of Example 8:

Example 11. *Using multi-bind to enter Persons*

```
personList :: Task [Person]                                                   1
personList                                                                    2
    = enterInformation "Please fill in the form" []                          3
      >?* [(Action "Add one", IfValid (λp → personList >>= λps → return [p:ps])) 4
          ,(Action "Done",     IfValid (λp → return [p]))                     5
          ,(ActionQuit,        Always (return []))                           6
          ]                                                                   7
```

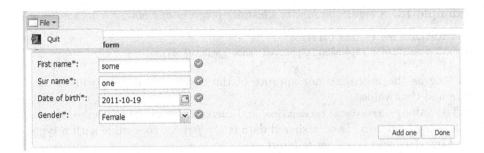

Fig. 7. Screenshot of Example 11: *Different Ways to Continue Work*

Exercise 14. *Repeat until approved revisited*
Change the repeatUntilApproved combinator from Example 9 such that it uses actions instead of the choice-construct with hidden continuation tasks.

Exercise 15. *Palindrome*
Use >?* to enhance a String editor task with three actions:

1. an action labeled "No text" that is enabled only if no text has been entered;
2. an action labeled "Palindrome!" that is enabled only if text has been entered *and* is a palindrome;
3. conversely, an action labeled "Nope!" that is enabled only if text has been entered *and* is not a palindrome.

■

5   Shared Data

In any workflow management system it is vital to keep track of time in order to enforce deadlines and coordinate work. Earlier, we have seen that Date is a predefined type in iTask. Similarly, Time and DateTime are predefined. You can obtain the current date and time as follows:

Example 12. *A task to obtain the current date and time*

```
getDateAndTime :: Task DateTime                                          1
getDateAndTime = get currentDateTime                                     2
```

In a similar way, get currentDate and get currentTime return the current date and time individually.

During execution of a workflow, time progresses. This is illustrated by turning Example 12 into a repetitive workflow:

Example 13. *A repetitive task to illustrate progress of time*

```
repeatDateAndTime :: Task DateTime                                          1
repeatDateAndTime = repeatUntilApproved (show getDateAndTime)               2
```

As long as the user does not approve of the current result, she will see new date and time values.

The values `currentDate`, `currentTime`, and `currentDateTime` are examples of *read-only shared data*. In iTask, a shared data is a *reference* to a value with a typed *read*-interface and typed *write*-interface.

Table 6. The shared data API

```
:: RWShared r w
:: Shared   a :== RWShared a a
:: ROShared a :== RWShared a Void

get    ::              (RWShared r w) → Task r | iTask r
set    :: w            (RWShared r w) → Task w | iTask w
update :: (r → w) (RWShared r w) → Task w | iTask r & iTask w
```

Table 6 enumerates the types and tasks that can be found in module `CoreTasks`. A shared data of type (`RWShared r w`) can be read with the `get` function, which returns of value of type `r`, and it can be overwritten with the `set` function, which takes a value of type `w`. Reading and writing can be done atomically with the function `update f`, when `f :: r → w`. A read-only shared data is a shared data in which the write-interface has type `Void`. Symmetric shared data have identical read-write interface types (see module `CoreTasks`).

Shared data is useful for two reasons: it can be used to serve as unstructured many-to-many communication between tasks that are evaluated in parallel, and for storing data persistently. The unstructured nature of shared data impedes reasoning. For this reason it has been 'tamed' when working with parallel tasks, as will be discussed in Section 8. In the remainder of this section, we discuss only its application for storing purposes. We do this by means of an example.

Example 14. *A persistent 'to-do list'*

```
:: ToDo = { name :: String, deadline :: Date, remark :: Maybe Note, done :: Bool }  1
derive class iTask ToDo                                                              2
                                                                                    3
toDoList       :: Shared [ToDo]                                                      4
toDoList       = sharedStore "My to-do list" []                                     5
                                                                                    6
updateToDoList :: Task [ToDo]                                                        7
updateToDoList =                    get toDoList                                     8
               >>= λoldList → updateInformation "Your to-do list" [] oldList         9
               >>= λnewList → set newList toDoList                                  10
```

First of all, we design a data type, ToDo, that contains a description of something to do (line 1) and generate a generic instance of the iTask class (line 2). Second, we need a reference to the store, which is created by the function sharedStore (line 5). In order to allow the user to update her to-do list, the task updateToDoList first reads the current content of the shared data (line 8), allow her to edit the list (line 9), and finally write it to persistent store (line 10).

Exercise 16. *Enhancing the to-do list*
Enhance the updateInformation task in Example 14 with the following actions:

1. sort the to-do list by name or deadline;
2. remove all to-do items which deadline has passed;
3. remove all to-do items that have been done.

∎

In Section 2 we have presented the basic editor tasks to show, enter, and update values generically. For each of these basic editors, a basic *shared* editor task exists.

Table 7. The basic shared editor tasks

```
viewSharedInformation
      :: d [ViewOn l r w] (RWShared  r  w) l → Task (r,l)
                                     | descr d & iTask l & iTask r & iTask w
updateSharedInformation
      :: d [ViewOn l r w] (RWShared  r  w) l → Task (r,l)
                                     | descr d & iTask l & iTask r & iTask w
enterSharedInformation
      :: d [ViewOn l r w] (RWShared  r  w) → Task (r,l)
                                     | descr d & iTask l & iTask r & iTask w
updateSharedChoice
      :: d [ChoiceView ChoiceType o] (RWShared (c o) w) o → Task o
                  | descr d & iTask o & iTask w & iTask (c o) & OptionContainer c
enterSharedChoice
      :: d [ChoiceView ChoiceType o] (RWShared (c o) w) → Task o
                  | descr d & iTask o & iTask w & iTask (c o) & OptionContainer c
updateSharedMultipleChoice
      :: d [ChoiceView MultiChoiceType o] (c o) [o] → Task [o]
                  | descr d & iTask o & iTask (c o) & OptionContainer c
enterSharedMultipleChoice
      :: d [ChoiceView MultiChoiceType o] (c o) → Task [o]
                  | descr d & iTask o & iTask (c o) & OptionContainer c
```

The main difference between editor tasks and shared editor tasks is that the latter operate on shared data in addition to a local value. Shared editor tasks can be enhanced with the >?* operator in the same way as editor tasks can (Section 4). As a consequence, the updateToDoList function in Example 14 can also be implemented with a one-liner:

Example 15. *A shared editor for a persistent 'to-do list'*

updateSharedToDoList :: Task ([ToDo],Void)
updateSharedToDoList = updateSharedInformation "Your to-do list" [] toDoList Void

viewSharedToDoList :: Task ([ToDo],Void)
viewSharedToDoList = viewSharedInformation "Your to-do list" [] toDoList Void

Because no local data is required we use value Void of type Void.

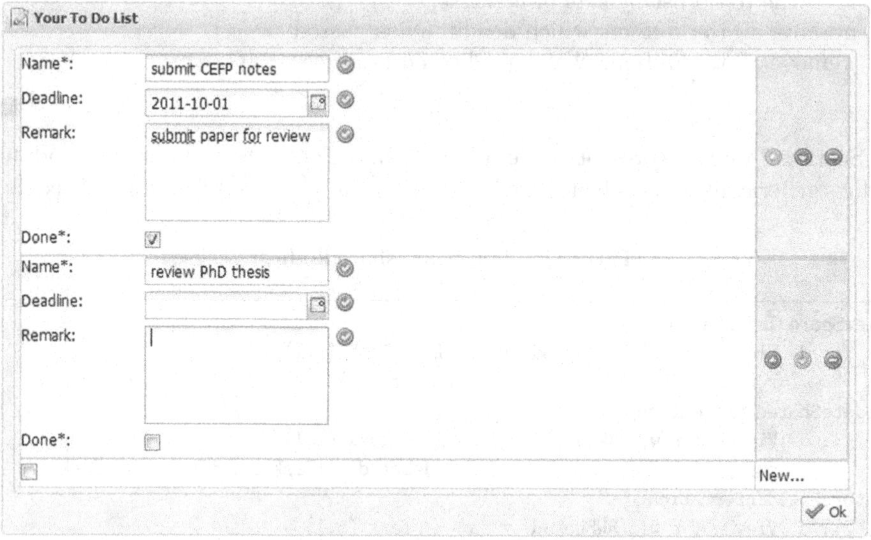

Fig. 8. Screenshot of Example 15: *An Editor on a Shared ToDo List*

It is important to notice that there is a big difference in behaviour between the two approaches. In updateToDoList a copy of the list is made first. This copy is edited by the end user. When the end user is happy with the changes made, the editing task is finished, and the result is written back to the shared state. In updateSharedToDoList no copy is made. Every change is applied directly to the shared to-do list, and therefore is also directly visible by any other task looking at the same to-do list (!). Hence, when one is working on a task, one can use shared data to communicate information with other tasks.

For example, if task viewSharedToDoList would be executed in parallel with updateSharedToDoList (see Section 8), any modification made in the todo-list with the editor is directly visible for someone viewing this to-do list at the same time. One can also imagine that several workers are working at the same time on the same shared to-do list. The iTask system will automatically report editing conflicts to the workers when they occur.

Fig. 9. Screenshot of Example 15: *A View on the Shared ToDo List*

6   Views on Local and Shared Data

The *view* parameter of the editors has been ignored so far. It makes it possible to present the information in the editor *model* in a desired format. Hence an editor is an instance of the *model-view* paradigm: the model is defined by the task type returned by an editor while the view is what is shown to the end-user. By default, when the view is defined as an empty list, model and view are identical. If one wants a different view, one has to think about what the format of the view has to be, which types can be used to express this, and one has to define a bidirectional transformation (*bimap*) between the view values and the model data the editor is actually applied on.

For example, an editor such as updateInformation allows the end user to modify data (of some type l) which is only locally available for the particular editor. When the editing task is finished, the final value is made public and passed to the next tasks to do. An editor such as updateSharedInformation allows to modify both local data and shared data. When shared data is being modified, the changes are automatically made visible to all other end users who are looking at the same shared data as well.

```
updateSharedInformation :: d [ViewOn l r w] (RWShared r w) l → Task (r,l)
                                   | descr d & iTask l & iTask r & iTask w
updateInformation       :: d [LocalViewOn l] l → Task l
                                   | descr d & iTask l

:: LocalViewOn a :== ViewOn a Void Void
```

By default, model and view are the same. In the case of updateInformation, by default an editable form is created for type l. In the case of updateSharedInformation, by default an additional editable form is created for the shared type r as well. Hence, in that case two editable forms are shown to the end user.

However, in particular when shared data is involved, this default view may not be very suitable. Let's have a look at the following example.

Example 16. *Twitter with an ill-chosen view*

```
:: Tweet :== (User,String)                                                    1
                                                                              2
twitterCEFP = get currentUser >>= join                                        3
where                                                                         4
    name    = "CEFP"                                                          5
    tweets  = sharedStore ("Twitter with " +++ name) []                      6
                                                                              7
    join :: User → Task Void                                                  8
    join user                                                                 9
        =     updateSharedInformation ("Tweets of " +++ name) view tweets ""  10
            >?* [ (ActionQuit, Always (return Void))                          11
                , (ActionOk,   IfValid (λ(_,message) → commit (user, message)))  12
                ]                                                             13
    where                                                                    14
        view = []                                                            15
                                                                              16
        commit :: Tweet → Task Void                                          17
        commit tweet = update (append tweet) tweets >>| join user            18
                                                                              19
append x xs = xs ++ [x]                                                       20
```

The function join (line 9) allows a user to follow messages (tweets) which are posted by someone or which are focussed on a certain topic area. In this case the topic is the "CEFP" summer school. Tweets are of type [(User, String)] which are stored in a shared store, tweets (line 6), that is initially empty.

In join a shared editor is created (updateSharedInformation, line 10) for the shared tweets as well as for entering a string. The idea is that the end user can see the tweets passing by which are being committed while she can type in a reaction as well. When the OK button is pressed (line 12), the entered message is committed, and the tweet store is updated by appending this message (line 18), after which this whole process is repeated by a recursive call of join. When a user no longer wants to follow the discussion, she can simply quit (line 11).

The updateSharedInformation editor, by default, provides an editor with which one can update both the shared value and the local value. In this case, this is not what we want (see Fig. 10). The shared value here are the tweets (of type [(User, String)]) being committed, which one actually only wants to see as text passing by, and one does not want to alter it at all. For entering a reaction, one would rather like to use a text box, as is being generated for type :: Note = Note String.

Example 17. *A proper view for Twitter*

```
view = [ DisplayView (GetShared id)                                          1
       , EnterView   (SetLocal (λ(Note reaction) _ _ → reaction))            2
       ]                                                                     3
```

Fig. 10. Screenshot of Example 16: *The Ill-Chosen View*

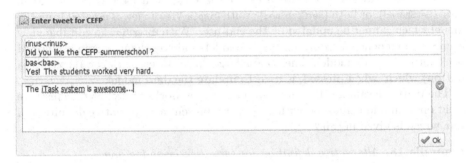

Fig. 11. Screenshot of Example 17: *A Well-Chosen View*

A proper representation (see Fig. 11) can be obtained by defining a dedicated *view* instead of the default view ([]) which states that the tweets have to be shown as text only (line 1 of view) while an editable textbox is created, which, when changed, will be copied back to the local string (line 2 of view). While looking at the screen or entering a reaction, the list of tweets being displayed will be updated constantly showing the new tweets committed by others.

```
:: ViewOn l r w   = ∃v: About        v                              & iTask v
                  | ∃v: EnterView   (SetFunc l r w v)              & iTask v
                  | ∃v: UpdateView  (GetFunc l r v, SetFunc l r w v) & iTask v
                  | ∃v: DisplayView (GetFunc l r v)                 & iTask v
                  |     UpdateTrigger String (UpdateFunc l r w)
:: GetFunc l r v  = GetLocal        (l     → v)
                  | GetShared       (r     → v)
                  | GetCombined     (l r   → v)
:: SetFunc l r w v = SetLocal       (v l r → l)
                  | SetShared       (v l r → w)
                  | SetCombined     (v l r → (Maybe l, Maybe w))
:: UpdateFunc l r w = UpdateLocal   (l     → l)
                  | UpdateShared    (r     → w)
                  | UpdateCombined  (l r   → (Maybe l, Maybe w))
```

The algebraic data type ViewOn defines how *views* can be defined on the data *model* of interaction tasks. Zero or more of these views can be defined as element in a list. If no views are defined (view = []) the identity is taken, and view and model will be the same. Each view presents a mapping ViewOn l r w between the local data of type l, the shared data of type r which can be read, and shared data of type w which can be written. A view can be of arbitrary type v, and is therefore existentially quantified ($\exists$ v) to allow these different view types v to be collected in a list.

With About additional information can be presented independent from the data model being used. With UpdateView one defines how to turn the model into a view, and one defines what the consequences are for the model when view values are modified. For turning a model into a view one can look at the current value of the local data (GetLocal), the global data (GetShared), or both (GetCombined). Any change made may have consequences for the local data (SetLocal), the global data (SetShared), or both (SetCombined). With DisplayView a view is created from the model which cannot be updated by the end-user. With EnterView an editable view is created independent from the current model, and any change made is mapped back into the data model. The UpdateTrigger introduces a trigger (typically a button) which, when pressed, is used to update the data model.

The twitter Example 16 with the adjusted view works nicely. To demonstrate what one can and cannot do with a view, we present an alternative definition of join which is given in join2.

Example 18. *Alternative definition for join, twittering too much*

```
join2 :: User → Task Void                                              1
join2 user                                                             2
    =    updateSharedInformation ("Enter tweet for " +++ name) view tweets ""  3
         >?* [ (ActionQuit,Always (return Void))                        4
             ]                                                          5
where                                                                  6
    view = [ UpdateView                                                7
             ( GetCombined (λtxt tweets                                8
                                    → (Display tweets, Note txt))       9
             , SetShared   (λ(_,Note reaction) _ tweets                 10
                                    → append (user,reaction) tweets)    11
             )                                                          12
           ]                                                            13
```

Even though the OK button is removed, and the definition is no longer recursive, tweets are added constantly. An UpdateView is defined which maps the model, the local value of type String and shared data of type [Tweet] into the desired view of type (Display [Tweet], Note) using GetCombined. The view is mapped back using SetShared which appends the entered text to the tweet store.

Although the view looks fine, the behaviour is unexpected: whenever a change is encountered, either in the shared data or in a view, the model is updated after which a new view is calculated and shown. As a result, while entering a string, parts of it are taken away and moved into the tweet store, even though the user has finished typing. This is clearly not what is wanted. So, when writing views one must be aware that mapping from model to view and backwards is happening regularly when changes are being made by someone in the underlying models.

Example 19. *Alternative definition for join*

```
join3 :: User → Task Void                                                1
join3 user                                                               2
   =    updateSharedInformation ("Enter tweet for " +++ name) view tweets ""  3
        >?* [ (ActionQuit, Always (return Void))                         4
            ]                                                            5
where                                                                    6
    view = [ DisplayView  (GetShared    id)                             7
           , UpdateView (GetLocal     Note                              8
                        ,SetLocal (λ(Note reaction) _ _ → reaction)     9
                        )                                               10
           , UpdateTrigger "Commit"                                     11
                        (UpdateData  (λreaction tweets →               12
                                     (Just ""                          13
                                     ,Just (append (user,reaction) tweets) 14
                                     )                                  15
                        ))                                              16
           ]                                                            17
```

A non-recursive version of join that exposes the desired behavior is given in Example 19 (join3). Here, to show the latest tweets, the shared tweet model is constantly displayed (DisplayView, line 7) while the local model of type String is constantly mapped (UpdateView, line 8-10) to and from a textbox of type Note. Only when the "Commit" button is hit, the reaction stored in the local model is added as tweet to the tweets store and this local store is reset to the empty string to allow a new reaction to be entered (UpdateTrigger, line 11-16).

7 Task Distribution

So far we have ignored the fact that tasks are typically *distributed* over several users working together on the internet. In this section we explain how tasks can be distributed over a number of workers.

Example 20. *Managing Multi-User Tasks*

```
module Section7                                                          1
                                                                         2
import iTasks                                                            3
derive bimap (,), Maybe                                                  4
                                                                         5
Start :: *World → *World                                                6
Start world = startEngine (manageWorkflows myWorkFlows) world           7
                                                                         8
myWorkFlows = [ workflow "view all users"  "view users" viewAllUserNames  9
              , workflow "edit to-do list" "edit to-do" updateSharedToDoList  10
              , workflow "view to-do list" "view to-do" viewSharedToDoList    11
              ]                                                          12
```

Clearly, if we want to do this, we need a different web interface. So far, an end user only had to handle one task. Now we need a web interface where every worker can work on several tasks and new tasks can be started and distributed to any other iTask worker working on the internet. Such a more fancy web interface can be defined "just" as an iTask task in the iTask system. It can be user defined as desired, but for doing so one needs more knowledge about the iTask system than we have explained so far, therefore we do not define such an iTask task here on this spot.

Instead, we simply make use of a task we have predefined for you. It is "just" an iTask task called manageWorkflows, which takes a list of tasks that can interactively be started by the end-user (see Example 20). For each task in the list a description is added which explains what the purpose of the task is.

In Fig. 12 this predefined task manager is shown with all CEFP exercises included. In the left-upper task pane all tasks which can be started are displayed in a tree structure. If one clicks on one of these tasks, it is displayed left-below what the purpose of that task is. The tasks to do are displayed in the right-upper pane, much alike incoming emails in an email application. These are task which the end-user either started herself or tasks to-do which are given to the end-user by someone else. The end-user can work on several tasks at the same time in the right-below pane, by choosing one of the tabs.

Before you enter the task manager, you have to login. In the beginning there is only one user administrated, the administrator named *root*. Before we start, you need to 'employ' a number of workers.

Exercise 17. *Setting up your user-base*
When logged in as *root*, you can start the *Admin/Users* task in the task pane which is only visible for the administrator. With this administrative task, you can add users to your workflow management system. This is needed for the remaining exercises of these lecture notes. Add a positive number of users to your workflow management system.   ■

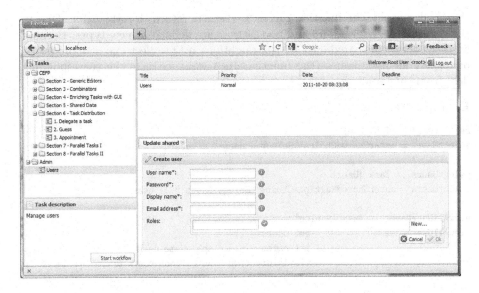

Fig. 12. The Predefined iTask Task Manager Task Showing All CEFP Examples

Once users are registered, you can access them with a number of operations. Just like date and time, as explained in Section 5, this is done via shared data.

Table 8. Accessing the user base

```
users              ::            ROShared [User]
usersWithRole      :: Role →     ROShared [User]
currentUser        ::            ROShared User
userDetails        :: User →     Shared UserDetails
currentUserDetails ::            ROShared (Maybe UserDetails)

:: UserDetails   = { userName     :: UserId
                   , password     :: Password
                   , displayName  :: String
                   , emailAddress :: EmailAddress
                   , roles        :: Maybe [Role]
                   }
:: UserId        :== String
:: Password      = Password    String
:: EmailAddress  = EmailAddress String
:: Role          :== String
```

Table 8 enumerates the functions with which (a subset of) the current users can be retrieved. For the purpose of the lecture notes, the User data type is not very interesting, but the UserDetails record is. It contains the information that you have entered in Exercise 17. Because you do not have to be logged in to use the iTask system, the function `currentUserDetails` returns a `Maybe` value. Due to their special status, `Password` and `EmailAddress` are defined as new types. Because access is done via shared data, it is straightforward to select one or more users, or display all user names (the function `displayName` extracts the corresponding field from the details record):

Example 21. *Tasks to access the user-base*

```
selectUser  :: Task User                                              1
selectUser  = enterSharedChoice "Select a user:" [] users            2
                                                                      3
selectUsers :: Task [User]                                            4
selectUsers = enterSharedMultipleChoice "Select users:" [] users     5
                                                                      6
viewAllUserNames :: Task [String]                                     7
viewAllUserNames =              get users                             8
                >>= λus → let names = map displayName us in           9
                        viewInformation "The current users are: " [] names  10
```

Exercise 18. *Reading your user-base*
Add the `viewAllUserNames` task as a workflow to your system and run it. This should display the names of the users that you have entered in Exercise 17. ■

With the `@:` operator, a task can be assigned to a user:

```
(@:) infix 3 :: User (Task a) → Task a | iTask a
```

As an example, consider the `delegate` workflow:

Example 22. *A delegate task pattern to distribute work*

```
delegate :: (Task a) → Task a | iTask a                              1
delegate task                                                        2
    =              selectUser                                        3
        >>= λuser   → user @: task                                   4
        >>= λresult → updateInformation "Check result" result        5
```

Exercise 19. *Question user*
Create a workflow that first selects an arbitrary user, then edits a question, and finally asks the selected user to answer the entered question. The answer must be displayed to the user who asked the question.

Exercise 20. *A 2-person number guessing game*
Use `delegate` to write a workflow that first asks the current user to enter a secret number, then to select two other users who are going to try and guess the secret number. The user who guesses the number first wins. Use one of the combinators of Table 3 to distribute the work in parallel.

Exercise 21. *A 2-person dialogue*
Write a workflow in which the current user contacts another user, and initiates a dialogue with that user. In turn, each user enters a line of text. The history of the conversation must be displayed, but should not be editable. The conversation is terminated as soon as either user enters an empty line of text. The result of the workflow must be a value of type [(User,String)] that collects the entire conversation, with the most recent line of text at the head of the list. ∎

8   Parallel Tasks I: A Fixed Number of Tasks

So far all examples involved at most two registered workflow users. Naturally, one wants to generalize over the number of users. The iTask system provides a single, *swiss army knife* combinator for this purpose, called parallel. In this section we explain how to use this versatile combinator for an arbitrary, yet constant, number of users. In Section 9 we continue our discussion and show how it can be used to accommodate a dynamic number of users.

The signature of parallel is:

```
parallel :: d s (ResultFun s a) [TaskContainer s] → Task a | iTask s & iTask a
                                                                    & descr d
```

We briefly discuss its parameters first. The first parameter is the usual *description* argument that we have encountered many times so far. It plays the same role here: a description to the user to inform her about the purpose of this particular parallel task in the workflow.

The second argument is the initial value of the *state* of the parallel task: the state is a shared data (as discussed in Section 5) that can be inspected and altered *only by* the tasks that belong to this parallel task.

The third argument is a function of type:

```
:: ResultFun s a   :== TerminationStatus s → a
:: TerminationStatus = AllRunToCompletion | Stopped
```

The purpose of the ResultFun function is to turn the value of the state of the parallel task at termination into the final value of the parallel task itself. They need not have the same type, so the state is converted to the final value when the parallel task is finished. The parallel combinator can terminate in two different ways. It can be the case that all subtasks are finished (AllRunToCompletion). But, as we will see later, a subtask can also explicitly kill the whole parallel construction (Stopped). This information can be used to create a proper final value of parallel.

Finally, the fourth argument is the initial list of *task (container)s* that constitute the parallel task. A task container consists of two parts: a task type representation (ParallelTaskType) defining how the subtask relates to its super-task, and the subtask itself (defined on shared state s) to be run in parallel with the others (ParallelTask s):

```
:: TaskContainer s :== (ParallelTaskType, ParallelTask s)
:: ParallelTaskType = Embedded
                    | Detached ManagementMeta
```

The ParallelTaskType is either one of the following:

- Embedded basically 'inlines' the task in the current task.
- Detached meta displays the task computed by the function as a distinct new
  task for the user identified in the worker field of meta. ManagementMeta is a
  straightforward record type that enumerates the required information:

```
:: ManagementMeta =
    { worker          :: Maybe User
    , role            :: Maybe Role
    , startAt         :: Maybe DateTime
    , completeBefore  :: Maybe DateTime
    , notifyAt        :: Maybe DateTime
    , priority        :: TaskPriority
    }
:: TaskPriority       = HighPriority | NormalPriority | LowPriority
```

It should be noted that the u @: combinator is simply expressed as a parallel
combination of two tasks. One of type Detached with the worker set, and another of type Embedded that displays progress information.

```
:: ParallelTask s :== (TaskList s) → Task ParallelControl
:: TaskList s
:: ParallelControl = Stop | Continue
```

The task creation function takes as argument an abstract type, TaskList s, where
s is the type of the data the subtasks share. Every subtask has to yield a task
of type ParallelControl to tell the system, when the subtask is finished, whether
the parallel task as a whole is also finished (by yielding Stop) or not (by yielding
Continue.)

As will be explained in Section 9, the number of subtasks in the task list can
change dynamically. One can enquire its status, using the following functions on
the abstract type TaskList s:

```
taskListState      :: (TaskList s) → Shared s | TC s
taskListProperties :: (TaskList s) → Shared [ParallelTaskInfo]
```

With the function taskListState one can retrieve the data shared between the
tasks of the parallel combinator. As discussed in Section 5, you can use get,
set, and update to access its value. There is another function, taskListProperties,
which can be used to retrieve detailed information about the current status of
the parallel tasks created. This can be used to control the tasks, and is explained
in more detail in the next section.

We first illustrate the static use of **parallel** by a number of examples. In the first example, we create a variant of Exercise 19.

Example 23. *Question N users*

```
questions :: Task [(User,String)]                                         1
questions                                                                 2
    =                   updateInformation "Pose a question" [] "...?"      3
      >>= λquestion → selectUsers                                         4
      >>= λusers    → parallel "parallel" [] (λ_ s → s)                   5
                        [ (DetachedTask (normalTask u), answer u question) 6
                        \\ u ← users                                       7
                        ]                                                  8
where                                                                     9
    answer u question tasks                                               10
        =               updateInformation question [] "...!"              11
          >>= λa → update (λanswers → [(u,a):answers]) (taskListState tasks) 12
          >>|       return Continue                                       13
                                                                          14
normalTask :: User → ManagerProperties                                    15
normalTask u = { worker   = u                                             16
               , priority = NormalPriority                                17
               , deadline = Nothing                                       18
               , status   = Active                                        19
               }                                                          20
```

Example 23 first asks the current user to enter a question (line 3), and then make a selection of the current set of registered users (line 4). For each user (line 7), a detached task is created (line 6) that asks the user to answer the question (line 10). This task simply adds the given answer to the shared data of the parallel construct (line 12) and returns Continue. The parallel construction therefore will end when all subtasks are finished in this way (yielding AllRunToCompletion). The function normalTask is a useful convenience function. Notice that an update of shared data is performed in one atomic action, such that no concurrency problems can occur when multiple subtasks are finishing up.

Finally, we develop a *chat* example in which an arbitrary number of people communicate with each other.

Example 24. *Chat infrastructure*

```
:: ChatState    :== [String]                                              1
                                                                          2
initChatState   :: ChatState                                              3
initChatState   = []                                                      4
                                                                          5
addLine         :: User String ChatState → ChatState                      6
addLine me line s = s ++ [me +++> ": " +++ line]                          7
```

The conversation is to be stored as a simple list of strings (of type ChatState), and there are two trivial access function to create an initial value, and to add a new line of text to the conversation. (The operators +++> and <+++ are convenient to convert the first and second argument respectively to text and concatenate it with their String argument.)

Example 25. *A naive parallel chat example without menus*

```
naive_chat :: Task ChatState                                                    1
naive_chat                                                                      2
    =                        get currentUser                                    3
        >>= λme      →  selectUsers                                             4
        >>= λothers →  let chatters = [me : others]                            5
                       in  parallel "Naive chat" initChatState (λ_ chats → chats) 6
                           [  (DetachedTask (normalTask who), chat who chatters)  7
                           \\ who ← chatters                                     8
                           ]                                                     9
where                                                                          10
    chat :: User [User] (TaskList ChatState) → Task ParallelControl            11
    chat me chatters tasks                                                     12
        = forever (                   get chatState                           13
            >>= λxs           → updateInformation header [] (Display xs, Note "") 14
            >>= λ(_,Note n) → update (addLine me n) chatState                 15
          )                                                                    16
        >>| return Stop                                                        17
    where                                                                      18
        chatState = taskListState tasks                                        19
        header    = "Chat with " +++ join "," (map toString chatters)         20
```

The chat example first selects a number of users (lines 3-4), and continues with the parallel creation of tasks (lines 6-9). These are created as menu-less detached chat tasks (normalTask was defined in Example 23). The chat task is an infinite task (using the forever combinator) that reads the current conversation (line 13), allows the current user to enter a new line of text (line 14), and that adds the new line of text to the current conversation (line 15). The forever constructor is followed by the task return Stop to ensure that the definition of chat is type correct yielding a value of type Task ParallelControl, even though it is known that this return will never be reached. The join function concatenates a list of strings, using an infix string given as first argument (it is actually overloaded, see Text.dcl).

Exercise 22. *Naive chat*
Run the naive chat Example 25, and test it with several users. Does the example run as you would expect? Adapt the example in such a way that the chat task is inlined for the me user, and displayed as detached task for the others users. What is changed in the interface?   ■

Running the naive chat example demonstrates that the shared state is only updated *after* a user has entered text. For a chat example, this does not make much sense: you want to *monitor* the shared value in order to be informed of changes to that value. In iTask, this can be achieved with the viewSharedInformation interaction task combinator:

```
viewSharedInformation :: d [ViewOn l r w]  (RWShared r w) l → Task (r,l)
                       | descr d & iTask l & iTask r & iTask w
```

We can use this in the task below to create a more realistic chat example.

Example 26. *A monitoring parallel chat example without menus*

```
monitor_chat :: Task ChatState                                            1
monitor_chat                                                              2
   = ...same body as naive chat ...                                       3
where                                                                     4
     chat :: User [User](TaskList ChatState) → Task ParallelControl       5
     chat me chatters tasks                                               6
        =  viewSharedInformation headerMonitor [] chatState Void          7
           ||-                                                            8
           forever enterLine                                              9
       >>| return Continue                                                10
     where                                                               11
        headerEditor    = "Chat with "        +++ join "," (map toString chatters) 12
        headerMonitor   = "Conversation of " +++ join "," (map toString chatters) 13
        enterLine       =            enterInformation headerEditor []     14
                    >>= λ(Note n) → update (addLine me n) chatState       15
                                                                         16
        chatState       = taskListState tasks                            17
```

The difference with the naive chat example is that we use the viewSharedInformation task combinator to display the current content of the conversation (line 10), and an infinite task for each user to enter text lines (lines 9 and 14-15).

9   Parallel Tasks II: A Dynamic Number of Tasks

Parallel tasks can inspect each other's status by applying the function taskList-Meta to the TaskList. It returns a shared data of type [ParallelTaskMeta]. This can be used to read the status (via a get), but also to change the properties (via a set or update) of the subtasks running in parallel.

Table 9. Parallel task meta-information

```
taskListMeta :: (TaskList s) → Shared [ParallelTaskMeta]

:: ParallelTaskMeta = { index                :: Int
                      , taskId               :: TaskId
                      , taskMeta             :: TaskMeta
                      , progressMeta         :: Maybe ProgressMeta
                      , managementMeta       :: Maybe ManagementMeta
                      }

:: ProgressMeta     = { issuedAt             :: DateTime
                      , issuedBy             :: User
                      , status               :: TaskStatus
                      , firstEvent           :: Maybe DateTime
                      , latestEvent          :: Maybe DateTime
                      }
:: TaskStatus       = Running | Finished | Excepted
```

In Table 9, ParallelTaskMeta is shared data which can be inspected by all tasks in the parallel construction to get meta-information of all tasks. This is comparable to a process table in an operating system, except that only the subtasks are shown which belong to this particular parallel combinator. This shared data structure provides useful information to monitor the running tasks, but also to change them. For example, the meta-data of a task, such as the ManagementMeta can be altered on-the-fly using a set. We will not pursue this further in these lecture notes.

In this section it is shown how the taskList can be used to dynamically alter the number of subtasks running in parallel. The following operations are offered to the programmer.

```
appendTask :: (TaskContainer s) (TaskList s) → Task Int  | TC s
removeTask :: Int              (TaskList s) → Task Void | TC s
```

Tasks can be appended to the list of tasks running under this parallel construction using appendTask. In a similar way, removeTask terminates the indicated task from the list of tasks, even if it has not run to completion.

Example 27. *A Petition Campaign*

```
:: Petition = { titlePetition      :: String              1
              , deadlineSubmission :: DateTime            2
              , description        :: Note                3
              }                                           4
:: Signer   = { name               :: String              5
              , profession         :: Maybe String        6
              , emailAddress       :: String              7
              , comments           :: Maybe Note          8
              }                                           9
derive class iTask Petition, Signer                      10
                                                         11
myPetition :: Task (Petition,[Signer])                   12
myPetition =          enterInformation "Describe the petition" []   13
           >>= λp → campaign p p.titlePetition p.deadlineSubmission 14
           >>=      viewInformation "The petition has been signed by:" []  15
```

To illustrate their use, we show as example a workflow for coordinating a petition campaign. In myPetition a concrete description (of type Petition) of the petition has to be given by the end user first (line 13). Then, the petition campaign is started (line 14). The idea of this campaign is to get the petition signed by as many people as possible before the specified deadline has been reached (see Figure 13).

When the campaign is finished, it is shown by whom the petition has been signed (line 17). To sign the petition, a supporter has to fill in a form, in this particular case of type Signer. All signed petitions are collected in a list which is returned by the campaign task, together with the petition itself.

```
campaign :: pet String DateTime → Task (pet,[signed]) | iTask pet & iTask signed 1
campaign pet title deadline                                                     2
   =              enterSharedMultipleChoice "Invite people to sign" [] users    3
   >>= λsigners → parallel ("Sign Petition: " +++ title) []                     4
                 (λ_ signed → (pet,signed))                                      5
                 [ (Embedded, waitForDeadline deadline)                         6
                 : [ (Detached (normalTask signer),sign pet)                    7
                   \\ signer ← signers                                          8
                 ]                                                              9
                 ]                                                             10
```

Notice that the campaign task can be used for any kind of petition as well as for any kind of form to be signed by the supporters. The campaign starts by letting the organizer select an initial set of users (line 3) who all in parallel will be asked to sign the petition (lines 7-9). The signed petitions are collected in the shared state of parallel, which is of type [Signed]. In addition also a hidden task is started to watch the deadline (line 6). When the parallel construct is finished, either because the deadline has been passed or all users who have been asked have finished signing, the signed petitions together with the petition itself is returned (line 5).

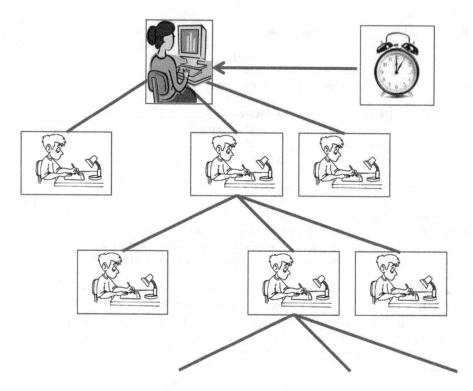

Fig. 13. A Petition Campaign

```
waitForDeadline dateTime list                                           1
    =       waitForDateTime dateTime                                    2
        >>| return Stop                                                 3
```

The subtask `waitForDeadline` waits until the indicated date and time are passed.
It returns `Stop` to indicate that the entire parallel construct ends. All users who
want to sign the petition after the deadline get a message that this task is no
longer needed.

```
sign :: pet (TaskList [signed]) → Task ParallelControl | iTask pet & iTask signed 1
sign pet list                                                                      2
    =       enterInformation ("Please sign the following petition:") [About pet]   3
        >?* [(Action "Decline", Always  (return Continue))                         4
            ,(Action "Sign",    IfValid signAndAskFriends)                         5
            ]                                                                       6
where                                                                              7
    signAndAskFriends signed                                                       8
        =       update (λlist → [signed:list]) (taskListState list)                9
            >>| viewInformation "Thanks for signing !" [] Void                    10
            >>| enterSharedMultipleChoice "Invite other people too" [] users      11
            >>= askSigners                                                        12
```

```
                                                                              13
  askSigners []      = return Continue                                        14
  askSigners [c:cs] = appendTask (Detached (normalTask c), sign pet) list     15
                   >>| askSigners cs                                          16
```

In task `sign` a user is first asked to sign the petition shown (line 3) by filling in
the presented form. She can decline (line 4) after which the subtask is ended.
She can also "`Sign`" the petition after filling in the presented form (line 5). After
being so supportive, she on her turn is asked to invite other people to sign as
well (line 11). For all people additionally invited in this way, `askSigners` appends
a new subtask for signing to the parallel construct.

To illustrate that the parallel construct can also be used to make a single user
multi-window web application, we show how a simple text editor can be defined.

Example 28. *Editor Application*

```
:: EditorState  = { mytext      :: String                                     1
                , replace    :: Bool                                           2
                , statistics :: Bool                                           3
                }                                                              4
initEditor text = { mytext     = text                                         5
                , replace    = False                                          6
                , statistics = False                                         7
                }                                                              8
updateText    f = update (λs → {s & mytext     = f s.mytext})                 9
updateReplace b = update (λs → {s & replace    = b})                          10
updateStat    b = update (λs → {s & statistics = b})                          11
                                                                              12
noReplace    s = not s.replace                                                13
noStatistics s = not s.statistics                                             14
                                                                              15
:: FileName    :== String                                                     16
readTextFile   ::  FileName        → Task (Bool, String)                      17
saveTextFile   ::  FileName String → Task Bool                                18
```

First we define some types and utility functions. In this example there are three
different windows offering three different views on the same text. In addition to
the main text editor, there are two additional, optional, windows. One can optionally be opened allowing to search for substrings to be replaced. Another one
can be opened to display statistics of the current text, such as the number of characters, words, and lines. The `EditorState` is used as shared data in which the text
being edited is stored (`mytext`). The state also administrates whether the `replace`
and `statistics` tasks are running. This is used to prevent the creation of multiple instances. There are utility functions for accessing (`noReplace`, `noStatistics`)
and updating the specific fields in the `EditorState` (`updateText`, `updateReplace`, and
`updateStat`). The tasks `saveTextFile` and `readTextFile` can be used for writing and
reading text to a file.

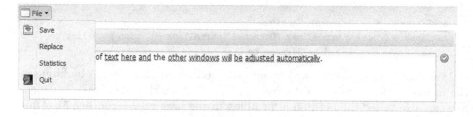

Fig. 14. Screenshot of Example 28: *A Simple Text Editor*

```
editorApplication ::  Task Void                                                    1
editorApplication                                                                  2
    =                   enterInformation "Give name file to edit..." []            3
        >>= λfileName → readTextFile fileName                                       4
        >>= λ(_,text) → parallel "Editor" (initEditor text) (_ _ → Void)           5
                                       [(BodyTask, editor fileName)]               6
```

In the editorApplication the end user is asked for the name of the file to edit (line
3), after which its content is read from disk (line 4). In the parallel (line 5-6) the
content is stored in the shared editor state, and initially just one task is created,
the editor itself.

```
editor fileName ls                                                                 1
    = updateSharedInformation (fileName,"Edit " +++ fileName) views myState Void    2
      >?* [(ActionSave,       IfValid   save)                                       3
          ,(ActionReplace,    Sometimes (onlyIf (noReplace    o fst) replace))      4
          ,(ActionStatistics, Sometimes (onlyIf (noStatistics o fst) statistics))   5
          ,(ActionQuit,       Always    quit)                                       6
          ]                                                                         7
where                                                                              8
    views = [UpdateView ( GetShared (λs              → Note s.mytext)               9
                        , SetShared (λ(Note text) _ s → {s & mytext = text})       10
                        )                                                          11
            ]                                                                      12
                                                                                  13
    save (val,_)                                                                  14
        =       saveTextFile fileName val.mytext                                 15
            >>| editor fileName ls                                               16
                                                                                  17
    replace _                                                                     18
        =       updateReplace True myState                                       19
            >>| appendTask ( Embedded                                            20
                           , replaceTask {search = "", replaceBy = ""}           21
                           ) ls                                                  22
            >>| editor fileName ls                                               23
                                                                                  24
    statistics _                                                                  25
        =       updateStat True myState                                          26
            >>| appendTask ( Embedded, statisticsTask) ls                        27
            >>| editor fileName ls                                               28
```

```
                                                                    29
quit                                                                30
    =        return Stop                                            31
                                                                    32
myState = taskListState ls                                          33
                                                                    34
ActionReplace    :== Action "File/Replace"                          35
ActionStatistics :== Action "File/Statistics"                       36
```

In the main parallel task, editor, the editing of the text stored in the shared
state is realized by the iTask editor updateSharedInformation (line 2). A value of
type Note is used as view on the shared text string and any update made by the
end-user is directly be mapped back in this shared state (lines 8-11). It provides
four options to the end user, labeled ActionSave, ActionReplace, ActionStatistics,
and ActionQuit (lines 3-7).

With ActionSave, she can choose to save the current text (line 3), after which
the text is stored to file and the editor is recursively called to allow to continue
editing (line 14-16). The update of the browser page is optimized such that such
recursive calls are not visually noticeable to the end user.

With ActionReplace, the end user can replace text (line 5). This creates a new
task, replaceTask, to run in parallel with the text editor (line 23). The option is
available only if the replaceTask task is not already running (line 5). If this is
indeed the case, the corresponding Boolean value is set in the shared state (line
21), to mark that a replacement task is created, after which this task is indeed
appended (line 21-24). After forking off this task, the editor is recursively called
to allow to continue editing.

```
:: Replace  = { search    :: String                                 1
              , replaceBy :: String                                 2
              }                                                      3
                                                                    4
replaceTask :: Replace (TaskList EditorState) → Task ParallelControl 5
replaceTask replacement ls                                          6
   = updateInformation ("Replace","Define replacement...") [] replacement  7
     >?* [(ActionOk,      IfValid replace)                          8
         ,(Action "Close", Always close)                            9
         ]                                                          10
where                                                               11
    replace repl                                                    12
        =      updateText (replaceSubString repl.search repl.replaceBy) myState  13
          >>| replaceTask repl ls                                   14
    close                                                           15
        =      updateReplace False myState                          16
          >>| return Continue                                       17
```

The replaceTask uses a local iTask editor on type Replace allowing the end user to
type in a string to search for with its replacement (line 7). When the OK button is
hit (line 8), the text in the shared state will be searched and updated (line 13),
after which replaceTask calls itself again (line 14) to allow more replacements to

Fig. 15. Screenshot of Example 28: *The Replace Dialogue*

be made. All other tasks looking at the shared state, such as the main editor and possibly the statistics task, immediately get the update made and change their view accordingly. When the end user chooses Close (line 9), it is administrated in the shared state that the task has ended (line 16), and this tasks ends (line 17).

Analogous to replacing text, ActionStatistics keeps track whether it is active or not, and triggers the statisticsTask if not (line 6, 27-30).

```
:: TextStatistics = { lines        :: Int                                       1
                    , words        :: Int                                       2
                    , characters :: Int                                         3
                    }                                                           4
                                                                                5
statisticsTask :: (TaskList EditorState) → Task ParallelControl                 6
statisticsTask ls                                                               7
    = viewSharedInformation ("Statistics","Statistics of your document")        8
                                             views (taskListState ls) Void      9
        >?* [(Action "Close", Always close)]                                    10
where                                                                           11
    views = [DisplayView (GetShared showStatistics)]                           12
                                                                                13
    showStatistics state                                                        14
        = { lines = length (split "\n" state.mytext)                            15
          , words = length (split " " (replaceSubString "\n" " " state.mytext)) 16
          , characters = textSize state.mytext                                  17
          }                                                                     18
    close                                                                       19
        =       updateStat False myState                                        20
            >>| return Continue                                                 21
                                                                                22
    myState = taskListState ls                                                  23
```

The statisticsTask has a read-only view on the text stored in the shared state (lines 8-9,13). Any change made in the shared text by the end user, either made by using the editor, or by using the replaceTask will directly lead to an update of the statistic information displayed. When the statistic window is closed, this is administrated (line 20) to allow it to be opened again in the main editor.

Fig. 16. Screenshot of Example 28: *The Statistics Dialogue*

Finally, with ActionQuit, the end user quits the application by Stopping the parallel construct which closes any remaining windows.

10   The Core Pillars of iTasks

The iTask system is a special combinator library written in Clean to support the construction of interactive applications with an emphasis on the task concept. In these lecture notes we have focussed on an important class of basic tasks, the iTask editors. Tasks can be composed from others using iTask combinators. Editors and combinators are two important concepts in the iTask system. Although we have seen many different editors and many different combinators, they are actually all variants of the same. In the core of the iTask system we have defined one function which can take care of all editor variants. For combining tasks, we only need two: the monadic bind for sequencing tasks and the parallel combinator for creating a dynamically extensible number of parallel tasks. From these functions all other editors and all other combinators shown can be derived. These core functions therefore form the pillars of the iTask core system. They deserve some special attention in this concluding section of the lecture notes.

The fact that we can express such a complicated functionality with only a few functions illustrates the expressive power of a functional language such as Clean. An advantage is that we need less code, errors are less likely to occur, and the maintenance effort is reduced significantly.

10.1   The Core iTask Editor

The core iTask editor interact (see below) has many similarities with update-SharedInformation, that we already have seen in Section 6. The main difference with updateSharedInformation is that interact is even more general and contains more information for the construction of views. In these lecture notes, many different variant of editors are presented, but they can all be expressed in terms of this core editor.

Table 10. The core interaction task

```
interact :: d (l r Bool → [InteractionPart l w]) l (RWShared r w) → Task (l,r)
                                 | descr d & iTask l & iTask r & iTask w

:: InteractionPart l w
   =∃v:  FormPart    (FormView v) ((Maybe v) → (l,Maybe w)) & iTask v
   |∃v:  DisplayPart v                                      & iTask v
   |     UpdatePart  String (l,Maybe w)

:: FormView v  = FormValue v
               | Blank
               | Unchanged (FormView v)
```

With interact, one can edit two different kinds of given values at the same time: a local value, which is only accessible for this specific editor, say of type l, and shared data, which can be accessed by other editors or systems at the same time as well. Reading and writing to shared data can be of different type, say a value of type r can be read, while a value of type w can be written. Different users of an iTask system can play a different role in an organization. One therefore needs to be able to present the information in a proper way, depending on the role to play. As usual one can therefore define different Views On the local and shared data. This actually means that one defines a *bidirectional map* between the demanded view v and the local data l and shared data r and w.

A view is just a value of some type. The iTask system presents the value to the browser which renders the information in such a way that the end user can do her work and edit the information. Any change made in any view is mapped back to a change in the local and shared data. These changes are communicated immediately to the other users or systems looking at this data and may lead to an update of their view. When the edit action is ended, the final values of local and shared data are communicated to the next tasks to be done.

The views to show can be defined as follows. The interactive rendering to create can be an editable form (FormPart), a non-editable form (DisplayPart), or it can be a trigger such as a button (UpdatePart). For a smooth interaction it needs to know what to do when a form is not yet filled in (Blank), changed (FormValue), or left unchanged (Unchanged). One can define as many views as wanted, such that certain information can be shown editable, and others not. Also the number and kind of views can be calculated dynamically using a function yielding the list of views to show, given the current value of local and shared state. The Boolean value which is given as additional parameter to this function is internally set by the iTask engine. It indicates whether the shared state has recently been altered by someone else, which is used to trigger a recalculation of the rendering, even though the end-user did not change anything with this editor.

10.2   The Core iTask Combinators

We already have explained the core iTask combinators in the previous sections. Here we summarize them once again.

```
(>>=) infixl 1 :: (Task a) (a → Task b)          → Task b | iTask a & iTask b
return        :: a                               → Task a | iTask a
```

The iTask library uses on the top level a monadic approach to hide the state transformation for the iTask programmer. The monad we use is called the Task monad. Internally, in the core implementation, however, uniqueness typing is being used instead [2]. This gives us the best of two worlds: internally it makes it easier to handle all the different kind of state information which has to be maintained, while on the top level this is all hidden.

One can define a sequence of two tasks with the monadic bind operator (>>=). As usual, the result of the first operand (of type Task a) is passed as argument to the second argument, a function of type a → Task b. With return any value can be lifted to the task domain.

```
parallel :: d s (ResultFun s a) [TaskContainer s] → Task a
                                      | iTask s & iTask a & descr d

:: TaskContainer s :== (ParallelTaskType, ParallelTask s)
:: ParallelTask s  :== (TaskList s)    → Task ParallelControl

taskListState      ::            (TaskList s) → Shared s | TC s
taskListProperties ::            (TaskList s) → Shared [ParallelTaskInfo]

appendTask         :: (TaskContainer s) (TaskList s) → Task Int  | TC s
removeTask         :: Int         (TaskList s) → Task Void | TC s
```

With parallel an arbitrary number of tasks can be created to work on in parallel. Each parallel task has two components: the task to do and a GUI container defining what the purpose of a task is, such that it can be presented to the end-user in the proper way.

It is observed that parallel tasks can be used for different purposes. One can use a task to take care of some computer system, device driver, web server or application. But a parallel task can also be used to handle multiple tasks to be performed by the same end user, or to handle some task to be performed by someone else. For all these different purposes, a suitable GUI container can be specified (see Section 8).

TaskList is an abstract type which manages a kind of process table administration. It is administrated which subtasks have been created for this particular parallel combinator. One can enquire the administration (using taskListProperties) and ask which processes (tasks) are known and what their status is. One can get hold of the shared state (using taskListState) the subtasks are using to communicate with each other. One can add new tasks (using appendTask) or kill existing ones (using removeTask). Hence the iTask system behaves much like an operating system where new processes can be created or stopped as demanded. Instead of one flat process administration as common in an operating system, the iTask system has a hierarchical one. A new level is made when a subtask uses the `parallel` combinator.

11   Related Work

The iTask system is a toolbox to create WFMS applications. These applications are distributed, multi-user, and persistent. The iTask system deploys contemporary web technology to create this as well as to generate rich content and GUI elements for the end-user. In Section 1, we have already compared the system with contemporary WFMS systems. The other core aspect of the iTask system, programming rich web applications in a functional style, has not been compared yet. This is the topic in this section. Many solutions that have been inspiring for our work have been proposed to program web applications. We mention just a few of them in a number of languages: the Haskell cgi library [14]; the Curry approach [8]; writing xml applications [6] in *SMLserver* [7], and the WashCGI [21], based on Haskell. In these lecture notes we have shown that programming interactive applications in iTask is generic, allowing application developers to focus on creating proper *models* of interactive programs, instead of *programming the visualization*. This is also the key difference with the above mentioned approaches.

Links [3] and formlets [4] were developed in roughly the same period as the iTask system. Links compiles to JavaScript for rendering html pages, and SQL to communicate with a back-end database. A Links program stores its session state at the client side. In a Links program, the keywords `client` and `server` force a top-level function to be executed at the client or server respectively. Both systems, as well as iTask, use Ajax technology to implement the communication between client and server. The iTask system generalizes the opportunity to perform client-side computation to arbitrary expressions of a workflow.

Finally, in the Hop [20,13] web programming language, only the GUI part is compiled to JavaScript, whereas the other part runs natively. Hop is a stratified language and maintains a strict separation between programming the user interface and the logic of an application. The programmer is forced to express the required functionality in the proper stratum. In contrast, in iTask there is no such distinction, and the client is, in principle, able to perform any server-side computation that does not rely on server-side properties such as access to back-end databases.

12   Conclusions

In these lecture notes we have presented the iTask system. Although originally designed to be a WFMS programming language, it has evolved gradually into a more general approach that is based on the concept of tasks. In our view, there are two key reasons for this development:

- *The use of a functional host programming language* stimulates abstraction and hence the creation of general purpose building blocks. In these lecture notes we have illustrated this approach by many examples and exercises to show how to apply well-known functional programming techniques such as polymorphism and higher-order functions to obtain such applications.
- *The use of generic programming techniques* increases the degree of abstraction even further and allows the specification of interactive programs in terms of *models* instead of *programming views*. This is illustrated extensively in these lecture notes in the way interactive applications are constructed.

We have shown in Section 10 that the entire system is founded on three primitive functions, viz. the `interact` task to handle *user-system-interaction*, the `parallel` combinator to *coordinate* cooperating tasks, and the monadic `>>=` combinator to *sequentially* compose tasks. Finally, the concept of *shared state* (Section 5) abstracts from handling persistent and volatile data. In short, a task-oriented language should liberate the programmer from these programming chores. We think that the iTask system is a first step towards achieving this goal.

Acknowledgements. The authors thank the anonymous referees for their constructive comments.

References

1. van der Aalst, W., ter Hofstede, A., Kiepuszewski, B., Barros, A.: Workflow patterns. Technical Report FIT-TR-2002-02, Queensland University of Technology (2002)
2. Barendsen, E., Smetsers, S.: Conventional and Uniqueness Typing in Graph Rewrite Systems (Extended Abstract). In: Shyamasundar, R.K. (ed.) FSTTCS 1993. LNCS, vol. 761, pp. 41–51. Springer, Heidelberg (1993)
3. Cooper, E., Lindley, S., Wadler, P., Yallop, J.: Links: Web Programming Without Tiers. In: de Boer, F.S., Bonsangue, M.M., Graf, S., de Roever, W.-P. (eds.) FMCO 2006. LNCS, vol. 4709, pp. 266–296. Springer, Heidelberg (2007)
4. Cooper, E., Lindley, S., Wadler, P., Yallop, J.: An idiom's guide to formlets. Technical report, The University of Edinburgh, UK (2007), http://-groups.inf.ed.ac.uk/links/papers/formlets-draft2007.pdf
5. Domoszlai, L., Bruël, E., Jansen, J.M.: Implementing a non-strict purely functional language in JavaScript. Acta Universitatis Sapientiae 3, 76–98 (2011)
6. Elsman, M., Larsen, K.F.: Typing XHTML Web Applications in ML. In: Jayaraman, B. (ed.) PADL 2004. LNCS, vol. 3057, pp. 224–238. Springer, Heidelberg (2004)
7. Elsman, M., Hallenberg, N.: Web Programming with SMLserver. In: Dahl, V. (ed.) PADL 2003. LNCS, vol. 2562, pp. 74–91. Springer, Heidelberg (2003)
8. Hanus, M.: High-Level Server Side Web Scripting in Curry. In: Ramakrishnan, I.V. (ed.) PADL 2001. LNCS, vol. 1990, pp. 76–92. Springer, Heidelberg (2001)
9. Jansen, J.M., Koopman, P., Plasmeijer, R.: Efficient interpretation by transforming data types and patterns to functions. In: Nilsson, H. (ed.) Proceedings of the 7th Symposium on Trends in Functional Programming, TFP 2006, Nottingham, UK, April 19-21, pp. 157–172 (2006) ISBN 978-1-84150-188-8

10. Jansen, J.M., Plasmeijer, R., Koopman, P.: iEditors: Extending iTask with Interactive Plug-ins. In: Scholz, S.-B., Chitil, O. (eds.) IFL 2008. LNCS, vol. 5836, pp. 192–211. Springer, Heidelberg (2011)
11. Koopman, P., Plasmeijer, R., Achten, P.: An Executable and Testable Semantics for iTasks. In: Scholz, S.-B., Chitil, O. (eds.) IFL 2008. LNCS, vol. 5836, pp. 212–232. Springer, Heidelberg (2011)
12. Lijnse, B., Jansen, J.M., Nanne, R., Plasmeijer, R.: Capturing the Netherlands coast guard's sar workflow with itasks. In: Mendonca, D., Dugdale, J. (eds.) Proceedings of the 8th International Conference on Information Systems for Crisis Response and Management, ISCRAM 2011, Lisbon, Portugal. ISCRAM Association (May 2011)
13. Loitsch, F., Serrano, M.: Hop client-side compilation. In: Proceedings of the 7th Symposium on Trends in Functional Programming, TFP 2007, New York, NY, USA, April 2-4, pp. 141–158. Interact (2007)
14. Meijer, E.: Server side web scripting in Haskell. Journal of Functional Programming 10(1), 1–18 (2000)
15. Michels, S., Plasmeijer, R., Achten, P.: iTask as a New Paradigm for Building GUI Applications. In: Hage, J., Morazán, M.T. (eds.) IFL 2010. LNCS, vol. 6647, pp. 153–168. Springer, Heidelberg (2011)
16. Plasmeijer, R., Achten, P., Koopman, P.: iTasks: executable specifications of interactive work flow systems for the web. In: Hinze, R., Ramsey, N. (eds.) Proceedings of the International Conference on Functional Programming, ICFP 2007, Freiburg, Germany, pp. 141–152. ACM Press (2007)
17. Plasmeijer, R., Achten, P., Koopman, P., Lijnse, B., van Noort, T., van Groningen, J.: iTasks for a change - Type-safe run-time change in dynamically evolving workflows. In: Khoo, S.-C., Siek, J. (eds.) Proceedings of the Workshop on Partial Evaluation and Program Manipulation, PEPM 2011, Austin, TX, USA, pp. 151–160. ACM Press (2011)
18. Plasmeijer, R., Jansen, J.M., Koopman, P., Achten, P.: Declarative Ajax and client side evaluation of workflows using iTasks. In: Proceedings of the 10th International Conference on Principles and Practice of Declarative Programming, PPDP 2008, Valencia, Spain, July 15-17, pp. 56–66 (2008)
19. Plasmeijer, R., Lijnse, B., Achten, P., Michels, S.: Getting a grip on tasks that coordinate tasks. In: Proceedings Workshop on Language Descriptions, Tools, and Applications (LDTA), Saarbrücken, Germany, March 26-27 (2011)
20. Serrano, M., Gallesio, E., Loitsch, F.: Hop, a language for programming the web 2.0. In: Proceedings of the 11th International Conference on Object-Oriented Programming, Systems, Languages, and Applications, OOPSLA 2006, Portland, Oregon, USA, October 22-26, pp. 975–985 (2006)
21. Thiemann, P.: WASH/CGI: Server-side Web Scripting with Sessions and Typed, Compositional Forms. In: Krishnamurthi, S., Ramakrishnan, C.R. (eds.) PADL 2002. LNCS, vol. 2257, pp. 192–208. Springer, Heidelberg (2002)
22. Wadler, P.: Comprehending monads. In: Proceedings of the Conference on Lisp and Functional Programming, LFP 1990, Nice, France, pp. 61–77 (1990)

Reasoning about I/O in Functional Programs

Andrew Butterfield*

Trinity College, University of Dublin
Andrew.Butterfield@scss.tcd.ie

Abstract. We look at formalisms for reasoning about the effects of I/O in pure functional programs, covering both the monadic I/O of Haskell and the uniqueness-based framework used by Clean. The material will cover comparative studies of I/O reasoning for Haskell, Clean and a C-like language, as well as describing the formal infrastructure needed and tool support available to do such reasoning.

1 Introduction

This tutorial focusses on techniques for reasoning about the input-output behaviour of pure functional programs, and is largely based on material published at IFL on the issue [BS01, BDS02].

The key points to be made are that: (1) ultimately users are only interested in the I/O behaviour of their programs; (2) it is possible to apply formal reasoning techniques to give useful results in this area; (3) and yes, it does require a considerable degree of "real-world" modelling.

As ever, it is the choice of a suitable abstraction that makes such reasoning both tractable and useful. The focus of this tutorial is on pure (lazy) functional languages with referentially transparent I/O, such as Haskell and Clean, but the ideas presented here (particularly in the latter part) are also applicable to impure languages such as Scheme or ML.

1.1 Motivation

An often cited advantage of functional programming languages is that they are supposed to be easier to reason about than imperative languages [BW88, p1],[PJ87, p1],[Bd87, p23],[BJLM91, p17],[Hen87, pp6–7],[Dav92, p5] with the property of *referential transparency* getting a prominent mention and the notion of *side-effect* being deprecated all round. For a long time, a major disadvantage of functional programming languages was their inability to adequately handle features where side-effects are an intrinsic component, such as file or other I/O operations [BJLM91, p139],[Gor94, p-xi]. However, two methodologies have emerged in the last two decades to combine the side-effect world of I/O with the referentially transparent world of functional programming, namely

---

* The material in this tutorial draft derives from joint work with Glenn Strong, Malcolm Dowse, and Marko van Eekelen.

V. Zsók, Z. Horváth, and R. Plasmeijer (Eds.): CEFP 2011, LNCS 7241, pp. 93–141, 2012.
© Springer-Verlag Berlin Heidelberg 2012

the *uniqueness type system* of the programming language Clean [BS96] and the use of *monads* in the Haskell language [Gor94],[BW88, Chp 10, pp326–359].

In [BS01, BDS02] we explored some of the consequences of these developments for formal reasoning about I/O behaviour.

Our first concern was that the technical machinery necessary to handle I/O in pure functional languages, may have led to a situation where correctness proofs would have the same difficulty as found in imperative programs. Fortunately, this proved not to be the case. In technical terms, the reason why reasoning about I/O in pure functional languages is still easier than for imperative ones is the fact that the variables in a Haskell "do" or Clean "#-let" are all different (look carefully at the scope rules for those language constructs) even if they have the same name, whereas the repeated use in C of the same variable name denotes successive side-effects to the same memory location. Despite appearances, Haskell's do-notation using "<-" is not a sequence of assignments, but a series of nested function-call bindings, and similarly for Clean's #-let. In essence, both monads and uniqueness-typing are designed to ensure that I/O does not break referential transparency.

A second issue concerns the relative ease of reasoning when using either of the two technical alternatives, namely uniqueness typing and/or monads. The uniqueness typing approach uses the type-system to ensure that the external "world" is accessed in a single-threaded fashion, so that an underlying implementation can safely implement operations on the world using side-effects, while still maintaining referential transparency. From the programmer's perspective nothing changes in the program, except that it must satisfy the type-checker. The monadic approach uses an abstract datatype which enforces single-threaded use of world resources, but which also requires the programmer to explicitly make use of this datatype and its operations. In effect, the monad acts as a wrapper around the potentially unsafe operations. We asked if the monad wrapper was a significant extra overhead, relative to the uniquely typed program when it came to doing formal reasoning. In [BS01] we concluded there was a small overhead. However, in subsequent work [BDS02], we discovered that the ability of monads to help in structuring I/O actions, and its well-documented facility for structuring large programs [Esp95, LHJ95, HK98], carried over to giving proofs a better structure. It also proved to be quite easy to carry over this aspect to the proofs about Clean I/O.

The focus in [BS01] was on comparing a simple program written in Haskell, Clean and C, while the work in [BDS02] looked at a more complex program — a simplified version of the unix **make** command. This was to explore the fact that real-world programs of interest typically combine I/O and computation in essential and non-trivial ways. The concern here was how to develop reasoning techniques that scale when applied to complex programs which perform arbitrary I/O actions. This has to be done carefully —we need to make intelligent use of abstraction, and ensure the continuing adequacy of the resulting simplified models.

Some of the approaches discussed used simplified or unified versions of the corresponding languages, but we also dealt with full-blown Clean and Haskell programs and deal explicitly with the issue of error and exception handling, rather than ignoring it.

This tutorial basically delivers evidence to back up the conclusions of [BS01, BDS02], as discussed above.

1.2   The Practicality of I/O Proofs

One issue raised at IFL'02 concerned the possibility or practicality of doing any kind of formal proofs involving I/O. This was on foot of our talk about proving the correctness of a simplified version of the Unix make utility, implemented in either Haskell or Clean. This seemed to accompany a concern regarding the lack of concurrency in our model. Here, for convenience, we reproduce the discussion about this matter in the IFL 2002 paper [BDS02].

The gist of the argument went as follows:

> On a real machine with a real OS there are many other processes running concurrently, so your I/O model needs to deal with these. In any case, some other process may make arbitrary changes to the filesystem while make is running so it becomes impossible to give a formal proof of any property, even in the unlikely event of having a complete formal model covering all possible concurrent processes.

We first address the issue of the impossibility/impracticality of doing formal proofs of the I/O behaviour of make (or any other similar program). First, consider the reaction of a make user if someone was to replace their make program with a broken version, or even go to such extremes as to substitute a completely different program (renaming cat to make, for example). The user would rapidly become aware that something was up. The point is, in typical uses of the make program, users have reasonable expectations for its behaviour, which are generally met, by and large. The main reason is that most users rely on an operating system to ensure that there aren't arbitrary and destructive changes to the collection of files being manipulated by make. Despite the theoretical possibility of concurrent processes making arbitrary changes to a user's files, the common practical use of make occurs in a much more controlled environment.

If informally we know what to expect of make, then it is possible to consider formal proofs of its properties. If arbitrary concurrent behaviour elsewhere in the system makes it impossible to reason formally about its behaviour, then it is just as impossible to reason informally about its behaviour, and its behaviour in that context will appear arbitrary.

A final comment is also required about the perception that formal proof is useless unless it is somehow "complete", i.e. covering every aspect of the system being modelled. This view was encouraged by early formal methods research which sought to produce systems which were completely verified "head-to-toe"

```
h <- openFile "a" ReadMode          h <- openFile "a" ReadMode
s <- hGetContents h                 s <- hGetContents h
i <- readIO s::IO Int               i <- readIO s::IO Int
hClose h                            hClose h
h <- openFile "a" WriteMode         h <- openFile "a" WriteMode
hPutStr h (show ((i+1)*(i-1)-1))    hPutStr h (show (i*i))
hClose h                            hClose h
```

              (a)   (b)

Fig. 1. Simple Haskell I/O Programs

(e.g. [Bjø92]). However formal proof is much more practical when it focuses on aspects of interest (usually safety critical), by exploiting suitable choices of abstractions.

1.3   Tutorial Structure

The remainder of this document is arranged as four sections, addressing the themes of formalisms for API modelling (Section 2), integration with language semantics (Section 3), increasing the modelling complexity (Section 4), and looking beyond the Haskell language and the $VDM^{\clubsuit}$ formalism discussed in the previous three sections (Section 5). The focus in Section 2 is on a brief description of a formalism called $VDM^{\clubsuit}$[Mac91], a functional dialect of VDM [Jon89], and its application to a simple filesystem API model. In Section 3, we explore how to formalise the connection between the API model, and a semantics for the programming language (in this case, Haskell). Here we introduce the use of monads as a key structuring concept. The emphasis switches in Section 4 into looking at examples of more realistic, and hence more complex filesystem APIs. Finally, in Section 5 we discuss broadening out from Haskell to other functional languages (most notably Clean), and also mention more powerful formalisms that are available, and point to a key challenge that remains: reasoning effectively about concurrency and state. Appendix A lists the class definitions and instances found in the Haskell implementation of the $VDM^{\clubsuit}$ toolkit.

2   Formalism and API Modelling

2.1   Motivation

Consider two Haskell programs whose top-level "do-actions" are shown in Figure 1. Both programs clearly have the same behaviour, because $(i+1)(i-1)-1 = i^2$, assuming we ignore any issues to do with overflow. We can prove this with varying degrees of rigour and formality in a number of ways.

For example, we can simply argue that the equality stated above holds, invoke the principle of referential transparency, and then convert one program above so its looks syntactically identical to the other. Given that I/O in general raises

$$n \in \mathbb{N} \;=\; \{0, 1, 2, \ldots\}$$
$$v \in Var \qquad \text{variables}$$
$$e \in E ::= n \mid v \mid plus(e,e) \mid mul(e,e) \mid app(f,e)$$
$$f \in F ::= v \hookrightarrow e$$

Fig. 2. The language E

concerns in Haskell about referential transparency, perhaps we might prefer to do a more rigourous proof, by using the monad laws (see Section 3.1), in which we can convert one program into the other, albeit by ending up invoking the above equality.

However, knowing that the two programs above have the same behaviour (in this case sequences of I/O action side-effects), is not the same as being able to demonstrate rigourously, that the effect of running either program is to:

- Open file "a" and read an integer from it
- Overwrite file "a" so it now contains only that integer squared.

The simple fact is that most users do not care if two programs are "equal":

$$prog_1 = prog_2,$$

or if one is an "improvement" or "refinement" of another:

$$spec \sqsubseteq prog.$$

Instead, their concern is that the program does the right thing, where "doing" covers the interactions of the program with its users and environment. However, most formal approaches to program correctness focus on relationships between "program design texts" (specifications, programs), rather than looking at the relationship between program and environment behaviours.

The focus in this tutorial is on techniques that support formal reasoning about the effects that functional programs have on their environments, via their I/O facilities. By the term environment we mean whatever is external to the program/system, which depends on context. Program/system environments may include: file-systems, network sockets, sensors or effectors, including keyboards, screens, or even other software artifacts: components, APIs, etc.

The key to all reasoning is Abstraction: *simplify, reduce, focus* on what is important. What we shall do here is demonstrate that it is possible to abstract I/O to an effective degree, simple enough to make formal reasoning possible, but complex enough to allow useful properties to be proven.

2.2   Formal Semantics

As we are going to be looking at developing formal semantics for I/O behaviours, it is worth exploring the key notions behind programming language semantics.

$$\rho \vdash n \rightarrow n \qquad\qquad \rho \vdash v \rightarrow \rho(v) \qquad\qquad \frac{\rho \vdash e_1 \rightarrow n_1 \qquad \rho \vdash e_2 \rightarrow n_2}{\rho \vdash plus(e_1, e_2) \rightarrow n_1 + n_2}$$

$$\frac{\rho \vdash e_1 \rightarrow n_1 \qquad \rho \vdash e_2 \rightarrow n_2}{\rho \vdash mul(e_1, e_2) \rightarrow n_1 \times n_2} \qquad\qquad \frac{\rho \vdash e_a \rightarrow n_a \qquad \rho \dagger \{v \mapsto n_a\} \vdash e_f \rightarrow n_f}{\rho \vdash app(v \hookrightarrow e_f, e_a) \rightarrow n_f}$$

Fig. 3. E : Natural Semantics

Program and I/O model semantics will have to be tied together in order to reason about a program's I/O behaviour. Specifically, we are looking at using mathematics to provide a rigourous meaning to our programs and models, to the extent that they are amenable to mechanized reasoning, at least in principle.

For program languages, formal semantics belong broadly to one of three distinctive "flavours": Operational, Denotational, or Axiomatic. We will illustrate these by using all three to give a semantics to a simple expression language (Figure 2).

Language E has numbers (n), variables (v), binary operators *plus* and *mul* and a function application operator *app*. Functions are described anonymously, using the binder notation $v \hookrightarrow e$, read as the "function taking v as input and returning e". We deliberately avoid using familiar notations such as $+$, $\times$ or $\lambda v \bullet e$ here, as we want to have these available to describe the semantics, not the syntax, and to keep these two aspects separate for clarity.

Operational Semantics. The key idea behind operational semantics, is to describe the meaning of a program by describing its execution on some form of symbolic mechanism that evaluates or runs the program. In many ways it is the most natural way to describe a programming language, as most programmers intuition is focussed on the effects of their programming language constructs. For this reason, it is also the favoured semantics for language implementors as it gives a clear specification of what the interpreter and/or compiled code must do.

Operational semantics comes in a number of varieties, of which the most prevalent today is the so-called Structural Operational Semantics (SOS), whose main principle is that the operational rules are defined inductively over the structure of the language syntax [Plo81, Hen90]. Another common distinction in operational semantics is the difference between big-step and small-step: the former describes the final outcome of running any fragment, whilst the latter describes the next single atomic action performed by any such fragment. SOS is typically small-step, whilst a large-step semantics based on the language structure is usually referred to as a Natural Semantics [Kah87].

A big-step (natural) semantics for language E is shown in Figure 3.

The natural semantics is defined as a set of inference rules about a judgement of the form

$$\rho \vdash e \rightarrow n$$

$$(\rho, v) \to (\rho, \rho(v)) \qquad (\rho, plus(n_1, n_2)) \to (\rho, n_1 + n_2)$$

$$(\rho, mul(n_1, n_2)) \to (\rho, n_1 \times n_2) \qquad \frac{(\rho, e_1) \to (\rho', e_1')}{(\rho, plus(e_1, e_2)) \to (\rho, plus(e_1', e_2))}$$

$$\frac{(\rho, e_2) \to (\rho', e_2')}{(\rho, plus(e_1, e_2)) \to (\rho, plus(e_1, e_2'))} \qquad \frac{(\rho, e_1) \to (\rho', e_1')}{(\rho, mul(e_1, e_2)) \to (\rho, mul(e_1', e_2))}$$

$$\frac{(\rho, e_2) \to (\rho', e_2')}{(\rho, mul(e_1, e_2)) \to (\rho, mul(e_1, e_2'))} \qquad \frac{(\rho, e_a) \to (\rho', e_a')}{(\rho, app(v \hookrightarrow e_f, e_a)) \to (\rho', app(v \hookrightarrow e_f, e_a'))}$$

$$\frac{(\rho \dagger \{v \mapsto n_a\}, e_f) \to (\rho', n_r')}{(\rho, app(v \hookrightarrow e_f, n_a)) \to (\rho, n_r')}$$

Fig. 4. E : SOS Semantics

which is read as saying: "Given environment ρ, expression e evaluates to number n". Here $\rho : Var \to \mathbb{N}$ is a mapping of variables to their values, and the rule for function application uses the notation $\rho \dagger \{v \mapsto n\}$ which describes map ρ having its value for v overwritten to now be n.

Note that this semantics defines function application as strict: arguments are evaluated before the call.

A small-step (SOS) semantics works with a different judgement:

$$(\rho, e) \to (\rho', e')$$

which asserts that a single step of the evaluation of e in environment ρ results in new environment ρ' and new expression e'. A small-step SOS semantics for E is shown in Figure 4. The main differences here are that small step semantics gives more control over evaluation order, and that we have to talk about the notion of when evaluation/execution halts, if at all. In this case it halts when none of the above rules apply, and the execution is successful if the final expression is a pure number. Note also that this semantics is non-deterministic, in that a *plus* or *mul* can evaluate each of its arguments using any interleaving of the small steps required. Non-determinism is not forced upon us here, but, for example, if we wanted to force operator *mul* argument evaluation in left to right order, then we could change the rules as follows:

$$\frac{(\rho, e_1) \to (\rho', e_1')}{(\rho, mul(e_1, e_2)) \to (\rho, mul(e_1', e_2))} \qquad \frac{(\rho, e_2) \to (\rho', e_2')}{(\rho, mul(n_1, e_2)) \to (\rho, mul(n_1, e_2'))}$$

We now only allow the second argument to evaluate when the first one is a number. Non-determinism in SOS is quite common, giving the implementor freedom to alter evaluation orders if that helps optimise the result. When reasoning about concurrent languages, non-determinism becomes an essential abstraction

$$\rho \in Env = Var \to \mathbb{N}$$
$$[\cdot] \; : \; E \to (Env \to \mathbb{N})$$
$$[n]_\rho \mathrel{\widehat{=}} n$$
$$[v]_\rho \mathrel{\widehat{=}} \rho(v)$$
$$[plus(e_1, e_2)]_\rho \mathrel{\widehat{=}} [e_1]_\rho + [e_2]_\rho$$
$$[mul(e_1, e_2)]_\rho \mathrel{\widehat{=}} [e_1]_\rho \times [e_2]_\rho$$
$$[app(v \hookrightarrow e_f, e_a)]_\rho \mathrel{\widehat{=}} [e_a]_{\rho \dagger \{v \mapsto [e_f]_\rho\}}$$

Fig. 5. Denotational Semantics of E

tool. Another advantage of the SOS semantics as formulated above, is that it effectively defines a labelled transition system (LTS) and these are the basis of a large number of automated analysis tools, of which model-checkers are probably the most important in contemporary industrial-scale verification [CGL92].

While good for specifying implementations, and animating or model-checking programs, operational semantics are not as well suited as denotational semantics when it comes to validating axiomatic semantics, nor are they good compared to axiomatic semantics for reasoning about general properties of a given program. This is because, typically, we are forced to prove properties via some form of induction over the language syntax or the SOS rules. and this does not scale well.

Denotational Semantics. The denotational approach to semantics [Sto77, Sch86] describes meaning as a function over an appropriate (often complex) mathematical structure ("domain"). A key principle here is that the meaning of composite language forms is as a function of the *meanings* of their subcomponents, so that the semantics is compositional (also a feature of SOS and natural semantics).

For our simple language E, the meaning of an expression is as a function from environments to numbers, and its denotational semantics is shown in Figure 5. From a functional programmers perspective, a denotational semantics seems a very natural way to talk about meaning, namely as a function. Admittedly, the denotational semantics of a pure functional language can appear almost trivial (it looks like the language "is" its own semantics), except that the treatment of recursion is decidedly non-trivial [Sto77]. For languages with recursion or iteration, the mathematical domain needs to have enough structure to allow the determination of solutions to fixed-point equations, and a whole sub-discipline of semantics called fixed-point theory has been developed to support this.

A denotational semantics can be viewed as a model (in the logical sense) for an operational semantics, which, with its inference rules, looks like a logical system. In general a denotational semantics can serve as a basis for proving the soundness of other semantic flavours. In particular, proving the soundness of an axiomatic semantics is often most easily done w.r.t. a denotational view.

$$plus(e, 0) = e$$
$$plus(e_1, plus(e_2, 1)) = plus(plus(e_1, e_2), 1)$$
$$plus(e_1, e_2) = plus(e_2, e_1)$$
$$plus(e_1, plus(e_2, e_3)) = plus(plus(e_1, e_2), e_3)$$
$$\text{similar for } mul$$
$$app(v \hookrightarrow e_f, e_a) = e_a[e_f/v]$$
$$plus(n_1, n_2) = n_1 + n_2$$
$$mul(n_1, n_2) = n_1 \times n_2$$

Fig. 6. Axiomatic Semantics for E

The main disadvantages of denotational semantics are: it can be very difficult to identify the proper domain, particularly in languages involving concurrency; the treatment of recursion can be problematical; there is often no obvious mapping to a language implementation, and like operational semantics, it is poor at reasoning about general properties of specific programs, when compared against axiomatic semantics.

Axiomatic Semantics. The third flavour, axiomatic semantics, gives a language meaning by providing laws that define relationships among program texts. These relationships may include some notion of equality (usually behavioural equivalence) or of inequality w.r.t to some ordering (typically refinement/reification). An axiomatic semantics for E is shown in Figure 6, that declares expressions to be equal if, for any environment, they always deliver the same result. In effect we obtain a set of "laws of E".

The notation $e[e'/v]$ denotes the substitution of e' for free v in e.

Axiomatic semantics are a series of laws relating program texts, and so are very useful for reasoning formally at that level, without having to change to some underlying semantic notation. We need to be careful, however, to ensure that the laws are consistent and sound. It is in this regard that a denotational semantics makes a good complement to an axiomatic one. Also difficult is the question of completeness: do we have enough laws to be able to prove/disprove the equality of any two arbitrary programs? For example, the axiomatic semantics in Figure 6 has more than a minimal set of laws: the top four laws can be proven given the last three, plus the laws of arithmetic. As each axiomatic law only captures a small aspect of a relationship between program texts, such a semantic flavour is not much help to language implementors.

Semantics Summary. We can summarise the strengths of the three main flavours of semantics as follows:

Operational. Intuitive capture of program execution; highly suited for language implementors; underlying LTS framework useful for automated exhaustive checking (where feasible).

Denotational. Solid basis for soundness proofs in other semantic flavours.

Axiomatic. Provides laws that allow reasoning about programs at the level of the program texts themselves.

For all languages we consider in this tutorial, we will use a suitable axiomatic semantics where possible For I/O systems of interest we will generally develop a semantics by:

1. constructing an appropriate mathematical "domain"
2. Building a denotational semantics of an I/O language ("API")
3. Formulating some I/O axioms on top of the denotation.

The development of a domain and the corresponding API denotation we cover under the term "Modelling".

Challenge 1. We are now going to set a challenge, to give focus to the rest of this section:

Problem 1. Build enough formal machinery to prove that program

```
main = do
        s <- readFile "a"
        let i = read s
        writeFile "a" (show (i*i))
```

opens file "a", reads an integer from it, and then overwrites "a" so it only contains that integer squared.

Solution 1. We shall solve Problem 1 by carrying out the following steps

1. Determine modelling assumptions
2. Choose appropriate mathematical constructions
3. Model API behaviour in the mathematics
4. Extend language semantics to cover API
5. State desired property
6. Prove it

We shall adopt a pre-existing modelling approach for the first 3 steps, namely the so-called "Irish School" of the VDM (*VDM♣*) [Mac91]. It is a variant of the Vienna Development Method (VDM) [Jon89] that is functional in style, rather than imperative, and uses equational reasoning in classical logic, rather than natural deduction in 3-valued logic. Its main modelling technique is based on invariant preserving functions, with pre-conditions, and refinements characterised by retrieval functions from concrete state spaces to more abstract ones. It employs a mathematical toolkit that provides definitions for sets, sequences, and maps, and makes extensive use of abstract algebra ideas, most notably monoids and their homomorphisms, as a basis for those definitions.

We now proceed to look at the toolkit in some more detail.

$\mathcal{P}$	type-constructor
$\mathcal{P}_1$	non-empty Sets
$\times$	Cross-Product
$\{a, b, c, \ldots\} : \mathcal{P}A$	Enumeration
$\{\}, \emptyset : \mathcal{P}A$	Empty
$\cap, \cup : \mathcal{P}A \times \mathcal{P}A \to \mathcal{P}A$	Intersection, Union
$\backslash, \triangle : \mathcal{P}A \times \mathcal{P}A \to \mathcal{P}A$	Difference, Symmettric
$\blacktriangleleft, \triangleleft : \mathcal{P}A \to \mathcal{P}A \to \mathcal{P}A$	Removal, Restriction
$\sqcup : \mathcal{P}A \times \mathcal{P}A \overset{p}{\to} \mathcal{P}A$	Disjoint Union
$\# : \mathcal{P}A \to \mathbb{N}$	Cardinality

Fig. 7. $VDM^{\clubsuit}$ Sets

2.3 Formal Toolkit

We give a brief introduction to the notation, of the $VDM^{\clubsuit}$ Toolkit which provides formal definitions for sets, sequences and maps. We shall spend a little more time on the latter as they are key, and our treatment of them is more extensive than most. How the mathematical toolkit is used for building formal models will be described later, when we use it to build our own theories of I/O.

Sets in $VDM^{\clubsuit}$. The notation used for sets is shown in Figure 7. A lot of the mathematical notation in $VDM^{\clubsuit}$ conforms to that of standard VDM. We will mainly focus on the non-standard notation and concepts here.

The most unusual operator in $VDM^{\clubsuit}$ is its so-called "disjoint union" ($\sqcup$), or "set extension operator". It is a partial operator, that captures the notion of a set being extended by adding on a new/disjoint part, and so $A \sqcup B$ is only defined if $A \cap B = \emptyset$. When defined, it behaves exactly like set union:

$$A \cap B = \emptyset \Rightarrow A \sqcup B = A \cup B$$

Its main use is in pattern-matching, to split a set, e.g.:

$$\#\emptyset \cong 0$$
$$\#(S \sqcup \{x\}) \cong \#S + 1 \qquad (1)$$

Here the pattern in (1) will match any non-empty set, with x being bound to an arbitrary element of that set, and S bound to the rest of the set. This latter binding results from the requirement that the pattern, when instantiated with that binding, is well-defined. So, for example, matching the above pattern against $\{a, b\}$ can result in the following two bindings:

$$x \mapsto a \,, S \mapsto \{b\}$$
$$x \mapsto b \,, S \mapsto \{a\}$$

as both $\{b\} \sqcup \{a\}$ and $\{a\} \sqcup \{b\}$ are well-defined, and equal to $\{a, b\}$. However the binding

$$x \mapsto a, S \mapsto \{a, b\} \qquad (2)$$

is not valid, because $\{a, b\} \sqcup \{a\}$ is not defined.

If by contrast, we had the pattern $S \cup \{x\}$, then the binding (2) would be acceptable, as $\{a, b\} \cup \{a\}$ is defined, and equal to $\{a, b\}$. However, such a pattern does not help, as the "definition"

$$\#(S \cup \{x\}) \mathrel{\widehat{=}} \#S + 1$$

can lead to an infinite regress, if S keeps matching the whole set, and in any case, if viewed as an assertion it is simply not true in general, holding only if $x \notin S$.

The importance of any pattern of the form $S \sqcup \{x\}$, is that none of its pattern variables can match the whole, with S necessarily being smaller that the set against which this match is made. We can say that the pattern is *well-founded* in some sense, whereas $S \cup \{x\}$ is not.

Note also, that unlike pattern matching in Haskell, which is essentially syntactic (i.e. over the structure of algebraic `datatype`), this pattern matching is against a (partial) binary operator, and so has to be viewed as a form of semantic pattern matching.

Such patterns are non-deterministic in general. The following defines a partial "function" that returns an arbitrary member of a non-empty set.

$$arbChoice \;:\; \mathcal{P}A \nrightarrow A$$
$$arbChoice(S \sqcup \{x\}) \mathrel{\widehat{=}} x$$

In general it is very hard to reason about such entities in a simple fashion. For example, we can no longer rely on the following apparently obvious truth:

$$e = e.$$

To see this, consider the following instance:

$$arbChoice\{1, 2\} = arbChoice\{1, 2\}$$

Do the two instances of $arbChoice$ above represent the same, or different calls? If the latter, then both calls can return different values, and so the above equality may, or may not hold. We also lose other nice laws—the above is no longer the same as

$$x = x \textbf{ where } x = arbChoice\{1, 2\}.$$

If we decide that both calls to $arbChoice$ above represent a single call, then we get our nice equality law, but now have the effect that all instances everywhere of the application of $arbChoice$ to the set $\{1, 2\}$ are that one call returning that one unknown value. If we are using $arbChoice$ extensively to model some system then we have a behaviour that is unfeasibly global.

Our use of this non-deterministic pattern will avoid this issue, by ensuring that, despite any non-determinism, the result of any call always results in the same result. This can happen if all that the non-determinism is doing is selecting the order in which sub-computations are carried out. If these computations are associative and commutative in some sense, then the final outcome will be the same, regardless of computation order. For example, looking at the rhs of (1), we see that we recurse over the remaining set (S), and add 1. This terminates because the remaining set is smaller, and defines a function because the order in which xs are pulled out is immaterial to the final result, due to the properties of $(+1)$ being used here. All our uses of partial non-deterministic pattern matching will be safe in this manner.

An important aspect to note here is that the $VDM^{\clubsuit}$ approach described here is based on the notion of sets (and sequences, and maps, see later) as being finite. This naturally raises the question of how this fits with, for example, the list datastructure of Haskell, which can be infinite, given the laziness of the language. We point out that will be using $VDM^{\clubsuit}$ here to model the relevant structures of the external world, and not to present a semantics for Haskell. We view these external structures as being finite, i.e. artifacts built up in a constructive fashion from basic building blocks. This approach is sufficiently powerful for most modelling purposes. If a model of an API behaviour requires infinite structures, then more powerful formalisms are required (co-algebraic, rather than algebraic), but these are beyond the scope of this tutorial.

The other operators that need explaining are the set removal ($\vartriangleleft$) and set restriction ($\vartriangleleft$) operators. In effect these are just recasting set difference and intersection in a different form:

$$\vartriangleleft_A B = B \setminus A$$
$$\vartriangleleft_A B = B \cap A$$

Why adopt this apparently redundant notation? The answer has two aspects: algebraically, an operator like set intersection, can be viewed as a binary operator $(\_ \cap \_ : \mathcal{P}A \times \mathcal{P}A \to \mathcal{P}A)$ that forms a monoid, but alternatively, in its curried form $(\vartriangleleft : \mathcal{P}A \to \mathcal{P}A \to \mathcal{P}A)$, as a monoid homomorphism. We shall see that this latter aspect captures a pattern that is common to not just sets, but also sequences and maps.

Definition 1. *Monoids*
A Monoid $(M, \oplus, \iota)$ is a carrier set M with a binary operator $\oplus : M \times M \to M$ and a special (identify) element $\iota \in M$ satisfying the following laws:

$$\iota \oplus m = m = m \oplus \iota \qquad \textit{Identity}$$
$$m_1 \oplus (m_2 \oplus m_3) \quad = \quad (m_1 \oplus m_2) \oplus m_3 \qquad \textit{Associativity}$$

Monoids are ubiquitous — almost all the common mathematical operators participate in some form of monoidal structure:

$$(\mathbb{N}, +, 0) \quad (\mathbb{Z}, \times, 1) \quad (\mathcal{P}A, \cup, \emptyset) \quad (\mathcal{P}A, \cap, A) \quad (\mathcal{P}A, \triangle, \emptyset) \quad (A^{\star}, \frown, \langle\rangle)$$

If $\oplus$ is partial, then we have a partial monoid. where laws hold when all uses of $\oplus$ are defined, e.g. $(\mathcal{P}A, \sqcup, \emptyset)$. Describing an operator with an element as a

$$
\begin{array}{ll}
\star & \text{type-constructor} \\
+ & \text{non-empty} \\
\langle a, b, c, \ldots \rangle : A^\star & \text{Enumeration} \\
\langle \rangle, \varLambda : A^\star & \text{Empty} \\
\quad : A \times A^\star \to A^+ & \text{Cons} \\
\frown \; : A^\star \times A^\star \to A^\star & \text{Concatenation} \\
\vartriangleleft, \vartriangleleft : \mathcal{P}A \to A^\star \to A^\star & \text{Removal, Restriction} \\
\mathtt{elems} : A^\star \to \mathcal{P}A & \text{Elements} \\
\mathtt{len} : A^\star \to \mathbb{N} & \text{Length}
\end{array}
$$

Fig. 8. *VDM*♣ Sequences

monoid is just a shorthand, so for example, the entry above asserting that union and the set form a monoid is shorthand for:

$$
S \cup \emptyset = S
$$
$$
\emptyset \cup T = T
$$
$$
S \cup (T \cup U) = (S \cup T) \cup U
$$

Definition 2. *Monoid Homomorphisms*
A monoid homomorphism $h : (M, \oplus, \iota) \to (N, \otimes, \epsilon)$ *is a function* $h : M \to N$ *satisfying the following laws:*

$$
h(\iota) = \epsilon
$$
$$
h(m_1 \oplus m_2) = h(m_1) \otimes h(m_2)
$$

Essential a monoid homomorphism is a function from the carrier set of one monoid to that of another, that respects the monoid structure. In other words identity elements are mapped to identities, and applying a binary operator and mapping the result is the same as mapping the two argument first, and applying the other operator afterwards. SO, for sets, we can identify the following homomorphisms:

$$
\vartriangleleft_A : (\mathcal{P}A, \cup, \emptyset) \to (\mathcal{P}A, \cup, \emptyset)
$$
$$
\vartriangleleft_A : (\mathcal{P}A, \cup, \emptyset) \to (\mathcal{P}A, \cup, \emptyset)
$$
$$
\# : (\mathcal{P}A, \sqcup, \emptyset) \to (\mathbb{N}, +, 0)
$$

The last one above is defined from a partial monoid, into a total one.

Sequences in *VDM*♣**.** The notation for lists and sequences is shown in Figure 8. Note that we overload operators ◁ and ◁ to act on sequences, where here they act as filters (here *filter* is analagous to Haskell's `filter`):

$$
\vartriangleleft_A s \mathrel{\widehat{=}} \mathit{filter} \; (\_ \notin A) \; s
$$
$$
\vartriangleleft_A s \mathrel{\widehat{=}} \mathit{filter} \; (\_ \in A) \; s
$$

Concatenation forms a monoid

$$
(A^\star, \frown, \langle \rangle)
$$

and we have a number of homomorphisms:

$$\texttt{len} : (A^\star, \frown, \langle\rangle) \to (\mathbb{N}, +, 0)$$
$$\texttt{sum} : (\mathbb{N}^\star, \frown, \langle\rangle) \to (\mathbb{N}, +, 0)$$
$$\texttt{elems} : (A^\star, \frown, \langle\rangle) \to (\mathcal{P}A, \cup, \emptyset)$$
$$\blacktriangleleft_A : (A^\star, \frown, \langle\rangle) \to (A^\star, \frown, \langle\rangle)$$
$$\vartriangleleft_A : (A^\star, \frown, \langle\rangle) \to (A^\star, \frown, \langle\rangle)$$

Note that $\texttt{sum}$ and $\texttt{len}$ on $\mathbb{N}^\star$ differ from each other in how they treat the singleton list:

$$\texttt{sum}\langle n\rangle = n$$
$$\texttt{len}\langle n\rangle = 1$$

Stating that a function is a homomorphism is just a shorthand for listing a collection of laws. So the line above regarding $\texttt{elems}$, for example, simply states that:

$$\texttt{elems} \langle\rangle = \{\} \tag{3}$$
$$\texttt{elems}(s \frown t) = \texttt{elems}\ s \cup \texttt{elems}\ t \tag{4}$$

If we add the following law, we then have a complete definition of $\texttt{elems}$:

$$\texttt{elems}\langle x\rangle = \{x\} \tag{5}$$

Exercise 1. Write out all the laws for $\texttt{len}$, and $\#$, and for each, an extra law similar to that in (5) above

Exercise 2 (tricky). Explain why the above three laws for $\texttt{elems}$ (3,4,5) define it completely. Does your line of reasoning generalise to say the same for $\texttt{len}$ and $\#$?

Our treatment of sequences is very similar to that of Haskell lists, so we do not elaborate further here.

Maps in *VDM*♣. A key concept in *VDM*♣, and indeed in theoretical computer science as a whole, is the notion we present here of maps. Maps are partial functions defined for a finite number of values, and are ideal for modelling keyed-data lookup-tables, environments, etc. The basic components of our view of maps are shown in Figure 9. Maps are functions, so any value to the left of $\mapsto$ can only occur once in any given map. The key aspect of maps is not so much that they are partial functions, but that we view them as being manipulable in a particular way. We use θ to denote the empty map, and $\{a \mapsto b\}$ to denote the singleton map from a to b. We can also enumerate maps by listing their mappings explicitly, e.g.

$$\{a \mapsto b, c \mapsto d, e \mapsto f\}$$

$$
\begin{array}{rcll}
& \overset{m}{\to} & & \text{type-constructor} \\
\{\}, \theta & : & A \overset{m}{\to} B & \text{Empty} \\
\{a \mapsto b\} & : & A \overset{m}{\to} B & \text{Singleton Map} \\
& & \{a_1 \mapsto b_1, a_2 \mapsto b_2, \ldots\} & \text{Enumeration} \\
\_(\_) & : & (A \overset{m}{\to} B) \to (A \mapsto B) & \text{Lookup} \\
(\mu \sqcup \{a \mapsto b\})(a') & \hat{=} & \textbf{if } a' = a \textbf{ then } b \textbf{ else } \mu(a') & \\
\textbf{dom} & : & (A \overset{m}{\to} B) \to \mathcal{P}A & \text{Domain} \\
\textbf{rng} & : & (A \overset{m}{\to} B) \to \mathcal{P}B & \text{Range} \\
\_\sqcup\_ & : & (A \overset{m}{\to} B) \times (A \overset{m}{\to} B) \to (A \overset{m}{\to} B) & \text{(Disjoint) Map Union} \\
\_\dagger\_ & : & (A \overset{m}{\to} B) \times (A \overset{m}{\to} B) \to (A \overset{m}{\to} B) & \text{Override}
\end{array}
$$

Fig. 9. VDM♣ Map Basics

Map application takes a map of type $A \overset{m}{\to} B$ and a value of type A, and returns the corresponding value of type B, and is written using the usual function application notation:

$$\{a \mapsto b, c \mapsto d, e \mapsto f\}(c) = d$$

If the argument value is not present, then the application result is undefined. Given a map $A \overset{m}{\to} B$, its domain is the set of all values from A that appear, while its range is the values of type B that are present:

$$\textbf{dom}\{a \mapsto b, c \mapsto d, e \mapsto f\} = \{a, c, e\}$$
$$\textbf{rng}\{a \mapsto b, c \mapsto d, e \mapsto f\} = \{b, d, f\}$$

There are various ways to combine two maps of the same type. We will look at the most important two. The first is disjoint map union, analagous to disjoint set union, which is undefined the domains of the two maps overlap:

$$\{a \mapsto b, e \mapsto f\} \sqcup \{c \mapsto d\} = \{a \mapsto b, c \mapsto d, e \mapsto f\}$$

It is most commonly used for pattern matching, as already described for sets.

The second is map override, where overlapping domain conflicts are resolved by taking the second map as having precedence:

$$\{a \mapsto b, c \mapsto d\} \dagger \{c \mapsto g, e \mapsto f\} = \{a \mapsto b, c \mapsto g, e \mapsto f\}$$

There are other ways to resolve overlap conflicts, but we do not need them here.

Analagously to both sets and sequences, we also ways to remove and restrict map elements by specify sets of domain values to be removed ($\lhd_A$) or kept ($\lhd_A$).

$$\lhd_{\{c\}}\{a \mapsto b, c \mapsto d, e \mapsto f\} = \{a \mapsto b, e \mapsto f\}$$
$$\lhd_{\{c\}}\{a \mapsto b, c \mapsto d, e \mapsto f\} = \{c \mapsto d\}$$

Table 1. Sets in Haskell (excerpt)

Name	$VDM^{\clubsuit}$	Haskell
Constructor	$\mathcal{P}A$	`Set a`
Empty or Null	$\emptyset$	`nullSet`
Singleton	$\{a\}$	`iSet a`
Extension	$\sqcup$	`sextend`
Characteristic Fn., Membership	$\chi, \in$	`chrf, mOf`
Subset	$\subseteq$	`subSet`
Cardinality	$\#$	`card`
Union	$\cup$	`union`
Restriction/Intersection	$\lhd, \cap$	`srestrict, intersect`
Set Filter	$\lhd[p]$	`sfilter`
Removal/Difference	$\lhd, \setminus$	`sremove, setdiff`
Symmetric Difference	$\triangle$	`symdiff`
Choice	$S \sqcup \{x\}$	`sChoose`

We can summarise the laws by stating that both disjoint union and override form monoids, and noting that domain, range, removal and restriction are all homomorphisms:

$$(A \overset{m}{\to} B, \sqcup, \theta) \quad (A \overset{m}{\to} B, \dagger, \theta)$$

$$\mathrm{dom} \; : \; (A \overset{m}{\to} B, \dagger, \theta) \to (\mathcal{P}A, \cup, \emptyset)$$

$$\mathrm{dom}\{a \mapsto b\} = \{a\}$$

$$\mathrm{rng} \; : \; (A \overset{m}{\to} B, \sqcup, \theta) \to (\mathcal{P}B, \cup, \emptyset)$$

$$\mathrm{rng}\{a \mapsto b\} = \{b\}$$

$$\lhd, \lhd \; : \; \mathcal{P}A \to (A \overset{m}{\to} B, \dagger, \theta) \to (A \overset{m}{\to} B, \dagger, \theta)$$

$$\lhd_R\{a \mapsto b\} = \textbf{if } a \in R \textbf{ then } \theta \textbf{ else } \{a \mapsto b\}$$

$$\lhd_R\{a \mapsto b\} = \textbf{if } a \in R \textbf{ then } \{a \mapsto b\} \textbf{ else } \theta$$

Exercise 3. Write out explicitly all the laws regarding $\lhd$ contained in the above set of equations. Explain why they are enough to completely define $\lhd$.

The single most important law of maps is that which connects override and lookup:

$$(\mu_1 \dagger \mu_2)(a) = \textbf{if } a \in \mathrm{dom}\mu_2 \textbf{ then } \mu_2(a) \textbf{ else } \mu_1(a)$$

Override can also be expressed with restrict, remove and extend:

$$\mu_1 \dagger \mu_2 = \lhd_{(\mathrm{dom}\mu_2)}\mu_1 \sqcup \mu_2$$

Assuming $a \neq a'$ and $\{a, a'\} \subseteq \mathrm{dom}\,\mu$, then we can see that maps obey the following laws:

Lookup after Override with same key :
$$(\mu \dagger \{a \mapsto b\})(a) = b$$
Lookup after Override with different key :
$$(\mu \dagger \{a \mapsto b\})(a') = \mu(a')$$
Later overrides overwrite earlier ones :
$$(\mu \dagger \{a \mapsto b\}) \dagger \{a \mapsto b'\} = \mu \dagger \{a \mapsto b'\}$$
Disjoint overrides commute :
$$(\mu \dagger \{a \mapsto b\}) \dagger \{a' \mapsto b'\} = (\mu \dagger \{a' \mapsto b'\}) \dagger \{a \mapsto b\}$$

Maps are basically just an abstract model of addressed memory, or of state change were state has independent named components. This is the reason they are so important in modelling.

2.4   VDM♣ in Haskell

There is a simple implementation of the VDM♣ toolkit in Haskell that: implements sets as ordered non-unique lists; implements sequences as lists; and implements maps as ordered key-unique association lists. Overloading similar to that shown above for the toolkit is implemented using the Haskell classes feature

This is done by defining four classes: Container ($\mathcal{CT}$), Sngl ($\mathcal{SL}$), Dbl ($\mathcal{DL}$) and Partition ($\mathcal{PT}$), that capture basic notions of containment, membership, singleton construction, and partitioning or splitting.

Definition 3. *A container type $\mathcal{CT}$ is a type-constructor, such that $\mathcal{CT}\ T$ denotes some form of structure containing elements drawn from type T, supporting notions of emptiness (θ), membership ($\in$), merging ($\uplus$) and underlying set (uset), satisfying laws as detailed below:*

$$\theta\ :\ \mathcal{CT}\ T$$
$$\_\in\_\ :\ T \times \mathcal{CT}\ T \to \mathbb{B}$$
$$\_\uplus\_\ :\ \mathcal{CT}\ T \times \mathcal{CT}\ T \to \mathcal{CT}\ T$$
$$uset\ :\ \mathcal{CT}\ T \to \mathcal{P}\ T$$
$$x \notin \theta$$
$$x \in (C \uplus D)\ \equiv\ x \in C \vee x \in D$$
$$uset\ \theta\ =\ \emptyset$$
$$uset(C \uplus D)\ =\ uset\ C \cup uset\ D$$

Definition 4. *A single-element singleton type $\mathcal{SL}$ is a $\mathcal{CT}$ type-constructor that supports the construction of a singleton from a single datum (ι), satisfying the laws:*

$$\iota\ :\ T \to \mathcal{CT}\ T$$
$$x \in \iota\ y \equiv x = y$$
$$uset(\iota x) = \{x\}$$

Table 2. Maps in Haskell (excerpt)

Name	$VDM^{\clubsuit}$	Haskell
Constructor	$A \overset{m}{\to} B$	Map a b
Empty or Null	θ	nullMap
Singleton	$\{a \mapsto b\}$	iMap a b
Extension	$\sqcup$	mextend
Application	$\mu(a)$	mApp m a
Domain	dom	dom
Range	rng	rng
Override	$\dagger$	override
Glueing	$\cup$	glue
Restriction	$\lhd$	mrestrict
Removal	$\ntriangleleft$	mremove

Definition 5. *A double-element singleton type $\mathcal{DL}$ is a 2-argument type-constructor that supports the construction of a singleton from a pair of datums (γ), satisfying the laws:*

$$\gamma : T_1 \to T_2 \to \mathcal{CT}_{T_2} T_1$$
$$x \sqsubseteq \gamma \; y \; z \equiv x = y$$
$$uset(\gamma \; x \; y) = \{x\}$$

Definition 6. *A partition type $\mathcal{PT}$ is a type-constructor that is an instance of $\mathcal{CT}$, such that $\mathcal{PT} \; T$ is a container supporting three ways of being split: by selecting a singleton component ($\_ \sqcup (\iota\_)$); or doing the same but with a predicate to limit the selection ($\_ \sqcup_p (\iota\_)$); or splitting into two smaller chunks, using a predicate ($\_ \sqcup_p \_$), satisfying laws as detailed below:*

$$x \sqsubseteq (C \sqcup D) = x \sqsubseteq C \wedge x \notin D \vee x \sqsubseteq D \wedge x \notin C$$
$$x \sqsubseteq (C \sqcup_p D) = p \; x \wedge x \sqsubseteq C \vee \neg p \; x \wedge x \sqsubseteq D$$

The instantiation of sets, lists and maps as these classes is shown in Table 3.

The Haskell implementation of these classes and instances is summarised in Appendix A.

In effect we are able to take an $VDM^{\clubsuit}$ model and transcribe it into a Haskell equivalent. This provides type-checking support, and then allows the models to be animated, by loading it into the GHCi interpeter and then applying the reelvant functions to examples. QuickCheck integration is also provided, for both QuickChecks I & II, so it can be used to test properties of any models developed in this way. However, no kind of proof or automated reasoning is supported.

It is not currently available on hackage/cabal, but can be accessed via a Mercurial repository hosted at: https://bitbucket.org/andrewbutterfield/irishvdm

Table 3. Instantiating Sets, Sequences and Maps

$\mathcal{CT}\ A$	$\mathcal{P}A$	A^*	$A \overset{m}{\to} B$
C	S	σ	μ
θ	$\emptyset$	$\langle\rangle$	$\{\}$
$a \sqsubseteq C$	$a \in S$	$a \in \mathtt{elems}\ \sigma$	$a \in \mathtt{dom}\ \mu$
$C_1 \uplus C_2$	$S_1 \cup S_2$	$\sigma_1 \frown \sigma_2$	$\mu_1 \dagger \mu_2$
$\mathtt{uset}\ C$	S	$\mathtt{elems}\ \sigma$	$\mathtt{dom}\ \mu$
$\iota\ x$	$\{x\}$	$\langle x \rangle$	
$\gamma\ x\ y$			$\{x \mapsto y\}$
$C \sqcup \iota x$	$S \sqcup \{x\}$	$s \frown \langle x \rangle$	$\mu \sqcup \{a \mapsto b\}$
$C \sqcup D$	$S \sqcup T$	$s \frown t$	$\mu \sqcup \nu$

2.5   Simple Filesystem, Formal Model

We now turn to building a formal model of a (Very) Simple Filesystem (*VSFS*). This file-system supports the following Haskell API functions:

```
readFile  :: FilePath -> IO String
writeFile :: FilePath -> String -> IO ()
```

The important question to be answered here is about the required level of detail. We want to be able to talk about the file contents, associated with the appropriate filename, and to understand the relationship between strings and integers.

VDM♣ provides some basic types, including characters: $\mathbb{A}$, so both file-paths and contents we can treat as character sequences

$$n \in FP = \mathbb{A}^\star$$
$$s \in Str = \mathbb{A}^\star$$

We start with a very simple filesystem, that maps file-paths to file contents:

$$\phi \in VSFS = FP \overset{m}{\to} Str$$

We assume that all API functions have the same general format:

$$Input \to VSFS \to VSFS \times Output$$

where *Input* and/or *Output* may be omitted. This shape embodies that of the state monad, and this is no coincidence (of this, *much* more later ...). We are going to adopt a principle here that there is no need for the API function and the corresponding formal model function to have their arguments in the same order, or even exactly the same number of input and output values. This is fine because we formally define the meaning of the API call in terms of the model function, and that will explicitly describe the relationship between the two.

$$
\begin{aligned}
rdF &: & FP &\to VSFS \to VSFS \times Str \\
rdF\ n\ \phi &\ \hat{=}\ & &\textbf{if } n \in \textbf{dom } \phi \textbf{ then } (\phi, \phi(n)) \textbf{ else } (\phi, \langle\rangle) \\
wrF &: & FP &\to Str \to VSFS \to VSFS \\
wrF\ n\ s\ \phi &\ \hat{=}\ & \phi &\dagger \{n \mapsto s\} \\
read &: & \mathbb{A}^* &\to \mathbb{Z} \\
show &: & \mathbb{Z} &\to \mathbb{A}^* \\
& & read &\circ show = id
\end{aligned}
$$

Fig. 10. VSFS Formal Model Functions

For our two file API functions, we provide the following formal model functions

$$
rdF : FP \to VSFS \to VSFS \times Str
$$
$$
wrF : FP \to Str \to VSFS \to VSFS
$$

The meanings of `readFile` and `writeFile` are given in terms of rdF and wrF respectively, as follows:

$$
[\![readFile\ fp]\!]\ \phi \hat{=} rdF\ [\![fp]\!]\ \phi
$$
$$
[\![writeFile\ fp\ str]\!]\ \phi \hat{=} wrF\ [\![fp]\!]\ [\![str]\!]\ \phi
$$

Why does ϕ suddenly appear here like this? Its use here is reasonable, in that we need to talk about applying the API model function to a file-system object, as required by their signatures. We shall justify this formally in Section 3.

We can now formally define the model functions, shown in Figure 10. We don't give a formal definition of either *read* or *show* but just assert they are total[1], and give the one property we require. For reading, we note:

- If a file is missing, we return an empty string
- The filesystem itself is unchanged
- The operation is viewed as atomic
- We note the following immediate law:

$$
\pi_1(rdF\ n\ \phi) = \phi
$$

(Here π_i selects the ith component of a tuple).

Similarly, for writing:

- If the file does not exist, it is created.
- If the file already exists, it is overwritten.
- The operation is viewed as atomic.

---

[1] This is just for simplicity, to avoid having a side condition in our challenge that requires the initial file to contain a string that does denote an integer.

We can state our desired property as:

$$\text{``a''} \in \mathbf{dom}\ \phi \qquad\qquad\qquad \text{provided the file is present}$$
$$\Downarrow$$
$$read(\phi''\ \text{``a''}) = (read(\phi\ \text{``a''}))^2 \qquad \text{reading after is square of reading before}$$

$\qquad\qquad$ **where**

$(\phi', s) = rdF\ \text{``a''}\ \phi$	read file
$i = read\ s$	get integer
$\phi'' = wrF\ \text{``a''}\ (show(i^2))\ \phi'$	write its square

We can prove this by transforming the lefthand-side (LHS) into the righthand-side (RHS):

$$read(\phi''\ \text{``a''})$$
$$= read((wrF\ \text{``a''}\ (show(i^2))\phi')\ \text{``a''})$$
$$= read(\phi' \dagger \{\text{``a''} \mapsto show(i^2)\})\ \text{``a''}$$
$$= read(show(i^2))$$
$$= i^2$$
$$= (read\ s)^2$$
$$= (read\ \pi_2(rdF\ \text{``a''}\ \phi))^2$$
$$= (read\ \pi_2(\mathbf{if}\ \text{``a''} \in \mathbf{dom}\ \phi\ \mathbf{then}\ (\phi, \phi(\text{``a''}))\ \mathbf{else}\ (\phi, \langle\rangle)))^2$$
$$= (read\ \pi_2(\phi, \phi(\text{``a''}))))^2$$
$$= (read\ (\phi\ \text{``a''}))^2$$

This is all a bit ad-hoc: the property statement looks right and the proof is formal, and fairly easy, but is harder than it needs to be. However, it is not fully formalised, because:

- We wrote the property in an ad-hoc manner by reading the program and "figuring it out". The proof is formal, but the link to the program is not.
- For full formality, we need to integrate our API model with the program language's formal semantics.

We should also build an "API Theory" that allows us to simplify the proofs— doing a number of ad-hoc proofs like the above will rapidly reveal a number of proof-step patterns, which can be encapsulated by appropriate formal laws[2].

We consider a theory here to be a collection of laws/properties about some subject, that are useful when doing proofs involving that subject. The laws are derived from the relevant formal model, and they allow us to reason at the API level without always having to unwrap/rewrap formal definitions.

We want to do this for our simple *VSFS* API, and what is of interest here are the various ways in which *rdF* and *wrF* can interact.

---

[2] No prizes for guessing that the monad laws may play a part here!

Assuming $n \neq n'$ and $\{n, n'\} \subseteq \mathbf{dom}\ \phi$, we posit the following set of laws:

$$\pi_1(rdF\ n\ \phi) = \phi \qquad\qquad \text{[FRFSID]}$$
$$\pi_2(rdF\ n\ (wrF\ n\ s\ \phi)) = s \qquad\qquad \text{[FWRSAME]}$$
$$\pi_2(rdF\ n'\ (wrF\ n\ s\ \phi)) = \pi_2(rdF\ n'\ \phi) \qquad\qquad \text{[FWRDIFF]}$$
$$(wrF\ n\ s') \circ (wrF\ n\ s) = wrF\ n\ s' \qquad\qquad \text{[FWWSAME]}$$
$$(wrF\ n\ s) \circ (wrF\ n'\ s') = (wrF\ n'\ s') \circ (wrF\ n\ s) \qquad\qquad \text{[FWWDIFF]}$$

Proof of [FWWDiff]

Goal:

$$(wrF\ n\ s) \circ (wrF\ n'\ s') = (wrF\ n'\ s') \circ (wrF\ n\ s)$$

Strategy: Apply extensionality, and rewrite $\circ$.

$$wrF\ n\ s\ (wrF\ n'\ s'\ \phi) = wrF\ n'\ s'\ (wrF\ n\ s\ \phi)$$

and transform LHS into RHS:

$$wrF\ n\ s\ (\underline{wrF\ n'\ s'\ \phi})$$
$$= \langle\ \text{defn. } wrF\ \rangle$$
$$\underline{wrF\ n\ s\ (\phi \dagger \{n' \mapsto s'\})}$$
$$wrF\ n\ s\ (\phi \dagger \{n' \mapsto s'\})$$
$$= \langle\ \text{defn. } wrF\ \rangle$$
$$(\phi \dagger \{n' \mapsto s'\}) \dagger \{n \mapsto s\}$$
$$= \langle\ \text{disjoint overrides commute}\ \rangle$$
$$(\phi \dagger \{n \mapsto s\}) \dagger \{n' \mapsto s'\}$$
$$= \langle\ \text{defn. } wrF, \text{ backwards}\ \rangle$$
$$wrF\ n'\ s'\ (\phi \dagger \{n \mapsto s\})$$
$$= \langle\ \text{defn. } wrF, \text{ backwards}\ \rangle$$
$$wrF\ n'\ s'\ (wrF\ n\ s\ \phi)$$

Exercise 4. Prove the remaining Laws.

3 Integration

We now turn our attention to exploring a more rigourous way to link any formal API model we may develop, to the formal semantics of the programming language we are using. The key to this turns out to be to use monads, regardless of what paradigm is used by the functional programming language itself. For Haskell we have a close match, but even for Clean, with its uniqueness types, and explicit state, it is possible for us to use the monadic framework.

$$
\begin{array}{rll}
\gg\!= & :: m\ a \rightarrow (a \rightarrow m\ b) \rightarrow m\ b & \\
\gg & :: m\ a \rightarrow m\ b \rightarrow m\ b & \\
return & :: a \rightarrow m\ a & \\
fail & :: \mathbb{A}^\star \rightarrow m\ a & \\
m \gg\!= return & = m & [\textsc{MonRId}] \\
return\ a \gg\!= f & = f\ a & [\textsc{MonLId}] \\
(m \gg\!= f) \gg\!= g & = m \gg\!= (\lambda x @ f\ x \gg\!= g) & [\textsc{MonAssoc}] \\
m \gg n & = m \gg\!= (\lambda _ @ n) & [\textsc{MonThen}]
\end{array}
$$

Fig. 11. Monads (as per Haskell)

3.1 Monads

Haskell uses the IO Monad to interact with its environment, and we will effectively "implement" IO using our *VSFS* model. In essence, we will implement IO as a state monad, using *VSFS* as the state. The `Monad` class in Haskell, and the laws that any instance should obey are shown in Figure 11. Symbol $\gg\!=$ is pronounced "bind" while $\gg$ is pronounced "then".

The Haskell "do-notation" is syntactic sugar for the most common usage of $\gg\!=$ and $\gg$:

$$
\begin{array}{rcl}
m & : & M\ A \\
d \in DO & ::= & \mathbf{do}\ \{act; act; \ldots\} \\
act & = & m \mid x \leftarrow m \mid \mathbf{let}\ x = e
\end{array}
$$

The meaning of do-notation is given as a translation into the appropriate combination of binds, seqs and returns:

$$
\begin{array}{rcl}
\mathbf{do}\, m & = & m \\
\mathbf{do}\, m\ ;\ acts & = & m \gg acts \\
\mathbf{do}\, x \leftarrow m\ ;\ acts & = & m \gg\!= (\lambda x \bullet\ \mathbf{do}\, acts) \\
\mathbf{do}\,\mathbf{let}\ x = e\ ;\ acts & = & \mathbf{let}\ x = e\ \mathbf{in}\ \mathbf{do}\, acts
\end{array}
$$

The monad laws can then be restated for do-notation, as laws over action sequences:

$$
\begin{array}{rcl}
x \leftarrow return\ a\ ;\ f\ x & = & f\ a \\
x \leftarrow m\ ;\ return\ x & = & m \\
\mathbf{let}\ x = e\ ;\ return\ x & = & return\ e \\
\mathbf{let}\ x = e\ ;\ f\ x & = & f\ e
\end{array}
$$

The associativity law works on full do-expressions:

$$
\mathbf{do}\, x \leftarrow (\mathbf{do}\, y \leftarrow m\ ;\ f\ y)\ ;\ g\ x = \mathbf{do}\, y \leftarrow m\ ;\ x \leftarrow f\ y\ ;\ g\ x
$$

In addition to bind, seq and return, common to all monads, any given monad instantiation will have its own bespoke monad action functions that take some input and return a monadic value:

$$
action : b \rightarrow m\ a
$$

3.2   State Monads

We can instantiate a monad that manages state change, the so-called *State Monad (ST)*. It is a function from an (initial) state to a pair consisting of a (final) state and the monad result type.

$$ST\ A = S \to S \times A$$

Here we take S to denote a constant type, that denotes the form of the state of interest. The precise nature of S will always be clear from context.

We define "return" and "bind" as follows:

$$(return\ a)\ s \quad \hat{=} \quad (s, a)$$
$$(m \ggg f)s \quad \hat{=} \quad f\ a'\ s'\ \textbf{where}\ (s', a') = m\ s$$

Exercise 5. Prove that *return* and $\ggg$ as defined above for ST obey the monad laws.

Sometimes we do not want to return a result from a monad, and are just interested in the hidden (state-change) effect. In Haskell the so-called "void" type[3] (), with one member, also written (), is used. In our mathematical notation we denote the type containing one element as **1**, and its sole value as $*$.

With the state monad two special actions are usually introduced to get and set the state, of which the following is a possible example, using functions g and p to get a part of the state or transform it respectively.

$$get\ :\ ST\ S$$
$$get\ g\ s \ \hat{=}\ (s,\ s)$$
$$put\ :\ (S \to S) \to ST\ \mathbf{1}$$
$$put\ p\ s \ \hat{=}\ (p\ s, *)$$

We supply function arguments to get and set simply for flexibility — in particular, for *put*, it makes it easier to describe state changes that depend on the old state. We should also point out that while the whole purpose of using a state-like monad for I/O is in order to hide the mutable state, here we are modelling those mutation effects in our formalism which why we are looking "under the hood". The programmers use of *get* and *put* would be limited to writing calls of the form *get g* and *put p* — the state parameter s would never appear explicitly. We cannot emphasise this enough: whilst the programmers use of *get* and *put* will never mention s explicitly, in order to reason about the effect of such a program on the environment, here we need not only to mention s, but to model its internals explicitly. If make our formal reasoning "monadic", in the sense that we cannot see the state, then we are back to only being able to prove that two

---

[3] It's not void, because it contains one value!

programs have the same I/O behaviour. We will be unable to reason about what effect that common behaviour has on the outside world.

If we are working in a state monad $M\ A = S \to S \times A$ then the following law holds:

$$(\textbf{do}\ x \leftarrow m; f\ x)s\quad =\quad (\textbf{do}\ f\ x')\ s' \qquad [\textsc{StateDo}]$$
$$\textbf{where}\qquad (s', x') = m\ s$$

In state monads, as used in programs, the state (before or after) is hidden, so there is no way to explicitly refer to the state at any point in time. The state monad "is" instead a function that describes the relevant state change. The IO monad in Haskell is inspired by the state monad, and in GHC it is implemented as

```
newtype IO a = IO (State# RealWorld -> (# State# RealWorld, a #))
```

The IO world is hidden from the programmer, so it cannot be mentioned, and so the (ordinary[4]) use of the IO monad in Haskell is referentially transparent and is part of the pure language (provided that the whole of the ordinary IO implementation actually obeys the monad laws!).

3.3   VSFS Monad Model

In order to "implement" the IO monad, we shall follow GHC's lead and define IO as a state monad over *VSFS*

$$IO_{VSFS}\ A \cong VSFS \to VSFS \times A$$

We immediately get $\ggeq$, $\gg$, etc for free.

We can now give the semantics of the program API calls in terms of our new IO monad and API model (here we model our API calls as monadic actions, rather than as pure functions which are then used with *put* and *get*):

$$rdFIO\ :\ FP \to IO_{VSFS}\ Str$$
$$rdFIO\ n \cong \lambda\phi \bullet rdF\ n\ \phi$$
$$wrFIO\ :\ FP \to Str \to IO\ \mathbf{1}$$
$$wrFIO\ n\ s \cong \lambda\phi \bullet (wrF\ n\ s\ \phi, *)$$

We note that the main program of type $IO_{VSFS}\ \mathbf{1}$ is now a function over *VSFS*

 - If ϕ is the initial filesystem, and ϕ' is the final filesystem, then we can now assert

$$\phi' = main\ \phi$$

At this point, those familiar with either Haskell's monadic I/O, or Clean's uniqueness type system may feel that the last assertion above makes no sense !

---

[4] The use of "unsafe" functions is not "ordinary".

The objection from a Haskell perspective is that you can't use the IO monad like that, as the whole point is that the state is hidden. As for Clean, the uniqueness type system is designed to explicitly forbid any expressions that require simultaneous access to both an original and modified state, so the assertion above does not typecheck.

However neither of the above objections is pertinent here. This is a *reasoning* framework, and in order to reason about changes to a hidden state, we have to make it visible, and be able to see both before- and after-states. Another way to view the above, is that it is a proposition about a program, and not itself a program, and hence not bound by the Haskell or Clean typing rules, and that it should be viewed as that IO_{VSFS} is a formal *specification* of IO.

3.4   Challenge 1, Formally

We can now conclude Challenge 1, as we have done the following:

- Determined modelling assumptions
- Chosen appropriate mathematical constructions
- Modelled API behaviour in the mathematics
- Extended language semantics to cover API

We now have to do the rest:

- State desired property
- Prove it

The program opens file "a", reads an integer from it, and then overwrites "a", so it only contains that integer squared.

Ad-Hoc statement:

$$a \in \mathbf{dom}\ \phi \Rightarrow read(\phi''\ a) = (read(\phi\ a))^2$$

Formal statement:

$$a \in \mathbf{dom}\ \phi$$
$$\Downarrow$$
$$read(\ (main\ \phi)(a)\ ) = (\ read(\phi(a))\ )^2$$

Our ad-hoc statement was quite close to the formal one, with the only change now being that we have a model function *main* that captures formally how the I/O infrastructure is plumbed in.

Challenge 1 : Formal Proof We transform

$$read(\ (main\ \phi)(a)\ )$$

into

$$(\ read(\phi(a))\ )^2$$

using assumption $a \in \mathbf{dom}\ \phi$ to simplify as required

First, we reduce *main* ϕ, as a lemma

$$main\ \phi$$
$$= \langle\ \text{defn}\ main\ \rangle$$
$$(\ \textbf{do}\ s \leftarrow rdFIO\ a$$
$$\qquad \textbf{let}\ i = read\ s$$
$$\qquad wrFIO\ a\ (show(i^2))\ )\ \phi$$
$$= \langle\ \text{defn}\ rdFIO, rdF, \text{assumption}, [\textsc{StateDo}]\ \rangle$$
$$(\ \textbf{do}\ \textbf{let}\ i = read\ (\phi(a))$$
$$\qquad wrFIO\ a\ (show(i^2))\ )\ \phi$$
$$= \langle\ \text{defn of}\ \textbf{let}\ \rangle$$
$$(\ \textbf{do}\ wrFIO\ a\ (show((read\ (\phi(a)))^2))\ )\ \phi$$
$$= \langle\ \text{defn}\ wrFIO, wrF, [\textsc{StateDo}]\ \rangle$$
$$\phi \dagger \{a \mapsto (show((read\ (\phi(a)))^2))\}$$

Now, the main property

$$read(\ (main\ \phi)(a)\ )$$
$$= \langle\ \text{previous lemma}\ \rangle$$
$$read((\phi \dagger \{a \mapsto (show((read\ (\phi(a)))^2))\})(a))$$
$$= \langle\ \text{map lookup}\ \rangle$$
$$read(\ (show((read\ (\phi(a)))^2))\ )$$
$$= \langle\ \text{read-show-identity}\ \rangle$$
$$(\ read(\phi(a))\ )^2$$

The proofs were quite short, but we did a lot of work to set it up. However this setup work only needs to be done once for any API, and the resulting laws can be reused for lots of program proofs, so it is a worthwhile investment, provided we get the abstraction right.

Exercise 6. Lab Challenge 1

1. Implement VSFS in Haskell
2. Implement new IO monad using VSFS as state
3. Use it to run that program on a simulated VSFS.

4   Increasing Realism

4.1   Using *VDM*♣

VDM♣ is more than just functions and equational reasoning, as it has an associated modelling approach, based on invariants. An invariant is a well-formedness property of a system, that should hold for a running/live system and which should be preserved by any system operation. In some sense invariants characterise the safe configurations of a system, and they form a hierarchy, from those that must hold at all times, e.g. keeping an aircraft within its safe performance envelop, to those that only need to hold at certain key points during system execution. Many of the latter are concerned with ensuring that system data-structures are consistent at the start and end of system operations, while allowing them to be in an inconsistent state during an operation, as it is typically impossible to maintain such invariants in the middle of certain changes. To see this, consider an example of a data-type consisting of a list along with its length (xs, len) with an invariant $length\ xs = len$. Adding an element x requires this to change to $(x : xs, len + 1)$, but in most sequential programming languages we cannot change both components simultaneously. The add operation will have an intermediate state, either $(x : xs, len)$ or $(xs, len + 1)$, where the invariant does not hold.

The $VDM^{\clubsuit}$ methodology supports this approach by allowing us to define invariants. Given a definition of some system type:

$$s \in System \mathbin{\widehat{=}} \ldots \text{some type}$$

we may choose to define well-structured ones with an invariant predicate

$$inv\text{-}System\ :\ System \to \mathbb{B}$$
$$inv\text{-}System(s) \mathbin{\widehat{=}} \ldots$$

A key property of interest is *Invariant Preservation* Consider an API operation on our system:

$$Op\ :\ Input \to System \to System \times Output$$
$$Op\ i\ s \mathbin{\widehat{=}} (s', o')\ \textbf{where} \ldots$$

We now have a proof obligation to show that Op *preserves* the invariant:

$$inv\text{-}System(s) \Rightarrow inv\text{-}System(\pi_1(Op\ i\ s))$$

This proof obligation is part of the model-building exercise, and supports the second level of hierarchy mentioned above.

Simple type systems, i.e. Hindley-Milner, are not rich enough in general to capture data-dependent well-formedness conditions, so some extra power is required. VDM and $VDM^{\clubsuit}$ use the invariant predicate approach just mentioned, whilst another very active area of research uses dependent types to allow invariant properties to be expressed as part of the operator types [McK06].

We shall illustrate the invariant approach using our existing model, and constraining it a little.

Example 1. Very Simple Integer File System (VSIFS) Imagine we want a file system to have file content strings restricted to those that can be *read* as valid integers. We shall define *VSIFS* to be such a filesystem:

$$\phi \in \mathit{VSIFS} = FP \xrightarrow{m} \mathit{Str}$$
$$\mathit{inv\text{-}VSIFS}\phi \,\hat{=}\, \forall s \in \mathbf{rng}\ \phi \bullet \mathit{valid}\ s$$
$$\mathit{valid}\ s \,\hat{=}\, s \neq \langle\rangle \wedge s = \mathit{takeWhile}\ \mathit{isDigit}\ s$$

The definitions of rdF and wrF look the same as before (we are using the non-monadic VSFS model here for illustrative purposes—the ideas extend to the monadic IO_{VSFS} model in the obvious way).

We now need to check that wrF preserves the VSIFS invariant, as it changes the state.

$$\mathit{inv\text{-}VSIFS}\phi \Rightarrow \mathit{inv\text{-}VSIFS}(wrF\ n\ s\ \phi)$$

We shall assume the antecedent $\mathit{inv\text{-}VSIFS}\phi$ is true, and seek to reduce the consequent to true:

$$\mathit{inv\text{-}VSIFS}(wrF\ n\ s\ \phi)$$
$$\equiv \quad \text{`` defn. } wrF \text{ ''}$$
$$\underline{\mathit{inv\text{-}VSIFS}(\phi \dagger \{n \mapsto s\})}$$
$$\equiv \quad \text{`` defn. } \mathit{inv\text{-}VSIFS} \text{ ''}$$
$$\forall f \in \underline{\mathbf{rng}(\phi \dagger \{n \mapsto s\})} \bullet \mathit{valid}\ f$$
$$\equiv \quad \text{`` } \mathbf{rng} \text{ applied to map override ''}$$
$$\forall f \in \mathbf{rng}(\vartriangleleft_{\{s\}}\phi) \cup \{s\} \bullet \mathit{valid}\ f$$
$$\equiv \quad \text{`` } \forall \text{ range split ''}$$
$$(\forall f \in \mathbf{rng}(\vartriangleleft_{\{s\}}\phi \bullet \mathit{valid}\ f) \wedge (\forall f \in \{s\}) \bullet \mathit{valid}\ f)$$
$$\equiv \quad \text{`` assumption's range covers } \vartriangleleft_{\{s\}}\phi \text{ ''}$$
$$\textsc{True} \wedge \underline{(\forall f \in \{s\}) \bullet \mathit{valid}\ f}$$
$$\equiv \quad \text{`` } x \in \{y\} \equiv x = y, \text{ one-point rule ''}$$
$$\textsc{True} \wedge \mathit{valid}\ s$$

After all that effort, the proof fails because we cannot show $\mathit{valid}\ s$[5]. Why not? Because, in order to ensure the invariant is preserved, either s must itself be valid, or wrF should check it and then take some appropriate action.

Just as we wanted/needed to associate invariants with systems, we need to attach *pre-conditions* to operations:

$$Op\ :\ \mathit{Input} \to \mathit{System} \to \mathit{System} \times \mathit{Output}$$
$$\mathit{pre\text{-}Op}\ :\ \mathit{Input} \to \mathit{System} \to \mathbb{B}$$
$$\mathit{pre\text{-}Op}\ i\ s \,\hat{=}\, \ldots$$
$$Op\ i\ s \,\hat{=}\, (s', o')\ \textbf{where} \ldots$$

---

[5] Should have `QuickChecked` first !

The proof obligation is changed to require the pre-condition:

$$inv\text{-}System(s) \land pre\text{-}Op\ i\ s \Rightarrow inv\text{-}System(\pi_1(Op\ i\ s))$$

Effectively we are describing the error-free usage for our API. We can now give a complete definition of wrF for our integer file-system:

$$wrF\ :\ FP \rightarrow Str \rightarrow VSIFS \rightarrow VSIFS$$
$$pre\text{-}wrF\ n\ s\ \phi \triangleq valid\ s$$
$$wrF\ n\ s\ \phi \triangleq \phi \dagger \{n \mapsto s\}$$

There is also an obvious pre-condition for rdF in either filesystem model:

$$pre\text{-}rdF\ n\ \phi \triangleq n \in \mathsf{dom}\ \phi$$

The file being read must already exist. In the above example, our antecedent would have been extended to assert $valid\ s$, and so the above proof could have been completed successfully.

Assume $inv\text{-}VSIFS\phi$ and $pre\text{-}wrF\ n\ s\ \phi$ and reduce:

$$inv\text{-}VSIFS(\underline{wrF\ n\ s\ \phi})$$

$$\vdots$$

$$\underline{\mathrm{TRUE} \land valid\ s}$$
$$\equiv\quad \text{`` pre-condition assumption, simplify ''}$$
$$\mathrm{TRUE}$$

The invariant and pre-conditions allows us to formally document key underlying correctness assumptions for our system. We can prove that our API functions work sensibly w.r.t. these assumptions. What does this say about situations were the conditions fail? VDM's proof system takes the view that system behaviour is unpredictable if invariants or pre-conditions fail. In most safety-critical applications major effort is taken to "design out" those situations—we do not rely on formal techniques to fix these situations, but instead rely on the application to detect and flag them if present, or confirm all is well if they are absent.

4.2   Real-World Filesystems

Just before we plunge into more realistic file-system models, it is worth noting that the real world is interested in fully formally verifying the correctness of a filesystems. As part of the Verified Software Initiative — a grand challenge to see software routinely formally verified in future real-world software engineering practise —NASA JPL suggested, as a mini-challenge, a full formal verification of a POSIX filesystem down to the underlying flash memory hardware [HJ05]. This was motivated by their experience of a close shave with 3rd-party FS software on the Mars rovers, which they hope not to have to repeat.

```
data Handle
data IOMode = ReadMode  |  WriteMode  ...
openFile :: FilePath -> IOMode -> IO Handle
hClose :: Handle -> IO ()
hIsEOF :: Handle -> IO Bool
hGetChar :: Handle -> IO Char
hPutChar :: Handle -> Char -> IO ()
```

Fig. 12. Extract from System.IO

Filesystems are built on top of operating systems, and NICTA in Australia did the first formal verification of an OS microkernel (sel4), from specification down to C code, using Haskell to model the specification level [KEH⁺09]. Another VSI mini-challenge is looking at verifying the freeRTOS (real-time) kernel[DGM09], and a book describing the verification of OpenComRTOS has just been published [VBF⁺11].

4.3   Modelling Handle-Based Filesystems

We now look at modelling a more realistic filesystem, in particular at a level of granularity that is more realistic than the read/write whole file view we have taken up to this point. Of particular interest is dealing with the situation where files are opened first, then read or written in an incremental manner, and finally closed once their contents have been processed. The challenge here will be coming up with a notion of open file handles, and being able to support the sharing of files as appropriate.

Our task now will be to build a formal model that covers the extract from Haskell's System.IO module shown in Figure 12. In addition to some new enumeration types like IOMode, we also have to decide just what is involved in defining the notion of Handle. A Handle records, for the corresponding open file (System.IO documentation on Hackage):

- whether it manages input or output or both;
- whether it is open, closed or semi-closed;
- whether the object is seekable;
- whether buffering is disabled, or enabled on a line or block basis;
- a buffer (whose length may be zero).

At this point we need to decide the level of detail we require. Some of the aspects recorded for handles are very low level (line/block buffering), while others are fairly high level and general (input/output direction). What level is appropriate for our needs?

In this case, we plan to model the extract of file I/O shown in Figure 12. We must describe input/output direction, because we have included the IOMode type covering those two aspects. However as the extract has no mention of types, parameters or API calls to do with buffering, there seems little point in modelling it. This is a useful general principle:

The level of detail used in a formal model should be just enough to reason about the behaviours covered by the subset of the relevant API.

Applying this principle here, we shall just focus on `Handles` that:

- are open or closed;
- manage input or output;
- note current position;
- support shared reading

4.4   HFS: Formal Model

The key decisions we have to make in modelling a Handle File System (HFS) are the precise nature of handles, and how they are manifested in a running system. The important observation is that handles are dynamic entities that come to life when a file is opened, and disappear once a file has been closed. They contain all the information about the opened file as already discussed. Their support for sharing is implicit—each shared access to one file has its own handle. An implication of this that we need a way to track sharing in a manner that is independent of each handle. We achieve this by associating meta-data about file-open status and sharing with the files themselves.

HFS Filesystem. We consider a file-system as a mapping between names and file-data:

$$\varphi \in HFS = FP \xrightarrow{m} FData$$

File-data (δ) is split into two portions, the file state (Ξ), and the data (s):

$$\delta, (\Xi, s) \in FData = (FState \times \mathbb{A}^{\star})$$

The file-state records the fact that a file is either closed, opened for reading by a number of readers, or opened exclusively for writing. If opened for (shared) reading, we record the number of read handles associated with that file.

$$\Xi \in FState = \text{CLSD} \mid \text{OPRD} \, \mathbb{N} \mid \text{OPWR}$$

HFS Handles. When a file is opened, the program gets a file handle (h), which records the filename, and the current state of the data. If the file is open for writing, then we record the characters written so far (HWR cs). For reading, we record what has been read so far, and what remains (HRD $sofar\ rest$), allowing us to have a notion of seek (even though the API shown doesn't provide this feature).

$$h \in Hndl = FP \times HData$$
$$\hbar \in HData = \text{HWR} \, \mathbb{A}^{\star} \mid \text{HRD} \, \mathbb{A}^{\star} \, \mathbb{A}^{\star}$$

HFS File Opening. When opening a file we need to specify a mode, either reading or writing:

$$m \in OMode = \text{MRD} \mid \text{MWR}$$

Opening a file requires supplying a name and mode:

$$\text{Opn} : FP \to OMode \to HFS \to HFS \times Hndl$$

Our pre-conditions are described by two (pattern-matching) cases, one for each $OMode$. We open a file for writing if it doesn't exist or is closed, for reading provided it exists and hasn't been opened for writing:

$$\text{pre-Opn } n \text{ MWR } \varphi \;\widehat{=}\; n \notin \varphi \vee \varphi(n) \simeq (\text{CLSD}, \_)$$
$$\text{pre-Opn } n \text{ MRD } \varphi \;\widehat{=}\; n \in \varphi \wedge \varphi(n) \not\simeq (\text{OPWR}, \_)$$

The notation $\varphi(n) \simeq (\text{CLSD}, \_)$ is a form of pattern matching, and is equivalent to $\pi_1(\varphi(n)) = \text{CLSD}$, with the underscore acting as a do-not-care pattern.

Opening a file for writing (it doesn't exist or is closed) involves updating the filesystem to record that file as open for writing, with contents initialised to empty $(\text{OPWR}, \langle \rangle)$. The handle returned also has empty contents $(\text{HWR } \langle \rangle)$.

$$\text{Opn } n \text{ MWR } (\varphi) \;\widehat{=}\; (\varphi \dagger \{n \mapsto (\text{OPWR}, \langle \rangle)\}, (n, \text{HWR } \langle \rangle))$$

Opening a file for reading (it exists and hasn't been opened for writing) involves updating the filesystem to record either the first read, or if another read is taking for that place, returning a file handle with the full file-contents to be read. The auxiliary function *incr* modifies the file-status appropriately, depending on if the file was closed or already opened for reading.

$$\text{Opn } n \text{ MRD } \varphi \;\widehat{=}\; (\varphi \dagger \{n \mapsto incr(\varphi(n))\}, (n, \text{HRD } \langle \rangle \; s))$$
$$\textbf{where} \quad s = \pi_2(\varphi(n))$$
$$incr(\text{CLSD}, s) = (\text{OPRD } 1, s)$$
$$incr(\text{OPRD } i, s) = (\text{OPRD } (i+1), s)$$

HFS File Closing. Closing a file requires the file-handle

$$\text{Cls} : Hndl \to HFS \to HFS$$

We close a file if it is open (in the appropriate mode):

$$\text{pre-Cls}(n, \text{HWR } \_)\varphi \;\widehat{=}\; n \in \varphi \wedge \varphi(n) \simeq (\text{OPWR}, \_)$$
$$\text{pre-Cls}(n, \text{HRD } \_\_)\varphi \;\widehat{=}\; n \in \varphi \wedge \varphi(n) \simeq (\text{OPRD } \_, \_)$$

Closing a file that is being written involves flushing the data in the handle into the filesystem, and then marking the file as closed:

$$\text{Cls}(n, \text{HWR } s)\varphi \;\widehat{=}\; \varphi \dagger \{n \mapsto (\text{CLSD}, s)\}$$

Closing a file that is being read simply means noting in the filesystem that one read handle has now gone, and marking the file as closed if the number of remaining handles drops to zero:

$$\text{Cls}(n, \text{HRD} \_\_)\varphi \cong \varphi \dagger \{n \mapsto decr(\varphi(n))\}$$
$$\textbf{where} \quad decr(\text{OPRD } 1, s) = (\text{CLSD}, s)$$
$$decr(\text{OPRD } (i + 1), s) = (\text{OPRD } i, s)$$

HFS End-of-File. We are at the end of file if the handle is reading and no data is left:

$$\text{EoF} \; : \; Hndl \to \mathbb{B}$$
$$\text{EoF}(\_, \text{HWR } \_) \cong \text{FALSE}$$
$$\text{EoF}(\_, \text{HRD} \_ \omega) \cong \omega = \langle\rangle$$

HFS Read. We can read from a file-handle if it is in reading mode, and there is data left:

$$\text{Rd} \; : \; Hndl \to Hndl \times \mathbb{A}$$
$$\text{pre-Rd}(n, \hbar) \cong \hbar \simeq \text{HRD} \_ \omega \wedge \omega \neq \langle\rangle$$
$$\text{Rd}(n, \text{HRD } \alpha \; \omega) \cong ((n, \text{HRD } (\alpha \frown \langle d\rangle) \; \omega'), \; d)$$
$$\textbf{where}$$
$$(\langle d\rangle \frown \omega') = \omega$$

HFS Write. We write to a file-handle if it is in writing mode:

$$\text{Wr} \; : \; \mathbb{A} \to Hndl \to Hndl$$
$$\text{pre-Wr}d(n, \hbar) \cong \hbar \simeq \text{HWR} \_$$
$$\text{Wr}d(n, \text{HWR } s) \cong (n, \text{HWR } (s \frown \langle d\rangle))$$

HFS Discussion

Question 1. Is the *HFS* model as just presented adequate ?

It is a good first approximation, however it is lacking in a few areas.

The first thing to note is that we did not give a system invariant. There were no constraints on the file contents, and as we did not have notation for "all the file handles" in the model, we could not talk about an invariant relating file handles to file states. Also, there is no notion of error returns, so the caller program has to just get it right.

Also there are various forms of abuse of file-handles that are possible. Once a file is closed, it cannot be accessed with an old handle because the pre-conditions forbid it, but if a file is re-opened in the same mode as used previously, old file handles for that mode will now be active once more. A key issue here is that the system doesn't have a global view of existing file handles or some way of marking them as stale.

We will not discuss error reporting further here, apart from noting that we can either add some error state components, a la the UNIX `errno` facility , and provide means to test these values, or we can decide to model exceptions. Modelling exceptions requires us to re-visit the programming language semantics and add in support for reasoning about exception raising and handling.

4.5   Improved Handle File System (IHFS)

Instead we shall focus on how to make our modelling of handles more robust. We do this by adding on a table as part of the filesystem that records and tracks file handles.

The Haskell Handle is now just a numeric reference to a hidden record

$$hn \in HndlNo = \mathbb{N}$$

A Handle table maintains a binding between handle numbers and handle records:

$$\varpi \in HTab = HndlNo \xrightarrow{m} Hndl$$

File opening in *IHFS* requires us to formalise the notion of generating new handle numbers. Ideally a handle number returned from file opening will not be one that has been seen before. At the very least, it should not be a number currently in use. There are a number of ways to do this, at various levels of abstraction, noting that preventing handle number re-use requires a notion of the history of all previous file openings. We shall adopt the simple approach of maintaining a seed number (hs) used to generate new handles—it effectively abstracts the history by declaring that no handle number equal to or greater than it has been used.

IHFS Invariant. Our file system brings together handles, the handle seed and files

$$(\varphi, hs, \varpi), \ H \in IHFS = HFS \times \mathbb{N} \times HTab$$

We expect that the seed is larger than any live handle number, every handle corresponds to a file in the appropriate mode, and for every file open for writing, there is only one handle

$$inv\text{-}IHFS(\varphi, hs, \varpi) \; \widehat{=} \; hs > \max(\mathbf{dom}\;\varpi)$$
$$\wedge \; (\forall hn \in \varpi \bullet validH(\varpi(hn), \varphi))$$
$$\wedge \; (\forall n \in \varphi \bullet \varphi(n) \simeq (\mathrm{OpWr}, \_) \Rightarrow hcount(n)\varpi = 1)$$
$$validH \; : \; Hndl \times HFS \to \mathbb{B}$$
$$validH((n, \mathrm{HWr}\;\_), \varphi) \; \widehat{=} \; n \in \varphi \wedge \varphi(n) \simeq (\mathrm{OpWr}, \_)$$
$$validH((n, \mathrm{HRd}\;\_\;\_), \varphi) \; \widehat{=} \; n \in \varphi \wedge \varphi(n) \simeq (\mathrm{OpRd}\_, \_)$$
$$hcount \; : \; FP \to HTab \to \mathbb{N}$$
$$hcount \; n \; \{\} \; \widehat{=} \; 0$$
$$hcount \; n \; (\varpi \sqcup \{hn \mapsto (n', \_)\}) \; \widehat{=} \; (hcount \; n \; \varpi) + (\text{if } n = n' \text{ then } 1 \text{ else } 0)$$

The invariant is complex, but the structure chosen does have the advantage of making pre-condition checks simpler. Checking for appropriate file-states and valid handles can now be separated, because the invariant ensures their mutual consistency.

In the HFS model, opening returned a handle which was retained by the caller and then used for subsequent file operations. In the IHFS model, we now get a new handle number back to the caller, which is used to de-reference the internal table. The main changes to the operation models are this extra layer of indirection for handles.

IHFS Initial State. Another part of the $VDM^{\clubsuit}$ methodology is to define the initial state of the system, and to show that it satisfies the invariant. We did not present this for HFS because, given the lack of any invariant, or rather the presence of the trivial invariant True, any instance of HFS would satisfy it. For IHFS we have a complex invariant, so demonstrating a simple initial system that satisfies it is important to show that the invariant isn't so strong as to be unsatisfiable.

We propose an initial system with no files, no handles and the seed set to 1:

$$IHFS_0 \; : \; IHFS$$
$$IHFS_0 \; \widehat{=} \; (\{\}, 1, \{\})$$

This may seem a little sparse, to say the least, but it satisfies an important technical objective. It establishes a file-system that satisfies the invariant. Since our operations are (hopefully) invariant-preserving, then we can ensure that any filesystem that results from any sequence of such operations starting with $IHFS_0$ also satisfies the invariant. We could propose a large, more complex (more "realistic") initial filesystem, but then we are left with a much harder job to show it satisfies the invariant.

We want to show $inv\text{-}IHFS_0$, by reducing it to true:

$inv\text{-}IHFS_0$

$\equiv$ " expand defns "

$1 > \max(\text{dom } \{\})$

$\wedge \, (\forall hn \in \{\} \bullet validH(\{\}(hn), \varphi))$

$\wedge \, (\forall n \in \{\} \bullet \{\}(n) \simeq (\text{OPWR}, \_) \Rightarrow hcount(n)\{\} = 1)$

$\equiv$ " $\forall$ on empty ranges reduce to true "

$1 > \max(\text{dom } \{\})$

$\equiv$ " max of empty set is 0 "

$1 > 0$

$\equiv$ " arithmetic "

TRUE

We now turn our attention to defining the API operators. We will overload the names used for HFS to avoid either yet another set of new names or the use of subscripts.

IHFS File Opening. We simply present the full definition in one go, noting the big change is the adding of the handle to the internal table and returning the seed value (post-incremented) as the handle identifier to the caller:

$$\text{Opn} \, : \, FP \to OMode \to IHFS \to IHFS \times HndlNo$$

$$pre\text{-}\text{Opn}(n) \, \text{MWR} \, (\varphi, hs, \varpi) \, \widehat{=} \, n \notin \varphi \vee \varphi(n) \simeq (\text{CLSD}, \_)$$

$$pre\text{-}\text{Opn}(n)\text{MRD}(\varphi, hs, \varpi) \, \widehat{=} \, n \in \varphi \wedge \varphi(n) \not\simeq (\text{OPWR}, \_)$$

$$\text{Opn}(n) \, \text{MWR} \, (\varphi) \, \widehat{=} \, (\, (\varphi \dagger \{n \mapsto (\text{OPWR}, \langle\rangle)\},$$
$$hs + 1, \varpi \sqcup \{hs \mapsto (n, \text{HWR} \, \langle\rangle)\})$$
$$, hs \,)$$

$$\text{Opn}(n)\text{MRD}(\varphi) \, \widehat{=} \, (\, (\varphi \dagger \{n \mapsto incr(\varphi(n))\},$$
$$hs + 1, \varpi \sqcup \{hs \mapsto (n, \text{HRD} \, \langle\rangle \, s)\}),$$
$$, hs \,)$$

$$\textbf{where} \quad incr(\text{CLSD}, s) = (\text{OPRD } 1, s)$$
$$incr(\text{OPRD } i, s) = (\text{OPRD } (i + 1), s)$$

The pre-conditions are unchanged, and the main complexity lies in updating the handle table, which is just a simple map extension with the new handle.

IHFS File Closing. When a file is closed, change the file state as appropriate, and remove the handle from the table. The pre-condition is simple—we just ensure the handle number is currently in the table. The consistency between handle and file is guaranteed by the invariant.

$$\text{Cls} \ : \ HndlNo \to IHFS \to IHFS$$

$$\text{pre-Cls } hn \ (\varphi, hs, \varpi) \ \widehat{=} \ hn \in \varpi$$

$$\text{Cls } hn \ (\varphi, hs, \varpi) \ \widehat{=} \ \text{Cls}' \ hn \ (\varpi(hn))(\varphi, hs, \varpi)$$

$$\text{Cls}' \ hn \ (n, \text{HWR } s)(\varphi, hs, \varpi) \ \widehat{=} \ (\varphi \dagger \{n \mapsto (\text{CLSD}, s)\}, hs, \triangleleft_{hn}\varpi)$$

$$\text{Cls}' \ hn \ (n, \text{HRD } \_ \_)(\varphi, hs, \varpi) \ \widehat{=} \ (\varphi \dagger \{n \mapsto decr(\varphi(n))\}, hs, \triangleleft_{hn}\varpi)$$

$$\textbf{where} \quad decr(\text{OPRD } 1, s) = (\text{CLSD}, s)$$

$$decr(\text{OPRD } (i+1), s) = (\text{OPRD } i, s)$$

IHFS End-of-File. In HFS, given the explicit file-handles returned to the caller, we were lazy in defining the end-of-file predicate, as there was no need to refer back to the filesystem. In IHFS we do not have that luxury:

$$\text{EoF} \ : \ HndlNo \to IHFS \to IHFS \times \mathbb{B}$$

$$\text{pre-EoF } hn \ (\varphi, hs, \varpi) \ \widehat{=} \ hn \in \varpi$$

$$\text{EoF } hn \ (\varphi, hs, \varpi) \ \widehat{=} \ ((\varphi, hs, \varpi), \varpi(hn) \simeq (\_, \text{HRD } \_ \ \omega) \wedge \omega = \langle\rangle)$$

We return true if the referenced handle matches a read handle, and the remaining data is empty. If the handle is for writing, or for reading with data left over we return false.

IHFS Read. Again, the revised definition for read is largely about plumbing to access the handle table:

$$\text{Rd} \ : \ HndlNo \to IHFS \to IHFS \times \mathbb{A}$$

$$\text{pre-Rd } hn \ (\varphi, hs, \varpi) \ \widehat{=} \ hn \in \varpi \wedge \varpi(hn) \simeq \text{HRD } \_ \ \omega \wedge \omega \neq \langle\rangle$$

$$\text{Rd } hn \ (\varphi, hs, \varpi) \ \widehat{=} \ \text{Rd}' \ hn \ (\varpi(hn))(\varphi, hs, \varpi)$$

$$\text{Rd}' \ hn \ (n, \text{HRD } \alpha \ (\langle d\rangle \frown \omega'))(\varphi, hs, \varpi) \ \widehat{=} \ ((\varphi, hs, \varpi \dagger hn(n, \text{HRD } (\alpha \frown \langle d\rangle) \ \omega')), d)$$

IHFS Write. Write is no different:

$$\text{Wr} \ : \ \mathbb{A} \to HndlNo \to IHFS \to IHFS \times 1$$

$$\text{pre-Wr } d \ hn \ (\varphi, hs, \varpi) \ \widehat{=} \ hn \in \varpi \wedge \varpi(hn) \simeq \text{HWR } \_$$

$$\text{Wr } d \ hn \ (\varphi, hs, \varpi) \ \widehat{=} \ \text{Wr}' \ d \ hn \ (\varpi(hn)) \ (\varphi, hs, \varpi)$$

$$\text{Wr}' \ d \ hn \ (n, \text{HWR } s) \ (\varphi, hs, \varpi) \ \widehat{=} \ ((\varphi, hs, \varpi \dagger \{hn \mapsto (n, \text{HWR } (s \frown \langle d\rangle))\}), *)$$

4.6 Summary

We have seen two handle-based models, one, HFS, is based on explicit handles and is quite simple, but exposed those handles in way that makes them very vulnerable to unsafe patterns of use. This does not mean that HFS has no utility. It is a useful model to get the basic processes of opening, reading/writing and closing worked out. It can also be used to do lightweight proofs of desired properties—for example proving that reading a file that was previously written results in the same data.

The second model, IHFS, protects handles by keeping the critical data inside the model, and only handing out references to that data. This comes with the price of extra model complexity. However we feel the complexity is manageable, as the model was developed by building on HFS and then folding the handle data in under the hood, as it were.

Exercise 7. Prove that all the IHFS operations preserve the invariant

Exercise 8. Encode the IHFS model in Haskell, which gives a means to animate the model for free, explore it, and then develop some suitable QuickCheck tests.

5   Beyond Haskell and *VDM*♣

Haskell is not the only lazy functional language that has pure I/O, and monads are not the only technique available for managing side-effects in a functional setting. In the programming language Clean there are explicit references to the external world, but purity is maintained by requiring such references to be *uniquely typed* [BS96]. This uniqueness typing ensures that the use of external resources is single-threaded, in that there is no simultaneous access to both the before- and after-values of the resource. The I/O API calls have been carefully annotated with appropriate uniqueness attributes (∗) and the type-checker ensures single-threadedness.

So, for example, a simplified[6] type signature for file-opening in Clean is

```
fopen :: String FileMode *World -> (Bool,*File,*World)
```

So `fopen` takes three arguments: a file name string, a read/write mode indicator, and a `unique` reference to the outside world. It returns a boolean success flag, a *unique* reference to a file (handle) and a *unique* reference to the "rest of the world". Any attempt to retain access to both before- and after-versions of the world results in a type error, e.g.:

```
let (ok,f,w') = fopen "a.txt" FReadText w in (w,w') // type-error !
```

So in Clean, the I/O objects (world, files) are explicitly mentioned, but type-checking prevents unsafe use, whereas Haskell's monads solve the problem of unsafe side-effects by making it impossible to mention the I/O objects at all —they are implicit, hidden under the hood in the IO monad. Another difference between Clean and Haskell becomes evident when we consider file reading (simplified type signature):

---

[6] `fopen` is in fact a class method, and we have left out strictness annotations.

```
freadc :: *File -> (Bool,Char,*File)
```

We take and return unique file references, but no mention is made of the world. —in Haskell, all I/O is done in the single global I/O monad. With Clean's uniqueness typing we can effectively partition I/O state and effectively encapsulate the handling of different state fragments. In Haskell, by contrast, every I/O access is against the global I/O monad, and hence such operations have to be over-sequentialised[PJ01] by comparison with Clean.

5.1   Clean Syntax

Clean syntax is similar to Haskell, with a few variations:

```
haskellFunction :: a -> b -> c -> d
cleanFunction :: a b c -> d
haskellCons = (x:xs)
cleanCons = [x:xs]
```

Clean does not have do-notation, but provides a special let syntax (#-let) designed to make I/O coding easier:

$$id, p, b \qquad \text{ident, patterns, boolexpr}$$
$$h \in HL ::= id\ p\ \{act; act; \ldots\} = e$$
$$act = \#p = e$$
$$| \quad |b = e$$

- $\#p = e$ evaluates e and binds variables in pattern p to the result. These variables are in scope in all subsequent act and the final e.
- $|c = e$ evaluates its condition, and if true, returns e, and all subsequent act and the final e are skipped. If condition c is false, we skip to the next act.
- When all act have been done, we evaluate the final e, with all the pattern bindings and return its value as the overall result.

Clean uses the offside syntax rule in a similar manner to Haskell, so a function to read the contents of an open file can be written as follows:

```
fileRead :: *File -> (String,*File)
fileRead f
   # (eof,f) = fend f
   | eof = ([],f)
   # (ok,c,f) = freadc f
   # (cs,f) = fileRead f
   = ([c:cs],f)
```

This function checks for end of file and quits, returning the empty string in that case, and otherwise, reads a character, recurses, and returns the final string. The (fully read) file is also returned, but as access to f is singly threaded, this function is safe (and pure). The important thing to note is that each of the lefthand side occurrences of f are distinct variables (nested scopes).

A program that reads character data from file "data.in" and outputs that data transformed to file "clean-data.out":

```
rdTxWr w
    # ((_,fin),w) = fileOpen "data.in" FReadText w
    # (indata,fin) = fileRead fin
    # (_,w) = fclose fin w
    # ((_,fout),w) = fileOpen "clean-data.out" FWriteText w
    # fout = fwrites (toString (transform indata)) fout
    # (_,w) = fclose fout w
    = w
```

Note that fileOpen "pulls" the file out of the world w. The file read only works on that file (w is not mentioned), and fclose "puts" the final file back "into" w.

5.2   Formalising Clean's I/O

The question now arises: how do we formalise I/O in Clean? It turns out that we can re-use almost all the work done up to this point. The first key thing to note is that all the I/O operation type signatures can be re-arranged slightly to match that of the state monad:

$$\text{open} :: \{\text{\#Char}\} \text{ Int *World } \text{->} \text{ (Bool,*File,*World)}$$
$$Opn \ : \ FP \to OMode \to IHFS \to IHFS \times (\mathbb{B} \times HndlNo)$$
$$\text{fclose} :: \text{*File *World } \text{->} \text{ (Bool,*World)}$$
$$Cls \ : \ HndlNo \to IHFS \to IHFS \times \mathbb{B}$$
$$\text{freadc} :: \text{*File } \text{->} \text{ (Bool,Char,*File)}$$
$$Rd \ : \ HndlNo \to IHFS \to IHFS \times (\mathbb{B} \times \mathbb{A} \times HndlNo)$$
$$\text{fwritec} :: \text{Char *File } \text{->} \text{ *File}$$
$$Wr \ : \ \mathbb{A} \to HndlNo \to IHFS \to IHFS \times HndlNo$$

The $HndlNo$ becomes a proxy for the file, hidden in $IHFS$. Essentially we can view the Clean and Haskell I/O models as essentially the same underneath, just with slightly different plumbing to make the connection to the programming language level. We can then take advantage of the monad laws to simplify reasoning for Clean programs as well. While there are some Clean programs that cannot be expressed in monadic style, and we lose some of the ability to encapsulate the reasoning about a small part of partitioned state, we find most Clean programs fit with the monadic style.

The #-let notation has a straightforward translation:

$$[\![id\ p\ acts{=}e]\!] \mathrel{\widehat{=}} id(p) = [\![acts, e]\!]$$
$$[\![\#p{=}e; acts, e]\!] \mathrel{\widehat{=}} \mathbf{let}\ p = e\ \mathbf{in}\ [\![acts, e]\!]$$
$$[\![\ |\ c{=}e; acts, e]\!] \mathrel{\widehat{=}} \mathbf{if}\ c\ \mathbf{then}\ e\ \mathbf{else}\ [\![acts, e]\!]$$
$$[\![\#p{=}e1, e]\!] \mathrel{\widehat{=}} \mathbf{let}\ p = e1\ \mathbf{in}\ e$$
$$[\![\ |\ c{=}e1, e]\!] \mathrel{\widehat{=}} \mathbf{if}\ c\ \mathbf{then}\ e1\ \mathbf{else}\ e$$

In effect we find that there is very little difference in the formalisms needed to reason about I/O for both Haskell and Clean, and indeed the monadic style of presentation can be fruitfully used for reasoning about both. Based on these observations, a prototype tool for reasoning about I/O was constructed using the Sparkle theorem prover [dMvEP01, dMvEP07, dM09] which developed a monadic framework that supported limited deterministic concurrency [DBvEdM04, DB06].

5.3   Process Algebras

VDM♣ is not the only formalism suited for reasoning about functional I/O. The material discussed to this point could equally well have been captured using other state-oriented imperative specification languages such as standard VDM (VDM-SL [Com92]), Z [Spi92] or B [Abr91]. However, so far we have avoided a discussion of concurrency, although we have nodded in that direction in *HFS* with its shared reads. Formalisms like *VDM*♣, VDM, Z, B are all sequential in character, and provide little or no support for concurrent behaviour modelling.

The best formalisms for concurrent reasoning are those developed with it in mind, most notably the so-called *Process Algebras*: CSP [Hoa90], CCS [Mil80], ACP [BK85], π-calculus [Mil99]. The strength of these formalisms lie in their ability to model and reason concurrent processes, with communication abstracted as events that denote the exchange of messages. Essentially systems can be viewed as so-called labelled transition systems (LTS) of states connected by transition arrows marked with events. However while process algebras are good for modelling concurrency, and also support good automated techniques for deadlock and livelock detection, their use for I/O modelling is a bit reminiscent of using the monad laws to reason about I/O. We can show that two system descriptions have the same behaviour, in terms of sequences of I/O events, but we cannot talk about the effect of those events on the I/O world state.

What is needed to reason about the effects of I/O on world state is a process algebra with support for state. Most have it to some degree, by allowing processes to be parameterised, but the formal semantics and tool support can be relatively weak. Model-checking, the automated proof technique that does exhaustive search of LTSs, has to deal with the state explosion problem, which gets exacerbated when extra state parameters are added. A full treatment of I/O's effects on the outside world, along with concurrency features as seen in Parallel Haskell, for example, still require further theoretical development, integrating process algebras with *VDM♣*-like state modelling. Recent work on so-called "state-rich" process algebras is in progress, of which *Circus*[OCW06] is a good exemplar.

References

[Abr91]   Abrial, J.-R., Lee, M.K.O., Neilson, D.S., Scharbach, P.N., Sørensen, I.H.: The B Method. In: Prehn, S., Toetenel, H. (eds.) VDM 1991. LNCS, vol. 552, pp. 398–405. Springer, Heidelberg (1991)

[Bd87]   Bird, R., de Moor, O.: Algebra of Programming. Series in Computer Science. Prentice Hall International, London (1987)

[BDS02]   Butterfield, A., Dowse, M., Strong, G.: Proving Make Correct: I/O Proofs in Haskell and Clean. In: Peña, R., Arts, T. (eds.) IFL 2002. LNCS, vol. 2670, pp. 68–83. Springer, Heidelberg (2003)

[BJLM91]   Banâtre, J.-P., Jones, S.B., Le Métayer, D.: Prospects for Functional Programming in Software Engineering. ESPRIT Research Reports, Project 302, vol. 1. Springer, Berlin (1991)

[Bjø92]   Bjørner, D.: Trusted computing systems: the procos experience. In: Proceedings of the 14th International Conference on Software Engineering, ICSE 1992, pp. 15–34. ACM, New York (1992)

[BK85]   Bergstra, J.A., Klop, J.W.: Algebra of communicating processes with abstraction. Theoretical Computer Science 37(1), 77–121 (1985)

[BS96]   Barendsen, E., Smetsers, S.: Uniqueness Typing for Functional Languages with Graph Rewriting Semantics. Mathematical Structures in Computer Science 6(6), 579–612 (1996)

[BS01]   Butterfield, A., Strong, G.: Proving Correctness of Programs with IO – A Paradigm Comparison. In: Arts, T., Mohnen, M. (eds.) IFL 2001. LNCS, vol. 2312, pp. 72–87. Springer, Heidelberg (2002)

[BW88]   Bird, R., Wadler, P.: Introduction to Functional Programming. Series in Computer Science. Prentice Hall International, London (1988)

[CGL92]   Clarke, E.M., Grumberg, O., Long, D.E.: Model checking and abstraction. In: Conference Record of the Nineteenth ACM SIGPLAN-SIGACT Symposium on Principles of Programming Languages, Albuquerque, New Mexico, January 19-22, pp. 343–354. ACM Press (1992)

[Com92]   VDM Standards Committee. VDM Specification Language — Proto-Standard. Technical report, VDM Standards Committee (1992)

[Dav92]   Davie, A.J.T.: An Introduction to Functional Programming Systems using Haskell. Cambridge Computer Science Texts. Cambridge University Press (1992)

[DB06]   Dowse, M., Butterfield, A.: Modelling deterministic concurrent I/O. In: Reppy, J.H., Lawall, J.L. (eds.) Proceedings of the 11th ACM SIGPLAN International Conference on Functional Programming, ICFP 2006, Portland, Oregon, USA, September 16-21, pp. 148–159. ACM (2006)

[DBvEdM04] Dowse, M., Butterfield, A., van Eekelen, M., de Mol, M.: Towards Machine Verified Proofs for I/O. Technical Report NIII-R0415, nijmeegs instituut voor informatica en informatiekunde (2004), http://www.cs.kun.nl/research/reports/

[DGM09]   Déharbe, D., Galvão, S., Moreira, A.M.: Formalizing FreeRTOS: First Steps. In: Oliveira, M.V.M., Woodcock, J. (eds.) SBMF 2009. LNCS, vol. 5902, pp. 101–117. Springer, Heidelberg (2009)

[dM09]   de Mol, M.: Reasoning about Functional Programs: Sparkle, a proof as-
            sistant for Clean. PhD thesis, Institute for Programming research and
            Algorithmics, Radboud University Nijmegen (2009)

[dMvEP01]   de Mol, M., van Eekelen, M., Plasmeijer, R.: Theorem Proving for Func-
            tional Programmers. In: Arts, T., Mohnen, M. (eds.) IFL 2001. LNCS,
            vol. 2312, pp. 55–71. Springer, Heidelberg (2002)

[dMvEP07]   de Mol, M., van Eekelen, M., Plasmeijer, R.: Proving Properties of Lazy
            Functional Programs with SPARKLE. In: Horváth, Z., Plasmeijer, R., Soós,
            A., Zsók, V. (eds.) CEFP 2007. LNCS, vol. 5161, pp. 41–86. Springer,
            Heidelberg (2008)

[Esp95]   Espinosa, D.A.: Semantic Lego. PhD thesis, University of Columbia (1995)

[Gor94]   Gordon, A.: Functional Programming and Input/Output. Distinguished
            Dissertations in Computer Science. Cambridge University Press (1994)

[Hen87]   Henson, M.C.: Elements of Functional Languages. Computer Science
            Texts. Blackwell Scientific Publications (1987)

[Hen90]   Hennessy, M.: The Semantics of Programming Languages: An elementary
            introduction using Structured Operational Semantics. Wiley (1990)

[HJ05]   Holzmann, G.J., Joshi, R.: Reliable Software Systems Design: Defect Pre-
            vention, Detection, and Containment. In: Meyer, B., Woodcock, J. (eds.)
            Verified Software. LNCS, vol. 4171, pp. 237–244. Springer, Heidelberg
            (2008)

[HK98]   Harrison, W.L., Kamin, S.N.: Modular compilers based on monad trans-
            formers. In: Proceedings of the IEEE International Conference on Com-
            puter Languages, pp. 122–131. Society Press (1998)

[Hoa90]   Hoare, C.A.R.: Communicating Sequential Processes. Intl. Series in
            Computer Science. Prentice Hall (1990)

[Jon89]   Jones, C.B.: Systematic Software Development using VDM. Series in Com-
            puter Science. Prentice Hall (1989)

[Kah87]   Kahn, G.: Natural Semantics. In: Brandenburg, F.J., Wirsing, M.,
            Vidal-Naquet, G. (eds.) STACS 1987. LNCS, vol. 247, pp. 22–39. Springer,
            Heidelberg (1987)

[KEH+09]   Klein, G., Elphinstone, K., Heiser, G., Andronick, J., Cock, D., Derrin,
            P., Elkaduwe, D., Engelhardt, K., Kolanski, R., Norrish, M., Sewell, T.,
            Tuch, H., Winwood, S.: Sel4: Formal verification of an os kernel. In: ACM
            Symposium on Operating Systems Principles, pp. 207–220. ACM (2009)

[LHJ95]   Liang, S., Hudak, P., Jones, M.: Monad transformers and modular inter-
            preters. In: Proceedings of the 22nd ACM Symposium on Principles of
            Programming Languages. ACM Press (1995)

[Mac91]   Macan Airchinnigh, M.: Tutorial Lecture Notes on the Irish School of the
            VDM. In: Prehn, S., Toetenel, H. (eds.) VDM 1991. LNCS, vol. 552, pp.
            141–237. Springer, Heidelberg (1991)

[McK06]   McKinna, J.: Why dependent types matter. In: Gregory Morrisett, J.,
            Peyton Jones, S.L. (eds.) POPL, p. 1. ACM (2006)

[Mil80]   Milner, R.: A Calculus of Communication Systems. LNCS, vol. 92.
            Springer, Heidelberg (1980)

[Mil99]   Milner, R.: Communicating and mobile systems - the Pi-calculus.
            Cambridge University Press (1999)

[OCW06]   Oliveira, M., Cavalcanti, A., Woodcock, J.: A denotational semantics for
            circus. In: REFINE 2006, pp. 1–16. ENTCS (2006)

[PJ87]   Peyton-Jones, S.L.: The Implementation of Functional Programming Lan-
            guages. Series in Computer Science. Prentice Hall International, London
            (1987)
[PJ01]   Peyton-Jones, S.L.: Tackling the awkward squad: monadic input/output,
            concurrency, exceptions, and foreign-language calls in haskell. In: Hoare,
            C.A.R., Broy, M., Steinbrueggen, R. (eds.) Engineering Theories of Soft-
            ware Construction. NATO ASI Series, pp. 47–96. IOS Press (2001);
            Marktoberdorf Summer School 2000
[Plo81]   Plotkin, G.: A structural approach to operational semantics. Technical Re-
            port DAIMI FN-19, Department of Computer Science, Aarhus University,
            Denmark (1981)
[Sch86]   Schmidt, D.A.: Denotational Semantics: A Methodology for Language De-
            velopment. Allyn and Bacon, Boston (1986)
[Spi92]   Spivey, J.M.: The Z Notation: A Reference Manual, 2nd edn. Series in
            Computer Science. Prentice Hall (1992)
[Sto77]   Stoy, J.E.: Denotational Semantics: The Scott-Strachey approach to pro-
            gramming language theory. MIT Press, Cambridge (1977)
[VBF⁺11]   Verhulst, E., Boute, R.T., Faria, J.M.S., Sputh, B.H.C., Mezhuyev, V.:
            Formal Development of a Network-Centric RTOS. Springer (2011)

A   Haskell Classes for *VDM*♣

Here we simply extract all the class and instance definitions from the IVDM
sources. They differ from the description in the main body of the tutorial, in
that we have two classes, Container and Partition

A.1   Classes

Basic Containers are types for which notions of membership, insertion and
merging are paramount.

```
class Container c where
  mof  :: Ord a => a -> c a -> Bool
  chrf :: Ord a => c a -> a -> Bool
  x 'mof' cs = chrf cs x
  chrf cs x  = x 'mof' cs
  nil :: c a
  isNil :: c a -> Bool
  distinctFrom :: Ord a => c a -> c a -> Bool
  union :: Ord a => c a -> c a -> c a
  forget :: Ord a => c a -> Set a
```

For some containers, singletons are defined on a single element type:

```
class Container c => Sngl c where
  sngl :: a -> c a
```

But for other containers, singletons are defined over pairs:

```
class Dbl m where
  dbl :: a -> b -> m b a
```

A Container belongs to the Partition class if it also supports ways of breaking it apart:

```
class Container c => Partition c where
  select :: c a -> (a, c a)
  pselect :: (a -> Bool) -> c a -> (a, c a)
  split :: (a -> Bool) -> c a -> (c a, c a)
  pRestrict, pRemove :: (a -> Bool) -> c a -> c a
  pRestrict p = fst . split p
  pRemove p = snd . split p
  sRestrict, sRemove :: Ord a => (Set a) -> c a -> c a
  sRestrict s = pRestrict (chrf s)
  sRemove s = pRemove (chrf s)
  cRestrict, cRemove :: (Ord a, Container d) => d a -> c a -> c a
  cRestrict c = sRestrict (forget c)
  cRemove c = sRemove (forget c)
```

We show the instances for sets, lists and maps below. See the sources and documentation at https://bitbucket.org/andrewbutterfield/irishvdm for details.

A.2   Set Instances

Sets as Containers

```
instance Container Set where
  -- mof = mOf
  chrf = sChrf
  nil = nullSet
  isNil = isNullSet
  sngl = iSet
  distinctFrom c1 c2 = isNullSet (c1 `intersect` c2)
  union = sUnion
  forget = id
```

Singleton Sets:

```
instance Sngl Set where
  sngl = iSet
```

Sets as splittable.

```
instance Partition Set where
  select = sChoose
  pselect = sPChoose
  split = sPSplit
```

A.3   List Instances

Lists as Containers

```
instance Container [] where
  mof = elem
  chrf = flip elem
  nil = []
  isNil = null
  s1 'distinctFrom' s2 = (elems s1) 'distinctFrom' (elems s2)
  union = (++)
  forget = elems
```

Singleton Lists

```
instance Sngl [] where
  sngl x = [x]
```

Lists as splittable.

```
instance Partition [] where
  select = lChoose
  pselect = lPChoose
  split = partition
```

A.4   Map Instances

Maps do not exactly fit the Container/Partition model, because of the way the map constructor takes two types, whose roles are asymmetrical.

However we shoehorn maps into these classes in the Haskell implementation to support overloading of features such a membership (so we can write a 'mof' mp rather than a 'mof' (dom mp)). In particular, we generally characterise membership in terms of domain elements, ignoring the range values, and consider splitting maps by partition entries according to their domains.

We want to define Container and Partition instances parameterised on the domain type, so we devise a type-constructor Pam that takes the range type argument first, and then define Map as a flipping of Pam:

```
newtype Pam r d = MkM [(d,r)]
type    Map d r = Pam r d
```

Maps as Containers, with a domain-centric bias:

```
instance Container (Pam r) where
  d 'mof' m = d 'mof' dom m
  chrf = flip mof
  nil = nullMap
  isNil = isNullMap
  distinctFrom = pre_mextend
  union = mextend
  forget = dom
```

We also find that a "singleton" map ($\{a \mapsto b\}$) actually has two components, so the Sngl class is not adequate. Instead we use the Dbl class.

```
instance Dbl Pam where
  dbl x y = iMap x y
```

Maps as splittable (lossy—loses range information).

```
instance Partition (Pam r) where
  select m = let (d,_,m') = mChoose m in (d,m')
  pselect p m = let (d,_,m') = mPChoose (p . fst) m in (d,m')
  split p = mPSplit (p . fst)
```

Eden – Parallel Functional Programming with Haskell

Rita Loogen

Fachbereich Mathematik und Informatik
Philipps-Universität Marburg, Germany
loogen@informatik.uni-marburg.de

Abstract. Eden is a parallel functional programming language which extends Haskell with constructs for the definition and instantiation of parallel processes. Processes evaluate function applications remotely in parallel. The programmer has control over process granularity, data distribution, communication topology, and evaluation site, but need not manage synchronisation and data exchange between processes. The latter are performed by the parallel runtime system through implicit communication channels, transparent to the programmer. Common and sophisticated parallel communication patterns and topologies, so-called algorithmic skeletons, are provided as higher-order functions in a user-extensible skeleton library written in Eden. Eden is geared toward distributed settings, i.e. processes do not share any data, but can equally well be used on multicore systems. This tutorial gives an up-to-date introduction into Eden's programming methodology based on algorithmic skeletons, its language constructs, and its layered implementation on top of the Glasgow Haskell compiler.

1 Introduction

Functional languages are promising candidates for effective parallel programming, because of their high level of abstraction and, in particular, because of their referential transparency. In principle, any subexpression could be evaluated in parallel. As this implicit parallelism would lead to too much overhead, modern parallel functional languages allow the programmers to specify parallelism explicitly.

In these lecture notes we present Eden, a parallel functional programming language which extends Haskell with constructs for the definition and instantiation of parallel processes. The underlying idea of Eden is to enable programmers to specify process networks in a declarative way. Processes evaluate function applications in parallel. The function parameters are the process inputs and the function result is the process output. Thus, a process maps input to output values. Inputs and outputs are automatically transferred via unidirectional one-to-one channels between parent and child processes. Programmers need not think about triggering low-level send and receive actions for data transfer between parallel processes. Furthermore, process inputs and outputs are always completely

V. Zsók, Z. Horváth, and R. Plasmeijer (Eds.): CEFP 2011, LNCS 7241, pp. 142–206, 2012.

evaluated before being sent in order to enable parallelism in the context of a host language with a demand-driven evaluation strategy. Algorithmic skeletons which specify common and sophisticated parallel communication patterns and topologies are provided as higher-order functions in a user-extensible skeleton library written in Eden. Skeletons provide a very simple access to parallel functional programming. Parallelization of a Haskell program can often simply be achieved by selecting and instantiating an appropriate skeleton from the skeleton library. From time to time, adaptation of a skeleton to a special situation or the development of a new skeleton may be necessary.

Eden is tailored for *distributed memory architectures*, i.e. processes work within disjoint address spaces and do not share any data. This simplifies Eden's implementation as there is e.g. no need for global garbage collection. There is, however, a risk of loosing sharing, i.e. it may happen that the same expression is redundantly evaluated by several parallel processes.

Although the automatic management of communication by the parallel runtime system has several advantages, it also has some restrictions. This form of communication is only provided between parent and child processes, but e.g. not between sibling processes. I.e. only hierarchical communication topologies are automatically supported. For this reason, Eden also provides a form of *explicit channel management*. A receiver process can create a new input channel and pass its name to another process. The latter can directly send data to the receiver process using the received channel name. An even easier-to-use way to define non-hierarchical process networks is the *remote data concept* where data can be released by a process to be fetched by a remote process. In this case a handle is first transferred from the owner to the receiver process (maybe via common predecessor processes). Via this handle the proper data can then directly transferred from the producer to the receiver process. Moreover, *many-to-one communication* can be modeled using a pre-defined (necessarily non-deterministic) merge function. These non-functional Eden features make the language very expressive. Arbitrary parallel computation schemes like sophisticated master-worker systems or cyclic communication topologies like rings and tori can be defined in an elegant way. Eden supports an equational programming style where recursive process nets can simply be defined using recursive equations. Using the recently introduced PA (parallel action) monad, it is also possible to adopt a monadic programming style, in particular, when it is necessary to ensure that series of parallel activities are executed in a given order.

Eden has been implemented by extending the runtime system of the Glasgow Haskell compiler [24], a mature and efficient Haskell implementation, for parallel and distributed execution. The parallel runtime system (PRTS) uses suitable middleware (currently PVM [52] or MPI [43]) to manage parallel execution. Recently, a special multicore implementation which needs no middleware has been implemented [48]. Traces of parallel program executions can be visualised and analysed using the Eden Trace Viewer EdenTV.

This tutorial gives an up-to-date introduction into Eden's programming methodology based on algorithmic skeletons, its language constructs, and its layered implementation on top of the Glasgow Haskell compiler. Throughout the tutorial, exercises are provided which help the readers to test their understanding of the presented material and to experiment with Eden. A basic knowledge of programming in Haskell is assumed. The Eden compiler, the skeleton library, EdenTV, and the program code of the case studies are freely available from the Eden web pages, see

http://www.mathematik.uni-marburg.de/~eden/

Plan of This Tutorial. The next section provides a quick start to Eden programming with algorithmic skeletons. Section 3 introduces the basic constructs of Eden's coordination language, i.e. it is shown how parallelism can be expressed and managed. The next section presents techniques for reducing the communication costs in parallel programs. Section 5 shows how non-hierarchical communication topologies can be defined. In particular, a ring and a torus skeleton are presented. Section 6 explains how master-worker systems can be specified. An introduction to explicit channel management in Section 7 leads to Section 8 which introduces Eden's layered implementation. Hints at more detailed material on Eden are given in Section 9. After a short discussion of related work in Section 10 conclusions are drawn in Section 11. Appendix A contains a short presentation of how to compile, run, and analyse Eden programs. In particular, it presents the Eden trace viewer tool, EdenTV, which can be used to analyse the behaviour of parallel programs. Appendix B contains the definitions of auxiliary functions from the Eden `Auxiliary` library that are used in this tutorial.

The tutorial refers to several case studies and shows example trace visualisations. The corresponding traces have been produced using the Eden system, version 6.12.3, on the following systems: an Intel 8-core machine (2 × Xeon Quadcore @2.5GHz, 16 GB RAM) machine and two Beowulf clusters at Heriot-Watt University in Edinburgh (Beowulf I: 32 Intel P4-SMP nodes @ 3 GHz 512MB RAM, Fast Ethernet and Beowulf II: 32 nodes, each with two Intel quad-core processors (Xeon E5504) @ 2GHz, 4MB L3 cache, 12GB RAM, Gigabit Ethernet).

2 Skeleton-Based Programming in Eden

Before presenting the Eden programming constructs we show how a quick and effective parallelization of Haskell programs can be achieved using pre-defined skeletons from the Eden skeleton library. (Algorithmic) skeletons [16] define common parallel computation patterns. In Eden they are defined as higher-order functions. In the following we look at two typical problem solving schemes for which various parallel implementations are provided in the Eden skeleton library: map-and-reduce and divide-and-conquer.

2.1 Map-and-Reduce

Map-and-reduce is a typical data-parallel evaluation scheme. It consists of a `map` and a subsequent `reduce`.

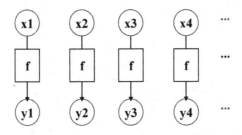

Fig. 1. Basic map evaluation scheme

Map, Parallel Map and Farm. The map function applies a function to each element of a list. In Haskell it can simply be expressed as follows

```
map :: (a → b) → [a] → [b]
map f []      = []
map f (x:xs) = (f x) : (map f xs)
```

The map function is inherently parallel because in principle all function applications (f x) can be evaluated in parallel. It presents a simple form of data parallelism, because the same function is applied to different data elements (see Figure 1).

Eden's skeleton library contains several parallel implementations of map. The simplest parallel version is parMap where a separate process is created for each function application, i.e. as many processes as list elements will be created. The input parameter as well as the result of each process will be transmitted via communication channels between the generator process and the processes created by parMap. Therefore parMap's type is

```
parMap :: (Trans a, Trans b) ⇒ (a → b) → [a] → [b]
```

The Eden-specific type context (Trans a, Trans b) indicates that both types a and b must belong to the Eden Trans type class of *transmissible* values. Most predefined types belong to this type class. In Haskell, type classes provide a structured way to define overloaded functions. Trans provides implicitly used communication functions.

If the number of list elements is much higher than the number of available processing elements, this will cause too much process creation overhead. Another skeleton called farm takes two additional parameter functions

distribute :: [a] → [[a]] and combine :: [[b]] → [b].

It uses the distribute-function to split the input list into sublists, creates a process for mapping f on each sublist and combines the result lists using the combine-function. Of course, a proper use of farm to implement another parallel version of map requires that the following equation is fulfilled[1]:

map f = combine ∘ (map (map f)) ∘ distribute.

---

[1] The programmer is responsible for guaranteeing this condition.

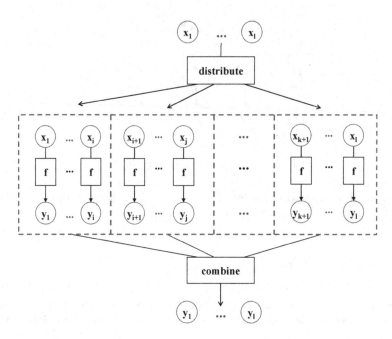

Fig. 2. Parallel `farm` evaluation scheme

Replacing the outer `map`-application with `parMap` leads to the definition of the `farm` skeleton in Eden:

```
farm :: (Trans a, Trans b) ⇒
          ([a] → [[a]])              -- ^ distribute
        → ([[b]] → [b])             -- ^ combine
        → (a → b) → [a] → [b]       -- ^ map interface
farm distribute combine f
  = combine ∘ (parMap (map f)) ∘ distribute
```

The `farm` skeleton creates as many processes as sublists are generated by the parameter function `distribute` (see Figure 2, dotted lines indicate processes). In Eden's `Auxiliary` library the following functions for distributing and (re-)combining lists are defined. For the reader's convenience we have also put together the pure Haskell definitions of these functions in Appendix B.

- `unshuffle :: Int → [a] → [[a]]` distributes the input list in a round robin manner into as many sublists as the first parameter indicates.
- `shuffle :: [[a]] → [a]` shuffles the given list of lists into the output list. It works inversely to `unshuffle`.
- `splitIntoN :: Int → [a] → [[a]]` distributes the input list blockwise into as many sublists as the first parameter determines. The lengths of the output lists differ by at most one. The inverse function of `splitIntoN` is the Haskell prelude function `concat :: [[a]] → [a]` which simply concatenates all lists in the given list of lists.

Eden provides a constant

```
noPe :: Int
```

which gives the number of available processing elements. Thus, suitable parallel implementations of map using farm are e.g.

```
mapFarmS , mapFarmB :: (Trans a, Trans b) ⇒
                       (a → b) → [a] → [b]
mapFarmS = farm (unshuffle  noPe) shuffle
mapFarmB = farm (splitIntoN noPe) concat
```

Reduce and Parallel Map-Reduce.   In many applications, a reduction is executed after the application of map, i.e. the elements of the result list of map are combined using a binary function. In Haskell list reduction is defined by higher-order fold-functions. Depending on whether the parameter function is right or left associative, Haskell provides folding functions foldr and foldl. For simplicity, we consider in the following only foldr:

```
foldr :: (a → b → b) → b → [a] → b
foldr g e []     = e
foldr g e (x:xs) = g x (foldr g e xs)
```

Accordingly, the following composition of map and foldr in Haskell defines a simple map-reduce scheme:

```
mapRedr :: (b → c → c) → c → (a → b) → [a] → c
mapRedr g e f = (foldr g e) ∘ (map f)
```

This function could simply be implemented in parallel by replacing map with e.g. mapFarmB, but then the reduction will completely and sequentially be performed in the parent process. If the parameter function g is associative with type b → b → b and neutral element e, the reduction could also be performed in parallel by pre-reducing the sublists within the farm processes. Afterwards only the subresults from the processes have to be combined by the main process (see Figure 3). The code of this parallel map-reduce scheme is a slight variation of the above definition of the farm-skeleton where the distribution and combination of values is fixed and mapRedr is used instead of map as argument of parMap:

```
parMapRedr :: (Trans a, Trans b) ⇒
              (b → b → b) → b → (a → b) → [a] → b
parMapRedr g e f
   = if noPe == 1 then  mapRedr g e f xs   else
     (foldr g e) ∘ (parMap (mapRed g e f)) ∘ (splitIntoN noPe)
```

Note that parallel processes are only created if the number of available processor elements is at least 2. On a single processor element the sequential scheme mapRedr is executed.

With this skeleton the input lists of the processes are evaluated by the parent process and then communicated via automatically created communication channels between the parent process and the parMap processes. In Eden, lists

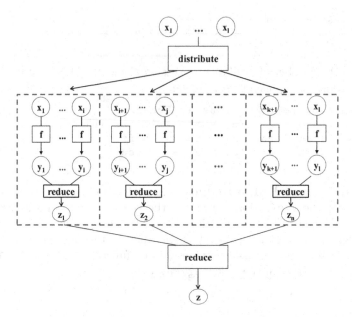

Fig. 3. Parallel map-reduce evaluation scheme

are transmitted as streams which means that each element is sent in a separate message. Sometimes this causes a severe overhead, especially for very long lists. The following variant `offline_parMapRedr` avoids the stream communication of the input lists at all. Only a process identification number is communicated and used to select the appropriate part of the input list. The whole (unevaluated) list is incorporated in the worker function which is mapped on the identification numbers. As each process evaluates now the (`splitIntoN noPe`) application, this may cause some redundancy in the input evaluation but it substantially reduces communication overhead. In Subsection 4.2, we discuss this technique in more detail.

```
offline_parMapRedr :: (Trans a, Trans b) ⇒
                      (b → b → b) → b → (a → b) → [a] → b
offline_parMapRedr g e f xs
  = if noPe == 1 then  mapRedr g e f xs  else
    foldr g e (parMap worker [0..noPe-1])
    where worker i = mapRed g e f ((splitIntoN noPe xs)!!i)
```

Example: The number π can be calculated by approximating the integral

$$\pi = \int_0^1 f(x)\ dx \text{ where } f(x) = \frac{4}{1+x^2}$$

in the following way:

$$\pi = \lim_{n\to\infty} pi(n) \text{ with } pi(n) = \frac{1}{n}\sum_{i=1}^{n} f\left(\frac{i-0.5}{n}\right).$$

```
module Main where

import System
import Control.Parallel.Eden
import Control.Parallel.Eden.EdenSkel.MapRedSkels

main :: IO ()
main = getArgs >>= \ (n:_) ->
        print (cpi (read n))

-- compute pi using integration
cpi     :: Integer -> Double
cpi n =  offline_parMapRedr (+) 0 (f o index) [1..n] /
            fromInteger n
  where
    f        :: Double -> Double
    f x      =  4 / (1 + x*x)
    index    :: Integer -> Double
    index i =  (fromInteger i - 0.5) / fromInteger n
```

Fig. 4. Eden program for parallel calculation of π

The function pi can simply be expressed in Haskell using our mapRedr function:

```
cpi     :: Integer -> Double
cpi n =  mapRedr (+) 0 (f o index) [1..n] / fromInteger n
  where
    f        :: Double -> Double
    f x      =  4 / (1 + x*x)
    index    :: Integer -> Double
    index i =  (fromInteger i - 0.5) / fromInteger n
```

The Haskell prelude function fromInteger converts integer numbers into double-precision floating point numbers.

A parallel version is obtained by replacing mapRed with offline_parMapRedr. The complete parallel program is shown in Figure 4. It is important that each Eden program imports the Eden module Control.Parallel.Eden. In addition, the program imports the part of the Eden skeleton library which provides parallel map-reduce skeletons. How to compile, run and analyse Eden programs is explained in detail in the appendix of this tutorial. Figure 5 shows on the left the visualisation of a trace file by EdenTV and on the right some statistical data of this program run also provided by EdenTV. The trace has been produced for the input 1000000 with the parallel MPI-based runtime system on the Beowulf II. When using MPI the start-up time of the parallel runtime system is incorporated in the trace. The start-up time depends on the number of processor elements which are started. In the program run underlying the trace in Figure 5 the start-up took 1.14 seconds. Thus, it dominates the overall runtime which has been 1.62 seconds. The actual parallel runtime of the program has been 0.48

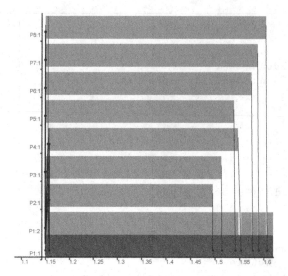

input size 1000000
total runtime 1.62s
start up time 1.14s
parallel runtime 0.48s
sequential runtime 3.74s
speedup 7.79 8 machines
9 processes
17 threads
29 messages

Fig. 5. Pi trace on 8 PEs, parallel map-reduce with 8 processes

seconds. The sequential program takes 3.74 seconds with the same input on the same machine. The fraction

$$\frac{\text{sequential runtime}}{\text{parallel runtime}}$$

is called the speed-up of the parallel evaluation. The speed-up is usually bounded by the number of processor elements. In this example the speed-up has been 7.79 which is very good on 8 PEs.

The trace visualisation on the left shows the parallel program behaviour. It consists of 9 horizontal bars, the timelines for the 9 processes that have been executed. On the x-axis the time is shown in seconds. On the y-axis the process numbers are given in the form P $i:j$ where i is the number of the processor element or machine, on which the process is executed and j is the local number of the process per machine. Note that the timelines have been moved to the left to omit the start-up time, i.e. the x-axis starts at 1.14 seconds.

The colours of the bars indicate the status of the corresponding process. Green (in grayscale: grey) means that the process is running. Yellow (light grey) shows that a process is runnable but not running which might be due to a garbage collection or another process running on the same PE. Red (dark grey) indicates that a process is blocked, i.e. waiting for input. Messages are shown as black lines from the sender to the receiver process where the receiver is marked by a dot at the end of the line. The program starts 9 processes. Process P 1:1, i.e. Process 1 on PE 1 executes the main program. The `offline_parMapRedr` skeleton starts `noPe = 8` processes which are placed by default in a round-robin manner on the available PEs, starting with PE 2. Thus, the last process has also been allocated on PE 1 and is numbered P 1:2.

The trace picture shows that the child processes are always running (green) while the main process is blocked (red) most of the time waiting for the results of the child processes. 17 threads have been generated: one thread runs in the 9 processes each to compute the process output. In addition, 8 (short-living) threads have been started in the main process to evaluate and send the input (identification numbers) to the 8 child processes. In total 29 messages have been sent: In the beginning, 8 process creation messages and 7 acknowledgement messages are exchanged. Messages between P 1:2 and P 1:1 are not counted because they are not really sent, as both processes are executed on the same PE. Moreover, the main process P 1:1 sends 7 input messages to the 7 remote processes. When the remote child processes terminate, they send their result back to the main process. Finally the main process computes the sum of the received values, divides this by the original input value and prints the result.   ◁

Exercise 1: The following Haskell function summePhi sums Euler's totient or ϕ function which counts for parameter value n the number of positive integers less than n that are relatively prime to n:

```
summePhi    :: Int  → Int
summePhi n =  sum (map phi [1..n])

phi  :: Int  → Int
phi n =  length (filter (relprime n) [1..(n-1)])

relprime     :: Int  → Int  → Bool
relprime x y = gcd x y == 1
```

sum and gcd are Haskell prelude function, i.e. predefined Haskell function. sum sums all elements of a list of numbers. It is defined as an instance of the folding function foldl', a strict variant of foldl:

```
sum :: Num a ⇒ [a]  → a
sum =  foldl' (+) 0
```

gcd computes the greated common divisor of two integers.
1. Define summePhi as instance of a map-reduce scheme.
2. Parallelise the program using an appropriate map-reduce skeleton of the Eden skeleton library.
3. Run your parallel program on i machines, where $i \in \{1, 2, 4, ...\}$ (runtime option -Ni) and use the Eden trace viewer to analyse the parallel program behaviour.

2.2 Divide-and-Conquer

Another common computation scheme is divide-and-conquer. Eden's skeleton library provides several skeletons for the parallelisation of divide-and-conquer algorithms. The skeletons are parallel variants of the following polymorphic higher-order divide-and-conquer function dc which implements the basic scheme: If a problem is *trivial*, it is *solved* directly. Otherwise, the problem is divided or

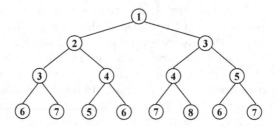

Fig. 6. Divide-and-conquer call tree with default process placement

(*splitted*) into two or more subproblems, for which the same scheme is applied.
The final solution is computed by *combining* the solutions of the subproblems.

```
type DivideConquer a b
   = (a → Bool) → (a → b)          -- ^ trivial? / solve
       → (a → [a]) → (a → [b] → b) -- ^ split / combine
       → a → b                     -- ^ input / result
dc :: DivideConquer a b
dc trivial solve split combine = rec_dc
   where
      rec_dc x = if trivial x then solve x
                 else combine x (map rec_dc (split x))
```

The easiest way to parallelise this `dc` scheme in Eden is to replace `map` with
`parMap`. An additional integer parameter `lv` can be used to stop the parallel
unfolding at a given level and to use the sequential version afterwards:

```
parDC :: (Trans a, Trans b) ⇒
           Int →   -- depth
           DivideConquer a b
parDC lv trivial solve split combine
 = pdc lv
 where
  pdc lv x
   | lv == 0 = dc trivial solve split combine
   | lv > 0 = if trivial x then solve x
              else combine x (parMap (pdc (lv-1)) (split x))
```

In this approach a dynamic tree of processes is created with each process connected to its parent. With the default round robin placement of child processes,
the processes are however not evenly distributed on the available processing elements (PEs). Note that each PE `i` places new locally created child processes in
a round-robin manner on the PEs (`i mod noPe)+1`, `((i+1) mod noPe)+1` etc.

Example: If 8 PEs are available and if we consider a regular divide-and-conquer
tree with branching degree 2 and three recursive unfoldings, then 14 child processes will be created and may be allocated on PEs 2 to 8 as indicated by the
tree in Figure 6. The main process on PE 1 places its two child processes on
PEs 2 and 3. The child process on PE2 creates new processes on PEs 3 and
4, the one on PE 3 accordingly on PEs 4 and 5. The second process on PE 3

allocates its children on PE 6 and 7, where we assume that the two processes on PE 3 create their child processes one after the other and not in an interleaved way. In total, PEs 3, 4 and 5 would get two processes each, three processes would be allocated on PEs 6 and 7, while only one process would be placed on PE 8. Thus, the default process placement leads to an unbalanced process distribution on the available PEs.   ◁

The Eden skeleton library provides more elaborated parallel divide-and-conquer implementations. In the following example, we use the disDC skeleton. In Subsection 3.3 we show the implementation of this skeleton in Eden. The disDC skeleton implements a so-called distributed expansion scheme. This works in a similar way like the above parallelization with parMap except for the following differences:

1. The skeleton assumes a fixed-degree splitting scheme, i.e. the split function always divides a problem into the same number of subproblems. This number, called the *branching degree*, is the first parameter of the disDC skeleton.
2. The creation of processes and their allocation is controlled via a list of PE numbers, called *ticket list*. This list is the second parameter of the skeleton. It determines on which PEs newly created processes are allocated und thus indirectly how many processes will be created. When no more tickets are available, all further evaluations take place sequentially. This makes the use of a level parameter to control parallel unfolding superfluous. Moreover, it allows to balance the process load on PEs. The ticket list [2..noPe] leads e.g. to the allocation of exactly one process on each PE. The main process starts on PE1 and noPe-1 processes are created on the other available PEs. If you want to create as many processes as possible in a round-robin manner on the available PEs, you should use the ticket list cycle ([2..noPe]++[1]). The Haskell prelude function cycle :: [a] → [a] defines a circular infinite list by repeating its input list infinitely.
3. Each process keeps the first subproblem for local evaluation and and creates child processes only for the other subproblems.

Example: A typical divide-and-conquer algorithm is mergesort which can be implemented in Haskell as follows:

```
mergeSort      :: Ord a ⇒ [a] → [a]
mergeSort []   =  []
mergeSort [x]  =  [x]
mergeSort xs   =  sortMerge (mergeSort xs1) (mergeSort xs2)
                  where [xs1,xs2] = splitIntoN 2 xs
```

The function mergeSort transforms an input list into a sorted output list by subsequently merging sorted sublists with increasing length. Lists with at least two elements are split into into their first half and their second half using the auxiliary function splitIntoN from Eden's Auxiliary library (see also Appendix B). The sublists are sorted by recursive instantiations of mergeSort processes. The sorted sublists are coalesced into a sorted result list using the function sortMerge which is an ordinary Haskell function. The context `Ord a` ensures that an ordering is defined on type `a`.

```
sortMerge :: Ord a ⇒ [a] → [a] → [a]
sortMerge []         ylist         = ylist
sortMerge xlist      []            = xlist
sortMerge xlist@(x:xs) ylist@(y:ys)
  | x ≤ y = x : sortMerge xs ylist
  | x > y = y : sortMerge xlist ys
```

In order to derive a simple skeleton-based parallelization one first has to define `mergeSort` as an instance of the `dc` scheme, i.e. one has to extract the parameter functions of the `dc` scheme from the recursive definition:

```
mergeSortDC   :: Ord a ⇒ [a] → [a]
mergeSortDC   =  dc trivial solve split combine
  where
    trivial    :: [a] → Bool
    trivial xs =  null xs || null (tail xs)

    solve :: [a] → [a]
    solve =  id

    split :: [a] → [[a]]
    split =  splitIntoN 2

    combine                    :: [a] → [[b]] → [b]
    combine _ (xs1:xs2:_) =  sortMerge xs1 xs2
```

A parallel implementation of `mergeSort` is now achieved by replacing `dc` in the above code with `disDC 2 [2..noPe]`. Figure 7 shows the visualisation of a trace produced by a slightly tuned version of this parallel program for an input list with 1 million integer numbers. The tuning concerns the communication of inputs and outputs of processes. We will discuss the modifications in Subsection 4.3 after the applied techniques have been introduced.

The trace picture shows that all processes have been busy, i.e. in mode running (green / grey), during all of their life time. Processes are numbered `P i:1` where `i` is the number of the PE on which the process is evaluated and the `1` is the local process number on each PE. As exactly one process has been allocated on each PE, each process has the local process number `1`. The whole evaluation starts with the main process on PE 1 whose activity profile is shown by the lowest bar. The recursive calls are evaluated on the PEs shown in the call tree on the left in Figure 8. With ticket list `[2..noPe]` seven child processes will be created. The main process is allocated on PE 1 and executes the skeleton call. It splits the input list into two halves, keeps the first half for local evaluation and creates a child process on PE 2 for sorting the second half. The remaining ticket list `[3..noPe]` is unshuffled into the two lists `[3,5,7]` and `[4,6,8]`. The first sublist is kept locally while the child process gets the second one. The main process and the child process on PE 2 proceed in parallel creating further subprocesses on PE 3 and PE 4, respectively, and unshuffling their remaining ticket lists into

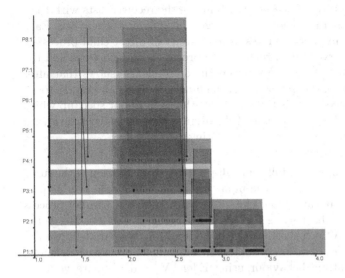

input size 1000000
runtime 3 s
8 machines
8 processes
22 threads
32 conversations
258 messages

Fig. 7. Parallel `mergeSort` trace on 8 PEs, `disDC` skeleton

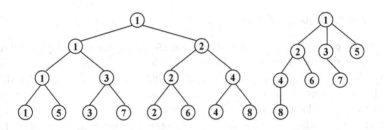

Fig. 8. Call tree (left) and process generation tree (right) of parallel `mergesort` execution

two sublists etc. The process generation tree on the right hand side in Figure 8 shows which process creates which other processes. As there is a one-to-one correspondence between processes and PEs processes are simply marked with the PE number.

In Figure 7 single messages are shown as black lines with a big dot at the receiver side while the communication of streams is shown as a shaded area. A stream communication consists of a series of messages. Only the last message of a stream is shown as a black line. The other messages are only indicated by a very short black line on the receiver side. In the statistics, messages and conversations are counted. A stream communication is counted as a single conversation and as many messages as have been needed to communicate the stream. Thus in this example, we have only 32 conversations but 258 messages.

After about half of their runtime the upper half of processes (i.e. the leaf processes of the process generation tree in Figure 8) start to return their results in streams to their generator processes which merge the received lists with their own results using sortMerge. The whole merge phase occurs level-wise. Each process performs as many merge phases as its number of direct child processes. This can clearly be observed when relating the process generation tree and the message flow in the trace picture. Moreover, the trace clearly shows that after half of the overall runtime, the upper half of the processes finish already. In total, the PEs are badly utilised. This is the reason for the rather poor speedup which is only about 3 with 8 PEs, the runtime of the original sequential mergeSort with input size 1000000 being 9 sec in the same setting.   ◁

Exercise 2: 1. Implement the following alternative parallelisation of the function mergeSort: Decompose the input list into as many sublists as processor elements are available. Create for each sublist a parallel process which sorts the sublist using the original mergeSort function. Merge the sorted sublists. Which skeleton(s) can be used for this parallelisation?

2. Run your parallel program on different numbers of processor elements, analyse the runtime behaviour using EdenTV, and compare your results with those achieved with the parallel divide-and-conquer version described before.

2.3   Eden's Skeleton Library

The functions parMap, farm, mapFarmS, mapFarmB, parMapRedr, and parDC defined above are simple examples for skeleton definitions in Eden. As we have seen, there may be many different parallel implementations of a single computation scheme. Implementations may differ in the process topology created, in the granularity of tasks, in the load balancing strategy, or in the communication policy. It is possible to predict the efficiency of skeleton instantiations by providing a *cost model* for skeleton implementations [38]. This aspect will however not be considered in this tutorial.

While many skeleton systems provide pre-defined, specially supported sets of skeletons, the application programmer has usually not the possibility of creating new ones. In Eden, skeletons can be *used*, *modified* and *newly implemented*, because (like in other parallel functional languages) skeletons are no more than polymorphic higher-order functions which can be applied with different types and parameters. Thus, programming with skeletons in Eden follows the same principle as programming with higher-order functions. Moreover, describing both the functional specification and the parallel implementation of a skeleton in the same language context constitutes a good basis for formal reasoning and correctness proofs, and provides greater flexibility.

In a way similar to the rich set of higher-order functions provided in Haskell's prelude and libraries, Eden provides a well assorted skeleton library
Control.Parallel.Eden.EdenSkel:

– Control.Parallel.Eden.EdenSkel.Auxiliary provides useful auxiliary functions like unshuffle and shuffle (see also Appendix B).

- `Control.Parallel.Eden.EdenSkel.DCSkels` comprises various divide and conquer skeletons like `parDC` or `disDC`.
- `Control.Parallel.Eden.EdenSkel.MapSkels` provides parallel map-like skeletons like `parMap`, `farm` or `offline_farm`.
- `Control.Parallel.Eden.EdenSkel.MapRedSkels` supplies parallel implementations of the map-reduce scheme like `parMapRedr` or a parallel implementation of Google map-reduce [6].
- `Control.Parallel.Eden.EdenSkel.TopoSkels` collects topology skeletons like pipelines or rings.
- `Control.Parallel.Eden.EdenSkel.WPSkels` puts together workpool skeletons like the master worker skeleton defined in Section 6.2.

3 Eden's Basic Constructs

Although many applications can be parallelised using pre-defined skeletons, it may be necessary to adjust skeletons to special cases or to define new skeletons. In these cases it is important to know the basic Eden coordination constructs for

- for defining and creating processes
- for generating non-hierarchical process topologies
- for modeling many-to-one communication.

Eden's basic constructs are defined in the Eden module `Control.Parallel.Eden` which must be imported by each Eden program.

3.1 Defining and Creating Processes

The central coordination constructs for the definition of processes are *process abstractions* and *instantiations*:

```
process  :: (Trans a, Trans b) ⇒  (a → b)     → Process a b
( # )    :: (Trans a, Trans b) ⇒  Process a b → a → b
```

The purpose of function `process` is to convert functions of type a → b into *process abstractions* of type `Process a b` where the type context (`Trans a`, `Trans b`) indicates that both types a and b must belong to the `Trans` class of *transmissible* values. Process abstractions are instantiated by using the infix operator (#). An expression (`process funct`) # `arg` leads to the creation of a remote process for evaluating the application of the function `funct` to the argument `arg`. The argument expression `arg` will be evaluated concurrently by a new thread in the parent process and will then be sent to the new child process. The child process will evaluate the function application `funct arg` in a demand driven way, using the standard lazy evaluation scheme of Haskell. If the argument value is necessary to complete its evaluation, the child process will suspend, until the parent thread has sent it. The child process sends back the result of the function application to its parent process. Communication is performed through *implicit*

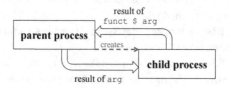

Fig. 9. Process topology after evaluating (`process funct`) # `arg`

1:1 channels that are established between child and parent process on process instantiation (see Figure 9). Process synchronisation is achieved by exchanging data through the communication channels, as these have non-blocking sending, but blocking reception. In order to increase the parallelism degree and to speed up the distribution of the computation, process in- and outputs will be evaluated to normal form before being sent (except for expressions with a function type, which are evaluated to weak head normal form). This implements a *pushing approach* for communication instead of a *pulling approach* where remote data would have to be requested explicitly.

Because of the normal form evaluation of communicated data, the type class `Trans` is a subclass of the class `NFData` (Normal Form Data) which provides a function `rnf` to force the normal form evaluation of data. `Trans` provides communication functions overloaded for `lists`, which are transmitted as streams, element by element, and for `tuples`, which are evaluated component-wise by concurrent threads in the same process. An Eden process can thus comprise a number of threads, which may vary during its lifetime. The type class `Trans` will be explained in more detail in Section 8. A channel is closed when the output value has been completely transmitted to the receiver. An Eden process will end its execution as soon as all its output channels are closed or are detected to be unnecessary (during garbage collection). Termination of a process implies the immediate closure of its input channels, i.e., the closure of the output channels in the corresponding producer processes, thus leading to a termination cascade through the process network.

The coordination functions `process` and (#) are usually used in combination as in the definition of the following operator for parallel function application:

```
( $# )     :: (Trans a, Trans b) ⇒ (a → b) → a → b
f $# x  =   process f # x      -- ( $# ) = ( # ) ∘ process
```

The operator (`$#`) induces that the input parameter `x`, as well as the result value, will be transmitted via channels. The types `a` and `b` must therefore belong to the class `Trans`.

In fact, this simple operator would be enough for extending Haskell with parallelism. The distinction of process abstraction and process instantiation may however be useful from a didactic point of view. A process abstraction defines process creation on the side of the child process while a process instantiation defines it on the side of the parent process. This is also reflected by the implementation of these constructs, shown in Section 8.

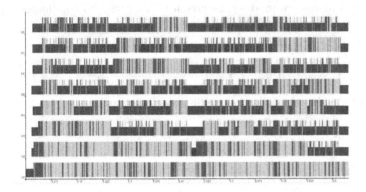

input size 1000
par. time 0.95s
seq. time 0,004s
8 machines
1999 processes
31940 messages

Fig. 10. Trace visualisation of simple parallel mergesort, machines view

It is tempting to parallelise functional programs simply by using this parallel application operator at suitable places in programs. Unfortunately, in most cases this easy approach does not work. The reasons are manyfold as shown in the following simple example.

Example: In principle, a simple parallelisation of mergeSort could be achieved by using the parallel application operator ($#) in the recursive calls of the original definition of mergeSort (see above):

```
mergeSort xs = sortMerge (mergeSort $# xs1)
                         (mergeSort $# xs2)
               where [xs1,xs2] = unshuffle 2 xs
```

In this definition, two processes are created for each recursive call as long as the input list has at least two elements. In Figure 10 the activity profile of the 8 processor elements (machines view of EdenTV, see Appendix B) is shown for the execution of this simple parallel mergesort for an input list of length 1000. The processor elements are either idle (small blue bar), i.e. they have no processes to evaluate, busy with system activity (yellow/light grey bar), i.e. there are runnable processes but no process is being executed or blocked (red/dark grey bar), i.e. all processes are waiting for input. The statistics show that 1999 processes have been created and that 31940 messages have been sent. The parallel runtime is 0.95 seconds, while the sequential runtime is only 0.004 seconds, i.e. the parallel program is much slower than the original sequential program. This is due to the excessive creation of processes and the enourmous number of messages that has been exchanged. Moreover, this simple approach has a demand problem, as the processes are only created when their result is already necessary for the overall evaluation. In the following sections, we will present techniques to cope with these problems.   ◁

Eden processes exchange data via unidirectional one-to-one communication channels. The type class Trans provides implicitly used functions for this purpose. As laziness enables infinite data structures and the handling of partially available data, communication streams are modeled as lazy lists, and circular topologies of processes can be created and connected by such streams.

Example: The sequence of all multiples of two arbitrary integer values n and m

$$\langle n^i m^j \mid i, j \geq 0 \rangle$$

can easily be computed using the following cyclic process network:

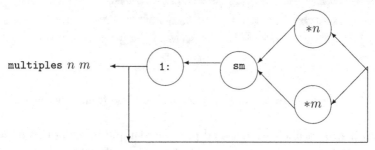

multiples $n\ m$

This network can be expressed in Eden as follows:

```
multiples :: Integer → Integer → [Integer]
multiples n m = ms
       where ms = 1: sm (map (*n) $# ms) (map (*m) $# ms)
```

The ordinary Haskell function sm works in a similar way as the sortMerge function used in the mergesort example but it eliminates duplicates when merging its sorted input lists:

```
sm :: [Int] →    [Int]    → [Int]
sm    [ ]       ys      = ys
sm    xs        [ ]     = xs
sm    xl@(x:xs) yl@(y:ys)
              | x < y     = x : sm xs yl
              | x == y    = x : sm xs ys
              | otherwise = y : sm xl ys
```

In this example two child processes will be created corresponding to the two applications of ($#). Each of these processes receives the stream of multiples from the parent process, multiplies each element with n or m, respectively, and sends each result back to the parent process. The parent process will evaluate the application of sm to the two result streams received from the two child processes. It uses two concurrent threads to supply the child processes with their input. Streaming is essential in this example to avoid a deadlock. The parallelism is rather fine-grained with a low ratio of computation versus communication. Thus, speedups cannot be expected when this program is executed on two processors.

◁

Exercise 3: Define a cyclic process network to compute the sorted sequence of Hamming numbers $\langle 2^i 3^j 5^k \mid i, j, k \geq 0 \rangle$. Implement the network in Eden and analyse its behaviour with EdenTV.

3.2 Coping with Laziness

The laziness of Haskell has many advantages when considering recursive process networks and stream-based communication as shown above. Even though, it is also an obstacle to parallelism, because pure demand-driven (lazy) evaluation will activate a parallel evaluation only when its result is already needed to continue the overall computation, i.e. the main evaluation will immediately wait for the result of a parallel subcomputation. Thus, sometimes it is necessary to produce additional demand in order to unfold certain process systems. Otherwise, the programmer may experience *distributed sequentialism*. This situation is illustrated by the following attempt to define `parMap` using Eden's parallel application operator (`$#`):

Example: Simply replacing the applications of the parameter function in the `map` definition with parallel applications leads to the following definition:

```
parMap_distrSeq            :: (Trans a, Trans b) ⇒
                              (a → b) → [a] → [b]
parMap_distrSeq f []     = []
parMap_distrSeq f (x:xs) = (f $# x) : parMap_distrSeq f xs
```

The problem with this definition is that for instance the expression
```
sum (parMap_distrSeq square [1..10])
```
will create 10 processes, but only one after the other as demanded by the `sum` function which sums up the elements of a list of numbers. Consequently, the computation will not speed up due to "parallel" evaluation, but slow down because of the process creation overhead added to the distributed, but sequential evaluation. Figure 11 shows the trace of the program for the parallel computation of π in which `parMap` has been replaced with `parMap_distrSeq` in the definition of the skeleton `offline_parMapRedr`. The input parameter has been 1000000 as in Figure 5. The distributed sequentialism is clearly revealed. The next process is always only created after the previous one has terminated. Note that the 8th process is allocated on PE 1. Its activity bar is the second one from the bottom.

◁

To avoid this problem the (predefined) Eden function `spawn` can be used to eagerly and immediately instantiate a complete list of process abstractions with their corresponding inputs. Neglecting demand control, `spawn` can be denotationally specified as follows:

```
spawn :: (Trans a, Trans b) ⇒ [Process a b] → [a] → [b]
spawn =  zipWith ( # ) -- definition without demand control
```

The actual definition is shown in Section 8. The variant `spawnAt` additionally locates the created processes on given processor elements (identified by their number).

```
spawnAt :: (Trans a, Trans b) ⇒
           [Int] → [Process a b] → [a] → [b]
```

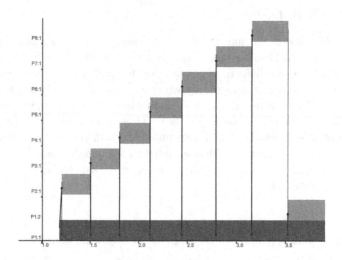

Fig. 11. Trace visualisation of pi program with `parMap_distrSeq`

In fact, `spawn` is defined as `spawnAt [0]`. The parameter `[0]` leads to the default round-robin process placement.

The counter part `spawnF` with a purely functional interface can be defined as follows:

```
spawnF :: (Trans a, Trans b) ⇒ (a → b) → [a] → [b]
spawnF =  spawn ∘ (map process)
```

The actual definition of `parMap` uses `spawn`:

```
parMap    :: (Trans a, Trans b) ⇒ (a→b) → [a] → [b]
parMap f =  spawn (repeat (process f))
```

The Haskell prelude function `repeat :: a → [a]` yields an infinite list by repeating its parameter.

Although `spawn` helps to eagerly create a series of processes, it may sometimes be necessary to add even more additional demand to support parallelism. For that purpose one can use the *evaluation strategies* provided by the library `Control.Parallel.Strategies` [41]. The next subsection and Section 5.2 contain examples.

3.3   Implementing the Divide-and-Conquer Skeleton `disDC`

The skeleton `disDC` which we have used in Section 2 to parallelise the `mergeSort` algorithm implements a *distributed expansion scheme*, i.e. the process tree expands in a *distributed* fashion: One of the tree branches is processed locally, while the others are instantiated as new processes, as long as processor elements (PEs) are available. These branches will recursively produce new parallel subtasks. Figure 12 shows the binary tree of task nodes produced by a divide-and-conquer

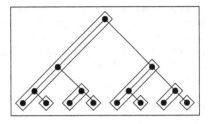

Fig. 12. Distributed expansion divide and conquer skeleton for a binary task tree

strategy splitting each non-trivial task into two subtasks, in a context with 8 PEs. The boxes indicate which task nodes will be evaluated by each PE. This tree corresponds with the call tree of the parallel `mergeSort` execution shown in Figure 8.

For the distributed expansion scheme explicit placement of processes is essential to avoid that too many processes are placed on the same PE while leaving others unused. Therefore `spawnAt` is used for process creation in the Eden implementation of the `disDC` skeleton shown in Figure 13.

Two additional parameters are used: the branching degree `k` and a `tickets` list with PE numbers to place newly created processes. As explained above, the leftmost branch of the task tree is solved locally (`myIn`), other branches (`theirIn`) are instantiated using the Eden function `spawnAt`.

The ticket list is used to control the placement of newly created processes: First, the PE numbers for placing the immediate child processes are taken from the ticket list; then, the remaining tickets are distributed to the children in a round-robin manner using the `unshuffle` function. Computations corresponding to children will be performed locally (`localIns`) when no more tickets are available. The explicit process placement via ticket lists is a simple and flexible way to control the distribution of processes as well as the recursive unfolding of the task tree. If too few tickets are available, computations are performed locally. Duplicate tickets can be used to allocate several child processes on the same PE.

The parallel creation of processes is explicitly supported using the explicit demand control function

```
childRes `pseq` rdeepseq myRes `pseq`
```

The function `pseq :: a -> b -> b` evaluates its first argument to weak head normal form before returning its second argument. Note that `pseq` denotes the infix variant of this function. The strategy function `rdeepseq` forces the complete evaluation of its argument (to normal form) [41]. Both functions are originally provided in the library `Control.Deepseq` but re-exported from the Eden module. The above construct has the effect that first the child processes are created because the expression `childRes` is an application of `spawnAt`. As soon as all processes have been created, the strategy `rdeepseq` forces the evaluation of `myRes`, i.e. the recursive unfolding and generation of further processes. Using `pseq` the

```
disDC :: (Trans a, Trans b) ⇒
         Int → [Int] →          -- ^ branch degree / tickets
         DivideConquer a b
disDC k tickets trivial solve split combine x
  = if null tickets then seqDC x
    else recDC tickets x
  where
    seqDC = dc trivial solve split combine
    recDC tickets x =
      if trivial x then solve x
      else childRes              'pseq'   -- explicit demand
           rdeepseq myRes        'pseq'   -- control
           combine x ( myRes:childRes ++ localRess )
      where
        -- child process generation
        childRes   = spawnAt childTickets childProcs procIns
        childProcs = map (process ∘ recDC) theirTs
        -- ticket distribution
        (childTickets , restTickets) = splitAt (k-1) tickets
        (myTs : theirTs) = unshuffle k restTickets
        -- input splitting
        (myIn:theirIn)  = split x
        (procIns , localIns)
                   = splitAt (length childTickets) theirIn
        -- local computations
        myRes      = recDC myTs myIn
        localRess  = map seqDC localIns
```

Fig. 13. Definition of distributed-expansion divide-and-conquer skeleton

evaluation order of subexpressions is explicitly determined. Only then, the standard Haskell evaluation strategy is used to evaluate the overall result expression combine x (myRes:childRes ++ localRess).

4   Controlling Communication Costs

In many cases, it is not sufficient to simply instantiate a skeleton like parMap, parMapRedr, farm or disDC to parallelise a program. Often it is necessary to apply some techniques to reduce the communication costs of parallel programs, especially, when big data structures have to be transmitted between processes. In the following subsections, we explain two such techniques. We use a simple case study, raytracer, to show the effectiveness of these techniques. Details on the case study, especially the complete programs, can be found on the Eden web pages.

4.1   Reducing Communication Costs: Chunking

The default stream communication in Eden produces a single message for each stream element. This may lead to high communication costs and severely delimit

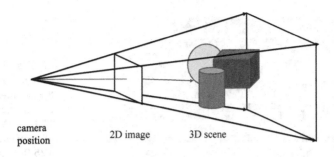

camera
position   2D image   3D scene

Fig. 14. Raytracing

the performance of the parallel program, as we have already mentioned in the examples discussed in Section 2.

Case Study (Raytracer): Ray tracing is a technique in computer graphics for generating a two-dimensional image from a scene consisting of three-dimensional objects. As the name indicates rays are traced through pixels of the image plane calculating their impacts when they encounter the objects (see Figure 14). The following central part of a simple raytracer program can easily be parallelised using the farm skeleton.

```
raytrace :: [Object] → CameraPos → [Impact]
rayTrace scene viewpoint
  = map impact rays
  where rays = generateRays viewPoint
        impact ray = fold earlier (map (hit ray) scene)
```

By replacing the outer `map` with `mapFarmS` (defined in Section 2, see page 147) we achieve a parallel ray tracer which creates as many processes as processing elements are available. Each process computes the impacts of a couple of rays. The rays will be computed by the parent process and communicated to the remote processes. Each process receives the `scene` via its process abstraction. If the `scene` has not been evaluated before process creation, each process will evaluate it.

Figure 15 shows the trace visualisation (processes' activity over time) and some statistics produced by our trace viewer EdenTV (see Section A.3). The trace has been generated by a program run of the raytracer program with input size 250, i.e. 250^2 rays on an Intel 8-core machine (2 × Xeon Quadcore @2.5GHz, 16 GB RAM) machine using the PVM-based runtime system. As PVM works with a demon which must be started before any program execution the startup time of the parallel program is neglectable. The result is disappointing, because most processes are almost always blocked (red/dark grey) and show only short periods of activity (green/grey). 9 processes (the main process and 8 farm processes) and 17 threads (one thread per farm process and 9 threads in the main process, i.e. the main thread and 8 threads which evaluate and send the input for the farm processes) have been created. Two processes have been allocated on machine 1 (see the two bottom bars with process numbers P 1:1 and P 1:2) .

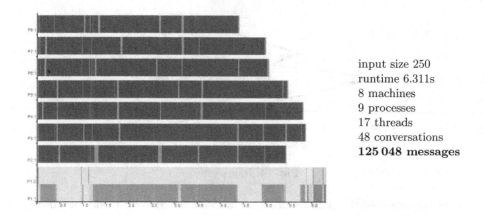

input size 250
runtime 6.311s
8 machines
9 processes
17 threads
48 conversations
125 048 messages

Fig. 15. Raytracer trace on 8 PEs, farm with 8 processes

Alarming is the enormous number of 125048 messages that has been exchanged between the processes. When messages are added to the trace visualisation, the graphic becomes almost black. It is obvious that the extreme number of messages is one of the reasons for the bad behaviour of the program. Most messages are stream messages. A stream is counted as a single conversation. The number of conversations, i.e. communications over a single channel, is 48 and thus much less than the number of messages. ◇

In such cases it is advantageous to communicate a stream in larger segments. Note that this so-called *chunking* is not always advisable. In the simple cyclic network shown before it is e.g. important that elements are transferred one-by-one — at least at the beginning — because the output of the network depends on the previously produced elements. If there is no such dependency, the decomposition of a stream into chunks reduces the number of messages to be sent and in turn the communication overhead. The following definition shows how chunking can be defined for parallel map skeletons like parMap and farm. It can equally well be used in other skeletons like e.g. disDC as shown in Subsection 4.3. The auxiliary function chunk decomposes a list into chunks of the size determined by its first parameter. See Appendix B for its definition which can be imported from the Auxiliary library. The function chunkMap applies chunk on the input list, applies a map skeleton mapscheme with parameter function (map f) and finally concatenates the result chunks using the Haskell prelude function concat :: [[a]] → [a].

```
chunkMap :: Int
        → (([a] → [b]) → (([[a]] → [[b]])))
        → (a → b) → [a] → [b]
chunkMap size mapscheme f xs
  = concat (mapscheme (map f) (chunk size xs))
```

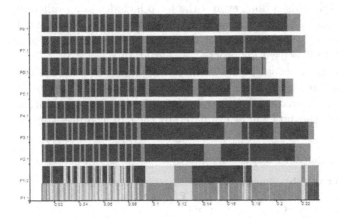

input size 250
chunk size 250
runtime 0.235s
8 machines
9 processes
17 threads
48 conversations
548 messages

Fig. 16. Raytracer trace on 8 PEs, farm with 8 processes and chunking

Case Study (Raytracer continued): In our raytracer case study, we replace the `mapFarmS` skeleton with `chunkMap chunksize mapFarmS` where `chunksize` is an extra parameter of the program. Chunking substantially reduces communication costs, as the number of messages drops drastically when chunking is used. With input size 250, which means that 250^2 stream elements have to be sent to the farm processes and to be returned to the main process, and chunk size 250 the number of messages drops from $125048(= 125000 + 48)$ downto $548(= 500 + 48)$. This leads to much better results (see Figure 16). It becomes clear that processes are more active, but still are blocked a lot of time waiting for input from the main process. Only the main process (see bottom bar) is busy most of the time sending input to the farm processes. The number of messages has drastically been reduced, thereby improving the communication overhead and consequently the runtime a lot. A speedup of 26,86 in comparison to the previous version could be achieved. Nevertheless, the program behaviour can still be improved.

◇

Exercise 4: Give an alternative definition of the `mapFarmB` skeleton using

`chunkMap size parMap`

with a suitable `size` parameter. Assume that the length of the input list is a multiple of the number of processor elements.

We can even act more radically and reduce communication costs further for data transfers from parent to child processes.

4.2   Communication vs. Parameter Passing: Running Processes Offline

Eden processes have disjoint address spaces. Consequently, on process instantiation, the process abstraction will be transferred to the remote processing element including its whole environment, i.e. the whole heap reachable from the process abstraction will be copied. This is done even if the heap includes non-evaluated parts which may cause the duplication of work. A programmer is able to avoid work duplication by forcing the evaluation of unevaluated subexpressions of a process abstraction before it is used for process instantiation.

There exist two different approaches for transferring data to a remote child process. Either the data is passed as a parameter or subexpression (without prior evaluation unless explicitly forced) or data is communicated via a communication channel. In the latter case the data will be evaluated by the parent process before sending.

Example: Consider the function fun2proc defined by

```
fun2proc     :: (Trans b, Trans c) ⇒
                (a → b → c) → a → Process b c
fun2proc f x =  process (\ y → f x y)
```

and the following process instantiation:

$$\underbrace{\text{fun2proc fexpr xarg}}_{\substack{\text{evaluated by child process} \\ \text{(lazy evaluation of fexpr and xarg)}}} \quad \# \quad \underbrace{\text{yarg}}_{\substack{\text{evaluated and sent} \\ \text{by parent process}}}$$

When this process instantiation is evaluated, the process abstraction

```
                 fun2proc fexpr xarg
```

(including all data referenced by it) will be copied and sent to the processing element where the new process will be evaluated. The parent process creates a new thread for evaluating the argument expression yarg to normal form and a corresponding outport (channel). Thus, the expressions fexpr and xarg will be evaluated lazily if the child process demands their evaluation, while the expression yarg will immediately be evaluated by the parent process.   ◁

If we want to evaluate the application of a function h :: a → b by a remote process, there are two possibilities to produce a process abstraction and instantiate it:

1. If we simply use the operator ($#), the argument of h will be evaluated by the parent process and then passed to the remote process.
2. Alternatively, we can pass the argument of h within the process abstraction and use instead the following *remote function invocation*.

```
rfi       :: Trans b ⇒ (a → b) →  a → Process () b
rfi h x =  process (\ () → h x)
```

Now the argument of h will be evaluated on demand by the remote process itself. The empty tuple () (unit) is used as a dummy argument in the process abstraction. If the communication network is slow or if the result of the argument evaluation is large, instantiation via rfi h x # () may be more efficient than using (h $# x). We say that the child process runs *offline*.

```
offline_farm :: Trans b =>
  Int              ->      -- ^ number of processes
  ([a] -> [[a]])   ->      -- ^ input distribution
  ([[b]] -> [b])   ->      -- ^ result combination
  (a -> b) -> [a] -> [b]   -- ^ map interface
offline\_farm np distribute combine f xs
  = combine $ spawn (map (rfi (map f))
                    [select i xs | i <- [0..np-1])
                  (repeat ())
  where select i xs = (distribute xs ++ repeat []) !! i
```

Fig. 17. Definition of `offline_farm` skeleton

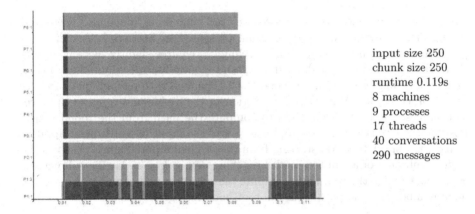

input size 250
chunk size 250
runtime 0.119s
8 machines
9 processes
17 threads
40 conversations
290 messages

Fig. 18. Raytracer trace on 8 PEs, offline farm with 8 processes and chunking

The same technique has been used in Section 2 to define the `offline_parMapRedr` skeleton. In a similar way, the previously defined `farm` can easily be transformed into the *offline farm* defined in Figure 17, which can equally well be used to parallelise `map` applications. In contrast to the `farm` skeleton, this skeleton needs to know the number of processes that has to be created. Note that the offline farm will definitely create as many processes as determined by the first parameter. If input distribution does not create enough tasks, the selection function guarantees that superfluous processes will get an empty task list.

Although the input is not explicitly communicated to an `offline_farm`, chunking may still be useful for the result stream.

Case Study (Raytracer continued 2): Using the offline farm instead of the farm in our raytracer case study eliminates the explicit communication of all input rays to the farm processes. The processes now evaluate their input by themselves. Only the result values are communicated. Thus, we save 8 stream communications and 258 messages. Figure 18 shows that the farm processes are now active during all their life time. The runtime could further be reduced by a factor of almost 2.   ◇

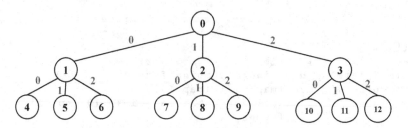

Fig. 19. Numbering of call tree nodes in offline divide-and-conquer skeleton

4.3 Tuning the Parallel Mergesort Program

The tuning techniques "offline processes" and "chunking" have also been used to tune the parallel mergesort program presented in Section 2. Avoiding input communication using the offline technique requires slightly more modifications which can however be defined as a stand-alone offline distributed-expansion divide-and-conquer skeleton `offline_disDC`. The idea is to pass unique numbers to the processes which identify its position in the divide-and-conquer call tree. The processes use these numbers to compute the path from the root to their positions and to select the appropriate part of the input by subsequent applications of the `split` function starting from the original input. Figure 19 shows the node numbering of a call tree with branching degree $k = 3$. Auxiliary functions `successors` and `path` are used to compute the successor node numbers for a given node number and the path from the root node to a given node:

```
successors :: Int → Int → [Int]
successors k n = [nk + i | let nk = n*k, i ← [1..k]]

path :: Int → Int → [Int]
path k n | n == 0    = []
         | otherwise = reverse (factors k n)

factors :: Int → Int → [Int]
factors k n
  | n ≤ 0     = []
  | otherwise = (n+k-1) 'mod' k : factors k ((n-1) 'div' k)
```

For the example tree in Figure 19 we observe that `successors 3 2 = [7,8,9]` and `path 3 9 = [1,2]`.

If we neglect the case that the problem size might not be large enough to supply each process with work, the offline divide-and-conquer skeleton can be defined as follows:

```
offline_disDC :: Trans b ⇒
                 Int → [Int] → DivideConquer a b
offline_disDC k ts triv solve split combine x
  = disDC k ts newtriv newsolve newsplit newcombine 0
  where
    seqDC      = dc triv solve split combine
```

```
offline_disDC :: Trans b ⇒
                 Int → [Int] → DivideConquer a b
offline_disDC k ts triv solve split combine x
  = snd (disDC k ts newtriv newsolve newsplit newcombine 0)
  where
    seqDC      = dc triv solve split combine
    newsplit   = successors k
    newtriv  n = length ts ≤ k^(length (path k n))
    newsolve n = (flag, seqDC localx)
      where (flag, localx) = select triv split x (path k n)
    newcombine n bs@((flag,bs1):_)
      = if flag then (True, combine localx (map snd bs))
                else (lab,  bs1)
      where (lab, localx) = select triv split x (path k n)

select :: (a → Bool) → (a → [a])    -- ^ trivial / split
              → a → [Int] → (Bool,a)
select trivial split x ys = go x ys
  where go x []      = (True , x)
        go x (y:ys) = if trivial x then (False, x)
                      else go (split x !! y) ys
```

Fig. 20. Offline version of the divide-and-conquer skeleton disDC

```
    newsplit   = successors k
    newtriv  n = length ts ≤ k^(length (path k n))
    newsolve n = seqDC  (select split x (path k n))
    newcombine n bs
      = combine (select split x (path k n)) bs

select :: (a → [a]) → a → [Int] → a
select split x ys = go x ys
  where go x []      = x
        go x (y:ys) = go (split x !! y) ys
```

The skeleton will create as many processes as the length of the ticket list. The successors function is used as split function for the offline divide-and-conquer skeleton. The initial input is set to zero, the root node number of the call tree. The predicate newtriv stops the parallel unfolding as soon as number of leaves in the generated call tree is greater than the length of the ticket list, i.e. the number of processes that has to be generated. When the parallel unfolding stops, the skeleton applies the normal sequential divide-and-conquer function dc to solve the remaining subproblems. The auxiliary function select computes the subproblem to be solved by node with number n. It successively applies the original split function and selects the appropriate subproblems with the Haskell list index operator (!!) :: [a] → Int → a, thereby following the path path k n from the root node to the current node. The combine function is also modified to locally select the current subproblem. In most cases this simplified version of the offline divide-and-conquer skeleton will work satisfactorily. However, the skeleton will bounce whenever the problem size is not large enough to allow for the series of split applications. Therefore, Figure 20 presents a modified version of the skeleton definition which checks whether splitting is still possible or not. If no more splitting is possible, the process has no real work to do, because one of its predecessor processes has the same problem to solve. In principle, it need not produce a result. Changing the internal result type of the skeleton to e.g. a Maybe type is however not advisable because this would e.g. de-activate chunking or streaming, if this is used for the result values in the original skeleton. Instead, the skeleton in Figure 20 internally produces two results, a flag that indicates whether the process created a valid subresult or whether it already the result its parent process simply can pass. In fact, all superfluous processes compute the result of a trivial problem which is assigned to one of its predecessor. The corresponding predecessor can then simply overtake the first of the (identical) results of its child processes. This offline divide-and-conquer skeleton has been used to produce the trace file in Figure 7. In addition, chunking of the result lists has been added by adapting the parameter functions of the offline_disDC skeleton, i.e. composing the function chunk size with the result producing parameter functions solve and combine and unchunking parameter list elements of combine as well as the overall result using concat. Note that the parameter functions trivial, solve, split, and combine are the same as in the definition of the function mergeSortDC (see Page 154, Section 2). Finally, the actual code of the parallel mergesort implementation is as follows:

```
par_mergeSortDC :: (Ord a, Trans a) ⇒ Int → [a] → [a]
par_mergeSortDC size
  = concat ∘
      (offline_disDC 2 [2..noPe] trivial
        ((chunk size) ∘ solve)    split
        (\ xs → (chunk size) ∘ (combine xs) ∘ (map concat)))
    where
      -- the same as in mergeSortDC
```

Exercise 5: Change the parallel mergesort implementation in such a way that the branching degree of the recursive call tree can be given as an additional parameter to the function par_mergeSortDC.

5 Defining Non-hierarchical Communication Topologies

With the Eden constructs introduced up to now, communication channels are only (implicitly) established during process creation between parent and child processes. These are called *static channels* and they build purely hierarchical process topologies. Eden provides additional mechanisms to define non-hierarchical communication topologies.

5.1 The Remote Data Concept

A high-level, natural and easy-to-use way to define non-hierarchical process networks like e.g. rings in Eden is the *remote data concept* [1]. The main idea is to

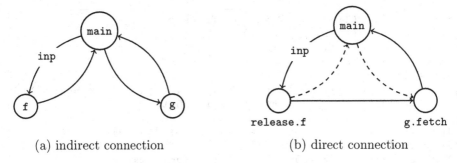

(a) indirect connection   (b) direct connection

Fig. 21. A simple process graph

replace the data to be communicated between processes by handles to it, called remote data. These handles can then be used to transmit the real data directly to the desired target. Thus, a remote data of type a is represented by a handle of type RD a with interface functions release and fetch. The function release produces a remote data handle that can be passed to other processes, which will in turn use the function fetch to access the remote data. The data transmission occurs automatically from the process that releases the data to the process which uses the handle to fetch the remote data.

The remote data feature has the following interface in Eden [20]:

```
type RD a    -- remote data

-- convert local data into remote data
release :: Trans a  ⇒ a → RD a

-- convert remote data into local data
fetch :: Trans a  ⇒ RD a → a
```

The following simple example illustrates how the remote data concept is used to establish a direct channel connection between sibling processes.

Example: Given functions f and g, the expression ((g ∘ f) a) can be calculated in parallel by creating a process for each function. One just replaces the function calls by process instantiations

$$(g \;\$\# \;(f \;\$\# \;inp)).$$

This leads to the process network in Figure 21 (a) where the process evaluating the above expression is called main. Process main instantiates a first process for calculating g. In order to transmit the corresponding input to this new process, main instantiates a second process for calculating f, passes its input to this process and receives the remotely calculated result, which is passed to the first process. The output of the first process is also sent back to main. The drawback of this approach is that the result of the process calculating f is not sent directly to the process calculating g, thus causing unnecessary communication costs.

```
ring         :: (Trans i, Trans o, Trans r) ⇒
                ((i,r) → (o,r))    --^ ring process function
                → [i] → [r]        --^ input - output mapping
ring f is = os
  where
    (os,ringOuts)   = unzip (parMap f (lazyzip is ringIns))
    ringIns         = rightRotate ringOuts

lazyzip                :: [a] → [b] → [(a,b)]
lazyzip [] _        = []
lazyzip (x:xs) ~(y:ys) = (x,y) : lazyzip xs ys

rightRotate     :: [a] → [a]
rightRotate [] = []
rightRotate xs = last xs : init xs
```

Fig. 22. Definition of `ring` skeleton

In the second implementation, we use remote data to establish a direct channel connection between the child processes (see Figure 21 (b)):

$$(g \circ fetch) \ \$\# \ ((release \circ f) \ \$\# \ inp)$$

The output produced by the process calculating `f` is now encapsulated in a remote handle that is passed to the process calculating `g`, and fetched there. Notice that the remote data handle is treated like the original data in the first version, i.e. it is passed via the main process from the process computing `f` to the one computing `g`.   ◁

5.2   A Ring Skeleton

Consider the definition of a process ring in Eden given in Figure 22. The number of processes in the ring is determined by the length of the input list. The ring processes are created using the `parMap` skeleton.

   The auxiliary function `lazyzip` corresponds to the Haskell prelude function `zip` but is lazy in its second argument (because of using the lazy pattern `~(y:ys)`). This is crucial because the second parameter `ringIns` will not be available when the `parMap` function creates the ring processes. Note that the list of ring inputs `ringIns` is the same as the list of ring outputs `ringOuts` rotated by one element to the right using the auxiliary function `rightRotate`. Thus, the program would get stuck without the lazy pattern, because the ring input will only be produced after process creation and process creation will not occur without the first input.

   Unfortunately, this elegant and compact ring definition will not produce a ring topology but a star (see Figure 23). The reason is that the channels for communication between the ring processes are not established in a direct way, but only indirectly via the parent process. One could produce the ring as a chain of processes where each ring process creates its successor but this approach would

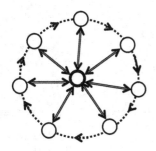 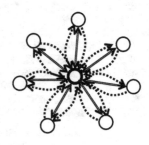

Fig. 23. Topology of process ring (left: intended topology, right: actual topology)

```
ringRD       :: (Trans i, Trans o, Trans r) ⇒
                ((i,r) → (o,r))       --^ ring process function
                → [i] → [r]           --^ input - output mapping
ringRD f is =  os
  where
  (os,ringOuts)  = unzip (parMap (toRD f)
                                 (lazyzip is ringIns))
  ringIns        = rightRotate ringOuts

toRD :: (Trans i, Trans o, Trans r) ⇒
        ((i,r) → (o,r))                 -- ^ ring process function
        → ((i, RD r) → (o, RD r)) -- ^ -- with remote data
toRD f (i, ringIn)  = (o, release ringOut)
  where (o, ringOut) = f (i, fetch ringIn)
```

Fig. 24. Ring skeleton definition with remote data

cause the input from and output to the parent process to run through the chain
of predecessor processes. Moreover it is not possible to close this chain to form
a ring.

Fortunately, the process ring can easily be re-defined using the remote data
concept as shown in Figure 24. The original ring function is embedded using the
auxiliary function toRD into a function which replaces the ring data by remote
data and introducing calls to fetch and release at appropriate places. Thus,
the worker functions of the parallel processes have a different type. In fact,
the star topology is still used but only to propagate remote data handles. The
proper data is passed directly from one process to its successor in the ring.
This transfer occurs via additional so-called *dynamic* channels, which are not
reflected in the worker function type. This is the mechanism used to implement
the remote data concept in Eden. We will introduce Eden's dynamic channels
and the implementation of remote data using dynamic channels in Section 7.
Before we present a case study with the ring skeleton ringRD.

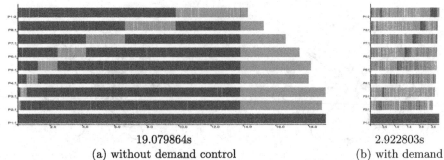

19.079864s   2.922803s

(a) without demand control   (b) with demand

Runtimes are shown above. The other statistics are the same for both versions:
input size 500, 8 machines, 9 processes, 41 threads, 72 conversations, 4572 messages

Fig. 25. Warshall trace on 8 PEs, ring with 8 processes and chunking

Case Study (Warshall's algorithm): Warshall's algorithm for computing shortest
paths in a graph given by an adjacency matrix can be implemented using the
ring skeleton. Each ring process is responsible for the update of a subset of rows.
The whole adjacency matrix is rotated once around the process ring. Thus,
each process sees each row of the whole adjacency matrix. The kernel of the
implementation is the iteration function executed by the ring processes for each
row assigned to them. Note that the final argument of this function is the one
communicated via the ring.

```
ring_iterate :: Int → Int → Int →
                [Int] → [[Int]] → ( [Int], [[Int]])
ring_iterate size k i rowk (rowi:xs)
    | i > size  =  (rowk, [])       -- Finish Iteration
    | i == k    =  (rowR, rowk:restoutput)  - send own row
    | otherwise =  (rowR, rowi:restoutput)  - update row
  where
    (rowR, restoutput) = ring_iterate size k (i+1) nextrowk xs
    nextrowk | i == k    = rowk -- no update, if own row
             | otherwise = updaterow rowk rowi (rowk!!(i-1))
```

In the kth iteration the process with row k sends this row into the ring. During
the other iterations each process updates its own row with the information of
the row received from its ring predecessor.

Unfortunately, a trace analysis reveals (see Figure 25(a)) that this program has
a demand problem. In a first part, an increasing phase of activity runs along the
ring processes, until the final row is sent into the ring. Then all processes start to
do their update computations. By forcing the immediate evaluation of `nextrowk`,
i.e. the update computation, the sequential start-up phase of the ring can be com-
pressed. The additional demand can be expressed by `rdeepseq nextrowk 'pseq'`
which has to be included before the recursive call to ring_iterate:

```
(rowR, restoutput) = rdeepseq nextrowk 'pseq'
                     ring_iterate size k (i+1) nextrowk xs
```

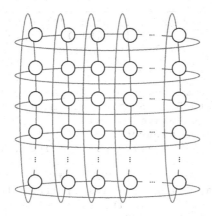

Fig. 26. Torus topology

This forces the evaluation of `nextrowk` to normal form before the second argument of `pseq` is evaluated. The effect of this small code change is enormous as shown in Figure 25(b). Note the different scaling on the x-axes in both pictures. The improved program version needs only a sixth of the runtime of the first version.

◇

Exercise 6: Define a ring skeleton in such a way that each process creates its successor processor. Use remote data to close the ring and to establish the communication with the process which executes the ring skeleton.

5.3   A Torus Skeleton

A torus is a two-dimensional topology in which each process is connected to its four neighbours. The first and last processes in each row and column are considered neighbours, i.e. the processes per row and per column form process rings (see Figure 26). In addition, each process has two extra connections to send and receive values to/from the parent. These are not shown in Figure 26. The torus topology can be used to implement systolic computations, where processes alternate parallel computation and global synchronisation steps. At each round, every node receives messages from its left and upper neighbours, computes, and then sends messages to its right and lower neighbours.

The implementation that we propose in Eden uses lists instead of synchronization barriers to simulate rounds. The remote data approach is used to establish direct connections between the torus nodes. The `torus` function defined in Figure 27 creates the desired toroidal topology of Figure 26 by properly connecting the inputs and outputs of the different `ptorus` processes. Each process receives an input from the parent, and two remote handles to be used to fetch the values from its predecessors. It produces an output to the parent and two remote handles to release outputs to its successors. The shape of the torus is determined by the shape of the input.

```
torus :: (Trans a, Trans b, Trans c, Trans d) ⇒
         ((c,[a],[b]) → (d,[a],[b])) --^ node function
         → [[c]] → [[d]]          --^ input-output mapping
torus f inss = outss
 where
   t_outss = zipWith spawn (repeat (repeat (ptorus f))) t_inss
   (outss,outssA,outssB) = unzip3 (map unzip3 t_outss)
   inssA   = map rightRotate outssA
   inssB   = rightRotate outssB
   t_inss  = lazyzipWith3 lazyzip3 inss inssA inssB

-- each individual process of the torus
ptorus :: (Trans a, Trans b, Trans c, Trans d) ⇒
          ((c,[a],[b]) → (d,[a],[b])) →
          Process (c,RD [a],RD [b])
                  (d,RD [a],RD [b])
ptorus f
 = process (\ (fromParent, inA, inB) →
             let (toParent, outA, outB)
                 = f (fromParent, fetch inA, fetch inB)
             in  (toParent, release outA, release outB))

lazyzipWith3 :: (a → b → c → d)
             → [a] → [b] → [c] → [d]
lazyzipWith3 f (x:xs) ~(y:ys) ~(z:zs)
             = f x y z : lazyzipWith3 f xs ys zs
lazyzipWith3 _ _ _ _ = []

lazyzip3 :: [a] → [b] → [c] → [(a,b,c)]
lazyzip3 = lazyzipWith3 (\ x y z → (x,y,z))
```

Fig. 27. Definition of torus skeleton

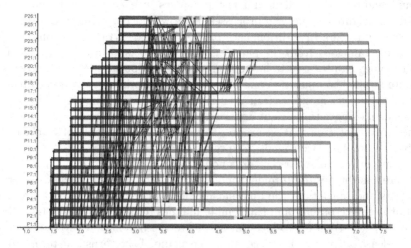

Fig. 28. Trace of parallel matrix multiplication with torus skeleton

The size of the torus will usually depend on the number of available processors (noPe). A typical value is e.g. $\lfloor \sqrt{noPe} \rfloor$. In this case each torus node can be placed on a different PE. The first parameter of the skeleton is the worker function, which receives an initial value of type c from the parent, a stream [a] from the left predecessor and a stream [b] from its upper predecessor, and produces a final result d for its parent as well as result streams of type [a] and [b] for its right and lower successors, respectively. Functions lazyzip3 and lazyzipWith3 are lazy versions of functions of the zip family, the difference being that these functions use irrefutable patterns for parameters, corresponding to the torus interconnections.

Case Study (Matrix Multiplication): A typical application of the torus skeleton is the implementation of a block-wise parallel matrix multiplication [23]. Each node of the torus gets two blocks of the input matrices to be multiplied sequentially. It passes its blocks to the successor processes in the torus, the block of the first matrix to the successor in the row and the block of the second matrix to the successor in the column. It receives corresponding blocks from its neighbour processes and proceeds as before. If each process has seen each block of the input matrices which are assigned to its row or column, the computation finishes. The torus can be instantiated with the following node function:

```
nodefunction :: Int                              --^ torus dimension
  → ((Matrix,Matrix), [Matrix], [Matrix])  --^ process input
  → ([Matrix],        [Matrix], [Matrix])  --^ process output
nodefunction n ((bA,bB), rows, cols)
  = ([bSum], bA:nextAs, bB:nextBs)
  where bSum = foldl' matAdd (matMult bA bB)
                            (zipWith matMult nextAs nextBs)
        nextAs = take (n-1) rows
        nextBs = take (n-1) cols
```

The result matrix block is embedded in a singleton list to avoid its streaming when being returned to the main process. Figure 28 shows a trace of the torus parallelisation of matrix multiplication created on the Beowulf cluster II for input matrices with dimension 1000. Messages are overlayed. In total, 638 messages have been exchanged. It can be seen that all communication takes place in the beginning of the computation. This is due to Eden's push policy. Data is communicated as soon as it has been evaluated to normal form. As the processes simply pass matrix blocks without manipulating them, communication occurs immediately. Afterwards, the actual computations are performed. Finally the processes return their local result blocks to the main process on PE 1 (bottom bar).   ◇

6   Workpool Skeletons

Workpool skeletons provide a powerful and general way to implement problems with irregular parallelism, which are decomposed into tasks of varying complexity. For such problems it is feasible to implement a task or work pool which is processed by a set of worker processes. The tasks are dynamically distributed among the workers to balance the work load. Often a master process manages the task pool, distributes the tasks to the worker processes, and collects the results. Then the work pool is organised as a master-worker system. In such systems it is important that the master reacts immediately on the reception of a worker result by sending a new task to the respective worker, i.e. the master must receive worker results as soon as they arrive. Thus, many-to-one communication is necessary for the communication from the workers to the master.

6.1 Many-to-One Communication: Merging Communication Streams

Many-to-one communication is an essential feature for many parallel applications, but, unfortunately, it introduces non-determinism and, in consequence, spoils the purity of functional languages. In Eden, the predefined function

```
merge :: [[a]] → [a]
```

merges (in a non-deterministic way) a list of streams into a single stream. In fact, merging several incoming streams guarantees that incoming values are passed to the single output stream as soon as they arrive. Thus, merging the results streams of the worker processes allows the master in a master-worker system to react quickly on the worker results which are also interpreted as requests for new tasks. As the incoming values arrive in an unpredictable order, merge introduces non-determinism. Nevertheless functional purity can be preserved in most portions of an Eden program. It is e.g. possible to use sorting in order to force a particular order of the results returned by a merge application and thus to encapsulate merge within a skeleton and save the deterministic context. In the next subsection we show how a determinstic master-worker skeleton is defined although the merge function is internally used for the worker-to-master communication.

6.2 A Simple Master-Worker Skeleton

The merge function is the key to enable dynamic load balancing in a master-worker scheme as shown in Figure 29. The master process distributes tasks to worker processes, which solve the tasks and return the results to the master.

The Eden function masterWorker (evaluated by the "master" process) (see Figure 30) takes four parameters: np specifies the number of worker processes that will be spawned, prefetch determines how many tasks will initially be sent by the master to each worker process, the function f describes how tasks have to be solved by the workers, and the final parameter tasks is the list of tasks that have to be solved by the whole system. The auxiliary pure Haskell function distribute :: Int → [a] → [Int] → [[a]] is used to distribute the tasks to the workers. Its first parameter determines the number of output lists, which become the input streams for the worker processes. The third parameter is the request list reqs which guides the task distribution. The request

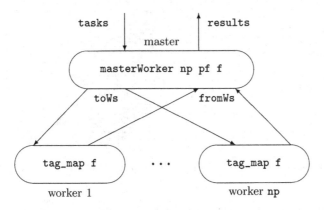

Fig. 29. Master-worker process topology

```
masterWorker  :: (Trans a, Trans b) ⇒
                 Int → Int → (a→b) → [a] → [b]
masterWorker np prefetch f tasks
  = orderBy fromWs reqs
  where
      fromWs    = spawn workers toWs
      workers   = [process (map f) | n ← [1..np]]
      toWs      = distribute np tasks reqs
      newReqs   = merge [ [i | r ← rs]
                        | (i,rs) ← zip [1..np] fromWs]
      reqs      = initReqs ++ newReqs
      initReqs  = concat (replicate prefetch [1..np])
```

Fig. 30. Definition of a simple master worker skeleton

list is also used to sort the results according to the original task order (function orderBy :: [[b]] → [Int] → [b]). Note that the functions distribute and orderBy can be imported from Eden's Auxiliary library. Their definitions are also given in Appendix B.

Initially, the master sends as many tasks as specified by the parameter prefetch in a round-robin manner to the workers (see definition of initReqs in Figure 30). The prefetch parameter determines the behaviour of the skeleton, between a completely dynamic (prefetch 1) and a completely static task distribution (prefetch $\geq \frac{\text{\# tasks}}{\text{\# workers}}$). Further tasks are sent to workers which have delivered a result. The list newReqs is extracted from the worker results which are tagged with the corresponding worker id. The requests are merged according to the arrival of the worker results. This simple master worker definition has the advantage that the tasks need not be numbered to re-establish the original task order on the results. Moreover, worker processes need not send explicit requests for new work together with the result values. Note that we have assumed

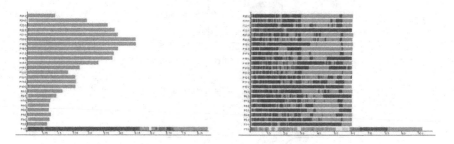

Fig. 31. Mandelbrot traces on 25 PEs, offline farm (left) vs master-worker (right)

a statically fixed task pool, which, in essence, results in another parallel map implementation with dynamic assignment.

Case Study (Mandelbrot): The kernel function of a program to compute a two-dimensional image of the Mandelbrot set for given complex coordinates `ul` (upper left) and `lr` (lower right) and the number of pixels in the horizontal dimension `dimx` as a string can be written as follows in Haskell:

```
image :: Double        -- ^ threshold for iterations
         → Complex Double → Complex Double
                       -- ^ coordinates
         → Integer   -- ^ size
         → String
image threshold ul lr dimx
  = header ++ (concat $ map xy2col lines)
  where
     xy2col :: [Complex Double] →   String
     xy2col line
       = concatMap (rgb.(iter threshold (0.0 :+ 0.0) 0)) line
     (dimy, lines) =   coord ul lr dimx
```

The first parameter is a threshold for the number of iterations that should be done to compute the color of a pixel.

The program can easily be parallelised by replacing `map` in the expression `map xy2col lines` with a parallel map implementation. Figure 31 shows two traces that have been produced on the Beowulf cluster I at Heriot-Watt University in Edinburgh. The Mandelbrot program was evaluated with an input size of 2000 lines with 2000 pixels each using 25 PEs.

The program that produced the trace on the left hand side replaced `map` by (`offline_farm noPe (splitInto noPe) concat`). The program yielding the trace on the right hand side replaced `map` by `masterWorker noPe 8`, where in both cases `noPe = 25`. In the offline farm, all worker processes are busy during their life time, but we observe an unbalanced workload which reflects the shape of the mandelbrot set. To be honest, the uneven workload has been enforced by using

version	number of processes	task transfer	task distribution
parMap	number of tasks	communication	one per process
mapFarm{S/B}	noPe	communication	static
offline_farm	mostly noPe	local selection	static
masterWorker	mostly noPe	communication	dynamic

Fig. 32. Classification of parallel map implementations

splitInto noPe for a block-wise task distribution instead of unshuffle 25. The latter would lead to a well-balanced workload with the farm which is however a special property of this example problem. In general, general irregular parallelism cannot easily be balanced. The master-worker system uses a dynamic task distribution. In our example a prefetch value of 8 has been used to initially provide 8 tasks to each PE. The trace on the right hand side in Figure 31 reveals that the workload is better balanced, but worker processes are often blocked waiting for new tasks. Unfortunately, the master process on machine 1 (lowest bar) is not able to keep all worker processes busy. In fact, the master-worker parallelisation needs more time than the badly balanced offline farm. In addition, both versions suffer from a long end phase in which the main or master process collects the results. ◇

Exercise 7: Define a master-worker skeleton mwMapRedr which implements a map-reduce scheme.

```
mwMapRedr :: Int             -- ^ number of processes
          → Int              -- ^ prefetch
          → (b → b → b)      -- ^ reduce function
          → b                -- ^ neutral element
          → (a → b)          -- ^ map function
          → [a] → b          -- ^ input - output mapping
```

The worker processes locally reduce their results using foldr and return requests to the master process to ask for new input values (tasks). When all tasks have been solved (how can this be detected?), the worker processes return their reduction result to the master who performs the final reduction of the received values.

6.3   Classification of Parallel Map Implementations

In Section 2 we have defined several parallel implementations of map, a simple form of data parallelism. A given function has to be applied to each element of a list. The list elements can be seen as tasks, to which a worker function has to be applied. The parallel map skeletons we developed up to now can be classified as shown in Figure 32. The simple parMap is mainly used to create a series of processes evaluating the same function. The static task distribution implemented in the farm variants is especially appropriate for regular parallelism, i.e. when all tasks have same complexity or can be distributed in such a way that the workload of the processes is well-balanced. The master worker approach with dynamic task distribution is suitable for irregular tasks.

Exercise 8: Write parallel versions of the Julia-Set program provided on the Eden web pages using the various parallel map skeletons. Use EdenTV to analyse and compare the runtime behavior of the different versions.

6.4   A Nested Master-Worker Skeleton

The master worker skeleton defined above is a very simple version of a workpool skeleton. It has a single master process with a central workpool, the worker processes have no local state and cannot produce and return new tasks to be entered into the workpool. Several more sophisticated workpool skeletons are provided in the Eden skeleton library. We will here exemplarily show how a hierarchical master worker skeleton can elegantly be defined in Eden. For details see [7,50]. As a matter of principle, a nested master-worker system can be defined by using the simple master worker skeleton defined above as the worker function for the upper levels. The simple master worker skeleton must only be modified in such a way that the worker function has type [a] → [b] instead of a → b. The nested scheme is then simply achieved by folding the zipped list of branching degrees and prefetches per level. This produces a regular scheme. The proper worker function is used as the starting value for the folding. Thus it is used at the lowest level of worker processes. Figure 33 shows the definition of the corresponding skeleton mwNested.

```
mwNested :: (Trans a, Trans b) ⇒
            [Int]          -- ^ branching degrees per level
          → [Int]          -- ^ prefetches per level
          → ([a] → [b])  -- ^ worker function
          → [a] → [b]     -- ^ tasks, results
mwNested ns pfs wf = foldr fld wf (zip ns pfs)
   where
     fld :: (Trans a, Trans b) ⇒
            (Int,Int) → ([a] → [b]) → ([a] → [b])
     fld (n,pf) wf = masterWorker' n pf wf
```

Fig. 33. Definition of nested workpool skeleton

Case Study (Mandelbrot continued): Using a nested master-worker system helps to improve the computation of Mandelbrot sets on a large number of processor elements. Figure 34 shows an example trace produced for input size 2000 on 25 PEs with a two-level master worker system comprising four submasters serving five worker processes each. Thus, the function mwNested has been called with parameters [4,5] and [64,8]. The trace clearly shows that the work is well-balanced among the 20 worker processes. Even the post-processing phase in the main process (top-level master) could be reduced, because the results are now collected level-wise. The overall runtime could substantially be reduced in comparison to the simple parallelisations discussed previously (see Figure 31). ◇

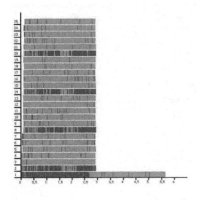

branching degrees [4,5]:
1 master, 4 submasters, 5 workers per
submaster
prefetches [64,8]:
64 tasks per submaster, 8 tasks per
worker

Fig. 34. Mandelbrot trace on 25 PEs with hierarchical master-worker skeleton (hierarchy shown on the right)

7   Explicit Channel Management

In Eden, process communication occurs via unidirectional one-to-one channels. In most cases, these channels are implicitly created on process creation. This mechanism is sufficient for the generation of hierarchical communication topologies. In Section 5, we have seen how non-hierarchical process topologies and corresponding skeletons like rings can easily be defined using the remote data concept. This concept is based on the lower-level mechanism of dynamically creating channels by receiver processes.

7.1   Dynamic Channels

Eden provides functions to explicitly create and use *dynamic* channel connections between arbitrary processes:

```
new     :: Trans a ⇒ (ChanName a → a → b) → b
parfill :: Trans a ⇒  ChanName a → a → b → b
```

By evaluating new (name val → e) a process creates a dynamic channel name of type ChanName a in order to receive a value val of type a. After creation, the channel should be passed to another process (just like normal data) inside the result expression e, which will as well use the eventually received value val. The evaluation of (parfill name e1 e2) in the other process has the side-effect that a new thread is forked to concurrently evaluate and send the value e1 via the channel. The overall result of the expression is e2.

These functions are rather low-level and it is not easy to use them appropriately. Let us suppose that process A wants to send data directly to some process B by means of a dynamic channel. This channel must first be generated by the

```
ringDC         :: (Trans i, Trans o, Trans r) ⇒
                  ((i,r) → (o,r))      -- ^ ring process function
                  → [i] → [r]          -- ^ input-output mapping
ringDC f is =  os
  where
    (os,ringOuts)  = unzip (parMap (plink f)
                                    (lazyzip is ringIns))
    ringIns        = leftRotate ringOuts

leftRotate        :: [a] → [a]
leftRotate []     = []
leftRotate (x:xs) = xs ++ [x]

plink :: (Trans i, Trans o, Trans r) ⇒
         ((i,r) → (o,r))       -- ^ ring process function
         → ((i, ChanName r) → (o, ChanName r))
                               -- ^ -- with dynamic channels
plink f (i, outChan)
  = new (\ inChan ringIn →
         parfill outChan ringOut (o, inChan))
  where (o, ringOut) = f (i, ringIn)
```

Fig. 35. Definition of ring skeleton with dynamic channels

process B and sent to A before the proper data transfer from A to B can take place. Hence, the dynamic channel is communicated in the direction opposite to the desired data transfer.

Example: It is of course also possible to define the ring skeleton directly using dynamic channels. Again, the ring function f is replaced with a modified version plink f which introduces dynamic channels to transfer the ring input. Instead of passing the ring data via the parent process, only the channel names are now passed via the parent process from successor to predecessor processes in the ring. The ring data is afterwards directly passed from predecessors to successors in the ring. Note the the orientation of the ring must now be changed which is done by using leftrotate instead of rightrotate in the definition of ringDC given in Figure 35.

Each ring process creates an input channel which is immediately returned to the parent process and passed to the predecessor process. It receives from the parent a channel to send data to the successor in the ring and uses this channel to send the ring output ringOut to its successor process using a concurrent thread created by the parfill function. The original ring function f is applied to the parent's input and the ring input received via the dynamic ring input channel. It produces the output for the parent process and the ring output ringOut for the successor process in the ring.

```
type RD a = ChanName (ChanName a)   -- remote data

-- convert local data into remote data
release :: Trans a  ⇒ a → RD a
release x = new (\ cc c → parfill c x cc)

-- convert remote data into local data
fetch :: Trans a  ⇒ RD a → a
fetch cc = new (\ c x → parfill cc c x)
```

Fig. 36. Definition of remote data with dynamic channels

Although this definition also leads to the intended topology, the correct and effective use of dynamic channels is not as obvious as the use of the remote data concept.   ◁

7.2 Implementing Remote Data with Dynamic Channels

Remote data can be implemented in Eden using dynamic channels [20] as shown in Figure 36.

Notice how the remote data approach preserves the direction of the communication (from process A to process B) by introducing another channel transfer from A to B. This channel will be used by B to send its (dynamic) channel name to A, and thus to establish the direct data communication. More exactly, to release local data x of type a, a dynamic channel cc of type RD a, i.e. a channel to transfer a channel name, is created and passed to process B. When process A receives a channel c (of type ChanName a) from B via cc, it sends the local data x via c to B. Conversely, in order to fetch remote data, represented by the remote data handle cc, process B creates a new (dynamic) channel c and sends the channel name via cc to A. The proper data will then be received via the channel c.

8 Behind the Scenes: Eden's Implementation

Eden has been implemented by extending the runtime system (RTS) of the Glasgow Haskell compiler (GHC) with mechanisms for process management and communication. In principle, it shares its parallel runtime system (PRTS) with Glasgow parallel Haskell [58] but due to the disjoint address spaces of its processes does not need to implement a virtual shared memory and global garbage collection in contrast to GpH. In the following, we abstract from low-level implementation details like graph reduction and thread management which are explained elsewhere [47,58,14,34] and describe Eden's implementation on top of the module

Control.Parallel.Eden.ParPrim.

This module provides primitive monadic operations which are used to implement the Eden constructs on a higher-level of abstraction [10].

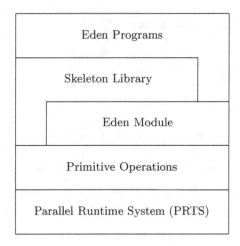

Fig. 37. Layer structure of the Eden system

8.1   Layered Parallel Runtime Environment

Eden's implementation has been organised in layers (see Figure 37) to achieve more flexibility and to improve the maintainability of this highly complex system. The main idea has been to lift aspects of the runtime system (RTS) to the level of the functional language, i.e. defining basic workflows on a high level of abstraction in the Eden module and concentrating low-level RTS capabilities in a couple of primitive operations. In this way, part of the complexity has been eliminated from the imperative RTS level.

Every Eden program must import the *Eden module*, which contains Haskell definitions of Eden's language constructs. These Haskell definitions use primitive operations which are functions implemented in C that can be accessed from Haskell. The extension of GHC for Eden is mainly based on the implementation of these primitive operations, which provide the elementary functionality for Eden and form a low-level coordination language by themselves.

The Eden module contains Haskell definitions of the high-level Eden constructs, thereby making use of the *primitive operations* shown in Figure 38. The primitive operations implement basic actions which have to be performed directly in the runtime system of the underlying sequential compiler GHC[2].

Each Eden channel connects an outport of the sender process to an inport of the receiver process. There is a one-to-one correspondence between the threads of a process and its outports. Each thread of a process evaluates some expression to normal form and sends the result via its outport. The primitive channels within the parallel runtime system are identified by three primitive integer values identifying the receiver side, i.e. the inport connecting a channel with a process.

---

[2] Note that, in GHC, primitive operations and types are distinguished from common functions and types by **#** as the last sign in their names.

Channel Administration:
- createC# creates a placeholder and an inport for a new communication channel
- connectToPort# connects a communication channel in the proper way

Communication:
- sendData# sends data on a communication channel

Thread Creation:
- fork# forks a concurrent thread

General:
- noPE#   determines number of processing elements in current setup
- selfPE# determines own processor identifier

Fig. 38. Primitive operations

The three integers are (1) the processor element number, (2) the process number and (3) a specific port number:

```
data ChanName ' a = Chan Int# Int# Int#
```

This type is only internally visible and used by the primitive channel administration functions. The wrapper functions of the primitive operations have the following types:

```
createC        :: IO ( ChanName ' a, a )
connectToPort :: ChanName ' a → IO ()
```

Note that the wrapper functions always yield a result in the IO monad. Function createC creates a primitive imput channel and a handle to access the data received via this channel. Function connectToPort connects the outport of the thread executing the function call to a given channel i.e. the corresponding inport.

There is only a primitive for sending data but no one for receiving data. Receiving is done automatically by the runtime system which writes data received via an inport immediately into a placeholder in the heap. The wrapper function of the primitive sendData# has the following type:

```
sendData   :: Mode → a → IO ()
data Mode =  Connect | Stream | Data | Instantiate Int
```

There are four send modi and corresponding message types. Note that the messages are always sent via the outport associated with the executing thread. A Connect message is initially sent to connect the outport to the corresponding inport. This makes it possible to inform a sender thread when its results are no longer needed, e.g. when the placeholders associated with the inport are identified as garbage.

A Data message contains a data value which is sent in a single message. The mode Stream is used to send the values of a data stream. The Instantiate i message is sent to start a remote process on PE i.

```
class NFData a ⇒ Trans a where
  write    :: a → IO ()
  write x  =  rnf x 'pseq' sendData Data x

  createComm :: IO (ChanName a, a)
  createComm = do (cx,x) ← createC
                  return (Comm (sendVia cx) , x)

-- Auxiliary send function
sendVia :: (NFData a, Trans a) ⇒
           (ChanName' a) → a → IO()
sendVia c d = do connectToPort c
                 sendData Connect d
                 write d
```

Fig. 39. Type class Trans

8.2   The Type Class Trans

As explained in Section 3, the type class Trans comprises all types which can be communicated via channels. It is mainly used to overload communication for streams and tuples. Lists are transmitted in a *stream*-like fashion, i.e. element by element. Each component of a tuple is communicated via a separate primitive channel. This is especially important for recursive processes which depend on part of their own output (which is re-fed as input).

On the level of the Eden module, a channel is represented by a communicator, i.e. a function to write a value into the channel:

```
newtype ChanName a = Comm (a → IO())
```

This simplifies overloading of the communication function for tuple types. The definition of the Trans class is given in Figure 39. The context NFData (normal form data) is needed to ensure that transmissible data can be fully evaluated (using the overloaded function rnf (reduce to normal form)) before sending it. An overloaded operation write :: a → IO () is used for sending data. Its default definition evaluates its argument using rnf and sends it in a single message using sendData with mode Data.

The function createComm creates an Eden channel and a handle to access the values communicated via this channel. The default definition creates a single primitive channel. The default communicator function is defined using the auxiliary function sendVia which connects to the primitive channel before sending data on it. Note that the communicator function will be used by the sender process while the channel creation will take place in the receiver process. The explicit connection of the sender outport to the inport in the receiver process helps to guarantee that at most one sender process will use a channel.

For streams, write is specialized in such a way that it evaluates each list element to normal form before transmitting it using sendData Stream. The corresponding instance declaration for lists is shown in Figure 40. For tuples (up to

```
instance Trans a ⇒ Trans [a] where
  write list@[] = sendData Data list
  write (x:xs)  = do rnf x 'pseq' sendData Stream x
                     write xs

instance (Trans a, Trans b) ⇒ Trans (a,b) where
  createComm = do (cx,x) ← createC
                  (cy,y) ← createC
                  return (Comm (write2 (cx,cy)),(x,y))

-- auxiliary write function for pairs
write2 :: (Trans a, Trans b) ⇒
          (ChanName' a, ChanName' b) → (a,b) → IO ()
write2 (c1,c2) (x1,x2) = do fork (sendVia c1 x1)
                            sendVia c2 x2
```

Fig. 40. Trans instance declarations for lists and pairs

9 components), channel creation is overloaded as shown exemplarily for pairs in Figure 40. Two primitive channels are created. The communicator function creates two threads to allow the concurrent and independent transfer of the tuple components via these primitive channels. For tuples with more than 9 components, the Eden programmer has to provide a corresponding Trans instance by himself or the default communicator will be used, i.e. a 10-tuple would be sent in a single message via a single channel.

For self-defined data structures that are input or output of processes, the Eden programmer must provide instance declarations for the classes NFData and Trans. In most cases, it is sufficient to use the default definition for the Trans class and to define a normal form evaluation function rnf.

Example: For binary trees the following declarations would be sufficient:

```
data Tree a = Leaf a | Node a (Tree a) (Tree a)

instance NFData a ⇒ NFData (Tree a) where
  rnf (Leaf x)     = rnf x
  rnf (Node x l r) = rnf x 'seq' rnf l 'seq' rnf r

instance Trans a ⇒ Trans (Tree a)
```

With these declarations, trees will be completely evaluated before being sent in a single message.   ◁

8.3   The PA Monad: Improving Control over Parallel Activities

The Eden module provides a parallel action monad which can be used to improve the control of series of parallel actions. The parallel action monad wraps the IO monad. In particular, it is advantageous to define a sequence of side-effecting operations within the PA monad and unwrap the parallel action only once. The

```
newtype PA a = PA { fromPA :: IO a }

instance Monad PA where
 return b       = PA $ return b
 (PA ioX) >>= f = PA $ do
   x   ← ioX
   fromPA $ f x


runPA :: PA a → a
runPA = unsafePerformIO ∘ fromPA
```

Fig. 41. PA monad definition

definition of the PA monad is given in Figure 41. Note that the data constructor PA of the PA monad is not exported from the Eden module. Thus, the ordinary programmer can only use **return** and **bind** to specify series of parallel actions.

In Section 7, the remote data concept has been implemented using Eden's dynamic channel operations. In fact, the implementation immediately uses the primitive operations and provides definition variants in the PA monad as shown in Figure 42.

In the PA variants of **fetch** and **release**, a channel is created, a thread is forked and in the **release** case the channel and in the **fetch** case the value received via the channel is returned.

The PA monad is especially advantageous when defining series of parallel activities like e.g. when each component of a data structure has to be released or fetched. In particular, this keeps the compiler from applying optimising transformations that are not safe for side-effecting operations.

Example: The following definitions transform a list of local data into a corresponding remote data list and vice versa:

```
releaseAll :: Trans a
              ⇒ [a]      -- ^ The original list
              → [RD a]   -- ^ List of Remote Data handles,
                         -- ^ one for each list element
releaseAll as = runPA $ mapM releasePA as

fetchAll :: Trans a
           ⇒ [RD a]  -- ^ The Remote Data handles
           → [a]     -- ^ The original data
fetchAll ras = runPA $ mapM fetchPA ras
```

Note that the predefined Haskell function

$$mapM :: (Monad\ m) \Rightarrow (a \to m\ b) \to [a] \to m\ [b]$$

lifts a monadic function to lists.   ◁

Exercise 9: Define functions **releaseTree** and **fetchTree** to release node-wise the data elements in binary trees:

```
type RD a = ChanName (ChanName a)

releasePA :: Trans a
             ⇒ a            -- ^ The original data
             → PA (RD a)    -- ^ The Remote Data handle
releasePA val = PA $ do
  (cc, Comm sendValC) ← createComm
  fork (sendValC val)
  return cc

release :: Trans a ⇒ a -- ^ The original data
           → RD a        -- ^ The Remote Data handle
release = runPA ∘ releasePA

fetchPA    :: Trans a ⇒ RD a → PA a
fetchPA (Comm sendValCC) = PA $ do
  (c,val) ← createComm
  fork (sendValCC c)
  return val

fetch    :: Trans a
            ⇒ RD a     -- ^ The Remote Data handle
            → a        -- ^ The original data
fetch = runPA ∘ fetchPA
```

Fig. 42. Implementation of Remote Data using the PA monad

```
data Tree a = Leaf a | Node a (Tree a) (Tree a)

releaseTree :: Trans a ⇒ Tree a       → Tree (Rd a)
fetchTree   :: Trans a ⇒ Tree (Rd a) → Tree a
```

8.4 Process Handling: Defining Process Abstraction and Instantiation

Process abstraction with **process** and process instantiation with (**#**) are implemented in the Eden module. While process abstractions define process creation on the side of the newly created process, process instantiation defines the activities necessary on the side of the parent process. Communication channels are explicitly created and installed to connect processes using the primitives provided for handling Eden's dynamic input channels.

A process abstraction of type **Process a b** is implemented by a function **f_remote** (see Figure 43) which will be evaluated remotely by a corresponding child process. It takes two arguments: the first is an Eden channel (comprising a communicator function **sendResult**) via which the result of the process should be returned to the parent process. The second argument is a primitive channel **inCC** (of type **ChanName' (ChanName a)**) to return its input channels (communicator function) to the parent process. The exact number of channels between parent

```
data (Trans a, Trans b) ⇒
     Process a b =
        Proc (ChanName b → ChanName ' (ChanName a) → ())
process     :: (Trans a, Trans b) ⇒
                (a → b) → Process a b
process f =   Proc f_remote
  where
    f_remote (Comm sendResult) inCC
      = do (sendInput , invals) = createComm
           connectToPort inCC
           sendData Data sendInput
           sendResult (f invals)
```

Fig. 43. Implementation of process abstraction

```
( # ) :: (Trans a, Trans b) ⇒ Process a b → a → b
pabs # inps
  = runPA $ instantiateAt   0  pabs inps

instantiateAt :: (Trans a, Trans b) ⇒
                  Int → Process a b → a → PA b
instantiateAt pe (Proc f_remote) inps
  = PA $
     do (sendresult, result)     ← createComm
        (inCC,  Comm sendInput)  ← createC
        sendData (Instantiate pe) (f_remote sendresult  inCC)
        fork  (sendInput inps)
        return result
```

Fig. 44. Implementation of process instantiation

and child process does not matter in this context, because the operations on dynamic channels are overloaded. The definition of process shows that the remotely evaluated function, f_remote, creates its input channels via the function createComm. Moreover, it connects to the primitive input channel of its parent process and sends the communicator function of its input channels to the parent. Finally the process output, i.e. the result of evaluating the function within the process abstraction f to the inputs received via its input channels invals. The communicator function sendResult will trigger the evaluation of the process result to normal form before sending it.

Process instantiation by the operator (#) defines process creation on the parent side. The auxiliary function instantiateAt implements process instantiation with explicit placement on a given PE which are numbered from 1 to noPe. Passing 0 as a process number leads to the default round robin placement policy for processes. Process creation on the parent side works somehow dually to the process creation on the child side, at least with respect to channel management. First a new input channel for receiving the child process' results is

```
spawnAt :: [Int] → [Process a b] → [a] → [b]
spawnAt pos ps is
   = runPA $ sequence
                [instantiateAt st p i |
                 (st,p,i) ← zip3 (cycle pos) ps is]

spawn = spawnAt [0]
```

Fig. 45. Definition of spawn

generated. Then a primitive channel for receiving the child process' input channel(s) is created. The process instantiation message sends the application of the process abstraction function f_remote applied to the created input channels to the processor element where the new child process should be evaluated. Finally a concurrent thread is forked which sends the input for the child process using the communicator function received from the child process. The result of the child process is returned to the environment.

The functions spawnAt and spawn can easily be defined using the PA monad and the primitive function instantiateAt, see Figure 45. Note that it is not necessary to provide a processor number for each process abstraction. The list with PE numbers is cycled to guarantee sufficient PE numbers.

Exercise 10: Define a function spawnTree to instantiate process abstractions given in a binary tree structure together with their inputs:

```
data Tree a = Leaf a | Node a (Tree a) (Tree a)

spawnTree :: (Trans a, Trans b) ⇒
             Tree (Process a b, a) → Tree b
```

9 Further Reading

Comprehensive and up-to-date information on Eden is provided on its web site

http://www.mathematik.uni-marburg.de/~eden.

Basic information on its design, semantics, and implementation as well as the underlying programming methodology can be found in [39,13]. Details on the parallel runtime system and Eden's concept of implementation can best be found in [8,10,4]. The technique of layered parallel runtime environments has been further developed and generalised by Berthold, Loidl and Al Zain [3,12]. The Eden trace viewer tool EdenTV is available on Eden's web site. A short introductory description is given in [11]. Another tool for analysing the behaviour of Eden programs has been developed by de la Encina, Llana, Rubio and Hidalgo-Herreo [21,22,17] by extending the tool Hood (Haskell Object Observation Debugger) for Eden. Extensive work has been done on skeletal programming in

Eden. An overview on various skeleton types (specification, implementation, and cost models) have been presented as a chapter in the book by Gorlatch and Rabhi [38,54]. Several parallel map implementations have been discussed and analysed in [33]. An Eden implementation of the large-scale *map-and-reduce* programming model proposed by Google [18] has been investigated in [6,4]. Hierarchical master-worker schemes with several layers of masters and submasters have been presented in [7]. A sophisticated distributed workpool has been presented in [19]. Definitions and applications of further specific skeletons can be found in the following papers: topology skeletons [9], adaptive skeletons [25], divide-and-conquer schemes [5,36]. Special skeletons for computer algebra algorithms are developed with the goal to define the kernel of a computer algebra system in Eden [37,35]. Meta-programming techniques have been investigated in [51]. An operational and a denotational semantics for Eden have been defined by Ortega-Mallén and Hidalgo-Herrero [28,29,27]. These semantics have been used to analyze Eden skeletons [31,30]. A non-determinism analysis has been presented by Segura and Peña [44,55].

10   Other Parallel Haskells (Related Work)

Several extensions of the non-strict functional language Haskell [26] for parallel programming are available. These approaches differ in the degree of explicitness when specifying parallelism and the control of parallel evaluations. The spectrum reaches from explicit low-level approaches where the programmer has to specify and to control parallel evaluations on a low level of abstraction to implicit high-level approaches where in the extreme the programmer does not have to bother about parallelism at all. Between the extremes there are approaches where the programmer has to specify parallelism explicitly but parallel execution is managed by sophisticated parallel runtime systems. It is a challenge to find the right balance between control and abstraction in parallel functional programming. The following enumeration sketches some parallel extensions of Haskell from explicit to implicit approaches:

Haskell plus MPI uses the foreign function interface (FFI) of Haskell to provide the MPI [43] functionality in Haskell [49]. It supports an SPMD style, i.e. the same program is started on several processing elements (PEs). The different instances can be distinguished using their MPI rank and may exchange serializable Haskell data structures via MPI send and receive routines.

The Par Monad [56] is a monad to express deterministic parallelism in Haskell. It provides a `fork` to create parallel processes and write-once mutable reference cells called `IVars` for exchanging data between processes. A skeleton-based programming style is advocated to abstract from the low-level basic constructs. It is notable that the Par monad is completely implemented as a Haskell library including a work-stealing scheduler written in Haskell.

Eden (the subject of these lecture notes) abstracts from low-level sending and receiving of messages. Communication via channels is automatically provided by the parallel runtime system. It allows, however, to define processes and communication channels explicitly and thus to control parallel activity and data distribution. Eden has been designed for distributed memory systems but can equally well be used on multicore systems.

Glasgow parallel Haskell (GpH) [58] and **Multicore Haskell** [42] share the same language definition (basic combinators par and pseq and evaluation strategies) but differ in their implementations. While GpH with its parallel runtime system GUM can be executed on distributed memory systems, Multicore Haskell with its threaded runtime system is tailored to shared-memory multicore architectures. The language allows to mark expressions using the simple combinator par for parallel evaluation. These expressions are collected as *sparks* in a spark pool. The runtime system decides which sparks will be evaluated in parallel. This is out of control of the programmer. Moreover, access to local and remote data is automatically managed by the runtime system. Evaluation strategies [57,41] abstract from low-level expression marking and allow to describe patterns for parallel behaviour on a higher level of abstraction.

Data Parallel Haskell [46] Data Parallel Haskell extends Haskell with support for nested data parallelism with a focus to utilise multicore CPUs. It adds parallel arrays and implicitly parallel operations on those to Haskell. This is the most implicit and easy-to-use approach, but restricted to the special case of data parallelism.

Note that we excluded from this overview approaches to concurrent programming like Concurrent Haskell [45] and distributed programming like Cloud Haskell [32] or HdpH [40]. Although not dedicated to parallel programming these languages can also be used for that purpose but on a rather low level of abstraction.

11   Conclusions

These lecture notes have given a comprehensive overview of the achievements and the current status of the Eden project with a focus on Eden's skeleton-based programming methodology. Eden extends Haskell with constructs for the explicit definition and creation of processes. Communication between these processes occurs via uni-directional one-to-one channels which will be established automatically on process creation between parent and child processes, but can also be explicitly created for direct data exchange between arbitrary processes. Eden provides an elaborated skeleton library with various parallel implementations of common computation schemes like map, map-reduce, or divide-and-conquer, as well as skeletons defining communication topologies and master-worker systems. Communication costs are crucial in distributed systems. Techniques like chunking, running processes offline and establishing direct communication channels using remote data or dynamic channels can be used to reduce communication costs substantially. Application programmers will typically find appropriate predefined skeletons for parallelising their Haskell programs, but also have the possibility to modify and adapt skeletons for their special requirements. The Eden project is ongoing. Current activities comprise the further development of the Eden skeleton library as well as the investigation of further high-level parallel programming constructs.

Acknowledgements. The author thanks the co-developers of Eden Yolanda Ortega-Mallén and Ricardo Peña from Universidad Complutense de Madrid for their friendship and continuing support. It is thanks to Jost Berthold that we have an efficient implementation of Eden in the Glasgow Haskell compiler. I am grateful to all other actual and former members of the Eden project for their manifold contributions: Alberto de la Encina, Mercedes Hildalgo Herrero, Christóbal Pareja, Fernando Rubio, Lidia Sánchez-Gil, Clara Segura, Pablo Roldan Gomez (Universidad Complutense de Madrid) and Silvia Breitinger, Mischa Dieterle, Ralf Freitag, Thomas Horstmeyer, Ulrike Klusik, Dominik Krappel, Oleg Lobachev, Johannes May, Bernhard Pickenbrock, Steffen Priebe, Björn Struckmeier, Nils Weskamp (Philipps-Universität Marburg). Last but not least, thanks go to Hans-Wolfgang Loidl, Phil Trinder, Kevin Hammond, and Greg Michaelson for many fruitful discussions, successful cooperations, and for giving us access to their Beowulf clusters.

Special thanks go to Yolanda Ortega-Mallén, Oleg Lobachev, Mischa Dieterle, Thomas Horstmeyer, and the anonymous reviewer for their valuable comments on a preliminary version of this tutorial.

References

1. Alt, M., Gorlatch, S.: Adapting Java RMI for grid computing. Future Generation Computer Systems 21(5), 699–707 (2004)
2. Batcher, K.E.: Sorting networks and their applications. In: Proc. AFIPS Spring Joint Computer Conference, vol. 32, pp. 307–314 (1968)
3. Berthold, J.: Towards a Generalised Runtime Environment for Parallel Haskells. In: Bubak, M., van Albada, G.D., Sloot, P.M.A., Dongarra, J. (eds.) ICCS 2004. LNCS, vol. 3038, pp. 297–305. Springer, Heidelberg (2004); Workshop on Practical Aspects of High-level Parallel Programming — PAPP 2004
4. Berthold, J.: Explicit and Implicit Parallel Functional Programming: Concepts and Implementation. PhD thesis, Philipps-Universität Marburg, Germany (2008)
5. Berthold, J., Dieterle, M., Lobachev, O., Loogen, R.: Distributed Memory Programming on Many-Cores A Case Study Using Eden Divide-&-Conquer Skeletons. In: ARCS 2009, Workshop on Many-Cores. VDE Verlag (2009)
6. Berthold, J., Dieterle, M., Loogen, R.: Implementing Parallel Google Map-Reduce in Eden. In: Sips, H., Epema, D., Lin, H.-X. (eds.) Euro-Par 2009. LNCS, vol. 5704, pp. 990–1002. Springer, Heidelberg (2009)
7. Berthold, J., Dieterle, M., Loogen, R., Priebe, S.: Hierarchical Master-Worker Skeletons. In: Hudak, P., Warren, D.S. (eds.) PADL 2008. LNCS, vol. 4902, pp. 248–264. Springer, Heidelberg (2008)
8. Berthold, J., Klusik, U., Loogen, R., Priebe, S., Weskamp, N.: High-Level Process Control in Eden. In: Kosch, H., Böszörményi, L., Hellwagner, H. (eds.) Euro-Par 2003. LNCS, vol. 2790, pp. 732–741. Springer, Heidelberg (2003)

9. Berthold, J., Loogen, R.: Skeletons for Recursively Unfolding Process Topologies. In: Parallel Computing: Current & Future Issues of High-End Computing, ParCo 2005. NIC Series, vol. 33, pp. 835–842 (2006)

10. Berthold, J., Loogen, R.: Parallel Coordination Made Explicit in a Functional Setting. In: Horváth, Z., Zsók, V., Butterfield, A. (eds.) IFL 2006. LNCS, vol. 4449, pp. 73–90. Springer, Heidelberg (2007)

11. Berthold, J., Loogen, R.: Visualizing Parallel Functional Program Runs – Case Studies with the Eden Trace Viewer. In: Parallel Computing: Architectures, Algorithms and Applications, ParCo 2007. NIC Series, vol. 38, pp. 121–128 (2007)

12. Berthold, J., Al Zain, A., Loidl, H.-W.: Scheduling Light-Weight Parallelism in ArTCoP. In: Hudak, P., Warren, D.S. (eds.) PADL 2008. LNCS, vol. 4902, pp. 214–229. Springer, Heidelberg (2008)

13. Breitinger, S.: Design and Implementation of the Parallel Functional Language Eden. PhD thesis, Philipps-Universität of Marburg, Germany (1998)

14. Breitinger, S., Klusik, U., Loogen, R.: From (Sequential) Haskell to (Parallel) Eden: An Implementation Point of View. In: Palamidessi, C., Meinke, K., Glaser, H. (eds.) ALP 1998 and PLILP 1998. LNCS, vol. 1490, pp. 318–334. Springer, Heidelberg (1998)

15. Bresenham, J.E.: Algorithm for computer control of a digital plotter. IBM Systems Journal 4(1), 25–30 (1965)

16. Cole, M.: Algorithmic Skeletons: Structured Management of Parallel Computation. MIT Press (1989)

17. de la Encina, A.: Formalizando el proceso de depuración en programación funcional paralela y perezosa. PhD thesis, Universidad Complutense de Madrid (Spain) (2008) (in Spanish)

18. Dean, J., Ghemawat, S.: MapReduce: Simplified Data Processing on Large Clusters. Communications of the ACM 51(1), 107–113 (2008)

19. Dieterle, M., Berthold, J., Loogen, R.: A Skeleton for Distributed Work Pools in Eden. In: Blume, M., Kobayashi, N., Vidal, G. (eds.) FLOPS 2010. LNCS, vol. 6009, pp. 337–353. Springer, Heidelberg (2010)

20. Dieterle, M., Horstmeyer, T., Loogen, R.: Skeleton Composition Using Remote Data. In: Carro, M., Peña, R. (eds.) PADL 2010. LNCS, vol. 5937, pp. 73–87. Springer, Heidelberg (2010)

21. Encina, A., Llana, L., Rubio, F., Hidalgo-Herrero, M.: Observing Intermediate Structures in a Parallel Lazy Functional Language. In: Principles and Practice of Declarative Programming (PPDP 2007), pp. 109–120. ACM (2007)

22. Encina, A., Rodríguez, I., Rubio, F.: pHood: A Tool to Analyze Parallel Functional Programs. In: Implementation of Functional Languages (IFL 2009), pp. 85–99. Seton Hall University, New York (2009), Technical Report, SHU-TR-CS-2009-09-1

23. Gentleman, W.M.: Some complexity results for matrix computations on parallel computers. Journal of the ACM 25(1), 112–115 (1978)

24. GHC: The Glasgow Haskell Compiler, http://www.haskell.org/ghc

25. Hammond, K., Berthold, J., Loogen, R.: Automatic Skeletons in Template Haskell. Parallel Processing Letters 13(3), 413–424 (2003)

26. Haskell: A non-strict functional programming language, http://www.haskell.org/

27. Hidalgo-Herrero, M.: Semánticas Formales para un Lenguaje Funcional Paralelo. PhD thesis, Universidad Complutense de Madrid (Spain) (2004) (in Spanish)

28. Hidalgo-Herrero, M., Ortega-Mallén, Y.: An Operational Semantics for the Parallel Language Eden. Parallel Processing Letters 12(2), 211–228 (2002)

29. Hidalgo-Herrero, M., Ortega-Mallén, Y.: Continuation Semantics for Parallel Haskell Dialects. In: Ohori, A. (ed.) APLAS 2003. LNCS, vol. 2895, pp. 303–321. Springer, Heidelberg (2003)
30. Hidalgo-Herrero, M., Ortega-Mallén, Y., Rubio, F.: Analyzing the Influence of Mixed Evaluation on the Performance of Eden Skeletons. Parallel Computing 32(7-8), 523–538 (2006)
31. Hidalgo-Herrero, M., Ortega-Mallén, Y., Rubio, F.: Comparing Alternative Evaluation Strategies for Stream-Based Parallel Functional Languages. In: Horváth, Z., Zsók, V., Butterfield, A. (eds.) IFL 2006. LNCS, vol. 4449, pp. 55–72. Springer, Heidelberg (2007)
32. Jeff Epstein, S.P., Black, A.P.: Towards Haskell in the cloud. In: Haskell 2011: Proceedings of the 4th ACM Symposium on Haskell, pp. 118–129. ACM (2011)
33. Klusik, U., Loogen, R., Priebe, S., Rubio, F.: Implementation Skeletons in Eden: Low-Effort Parallel Programming. In: Mohnen, M., Koopman, P. (eds.) IFL 2000. LNCS, vol. 2011, pp. 71–88. Springer, Heidelberg (2001)
34. Klusik, U., Ortega, Y., Peña, R.: Implementing Eden - or: Dreams Become Reality. In: Hammond, K., Davie, T., Clack, C. (eds.) IFL 1998. LNCS, vol. 1595, pp. 103–119. Springer, Heidelberg (1999)
35. Lobachev, O.: Implementation and Evaluation of Algorithmic Skeletons: Parallelisation of Computer Algebra Algorithms. PhD thesis, Philipps-Universität Marburg, Germany (2011)
36. Berthold, J., Dieterle, M., Lobachev, O., Loogen, R.: Parallel FFT with Eden Skeletons. In: Malyshkin, V. (ed.) PaCT 2009. LNCS, vol. 5698, pp. 73–83. Springer, Heidelberg (2009)
37. Lobachev, O., Loogen, R.: Towards an Implementation of a Computer Algebra System in a Functional Language. In: Autexier, S., Campbell, J., Rubio, J., Sorge, V., Suzuki, M., Wiedijk, F. (eds.) AISC/Calculemus/MKM 2008. LNCS (LNAI), vol. 5144, pp. 141–154. Springer, Heidelberg (2008)
38. Loogen, R., Ortega-Mallén, Y., Peña, R., Priebe, S., Rubio, F.: Parallelism Abstractions in Eden. In: [53], ch. 4, pp. 95–128. Springer (2003)
39. Loogen, R., Ortega-Mallén, Y., Peña-Marí, R.: Parallel Functional Programming in Eden. Journal of Functional Programming 15(3), 431–475 (2005)
40. Maier, P., Trinder, P., Loidl, H.-W.: Implementing a High-level Distributed-Memory parallel Haskell in Haskell. In: IFL 2011: 23rd Int. Workshop on the Implementation of Functional Languages. LNCS, vol. 7257. Springer (2012) (to appear)
41. Marlow, S., Maier, P., Loidl, H.-W., Aswad, M.K., Trinder, P.W.: Seq no more: Better strategies for parallel Haskell. In: Haskell Symposium 2010. ACM Press (2010)
42. Marlow, S., Peyton-Jones, S.L., Singh, S.: Runtime support for multicore Haskell. In: ICFP 2009 — Intl. Conf. on Functional Programming, pp. 65–78. ACM Press (2009)
43. MPI: The Message-Passing Interface, http://www.open-mpi.org/
44. Peña, R., Segura, C.: Non-determinism Analysis in a Parallel-Functional Language. In: Mohnen, M., Koopman, P. (eds.) IFL 2000. LNCS, vol. 2011, pp. 1–18. Springer, Heidelberg (2001)
45. Peyton Jones, S., Gordon, A., Finne, S.: Concurrent Haskell. In: Proceedings of POPL 1996, pp. 295–308. ACM Press (1996)
46. Peyton Jones, S., Leshchinskiy, R., Keller, G., Chakravarty, M.: Harnessing the Multicores: Nested Data Parallelism in Haskell. In: Foundations of Software Technology and Theoretical Computer Science, FSTTCS 2008 (2008)
47. Peyton Jones, S.L.: Implementing lazy functional languages on stock hardware: the Spineless Tagless G-machine. Journal of Functional Programming 2(2), 127–202 (1992)

48. Pickenbrock, B.: Developing a Multicore Implementation of Eden. Bachelor thesis, Philipps-Universität Marburg (2011) (in German)
49. Pope, B., Astapov, D.: Haskell-mpi, Haskell bindings to the MPI library (2010), https://github.com/bjpop/haskell-mpi
50. Priebe, S.: Dynamic Task Generation and Transformation Within a Nestable Workpool Skeleton. In: Nagel, W.E., Walter, W.V., Lehner, W. (eds.) Euro-Par 2006. LNCS, vol. 4128, pp. 615–624. Springer, Heidelberg (2006)
51. Priebe, S.: Structured Generic Programming in Eden. PhD thesis, Philipps-Universität Marburg, Germany (2007)
52. PVM: Parallel Virtual Machine, http://www.epm.ornl.gov/pvm/
53. Rabhi, F.A., Gorlatch, S. (eds.): Patterns and Skeletons for Parallel and Distributed Computing. Springer (2003)
54. Rubio, F.: Programación Funcional Paralela Eficiente en Eden. PhD thesis, Universidad Complutense de Madrid, Spain (2001) (in Spanish)
55. Segura, C.: Análisis de programas en lenguajes funcionales paralelos. PhD thesis, Universidad Complutense de Madrid, Spain (2001) (in Spanish)
56. Simon Marlow, S.P., Newton, R.: A monad for deterministic parallelism. In: Haskell 2011: Proceedings of the 4th ACM Symposium on Haskell, pp. 71–82. ACM (2011)
57. Trinder, P., Hammond, K., Loidl, H.-W., Peyton Jones, S.: Algorithm + Strategy = Parallelism. Journal of Functional Programming 8(1), 23–60 (1998)
58. Trinder, P.W., Hammond, K., Mattson Jr., J.S., Partridge, A.S., Peyton Jones, S.L.: GUM: a portable implementation of Haskell. In: Proceedings of Programming Language Design and Implementation (1996)

A Compiling, Running, Analysing Eden Programs

The Eden compiler, an extension of the Glasgow Haskell compiler (GHC), is available from the Eden homepage under URL

> http://www.mathematik.uni-marburg.de/~eden

Prerequisites and installation instructions are provided.

Typical command lines for compiling, running and analysing the simple program for computing π shown in Figure 4 are e.g.

```
prompt> ghc -parmpi --make -O2 -eventlog pi.hs
prompt> pi 1000000 +RTS -N8 -ls
prompt> edentv loogen=pi_1000000_+RTS_-N8_-ls.parevents
```

Because of the option -parmpi code for the MPI version of the parallel runtime system (PRTS) is produced. The option -eventlog enables the code to produce traces at runtime. The code is then run with input parameter 1000000. The runtime system options after +RTS have the effect that the runtime system is started on 8 processing elements (option -N8) and that a trace file is produced (option -ls). Finally the trace viewer EdenTV (see Section A.3) is started to visualise and analyse the produced trace file.

A.1 Compile Time Options

To compile Eden programs with parallel support one has to use the options -parpvm to use PVM [52] or -parmpi to use MPI [43] as middleware. The option

-eventlog allows for the production of trace files (event logs) when compiled
Eden programs are executed. All GHC options, e.g. optimisation flags like -O2,
can equally well be used with the Eden version of GHC.

A.2 Runtime Options

A compiled Eden program accepts in addition to its arguments *runtime system
options* enclosed in

$$+RTS <your options> -RTS$$

With these options one can control the program setup and behaviour, e.g. on
how many (virtual) processor elements (PEs) the program should be executed,
which process placement policy should be used etc. The following table shows
the most important Eden specific runtime options. All GHC RTS options can
also be used. By typing ./myprogram +RTS -? a complete list of available RTS
options is given.

RTS option	effect	default
-N<n>	set number of PEs	number of PVM/MPI nodes
-MPI@<file>	specify MPI hostfile	mpihosts
-qQ<n>	set buffer size for messages	32K
-ls	enable event logging[3]	
-qrnd	random process placement	round-robin placement

A.3   EdenTV: The Eden Trace Viewer

The Eden trace viewer tool (EdenTV) [11] provides a *post-mortem analysis* of
program executions on the level of the computational units of the parallel runtime system (PRTS). The latter is instrumented with special trace generation
commands activated by the compile-time option -eventlog and the run-time
option +RTS -ls. In the space-time diagrams generated by EdenTV, machines
(i.e. processor elements), processes or threads are represented by horizontal bars,
respectively, with time on the x-axis.

The machines diagrams correspond to the view of profiling tools observing
the parallel machine execution, if there is a one-to-one correspondence between
virtual and physical processor elements which will usually be the case. The
processes per machine diagrams show the activity of Eden processes and their
placement on the available machines. The threads diagrams show the activity
of all created threads, not only the threads of Eden processes but also internal
system threads.

The diagram bars have segments in different colours, which indicate the activities of the respective logical unit (machine, process or thread) in a period
during the execution. Bars are

- green when the logical unit is running,
- yellow when it is runnable but currently not running, and
- red when the unit is blocked.

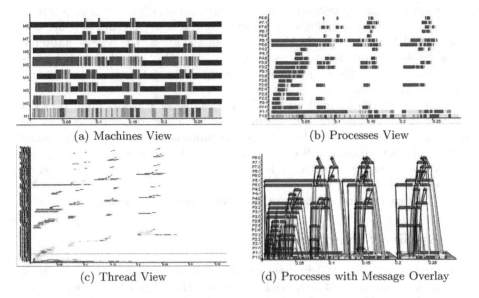

(a) Machines View

(b) Processes View

(c) Thread View

(d) Processes with Message Overlay

Fig. 46. Examples of EdenTV diagrams

If trace visualisations are shown in greyscale, the colors have the following correspondences: light grey = yellow, grey = green, dark grey = red. In addition, a machine can be idle which means that no processes are allocated on the machine. Idleness is indicated by a small blue bar. The thread states are immediately determined from the thread state events in the traces of processes. The states of processes and machines are derived from the information about thread states.

Figure 46 shows examples of the machines, processes and threads diagrams for a divide-and-conquer program implementing the bitonic-merge-sort algorithm [2]. The trace has been generated on 8 Linux workstations connected via fast Ethernet. The program sorted a list of 1024 numbers with a recursion depth limit of 4.

The example diagrams in Figure 46 show that the program has been executed on 8 machines (virtual processor elements). While there is some activity on machine 1 (where the main program is started) during the whole execution, machines 6 to 8 are idle most of the time (smaller blue bar). The corresponding processes graphic (see Figure 46(b)) reveals that several Eden processes have been allocated on each machine. The activities in Machine 2 have been caused by different processes. The diagrams show that the workload on the parallel machines was low — there were only small periods where threads were running. The yellow-colored periods indicate system activity in the diagrams. The threads view is not readable because too many threads are shown. It is possible to zoom the diagrams to get a closer view on the activities at critical points during the execution.

Messages between processes or machines are optionally shown by grey arrows which start from the sending unit bar and point at the receiving unit bar (see Figure 46(d)). Streams can be shown as shadowed areas. The representation of messages is very important for programmers, since they can observe hot spots and inefficiencies in the communication during the execution as well as control communication topologies.

When extensive communication takes places, message arrows may cover the whole activity profile. For this reason, EdenTV allows to show messages selectively, i.e. between selectable (subsets of) processes. EdenTV provides many additional information and features, e.g. the number of messages sent and received by processes and machines is recorded. More information is provided on the web pages of EdenTV:

`http://www.mathematik.uni-marburg.de/~eden/?content=trace_main&navi=trace`

B   Auxiliary Functions

This section contains the definitions of the auxiliary functions which have been used in the examples of this tutorial. These pure Haskell functions are provided in the Eden module `Control.Parallel.Eden.EdenSkel.Auxiliary`.

B.1   Unshuffle and Shuffle

The function `unshuffle :: Int → [a] → [[a]]` distributes the input list in a round robin manner into as many sublists as the first parameter determines.

```
unshuffle :: Int       -- ^ number of sublists
             → [a]      -- ^ input list
             → [[a]]    -- ^ distributed output
unshuffle n xs = [takeEach n (drop i xs) | i ← [0..n-1]]

takeEach :: Int → [a] → [a]
takeEach n []     = []
takeEach n (x:xs) = x : takeEach n (drop (n-1) xs)
```

The inverse function `shuffle :: [[a]] → [a]` shuffles the given list of lists into the output list.

```
shuffle :: [[a]]    -- ^ sublists
           → [a]    -- ^ shuffled sublists
shuffle = concat ∘ transpose
```

Note that the function `transpose` is predefined in the standard library `Data.List`. The Haskell prelude function `concat :: [[a]] → [a]` simply concatenates all lists of the given list of lists.

The function `unshuffle` has the advantage that the result lists grow uniformly. Consequently, the function works *incrementally* in the sense that it produces values on all output lists even if the input list is not completely available or an infinite stream. In the same way, `shuffle` is able to produce output even if the input lists are incomplete or infinite.

B.2   SplitIntoN and Chunk

The function splitIntoN :: Int → [a] → [[a]] distributes the input list block-wise into as many sublists as the first parameter determines. The lengths of the output lists differ by at most one. This property is achieved by using the following function bresenham which follows an idea from the Bresenham algorithm from computer graphics [15]. The function bresenham computes takes two integer parameters n and p and computes $[i_1, ..., i_p]$ such that $i_1 + ... + i_p = n$ and $|i_j - i_k| \leq 1$ for all $1 \leq j, k \leq n$.

```
bresenham :: Int      -- ^n
          → Int       -- ^p
          → [Int]     -- ^[i1,...,ip]
bresenham n p = take p (bresenham1 n)
  where
    bresenham1 m = (m 'div' p) : bresenham1 ((m 'mod' p)+ n)


splitIntoN :: Int      -- ^ number of blocks
           → [a]       -- ^ list to be split
           → [[a]]     -- ^ list of blocks
splitIntoN n xs = f bh xs
  where bh = bresenham (length xs) n
        f [] [] = []
        f [] _  = error "some␣elements␣left␣over"
        f (t:ts) xs = hs : (f ts rest)
          where (hs,rest) = splitAt t xs
```

The Haskell prelude function splitAt :: Int → [a] → ([a],[a]) splits a list into a prefix of the length determined by its first parameter and the rest list.

Note that splitIntoN works only for finite lists. Moreover, it does not work incrementally, i.e. the whole input list must be available before any output will be produced.

While splitIntoN divides a list into the given number of sublists, the following function chunk decomposes a list into sublists of the size given as first parameter. All sublists except of the last one have the given size.

```
chunk      :: Int → [a] → [[a]]
chunk k [] =  []
chunk k xs =  ys : chunk k zs
  where (ys,zs) = splitAt k xs
```

In contrast to splitIntoN, chunk works incrementally and can also be applied to incomplete or infinite lists.

Note that the inverse function to splitIntoN and to chunk is the Haskell prelude function concat :: [[a]] → [a].

B.3   Distribute and OrderBy

The functions distribute and orderBy are used in the definition of the master-worker skeleton (see Section 6.2). The function distribute distributes a task

list into several task lists for the worker processes in the order determined by a
stream of worker id's which are the workers' requests for new tasks.

```
distribute :: Int          -- ^ number of workers
             → [Int]  -- ^ request stream  with worker IDs
             → [t]    -- ^ task list
             → [[t]]  -- ^ each inner list for one worker
distribute np reqs tasks
  = [taskList reqs tasks n | n← [1..np]]
    where taskList (r:rs) (t:ts) pe
                            | pe == r   = t:(taskList rs ts pe)
                            | otherwise =    taskList rs ts pe
          taskList _          _          _ = []
```

The function orderBy combines the worker results in the order determined by a
stream of worker id's.

```
orderBy :: [[r]]        -- ^ nested input list
           → [Int]  -- ^ request stream gives distribution
           → [r]    -- ^ ordered result list
orderBy rss [] = []
orderBy rss (r:reqs)
  = let (rss1,(rs2:rss2)) = splitAt r rss
    in (head rs2): orderBy (rss1 ++ ((tail rs2):rss2)) reqs
```

Single Assignment C (SAC)
High Productivity Meets High Performance

Clemens Grelck

University of Amsterdam, Institute of Informatics
Science Park 904, 1098 XH Amsterdam, Netherlands
c.grelck@uva.nl

Abstract. We present the ins and outs of the purely functional, data parallel programming language SAC (Single Assignment C). SAC defines state- and side-effect-free semantics on top of a syntax resembling that of imperative languages like C/C++/C# or Java: functional programming with curly brackets. In contrast to other functional languages data aggregation in SAC is not based on lists and trees, but puts stateless arrays into the focus.

SAC implements an abstract calculus of truly multidimensional arrays that is adopted from interpreted array languages like APL. Arrays are abstract values with certain structural properties. They are treated in a holistic way, not as loose collections of data cells or indexed memory address ranges. Programs can and should be written in a mostly index-free style. Functions consume array values as arguments and produce array values as results. The array type system of SAC allows such functions to abstract not only from the size of vectors or matrices but likewise from the number of array dimensions, supporting a highly generic programming style.

The design of SAC aims at reconciling high productivity in software engineering of compute-intensive applications with high performance in program execution on modern multi- and many-core computing systems. While SAC competes with other functional and declarative languages on the productivity aspect, it competes with hand-parallelised C and Fortran code on the performance aspect. We achieve our goal through stringent co-design of programming language and compilation technology.

The focus on arrays in general and the abstract view of arrays in particular combined with a functional state-free semantics are key ingredients in the design of SAC. In conjunction they allow for far-reaching program transformations and fully compiler-directed parallelisation. From literally the same source code SAC currently supports symmetric multi-socket, multi-core, hyperthreaded server systems, CUDA-enables graphics accelerators and the MicroGrid, an innovative general-purpose many-core architecture.

The CEFP lecture provides an introduction into the language design of SAC, followed by an illustration of how these concepts can be harnessed to write highly abstract, reusable and elegant code. We conclude with outlining the major compiler technologies for achieving runtime performance levels that are competitive with low-level machine-oriented programming environments.

V. Zsók, Z. Horváth, and R. Plasmeijer (Eds.): CEFP 2011, LNCS 7241, pp. 207–278, 2012.
© Springer-Verlag Berlin Heidelberg 2012

1   Introduction and Motivation

The on-going multi-core/many-core revolution in processor architecture has arguably more radically changed the world's view on computing than any other innovation in microprocessor architecture. For several decades the same program could be expected to run faster on the next generation of computers than on the previous. The trick that worked so well and so cheaply all the time is clock frequency scaling. Gordon Moore's famous prediction (also known as Moore's law) says that the number of transistors in a chip doubles every 12–24 months [1]. In other words, the number of transistors on a single chip was predicted to grow exponentially. Surprisingly, this prediction has been fairly accurate since the 1960s. Beyond all clever tricks in microprocessor architecture that were enabled by ever growing transistor counts the probably most important impact of Moore's law lies in the miniaturisation of the logical structures within a processor. The time it takes for an electrical signal to advance from one gate to the next is linear in the distance. With the distance shrinking exponentially, processors were able to run on higher and higher clock frequencies, moving from kilo-Hertz to giga-Hertz.

But now this "free lunch" of programs automatically running faster on a new machine is over [2]. What has happened? Unlike Moore's law, which is rather a prediction than a law, there are also true laws of physics, and according to them the energy consumption of a processor grows quadratically with the clock frequency. Consequently, energy cost has become a relevant factor in computing these days. Another law of physics, the law of conservation of energy, says that energy neither appears from nothing nor does it disappear to nothing; energy only changes its physical condition. In the case of processors, the electrical energy consumed is mostly dissipated as heat, thus requiring even more energy for cooling. These cause the technical and economic challenges we face today.

Circumstances have fostered two technological developments: the multi-core revolution and the many-core revolution. The former means that general-purpose processors do not run at any higher clock frequency than before, but the continuing miniaturisation of structures is used to put multiple cores, fully-fledged processors by themselves, into a single chip. While quad-core processors are already common place in the consumer market, server processors often have already 6, 8 or even 12 cores today. It is generally anticipated that Moore's law of exponential growth will continue for the foreseeable future, but that instead of the clock frequency the number of cores will benefit.

The many-core revolution has its origin in a similar technological progress in the area of graphics cards. With their specialised designs graphics cards have developed into highly parallel, extremely powerful co-processors. They can compute fitting workloads much faster than state-of-the-art general-purpose processors. And, increasingly relevant, they can do this with a fraction of the energy budget. With the fairly general-purpose CUDA programming model, particularly NVidia graphics cards have become integral parts of many high-performance computing installations [3]. But even on the other end of the scale, in the personal computing domain, GPGPUs (or general-purpose graphics processing units) have become relevant for computing beyond computer graphics. After all, every computer does have a graphics card, and its full potential is not always needed for merely controlling the display.

Looking into the future (which is always dangerous) one can anticipate a certain symbiosis of general-purpose multi-core processors and GPU-style accelerators into unified processor designs with a few general-purpose *fat* cores and a large number of restricted *thin* cores. AMD's Fusion and Intel's Knights Ferry architectures are precursors of this development.

The radical paradigm shift in computer architecture from increasing clock frequencies to duplicating computing devices on chip incurs a paradigm shift in software engineering that is at least as revolutionary. As said before, programs no longer automatically benefit from a new generation of computers. A sequential program does not run any faster on a quad-core system than on a uni-core system, and it is very unlikely that it takes advantage of a computer's graphics card. Software at any level must be parallelised to effectively take advantage of today's computers. Harnessing the full power of increasingly concurrent, increasingly diverse and increasingly heterogeneous chip architectures is a challenge for future software engineers.

The multicore revolution must have a profound impact on the practice of software engineering. While parallel programming per sé is hardly new, until very recently it was largely confined to the supercomputing niche. Consequently, programming methodologies and tools for parallel programming are geared towards the needs of this domain: squeezing the maximum possible performance out of an extremely expensive computing machinery through low-level machine-specific programming. Programming productivity concerns are widely ignored as running code is often more expensive than writing it.

What has changed with the multi-/many-core revolution is that any kind of software and likewise any programmer is affected, not only specialists in high performance computing centers with a PhD in computer science.

What has also changed thoroughly is the variety of hardware. Until recently, the von-Neumann model of sequential computing was all that most software engineers would need to know about computer architecture. Today's computer landscape is much more varied and with existing programming technology this variety immediately affects programming. A computer today may just have a single dual-core or quad-core processor, but it may likewise be a 4-processor system with 4, 6 or 12 cores per processor [4,5]. So, already today the number of cores in a general-purpose system can differ by more than one order of magnitude. Technologies such as Intel's hyperthreading [6] further complicate the situation: they are often presented as real cores by the operating system, yet they require a different treatment.

Non-x86 based processor architectures like Oracle's Niagara range offer even more parallelism. The T3-4 server system [7,8] shipped in 2011, for instance, features 4 processors with 16 cores each while each core supports 8 hardware threads. Such a system totals in 512 hardware threads and adds another order of magnitude to the level of parallelism that software needs to effectively take advantage of. A similar variety of technologies can be seen in the GPGPU market.

Now any multi-core system can freely be combined with one or even multiple GPGPU accelerators leading to a combinatorial explosion of possibilities. This, at the latest, makes it technologically and economically challenging to write software that makes decent use of a large variety of computing systems.

The quintessential goal of the SAC project lies in the co-design of programming language technology and the corresponding compiler technology that effectively and efficiently maps programs to a large variety of parallel computing architectures [9,10]. In other words, SAC aims at reconciling programming productivity with execution performance in the multi-/many-core era.

Our fundamental approach is *abstraction*. In analogy to the von Neumann architecture of sequential computing machines SAC abstracts from all concrete properties of computing systems and merely allows the specification of concurrent activities without any programmer control as to whether two concurrent activities are actually evaluated in parallel or sequentially. This decision is entirely left to the compiler and runtime system. The guiding principle is to let the programmer define *what* to compute, not *how* exactly this is done. Our goal is to put expert knowledge, for instance on parallel processing or computer architecture, once into compiler and runtime system and not repeatedly into low-level implementations of many application programs. This approach is particularly geared towards the overwhelming number of software engineers who are neither experts in parallel programming nor appreciate being forced to develop such skills. Nonetheless, it is particularly this target group that wants or must exploit the capabilities of modern multi-core and many-core computing systems with limited software engineering effort.

Specifying *what* to compute, not exactly *how* to compute sounds very familiar to functional programmers. And indeed, SAC is a purely functional language with a state- and side-effect-free semantics. Thus, SAC programs deal with values, and program execution computes new values from existing values in a sequence of context-free substitution steps. How values actually manifest in memory, how long they remain in memory and whether they are created at all is left to the language implementation. Abstracting from all these low-level concerns makes SAC programs expose the algorithmic aspects of some computation because they are not interspersed with organisational aspects of program execution on some concrete architecture.

In order to make exclusively compiler-directed parallelisation feasible, SAC embraces a data-parallel agenda. More precisely, SAC is an *array programming language* in the tradition of APL [11,12], J [13] or Nial [14]. In fact, multi-dimensional arrays are the basic data aggregation principle in SAC. Operations on arrays are defined not exclusively but overwhelmingly following a data-parallel approach. Before we look closer into SAC, let us first illustrate why the data-parallel approach is crucial for our goal of supporting a wide range of parallel architectures solely through compilation. We do this by means of an example algorithm that clearly is none of the usual suspects in (data-)parallel computing. Fig. 1 shows three different implementations of the factorial function: an imperative implementation using C, a functional implementation in OCAML and a data-parallel implementation in SAC. It is characteristic for both the imperative and the functional definition of the factorial function that they do not expose any form of concurrency suitable for compiler-directed parallelisation. The imperative code is sequential by definition, but its functional counterpart likewise leads to a purely sequential computation.

```
int fac( int n)
{
  f = 1;
  while (n > 1) {
    f = f * n;
    n = n - 1;
  }
  return f;
}
```

```
fac n = if n <= 1
        then 1
        else n * fac (n - 1)
```

```
int fac( int n)
{
  return prod( 1 + iota( n));
}
```

Fig. 1. Three definitions of the factorial function: imperative using C (top), functional using OCAML (middle) and data-parallel using SAC (bottom)

In contrast, the array-style SAC implementation of the factorial function does expose a wealth of concurrency to compiler and runtime system to exploit for automatic parallelisation. However, this admittedly warrants some explanation of the SAC code in Fig. 1. The iota function (the name is inspired by the corresponding APL operation) yields a vector (a one-dimensional array) of n elements with the values 0 to n-1. Adding the value 1 to this vector yields the n-element vector with the numbers 1 to n. Computing the product of all elements of this vectors yields the factorial of n. While this definition of the factorial function may be unusual at first glance, it offers one significant advantage over the other definitions of Fig. 1: it exposes concurrency. Each of the three conceptual steps is a data-parallel operation. For appropriate values of n the data-parallel formulation of the factorial function exposes a high degree of fine-grained concurrency.

Fig. 2 illustrates why this is highly relevant. In the example we compute the factorial of 10. The data-parallel specification based on iota, element-wise addition and prod exposes a 10-fold concurrency in computing the factorial number. This, however, does not mean that the computation is split into 10 independent tasks, processes or threads. It is merely an option for the compiler and runtime system to exploit this fine-grained concurrency. Depending on the target

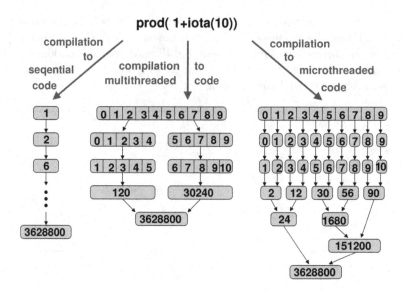

Fig. 2. Design choices in compiling a data-parallel program

architecture this may or may not be the case. If the target architecture, for instance, supports very light-weight concurrent activities, the compiler may indeed decide to expose the full amount of concurrency to the hardware. The MicroGrid many-core architecture [15] is such an example.

On the other end of the spectrum compiler and runtime system may equally well decide to run the entire computation sequentially. Maybe we utilise sequential legacy hardware; maybe we have already exhausted our parallel computing capabilities on an outer application level. If so, it is fairly simple *not* to make use of the apparent concurrency and generate sequential binary code instead.

Between these two extremes, exploiting all concurrency available or exploiting no concurrency at all, we find an almost contiguous design space for compiler and runtime system to make appropriate decisions. The right choice depends on a variety of concerns including properties of the target architecture, characteristics of the code and attributes of the data being processed. For example, in the center of Fig. 2 we can identify a solution that is presumably well-suited for a dual-core system. The compiler generates two independent tasks that each take care of one half of the intermediate vector. Both threads can run without synchronisation until the final multiplication of the partial reduction results.

A compiler could even generate multiple alternative code versions and postpone any decision until runtime when complete information about hardware capacities, data sizes, etc, are available to make a much more educate choice.

Of course, the factorial function is merely an example to illustrate the principle of data-parallel array programming, not at all a relevant application. Neither is the factorial function particularly interesting to be computed in parallel for large argument numbers, nor do the concrete implementations of Fig. 1, based on machine-width integer representations, support sufficiently large values.

As the name Single Assignment C suggests and the factorial example already reveals to some extent, SAC does not follow regular syntactic conventions of established functional languages. Neither do we invent a completely new syntax from scratch. Instead, we aim at providing imperative programmers with the warm feeling of a familiar programming environment. After all, the majority of programmers suddenly confronted with the multi-core revolution has not used HASKELL, OCAML or CLEAN before but rather C, C++, C# or JAVA. We will later see how imperative appearance and functional semantics can make a very beneficial symbiosis.

Last but certainly not least, SAC aims at combining high-level, problem-oriented programming not only with fully automatic parallelisation but likewise with competitive sequential performance. And competition here means established imperative programming languages, not high-level, declarative or functional ones. If we aim at converting imperative programmers to SAC, we must be able to generate absolute performance gains through automatic parallelisation. In other words SAC aims at outperforming sequential imperative codes on parallel hardware. For that it is paramount to deliver sequential performance that is close to imperative programs. After all, we cannot expect more than a linear performance increase from parallelisation. To support the performance demands, SAC dispenses with a number of programming features typical for main-stream, general-purpose functional languages. For instance, SAC neither supports higher-order functions, nor currying or partial applications. SAC also follows a strict evaluation regime.

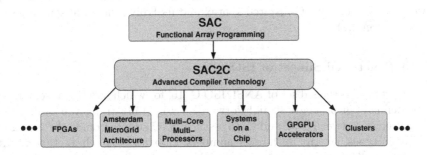

Fig. 3. The SAC compilation challenge: past, present and future work

Fig. 3 illustrates the compilation challenge taken by SAC. Based on competitive sequential performance, we aim at compiling a single SAC source program to a variety of computing architectures. At the moment SAC supports symmetric (potentially hyper-threaded) multi-core multi-processor systems with shared memory, i.e. today's bread-and-butter server systems. Moreover, SAC also supports general-purpose graphics processing units (GPGPUs) as accelerators as well as the MicroGrid [15], an innovative general-purpose many-core processor architecture developed at the University of Amsterdam. Work is currently on-going to combine multi-core and many-core code generators to support hybrid systems-on-chip. Support for reconfigurable hardware on one end of the spectrum and network-interconnected clusters of multi-core servers with accelerators on the other mark up-coming challenges that we have only started exploring.

The rest of the article is organised as follows: We begin with the core language design of SAC and explain the relationship between imperative syntax and functional semantics in Section 2. Section 3 elaborates on the calculus of multi-dimensional arrays and discusses its implementation by SAC. We then introduce the array type system of SAC and the associated programming methodology in Section 4. Sections 5 and 6 illustrate programming in SAC by means of two case studies: variations of convolution and numerical differentiation. Sections 7, 8 and 9 complete the introductory text on SAC and explain the module system, SAC's approach to functionally sound input/output and the foreign language interfaces, respectively. Last not least, we discuss essential aspects of the SAC compiler and runtime system in Section 10. A small selection of related work is sketched out in Section 11 before we conclude with a short summary and outlook on current and future research directions in Section 12.

2   Core Language Design

In this section we describe the core language design of SAC. First, we identify the syntactical subset of C for which we can define a functional semantics as language kernel for SAC (Section 2.1). Afterwards, we explain the relationship between the imperative, C-inspired syntax and its truly functional semantics in detail (Section 2.2).

2.1   A Functional Subset of ISO C

The core of SAC is the subset of ANSI/ISO C [16] for which functional semantics can be defined (surprisingly straightforwardly). Fig. 4 illustrates the similarities and differences between SAC and C. In essence, SAC adopts from C the names of the built-in types, i.e. int for integer numbers, char for ASCI characters, float for single precision and double for double precision floating point numbers. Conceptually, SAC also supports all variants derived by type specifiers such as short, long or unsigned, but for the time being we merely implements the above standard types. Unlike C, SAC properly distinguishes between numerical, character and Boolean values and features a built-in type bool for the latter.

As a functional language SAC uses type inference instead of C-style type declarations. This requires a strict separation of values of different basic types. While type bool is, as expected, inferred for the Boolean constants true and false and character constants like 'a' are obviously of type char, the situation is less clear for numerical constants. Here, we decide that any number constant without decimal point or exponent specification is of type int. Any floating

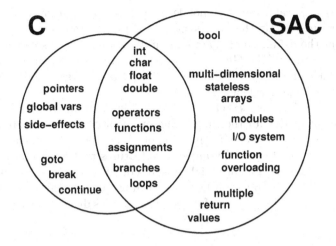

Fig. 4. Similarities and differences between SAC and C

point constant with decimal point or exponent specification is by default of type `double`. A trailing `f` character makes any numerical constant a single precision floating point constant, and a trailing `d` character a double precision floating point constant. For example, 42 is of type `int`, 42.0 is of type `double`, 42.0f and 42f are of type `float` and 42d is again of type `double`. SAC requires explicit conversion between values of different basic types by means of the overloaded conversion functions `toi` (conversion to integer), `toc` conversion to character, `tof` (conversion to single precision floating point), `tod` (conversion to double precision floating point) and `tob` (conversion to Boolean).

Despite these minor differences in details, SAC programs generally look intriguingly similar to C programs. SAC adopts the C syntax for function definitions and function applications that clearly distinguishes between functions and values. Function bodies are essentially sequences of assignments of expressions to variables. While C-style variable declarations are superfluous due to type inference, they are nonetheless permitted and may serve documentation purposes. If present declared types are checked against inferred types.

In addition to constants as explained above, expressions are made up of identifiers, function applications and operator applications. SAC supports most operators from C, among them all arithmetic, relational and logical operators. As usual, Boolean conjunction and disjunction only evaluate their right operand expression if necessary. Furthermore, SAC does also support the tertiary conditional expression operator from C (question mark and colon, in other words a proper functional conditional), operator assignments (e.g. `+=` and `*=`) as well as pre and post increment and decrement operators (i.e. `++` and `--`). For the time being, SAC does not support the bitwise operations of C.

SAC adopts almost all of C's structured control flow constructs: branches with and without alternative (`else`), loops with leading (`while`) and with trailing (do...while) predicate and, last not least, counted loops (for). All of these constructs feature exactly the same syntax as C proper. In case of the for-loop we even adopt the definition of exact semantics as a (preprocessor) transformation into a while-loop [17]. Given the proper separation between Boolean and numerical values, predicates in branches, conditional expressions and loops must be expressions of type bool, not int as in C.

We do not mention C's switch-construct in Fig. 4. While the SAC compiler does not implement this for the time being, our choice is not motivated by any conceptual issues, but solely by engineering effort concerns. In contrast, C does have a number of quintessentially imperative features that we definitely do not want to adopt: pointers, global variables and side effects in general. Moreover, C-style control flow manipulation features, such as goto, break and continue, make no sense in SAC because the functional semantics dispenses with any form of control flow.

```
int gcd( int high, int low)
{
  if (high < low) {
    mem  = low;
    low  = high;
    high = mem;
  }

  while (low != 0) {
    quotient, remainder = diffmod( high, low);
    high = low;
    low  = remainder;
  }

  return high;
}

int, int diffmod( int x, int y)
{
  quot   = x / y;
  remain = x % y;
  return (quot, remain);
}

int main()
{
  return gcd( 22, 27);
}
```

Fig. 5. Example of a core SAC program that illustrates the similarities and differences between SAC and C: greatest common denominator following Euclid's algorithm

The language kernel of SAC is enriched by a number of features as illustrated in Fig. 4. Some of these features are characteristic for SAC, e.g. the multi-dimensional, stateless arrays. Others are mere programming conveniences or state-of-the-art modernisations of C, e.g. a proper module system with information hiding or an I/O system that combines the simplicity of imperative I/O (e.g. simply adding a print statement where one is needed) with a save integration of state manipulation into the purely functional context of SAC "under the hood". Unlike C but in the tradition of C++ SAC also supports function and operator overloading (ad-hoc polymorphism). Syntactically, SAC allows functions to instantaneously yield multiple values. As functions can (of course) take multiple arguments, support for multiple return values creates a nice symmetry between domain and codomain.

Fig. 5 illustrates the (scalar) language kernel of SAC by means of a simple example: Euclid's algorithm to determine the greatest common denominator of two natural numbers. The code in Fig. 5 mainly highlights the syntactical similarity (if not identity) between SAC and C (at least for such simple programs). The code, nonetheless, is not legal C code as it also showcases a SAC-specific language feature: functions with multiple return values. The auxiliary function diffmod instantaneously yields the quotient and the remainder of two integers. Consequently, the function diffmod is defined to yield two integer values and its return-statement contains two expressions. Parentheses are required around multiple return expressions. The application of diffmod demonstrates instantaneous variable binding. Like in C and other languages, a function with the reserved name main defines the starting point of program execution. One may note the complete absence of local variable declarations in Fig. 5.

2.2   Functional Semantics vs. C-Like Syntax

Despite its imperative appearance, SAC is a purely functional programming language. While we refrain from any attempt to define a formal functional semantics for the language kernel, we nonetheless illustrate the main ideas behind combining an imperative syntax with a purely functional semantics. The examples in Figs. 6, 7 and 8 show relevant fragments of SAC code and explain their exact meaning by semantically equivalent OCAML code.

```
int add1( int a, int b)
{                                    let add1 (a,b) =
    c = a + b;                          let c = a + b
    x = 1;              ⟷               in let x = 1
    c = c + x;                          in let c = c + x
    return c;                           in c
}
```

Fig. 6. Semantic equivalence between SAC and OCAML: simple function definitions

Fig. 6 shows a very simple SAC function **add1** whose body merely consists of a sequence of assignments of expressions to variables and a trailing **return**-statement. Semantically, we interpret a sequence of assignments as a sequence of nested **let**-expressions with the return expression serving as the final goal expression of the **let**-cascade. This transformational semantics easily clarifies why and how SAC, despite prominently featuring the term *single assignment* in its name, does actually allow repeated assignment to the "same" variable. Any assignment to a previously defined variable or function parameter is actually an assignment to a fresh variable that merely happens to bear the same name as the variable defined earlier. Standard scoping and visibility rules, even familiar to imperative programmers, clarify that the previously assigned variable can no longer be accessed.

```
int fac( int n)
{
   if (n>1) {
      r = fac( n-1);
      f = n * r;
   }
   else {
      f = 1;
   }
   return f;
}
```

$$\Longleftrightarrow$$

```
let fac n =
   if n>1
   then let r = fac (n-1)
        in let f = n * r
           in f
   else let f = 1
        in f
```

Fig. 7. Semantic equivalence between SAC and OCAML: branching

The functional interpretation of imperative branching constructs is shown in Fig. 7 by means of a recursive definition of the factorial function. In essence, we "copy" the common code following the branching construct including the trailing **return**-statement into both branches. By doing so we transform the C branching statement into a functional OCAML conditional expression. For consistency with the equivalence defined in Fig. 6 we also transform both branches into cascading **let**-expressions.

The functional interpretation of loops requires slightly more effort, but it is immediately apparent that imperative loops are mainly syntactic sugar for tail recursion. Fig. 8 demonstrates this analogy by means of a standard imperative definition of the factorial function using a **while**-loop. Here, we need to turn the loop into a tail-recursive auxiliary function (**fwhile**) that is applied to the argument **n** and the start value **f**. Upon termination the auxiliary function yields the factorial.

```
int fac( int n)
{
    f = 1;

    while (n>1) {
        f = f * n;
        n = n - 1;
    }

    return f;
}
```

$\Longleftrightarrow$

```
let fac n =
    let f = 1
    in let fwhile (f,n) =
        if n>1
        then let f = f * n
            in let n = n - 1
                in fwhile (f,n)
        else f
    in let f = fwhile (f,n)
        in f
```

Fig. 8. Semantic equivalence between SAC and OCAML: while-loops

3   Multidimensional Stateless Arrays

On top of the scalar kernel SAC provides genuine support for truly multidimensional stateless arrays. The section begins with introducing the array calculus and its incorporation into a concrete programming language (Section 3.1) and proceeds to the built-in array functions supported by SAC (Section 3.2). The rest of the section is devoted to WITH-loops, the SAC array comprehension construct. We first introduce the principles (Section 3.3), then we show a complete example (Section 3.4) and finally we provide a complete reference of features (Section 3.5).

3.1   Array Calculus

On top of this language kernel SAC provides genuine support for truly multi-dimensional arrays. In fact, SAC implements an array calculus that dates back to the programming language APL[18,11]. This calculus was later adopted by other array languages, e.g. J[19,13,20] or NIAL[14,21] and also theoretically investigated under the name ψ-calculus [22,23]. In this array calculus any multidimensional array is represented by a natural number, named the *rank*, a vector of natural numbers, named the *shape vector*, and a vector of whatever data type is stored in the array, named the *data vector*. The rank of an array is another word for the number of dimensions or axes. The elements of the shape vector determine the extent of the array along each of the array's dimensions. Hence, the rank of an array equals the length of that array's shape vector, and the product of shape vector elements equals the length of the data vector and, thus, the number of elements of an array. The data vector contains the array's elements along ascending axes with respect to the shape vector, sometimes referred to as *row-major* ordering. Fig. 9 shows a number of example arrays and illustrates the relationships between rank, shape vector and data vector.

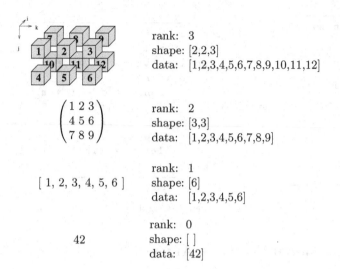

rank: 3
shape: [2,2,3]
data: [1,2,3,4,5,6,7,8,9,10,11,12]

$$\begin{pmatrix} 1\ 2\ 3 \\ 4\ 5\ 6 \\ 7\ 8\ 9 \end{pmatrix}$$

rank: 2
shape: [3,3]
data: [1,2,3,4,5,6,7,8,9]

[1, 2, 3, 4, 5, 6]

rank: 1
shape: [6]
data: [1,2,3,4,5,6]

42

rank: 0
shape: [ ]
data: [42]

Fig. 9. Truly multidimensional arrays in SAC and their representation by data vector, shape vector and rank scalar

More formally, let A be an n-dimensional array represented by the rank scalar n, the shape vector $s_A = [s_0, \ldots, s_{n-1}]$ and the data vector $d_A = [d_0, \ldots, d_{m-1}]$. Then the equation

$$m = \prod_{i=0}^{n-1} s_i$$

describes the correspondence between the shape vector and the length of the data vector. Moreover, the set of legal index vectors of the array A is defined as

$$\mathcal{IV}_A := \{ [iv_0, \ldots, iv_{n-1}] \mid \forall j \in \{0, \ldots, n-1\} : 0 \leq iv_j < s_j \} .$$

An index vector $iv = [iv_0, \ldots, iv_{n-1}]$ denotes the element d_k of the data vector d_A of array A if iv is a legal index vector of A, i.e. $iv \in \mathcal{IV}_A$, and the equation

$$k = \sum_{i=0}^{n-1} \left(iv_i * \prod_{j=i+1}^{n-1} s_j \right)$$

holds. Two arrays A and B are *conformable* iff they have the same element type and the same number of elements:

$$|d_A| = |d_B|$$

A vector of natural numbers s is *shape-conformable* to an array A iff the product of the elements of the vector equals the number of elements of the array:

$$\prod_{i=0}^{n-1} s_i = |d_A|$$

As already shown in Fig. 9 the array calculus nicely extends to scalars. A scalar value has the rank zero and the empty vector as shape vector; the data vector contains a single element, the scalar value itself. This is completely consistent with the rules sketched out before. The rank determines the number of elements in the shape vector. As the rank of a scalar is zero, so is the number of elements in the shape vector. The product of all elements of the shape vector determines the number of elements in the data vector. The product of an empty sequence of values is one, i.e. the neutral element of multiplication.

Unifying scalars and arrays within a common calculus allows us to say that any value in SAC is an array, and as such it has a rank, a shape vector and a data vector. Furthermore, we achieve a complete separation between data and structural information (i.e. rank and shape).

3.2   Built-In Operations on Arrays

In contrast to all its ancestors, from APL to the ψ-calculus, SAC only defines a very small number of built-in operations on multidimensional arrays. They are directly related to the underlying calculus:

- dim(a)
  yields the rank scalar of array a;
- shape(a)
  yields the shape vector of array a;
- sel(iv, a)
  yields the element of array a at index location iv, provided that iv is a legal index vector into array a according to the definition above;
- reshape(sv, a)
  yields an array that has shape sv and the same data vector as array a, provided that sv and a are shape-conformable;
- modarray(a, iv, v)
  yields an array with the same rank and shape as array a, where all elements are the same as in array a except for index location iv where the element is set to value v.

For the convenience of programmers SAC supports some syntactic sugar to express applications of the sel and modarray built-in functions:

$$\text{sel(} iv, \ a \text{)} \quad \equiv \quad a\,[iv]$$
$$a \ = \ \text{modarray(} a, \ iv, \ v \text{)}; \quad \equiv \quad a\,[iv] \ = \ v\,;$$

Fig. 10 further illustrates the SAC array calculus and its built-in functions by a number of examples. Most notably, selection supports any prefix of a legal index vector. The rank of the selected subarray equals the difference between the rank of the argument array and the length of the index vector. Consequently, if the length of the index vector coincides with the rank of the array, the rank of the result is zero, i.e. a single element of the array is selected.

$$
\begin{aligned}
\texttt{vec} &\equiv \texttt{[4,5,6,7]} \\
\texttt{mat} &\equiv \begin{pmatrix} 0 & 1 & 2 & 3 \\ 4 & 5 & 6 & 7 \\ 8 & 9 & 10 & 11 \end{pmatrix} \\
\texttt{dim(mat)} &\equiv \texttt{2} \\
\texttt{shape(mat)} &\equiv \texttt{[3,4]} \\
\texttt{dim(vec)} &\equiv \texttt{1} \\
\texttt{shape(vec)} &\equiv \texttt{[4]} \\
\texttt{mat[[1,2]]} &\equiv \texttt{6} \\
\texttt{vec[[3]]} &\equiv \texttt{7} \\
\texttt{mat[[]]} &\equiv \texttt{mat} \\
\texttt{mat[[1]]} &\equiv \texttt{vec} \\
\texttt{mat} &\equiv \texttt{reshape([3,4], [0,1,2,3,4,5,6,7,8,9,10,11])} \\
\texttt{[[4,5],[6,7]]} &\equiv \texttt{reshape([2,2], vec)}
\end{aligned}
$$

Fig. 10. SAC built-in functions in the context of the array calculus

3.3   With-Loop Array Comprehension

With only five built-in array operations (i.e. **dim**, **shape**, **sel**, **reshape** and **modarray**) SAC leaves the beaten track of array-oriented programming languages like APL and FORTRAN-90 and their derivatives. Instead of providing dozens if not a hundred or more hard-wired array operations such as element-wise extensions of scalar operators and functions, structural operations like shift and rotate along one or multiple axes and reduction operations with eligible built-in and user-defined operations like sum and product, SAC features a single but versatile array comprehension construct: the WITH-loop.

WITH-loops can be used to implement all the above and many more array operations in SAC itself. We make intensive use of this feature and provide a comprehensive standard library of array operations. Compared to hard-wired array support this approach offers a number of advantages. For instance, we can keep the language design of SAC fairly lean, the library implementations of array operations do not carve their exact semantics in stone and SAC users can easily extend and adapt the array library to their individual needs.

WITH-loops facilitate the specification of **map**- and **reduce**-like aggregate array operations. They come in three variants, named **genarray**, **modarray** and **fold**, as illustrated by means of simple examples in Figs. 11, 12 and 13, respectively. Since the WITH-loop is by far the most important and most extensive syntactical extension of SAC, we also provide a formal definition of the syntax in Fig. 14. For didactic purposes we begin with a simplified form of WITH-loops here and discuss a number of extensions in the following section.

We start with the **genarray**-variant in Fig. 11. Any WITH-loop array comprehension expression begins with the key word **with** (line 1) followed by a *partition* enclosed in curly brackets (line 2), a colon and an *operator* that defines the WITH-loop variant, here the key word **genarray**. The **genarray**-variant is an array comprehension that defines an array whose shape is determined by the first expression following the key word **genarray**. By default all element values

```
A = with {
     ([1,1] <= iv < [4,4]) : e(iv);
   }: genarray( [5,4],  def );
```

[0,0]	[0,1]	[0,2]	[0,3]
[1,0]	[1,1]	[1,2]	[1,3]
[2,0]	[2,1]	[2,2]	[2,3]
[3,0]	[3,1]	[3,2]	[3,3]
[4,0]	[4,1]	[4,2]	[4,3]

$\Longrightarrow$

$[\![def]\!]$	$[\![def]\!]$	$[\![def]\!]$	$[\![def]\!]$
$[\![def]\!]$	$[\![e[iv \leftarrow [1,1]]]\!]$	$[\![e[iv \leftarrow [1,2]]]\!]$	$[\![e[iv \leftarrow [1,3]]]\!]$
$[\![def]\!]$	$[\![e[iv \leftarrow [2,1]]]\!]$	$[\![e[iv \leftarrow [2,2]]]\!]$	$[\![e[iv \leftarrow [2,3]]]\!]$
$[\![def]\!]$	$[\![e[iv \leftarrow [3,1]]]\!]$	$[\![e[iv \leftarrow [3,2]]]\!]$	$[\![e[iv \leftarrow [3,3]]]\!]$
$[\![def]\!]$	$[\![def]\!]$	$[\![def]\!]$	$[\![def]\!]$

Fig. 11. The `genarray`-variant of the WITH-loop array comprehension

are defined by the second expression, the so-called *default expression*. The *shape expression* (i.e. the first expression after the key word `genarray`) must evaluate to a non-negative integer vector. The example WITH-loop in Fig. 11, hence, defines a matrix with 5 rows and 4 columns.

The middle part of the WITH-loop, the *partition* (line 2 in Fig. 11), defines a rectangular index subset of the defined array. A partition consists of a *generator* and an *associated expression*. The generator defines a set of index vectors along with an *index variable* representing elements of this set. Two expressions, which must evaluate to non-negative integer vectors of the same length as the value of the shape expression, define lower and upper bounds of a rectangular range of index vectors. For each element of this index vector set defined by the generator, the associated expression is evaluated with the index variable instantiated according to the index position. In the case of the `genarray`-variant the resulting value defines the element value at the corresponding index location of the array.

The default expression itself is optional with an element type dependent default default value, i.e. the fitting variant of zero (`false`, `'\0'`, 0, 0f, 0d for types `bool`, `char`, `int`, `float`, `double`, respectively). If possible the compiler adds the appropriate value. A default expression may not even be needed if the generator already covers the entire index set.

The second WITH-loop-variant is the `modarray`-variant illustrated in Fig. 12. While the partition (line 2) is syntactically and semantically equivalent to the `genarray`-variant, the definition of the array's shape and the default rule for element values that are not contained in the generator-defined index set are different. The key word `modarray` is followed by a single expression. The newly defined array takes its shape from the value of that expression, i.e. we define an array that has the same shape as a previously defined array. Likewise, the element values at index positions not covered by the generator are obtained from the corresponding elements of that array. It is important to note that the `modarray`-WITH-loop does not destructively overwrite the element values of the existing array, as it would be common in the imperative world. Since SAC is a purely functional language, we semantically define a new array value that lives aside the existing one.

```
B = with {
      ([1,1] <= iv < [4,4]) : e(iv);
    }: modarray( A);
```

[0,0]	[0,1]	[0,2]	[0,3]
[1,0]	[1,1]	[1,2]	[1,3]
[2,0]	[2,1]	[2,2]	[2,3]
[3,0]	[3,1]	[3,2]	[3,3]
[4,0]	[4,1]	[4,2]	[4,3]

$\Longrightarrow$

$[\![A[[0,0]]]\!]$	$[\![A[[0,1]]]\!]$	$[\![A[[0,2]]]\!]$	$[\![A[[0,3]]]\!]$
$[\![A[[1,0]]]\!]$	$[\![e[iv \leftarrow [1,1]]]\!]$	$[\![e[iv \leftarrow [1,2]]]\!]$	$[\![e[iv \leftarrow [1,3]]]\!]$
$[\![A[[2,0]]]\!]$	$[\![e[iv \leftarrow [2,1]]]\!]$	$[\![e[iv \leftarrow [2,2]]]\!]$	$[\![e[iv \leftarrow [2,3]]]\!]$
$[\![A[[3,0]]]\!]$	$[\![e[iv \leftarrow [3,1]]]\!]$	$[\![e[iv \leftarrow [3,2]]]\!]$	$[\![e[iv \leftarrow [3,3]]]\!]$
$[\![A[[4,0]]]\!]$	$[\![A[[4,1]]]\!]$	$[\![A[[4,2]]]\!]$	$[\![A[[4,3]]]\!]$

Fig. 12. The modarray-variant of the WITH-loop array comprehension

The third WITH-loop-variant supports the definition of reduction operations. It is characterised by the key word fold followed by the name of an eligible reduction function or operator and the neutral element of that function or operator. For certain built-in functions and operators the compiler is aware of the neutral element, and an explicit specification can be left out. SAC requires fold functions or operators to expect two arguments of the same type and to yield one value of that type. Fold functions must be associative and commutative. These requirements are stronger than in other languages with explicit reductions (e.g. foldl and foldr in many mainstream functional languages). This is motivated by the absence of an order on the generator defined index subset and ultimately by the wish to facilitate parallel implementations of reductions.

```
B = with {
      ([1,1] <= iv < [4,4]) : e(iv);
    }: fold( ⊕, neutr);
```

[1,1]	[1,2]	[1,3]
[2,1]	[2,2]	[2,3]
[3,1]	[3,2]	[3,3]

$\Longrightarrow$

$[\![neutr]\!] \oplus [\![e[iv \leftarrow [1,1]]]\!] \oplus [\![e[iv \leftarrow [1,2]]]\!] \oplus [\![e[iv \leftarrow [1,3]]]\!]$
$\oplus [\![e[iv \leftarrow [2,1]]]\!] \oplus [\![e[iv \leftarrow [2,2]]]\!] \oplus [\![e[iv \leftarrow [2,3]]]\!]$
$\oplus [\![e[iv \leftarrow [3,1]]]\!] \oplus [\![e[iv \leftarrow [3,2]]]\!] \oplus [\![e[iv \leftarrow [3,3]]]\!]$

Fig. 13. The fold-variant of the WITH-loop array comprehension

Note that the SAC compiler cannot verify associativity and commutativity of user-defined functions. It is the programmer's responsibility to ensure these properties. Using a function or operator in a fold-WITH-loop acts as an implicit assertion of the required properties. To be precise, neither floating point nor integer machine arithmetic is strictly speaking associative. It is up to the programmer to judge whether or not overflow/underflow in integer computations or numerical stability issues in floating point computations are relevant. If so and the exact order in which a reduction is performed does matter, the fold-WITH-loop is not the right choice. Instead, sequential loops as in C should be used. This is not a specific problem of SAC, but is owed to parallel reduction in general. The same issues appear in all programming environments that support parallel reductions, e.g. the reduction clause in OPENMP[24,25] or the collective operations in MPI[26].

WithLoopExpr	$\Rightarrow$	**with**	$\{$ *Partition* $\}$	:	*Operator*
Partition	$\Rightarrow$	*Generator*	:	*Expr*	;
Generator	$\Rightarrow$	(*Expr RelOp Identifier RelOp Expr*)			
RelOp	$\Rightarrow$	<=	<			
Operation	$\Rightarrow$	**genarray** (*Expr* [, *Expr*])			
			modarray (*Expr*)		
			fold (*FoldOp* [, *Expr*])		
FoldOp	$\Rightarrow$	*Identifier*	*BinOp*			

Fig. 14. Formal definition of the (simplified) syntax of WITH-loop expressions

3.4 With-Loop Examples

Following the rather formal introduction of WITH-loops in the previous section we now illustrate the concept and its use by a series of examples. For instance, the matrix

$$A = \begin{pmatrix} 0 & 1 & 2 & 3 & 4 & 5 & 6 & 7 & 8 & 9 \\ 10 & 11 & 12 & 13 & 14 & 15 & 16 & 17 & 18 & 19 \\ 20 & 21 & 22 & 23 & 24 & 25 & 26 & 27 & 28 & 29 \\ 30 & 31 & 32 & 33 & 34 & 35 & 36 & 37 & 38 & 39 \\ 40 & 41 & 42 & 43 & 44 & 45 & 46 & 47 & 48 & 49 \end{pmatrix}$$

can be defined by the following WITH-loop:

```
A = with {
    ([0,0] <= iv < [5,10]) : iv[[0]] * 10 + iv[[1]];
}: genarray( [5,10]);
```

Note here that the generator variable iv denotes a 2-element integer vector. Hence, the scalar index values need to be extracted through selection prior to computing the new array's element value.

The following `modarray`-WITH-loop defines the new array B that like A is a 5×10 matrix where all inner elements equal the corresponding values of A incremented by 50 while the remaining boundary elements are obtained from A without modification:

```
B = with {
    ([1,1] <= iv < [4,9]) : A[iv] + 50;
}: modarray( A );
```

This example WITH-loop defines the following matrix:

$$B = \begin{pmatrix} 0 & 1 & 2 & 3 & 4 & 5 & 6 & 7 & 8 & 9 \\ 10 & 61 & 62 & 63 & 64 & 65 & 66 & 67 & 68 & 19 \\ 20 & 71 & 72 & 73 & 74 & 75 & 76 & 77 & 78 & 29 \\ 30 & 81 & 82 & 83 & 84 & 85 & 86 & 87 & 88 & 39 \\ 40 & 41 & 42 & 43 & 44 & 45 & 46 & 47 & 48 & 49 \end{pmatrix}$$

Last not least, the following fold-WITH-loop computes the sum of all elements of array B:

```
sum =   with {
            ([0,0] <= iv < [5,10]) : B[iv];
        }: fold( +, 0);
```
which yields 2425.

3.5   Advanced Aspects of With-Loops

So far, we have focussed on the principles of WITH-loops and restricted ourselves to a simplified view. In fact, WITH-loops are much more versatile; Fig. 15 defines the complete syntax that we now explain step by step.

We begin with a major extension: a WITH-loop may have multiple partitions instead of a single one. With multiple partitions, disjoint index subsets of an array may be computed according to different specifications. For example, the WITH-loop

```
A = with {
        ([0,0] <= iv < [5, 8]) : iv[[0]] * 10 + iv[[1]];
        ([0,8] <= iv < [5,10]) : iv[[0]] + iv[[1]];
    }: genarray( [5,10], 0);
```
yields the matrix

$$A = \begin{pmatrix} 0 & 1 & 2 & 3 & 4 & 5 & 6 & 7 & 8 & 9 \\ 10 & 11 & 12 & 13 & 14 & 15 & 16 & 17 & 9 & 10 \\ 20 & 21 & 22 & 23 & 24 & 25 & 26 & 27 & 10 & 11 \\ 30 & 31 & 32 & 33 & 34 & 35 & 36 & 37 & 11 & 12 \\ 40 & 41 & 42 & 43 & 44 & 45 & 46 & 47 & 12 & 13 \end{pmatrix}$$

where the left 8 columns are defined according to the first partition and the right 2 columns according to the second partition. One question that immediately arises when defining multiple partitions is what happens if the index sets defined by the generators are not pairwise disjoint. Since this question is generally undecidable for the compiler, we define that the in textual order last partition that covers a certain index defines the corresponding value.

$WithLoopExpr$ $\Rightarrow$ **with** $\{$ $\big[$ *Partition* $\big]+$ $\}$: *OperatorList*

$Partition$ $\Rightarrow$ *Generator* $\big[$ *Block* $\big]$: *ExprList* ;

$Generator$ $\Rightarrow$ (*Bound RelOp GenVar RelOp Bound* $\big[$ *Filter* $\big]$)

$Bound$ $\Rightarrow$ *Expr* | .

$RelOp$ $\Rightarrow$ **<=** | **<**

$GenVar$ $\Rightarrow$ *Identifier*
| *IdentifierVector*
| *Identifier* **=** *IdentifierVector*

$IdentifierVector$ $\Rightarrow$ **[** $\big[$ *Identifier* $\big[$ **,** *Identifier* $\big]^*$ $\big]$ **]**

$Filter$ $\Rightarrow$ **step** *Expr* $\big[$ **width** *Expr* $\big]$

$ExprList$ $\Rightarrow$ *Expr* $\big[$ **,** *Expr* $\big]^*$

$OperatorList$ $\Rightarrow$ *Operator*
| (*Operator* $\big[$ **,** *Operator* $\big]^*$)

$Operator$ $\Rightarrow$ **genarray** (*Expr* $\big[$ **,** *Expr* $\big]$)
| **modarray** (*Expr*)
| **fold** (*FoldOp* $\big[$ **,** *Expr* $\big]$)

$FoldOp$ $\Rightarrow$ *Identifier* | *BinOp*

Fig. 15. Formal definition of the full syntax of WITH-loop-expressions

As in the previous example, it is often handy to access the scalar elements of the generator variable directly, instead of explicitly selecting elements inside the associated expression:

```
A = with {
      ([0,0] <= [i,j] < [5, 8]) : i * 10 + j;
      ([0,8] <= [i,j] < [5,10]) : i + j;
    }: genarray( [5,10]);
```

In fact, one can even use the generator variable in vector and scalar form in the same partition.

A significant extension of all WITH-loop variants concerns the generators. Rather than defining dense rectangular index spaces, extended generators may also define sparse periodic patterns of indices. For example, the WITH-loop

```
A = with {
      ([0,0] <= [i,j] < [5,10] step [1,2]) : i * 10 + j;
    }: genarray( [5,10], 0);
```

yields the matrix

$$\begin{pmatrix} 0\,0 & 20 & 40 & 60 & 80 \\ 10\,0 & 12\,0 & 14\,0 & 16\,0 & 18\,0 \\ 20\,0 & 22\,0 & 24\,0 & 26\,0 & 28\,0 \\ 30\,0 & 32\,0 & 34\,0 & 36\,0 & 38\,0 \\ 40\,0 & 42\,0 & 44\,0 & 46\,0 & 48\,0 \end{pmatrix}$$

An additional *width* specification allows generators to define generalised periodic grids as in the following example where

```
A = with {
        ([0,0] <= iv < [5,10] step [4,4] width [2,2]) : 9;
        ([0,2] <= iv < [5,10] step [4,4] width [2,2]) : 0;
        ([2,0] <= iv < [5,10] step [4,1] width [2,1]) : 1;
    }: genarray( [5,10]);
```

yields

$$\begin{pmatrix} 9\,9\,0\,0\,9\,9\,0\,0\,9\,9 \\ 9\,9\,0\,0\,9\,9\,0\,0\,9\,9 \\ 1\,1\,1\,1\,1\,1\,1\,1\,1\,1 \\ 1\,1\,1\,1\,1\,1\,1\,1\,1\,1 \\ 9\,9\,0\,0\,9\,9\,0\,0\,9\,9 \end{pmatrix}$$

Expressions that define step and width vectors must evaluate to positive integer vectors of the same length as the other vectors of the generator. The full range of generators can be used with all WITH-loop variants.

In order to give a formal definition of index sets, let a, b, s, and w denote expressions that evaluate to appropriate vectors of length n. Then, the generator

$$(\ a \ \text{<=} \ \text{iv} \ \text{<} \ b \ \text{step} \ s \ \text{width} \ w \ )$$

defines the following set of index vectors:

$$\{ \ iv \ | \ \forall_{j \in \{0,\dots,n-1\}} : a_j \le iv_j < b_j \ \wedge \ (iv_j - a_j) \ \bmod \ s_j < w_j \ \} \quad .$$

The last major extension concerns the operator. Actually, WITH-loops may come with a list of operators, and a single WITH-loop may combine multiple variants. For instance the WITH-loop

```
mini , maxi = with {
                ([0,0] <= iv < [5,10]) : A[iv], A[iv];
            }: (fold( min), fold( max));
```

simultaneously defines the minimum and the maximum value of the previously defined array A. Each generator is associated with a comma-separated list of expressions that correspond to the comma-separated list of operators. As this example illustrates, it is often handy to have the generator-associated expressions be preceded by a local block of assignments to abstract away complex or common subexpressions. Hence, the above example could also be written as

```
mini , maxi = with {
                ([0,0] <= iv < [5,10]) {
                                        a = A[iv];
                                    }: a, a;
            }: (fold( min), fold( max));
```

In practice, WITH-loops are often much simpler than they could be. Quite commonly they define homogeneous array operations where all elements of the index space are treated in the same way: a single generator covers the whole index space. To facilitate specification of the common case, dots may replace the bound expressions in generators. A dot as lower bound represents the least and a dot as upper bound represents the greatest legal index vector with respect to the shape vector of a genarray-WITH-loop or the shape of the referenced array in a modarray-WITH-loop. The lack of a reference shape restricts this feature in the case of a fold-WITH-loop to the lower bound. Here, a dot represents a vector of zeros with the same length as the vector defining the upper bound.

4 Programming Methodology

So far we have introduced the most relevant language features of SAC. In this section, we explain the methodology of programming in SAC, i.e. how the language features can be combined to write actual programs. We begin with the array type system of SAC (Section 4.1) and proceed to explain overloading (Section 4.2) and user-defined types (Section 4.3). At last, we explain the two major software engineering principles advocated by SAC: the principle of abstraction (Section 4.4) and the principle of composition (Section 4.5).

4.1 Array Type System

In Section 2 we introduced the basic types mostly adopted from C (i.e. int, float, double, char and bool). In Section 3 we discussed how to create arrays, but we carefully avoided any questions regarding the exact type of some integer matrix or double vector. We catch up with this deficit now.

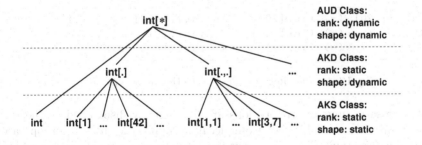

Fig. 16. The SAC array type system with the subtyping hierarchy

While SAC is monomorphic in scalar types including the base types of arrays, any scalar type immediately induces a hierarchy of array types with subtyping. Fig. 16 illustrates this type hierarchy for the example of the base type int. The shapely type hierarchy has three levels characterised by different amounts of compile time knowledge about shape and rank. On the lowest level of the subtyping hierarchy (i.e. the most specific types) we have complete compile time knowledge on the structure of an array: both rank and shape are fixed. We call this class *AKS* for *array of known shape.*

On an intermediate level of the subtyping hierarchy we still know the rank of an array, but abstract from its concrete shape. We call this class *AKD* for *array of known dimension.* For example, a vector of unknown length or a matrix of unknown size fall into this category. Note the special case for arrays of rank zero (aka scalars). Since there is only one vector of length zero, the empty vector, the shape of a rank-zero array is automatically known and the type int[] is merely an uncommon synonym for int.

Each type hierarchy also has a most common supertype that neither prescribes shape nor rank at compile time. We call such types *AUD* for *array of unknown dimension.* The syntax of array types is motivated by the common syntax for regular expressions: the Kleene star in the AUD type stands for any number of dots, including none.

4.2   Overloading

SaC supports overloading with respect to the array type hierarchy. The example in Fig. 17 shows three overloaded instances of the subtraction operator, one for 20×20-matrices, one for matrices of some shape and one for arrays of any rank and shape. As usual in subtyping there is a monotony restriction. For any two instances F_1 and F_2 of some function F with the same number of parameters and the same base types for each parameter either each parameter type of F_1 is a subtype of the corresponding parameter type of F_2 or vice versa. Function instances with different numbers of parameters are distinguished syntactically and there is no such restriction.

```
int[20,20]  (-) (int[20,20] A, int[20,20] B) {...}
int[.,.]    (-) (int[.,.]   A, int[.,.]   B) {...}
int[*]      (-) (int[*]     A, int[*]     B) {...}
```

Fig. 17. Overloading with respect to the array type hierarchy

If necessary, function applications are dynamically dispatched to the most specific instance available. For example, if we apply the subtraction operator, under the definition of Fig. 17, to two integer matrices of unknown shape (AKD class), we can statically rule out the third instance because the second instance fits and is more specific. However, we can not rule out the first instance as the argument matrices at runtime could turn out to be of shape 20×20 and then the more specific first instance must be preferred over the more general second instance.

4.3   User-Defined Types

SAC supports user-defined types in very much the same way as many other languages: any type can be abstracted by a name. Following our general design principles, SAC adopts the C syntax for type definitions. For example, a type complex for complex numbers can be defined as a two-element vector by the following type definition:

```
typedef double[2] complex;
```

This type definition induces a further complete subtyping hierarchy with overloading. In contrast to C, however, SAC user-defined types are real data types and not just type synonyms. Values require explicit conversion between the defining type and the defined type or vice versa. Such conversions use the familiar syntax of C type casts. In fact, this notation is mainly intended as an implementation vehicle for proper conversion functions. Fig. 18 illustrates programming with user-defined types by an excerpt from the standard library's module for complex arithmetic.

```
typedef double[2] complex;

complex toc( double real, double imag)
{
  return (complex) [real, imag];
}

double real( complex cpx)
{
  return ((double[2])cpx)[[0]];
}

double imag( complex cpx)
{
  return ((double[2])cpx)[[1]];
}

complex (+) (complex a, complex b)
{
  return toc( real(a) + real(b), imag(a) + imag(b));
}

complex (*) (complex a, complex b)
{
  return toc( real(a) * real(b) - imag(a) * imag(b),
              real(a) * imag(b) + imag(a) * real(b));
}
```

Fig. 18. Basic definitions for complex numbers: type definition, conversion functions making use of the type cast notation and overloaded definitions of arithmetic operators based on the conversion functions introduced before

A few restrictions apply to user-defined types. The defining type must be an AKS type, i.e. another scalar type or a type with static shape, as in the case of type `complex` defined above. We have been working on removing this restriction and supporting truly nested arrays, i.e. arrays where the elements are again arrays of different shape and potentially different rank. For now, however, this is an experimental feature of SAC; details can be found in [27].

4.4   The Principle of Abstraction

As pointed out in Section 3.2 SAC only features a very small set of built-in array operations. Commonly used aggregate array operations are defined in SAC itself in a completely generic way. Although not built-in, aggregate array operations are applicable to arguments of any rank and shape. A prerequisite for this design are the shape-generic programming capabilities of WITH-loops. As introduced in Sections 3.3 and 3.5, all relevant syntactic positions of WITH-loops may host arbitrary expressions. In the examples so far we merely used constant vectors for the purpose of illustration. In practice, WITH-loops are key to shape- and rank-generic definitions of array operations.

Fig. 19 demonstrates the transition from a shape-specific implementation over a shape-generic implementation to a rank-generic implementation taking element-wise subtraction of two arrays as a running example. The first (overloaded) instance of the subtraction operator is defined for 20×20 integer matrices. It makes use of a single WITH-loop and essentially maps the built-in scalar subtraction operator to all corresponding elements of the two argument arrays. As the shape of the matrix is fixed, we can simply use constant vectors in the syntactic positions for result shape, lower bound and upper bound.

Of course, it is neither productive nor elegant or even possible to explicitly overload the subtraction operator for each potential argument array shape. The second instance in Fig. 19 sticks to the two-dimensional case, but abstracts from the concrete size of argument matrices. This generalisation immediately raises an important question: how to deal with argument arrays of different shape? There are various plausible answers to this question, and the solution adopted in our example is to compute the element-wise minimum of the shape vectors of the two argument arrays. With this solution we safely avoid out-of-bound indexing while at the same time restricting the function domain as little as possible. The resulting vector `shp` is used both in the shape expression of the `genarray`-WITH-loop and as upper bound in the generator. Since indexing in SAC always starts at zero, we can stick to a constant vector as lower bound. Note that the generator-associated expression remains unchanged from the shape-specific instance.

One could argue that in practice, it is very rare to encounter problems that require more than 4 dimensions, and, thus, we could simply define all relevant operations for one, two, three and four dimensions. However, for a binary operator that alone would already require the definition of 16 instances. Hence, it is of practical relevance and not just theoretical beauty to also abstract from the rank of argument arrays, not only the shapes, and to support fully rank-generic programming.

```
int [20,20] (-) (int [20,20] A, int [20,20] B)
{
  res = with {
          ([0,0] <= iv < [20,20]) : A[iv] - B[iv];
        }: genarray( [20,20], 0);
  return res;
}

int [.,.] (-) (int [.,.] A, int [.,.] B)
{
  shp = min( shape(A), shape(B));
  res = with {
          ([0,0] <= iv < shp) : A[iv] - B[iv];
        }: genarray( shp, 0);
  return res;
}

int [*] (-) (int [*] A, int [*] B)
{
  shp = min( shape(A), shape(B));
  res = with {
          (0*shp <= iv < shp) : A[iv] - B[iv];
        }: genarray( shp, 0);
  return res;
}
```

Fig. 19. Three overloaded instances of the subtraction operator for arrays of known shape (AKS, top), arrays of known dimension (AKD, middle) and arrays of unknown dimension (AUD, bottom)

The third instance of the subtraction operator in Fig. 19 demonstrates this further abstraction step. Apart from using the most general array type int [*], the rank-generic instance is surprisingly similar to the rank-specific one. The main issue is an appropriate definition of the generator's lower bound, i.e. a vector of zeros whose length equals that of the shape expression. We achieve this by multiplying the shape vector with zero.

So far, we expected argument arrays to be at least of the same shape. With a rank-generic type, however, we must also consider argument arrays of different rank. What would happen if we apply the subtraction operator to a 10-element vector and a 5 × 5-matrix? The shapes of the argument arrays are, consequently, [10] and [5,5], respectively. Assuming an implementation of the minimum function along the lines of the subtraction operator discussed here, we obtain [5] as the minimum of the two vectors. Thus, the WITH-loop defines a 5-element vector whose elements are homogeneously defined as the subtraction of the corresponding elements from the argument arrays A and B. Since A is a vector and we select using a 1-element index vector, selection yields a scalar. As array B is a matrix, selection with a 1-element index vector yields a (row) vector. As a consequence, the subtraction in the body of the WITH-loop does not refer to the built-in scalar subtraction, but recursively back to the rank-generic instance. Whereas the type of this instance suggests to support a scalar and a vector argument, the definition inevitably leads to non-terminating recursion. We can easily avoid this by defining two more overloaded instances of the subtraction operator that cover the cases where one argument is scalar, as shown in Fig. 20.

```
int [*]  (-)  (int  A ,  int [*]  B)
{
  shp = shape(B);
  res = with {
          (0*shp <= iv < shp)  :  A - B[iv];
        }: genarray( shp, 0);
  return res;
}

int [*]  (-)  (int [*]  A ,  int  B)
{
  shp = shape(A);
  res = with {
          (0*shp <= iv < shp)  :  A[iv] - B;
        }: genarray( shp, 0);
  return res;
}
```

Fig. 20. Additional overloaded instances of the subtraction operator as they are found in the SAC standard library

It is one of the strengths of SAC that the exact behaviour of array operations is not hard-wired into the language definition. This sets SAC apart from all other languages with dedicated array support. Alternative to our above solution with the minimum shape, one could argue that any attempt to subtract two argument arrays of different shape is a programming error as in FORTRAN-90 or APL. The same could be achieved in SAC by comparing the two argument shapes and raising an exception if they differ. The important message here is that SAC does not impose a particular solution on its users: anyone can provide an alternative array module implementation with the desired behaviour.

A potential wish for future versions of SAC is support for a richer type system, in which shape relations like equality can be properly expressed in the array types. For example, matrix multiplication could be defined with a type signature along the lines of

```
double[a,c] matmul( double[a,b] X, double[b,c] Y)
```

This leads to a system of dependent array types that we have studied in the context of the dependently typed array language Qube [28,29]. However, how to carry these ideas over to SAC in the presence of overloading and dynamic dispatch requires a plethora of future research.

4.5 The Principle of Composition

The generic programming examples of the previous section open up an avenue to define a large body of array operations by means of WITH-loops. For instance, Fig. 21 shows the definition of a generic convergence check. Two argument arrays new and old are deemed to be convergent if for every element (reduction with logical conjunction) the absolute difference between the new and the old value is less than a given threshold eps.

```
bool is_convergent (double[*] new, double[*] old, double eps)
{
    shp = min( shape(new), shape(old));
    res = with {
            (. <= iv < shp) : abs(new[iv] - old[iv]) < eps;
          }: fold( &&);
    return res;
}
```

Fig. 21. Rank-generic definition of a convergence check

While defining the convergence check as in Fig. 21 is a viable approach, it lacks a certain elegance: we indeed re-invent the wheel with the minimum shape computation, that is actually only needed for the element-wise subtraction, for which we have already solved the issue with the code shown in Fig. 20. A closer look into the WITH-loop quickly reveals that we deal with a computational pipeline of basic operations on array elements. This can be much more elegantly and concisely expressed following the other guiding software engineering principle in SAC: the *principle of composition*.

```
bool is_convergent (double[*] new, double[*] old, double eps)
{
    return all( abs( new - old) < eps);
}
```

Fig. 22. Programming by composition: specification of a generic convergence check

As demonstrated in Fig. 22, the compositional specification of the convergence check is entirely based on applications of predefined array operations from the SAC standard library: element-wise subtraction, absolute value, element-wise comparison and reduction with Boolean conjunction. This example demonstrates how application code can be designed in an entirely index-, loop-, and comprehension-free style.

Ideally the use of WITH-loops as versatile but accordingly complex language construct would be confined to defining basic array operations like the ones used in the definition of the convergence check. And, ideally all application code would solely be composed out of these basic building blocks. This leads to a highly productive software engineering process, substantial code reuse, good readability of code and, last not least, high confidence into the correctness of programs. The case study on generic convolution developed in Section 5 further demonstrates how the principle of composition can be applied in practice.

5   Case Study: Convolution

In this section we illustrate the ins and outs of SAC programming by means of a case study: convolution. Following a short introduction to the algorithmic principle (Section 5.1) we show a variety of implementations of individual convolution steps that illustrate the principles of abstraction and composition. (Sections 5.2–5.5). Finally, we extend our work to an iterative process (Section 5.6).

5.1   Algorithmic Principle

Convolution follows a fairly simple algorithmic principle. Essentially, we deal with a regular, potentially multidimensional grid of data cells, as illustrated in Fig. 23. Convolution is an iterative process on this data grid: in each iteration (often referred to as *temporal dimension* in contrast to the *spatial dimensions* of the grid) the value at each grid point is recomputed as a function of the existing old value and the values of a certain neighbourhood of grid points. This neighbourhood is often referred to as *stencil*, and it very much characterises the convolution.

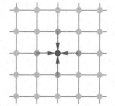 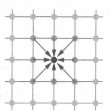

Fig. 23. Algorithmic principle of convolution, shown is the 2-dimensional case with a 5-point stencil (left) and a 9-point stencil (right)

In Fig. 23 we show two common stencils. With a *five-point stencil* (left) only the four direct neighbours in the two-dimensional grid are relevant. By including the four diagonal neighbours we end up with a *nine-point stencil* (right) and so on. In the context of cellular automata these neighbourhoods are often referred to as *von Neumann neighbourhood* and *Moore neighbourhood*, respectively. With higher-dimensional grids, we obtain different neighbourhood sizes, but the principle can straightforwardly be carried over to any number of dimensions.

Since any concrete grid is finite, boundary elements leaves essentially two choices: *cyclic boundary conditions* and *static boundary conditions*. In the former case the neighbourship relation is defined round-robin, i.e., the left neighbour of the leftmost element is the rightmost element and vice versa. In the latter case the grid is surrounded by a layer of elements that remain constant throughout the convolution process.

In principle, any function from a set of neighbouring data points to a single new one is possible, but in practice variants of weighted sums prevail. The algorithmic principle of convolution has countless applications in image processing, computational sciences, etc.

5.2 Convolution Step with Cyclic Boundary Conditions

As a first step in our case study of implementing various versions of convolution in SAC, we restrict ourselves to nearest neighbours and to the arithmetic mean of these neighbour values as the compute function, i.e. a weighted sum where all weights are identical. Furthermore, we use cyclic boundary conditions for now and leave static boundary conditions for later. With these fairly simple convolution parameters, we aim at shape- and rank-generic SAC implementations that are based on the software engineering principles of abstraction and composition. Whenever possible we employ an index-free programming style that treats arrays in a holistic way rather than as loose collections of elements.

```
double[.] convolution_step (double[.] A)
{
   R = A + rotate( 1, A) + rotate( -1, A);
   return R / 3.0;
}
```

Fig. 24. 1-dimensional index-free convolution step

With the code example in Fig. 24 we start with an index-free and shape- but not rank-generic implementation of a single convolution step. The function convolution_step expects a vector of double precision floating point numbers and yields a (once) convolved such vector. The implementation is based on the rotate function from the SAC standard library. It rotates a given vector by a certain number of elements towards ascending or descending indices. Rotation towards ascending indices means moving the rightmost element of the vector (the one with the greatest index) to the leftmost index position (the one with the least index). This implements cyclic boundary conditions almost for free. Adding up the original vector, the left-rotated vector and the right-rotated vector yields the convolved vector. The only task left is the division of each element by 3.0 to obtain the arithmetic mean. This implementation of 1-dimensional convolution makes use of a total of five data-parallel operations: two rotations, two element-wise additions and one element-wise division.

```
double[*] convolution_step (double[*] A)
{
  R = A;
  for (i=0; i<dim(A); i++) {
    R = R + rotate( i, 1, A) + rotate( i, -1, A);
  }
  return R / tod( 2 * dim(A) + 1);
}
```

Fig. 25. Rank-generic convolution step

We now generalise the one-dimensional convolution to the rank-generic convolution shown in Fig. 25. We use the same approach with rotation towards ascending and descending indices, but now we are confronted with a variable number of axes along which to rotate the argument array. We solve the problem by using a for-loop over the number of dimensions of the argument array A, which we obtain through the built-in function dim. In each dimension we rotate A by one element towards ascending and towards descending indices. Here, we use an overloaded, rank-generic version of the rotate function that takes the rotation axis as the first argument in addition to the rotation offset and the array to be rotated as second and as third argument, respectively.

The original argument array and the various rotated arrays are again summed up as in the one-dimensional solution. To eventually compute the arithmetic mean we still need to divide array R by the number of arrays we summed up. This number can easily be obtained through the dim function, as shown in Fig. 25. Since the SAC standard library currently restricts itself to defining arithmetic operators on identical argument types, we must explicitly convert the resulting integer to double using the conversion function tod. Of course, we could extend the standard library by all kinds of type combinations, but we refrain from this for two reasons. Firstly, it would substantially increase the size of the corresponding module due to combinatorial explosion. Secondly, it would reduce the programmer's reflection on the types involved.

5.3   Convolution Step with Static Boundary Conditions

With a rank-generic, index-free convolution step for cyclic boundary conditions at hand we aim at carrying over these ideas to the case of static boundary conditions. For didactic purposes we again begin with the one-dimensional case shown in Fig 26. While the signature of the convolution_step function remains as before, we now consider only the inner elements of the argument array A to be proper grid points and all boundary elements to form the constant halo.

Implementation-wise, we simply replace the applications of the rotate function in the code of Fig. 24 by corresponding applications of the shift function. The shift function is very similar to the rotate function with the exception that vector elements are not moved round-robin. Instead, elements moved out of the vector on one side are discarded while default values are moved into the vector

```
double[.] convolution_step (double[.] A)
{
  conv = (A + shift( 1, A) + shift( -1, A)) / 3.0;

  inner = tile( shape( conv) - 2, [1], conv);
  res   = embed( inner, [1], A);

  return res;
}
```

Fig. 26. 1-dimensional convolution step with static boundary conditions

from the other side. The default value in the version of shift used here is zero; other overloaded variants of the shift function in the SAC standard library allow the programmer to explicitly provide a default value.

Unlike the cyclic boundary case, however, we are not yet done with the computation in line 3. Treating all arrays in a holistic way, that computation includes the boundary elements of the arrays in the computation. This is algorithmically wrong as the halo elements shall remain constant throughout all iterations. To achieve this, we explicitly "correct" the boundary elements in lines 5 and 6. We do this by first creating the array of all inner elements (i.e. the "real" grid points) and then embedding this array within the original array A. We make use of two more functions from the SAC standard array library:

- double[*] tile(int[.] *shp*, int[.] *offset*, double[*] *array*)
  yields the subset of *array* of shape *shp* beginning at index *offset*;
- double[*] embed(double[*] *small*, int[.] *offset*, double[*] *big*)
  yields an array of the same shape as *big*. The elements are those of *big* except for the elements from index *offset* onwards for the shape of *small* which are taken from *small*.

In Fig. 27 we generalise the one-dimensional convolution kernel with static boundary conditions to a rank-generic implementation. We adopt the same approach as in the case of cyclic boundary conditions in Section 5.2 and make use of a for-loop over the rank of the argument array. The 3-ary, multidimensional variant of the shift function is an extension of the 2-ary, one-dimensional function used so far that is fully analogous to the corresponding extension of the rotate function used previously.

The correction of the boundary elements can be carried over from the one-dimensional to the multidimensional case with almost no change, thanks to the rank-invariant definitions of the library functions tile and embed. The only modification stems from the need to use a vector of ones whose length equals the rank of the argument array. For any rank-specific implementation we could simply use the corresponding vector constant as in Fig. 26, but for a rank-generic solution we need a small trick: we multiply the shape vector of the argument array by zero, which yields an appropriately sized vector of zeros, and then add one to obtain the desired vector of ones.

```
double[*] convolution_step (double[*] A)
{
  conv = A;
  for (i=0; i<dim(A); i++) {
    conv = conv + shift( i, 1, A) + shift( i, -1, A);
  }
  conv = conv / tod( 2 * dim(A) + 1));

  vector_of_ones = shape(conv) * 0 + 1;
  inner = tile( shape(conv) - 2, vector_of_ones, conv);
  res   = embed( inner, vector_of_ones, A);

  return res;
}
```

Fig. 27. Rank-generic convolution step with static boundary conditions

5.4   Red-Black Convolution

An algorithmic variant of convolution is called *red-black* convolution. In red-black convolution the grid is bipartite with each grid point either belonging to the red or to the black set. Convolution is then computed alternatingly on the red and on the black grid points while the other values are simply carried over from the previous iteration. Typically, the red and black sets are not randomly distributed over the index set of the grid, but themselves follow some regular alternating pattern along one or multiple axes.

```
double[*] redblack_step (bool[*] mask, double[*] A)
{
  A = where(  mask, convolution_step( A), A);
  A = where( !mask, convolution_step( A), A);

  return A;
}
```

Fig. 28. Red-black convolution

Fig. 28 shows a highly generic SAC implementation of a red-black convolution step where the choice of red and black grid points is abstracted into an additional parameter in form of a Boolean mask. We consecutively apply the convolution_step function to the red and to the black elements by restricting its effect using the where function from the SAC standard library:

- double[*] where(bool[*] *mask*, double[*] *then*, double[*] *else*)
  yields the array of the same shape as the Boolean array *mask* whose elements are taken from the corresponding elements of array *then* where the mask is true and from *else* where not.

The **where** function resembles the FORTRAN-90 language construct of the same name: Our implementation of red-black convolution can easily be combined with static and with cyclic boundary conditions.

5.5   Stencil-Generic Convolution

In all examples so far we have anticipated a direct-neighbour stencil, i.e., we had two neighbours in the one-dimensional case, four neighbours in the two-dimensional case, six neighbours in the three-dimensional case and so on. In this final escalation step we aim at abstracting from the concrete shape of the stencil and support arbitrary dynamic neighbourhoods. We return to cyclic boundary conditions for simplicity, but the idea for correcting the boundary elements for static boundary conditions, as introduced in Section 5.3 can be carried over straightforwardly.

```
double [*]  convolution_step  (double [*] A,  double [*] weights)
{
  R = with {
    ( 0*shape(weights) <= iv < shape(weights) ) :
      weights[iv] * rotate( shape(weights)/2-iv, A);
    } : fold( +);
  return R;
}
```

Fig. 29. Neighbourhood-generic, rank-generic convolution step

The `convolution_step` function shown in Fig. 29 is parameterised over a multidimensional array of weights. Although the type system of SAC does not allow us to express this restriction formally, we anticipate that the argument array A and the array **weights** have the same rank. For example, let us consider to convolve a matrix. Then the weight matrix

$$\begin{pmatrix} 0.0 & 0.2 & 0.0 \\ 0.2 & 0.2 & 0.2 \\ 0.0 & 0.2 & 0.0 \end{pmatrix}$$

would represent the 5-point stencil that we have used so far. The weight matrix allows us to easily define any neighbourhood and, of course, to give different weights to different neighbourship relations. The weight array is also not restricted to three elements per axis; we could easily include neighbourship relations including the left-left neighbour, etc.

The algorithmic idea behind the code in Fig. 29 is a generalisation of the approach taken so far using a **for**-loop over the rank of the argument array. We use a WITH-loop over the shape of the weight array. For instance, the weight matrix above would induce a 3×3 index space for the **fold**-WITH-loop. For each element of this index space (i.e. for each element of the weight array) we rotate the argument array into the direction of that weight's position in the array of weights. Returning to the above example, we rotate the argument array one element up and one element left for the upper left element of the weight matrix. For the central element of the weight matrix (index [1,1]) we do not rotate the argument at all, etc.

```
double[*] rotate( int[.] offsets, double[*] A)
{
  for (i=0; i < min( shape(offsets)[0], dim(A))) {
    A = rotate( i, offsets[i], A);
  }

  return A;
}
```

Fig. 30. Generically defined multidimensional rotation

The alert reader will have noticed that the rotation function used in Fig. 29 is again an overloaded variant of the rotation functions used so far; we show its definition in Fig. 30. This function makes use of a vector of rotation offsets. The first element of the offset vector determines the rotation offset along the first axis of the argument array and so on. Accordingly, we use a for-loop over the minimum of the length of the offset vector and the argument array rank. For each rotation offset we apply the previous version of rotate on the corresponding array axis. If the offset vector length is less than the argument array rank, trailing axes of the argument array remain unrotated; surplus offsets are ignored. We end up with a total of nine rotated and weighted arrays. The fold-WITH-loop eventually sums them up using the overloaded element-wise plus operator on arrays, which yields the convolved array.

5.6   Multiple Convolution Steps

Until now we have only looked at individual convolution steps. Convolution, however, is an iterative process of such steps. In the simplest case the number of iterations is given and thus known a-priori. Fig. 31 shows the SAC implementation of this scenario: we simply employ a for-loop to repeatedly apply individual convolution steps to the grid.

Computing an a-priori known number of convolution steps is a typical benchmark situation. In practice, it is often relevant to continue with the convolution until a certain fixed point is reached, i.e. continue until for no grid point the current iteration's value differs from the previous iteration's value by more than a given threshold. Fig. 32 shows our SAC implementation. As the number of convolution steps to be performed is a-priori unknown, we use a do-while-loop.

```
double [*] convolution (double [*] A, int iter)
{
  for (i=0; i<iter; i++) {
    A = convolution_step ( A);
  }

  return A;
}
```

Fig. 31. Convolution with given number of iteration steps

Of course, the argument array could in principle meet the convergence criterion right away, which would call for a while-loop instead of a do-while-loop,
but we consider this a pathological case and, hence, stick to the do-while-loop.
As the loop predicate we use the is_convergent function introduced in Section 4.5. The convergence test needs to refer to both the old and the new version
of the data grid, hence we introduce the local variable A_old.

```
double [*] convolution (double [*] A, double eps)
{
  do {
    A_old = A;
    A = convolution_step ( A_old);
  }
  while (!is_convergent ( A, A_old, eps));

  return A;
}
```

Fig. 32. Convolution with convergence test

6   Case Study: Differentiation

Our second case study looks into numerical differentiation along one or two axes.
We begin with simple SAC definitions (Section 6.1). They motivate a language
extension of SAC called the *axis control notation* (Section 6.2). Finally, we apply
this notation to numerical differentiation (Section 6.3).

6.1   Differentiation in 1 and 2 Dimensions

In its simplest form numerical differentiation is based on a function, given as
a vector of function values, and the constant difference between two argument
values. The first derivation of the function is then defined as a vector that is one
element shorter than that representing the function itself. The values are the
differences between neighbouring function values divided by their distance.

```
double[.] dfDx( double[.] vec, double delta)
{
   return ( drop( [1], vec) - drop( [-1], vec) ) / delta;
}
```

Fig. 33. 1-dimensional numerical differentiation

Fig. 33 shows a straightforward implementation of 1-dimensional differentiation as a SAC function dfDx. Rather than making use of a WITH-loop for its
definition we follow the SAC methodology and apply the principles of abstraction (Section 4.4) and composition (Section 4.5). The principle of abstraction
mainly materialises itself in the form of the function drop that we introduce
alongside its counterpart, the take function:

- double[*] drop(int[.] dv, double[*] a)
  drops as many elements from each axis of the argument array a as given
  by the *drop vector dv*. The first element of the drop vector determines how
  many elements to drop from the outermost axis of the array and so on.
  Positive drop values drop leading elements while negative drop values drop
  trailing elements. If the length of the drop vector exceeds the rank of the
  array, excess drop values are ignores; if the drop vector is shorter than the
  rank of the array, trailing axes of the array remain untouched. Dropping
  more elements than an array has along any axis results in zero elements
  alongside that axis and in an overall empty result array.
- double[*] take(int[.] tv, double[*] a)
  takes as many elements from each axis of the argument array a as given
  by the *take vector tv*. All small prints are equivalent to those of the drop
  function.

```
double[.,.] dfDy( double[.,.] mat, double delta)
{
   return with {
            (. <= xv <= .): dfDx( mat[xv], delta);
          }: genarray( take( [1], shape( mat)));
}

double[.,.] dfDx( double[.,.] mat, double delta)
{
   return transpose( dfDy( transpose( mat), delta));
}
```

Fig. 34. 2-dimensional numerical differentiation

In the same way as a unary function can be represented as a vector of function values, a binary function can be represented as a matrix of values. This gives us two directions for numerical differentiation, typically referred to as x and y. Fig. 34 shows SAC functions to differentiate a binary function with respect to the first parameter (dfDx) and the second parameter (dfDy).

Differentiating a binary function with respect to the second parameter means computing differences alongside the inner dimension of the matrix mat. In other words we interpret the matrix as a column vector of row vectors, apply our 1-dimensional differentiation function dfDx (Fig. 33) to each row vector and end up with a column vector of derivatives. Differentiating a binary function with respect to the first parameter (dfDx in Fig. 34) could be achieved in a similar way, but we instead advertise the SAC methodology and define it based on the dfDy function and matrix transposition.

6.2 Axis Control Notation

The definition of the function dfDy in the previous section represents a common pattern in array programming that can be generalised as a three step process:

1. interpret a rank k array as an array of rank m of (equally shaped) arrays of rank n with $m + n = k$;
2. individually apply some function to each of the inner arrays;
3. laminate the partial results to form the overall result array.

Fig. 35 illustrates this pattern by a 3-dimensional example. We start with a $4 \times 4 \times 4$-cube of elements. We then (re-)interpret this cube as 4×4-matrix of 4-element vectors, apply some function individually to each of the 16 vectors and laminate the 16 result vectors back into a $4 \times 4 \times 4$-cube.

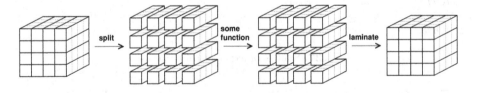

Fig. 35. The split-compute-laminate algorithmic pattern

In Fig. 35 we assume the function to be *uniform*, i.e. shape-preserving. This is not required, and Fig. 36 illustrates the split-compute-laminate principle with a reduction operation. In this example we interpret the $4 \times 4 \times 4$-cube as a vector of four 4×4-matrices. In the second step each matrix is individually reduced to a scalar value, and in the third step these scalar values are laminated into a 4-element vector. While compute functions do not need to preserve the shape of

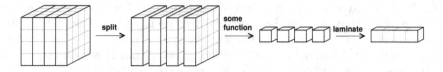

Fig. 36. The split-compute-laminate pattern with non-uniform function

the argument, they are nonetheless restricted: the shape of the result must not depend on anything but the shape of the argument.

SAC provides specific support for the common algorithmic pattern of split-compute-laminate through the *axis control notation* [30]. We sketch out the two syntactic extensions in Fig. 37. First, we extend array selection such that an index vector may contain dots instead of expressions. Semantically, a dot in an index vector means to select all elements in the corresponding dimension of the array selected from. This extension allows us to select entire subarrays of an array not only in trailing dimensions (as with index vectors that are shorter than the array's rank), but in any choice of dimension. Note that vectors containing dots are not first-class values, but are exclusively permitted in index position.

Expr	$\Rightarrow$ *...*
		Expr **[** *SelVec* **]**
		{ *FrameVec* **->** *Expr* **}**
SelVec	$\Rightarrow$ **[** *DotOrExpr* **[,** *DotOrExpr* **]*** **]**
FrameVec	$\Rightarrow$ *Id* **|** **[** *DotOrId* **[,** *DotOrId* **]*** **]**
DotOrExpr	$\Rightarrow$ **.** **|** *Expr*
DotOrId	$\Rightarrow$ **.** **|** *Id*

Fig. 37. Syntax of axis control notation

The other extension shown in Fig. 37 is an expression in curly brackets that defines a particular mapping from a set of indices represented by the vector left of the arrow to a set of values defined by the expression on the right hand side of the arrow. The extent of the index set is implicitly derived from the corresponding variables appearing in index position in the right hand side expression.

We illustrate the axis control notation the very concise definition of the `transpose` function shown in Fig. 38. The frame vector `[i,j]` defines a 2-dimensional index space whose boundaries are given by the reversed shape of `mat` through `i` and `j` appearing in index position on the right hand side. A complete account of the axis control notation can be found in [30].

```
double[.,.] transpose( double[.,.] mat)
{
  return {[i,j] -> mat[[j,i]]};
}
```

Fig. 38. Definition of matrix transpose with axis control notation

6.3 Differentiation with Axis Control Notation

In this section we demonstrate how the definitions of our differentiation functions from Section 6.1 benefit from the axis control notation as shown in Fig. 39. Both functions, dfDY and dfDx, clearly benefit from the axis control notation that enables much conciser and more readable definitions. In particular, the definitions now expose the same symmetries as the underlying mathematical problem they implement. In dfDy we interpret the argument matrix as a column vector of row vectors and apply 1-dimensional differentiation to each row vector. In dfDx we interpret the argument matrix as row vector of column vectors and accordingly apply 1-dimensional differentiation to each column vector.

```
double[.,.] dfDy( double[.,.] mat, double delta)
{
  return {[i,.] -> dfDx( mat[[i,.]], delta)};
}

double[.,.] dfDx( double[.,.] mat, double delta)
{
  return {[.,j] -> dfDx( mat[[.,j]], delta)};
}
```

Fig. 39. 2-dimensional differentiation with axis control notation

7 Modules

This section introduces the module system of SAC, that provides the necessary features for programming-in-the-large. Since SAC only provides very few built-in operations, the SAC standard library with its extensive support for high-level array operations is instrumental for writing even short programs. Hence, some familiarity with the module system is essential. We start with introducing the concept of name spaces (Section 7.1). We proceed with explaining several ways of making symbols from other name spaces available and discuss their differences in the context of function overloading (Sections 7.2 and 7.3). At last, we show how to write modules and make symbols available to other name spaces (Section 7.4).

7.1   Name Spaces

Name spaces are a common mechanism to resolve name clashes when symbols with the same name are defined in different modules of an application. In SAC every module defines a name space. Any program (featuring a `main` function), adds a name space `main`. In a multi-module application any symbol can uniquely be identified by its qualified name consisting of the name space and the symbol name connected by a double colon (as in C++).

```
double, double sincos( double val)
{
   return (Math::sin(val), Math::cos(val));
}
```

Fig. 40. Using symbols from other name spaces with qualified identifiers

Fig. 40 shows a simple example: we define a function `sincos` that simultaneously yields the sine and the cosine of a given value by applying the corresponding individual functions from the SAC standard library, more precisely the `Math` module. Functions `sin` and `cos` are identified by their qualified names.

7.2   The Use Directive

Qualified names quickly become unhandy if symbols are frequently used, in particular when names are not as short as in the previous example. Therefore, SAC supports ways to automatically resolve name spaces and let the compiler generate qualified identifiers internally. The programmer, still, needs to define a search space for the compiler to look for symbols. By means of the directive

```
use name_space all;
```

preceding all definitions in a module/program all symbols defined in the given module are made known locally. With this technique our `sincos` function can be re-written as in Fig. 41.

```
use Math: all;

double, double sincos( double val)
{
   return (sin(val), cos(val));
}
```

Fig. 41. Making all symbols from another module available in the current name space with the `use` directive

Symbols must not have multiple definitions within the search space as that would make their resolution ambiguous. An exception are functions with different argument counts or different argument base types. In the presence of overloading such functions are considered different symbols.

Nonetheless, more stringent control over which symbols to make available from what modules is required in practice. Therefore, the key word `all` in the use-directive can be replaced by a comma-separated list of identifiers embraced in curly brackets. Alternatively, the key words `all except` followed by a list of symbols allows us to explicitly exclude a set of named symbols from the search space. Fig. 42 illustrates these features by a further variation of the running example. We now explicitly choose the symbols `sin` and `tan` from the `Math` module while all other math support comes from an alternative `FastMath` module.

```
use Math: {sin, tan};
use FastMath: all except {sin, tan};

double, double sincos( double val)
{
   return (sin(val), cos(val));
}
```

Fig. 42. Making specific symbols from different name spaces available in the current name space with the qualified `use` directive

Functions can only be added to or removed from the symbol search space by their name. The module system does currently not distinguish overloaded instances of a function based on the number or the types of parameters.

7.3   The Import Directive

The use-directive adds symbols to the search space of the SAC compiler. While very handy in practice, it needs to be used with some care in order to avoid ambiguities (and thus compiler error messages) in the resolution of function symbols. Such an ambiguity arises whenever the same function name is defined in two name spaces, and both are *used* from a third name space. If the two function definitions differ in the number or the base types of parameters, function applications in the third name space can still be disambiguated. In contrast, purely shapely overloading can generally not be resolved at compile time, but warrants a runtime decision. Combining multiple shapely overloaded instances of the same function across name space boundaries, thus, may change the meaning of a function a-posteriori, potentially violating the intentions of the developers of the original modules. Therefore, we disallow *using* shapely overloaded functions.

Nonetheless, shapely overloading across module boundaries when used correctly and consciously, can be a very powerful mechanism, and the import-directive supports exactly this. Whereas the use-directive makes symbols from another name spaces accessible in the current name space, the import-directive clones symbols from other name spaces in the current name space. As a consequence, the compiler constructs a completely new dispatch tree that takes all *imported* instances as well as the locally defined instances equally into account.

```
import foomod: {foo};

int [42] foo( int [42] x) { ... }
int [.] foo( int [.] x) { ... }

int bar( int [*] a)
{
   ...
   b = foo( a);
   ...
}
```

Fig. 43. Shapely overloading across name spaces with the import-directive

Fig. 43 illustrates this be means of a small example. We first *import* the potentially already overloaded definition of foo from the name space foomod. Afterwards, we further overload the function foo with two more definitions, one for integer vectors of length 42 and one for integer vectors of arbitrary length. When we dispatch the application of foo in the body of function bar all instances of foo are equally considered, regardless whether they are locally defined or imported. The import-directive supports the same syntactic variations as the use-directive; both directives can be freely interspersed.

7.4   Defining Modules

A SaC module differs from a program in two aspects: the absence of a main function and a module header consisting of the key word module, the module name and a semicolon. Fig. 44 shows a simple example. We pick our convolution case study from Section 5 up and provide a module Convolution defining two overloaded instances of a function convolution computing either a fixed number of iterations or a variable number of iterations with convergence check as in Figs. 31 and 32, respectively. Before actually defining the new function instances, however, we need to make a number of functions defined elsewhere available that we need to define convolution, e.g. the various implementations of individual convolution steps or the convergence check. And of course, we require the basic array support from the standard library. The choice of selective or general use or import of symbols into the current name space is mainly motivated to showcase the various syntactic options.

The most interesting aspect of a module is the question which symbols are made available outside and which are kept hidden within the module . Two directive, provide and export, give programmers fine-grained control over this question. By default any symbol defined in a module is only accessible in the module itself. The provide directive makes symbols available to be *used* in other name spaces; the export directive makes symbols available for both *use* or *import*. Thus, the owner of a module decides whether or not functions can be shapely overloaded later with all consequences on semantics. The provide

```
module Convolution;

use Array: all;
import ConvolutionStep: all;
use Convergence: {is_convergent};

provide all except {convolution};
export {convolution};

double[*] convolution (double[*] A, int iter)    {...}
double[*] convolution (double[*] A, double eps) {...}
```

Fig. 44. Example of a module implementation that bundles the two generic convolution functions developed in Section 5.6

and **export** directives support the same features for symbol selection as the corresponding **use** and **import** directives.

In the example of Fig. 44 we export the two instances of the convolution function. More for didactic purposes we choose also to provide all other symbols defined in the current module. Note that we import (not use) the symbols from module ConvolutionStep. As a consequence, they are cloned in the current module and hence can be provided as genuine symbols of module Convolution. Again, our example rather illustrates the various options our module system provides; in practice one would rather only provide the convolution functions.

8   Input and Output

In this chapter we sketch out the principles of SAC's support for input/output in particular and for stateful computations in general. We begin with the user perspective on basic file I/O (Section 8.1), then shown how imperative-appearing I/O constructs can safely be integrated into the functional context of SAC (Section 8.2) and conclude with a complete I/O example with proper error checking and handling (Section 8.3).

8.1   Basic File I/O

Integration of I/O facilities into SAC is guided by two seemingly conflicting design principles. On the one hand, we aim at extending to look-and-feel of C programming to I/O-related SAC code; on the other hand, it is crucial to retain SAC's status as a pure functional language on the semantic level and not to restrain any optimisation potential.

Just as with the language kernel, programmers with a background in imperative programming should not be bothered by the conceptual troubles of manipulating the state of devices in a state-free environment. We certainly do not want our programmers to familiarise themselves with theoretically demanding concepts such as monads [31,32] and uniqueness types [33,34]. And we definitely do not want to rely on our programmers being experts in category theory to write a *hello world* program in SAC. Instead, any C programmer should be able to write I/O-related code in SAC even without the need to learn a new API.

```
import StdIO: all;
import ArrayIO: all;

int main()
{
  a = 42;
  b = [1,2,3,4,5];

  errcode, outfile = fopen( "filename", "w");

  fprintf( outfile, "a = %d\n", a);
  fprint( outfile, b);

  fclose( outfile);

  return 0;
}
```

Fig. 45. Example for doing file input/output in SAC

Fig. 45 shows a simple file I/O example written in SAC. For now, we ignore all potential semantic issues of the code and merely emphasise the similarities between SAC and C proper. First, we import all symbols from the two relevant SAC modules of the standard library. In the **main** function we begin with opening a file using a clone of C's **fopen** function. Like its C counterpart **fopen** expects two character strings as arguments. The first denotes the name of the file to be opened, and the second determines the file mode. In the example, we open the file **filename** for writing. The supported file modes are identical with C proper. In fact, the SAC **fopen** function is merely a wrapper for the C **fopen** function called through SAC's foreign language interface [35].

Unlike C, the SAC **fopen** function makes use of the support for multiple return values and yields two values: a file handle (**outfile**) and an error code (**errcode**). For the sake of simplicity, we expect the opening of the file to succeed and ignore the error code for now. We will discuss a complete example with proper error checking in Section 8.3.

Having opened the file, we write some text and a scalar value to the file using the **fprintf** function, that again is a clone of the corresponding C function. Next we write an entire array to the file using the SAC-specific function **fprint**. Since the C **fprintf** family of functions have no support for array-related conversion specifiers, we add the **fprint** family of functions for array output. Finally, we close the file using the usual `fclose` function. The example demonstrates how well we achieve our first aim: supporting I/O in way that is familiar to C programmers.

8.2 Imperative I/O vs Functional Semantics

Right now, it seems much less clear how we achieve our second aim: functionally sound I/O. After all, many I/O functions do not even yield a value and would be dead code in a purely functional interpretation. Worse, the textual order of statements now matters: there is an implicit execution order not enforced by data dependencies. The solution is surprisingly simple, nonetheless. In analogy to the interpretation of C-style loops as syntactic sugar for tail recursion code like in Fig. 45 is nothing but an imperative illusion of a purely functional code. Fig. 46 shows its *functional interpretation*. In essence, the compiler automatically establishes the necessary data dependencies that describe the intended execution order in a functionally sound way.

```
FileSystem, int main( FileSystem theFileSystem)
{
   a = 42;
   b = [1,2,3,4,5];

   theFileSystem, errcode, outfile
      = fopen( theFileSystem, "file_name", "w");

   outfile = fprintf( outfile, "a = %d\n", a);
   outfile = fprint( outfile, b);

   theFileSystem = fclose( theFileSystem, outfile);

   return (theFileSystem, 0);
}
```

Fig. 46. Functional interpretation of the I/O code in Fig. 45, compiler-inserted intermediate code typeset in italics

The `main` function has an extended signature: it now receives a representation of the file system and yields, in addition to the usual integer return code, a potentially modified representation of the file system. Likewise, all I/O-related functions in the body of `main` receive additional arguments and yield additional values. The `fopen` function takes the file system as an additional argument and yields a modified file system (representation). Assuming opening of the file succeeds, the new file system differs from the old file system in exactly this property: the named file was closed and is now open for writing.

The two output functions `fprintf` and `fprint` take the file handle as before, but additionally return the file handle. This creates a data dependency from the call to `fopen` over `fprintf` and `fprint` to the final closing of the file by `fclose`. In analogy to `fopen`, the `fclose` function takes the file system as an additional parameter and yields a modified file system, in which the file is no longer open but closed. This final state of the file system is eventually returned to the execution environment.

The SAC compiler actually does these transformations to deal with a proper functional representation of code when it comes to optimisation. Conceptually and technically, our solution is based on a variant of *uniqueness types* [34,36] as developed for I/O in the functional language Clean. The types of `theFileSystem` and `outfile` are uniqueness types, and one can easily verify that every definition (left hand side use) of one these variables has exactly (at most) one reference (right hand side use). The main difference to uniqueness types in Clean lies in the fact that the entire conceptual complexity of dealing with state in a functional context is hidden in a number of modules from the SAC standard library (and of course corresponding compiler support). Actually doing I/O in an application program is as simple as in imperative languages while under the hood everything is safe and clean. The non-expert programmer does not need to understand the ins and outs of safe functional I/O.

The SAC compiler does check the uniqueness property, but for the normal user it is close to impossible to produce a uniqueness violation. As long as a programmer merely makes use of the various I/O modules of the SAC standard library, the automatic (internal) expansion of code along the lines of Fig. 46 prior to uniqueness checking almost inevitably leads to correct code. Thus, programmers are usually not bothered with cryptic uniqueness-related error messages. In some cases the uniqueness checker can, however, detect common programming errors, e.g. missing or repeated closing of files. A more complete coverage of SAC I/O can be found in [36].

A particular issue is the combination of input/output, where a particular execution order is important, with SAC's data-parallel WITH-loops, where a concrete execution order is deliberately not guaranteed, nor even defined. Due to space limitations we refer the interested reader to [37] for a comprehensive discussion of this aspect of SAC.

8.3   File I/O with Error Checking

In our initial I/O example in Fig. 45 we deliberately skipped all error checking and crossed fingers that opening the file succeeds. We now extend the simple file I/O example with proper error checking making use of the `SysErr` module from the standard library. This module essentially replaces C's `errno` variable. Fig. 47 shows the complete example.

We remember that the `fopen` function yields an error code in addition to the file handle Unlike in Fig. 45, we now check this error code before making use of the file handle. The `fail` function discriminates success codes from failure

```
import StdIO: all;
import ArrayIO: all;
import SysErr: all;

int main()
{
  a = 42;
  b = [1,2,3,4,5];

  errcode, outfile = fopen( "file_name", "w");

  if (fail(errcode)) {
    fprintf( stderr, "%s\n", strerror( errcode));
  }
  else {
    fprintf( outfile, "a = %d\n", a);
    fprint( outfile, b);

    fclose( outfile);
  }

  return 0;
}
```

Fig. 47. Complete I/O example with error checking

codes and yields a Boolean value suitable for use in a predicate. Upon failure we print a message to `stderr`. Just as in C, `stdout`, `stdin` and `stderr` are file handles that are always open for writing or reading. In SAC they are so-called *global objects*: stateful entities that follow the same visibility and scoping rules as functions. They can be accessed anywhere in function bodies and are subject to use/import from other name spaces and provide/export to other name spaces. For more information on global objects we refer the interested reader to [36]. The `strerror` function is identical to its C counterpart and yields a problem description in the string form. Note that we do not close the file in the first branch as we have not (successfully) opened it either. The second branch is analogous to Fig. 45.

9   Foreign Language Interfaces

This section describes SAC's foreign language interfaces. They allow SAC code to interoperate with existing or yet to be developed C code. Two such interfaces exist that are equally important in practice: the c4sac interface allows SAC code to call C functions (Section 9.1) while the sac4c interface supports the compilation of SAC modules such that they can be embedded within larger C applications (Section 9.2).

9.1 Calling C from SAC

The c4sac interface is an indispensable feature for making SAC communicate with the outside world. Most I/O functions introduced in Section 8 are merely SAC wrappers for the corresponding C functions. It would not only be very cumbersome to re-implement I/O support from scratch in SAC, we would also inevitably re-invent the wheel and simply waste engineering effort. Instead, we aim at reusing existing implementations as much as possible and seek to excel in core areas of SAC.

```
external double cos( double x );
  #pragma linkwith "m"
  #pragma linksign [0,1]

external double, double sin_cos( double x );
  #pragma linksign [1,2,3]
  #pragma linkobj "src/Math/mymath"

external syserr, File fopen( string filename, string mode );
  #pragma linkobj "src/File/fopen.o"
  #pragma effect theFileSystem
  #pragma linkname "SACfopen"
  #pragma linksign [0,1,2,3]

external int, ... scanf( string format );
  #pragma linkobj "src/File/scanf.o"
  #pragma effect stdin

external void fprint( File &file,
                      int dim, int[.] shp, int[*] array )
  #pragma refcounting [4]
```

Fig. 48. Examples of foreign function declarations from the SAC standard library

Fig. 48 illustrates the c4sac foreign language interface by three examples from different modules of the SAC standard library. Foreign function declarations like the ones in Fig. 48 may appear interspersed with SAC function definitions throughout SAC modules. In principle, a pure declaration starting with the key word **external** followed by standard SAC function header and terminated by a semicolon suffices. In practice, the SAC compiler often needs some more information to seamlessly integrate an imperative foreign function into the functional world of SAC. Several pragmas serve this purpose.

Our first example is the cos function from SAC's **Math** module, obviously a foreign declaration for the corresponding cos function from the C math library **libm**. Most math functions are easy targets for SAC's foreign language interface as they directly expose a functional interface computing a new scalar value from an existing scalar value with call-by-value parameter passing. Nonetheless, someone needs to tell the SAC compiler to link an executable program with libm as soon as the cos function is used anywhere. This is done with the linkwith-pragma.

The linksign-pragma is more complex. It describes a mapping of SAC parameters and results to those of the corresponding C function. A vector defines for each result and parameter in textual order from left to right onto which position of the C function it is mapped. This pragma allows us to map C functions that return multiple values through reference parameters into proper SAC functions with multiple return values. The numbers in the vector stand for the positional parameters of the corresponding C function, where zero represents the explicit return position.

So, in the case of the sin function the linksign-pragma merely specifies the expected, i.e. the SAC function is mapped to a C function with the same function type. To illustrate the linksign-pragma Fig. 48 also contains a foreign declaration of an artificial function sin_cos that simultaneously yields the sine and the cosine of a given value. While in SAC this can elegantly by expressed with two return types, there is no equivalent C type. The linksign-pragma makes the SAC compiler expect the existence of a C function

```
    void sin_cos( double *sin, double *cos, double x)
```
and generate corresponding function calls. It is even possible to map one return value and one parameter onto the same parameter location of the C function. In this way C functions that take a pointer and manipulate the data behind the pointer can properly be used from SAC.

Unlike sin and cos, no function sin_cos is defined in libm. Hence, the SAC compiler needs to be informed where to locate code order to generate appropriate linker calls. This is the purpose of the linkobj-pragma.

The third declaration in Fig. 48 makes the fopen function, extensively discussed in Section 8.1, available in SAC. The effect-pragma tells the SAC compiler that this function makes an implicit side effect on the global object theFileSystem. This information is essential for the compiler to generate explicit data dependencies as shown in Section 8.2.

More adaptation between C and SAC is required due to the different approaches to error reporting. The SAC fopen function explicitly yields an error condition while the C fopen function yields NULL and sets the global errno variable. This difference requires a thin wrapper layer implemented in C. This wrapper can obviously not be named fopen. Thus, the linkname-pragma allows us to manipulate the name of the function that is actually called by the SAC compiler in place of fopen. The linksign-pragma again merely describes the default: the error condition is returned via the C function's result while the file handle is implemented as a reference parameter in the first parameter position and the other parameters follow in order.

The foreign declaration of the scanf function demonstrates how variable argument lists from C are mapped to SAC. Three dots on the left hand side indicate that scanf yields an unknown number of results in addition to the usual integer value returned by C's scanf function. These are always mapped to trailing reference parameters of the corresponding C function and, thus, to the expected type signature of scanf in C.

Our last example shows the declaration of a rank-generic print function for arrays. We use a function like this to implement the fprint function for arrays that we used throughout our examples in Section 8. Here, we expose the structural properties of the argument array explicitly. The ampersand marks the first parameter as a *reference parameter*. This triggers the addition of a corresponding result value as explained in Section 8.2. The refcounting-pragma declares the function to take care of reference counting for the fourth argument, i.e. the array to be printed. In this case the anticipated prototype of the C function changes such that 2 C parameters implement the one SAC parameter, the first being a pointer to the array itself (in flat, contiguous representation), the other being a pointer to an integer number that exposes the reference counter of the array. While this feature obviously requires in-depth understanding of the SAC memory management subsystem, it allows the expert user to safely implement destructive array updates and take similar advantages of reference counting as the SAC compiler itself does. In Section 10.4 we explain SAC memory management in greater detail.

With the facilities of the c4sac language interface we have made most of the standard C library functions from libc and libm available in SAC. These are extended by a range of array-specific functions implemented in C, e.g. for inout and output of arrays.

9.2   Calling SAC from C

Equally important to the c4sac interface, though for different reasons, is the sac4c interface that makes entire SAC modules available within otherwise C-implemented applications. Of course, we promote to use SAC to implement whole applications, but we must acknowledge that transition to SAC is substantially eased if programmers can choose to only implement parts of an application in SAC. This also allows us to concentrate on application aspects like compute-intensive kernels, for which SAC is tailor-made, and avoid engineering effort to be directed into directions that are not the core of our research, say for example support for GUI-based applications.

In principle, any standard SAC module can be used from C code, but it needs some mending to expose and publish a C-compatible interface. For this purpose we provide a separate tool as part of the SAC installation: sac4c. This tool takes a compiled SAC module as an argument and generates among others a C header file with the type and function declarations exposed by the module. Furthermore, sac4c generates the necessary linker information regarding all directly and indirectly needed SAC modules as well as all further object files dependent through the c4sac interface.

Fig. 49 shows a simple example of C code making use of the Convolution module defined in Section 7.4. At first, we include two header files, one providing the necessary generic declarations of the sac4c interface, the other being generated by the sac4c tool. In the example we compute 99 convolution steps

```
#include "sac4c.h"
#include "Convolution.h"

int main( int argc, char *argv[])
{
  double *matrix;
  SACarg *arg, *iter, *res;
  int rank;

  matrix = C_code_that_creates_matrix( 1024, 1024);

  SACinit( argc, argv);

  arg  = SACARGconvertFromDoublePointer( matrix, 2, 1024, 1024);
  iter = SACARGconvertFromIntScalar( 99);

  Convolution__convolution2( &res, arg, iter);

  rank = SACARGgetDim( res);
  assert( rank==2);

  matrix = SACARGconvertToDoubleArray( res);
  plot( matrix);

  SACfinalize();
  return 0;
}
```

Fig. 49. Example C code making use of the sac4c foreign language interface

on a 1024×1024 double precision floating point matrix. Before starting any computations, however, we must initialise the SAC runtime system by a call to the SACinit function; upon completion the runtime system should be shutdown by a call to SACfinalize.

At the center of Fig. 49 we can identify the call to our SAC-implemented convolution function. The C function name has automatically been derived from the SAC module name and the SAC function name with two underscores in between (double underscores are not permitted in SAC identifiers). The trailing number 2 helps to resolve SAC function overloading with different arity and declares the function to be binary. The C prototype of the function is

```
void Convolution__convolution2(
    SACarg **res, SACarg *mat, SACarg *iter);
```

Functions made available through the sac4c interface are always void-functions and exchange arguments and results with the C world through a dedicated abstract type SACarg. This type helps us to expose SAC overloading both on base type and on shape to the C world. The sac4c interface comes with a range of functions that convert C arrays (contiguous, uniform chunks of memory) into SAC arrays and vice versa. Towards SAC the naked C pointer is equipped with SAC-style multidimensional shape information. On the way back structural properties of result arrays can be queried and, eventually, flat C arrays extracted for further analysis or processing. C arrays handed over to SAC must not be touched thereafter; C arrays obtained from SAC are guaranteed to be alias-free.

10   Compilation Technology

In this section we discuss the fundamental challenges of compiling SAC source code into competitive executable code for a variety of parallel computing architectures and outline how compiler and runtime system address these issues. Following an overview of the compiler architecture (Section 10.1) we concentrate on type inference and specialisation (Section 10.2), optimisation (Section 10.4) and code generation for various parallel architectures (Section 10.5). In place of a proper evaluation, Section 10.6 provides an annotated bibliography covering programmability, productivity and performance issues across a wide range of problems and target architectures.

10.1   The SAC Compiler at a Glance

Despite the intentional syntactic similarities, SAC is far from merely being a variant of C. SAC is a complete programming language, that only happens to resemble C in its look and feel. A fully-fledged compiler is needed to implement the functional semantics and to address a series of challenges when it comes to achieving high performance.

Fig. 50 shows the overall internal organisation of the SAC compiler sac2c. It is a many-pass compiler around a central slowly morphing abstract intermediate code representation. We chose this design to facilitate concurrent compiler engineering across multiple individuals and institutions. Today, we have around 200 compiler passes, and Fig. 50 only shows a macroscopic view of what is really going on behind the scenes. The SAC compiler, however, is very verbose with respect to its efforts: the interested programmer can stop compilation after any pass and have the internal representation printed as annotated SAC source code.

As a first step, usual lexicographic and syntactic analyses transform textual source code into an abstract syntax tree. All remaining compilation steps work on this internal representation, that is subject to a number of lowering steps. Over the years, we have developed a complete, language-independent compiler engineering tool suite, that has successfully been re-used in other projects [38] as well as in a series of courses on compiler construction at the University of Amsterdam. In the following, however, we leave out such engineering concerns and rather take a conceptual view on the SAC compilation process.

The first major code transformation shown in Fig. 50 is named *functionalisation*. Here, we turn the imperative(-looking) source code into a more functional representation. For instance, C-style branches turn into functional conditionals, and C-style loops become proper tail-recursive functions, as explained in

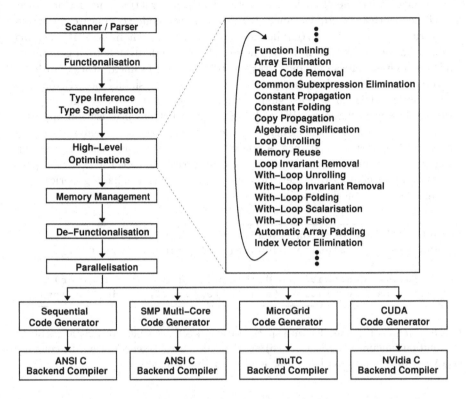

Fig. 50. Organisation of the compilation process

Section 2.2. Likewise, we augment state-based code with the missing data dependencies, as outlined in Section 8.2. All these transformations are eventually undone prior to code generation in a *de-functionalisation* step.

10.2 Type Inference and Specialisation

This part of the compiler implements the array type system outlined in Section 4.1. It annotates types to local variables and checks type declarations provided. Furthermore, the type inference system resolves function dispatch in the context of subtyping and overloading. Where possible function applications are dispatched statically; where necessary appropriate code is generated to make the decision at runtime. More information on this aspect of the SAC compiler can be found in [39].

The other important aspect handled by this part of the compiler is *function specialisation*. Shape- and rank-invariant specifications are a key feature of SAC. It is sort of obvious that the less we know at compile time about structural properties of arrays, the less efficiently will the generated code perform at runtime.

We are faced with the classical trade-off between abstraction and performance. Specific concerns are, for instance, how to generate code to operate on arrays whose rank is unknown at compile time and, hence, for whom no static nesting of loops can be derived, or how to generate efficient code from lists of generators when cache hierarchies demand arrays to be traversed in linear storage order.

From a software engineering point of view, all code should be written in a rank-generic (AUD) or at least shape-generic (AKS) way. From a compiler perspective, however, shape-specific code offers much better optimisation opportunities, can do with a much leaner runtime representation and generally shows considerably better performance. A common trick to reconcile abstract programming with high runtime performance is specialisation. In fact, the SAC compiler aggressively specialises rank-generic code to rank-specific (shape-generic) code and again shape-generic code into shape-specific code.

```
double[*]  convolution  (double[*]  A,  int iter)     {...}
double[*]  convolution  (double[*]  A,  double eps)  {...}

specialize  convolution  (double[1024,1024]  A,  int iter)
specialize  convolution  (double[1024,1024]  A,  double eps)
```

Fig. 51. Helping the compiler with specialisation directives: while both instances of the convolution function (see Section 5.6) are defined in a rank-generic way, the compiler is advised to generate specialisations for 1024 × 1024-matrices

Specialisation can only be effective to the extent that rank and shape information is somehow accessible by the compiler. While **sac2c** makes every effort to infer the shapes needed, there are scenarios in which the required information is simply not available in the code. For instance, argument arrays could be read from files. Other common examples arise from any use of the sac4c foreign language interface described in Section 9.2. Hence, full compiler support for generating shape-generic and rank-generic executable code cannot be avoided.

More than occasionally, however, programmers do know or can at least make an educated guess as to which array shapes will be relevant at runtime. Specialisation directives, as shown in Fig. 51, allow us to give hints to the compiler which shapes will be relevant at runtime without compromising the rank- and shape-generic programming methodology and code base. The compiler creates the recommended specialisations in addition to those that it would generate by itself and transparently integrates them into the function dispatch mechanism.

The code in Fig. 51 completes our running example on convolution. Starting out in Section 5.6 we defined the two instances of the convolution function that either compute a given number of iterations or continue to iterate until a given convergence threshold is reached. In Section 7.4 we showed how these functions can be abstracted into a SAC module. We then demonstrated in Section 9.2 how this SAC module can be made available to be used from a C-implemented application. In the example of Fig. 49 we ran convolution on 1024×1024-matrices.

In this scenario the shape of the array to be convolved is statically known in the
C code, but there is no way for the SAC compiler to know. Hence, it is forced to
execute a rank-generic implementation of convolution, which is likely to deliver
poor performance. The specialisation directives of Fig. 51 turn the tide and make
the sac4c interface dynamically select the highly optimised binary convolution
code for 1024 × 1024-matrices.

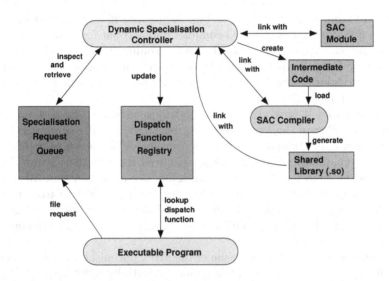

Fig. 52. Architecture of the SAC adaptive compilation framework

There are a number of scenarios, however, that rule out the helping hand of
the programmer as well. For instance, the provider of some module and the user
of that module could simply be distinct, or the nature of an application rules
out the availability of shape information until the application is actually run.
To address these cases we have devised the adaptive compilation infrastructure
sketched out in Fig. 52.

The essential idea is to postpone specialisations until application runtime.
When generic functions execute, they file a specialisation request that includes
the full set of array shapes appearing in the concrete application. One or more
specialisation controllers asynchronously take care of such requests, retrieve the
partially compiled intermediate code from the corresponding SAC (binary) modules, run essential parts of the SAC compilation tool chain with all knowledge
available at application runtime and eventually generate a specialised and highly
optimised binary implementation of the function that initiated the request.

The running application is then dynamically linked with that new code, and
the function dispatch mechanism is updated to include the new specialisation.
When the same function is applied again to arguments of the same shapes, the
specialised implementation will be chosen by the dispatch mechanism instead of
the generic one. The whole approach is based on the (realistic) assumption that

in many applications the number of different array shapes actually appearing is limited, even though at compile time no educated guess can be made on which shapes may and may not be relevant. A complete description and evaluation of our adaptive compilation framework can be found in [40]

10.3   High-level Optimisations

As apparent from a short glimpse at Fig. 50, high-level program optimisations constitute a major part of the SAC compiler and account for a substantial fraction of compiler engineering. Only the most prominent and/or relevant transformations are actually included in Fig. 50. They can coarsely be classified into two groups: (variations of) standard textbook optimisations and SAC-specific optimisations related to arrays.

The compositional programming methodology advocated by SAC creates a particular compilation challenge. Without dedicated compiler support it inflicts the creation of many temporary arrays at runtime, which adversely affects performance: large quantities of data must be moved through the memory hierarchy to perform almost negligible computations per array element. We quickly hit the memory wall and see our cores mainly waiting for data from memory rather than computing. With individual WITH-loops as basis for parallelisation, compositional specifications also incur high synchronisation and communication overhead.

As a consequence, the major theme of the array optimisation lies in condensing many light-weight array operations, more technically WITH-loops, into much fewer heavy-weight WITH-loops. Such techniques universally improve a number of ratios that are crucial for performance: the ratio between computations and memory operations, the ratio between computations and loop overhead and, in case of parallel execution, the ratio between computations and synchronisation and communication overhead. We identified three independent optimisation cases and address each one with a tailor-made program transformation:

– WITH-*loop-folding* [41] identifies computational pipelines where the result of one WITH-loop is referenced in a subsequent WITH-loop. If so, the reference in the second WITH-loop is replaced by the corresponding element definition from the first WITH-loop. Multi-generator WITH-loops and offset computations on index vectors make this a non-trivial undertaking. A good example is the convergence check in Fig. 22. Naive compilation would yield three temporary intermediate arrays before the final reduction is computed. WITH-loop-folding transforms the code into a single WITH-loop similar to the one shown in Fig. 21.

– WITH-*loop-fusion* [42] aims at WITH-loops that compute (data-)independent values based on a common or overlapping argument set. A typical example would be searching for the least and for the greatest value in an array. Naive compilation would yield one WITH-loop each, and the common argument array would be pumped through the entire memory hierarchy twice. WITH-loop-fusion, as the name suggests, fuses such WITH-loops into a single multi-operator WITH-loop traversing argument arrays only once. For instance, WITH-loop-fusion manages to fuse the convolution step and the convergence check in Fig. 32 into a single WITH-loop after properly resolving the data dependency between the convolution step and the convergence check

- WITH-loop-scalarisation [43] joins nested WITH-loops, where the element value of an outer WITH-loop is itself a WITH-loop-defined array. Naive compilation would materialise a temporary array for each index of the outer WITH-loop. Arrays of complex numbers, for instance, lead to this situation as each complex number itself again is an array, i.e. a 2-element vector (see Section 4.3).

These optimisations are essential for making the compositional programming style advocated by SAC feasible in practice; a survey can be found in [44].

Other array-specific optimisations aim at avoiding the creation of small vectors used for indexing purposes (*index vector elimination* [45]) or optimise the cache utilisation in the context of densely stored multi-dimensional arrays (*array padding* [46]) to name just two. Moreover, the SAC compiler puts considerable effort into compiling complex generator sets of WITH-loops, potentially with multiple strided generators, etc, into an abstract representation that traverses the involved arrays in linear storage order whenever possible. This technique [47] is crucial to effectively utilise cache hierarchies essential for achieving good performance on modern systems.

The textbook optimisations first and foremost act as enablers of the array-specific optimisations. They create larger optimisation contexts (e.g. function inlining, loop unrolling), do all sorts of partial evaluation (e.g. constant folding and propagation, loop unrolling, algebraic simplification) or aim at avoiding superfluous computations (e.g. dead code removal, common subexpression elimination, loop invariant removal). While these optimisations are common in industrial-strength C compilers, the functional semantics of SAC allows us to apply them much more aggressively than what is possible in imperative environments.

10.4   Memory Management

Stateless arrays require memory resources to be managed automatically at runtime. This is a key ingredient of any functional language, and it is well understood how to design and implement efficient garbage collectors [48,49,50]. So, the stress here is rather on *arrays*. In serious applications arrays often require large contiguous chunks of memory, easily hundreds of MegaBytes and more. Such sizes require many design decisions in memory management to be reconsidered, e.g. they rule out copying garbage collectors.

On a more conceptual level we need to deal with the *aggregate update problem* [51]. Often an array is computed from an existing array by only changing a few elements. Or, imagine a recurrence relation where vector elements are computed in ascending index order based on their left neighbour. A straightforward functional implementation would need to copy large quantities of data unchanged from the "old" to the "new" array. As any imperative implementation would simply overwrite array elements as necessary, the functional code could never achieve competitive performance. Of course, one could also question the unboxed, dense in-memory representation silently assumed here, but this is likewise well known to be no solution.

As a domain-specific solution for array processing, SAC uses *non-deferred reference counting* [52] for garbage collection. Each array is augmented with a reference counter, and the generated code is likewise augmented with reference counting instructions that dynamically keep track of how many conceptual copies of an array exist. Compared with other garbage collection techniques non-deferred reference counting has the unique advantage that memory can immediately be reclaimed as soon as it turns into garbage. All other techniques in one way or another decouple the identification and reclamation of dead data from the last operation that makes use of the data.

Only non-deferred reference counting supports a number of optimisations that are crucial for achieving high performance in functional array programming. The ability to dynamically query the number of references of an array prior to some eligible operation creates opportunities for immediate memory reuse. Take for example a simple arithmetic operator overloaded for arrays like subtraction as discussed in Section 4.4. The definition of subtraction on arrays is point-wise and the result array requires exactly the same amount of memory as any of the two argument arrays. If one of them shows a reference counter value of one prior to computing subtraction, that argument array's memory can immediately be reused to store the result array. As a consequence, not only a costly memory allocation is avoided, but also the memory footprint of the operation is reduced by one third leading to much better cache hierarchy utilisation on typical cache-based computing systems.

In other cases we may not only be able to reuse memory but also to reuse the data already present in that memory. Consider a WITH-loop as in the following SAC code fragment:

```
b = with {
      (. <= iv < shape(a) / 2) : a[iv] + 1;
    }: modarray(a);
```

Here, an array b is computed from an existing array a such that the upper left corner (in the 2-dimensional case) is incremented by one while the remaining elements are copied from a proper. If we can reuse the memory of a to store b, we can effectively avoid to copy all those elements that remain the same in b as in a. Such techniques are important prerequisites to compete with imperative languages in terms of performance. A survey on SAC memory management can be found in [53].

Unlike other garbage collection techniques, non-deferred reference counting still relies on a heap manager for allocations and de-allocations. Standard heap managers are typically optimised for memory management workloads characterised by many fairly small chunks. In array processing, however, extremely large chunks are common, and they are often handled inefficiently by standard heap managers. Therefore, SAC comes with its own heap manager tightly integrated with compiler and runtime system and properly equipped for multithreaded execution [54].

10.5   Parallelisation and Code Generation

An important (non-coincidental) property of WITH-loops is that evaluation of the associated expression for any element of the union of index sets is completely independent of all others. This allows the compiler to freely choose any suitable evaluation order. We thoroughly exploit this property in the various WITH-loop-optimisations described above, but in the end the main motivation for this design is ease of parallelisation.

In contrast to auto-parallelisation in the imperative world, our problem is not to decide *where* code can safely be executed in parallel, but we still need to decide *where* and *when* parallel execution is beneficial to reduce program execution times. The focus on data-parallel computations and arrays helps here (which is among others why we chose this path in the first place). We do know the index space size of an operation before actually executing it, which is better than in typical divide-and-conquer scenarios.

It is crucial to understand, the WITH-loop does not prescribe parallel execution, it merely opens up opportunities for compiler and runtime system. They still need to make an autonomous decision as whether to make use of this opportunity or not. This sets us apart from many other approaches, may they be as explicit as OPENMP directives or as implicit as par and seq in HASKELL.

Different target architectures require entirely different code generators. In all cases, the SAC compiler does not generate architecture-specific machine code but rather architecture-specific variations of C code. The final step of machine code generation is left to a highly customisable backend compiler tailor-made for a given computing platform. While this design choice foregoes certain machine-level optimisation opportunities, we found it to be a reasonable compromise between engineering effort and support for a variety of computing architectures and operating systems.

The SAC compiler currently supports four different compilation targets. The default target is plain sequential execution. Any ISO/ANSI-compliant C compiler may serve as backend code generator. This flexibility allows us to choose the best performing C compiler on each target architecture, e.g. the Intel compiler for Intel processors, the Oracle compiler for Niagara systems or GNU gcc for AMD Opteron based systems. It would be extremely challenging to compete with these compilers in terms of binary code quality.

For symmetric multi-core multi-processor systems we again target standard ANSI/ISO C with occasional calls to the PThread library. Conceptually, the SAC runtime system follows a fork-join approach, where a program is generally executed by a single *master thread.* Only computationally-intensive kernels, in intermediate SAC code conveniently represented by WITH-loops already enhanced and condensed through high-level optimisation, are effectively run in parallel by temporarily activating a set of a-priori created *worker threads.* The synchronisation and communication mechanisms implementing the transition between single-threaded and multi-threaded execution modes and vice versa are highly optimised to exploit properties of cache coherence protocols found in today's multi-core multi-processor systems. Compilation for these kinds of parallel systems is thoroughly described in [55,56].

As our approach to organising multithreaded execution is not dissimilar from implementations of OPENMP, we recently experimented with alternatively generating C code with OPENMP directives [57]. One result of this work is that (maybe not surprisingly) the tailor-made and highly tuned synchronisation mechanisms of the PThread-based implementation yield slightly better performance. The OPENMP-based code generator may still prove handy for supporting future chip architectures that may not meet our assumptions on cache coherence and memory consistency, but are supported by OPENMP. In either case, PThread- or OPENMP-based code generation, we benefit from the same range of choices to select the most appropriate backend C compiler for binary code generation.

Our support for GPGPUs, the SAC compiler's third target architecture, is based on the CUDA framework [58]. In this case, our design choice to leave binary code generation to an independent C compiler particularly pays off: one is effectively bound to NVidia's custom-made CUDA compiler for code generation.

A number of issues need to be taken into account when targeting graphics cards in general and the CUDA framework in particular that are quite different from generating multithreaded code as before. First CUDA kernels, i.e. the code fragments that actually run on the accelerator, are restricted by the absence of a runtime stack. Consequently, WITH-loops whose bodies contain function applications that cannot be eliminated by the compiler, e.g. through inlining, disqualify for being run on the graphics hardware. Likewise, there are tight restrictions on the organisation of C-style loop nestings that rule out the transformations for traversing arrays in linear order that are vital on standard multi-core systems. This requires a fairly different path through the compilation process early on. Last but certainly not least, data must be transferred from *host memory* to *device memory* and vice versa before the GPU can participate in any computations, effectively creating a distributed memory. It is crucial for achieving good performance to avoid superfluous memory transfers. The SAC compiler takes all this into account and drastically facilitates the utilisation of many-core graphics accelerators in practice. Details can be found in [59].

The fourth and final target architecture currently supported by the SAC compiler is the MicroGrid architecture [15]. While fairly different from GPGPUs from a computer architecture point of view, it is not dissimilar to CUDA from a code generator perspective. Like CUDA it comes with an architecture-specific programming language embedded into the C language, named μTC, and the corresponding compiler toolchain [60]. The MicroGrid exposes less restrictions on generated C code, but it requires us to expose fine-grained concurrency to the hardware. In essence, the right hand side of Fig. 2 can be seen to illustrate this approach. Whereas in the multithreaded approach the SAC compiler takes considerable effort to adapt the fine-grained concurrency exposed on the program level to the generally much coarser-grained actually available concurrency on the executing hardware platform, the MicroGrid efficiently deals with fine-grained concurrency in hardware. Details can be found in [61,62].

10.6 Experimental Evaluation

To the potential disappointment of our readers space limitations prevent us from any decent analysis as to what extent the SAC compiler achieves its aim of competing with C and FORTRAN in terms of runtime performance. Instead we refer the interested reader to a number of publications that have exactly this intention. Typically, they put software engineering concerns into context with runtime performance on diverse computing machinery comparing SAC with various other programming languages.

[63] experiments with anisotropic filters and single-class support vector machines from an industrial image processing pipeline. Performance figures are reported from standard commodity multi-core servers and GPGPUs and show competitive performance with respect to hand-coded C implementations and highly customised image processing libraries. [64] investigates scalability issues of the SAC multithreaded runtime system for a number of smaller benchmarks on the Oracle T3-4 server with up to 512 hardware threads. [59] analyses the performance of the GPGPU code generator for a variety of benchmarks.

[65] compares SAC with FORTRAN-90 in terms of programming productivity and performance on multi-core multi-processor systems for unsteady shock wave interactions. [66] again compares SAC with FORTRAN-90, this time based on the Kadomtsev-Petiviashvili-I equations (KP-I) that describe the propagation of non-linear waves in a dispersive medium. Last not least, [67] and [68] describe SAC implementations of the NAS benchmarks [69] FT (3-dimensional fast-Fourier transforms) and MG (multigrid), respectively. They show sequential performance for the SAC code that is competitive with the hand-optimised FORTRAN-77 reference implementations of the two benchmarks and good scalability on multi-processor systems of the pre-multi-core era.

11 Related Work

Given the wide range of topics around the design and implementation of SAC that we have covered in this article, there is a plethora of related work that is impossible to do justice in this section. Hence, the selection inevitably is subjective and incomplete.

General-purpose functional languages such as HASKELL, CLEAN, SML or OCAML all support arrays in one way or another on the language level. Or more precisely, they support (potentially nested) vectors (1-dimensional arrays) in our terminology. However, as far as implementations are concerned, arrays are rather side issues and design decisions are taken in favour of list- and tree-like data structures. This rules out to achieve competitive performance on array-based compute-intensive kernels.

The most radical step is taken by the ML family of languages: arrays come as stateful, not as functional data structures. To the same degree as this choice facilitates compilation, it looses most appealing characteristics of a functional approach. The lazy functional languages HASKELL and CLEAN both implement fully functional arrays, but investigations have shown that in order to achieve acceptable runtime performance arrays must not only be strict and unboxed (as in SAC), but array processing must also adhere to a stateful regime [70,71,72], i.e. state monads[31] or uniqueness types[33]. While conceptually more elaborate than the ML approach to arrays, monads and uniqueness types likewise enforce an imperative programming style where arrays are explicitly created, copied and removed.

Data Parallel Haskell [73] is an extension of vanilla HASKELL with particular support for nested vectors (arrays in HASKELL speak). Data Parallel Haskell mainly aims at irregular and sparse array problems and inhomogeneous nested vectors in the tradition of NESL[74]. Likewise, it adopts NESL's flattening optimisation that turns nested vectors into flat representations.

One project that must be acknowledged in the context of SAC is SISAL[75,76]. SISAL was the first approach to high-performance functional array programming, and, arguably, it is the only other approach that aims at these goals as stringently as SAC. SISAL predates SAC by about a decade, and consequently, we studied SISAL closely in the early years of the SAC project. Unfortunately, the development of SISAL effectively ended with version 1.1 around the time the first SAC implementation was available. Further developments, such as SISAL 2.0[77] and SISAL-90 [78], were proposed, but have never been implemented.

SAC adopted several ideas of SISAL, e.g. the dispense of many great but implementation-wise costly functional features from currying to higher-order functions and lazy evaluation or non-deferred reference counting to address the aggregate update problem. In many aspects, however, SAC goes far beyond SISAL. Examples are support for truly multi-dimensional arrays instead of 1-dimensional vectors (where only vectors of the same length can be nested in another vector), the ability to define generic abstractions on array operations or the compositional programming style. This list could be extended, but then the comparison is in a sense both unfair and of limited relevance given that development of SISAL ended many years ago.

An interesting offspring from the SISAL project is SAC's namesake SA-C also called Sassy[79,80]. Independently of us and around the same time the originators of SA-C had the idea of a functional language in the spirit of SISAL but with a C-inspired syntax. Thus, we came up with same name: Single Assignment C. Here, the similarities end, even from a syntactic perspective. Despite the almost identical name, SAC and SA-C are very different programming languages.

SAC's implementation of the calculus of multi-dimensional arrays is closely related to interpreted array languages like APL[11,12], J [13] or NIAL[14]. In [81] Bernecky argues that array languages are in principle well suited for data parallel execution and thus should be appropriate for high-performance computing. In practice, language implementations have not followed this path. The main show stopper seems to be the interpretive nature of these languages that hinders code-restructuring optimisations as prominently featured by SAC (Section 10.3). While individual operations could be parallelised, the ratios between productive computation and organisational overhead are often infavourable.

Dynamic (scripting) languages like PYTHON are very popular these days. Consequently, there are serious attempts to establish such languages for compute-intensive applications[82,83]. Here, however, it is very difficult to achieve high performance. Like the APL-family of languages the highly dynamic nature of programs renders static analysis ineffective. It seems that outside the classical high-performance community, programmers are indeed willing to sacrifice performance in exchange for a more agile software engineering process. Often this is used to explore the design space, and once a proper solution is identified, it is re-implemented with low-level techniques to equip production code with the right performance levels. This is exactly where we see opportunities for SAC: combine agile development with high runtime performance through compilation technology and save the effort of re-implementation and the corresponding consistency issues. Much of the above likewise holds for the arguably most used array language of our time: MatLab and its various clones.

12   Conclusions and Perspectives

We have presented the ins and outs of the programming language Single Assignment C (SAC), covering the whole range of issues from general motivation over language design to programming methodology. In essence, SAC combines array programming technology with functional programming principles and a C-like look-and-feel. In two cases studies on convolution and numerical differentiation we have demonstrated how the SAC methodology supports the engineering of concise, abstract, high-level, reusable code.

However, language design is just one side of the coin. One may even say that this is the easy part. The flip side of the coin is do develop the necessary compiler technology to meet our over-arching objective: competing with the performance of C and FORTRAN throughout a variety of parallel computing platforms. How to achieve this goal is the real research question behind the SAC project.

An important insight to this end is that before even looking into generating parallel code competitive sequential performance is of paramount importance. Sequential performance is crucial because we aim at exploiting parallel hardware to generate actual performance gains over existing implementations, not to overcome our own shortcomings in sequential performance. While this sounds more than plausible, it truly is a challenge, and a challenge more often avoided than one may think.

Nonetheless, the ability to fully automatically generate code for various parallel architectures, from symmetric multi-core multi-processors to GPGPU accelerators is arguably one of SAC's major assets. In a standard software engineering process the job is less than half done when a first sequential prototype yields

correct results. Every targeted parallel architecture requires a different parallelisation approach using different APIs, tools and expertise. Explicit parallelisation is extremely time-consuming and error-prone. Typical programming errors
manifest themselves in a non-deterministic way that makes them particularly
hard to find. Targeting different kinds of hardware, say multi-core systems and
GPGPU-accelerators inevitably clutters the code and creates particular maintenance issues. With SAC the job is done as soon as a sequential program is ready.
Multiple parallel target architectures merely require recompilation of the same
source code base with different compiler flags.

Much has been achieved since the principal ideas of SAC were first proposed [84]. In Section 10 we sketched out the most important aspects of compilation technology that we have developed to the present day. A series of case
studies, further more, A lot of work, nonetheless, lies ahead of us. The continuous development of new parallel architectures keeps us busy just as further
improvements of the language and of our compilation infrastructure. Work is
currently on-going in many directions, small and large. We conclude this article
with sketching out a few of them.

For now, the choice of a target architecture is exclusive. We can either generate code to make use of multiple CPU cores or code to exploit a single GPGPU
accelerator. One of our current threads of work is to combine these technologies to make use of multiple GPGPUs and multi-core CPUs at the same time.
This work also accounts for current hardware trends to combine CPU and GPU
technologies on-chip.

Another area of on-going work is to exploit the capabilities of vector registers and vector operations available in most of today's processors. The most
prominent example are Intel's Streaming SIMD Extensions (SSE) for the x86
architecture, but similar features are included in all modern processor designs.
At the moment, SAC does not explicitly exploits these facilities and leaves their
potential to be exploited by the backend compiler. Since the SAC compiler has
a much better understanding of its intermediate code than any backend C compiler could ever derive from the generated code, it would be desirable to generate
vector instructions explicitly in sac2c. Unfortunately, the multitude of ISA extensions and APIs is rather cumbersome. We also need to extend the set of SAC
base types to take full advantage of vector registers. Currently, we explore ways
to support user-defined bit widths for numerical values.

Fig. 3 in the very beginning of this article already outlined two directions of
on-going work. As of now, SAC does not support network-interconnected clusters
or, generally, distributed memory architectures. Despite the multicore revolution,
it is always attractive to combine multiple complete systems for even larger computational tasks. On the other end of the design space we envision a growing
relevance of reconfigurable hardware to address tomorrow's demands on energy
efficiency. One can even think of reconfigurable areas in general-purpose processors. Right now, programming reconfigurable hardware requires a completely
different tool and mind set than conventional software engineering. However,
SAC intermediate code appears to be a suitable starting point for compilation.

Our namesake SA-C/Sassy (see Section 11) took a similar approach about a decade ago, but was presumably ahead of its time. It is fair to say that our efforts into both directions are still in their infancy.

On the language level a number of features are highly desirable. As the participants of the CEFP summer school (painfully) learned during the lab sessions, the monomorphic type system for array base types is suboptimal. While it is easy to define new types in SAC, dealing with arrays of user-defined types is less easy. All support for our advocated compositional programming methodology is based on shape-generic but base-type-monomorphic function definitions in the SAC standard library. These are, of course, not available to (arrays of) user-defined types and need to be provided for each such type by its originator. Polymorphism on base types would immediately solve this issue, but realisation in the context of shapely polymorphism, overloading and the strong desire not to loose on the performance side of the coin create a challenging research question that is currently under investigation.

Another type system issue has been discussed already: the SAC array type system does not support the specification of relationships of the shapes of function arguments and results. For example, matrix multiplication can only be specified for 2-dimensional arrays of any shape, whereas the algorithm requires the y-axis extent of the first argument to coincide with the x-axis extent of the second argument. Furthermore, the algorithm reveals that the result matrix has the same size along the x-axis as the first argument matrix and the same size on the y-axis as the second argument matrix. This knowledge is lost in the type system due to a lack of expressiveness. Similar shape relations are common place across SAC standard array operations, e.g. take, drop or where. Capturing such shape relations in the type system leads to dependent array types that we have studied in the context of (more experimental) array language Qube [28,29]. However, how to carry these ideas over to SAC in the presence of overloading and dynamic dispatch is non-trivial.

Of course, as functional programmers we have a longer wish list for the feature set of SAC. While SAC will always put the emphasis on arrays, it would be highly desirable to support tuples, lists and trees, nonetheless. Likewise, higher-order functions are certainly worthwhile some implementation effort. Currently, the fold-WITH-loop are the only place where functions appear in an (almost) expression position, but this is very restricted and does not allow for abstractions like a general reduction function or operator. Not adopting the general concept of higher-order functions was an early design decisions to facilitate compilation into efficient code. However, restricted support for higher-order functions such that the compiler could in practice resolve them may nonetheless bring a considerable gain in expressiveness.

Acknowledgements. The work described in this paper is the result of more than 15 years of research and development conducted by an ever changing group of people working at a variety of places. From the nucleus at the University of Kiel, Germany, in the mid-1990s the virus spread to the University of Lübeck, Germany, the University of Hertfordshire, England, the University of Toronto,

Canada, the University of Amsterdam, Netherlands, and recently to Heriot-Watt University, Scotland. Apart from the internal funds of these universities, three European projects have been instrumental in supporting our activities: ÆTHER, APPLE-CORE and ADVANCE.

First and foremost, I would like to thank Sven-Bodo Scholz for many years of intense and fruitful collaboration. The original proposal of a no-frills functional language with a C-like syntax and particular support for arrays was his [84]. Apart from the name and these three design principles not too much in today's SAC resembles the original proposal, though.

My special thanks go to those who helped to shape SAC by years of continued work: Dietmar Kreye, Robert Bernecky, Stephan Herhut and Kai Trojahner. Over the years many more have contributed to advancing SAC to its current state. I take the opportunity to thank (in roughly temporal order) Henning Wolf, Arne Sievers, Sören Schwartz, Björn Schierau, Helge Ernst, Jan-Hendrik Schöler, Nico Marcussen-Wulff, Markus Bradtke, Borg Enders, Michael Werner, Karsten Hinckfuß, Steffen Kuthe, Florian Massel, Andreas Gudian, Jan-Henrik Baumgarten, Theo van Klaveren, Daoen Pan, Sonia Chouaieb, Florian Büther, Torben Gerhards, Carl Joslin, Jing Guo, Hraban Luyat, Abhishek Lal, Artem Shinkarov, Santanu Dash, Daniel Rolls, Zheng Zhangzheng, Aram Visser, Tim van Deurzen, Roeland Douma, Fangyong Tang, Pablo Rauzy and Miguel Diogo for their invaluable work.

References

1. Moore, G.E.: Cramming more components onto integrated circuits. Electronics 38 (1965)
2. Sutter, H.: The free lunch is over: A fundamental turn towards concurrency in software. Dr. Dobb's Journal 30 (2005)
3. Meuer, H., Strohmaier, E., Simon, H., Dongarra, J.: 38th top500 list (2011), www.top500.org
4. Intel: Product Brief: Intel Xeon Processor 7500 Series. Intel (2010)
5. AMD: AMD Opteron 6000 Series Platform Quick Reference Guide. AMD (2011)
6. Koufaty, D., Marr, D.: Hyperthreading technology in the netburst microarchitecture. IEEE Micro 23, 56–65 (2003)
7. Sun/Oracle: Oracle's SPARC T3-1, SPARC T3-2, SPARC T3-4 and SPARC T3-1B Server Architecture. Whitepaper, Oracle (2011)
8. Shin, J.L., Huang, D., Petrick, B., et al.: A 40 nm 16-core 128-thread SPARC SoC processor. IEEE Journal of Solid-State Circuits 46, 131–144 (2011)
9. Grelck, C., Scholz, S.B.: SAC: A functional array language for efficient multi-threaded execution. Int. Journal of Parallel Programming 34, 383–427 (2006)
10. Grelck, C., Scholz, S.B.: SAC: Off-the-Shelf Support for Data-Parallelism on Multicores. In: Glew, N., Blelloch, G. (eds.) 2nd Workshop on Declarative Aspects of Multicore Programming (DAMP 2007), Nice, France, pp. 25–33. ACM Press (2007)
11. Falkoff, A., Iverson, K.: The Design of APL. IBM Journal of Research and Development 17, 324–334 (1973)
12. International Standards Organization: Programming Language APL, Extended. ISO N93.03, ISO (1993)

13. Hui, R.: An Implementation of J. Iverson Software Inc., Toronto (1992)
14. Jenkins, M.: Q'Nial: A Portable Interpreter for the Nested Interactive Array Language Nial. Software Practice and Experience 19, 111–126 (1989)
15. Bousias, K., Guang, L., Jesshope, C., Lankamp, M.: Implementation and Evaluation of a Microthread Architecture. J. Systems Architecture 55, 149–161 (2009)
16. Schildt, H.: American National Standards Institute, International Organization for Standardization, International Electrotechnical Commission, ISO/IEC JTC 1: The annotated ANSI C standard: American National Standard for Programming Languages C: ANSI/ISO 9899-1990. McGraw-Hill (1990)
17. Kernighan, B., Ritchie, D.: The C Programming Language. Prentice-Hall (1988)
18. Iverson, K.: A Programming Language. John Wiley (1962)
19. Iverson, K.: Programming in J. Iverson Software Inc., Toronto (1991)
20. Burke, C.: J and APL. Iverson Software Inc., Toronto (1996)
21. Jenkins, M., Jenkins, W.: The Q'Nial Language and Reference Manual. Nial Systems Ltd., Ottawa (1993)
22. Mullin, L.R., Jenkins, M.: A Comparison of Array Theory and a Mathematics of Arrays. In: Arrays, Functional Languages and Parallel Systems, pp. 237–269. Kluwer Academic Publishers (1991)
23. Mullin, L.R., Jenkins, M.: Effective Data Parallel Computation using the Psi Calculus. Concurrency — Practice and Experience 8, 499–515 (1996)
24. Dagum, L., Menon, R.: OpenMP: An Industry-Standard API for Shared-Memory Programming. IEEE Transactions on Computational Science and Engineering 5 (1998)
25. Chapman, B., Jost, G., van der Pas, R.: Using OpenMP: Portable Shared Memory Parallel Programming. MIT Press (2008)
26. Gropp, W., Lusk, E., Skjellum, A.: Using MPI: Portable Parallel Programming with the Message Passing Interface. MIT Press (1994)
27. Douma, R.: Nested Arrays in Single Assignment C. Master's thesis, University of Amsterdam, Amsterdam, Netherlands (2011)
28. Trojahner, K., Grelck, C.: Dependently Typed Array Programs Don't Go Wrong. Journal of Logic and Algebraic Programming 78, 643–664 (2009)
29. Trojahner, K.: QUBE — Array Programming with Dependent Types. PhD thesis, University of Lübeck, Lübeck, Germany (2011)
30. Grelck, C., Scholz, S.B.: Axis Control in SAC. In: Peña, R., Arts, T. (eds.) IFL 2002. LNCS, vol. 2670, pp. 182–198. Springer, Heidelberg (2003)
31. Wadler, P.: Comprehending Monads. Mathematical Structures in Computer Science 2 (1992)
32. Peyton Jones, S., Launchbury, J.: State in Haskell. Lisp and Symbolic Computation 8, 293–341 (1995)
33. Smetsers, S., Barendsen, E., van Eekelen, M., Plasmeijer, M.: Guaranteeing Safe Destructive Updates through a Type System with Uniqueness Information for Graphs. Technical report, University of Nijmegen, Nijmegen, Netherlands (1993)
34. Achten, P., Plasmeijer, M.: The ins and outs of Clean I/O. Journal of Functional Programming 5, 81–110 (1995)
35. Grelck, C.: Integration eines Modul- und Klassen-Konzeptes in die funktionale Programmiersprache SAC – Single Assignment C. Master's thesis, University of Kiel, Germany (1996)
36. Grelck, C., Scholz, S.B.: Classes and Objects as Basis for I/O in SAC. In: 7th International Workshop on Implementation of Functional Languages (IFL 1995), Båstad, Sweden, pp. 30–44. Chalmers University of Technology, Gothenburg (1995)

37. Herhut, S., Scholz, S.B., Grelck, C.: Controlling Chaos — On Safe Side-Effects in Data-Parallel Operations. In: 4th Workshop on Declarative Aspects of Multicore Programming (DAMP 2009), Savannah, USA, pp. 59–67. ACM Press (2009)

38. Grelck, C., Scholz, S., Shafarenko, A.: Asynchronous Stream Processing with S-Net. International Journal of Parallel Programming 38, 38–67 (2010)

39. Scholz, S.B.: Single Assignment C — efficient support for high-level array operations in a functional setting. Journal of Functional Programming 13, 1005–1059 (2003)

40. Grelck, C., van Deurzen, T., Herhut, S., Scholz, S.B.: Asynchronous Adaptive Optimisation for Generic Data-Parallel Array Programming. Concurrency and Computation: Practice and Experience (2011)

41. Scholz, S.-B.: WITH-Loop-Folding in SAC - Condensing Consecutive Array Operations. In: Clack, C., Hammond, K., Davie, T. (eds.) IFL 1997. LNCS, vol. 1467, pp. 72–92. Springer, Heidelberg (1998)

42. Grelck, C., Hinckfuß, K., Scholz, S.B.: With-Loop Fusion for Data Locality and Parallelism. In: Butterfield, A., Grelck, C., Huch, F. (eds.) IFL 2005. LNCS, vol. 4015, pp. 178–195. Springer, Heidelberg (2006)

43. Grelck, C., Scholz, S.-B., Trojahner, K.: With-Loop Scalarization – Merging Nested Array Operations. In: Trinder, P., Michaelson, G.J., Peña, R. (eds.) IFL 2003. LNCS, vol. 3145, pp. 118–134. Springer, Heidelberg (2004)

44. Grelck, C., Scholz, S.B.: Merging compositions of array skeletons in SAC. Journal of Parallel Computing 32, 507–522 (2006)

45. Bernecky, R., Herhut, S., Scholz, S.-B., Trojahner, K., Grelck, C., Shafarenko, A.: Index Vector Elimination – Making Index Vectors Affordable. In: Horváth, Z., Zsók, V., Butterfield, A. (eds.) IFL 2006. LNCS, vol. 4449, pp. 19–36. Springer, Heidelberg (2007)

46. Grelck, C.: Improving Cache Effectiveness through Array Data Layout Manipulation in SAC. In: Mohnen, M., Koopman, P. (eds.) IFL 2000. LNCS, vol. 2011, pp. 231–248. Springer, Heidelberg (2001)

47. Grelck, C., Kreye, D., Scholz, S.B.: On Code Generation for Multi-Generator WITH-Loops in SAC. In: Koopman, P., Clack, C. (eds.) IFL 1999. LNCS, vol. 1868, pp. 77–94. Springer, Heidelberg (2000)

48. Wilson, P.R.: Uniprocessor Garbage Collection Techniques. In: Bekkers, Y., Cohen, J. (eds.) IWMM 1992. LNCS, vol. 637, pp. 1–42. Springer, Heidelberg (1992)

49. Jones, R.: Garbage Collection: Algorithms for Automatic Dynamic Memory Management. John Wiley (1999)

50. Marlow, S., Harris, T., James, R.P., Peyton Jones, S.: Parallel generational-copying garbage collection with a block-structured heap. In: 7th Int. Symposium on Memory Management (ISMM 2008), Tucson, AZ, USA, pp. 11–20. ACM (2008)

51. Hudak, P., Bloss, A.: The Aggregate Update Problem in Functional Programming Systems. In: 12th ACM Symposium on Principles of Programming Languages (POPL 1985), New Orleans, USA, pp. 300–313. ACM Press (1985)

52. Collins, G.E.: A Method for Overlapping and Erasure of Lists. CACM 3, 655–657 (1960).

53. Grelck, C., Trojahner, K.: Implicit Memory Management for SaC. In: 16th International Workshop on Implementation and Application of Functional Languages, IFL 2004, Lübeck, Germany, pp. 335–348. University of Kiel, Institute of Computer Science and Applied Mathematics (2004); Technical Report 0408

54. Grelck, C., Scholz, S.B.: Efficient Heap Management for Declarative Data Parallel Programming on Multicores. In: 3rd Workshop on Declarative Aspects of Multicore Programming (DAMP 2008), San Francisco, CA, USA, pp. 17–31. ACM Press (2008)

55. Grelck, C.: A Multithreaded Compiler Backend for High-Level Array Programming. In: 2nd International Conference on Parallel and Distributed Computing and Networks (PDCN 2003), Innsbruck, Austria, pp. 478–484. ACTA Press (2003)

56. Grelck, C.: Shared memory multiprocessor support for functional array processing in SAC. Journal of Functional Programming 15, 353–401 (2005)

57. Zhangzheng, Z.: Using OpenMP as an Alternative Parallelization Strategy in SAC. Master's thesis, University of Amsterdam, Amsterdam, Netherlands (2011)

58. Kirk, D., Hwu, W.: Programming Massively Parallel Processors: A Hands-on Approach. Morgan Kaufmann (2010)

59. Guo, J., Thiyagalingam, J., Scholz, S.B.: Breaking the GPU programming barrier with the auto-parallelising SAC compiler. In: 6th Workshop on Declarative Aspects of Multicore Programming (DAMP 2011), Austin, TX, USA. ACM Press (2011)

60. Bernard, T., Grelck, C., Jesshope, C.: On the compilation of a language for general concurrent target architectures. Parallel Processing Letters 20, 51–69 (2010)

61. Herhut, S., Joslin, C., Scholz, S.B., Grelck, C.: Truly Nested Data-Parallelism: Compiling SAC to the Microgrid Architecture. In: 21st Symposium on Implementation and Application of Functional Languages (IFL 2009), South Orange, NJ, USA. Seton Hall University (2009)

62. Herhut, S., Joslin, C., Scholz, S.-B., Poss, R., Grelck, C.: Concurrent Non-deferred Reference Counting on the Microgrid: First Experiences. In: Hage, J., Morazán, M.T. (eds.) IFL 2010. LNCS, vol. 6647, pp. 185–202. Springer, Heidelberg (2011)

63. Wieser, V., Grelck, C., Haslinger, P., Guo, J., Korzeniowski, F., Bernecky, R., Moser, B., Scholz, S.: Combining high productivity and high performance in image processing using Single Assignment C on multi-core cpus and many-core gpus. Journal of Electronic Imaging (to appear)

64. Grelck, C., Douma, R.: SAC on a Niagara T3-4 Server: Lessons and Experiences. In: 15th Int. Conference on Parallel Computing (ParCo 2011), Ghent, Belgium (2011)

65. Rolls, D., Joslin, C., Kudryavtsev, A., Scholz, S.-B., Shafarenko, A.: Numerical Simulations of Unsteady Shock Wave Interactions Using SAC and Fortran-90. In: Malyshkin, V. (ed.) PaCT 2009. LNCS, vol. 5698, pp. 445–456. Springer, Heidelberg (2009)

66. Shafarenko, A., Scholz, S.B., Herhut, S., Grelck, C., Trojahner, K.: Implementing a Numerical Solution of the KPI Equation using Single Assignment C: Lessons and Experiences. In: Butterfield, A., Grelck, C., Huch, F. (eds.) IFL 2005. LNCS, vol. 4015, pp. 160–177. Springer, Heidelberg (2006)

67. Grelck, C., Scholz, S.B.: Towards an Efficient Functional Implementation of the NAS Benchmark FT. In: Malyshkin, V.E. (ed.) PaCT 2003. LNCS, vol. 2763, pp. 230–235. Springer, Heidelberg (2003)

68. Grelck, C.: Implementing the NAS Benchmark MG in SAC. In: Prasanna, V.K., Westrom, G. (eds.) 16th International Parallel and Distributed Processing Symposium (IPDPS 2002), Fort Lauderdale, USA. IEEE Computer Society Press (2002)

69. Bailey, D., et al.: The NAS Parallel Benchmarks. International Journal of Supercomputer Applications 5, 63–73 (1991)

70. van Groningen, J.: The Implementation and Efficiency of Arrays in Clean 1.1. In: Kluge, W.E. (ed.) IFL 1996. LNCS, vol. 1268, pp. 105–124. Springer, Heidelberg (1997)

71. Zörner, T.: Numerical Analysis and Functional Programming. In: 10th International Workshop on Implementation of Functional Languages (IFL 1998), London, UK, University College, pp. 27–48 (1998)
72. Chakravarty, M.M., Keller, G.: An Approach to Fast Arrays in Haskell. In: Jeuring, J., Jones, S.L.P. (eds.) AFP 2002. LNCS, vol. 2638, pp. 27–58. Springer, Heidelberg (2003)
73. Peyton Jones, S., Leshchinskiy, R., Keller, G., Chakravarty, M.: Harnessing the multicores: Nested data parallelism in Haskell. In: IARCS Annual Conference on Foundations of Software Technology and Theoretical Computer Science (FSTTCS 2008), Bangalore, India, pp. 383–414 (2008)
74. Blelloch, G., Chatterjee, S., Hardwick, J., Sipelstein, J., Zagha, M.: Implementation of a Portable Nested Data-Parallel Language. Journal of Parallel and Distributed Computing 21, 4–14 (1994)
75. McGraw, J., Skedzielewski, S., Allan, S., Oldehoeft, R., et al.: Sisal: Streams and Iteration in a Single Assignment Language: Reference Manual Version 1.2. M 146. Lawrence Livermore National Laboratory, Livermore (1985)
76. Cann, D.: Retire Fortran? A Debate Rekindled. CACM 35, 81–89 (1992)
77. Oldehoeft, R.: Implementing Arrays in SISAL 2.0. In: 2nd SISAL Users Conference, San Diego, CA, USA, pp. 209–222. Lawrence Livermore National Laboratory (1992)
78. Feo, J., Miller, P., Skedzielewski, S.K., Denton, S., Solomon, C.: Sisal 90. In: Conference on High Performance Functional Computing (HPFC 1995), Denver, CO, USA, pp. 35–47. Lawrence Livermore National Laboratory, Livermore (1995)
79. Hammes, J., Draper, B., Böhm, A.: Sassy: A Language and Optimizing Compiler for Image Processing on Reconfigurable Computing Systems. In: Christensen, H.I. (ed.) ICVS 1999. LNCS, vol. 1542, pp. 83–97. Springer, Heidelberg (1999)
80. Najjar, W., Böhm, W., Draper, B., Hammes, J., et al.: High-level Language Abstraction for Reconfigurable Computing. IEEE Computer 36, 63–69 (2003)
81. Bernecky, R.: The Role of APL and J in High-Performance Computation. APL Quote Quad. 24, 17–32 (1993)
82. van der Walt, S., Colbert, S., Varoquaux, G.: The numpy array: A structure for efficient numerical computation. Computing in Science & Engineering 13 (2011)
83. Kristensen, M., Vinter, B.: Numerical Python for scalable architectures. In: 4th Conference on Partitioned Global Address Space Programming Model (PGAS 2010). ACM Press, New York (2010)
84. Scholz, S.B.: Single Assignment C – Functional Programming Using Imperative Style. In: 6th International Workshop on Implementation of Functional Languages (IFL 1994), pp. 21.1–21.13. University of East Anglia, Norwich (1994)

Reasoning about Multi-process Systems with the Box Calculus

Greg Michaelson[1] and Gudmund Grov[2]

[1] Heriot-Watt University
[2] University of Edinburgh

Abstract. The box calculus is a formalism for reasoning about the properties of multi-process systems which enables account to be taken of pragmatic as well as computational concerns. It was developed for the programming language Hume which explicitly distinguishes between coordination, based on concurrent boxes linked by wires, and expressions, based on polymorphic recursive functions. This chapter introduces Hume expressions and surveys classic techniques for reasoning about functional programs. It then explores Hume coordination and the box calculus, and examines how Hume programs may be systematically transformed while maintaining computational and pragmatic correctness.

1 Overview

Having constructed programs that meet their specifications, we often want to change them to take advantage of changing operating environments. For example, we might want to migrate a program from environments with smaller to larger numbers of processors to improve performance, in particular as the number of cores grows in new generations of the same CPU architecture. In changing programs, we want to ensure not only they still meet their original specifications, but also that their *pragmatic* (i.e. time, space, sequencing) behaviours change in well understood ways. In particular, in making what appear to be local improvements to a program, for example by introducing parallelism, we want to avoid unexpected global impacts that make overall performance worse, for example as a result of unanticipated additional communication or scheduling costs. Thus, we need some means of *reasoning* about changes to programs that can account for pragmatic as well as computational program properties.

Most software is constructed in imperative programming languages; abstractions from von Neumann architectures[1] based on sequences of state changes mediated by mutable memory. Here, different program components interact by manipulating the same memory areas. Thus, changing the order of component execution often changes the sequence of memory manipulation, changing what the program does. This complicates reasoning about imperative programs because the state change sequencing must be made explicit in the reasoning

---

[1] And also Harvard architectures.

V. Zsók, Z. Horváth, and R. Plasmeijer (Eds.): CEFP 2011, LNCS 7241, pp. 279–338, 2012.
© Springer-Verlag Berlin Heidelberg 2012

rules. While there are mature systems like Floyd-Hoare logic[Hoa69] and weakest preconditions[Dij75] for establishing properties of imperative programs, they require considerable mathematical sophistication, scale poorly with program size and lack mature automated or semi-automated tool support.

In contrast, declarative languages do not have any notion of state change through mutable memory. Instead, program components interact by passing each other values. Thus, in principle, components may be executed in arbitrary order without changing what the program does. This is alleged to make it simpler to reason about declarative programs, compared with imperative ones, as the reasoning rules do not require any notion of sequenced state change. Nonetheless, reasoning about functional programs is not really much easier than for imperative programs: once again, the mathematics is hard, scalability is poor and tools are lacking.

The introduction of parallelism further complicates reasoning about programs. Parallelism requires interaction between processors, either through shared mutable memory access or distributed memory message passing, and that interaction must take place in some order and at some additional performance cost. The development of tools and technologies for reasoning about parallelism is hampered by factors quite orthogonal to those constraining reasoning about sequential programs.

In particular, despite the explosive growth in deployment of multi-processor architectures, there is effectively no standardisation of parallel programming languages. This is hardly surprising. Given the vast investments in software tools and technologies for sequential imperative languages, it is really hard to make a commercial case for adapting unproven extensions to extant languages, let alone new parallel languages: the rise and fall of occam[Inm88] is an object lesson. Instead, extant languages tend to be augmented with libraries like MPI[MF94], for message passing, and OpenMP[CJP07], for shared memory. As yet, there is little formalisation of these libraries and so scant theoretical or practical support for formal reasoning about practical parallelism.

There are, of course, mature formalisms for reasoning about abstract parallelism, for example CSP[Hoa78], CCS[Mil82] and the π calculus[Mil99]. However, while well suited to reasoning about coordination, these take little account of the computations that are being coordinated, and share the same constraints as sequential formalisms.

It has long been claimed [Weg68] that declarative programs are ideal for parallelism as the absence of sequences state change enables implicit parallelism at all levels of programs. Indeed, parallelism formalisms share strong roots with declarative languages. In practice, such implicit parallelism is almost invariably too fine grain to be exploited efficiently. That is, the cost of the interaction between newly parallel program components outweighs any benefit from executing them in parallel. Thus, there is considerable research into developing new declarative languages for parallelism, such as Eden[BLOMP97], or extending extant languages, such as Haskell[eAB+99], again without any wide adoption of a single language or stable standardisation of extensions. Nonetheless, as we shall see, declarative languages do offer valuable abstractions for parallelism in *higher order functions (HOFS)* which generalise common patterns of computation enabling their efficient realisation as standard patterns of coordination.

Hume[HM03] is a general purpose programming language which was designed to enable the construction and analysis of systems where strong assurances are required that resource bounds are met. This language has deep roots in contemporary functional languages and is based on concurrent finite state automata with transitions controlled by pattern matching over inputs to invoke recursive expressions to generate outputs.

To meet Hume's design objectives, an explicit distinction is made amongst the expression, coordination and control *layers*:

- The *expression* layer is based on a strict, polymorphic functional language with a rich type system, reminiscent of Standard ML[MTHM97] or Haskell. This layer is used to define computations that return values for use in box transitions.
- The *coordination* layer is based on concurrent generalised finite state automata consisting of *boxes* linked by *wires*. This layer is used to define boxes and wiring, and box and wiring templates.
- The *declaration* layer is used to define common auxiliary constructs for use throughout programs, for example: constants; functions; type aliases; type signatures; exceptions and constructed data types.

To further facilitate resource analysis complementing system development, Hume supports the notion of *language level* with different formal properties, depending on the types of values on wires between boxes, and the forms of expressions within boxes. Thus:

- *full Hume* is a Turing complete language with undecidable time and space behaviour;
- *PR-Hume* restricts recursion to primitive recursion. Thus, time and space are decidable though not necessarily well bound;
- Template-Hume prohibits user defined recursion but provides a repertoire of higher order functions with well characterised behaviours. Here, time and space bounds may be well bound.
- *FSM-Hume* corresponds to a richly typed finite state machine abstraction. There is no recursion and all repetition is through iteration over boxes. Furthermore, only types of known size may be passed on wires. FSM-Hume enables accurate time and space analysis.
- *HW-Hume* is an impoverished language oriented to hardware at the bit levels, supporting pattern matching on tuples of bits to produce tuples of bits. HW-Hume enables precise time and space analysis.

It is unrealistic to expect programmers to restrict themselves to one level. Instead, Hume supports a methodology of transformational software development. An initial system is built and analysed. If satisfactory bounds cannot be established then problematic loci may be changed into a lower level, typically by moving activity from within boxes to between boxes. Clearly, reasoning about and changing programs at the coordination layer almost invariably requires reasoning and change at the expression layer. Thus, the box calculus strongly reflects this language design, and is novel in enabling movements between layers in search of optimal programs.

In the rest of this chapter we will:

- introduce the Hume expression layer;
- survey classical techniques for reasoning about functional programs;
- introduce the Hume coordination layer;
- explore the foundations of the box calculus;
- apply the box calculus to systematically deriving a range of multi-box programs from single box programs.

2   Hume Expression Language

2.1   Base Types and Expressions

Base Types. For our purposes, the main Hume base types are integer, floating points, words, characters and booleans. All base types are *sized*, that is they have fixed ranges of values which are related to the number of bits that instances occupy. For numeric types, the size is specified explicitly. For example, the integer type constructor is:

- int *size* - signed integer;

where *size* is some multiple of 8^2.

Type Aliases. In practice, it is usual to use *type aliases*, rather than raw type constructors, of the form:

type *id* = *type*;

where *id* is an identifier composed of upper and lower case letters and digits, starting with a letter or _, and *type* is a type expression, in the first instance a type constructor. Thereafter, *id* may be used in any context where a type expression is appropriate. For example:

type integer = int 64;

defines integer to be an alias for int 64.

Base Values. Hume has the standard base value representations:

- integers are sequences of possibly negative decimal digits: e.g. 12345, -678910;
- floats are sequences of decimal digits separated by a decimal point: e.g. 123.456, -789.1011;
- words are sequences of hexadecimal digits preceded by 0x: e.g. 0xabcdef;
- characters are letters or escaped letters within single quotes: e.g. 'a', '\n' (newline);
- booleans are true or false.

---

[2] In practice, current Hume implementations tie all sizes to some C equivalent.

Base Expressions. All expressions may be structured by brackets (...).
The integer infix operators are + (addition), - (subtraction), * (multiplication), div (division) and mod (remainder). All integer operators take two integer operands. The precedence, in descending order, is: (...); unary -; +, -; *, mod, div.

The float infix operators are + (addition), - (subtraction), * (multiplication) and / (division). All float operators take two float operands. The precedence, in descending order, is: (...); unary -; +, -; *, /.

The boolean operators are not (prefix negation), && (infix conjunction) and || (infix disjunction). All boolean operators take boolean operands. The precedence, in descending order, is: (...), not, ||, &&.

The comparison operators are == (equals), != (not equals), < (less than), <= (less than or equal), >= (greater than or equal) and > (greater than). All comparison operators take operands of the same type.

Constant Declaration. Constants may be declared by:

id = $expression$;

Here, id is associated with the value of $expression$ and may be used in subsequent $expressions$. For example:

```
cost = 35;
quantity = 12;
total = cost * quantity;
```

associates cost with 35, quantity with 12 and total with 420.

2.2   Functions

Function Declaration. At simplest, Hume functions are declared as:

id $pattern$ = $expression$;

where id names the function, $pattern$ introduces formal parameters and $expression$ is the function body. To begin with, a $pattern$ may just be an id. For example:

```
inc x = x+1;
isZero y = y==0;
```

declares inc to be function that increments its argument x and isZero to be a function that checks if it's argument y is zero.

Function Type and Type Signature. If $pattern$ is $type_1$ and $expression$ is $type_2$ then id is: $type_1$ -> $type_2$.

Types may be nominated explicitly through a $type$ $signature$ of the form:

id :: $type$;

For example, we could make the types of inc and isZero explicit as:

```
inc :: int 32 -> int 32
isZero :: int 32 -> bool
```

Hume supports polymorphic type inference and it is not a requirement to specify the function type if it is inferable from the context of declaration or use. However, it may be necessary to provide a type signature to disambiguate overloaded operators which may appear in different type contexts. For example:

```
sq :: integer -> integer;
sq x = x*x;
```

In sq, * is overloaded so x's type cannot be inferred. Here, the type signature makes it explicit that sq operates on integers so * must be an integer operator.

Explicit Parameter Type. An alternative to deploying a type signature is to explicitly nominate the type of a formal parameter using:

(*pattern*::*type*)

instead of *pattern*. For example:

```
sq (x::integer) = x*x;
```

makes it explicit that x is integer in sq.

Function Call. Functions are called with expressions of the form:

id expression

Here, *id* is a name associated with a function and *expression* is the actual parameter. If *id* is associated with a $type_1$->$type_2$ function and *expression* is $type_1$ then the call returns a value of $type_2$.

For a function call: where *id*'s function has formal parameter *pattern*, consisting in the first instance of a single id_1, and body $expression_1$, then:

- the actual parameter *expression* is evaluated to *value*;
- *value* is matched with *pattern* i.e. id_1 is bound to *value*;
- the function body $expression_1$ is evaluated with all free occurrences of the formal parameter id_1[3] replaced by *value*.

Note that Hume does not support anonymous functions.

Note that this is a *substitutive* model of function call evaluation. For example:

1. inc 41
2. → x+1 with x bound to 41
3. → 41+1
4. → 42

---

[3] i.e. occurrences outwith the scope of some other declaration of id_1 in $expression_1$.

For example:

1. `isZero (inc 3)`
2. $\rightarrow$ x+1 with x bound to 3
3. $\rightarrow$ 3+1
4. $\rightarrow$ 4
5. $\rightarrow$ y==0 with y bound to 4
6. $\rightarrow$ 4==0
7. $\rightarrow$ `false`

A function call has precedence higher than numeric operators and lower than $(\ldots)$.

2.3 Tuples

Tuple Form. A tuple is a fixed sized sequence of elements of possibly different types. A tuple has the form:

$$(exp_1, exp_2 \ldots exp_N)$$

If exp_i is of $type_i$ then this tuple has type:

$$(exp_1, exp_2 \ldots exp_N) \ :: \ (type_1, type_2, \ldots type_N)$$

For example:

```
(1,2.0,true) :: (int 32,float 32,bool)
(1,(2,3),4) :: (int 32,(int 32,int 32),int 32)
```

Tuple Pattern. Tuple patterns may be used for multi-parameter functions. These take the form:

$$(patt_1, patt_2 \ldots patt_N)$$

In:

$$id \ (patt_1, patt_2 \ldots patt_N) = expression$$

if $patt_i$ is $type_i$ and $expression$ is $type_{N+1}$ then the function type is:

$$(type_1, type_2 \ldots type_N) \ \text{->} \ type_{N+1}$$

Then, a function call:

$$id \ expression_1$$

proceeds as:

- evaluate $expression_1$ to:
    $$(value_1, value_2 \ldots value_N)$$
- match $patt_i$ with $value_i$ i.e. bind id_i from $patt_i$ to $value_i$;
- evaluate the body $expression$ with these bindings.

For example, given:

```
quad :: (integer,integer,integer,integer) -> integer;
quad (a,b,c,x) = a*x*x+b*x+c;
```

then:

1. quad (1,2,1,3)
2. → a*x*x+b*x*c with a=1, b=2, c=1 and x=3
3. → 1*3*3+2*3+1
4. → 16

2.4   Multi-case Functions

Multi-case Function Declaration. Multi-case functions may be declared as:

id $pattern_1$ = $expression_1$;
id $pattern_2$ = $expression_2$;
...
id $pattern_N$ = $expression_N$;

All cases must have same id. All $pattern_i$ must be same $type_1$. All $expression_i$ must be the same $type_2$. The function then has type: $type_1$->$type_2$.

As we shall see, case order is significant. The $pattern_i$ should be disjoint and cover all possible values of $type_1$. Thus, it is usual, for functions that do not have exhaustive cases, to provide a final case with a catch-all id pattern.

Constant Pattern. Patterns may include constant values in any positions where id may appear. For example, we might define boolean negation as:

```
Not false = true;
Not true = false;
```

and natural number decrement as:

```
natDec 0 = 0;
natDec x = x-1;
```

For a constant pattern match to succeed, the same constant must appear in the same structural position in the formal parameter pattern and actual parameter value.

Multi-case Function Call. For:

id $expression$

- $expression$ is evaluated to some $value$;
- $value$ is matched against each $pattern$ in turn from first to last.
- if a match with $pattern_i$ succeeds then $expression_i$ is evaluated;

For example, for:

    Not true

then:

1. try Not false - false does not match true;
2. try Not true - true matches true;
3. → false

For example, for:

    natDec 3

then:

1. try natDec 0 - 0 does not match 3;
2. try natDec x - x binds to 3;
3. → x-1
4. → 3-1
5. → 2

2.5   Recursion

Recursive Function Declaration. As in all functional languages, Hume functions may call themselves. At simplest, a recursive function has the typical structure:

- **base case** match constant and return final value;
- **recursion case** match *id* and call function again with modified *id*.

The recursion case should make progress towards the base case by changing the recursion parameter *id*.

For example, consider summing a sequence of integers from N to 0:

$$N + (N - 1) + ... + 2 + 1 + 0$$

We can write this as:

    sum 0;
    sum N = n+sum (N-1);

so:

    sum 3 → 3+sum 2 → 3+2+sum 1 → 3+2+1+sum 0 → 3+2+1+0 → 6

For example, consider summing a sequence of squares from N to 0:

$$N^2 + (N - 1)^2 + ... + 2^2 + 1^2 + 0$$

We can write this as:

    sumSq 0;
    sumSq N = sq n+sumSq (N-1);

so:

    sumSq 3 → sq 3+sumSq 2 → sq 3+sq 2+sumSq 1 →
    sq 3+sq 2+sq 1+sumSq 0 → sq 3+sq 2+sq 1+0 → 9+4+1+0 → 14

2.6   Higher Order Functions 1

As a first definition, a higher order function takes other functions as parameters. For example, consider summing some function f over the range from N to 0:

$$f\ N + f\ (N-1) + ...f\ 2 + f\ 1 + 0$$

We may write this as:

```
sumF :: (integer->integer,integer)->integer;
sumF (f,0) = 0;
sumF (f,N) = f N+sumF (f,n-1);
```

Then we may sum squares from N to 0 with:

sumF (sq,3) $\rightarrow$ sq 3+sumF (sq,2) $\rightarrow$ sq 3+sq 2+sumF (sq,1) $\rightarrow$
sq 3+sq 2+sq 1+sumF (sq,0) $\rightarrow$ sq 3+sq 2+sq 1+0 $\rightarrow$ 9+4+1+0 $\rightarrow$
14

2.7   Curried Functions

Functions with tuple formal parameters may be written as nested or *Curried* functions. Thus:

id::$(type_1,type_2...type_N)$->$type$;
$id\ (patt_1,pat_2...patt_N)$ = $expression$;

has equivalent nested function:

id::$type_1$->$type_2...type_N$->$type$;
$id\ patt_1\ patt_2\ ...\ patt_N$ = $expression$;

For example:

```
quad::(integer,integer,integer,integer)->integer;
quad (a,b,c,x) = a*x*x+b*x+c;
```
$\Leftrightarrow$
```
quadC::integer->integer->integer->integer->integer;
quadC a b c x = a*x*x+b*x+c;
```

Curried functions are called as:

$id\ exp_1\ exp_2\ ...\ exp_N$

For example:

```
quadC 1 2 1 3;
```

Currying is a matter of style. Its use lies in support for *partial application* where a function of N parameters is applied to $M < N$ parameters to return a function of $N - M$ parameters with the first M parameters bound to specific values. However, Hume does not support partial application.

2.8   Constructed Types 1

New types with distinct constant values may be declared by:

```
data id = id₁ | id₂ | ... ;
```

Here, id is the new type, and the id_i are new constructors returning values id_i of type id.

For example:

```
data STATE = ON | OFF;
```

declares a new type STATE with values ON and OFF.

Type constructors may be used as constants in patterns. For example, to flip STATE:

```
change ON = OFF;
change OFF = ON;
```

Here, change has type STATE->STATE.

2.9   Higher Order Functions 2

A second definition of a higher order function is one that returns a function. For example, consider:

```
data FN = INC | SQ;
getFN :: FN -> (integer->integer);
getFN INC = inc;
getFN SQ = sq;
```

Here, getFN returns either inc or sq, depending on the actual parameter. Thus:

getFn SQ 3 $\rightarrow$ sq 3 $\rightarrow$ 9

As always, the functions returned in different cases must have the same type, in this instance integer->integer.

2.10   Polymorphism

The ability to abstract over types is termed *polymorphism*, from the Greek for "many forms". In Hume, type expressions may include *type variables* with single lower-case letter identifiers: a, b, c etc.

In a type expression, all occurrences of a type variable must be capable of being replaced consistently with the same type. For example, consider the identity function:

```
identity :: a -> a;
identity x = x;
```

In:

identity 42 $\rightarrow$ 42

the type variable a is replaced consistently by int 32. In:

    identity ('a','b','c') → ('a','b','c')

the type variable a is replaced consistently by (char,char,char).

2.11   Lists

List Representation. A *list* is an arbitrary length sequence of the same type. A list whose elements are of *type* has type [*type*].

Lists are formed using the infix concatenation operator : of effective type (a,[a])->[a]. That is, if exp_1 is of *type* and exp_2 is a list of *type*, i.e. [*type*], then $exp_1:exp_2$ is of type [*type*].

The *empty list* is [] of effective type [a] and must end every list.

For example:

```
1:2:3:[] :: [int 32]
('a',true):('b',false):('c',false):[] :: [(char,bool)]
inc:sq:[] :: [int 32->int 32]
```

In $exp_1:exp_2$, exp_1 is called the list *head* and exp_2 the list *tail*.

The simplified notation:

$$exp_1:exp_2:\ldots:exp_N:[] \Leftrightarrow [exp_1,exp_2,\ldots,exp_N]$$

is often used. For example:

```
1:2:3:[] ⇔ [1,2,3]
('a',true):('b',false):('c',false):[] ⇔
    [('a',true),('b',false),('c',false)]
inc:sq:[] ⇔ [inc,sq]
```

Note that:

$$[exp] \Leftrightarrow exp:[]$$

List Pattern and List Recursion. Formal parameter patterns may include the forms:

  $patt_1:patt_2$
  $[exp_1,exp_2\ldots exp_N]$

For both forms, the actual parameters must have corresponding structures. Then, elements of the list pattern are matched against corresponding values in the actual parameter.

List recursion then has the typical structure:

- **base case** [] - return final value;
- **recursion case** $(id_1:id_2)$ - recurse on id_2 and combine with modified id_1.

For example, to find the length of a list:

```
Length :: [a] -> integer;
Length [] = 0;
Length (h:t) = 1+Length t;
```

so:

Length [1,2,3] $\rightarrow$ 1+Length [2,3] $\rightarrow$ 1+1+Length [3] $\rightarrow$ 1+1+1+
Length [] $\rightarrow$ 1+1+1+0 $\rightarrow$ 3

For example, to sum the elements of a list:

```
sumL [] = 0;
sumL (h:t) = h+sumL t;
```

so:

sumL [1,2,3] $\rightarrow$ 1+sumL [2,3] $\rightarrow$ 1+2+sumL [3] $\rightarrow$ 1+2+3+sumL []
$\rightarrow$ 1+2+3+0 $\rightarrow$ 6

To square all in a list:

```
sqList [] = [];
sqList (h:t) = sq h:sqList t;
```

so:

sqList [1,2,3] $\rightarrow$ sq 1:sqList [2,3] $\rightarrow$ sq 1:sq 2:sqList [3] $\rightarrow$
sq 1:sq 2:sq 3:sqList [] $\rightarrow$ sq 1:sq 2:sq 3:[] $\rightarrow$ 1:4:9:[] $\rightarrow$
[1,4,9]

2.12   List Higher Order Functions

We will now survey a number of list higher order functions which we will use in later sections.

Sum Function over List. To sum a function over a list:

```
sumFL :: (a->integer)->[a]->integer;
sumFL f [] = 0;
sumFL f (h:t) = f h+sumFL f t;
```

so:

sumFL sq [1,2,3] $\rightarrow$ sq 1+sumFL sq [2,3] $\rightarrow$ sq 1+sq 2+sumFL sq
[3] $\rightarrow$ sq 1+sq 2+sq 3+sumFL sq [] $\rightarrow$ sq 1+sq 2+sq 3+0 $\rightarrow$ 1+4+9
$\rightarrow$ 14

Map. To *map* a function over a list, that is apply a function to every element:

```
map :: (a->b)->[a]->[b];
map f [] = [];
map f (h:t) = f h:map f t;
```

so to square every element in a list:

> map sq [1,2,3] → sq 1:map sq [2,3] → sq 1:sq 2:map sq [3] →
> sq 1:sq 2:sq 3:map sq [] → sq 1:sq 2:sq 3:[] → 1:4:9:[] →
> [1,4,9]

Append. To *append* one list onto another, that is join the lists end to end:

```
append :: [a]->[a]->[a];
append [] 12 = 12;
append (h1:t2) 12 = h1:append t1 12;
```

For example:

> append [1,2,3] [4,5,6] → 1:append [2,3] [4,5,6] → 1:append
> [2,3] [4,5,6] → 1:2:append [3] [4,5,6] → 1:2:3:append [] [4,5,6]
> → 1:2:3:[4,5,6] → [1,2,3,4,5,6]

append $l1$ $l2$ may be written $l1$++$l2$.

2.13 String

A *string* is a sequence of letters within "...". For example:

> "this is not a string"

The string type constructor is **string**. A string is the same as a list of **char** so:

> "hello" ⇔ 'h':'e':'l':'l':'o':[] ⇔ ['h','e','l','l','o']

and:

> "hello"++" "++"there" ⇔ "hello there"

2.14 Conditional Expression

Pattern matching can only determine the presence or absence of a constant value. To establish other properties of values a *conditional expression* may be used:

> if *expression*$_1$ then *expression*$_2$ else *expression*$_3$

expression$_1$ must return a **bool**, and *expression*$_2$ and *expression*$_3$ must return the same type.

expression$_1$ is evaluated. If it is **true** then *expression*$_2$ is evaluated. Otherwise *expression*$_3$ is evaluated.

For example, to select all the even values in an integer list:

```
isEven y = y div 2==0;
getEven [] = [];
getEven (h:t) =
 if isEven h
 then h:getEven t
 else getEven t;
```

so:

```
getEven [1,2,3,4] → getEven [2,3,4] → 2:getEven [3,4] →
2:getEven[4] → 2:4:getEven [] → 2:4:[] → [2,4]
```

Filter. For example, to find all the elements of a list satisfying some property:

```
filter :: (a->bool)->[a]->[a];
filter p [] = [];
filter p (h:t) =
 if p h
 then h:filter p t
 else filter p t;
```

so:

```
filter isEven [1,2,3,4] → filter isEven [2,3,4] → 2:filter
isEven [3,4] → 2:filter isEven[4] → 2:4:filter isEven [] →
2:4:[] → [2,4]
```

2.15 Case Expression

The *case expression* provides an expression form which is equivalent to a multi-case function declaration. For:

```
case expression of
```
$pattern_1$ -> $expression_1$ |
$pattern_2$ -> $expression_2$ |
$\ldots$
$pattern_N$ -> $expression_N$

expression and all *pattern_i* must have the same type, and all *expression_i* must have the same type. As with multi-case functions, the *pattern*s should be disjoint and there should be full coverage for the corresponding type, so a final case with a catch-all variable pattern is common.

expression is evaluated and matched against each *pattern* in turn from 1 to N. If the match with *pattern_i* succeeds then the value of *expression_i* is returned. For example:

```
fib 0 = 1;
fib 1 = 1;
fib n = fib (n-1)+fib (n-2);
⇔
fib n =
 case n of
 0 -> 1 |
 1 -> 1 |
 n -> fib (n-1)+fin (n-2);
```

As we will see, the case expression is used in the box calculus to move activity between functions and boxes.

2.16   Constructed Types 2

The constructed type form is generalised to enable the declaration of structured types. For:

data $id = id_1\ type_1$ | $id_2\ type_2$ | ... $id_N\ type_N$;

each $id_i\ type_i$ is a type constructor of $type_i$->id.

The equivalent form $id_i\ pattern_i$ may then be used in patterns. For a match to succeed, the actual parameter $id_j\ expression_j$ must have the same constructor id_j as id_i and the $expression_j$ must match $pattern_i$.

For example, to declare integer lists:

data LIST = NIL | CONS (integer,LIST);

Here, the new type is LIST with constant value NIL and structured values of the form CONS (h,t) where h is an integer and t is a LIST. For example:

CONS(1,CONS(2,CONS(3,NIL)))

Then, we might declare a function to flatten a LIST into a [integer] as:

flatten NIL = [];
flatten (LIST(h,t)) = h:flatten t;

so:

flatten (CONS (1,CONS(2,CONS(3,NIL)))) →
1:flatten (CONS (2,CONS(3,NIL))) →
1:2:flatten (CONS(3,NIL)) →
1:2:3:flatten NIL → 1:2:3:[] → [1,2,3]

3   Reasoning about Functional Programs

3.1   Introduction

Our starting point was that we have a correct program, that is one that satisfies its specification, and we wish to change it in various ways without compromising that correctness. In the widely used Floyd-Hoare paradigm, we assume that we have *proved* that:

$$\{P\}program\{Q\}$$

That is, for some *program*, given a precondition P, which is true at the start of the program, then we can prove that some post-condition Q is true at the end of the program, using an appropriate proof theory. If we then change *program* to *program'* we then need to prove:

$\{P\}program'\{Q\}$

That is we must prove that the new program still satisfies the original specification.

Proving program correctness requires considerable sophistication in both constructing the specification and deriving the proof. This is a very time consuming process, despite partial automation through theorem provers.

An alternative is to deploy formal program *transformation*, using rules that are known to preserve correctness. That is, given a transformation T, if we can prove that:

$$\forall\ P,Q,program:\ \{P\}program\{Q\} \Rightarrow \{P\}T(program)\{Q\}$$

then we can deploy T to change programs without any further need to re-prove the changes.

In practice, the deployment of transformation assumes *referential transparency* [Qui64], that is that *substitution of equalities* preserves meaning. So, mathematical or logical techniques are used to establish that transformations establish equality and then the transformations may be applied to localised program fragments.

For functional programs, reasoning about program transformation draws on classical propositional and predicate calculi, set theory, Peano arithmetic and the theory of computing. We will next survey these sources and then carry out a number of proofs of basic transformations for use when we meet the box calculus proper.

3.2   Propositional Calculus

Inference. Propositional calculus[Nid62] is a system for reasoning about truth formula made up of:

- constants `true` and `false`;
- variables;
- operators such as: $\neg$ (not), $\wedge$ (and), $\vee$ (or), $\Rightarrow$ (implies), $\equiv$ (equivalent);
- ($\ldots$) (brackets)

Proofs are based on *axioms*, that is formula that are always true and *rules of inference* of the form: $\dfrac{assumptions}{conclusion}$

The proof that a *proposition* is a *theorem*, that is always true, then proceeds by starting from axioms, and established theorems, which have already been proved to be true, and applying rules of inference until the truth or falsity of the proposition is established.

Truth Tables. We may give semantics to propositional operators in terms of truth tables that spell out explicitly their values for all possible combinations of operands. Figure 1 shows the tables for $\neg$, $\wedge$, $\vee$ and $\Rightarrow$.

X	Y	$\neg X$	$X \wedge Y$	$X \vee Y$	$X \Rightarrow Y$
false	false	true	false	false	true
false	true		false	true	true
true	false	false	false	true	false
true	true		true	true	true

Fig. 1. Truth tables for $\neg$, $\wedge$, $\vee$ and $\Rightarrow$

We may then prove a theorem by constructing the truth table to demonstrate that it is true for all combinations or arguments. For example, Figure 2 shows a proof that:

$$X \Rightarrow Y \equiv \neg X \vee Y$$

X	Y	$\neg X$	$\neg X \vee Y$	$X \Rightarrow Y$
false	false	true	true	true
false	true	true	true	true
true	false	false	false	false
true	true	false	true	true

Fig. 2. $X \Rightarrow Y \equiv \neg X \vee Y$

Rewriting. Rewriting involves using proven equivalences of the form:

$$formula_1 \equiv formula_2$$

by substituting instances of $formula_2$ for $formula_1$ and vice versa, consistently replacing common meta-variables. There are many well known equivalences for cancelling out, reordering and expanding/grouping terms - see Figure 3.

We will meet many of these forms again when we consider other roots for reasoning about functional programs.

3.3   Predicate Calculus

Where propositional calculus is concerned with properties of propositions about truth values, *predicate calculus*[Hod77] is used to reason about properties of some universe of discourse. It extends propositional calculus with:

- constant values from a universe of some *type*;
- predicates capturing properties of values from the universe, from that *type* to boolean;
- functions between values in the universe, from *type* to *type*;

Most important, predicate calculus introduces *quantifiers* for expressing properties of the entire universe. *Universal* quantification (all):

$$\forall var : P(var)$$

states that P holds for all *var* from the universe. *Existential* quantification (exists):

$$\exists var : P(var)$$

states that P holds for some *var* from the universe.

Constant	Negation
$P \wedge \textbf{true} \equiv P$	$P \vee \neg P \equiv \textbf{true}$
$P \wedge \textbf{false} \equiv \textbf{false}$	$P \wedge \neg P \equiv \textbf{false}$

	Idempotency
$P \vee \textbf{true} \equiv \textbf{true}$	
$P \vee \textbf{false} \equiv P$	$P \vee P \equiv P$
	$P \wedge P \equiv P$

Associativity	Commutativity
$P \vee (Q \vee R) \equiv (P \vee Q) \vee R$	$P \vee Q \equiv Q \vee P$
$P \wedge (Q \wedge R) \equiv (P \wedge Q) \wedge R$	$P \wedge Q \equiv Q \wedge P$
	$(P \equiv Q) \equiv (Q \equiv P)$

Distributivity	De Morgan's Laws
$P \wedge (Q \vee R) \equiv (P \wedge Q) \vee (P \wedge R)$	$\neg(P \wedge Q) \equiv \neg P \vee \neg Q$
$P \vee (Q \wedge R) \equiv (P \vee Q) \wedge (P \vee R)$	$\neg(P \vee Q) \equiv \neg P \wedge \neg Q$

Implication	Equivalence
$P \Rightarrow Q \equiv \neg P \vee Q$	$(P \equiv Q) \equiv (P \Rightarrow Q) \wedge (Q \Rightarrow P)$
$P \Rightarrow Q \equiv \neg Q \Rightarrow \neg P$	$(P \equiv Q) \equiv (P \wedge Q) \vee (\neg P \wedge \neg Q)$
$P \wedge Q \Rightarrow R \equiv P \Rightarrow (Q \Rightarrow R)$	$(P \equiv Q) \equiv (P \Rightarrow Q) \wedge (\neg P \Rightarrow \neg Q)$

Fig. 3. Propositional equivalences

Pure predicate calculus is used to establish properties of arbitrary universes and we will not consider it further here. However, we will look at *applied* predicate calculus in more detail.

3.4   Set Theory

Set theory[Hal60] formalise properties of sets of constants, characterised either exhaustively or by some predicate. Finite sets are written as:

$\{element_1, element_2, ...element_N\}$

where each *element$_i$* is some atomic entity. The empty set is $\{\}$. The principle set operations are: $\in$ (member), $\cup$ (union), $\cap$ (intersection), $\subset$ and $\subseteq$ (subset) and $\backslash$ (difference).

Set theory also offers a rich collection of equivalences for cancelling, reordering, expanding and grouping terms in set expressions, summarised in Figure 4.

Set Theoretic Predicate Calculus. Quantification may be specialised to specific sets, so:

$\forall var \in S : P(var)$

states that P holds for all *var* in S, and:

$\exists var \in S : P(var)$

states that P holds for some *var* in S.

Constant	Idempotency
$X \cup \{\} \equiv X$	$A \cup A \equiv A$
$X \cap \{\} \equiv \{\}$	$A \cap A \equiv A$
$X \backslash \{\} \equiv X$	

Associativity	Commutativity
$A \cup (B \cup C) \equiv (A \cup B) \cup C$	$A \cup B \equiv B \cup A$
$A \cap (B \cap C) \equiv (A \cap B) \cap C$	$A \cap B \equiv B \cap A$

Distributivity
$$A \cap (B \cup C) \equiv (A \cap B) \cup (A \cap C)$$
$$A \cup (B \cap C) \equiv (A \cup B) \cap (A \cup C)$$

Fig. 4. Set equivalences

We may then note the equivalence:

$$\forall var \in S : P(var) \wedge P(s) \equiv \forall var \in S \cup \{s\} : P(var)$$

which states that if P holds for all in S and for s, then P holds for all of S augmented with s.

Similarly

$$\exists var \in S : P(var) \vee P(s) \equiv \exists var \in S \cup \{s\} : P(var)$$

which states that if P holds for some member of S or for s, then P holds for some member of S augmented with s.

3.5   Peano Arithmetic

We come even closer to functional reasoning with *Peano arithmetic*[Kne63] which formalises properties of natural numbers, that is numbers greater than or equal to zero. Peano arithmetic is based on constructing numbers from 0 and the successor function *succ* i.e. $succ(X) = X + 1$. The axioms are:

1. 0 is a natural number;
2. if N is a natural number then $succ(N)$ is a natural number;
3. if N is a natural number then $\neg(0 = succ(N))$;
4. if M and N are natural numbers and if $M = N$ then $succ(M) = succ(N)$.

Note that here we use the numeric notion of *equality* rather than boolean equivalence.

Induction. Peano arithmetic introduces the fundamental technique of *proof by induction* which underlies all recursive proof techniques. If:

- $P(0)$ can be proved;
- assuming $P(N)$ then $P(succ(N))$ can be proved.

then it may be concluded that P holds for all natural numbers.

Recursion. Complementing inductive proof, Peano arithmetic also introduces *recursion* already familiar from functional programming. That is, a recursive function may be defined in terms of:

- *base case* where the argument is 0 and some value is returned;
- *recursion case* where the argument is $succ(N)$ and the function is called with possibly modified N.

For example, we define addition and multiplication in Figure 5.

$$X + 0 = X \qquad\qquad\qquad X * 0 = 0$$
$$X + succ(Y) = succ(X + Y) \qquad X * succ(Y) = X + X * Y$$

Fig. 5. Addition and multiplication

Inductive Proof. We may then use *inductive proof* to establish properties of recursive functions. We first number and state the theorem. We next state and prove the base case, where one argument is 0. Then, we state the recursion case and the assumed *induction hypothesis*, where one argument involves *succ*, before proving the recursion case. We write proof steps systematically from one side of the equality to the other of the equality we wish to establish, one step to a line, noting the justification for the step. The justification is usually a reference to the definition of a function, the induction hypothesis or a theorem.

For example:

Theorem 1. $0 + X = X$

Proof. By induction on X

Base case: $\qquad 0 + 0 = 0$
$\qquad\qquad\qquad\quad 0 \qquad\qquad\qquad\qquad \rightarrow (+\ )$
$\qquad\qquad\qquad\quad 0 + 0$
Recursion case: $0 + succ(X) = succ(X)$
Assumption $\qquad 0 + X = X$ $\qquad\qquad\qquad$ [induction hyp.]
$\qquad\qquad\qquad\quad 0 + succ(X) \qquad\qquad\quad \rightarrow (+\ )$
$\qquad\qquad\qquad\quad succ(0 + X) \qquad\qquad\quad \rightarrow$ (induction hyp.)
$\qquad\qquad\qquad\quad succ(X)$

For example:

Theorem 2. $X + succ(Y) = succ(X) + Y$

Proof. By induction on Y

Base case: $\qquad X + succ(0) = succ(X) + 0$
$\qquad\qquad\qquad\quad X + succ(0) \qquad\qquad\qquad\qquad \rightarrow (+\ )$
$\qquad\qquad\qquad\quad succ(X + 0) \qquad\qquad\qquad\qquad \rightarrow (+\ )$
$\qquad\qquad\qquad\quad succ(X) \qquad\qquad\qquad\qquad\qquad \rightarrow (+\ )$
$\qquad\qquad\qquad\quad succ(X) + 0$
Recursion case: $X + succ(succ(Y)) = succ(X) + succ(Y)$
Assumption $\qquad X + succ(Y) = succ(X) + Y$ $\qquad$ [induction hyp.]
$\qquad\qquad\qquad\quad X + succ(succ(Y)) \qquad\qquad \rightarrow (+\ )$
$\qquad\qquad\qquad\quad succ(X + succ(Y)) \qquad\qquad \rightarrow$ (induction hyp.)
$\qquad\qquad\qquad\quad succ(succ(X) + Y) \qquad\qquad \rightarrow (+\ )$
$\qquad\qquad\qquad\quad succ(X) + succ(Y)$

Theorem 3. $X + Y = Y + X$:

Proof. By induction on Y

Base case:	$X + 0 = 0 + X$	
	$X + 0$	$\to (+\ )$
	X	$\to$ (Theorem 1)
	$0 + X$	
Recursion case:	$X + succ(Y) = succ(Y) + X$	
Assumption	$X + Y = Y + X$	[induction hyp.]
	$X + succ(Y)$	$\to (+\ )$
	$succ(X + Y)$	$\to$ (induction hyp.)
	$succ(Y + X)$	$\to (+\ )$
	$Y + succ(X)$	$\to$ (Theorem 2)
	$succ(Y) + X$	

Non-inductive. Peano arithmetic does not require us to stick to the induction form for defining functions. For example, we give recursive definitions of *comparison* operators in Figure 6, and could prove the usual transitive properties:

$$0 < succ(N) \qquad\qquad succ(N) > 0$$
$$succ(X) < succ(Y) = X < Y \qquad succ(X) > succ(Y) = X > Y$$

Fig. 6. Comparison

$$A = B \wedge B = C \Rightarrow A = C$$
$$A < B \wedge B < C \Rightarrow A < C$$
$$A > B \wedge B > C \Rightarrow A > C$$

We may then use the comparison operators to qualify other definitions. For example, we define subtraction and division in Figure 7[4].

$$X \leq Y \Rightarrow X - Y = 0 \qquad\qquad X < Y \Rightarrow X/Y = 0$$
$$X - 0 = X \qquad\qquad X/0 = 0$$
$$succ(X) - succ(Y) = X - Y \qquad X/Y = succ((X - Y)/Y)$$

Fig. 7. Subtraction and division

Arithmetic Equivalences. We could then prove the standard arithmetic equalities shown in Figure 8, using $1 \equiv succ(0)$.

3.6 λ Calculus

With recursive function theory[Pet67], Church's λ calculus[Chu36] is the bedrock of functional programming. λ calculus is based on pure abstractions over names, with three very simple expression forms:

---

[4] Note that, to make / total, we define division by 0 to be 0 not $\bot$.

Constant

$X + 0 = X$

$X - 0 = X$

$X * 0 = 0$

$X * 1 = X$

$X/1 = X$

$X/X = 1$

$-(-X) = X$

Associativity

$(A + B) + C = A + (B + C)$

$(A * B) * C = A * (B * C)$

Commutativity

$A + B = B + A$

$A * B = B * A$

Distributivity

$A * (B + C) = A * B + A * C$

$A * (B - C) = A * B - A * C$

Fig. 8. Arithmetic equivalences

- id - variable;
- $(\lambda id.expression)$ - function abstraction: id is the bound variable (formal parameter) and $expression$ is the body;
- $expression_1\ expression_2$ - function application: $expression_1$ is a function and $expression_2$ is the argument (actual parameter).

β Reduction. λ expressions are evaluated through a process of substitution of argument expressions for bound variables in function bodies called β reduction. Before we can formulate this, we need to clarify the notions of a variable being *bound* or *free* in an expression.

A variable id is bound in an expression if the expression is:

- $(\lambda id'.expressions)$ - id is the bound variable id' or id is bound in the body $expression$;
- $expression_1\ expression_2$ - id is bound in $expression_1$ or in $expression_2$.

A variable id is free in an expression if the expression is:

- id' - id is id';
- $(\lambda id'.expressions)$ - id is not id' and id is free in the $expression$;
- $expression_1\ expression_2$ - id is free in $expression_1$ or in $expression_2$.

Then to β reduce:

$(\lambda id.expression_1)\ expression_2$

in *normal order*, where the actual parameter $expression_2$ is not evaluated:

- replace all free occurrences of id in $expression_1$ with $expression_2$;
- β reduce the resulting expression.

We indicate a β reduction step with $\rightarrow_\beta$.
For example:

$((\lambda x.\lambda y.x\ y)\ (\lambda s.s\ s))\ (\lambda z.z) \rightarrow_\beta$
$(\lambda y.(\lambda s.s\ s)\ y)\ (\lambda z.z) \rightarrow_\beta$
$(\lambda s.s\ s)\ (\lambda z.z) \rightarrow_\beta$
$(\lambda z.z)\ (\lambda z.z) \rightarrow_\beta$
$\lambda z.z$

For *applicative order* β reduction, the argument $expression_2$ is evaluated before substitution in the body $expression_1$.

α **Renaming.** A potential problem with β reduction lies in *free variable capture* where a free variable in an argument expression, which should not be the site of further substitutions, is moved into the scope of a bound variable with the same identifier, where it may subsequently be replaced. For example, in:

$((\lambda x.\lambda y.x)\ y)\ (\lambda x.x) \rightarrow_\beta (\lambda y.y)\ (\lambda x.x) \rightarrow_\beta (\lambda x.x)$

y was free in the original expression but is bound in the reduced expression $\lambda y.y$ and so is replaced by $\lambda x.x$.

To α rename an expression $(\rightarrow_\alpha)$, all *id* free in an expression are replaced with a new unique *id'*. For example:

$((\lambda x.\lambda y.x)\ y)\ (\lambda x.x) \rightarrow_\alpha ((\lambda x.\lambda y.x)\ a)\ (\lambda x.x) \rightarrow_\beta (\lambda y.a)\ (\lambda x.x) \rightarrow a$

Here, $\lambda x.x$ is discarded as there are now no occurrences of the bound variable y in the renamed body a.

α renaming assumes that we have an inexhaustible supply of new names.

η **Reduction.** η reduction is a common special case of β reduction:

$\lambda\ x.f\ x \rightarrow_\eta f$

where abstracting over applying some function f to some argument x is simply equivalent to just the function f.

Example Proof. We may use β reduction to carry out equivalence proofs for the λ calculus. For example, given functions to convert between Curried and un-Curried forms:

```
curry f x y = f (x,y)
uncurry f (x,y) = f x y
```

we may show:

Theorem 4. curry(uncurry$f$) = f

Proof.

$$
\begin{aligned}
&\text{curry}(\text{uncurry} f) && \to \ (\text{uncurry }) \\
&\text{curry}((\lambda f.\lambda(x,y).f \ x \ y) \ f) && \to_\beta \\
&\text{curry}(\lambda(x,y).f \ x \ y) && \to \ (\text{curry }) \\
&(\lambda f.\lambda x.\lambda y.f \ (x,y))(\lambda(x,y).f \ x \ y) && \to_\beta \\
&\lambda x.\lambda y.(\lambda(x,y).f \ x \ y)(x,y) && \to_\beta \\
&\lambda x.\lambda y.f \ x \ y && \to_\eta \\
&\lambda x.f \ x && \to_\eta \\
&f
\end{aligned}
$$

and:

Theorem 5. $\text{uncurry}(\text{curry} f) = f$

Proof.

$$
\begin{aligned}
&\text{uncurry}(\text{curry} \ f) && \to \ (\text{curry }) \\
&\text{uncurry}((\lambda f.\lambda x.\lambda y.f \ (x,y)) \ f) && \to_\beta \\
&\text{uncurry}(\lambda x.\lambda y.f \ (x,y)) && \to \ (\text{uncurry definitiion}) \\
&(\lambda f.\lambda(x,y).f \ x \ y)(\lambda x.\lambda y.f \ (x,y)) && \to_\beta \\
&\lambda(x,y).(\lambda x.\lambda y.f \ (x,y)) \ x \ y && \to_\beta \\
&\lambda(x,y).(\lambda y.f \ (x,y)) \ y && \to_\beta \\
&\lambda(x,y).f \ (x,y) && \to_\eta \\
&f
\end{aligned}
$$

3.7   Structural Induction

Burstall's widely used *structural induction*[Bur69] is a generalisation of Mc-Carthy's recursion induction on recursive functions[McC62] to *compositional* recursive structures, that is structures whose properties may be characterised in terms of properties of their components. For example, lists are defined in terms of the empty list ([]) and the concatenation of a head and a tail $(h : t)$, so proving $P(h : t)$ by structural induction involves:

– base case: prove $P([])$;
– recursion case: assume $P(t)$ and prove $P(h : t)$.

As we shall see, structural induction is a mainstay of reasoning about functional programs.

3.8   Fold and Unfold

The other mainstay of reasoning about functional programs is Burstall and Darlington's fold/unfold approach[BD77]. This is based on five rules:

1. *instantiation*: substitute for actual parameter in function body;
2. *unfolding*: replace function call in expression by equivalent instantiation of function body;

3. *folding*: replace instance of function body by equivalent function call;
4. *abstraction*: introduce let (or where) by replacing instance with variable and defining variable to be instance.

Rules 1. and 2. are reminiscent of β reduction and rule 3. of its reverse. Of their fifth rule, termed *laws*, they say:

"We may transform an equation by using on its right hand side any laws we have about the primitives K,l...(associativity, commutativity etc)...." (p48)

thus advocating use of the equivalences and equalities we have already surveyed.

3.9   Bird-Meertens Formalism

The Bird-Meertens Formalism (BMF)[BdM97] is a general calculi of functional programs. Here we will consider the theory of lists[Bir87], which applies rules drawn from fold/unfold and structural induction to programs built from higher order functions like map, fold, append and compose. [5]
For example, to prove the associativity of ++:

Theorem 6. $a++(b++c) = (a++b)++c$

Proof. By induction on a

Base case: $[]++(b++c) = ([]++b)++c$
                 $[]++(b++c)$ $\rightarrow$ (++)
                 $b++c$ $\rightarrow$ (++)
                 $([]++b)++c$
Recursion case: $(h:t)++(b++c) = ((h:t)++b)++c$
Assumption $t++(b++c) = (t++b)++c$ [induction hyp.]
                $(h:t)++(b++c)$ $\rightarrow$ (++)
                $h:(t++(b++c))$ $\rightarrow$ (induction hyp.)
                $h:((t++b)++c)$ $\rightarrow$ (++)
                $(h:(t++b))++c$ $\rightarrow$ (++)
                $((h:t)++b)++c$

We will now carry out a number of proofs which we will use when we explore the box calculus.
We start with a generic definition of fold which applies some function f to the head of a list and the result of doing so recursively to the tail of the list, given some initial value r:

```
fold :: (b->a->b)->b->[a]->b
fold f r [] = r
fold f r (x:xs) = fold f (f r x) xs
```

---

[5] Note that in presenting proofs we assume that all variables are universally quantified.

We assume that f is associative so:

$$f\ a\ (f\ b\ c) = f\ (f\ a\ b)\ c$$

We next introduce additional functions to take the first n elements of a list:

```
take _ [] = []
take 0 xs = []
take (1+n) (x:xs) = x:take n xs
```

drop the first n elements of a list:

```
drop _ [] = []
drop 0 xs = xs
drop (1+n) (x:xs) = drop n xs
```

There now follow a number of simple BMF proofs which we will use when we come to consider a substantive box calculus example below.

First of all, we show that take and drop cancel:

Theorem 7. take n xs++drop n $xs = xs$

Proof. By induction on xs

Base case:	take n $[]$++drop n $[] = []$	
	take n $[]$++drop n $[]$	$\rightarrow$ (take/drop)
	$[]$++$[]$	$\rightarrow$ (++)
	$[]$	
Recursion case:	take n $(x:xs)$++drop n $(x:xs) =$	
	$x:xs$	
Assumption	take n xs++drop n $xs = xs$	[induction hyp.]
By induction on n		
Base case:	take 0 $(x:xs)$++drop 0 $(x:xs) =$	
	$x:xs$	
	take 0 $(x:xs)$++drop 0 $(x:xs)$	$\rightarrow$ (take/drop)
	$[]$++$(x:xs)$	$\rightarrow$ (++)
	$x:xs$	
Recursion case:	take $(y+1)$ $(x:xs)$++	
	drop $(y+1)$ $(x:xs) = x:xs$	
	take $(y+1)$ $(x:xs)$++	
	drop $(y+1)$ $(x:xs)$	$\rightarrow$ (take/drop)
	$(x:$take y $xs)$++	
	drop y xs	$\rightarrow$ (++)
	$x:($take y xs++	
	drop y $xs)$	$\rightarrow$ (induction hyp.)
	$x:xs$	

Note that we could have established the second induction by case analysis with n equal to 0.

We also show:

Theorem 8. $f\ a\ (\text{fold}\ f\ r\ b) = \text{fold}\ f\ a\ (r : b)$

Proof. By induction on b

Base case: $f\ a\ (\text{fold}\ f\ r\ [\,]) = \text{fold}\ f\ a\ (r : [\,])$

$\qquad\qquad\ \ f\ a\ (\text{fold}\ f\ r\ [\,])$ $\qquad\qquad\qquad\qquad\ \ \to (\text{fold}\ )$

$\qquad\qquad\ \ f\ a\ r$ $\qquad\qquad\qquad\qquad\qquad\qquad\ \to (\text{fold}\ )$

$\qquad\qquad\ \ \text{fold}\ f\ (f\ a\ r)\ [\,]$ $\qquad\qquad\qquad\quad\ \ \to (\text{fold}\ )$

$\qquad\qquad\ \ \text{fold}\ f\ a\ (r : [\,])$

Recursion case: $f\ a\ (\text{fold}\ f\ r\ (x : b)) =$

$\qquad\qquad\qquad\ \text{fold}\ f\ a\ (r : (x : b))$

Assumption $f\ a\ (\text{fold}\ f\ r\ b) = \text{fold}\ f\ a\ (r : b)$ $\qquad$ [induction hyp.]

$\qquad\qquad\ \ f\ a\ (\text{fold}\ f\ r\ (x : b))$ $\qquad\qquad\qquad\ \to (\text{fold}\ )$

$\qquad\qquad\ \ f\ a\ (\text{fold}\ f\ (f\ r\ x)\ b)$ $\qquad\qquad\quad\ \to (\text{induction hyp.})$

$\qquad\qquad\ \ \text{fold}\ f\ a\ ((f\ r\ x) : b)$ $\qquad\qquad\quad\ \ \to (\text{fold}\ )$

$\qquad\qquad\ \ \text{fold}\ f\ (f\ a\ (f\ r\ x))\ b$ $\qquad\qquad\ \ \to (\text{f associativity})$

$\qquad\qquad\ \ \text{fold}\ f\ (f\ (f\ a\ r)\ x)\ b$ $\qquad\qquad\ \ \to (\text{fold}\ )$

$\qquad\qquad\ \ \text{fold}\ f\ (f\ a\ r)\ (x : b)$ $\qquad\qquad\quad\ \to (\text{fold}\ )$

$\qquad\qquad\ \ \text{fold}\ f\ a\ (r : (x : b))$

Finally, we show that fold distributes over ++, assuming that e is an identity element for f so:

$$f\ e\ x\ =\ x\ =\ f\ x\ e$$

Theorem 9. $\text{fold}\ f\ r\ (a\text{++}b)\ =\ f\ (\text{fold}\ f\ r\ a)\ (\text{fold}\ f\ e\ b)$

Proof. By induction on a

Base case: $\text{fold}\ f\ r\ ([\,]\text{++}b)\ =$

$\qquad\qquad\ \ f\ (\text{fold}\ f\ r\ [\,])\ (\text{fold}\ f\ e\ b)$

$\qquad\qquad\ \ \text{fold}\ f\ r\ ([\,]\text{++}b)$ $\qquad\qquad\qquad\quad\ \to (\text{++}\ )$

$\qquad\qquad\ \ \text{fold}\ f\ r\ b$ $\qquad\qquad\qquad\qquad\quad\ \to (\text{e identity})$

$\qquad\qquad\ \ \text{fold}\ f\ (f\ r\ e)\ b$ $\qquad\qquad\qquad\ \to (\text{fold}\ )$

$\qquad\qquad\ \ \text{fold}\ f\ r\ (e : b)$ $\qquad\qquad\qquad\quad\ \to (\text{Theorem 8})$

$\qquad\qquad\ \ f\ r\ (\text{fold}\ f\ e\ b)$ $\qquad\qquad\qquad\quad\ \to (\text{fold}\ )$

$\qquad\qquad\ \ f\ (\text{fold}\ f\ r\ [\,])\ (\text{fold}\ f\ e\ b)$

Recursion case: $\text{fold}\ f\ r\ ((x : a)\text{++}b)\ =$

$\qquad\qquad\qquad\ f\ (\text{fold}\ f\ r\ (x : a))\ (\text{fold}\ f\ e\ b)$

Assumption $\text{fold}\ f\ r\ (a\text{++}b)\ =$

$\qquad\qquad\ \ f\ (\text{fold}\ f\ r\ a)\ (\text{fold}\ f\ e\ b)$ $\qquad\qquad$ [induction hyp.]

$\qquad\qquad\ \ \text{fold}\ f\ r\ ((x : a)\text{++}b)$ $\qquad\qquad\qquad\ \to (\text{++}\ )$

$\qquad\qquad\ \ \text{fold}\ f\ r\ (x : (a\text{++}b))$ $\qquad\qquad\qquad\ \to (\text{fold}\ )$

$\qquad\qquad\ \ \text{fold}\ f\ (f\ r\ x)\ (a\text{++}b)$ $\qquad\qquad\qquad\ \to (\text{induction hyp.})$

$\qquad\qquad\ \ f\ (\text{fold}\ f\ (f\ r\ x)\ a)\ (\text{fold}\ f\ e\ b)\ \to (\text{fold}\ )$

$\qquad\qquad\ \ f\ (\text{fold}\ f\ r\ (x : a))\ (\text{fold}\ f\ e\ b)$

We will see in subsequent sections both how the BMF enables us to reason about computational aspects of parallel programs and its limitations in accounting for pragmatic effects of parallel program transformation.

4   Hume Coordination Layer

We have met the Hume expression layer as a pure functional programming language and surveyed techniques for reasoning about functional programs. We will now look at the Hume coordination layer before considering requirements for reasoning about coordination in the next section.

4.1   Boxes and Wires

As we noted above, Hume programs are built from *boxes* connected to each other, the wider environment and themselves by input and output *wires*.

Boxes are generalised finite state automata which pattern match on their inputs and generate corresponding outputs with expression layer constructs. Boxes are repeated one-shot and stateless. So a box can be thought of as a non-terminating while loop which loses all the values of its local variables on each iteration.

Wires connect input and output *links* on boxes and *streams* to the operating environment. Wires are uni-directional, single buffered FIFOs which can hold any matchable construct. They retain information between box iterations and so are the sole locus of state in Hume programs.

4.2   Execution Model

Boxes execute repeatedly for ever in a two-phase execution cycle. In the *local* phase, each box attempts to match its inputs and generate outputs. Then in the *global* super-step phase, the consumption of input values from, and assertion of output values to, wires is resolved.

At the start of each execution cycle a box may be:

- *READY*: all outputs from the previous cycle have been consumed and so new inputs may be sought;
- *BLOCKED*: some outputs from the previous cycle have not been consumed and so new outputs cannnot be generated.

Then the execution model is:

    for each box:
    STATE ← READY
    forever
      for each READY box:
       if match inputs then:
         consume inputs from wires
         generate and buffer outputs
         STATE ← BLOCKED
      for each BLOCKED box:
       if previous outputs consumed then:
         assert outputs from buffer on wires
         STATE ← READY

In the model, the local and global phases may be conducted concurrently with an intervening barrier synchronisation.

4.3   Box, Wire and Steam Declarations

Box Declaration. A box is declared by:

```
box id
in (idᵢ₁::typeᵢ₁,...idᵢₘ::typeᵢₘ)
out (id_O1::type_O1,...id_ON::type_ON)
match
    pattern₁ -> expression₁ |
    ...
    patternₚ -> expressionₚ ;
```

id is the name of the box, and $id_{Ix}/type_{Ix}$ and $id_{Oy}/type_{Oy}$ are the names and types of the input and output links.

All the $pattern_i$ must have the same type as the input links and all the $expression_i$ must have the same type as the output links.

Note that the link name space and the pattern name space are disjoint so the same identifiers may be used in both.

Wire Declaration. A wire declaration takes the form:

```
wire id (linkᵢ₁,...linkᵢₘ) (link_O1,...link_ON);
```

id is the name of the box, and $link_{Ix}$ and $link_{Oy}$ are the names of the links (and streams) to which the corresponding box inputs and outputs are connected.

A link name may be $box_{id}.in - out_{id}$, where box_{id} is the name of a box and $in - out_{id}$ is the name of one of that box's input or output links, or the name of a stream $stream_{id}$.

All wires must make type-consistent connections.

Wire Initialisation. Wires which are not connected to an environmental input may require an initial value to enable pattern matching to commence. This may be achieved by using a wiring link of the form:

```
id.id initially constant
```

Stream Declaration. Streams convey character sequences from and to the operating environment. In principle they may be associated with arbitrary sources and sinks but currently only files and sockets are supported.

Streams are declared by:

```
input stream: stream id from "path";
output stream: stream id to "path";
```

where id is the stream name and $path$ is a path.

Automatic Input/Output. Stream text is automatically converted to and from appropriate representations for any bounded type associated with a box link. For an input stream, the type is used as a grammar to parse the text to the corresponding value. For an output stream, the type is used to guide flat, unbracketed pretty printing of the value. The conventions are the same as for the expression layer type conversion: *expression* as string.

4.4 Examples

Consider a box that copies input from the keyboard to output on the display without change:

```
1. type integer = int 32;

2. box identity
3. in (x::integer)
4. out (y::integer)
5. match
6.  p -> p;

7. stream input from "std_in";
8. stream output to "std_out";

9. wire identity (input) (output);
```

where line numbers are purely to aid narrative.

Lines 2 to 6 declare a box called identity with input link x and output link y which both carry integers as declared in line 1. The match in line 6 indicates that pattern p matches input on x to generate the corresponding value on output y.

Lines 7 and 8 declare the streams input and output connected to standard input and standard output respectively.

Line 9 wires link identity.x to input and identity.y to output.

When the program is run, the interaction is as follows:

```
$ identity
1
1 2
2 3
3...
```

We may next change the program to generate squares of successive outputs on new lines:

```
1. type integer = int 32;

2. sq::integer -> integer;
3. sq x = x*x;
```

```
 4. box square2
 5. in (x::integer)
 6. out (y::(integer,char))
 7. match
 8.  p -> (sq p,'\n');

 9. stream input from "std_in";
10. stream output to "std_out";

11. wire square2 (input) (output);
```

Now, output from line 8 is a tuple of a square and a newline character so the type of the output link on line 6 changes accordingly.

Interaction is now as:

```
$ square2
1
1
2
4
3
9...
```

Finally, consider inputting a simple sum of the form: *number operator number* where *operator* is one of +,-,* or /, and displaying the sum and result:

```
box sums
in (xy::integer,char,integer)
out (s::(integer,char))
match
  (x,'+',y) -> (x+y,'\n') |
  (x,'-',y) -> (x-y,'\n') |
  (x,'*',y) -> (x*y,'\n') |
  (x,'/',y) -> (x div y,'\n') ;
```

so interaction is as:

```
$ sums
1 + 1
2
6 / 2
3
4 * 8
32 ...
```

4.5   Feedback Wiring

It is often useful to wire a box back to itself to maintain intermediate state.
For example, to generate successive integers from 0:

```
box gen
in (n::integer)
out (n'::integer,s::(integer,char))
match
  (x) -> (x+1,(x,'\n'));

wire gen (gen.n' initially 0) (gen.n,output);
```

Here, input **n** is wired to **n'** and initialised to 0. Note that output **n'** is also wired back to **n**.

On each execution cycle, **n** gets the next integer from **n'**, sends **n+1** to **n'** and outputs **n**:

```
$ gen
0
1
2
...
```

For example, consider parity checking a sequence of bits to show at each stage if there is an odd or even number of 1s:

```
type BIT = word 1;

data STATE = ODD | EVEN;
```

```
box parity
in (oldstate::STATE,input::BIT)
out (newstate::STATE,output::string)
match
  (ODD,0) -> (ODD,"ODD\n") |
  (ODD,1) -> (EVEN,"EVEN\n") |
  (EVEN,0) -> (EVEN,"EVEN\n") |
  (EVEN,1) -> (ODD,"ODD\n") ;
```

```
wire parity
(parity.newstate initially EVEN, input)
(parity.oldstate, output);
```

Here, **oldstate** and **newstate** are wired reflexively to each others, with **newstate** initialised to EVEN.

On each execution cycle, the output to **newstate** flips if the input value is a 1. This which runs as:

```
$ parity 1 0 1 1 0
ODD
ODD
EVEN
ODD
```

ODD

. . .

4.6   From One Box to Multiple Boxes

Consider a box to find X *NAND* Y:

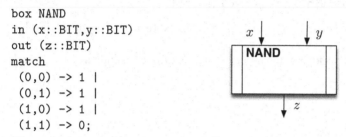

```
box NAND
in (x::BIT,y::BIT)
out (z::BIT)
match
  (0,0) -> 1 |
  (0,1) -> 1 |
  (1,0) -> 1 |
  (1,1) -> 0;
```

We could wire this into a test program that receives a pair of bits from a single wire from standard input and passes them on two wires to NAND:

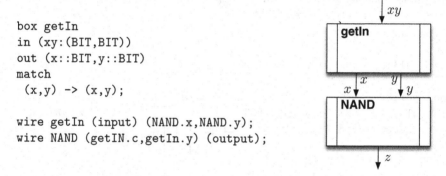

```
box getIn
in (xy:(BIT,BIT))
out (x::BIT,y::BIT)
match
  (x,y) -> (x,y);

wire getIn (input) (NAND.x,NAND.y);
wire NAND (getIN.c,getIn.y) (output);
```

We might, as an alternative, implement this as an *AND* box:

```
box AND
in (x::BIT,y::BIT)
out (z::BIT)
match
  (0,0) -> 0 |
  (0,1) -> 0 |
  (1,0) -> 0 |
  (1,1) -> 1;
```

feeding a *NOT* box:

```
box NOT
in (x::BIT)
out (y::BIT)
match
  0 -> 1 |
  1 -> 0;
```

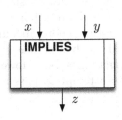

wired with:

```
wire getIn (input) (And.x,AND.y);
wire AND(getIn.x,getIn.y) (NOT.x);
wire NOT (AND.x) (output);
```

In a later section, we will look at using the box calculus to justify this change.

Now, consider a program for *IMPLIES*:

```
box IMPLIES
in (x::BIT,y::BIT)
out (z::BIT)
match
  (0,0) -> 1 |
  (0,1) -> 1 |
  (1,0) -> 0 |
  (1,1) -> 1;
```

$X \Rightarrow Y$ is equivalent to $\neg X \vee Y$, so we could also implement this as an *OR* box fed with a *NOT*ed X and unchanged Y:

```
box OR
in (x::BIT,y::BIT)
out (z::BIT)
match
  (0,0) -> 0 |
  (0,1) -> 1 |
  (1,0) -> 1 |
  (1,1) -> 1;

wire getIn (input) (NOT.x,OR.y);
wire NOT (getIn.x) (OR.x);
wire OR (NOT.y,getIN.y) (output);
```

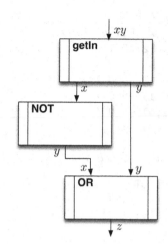

Again, in a later section, we will look at using the box calculus to justify this change.

4.7   * Pattern and Expression

The programs we've considered so far are synchronous where boxes execute in locked-step. To enable asynchronicity, Hume introduces the * pattern and expression.

The * pattern ignores its input. If there is no input then the match succeeds and if there is input then the match succeeds but the input is not consumed. The * pattern may only be used in box matches, not in functions.

Similarly, the * expression ignores its output. This may be used in expressions returning final values from box transitions, including in conditional and case expressions, and in function bodies. However, there is no associated value and so it is meaningless to attempt to pass a * as, say, an actual parameter to a function call.

4.8   Recursive Functions and Iterative Boxes

An important feature of boxes is that all space is retrieved on each execution cycle. If space is at a premium, for example in an embedded application, then it may be advantageous to convert stack consuming recursion within a box to constant space iteration using a feedback wire.

For example, consider finding the sum of the integers from 1 to N:

```
sum 0 = 0;
sum N = N+sum (N-1);
```

This may be re-written to use an accumulation variable:

```
sum' s 0 = s;
sum' s N = sum' (s+N) (N-1);
```

```
sum N = sum' 0 N;
```

where the partial sum s is passed from call to call. In turn, this is equivalent to the iteration:

```
sum(N)
{  int s;
   s = 0;
   while(N>0)
   {  s = s+N;
      N = N-1;
   }
   return s;
}
```

where s is the partial sum and N is the next value to be summed.

We may reformulate this as a box with feedback wires for the partial sum and the next value. Suppose the inputs are i for the original input, s for the partial sum and N for the next value. Suppose the outputs are o for the final result, s' for the incremented partial sum and N' for the decremented next value. Then we may distinguish three possibilities:

1. there is a new initial value with no partial sum or current value. The sum is initialised to 0, the current value is initialised to the initial value, and there is no final output:
   ```
   (i,*,*) -> (*,0,i)
   ```
2. the current value is 0. Any next initial value is ignored. The partial sum is the final output and there are no new values for the partial sum or current value:
   ```
   (*,s,0) -> (s,*,*)
   ```
3. the current value is not 0. Any next initial value is ignored. The current value is added to the partial sum and the current value is decremented, with no final output:
   ```
   (*,s,N) -> (*,s+N,N-1)
   ```

Thus, the final program is:

```
box itersum
in (i::integer,s::integer,N::integer)
out (o::integer, s'::integer,N::integer)
match
  (*,s,0) -> (s,*,*) |
  (*,s,N) -> (*,s+N,N-1) |
  (i,*,*) -> (*,0,i);

wire itersum
(input,itersum.s',itersum.N')
(output,itersum.s,itersum.N);
```

Note the order of the matches. We start with the "termination case" when N is 0, followed by the "iteration case" when N is non-zero, followed by the case for a new input.

5   The Box Calculus

The box calculus[GM08, Gro09, GM11] contains rules for transforming the coordination layer of a Hume program. In most cases this involves changes to the expression layer through functional reasoning techniques, especially rewriting.

5.1   Rules of the Calculus

We will now describe the rules used in the examples in the next section. Some of these rules are atomic, i.e. they can be seen as the axioms, while other are derived. Note that some of them have rather complicated formulations for which we will not give the formal syntax and semantics in full detail – for this we refer to [GM11].

Rename. The simplest family of rules are those that just rename a component. The calculus has two such rules: **Rename** which renames a box; and **RenameWire** which renames a given input or output wire of a box. Renaming of functions is considered to be independent of the calculus, and can be incorporated by the **ESub** rule.

Expression Substitution (ESub). The first rule of the calculus enables the use of the BMF reasoning discussed in Section 3.9. For any match

    p -> e1

if we can show that

$$e1 = e2 \,^6$$

then we can replace e1 with e2, which results in the following new match

    p -> e2

Expression/Function Folding. A special, but very common, case of the **ESub** rule is folding and unfolding as discussed in 3.8. Here we may create or delete functions during this process. Assume you have a match of the following form:

    p -> e p

We then fold e into a function f (with a parameter x):

    f x = e x;

It is then trivial to show that $f\ x = e\ x$, thus creating the new match:

    p -> f p

---

[6] We rely on extensional equality, meaning that two function f and g are the same if they return the same values: $\forall x.\ e1\ x = e2\ x$.

This rule, which creates a new function f from the expression and replaces the expression with a call to f, is called **expression folding introduction (EFoldI)**.

Its dual, which unfold the function definition of f in the expression is called **expression folding elimination (EFoldE)**.

Note that in applications where **EFoldI** creates a function which is equivalent to an existing function, then a new function is created. A subsequent step can then replace this new function with the existing one using **ESub** and BMF reasoning.

Match Composition. We can fold a set of adjacent matches

p1 -> e1 | p2 -> e2 | ... | pn -> en

into one match with a case expression for each match

p -> case p of p1 -> e1 | p2 -> e2 | ... | pn -> en

if and only if p will always match (and consume) whenever $p1, \cdots, pn$ will. This rule is called **match composition introduction (MCompI)**. A special case of this rule is when the * pattern is not used in any pattern, and the matches are *total* (will never fail if input are available on all wires). In this case we can fold all matches into one match,which we will do in several of the example below.

The dual of this rule, **match composition elimination (MCompE)** turns a case expression into a match for each case. The same precondition applies to this rule.

Tuple Composition. If there are more than one wire from a box to another then these wires can be combined into a single wire containing a tuple, where each element of this wire correspond to one of the original wires. A proviso for this is that the * pattern is used either for each or none of the tuple elements for each expression/pattern. This rule is called **tuple composition introduction (TupleI)**, and is illustrated on the left below:

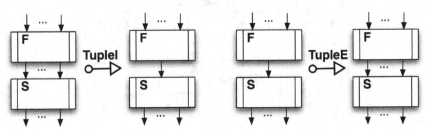

In order to apply the rule the patterns of S must change accordingly, and so must the expression of F. For simplicity, we can only apply this rule when each expression of F can be decomposed syntactically (e.g. the expression cannot be a function application)

Dually, **tuple composition elimination (TupleE)** is the process of splitting a tuple into mant wires – one for each element of the tuple. This is illustrated on the right above.

Vertical Box Composition. Vertical box composition introduction **(VCompI)** lifts function composition to the box level, and dually, **vertical box composition elimination) (VCompE)** lifts function de-composition into the box level.

VCompI takes two connected boxes and turn them into one. A proviso for such transformation is that all outputs of the first box are connected to the inputs of the second[7]. This is shown on the left hand side below:

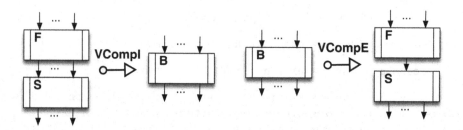

The proviso for it's dual, **VCompE**, is that the box being transformed only has one match which is of the form of a function composition (i.e. f 0 g). This is illustrated on the r.h.s. above.

Horizontal Box Composition. Two independent boxes can be joined together if it is never the case that one of them is blocked when the other is not. This is illustrated on the top below, where A and B are composed into box C. This rule is called **horizontal box composition introduction (HCompI)**.

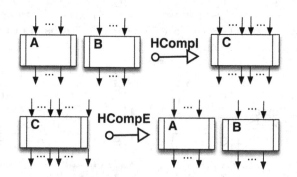

Its dual, **horizontal box composition elimination (HCompE)**, shown on the bottom above, decomposes a box C into two separate boxes A and B. In order to do this, we need to be able decompose input/output wires of the box so that

---

[7] This can in principle be relaxed but will add more complexities.

they are independent of each others, as well as ensuring that the boxes blocks at the same time. This principle is best illustrated by example, which we will show in the following section.

Identity Boxes. An identity box is a box with one input and one output with one match of the form `x -> x`, that is a box which introduces a one step latency for one wire. If such delay has no impact on the rest of the program, an arbitrary number of identity boxes can be introduced and eliminated, called **identity box introduction (IdI)** and **identity box elimination (IdE)** respectively:

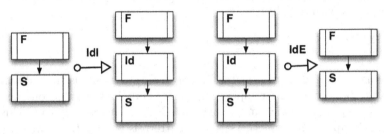

Introducing Wires. Wires which does 'nothing' can be eliminated. Syntactically, these are cases where all the source expressions and target patterns only contains *. Semantically, this can be generalised to cases where there are not only *, but it is provable that this behaves like *. This rule is known as **wire elimination (WireE)** and is shown on the right below.

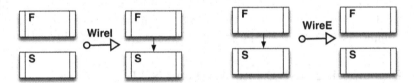

Dually, we can introduce a wire where both the source and targets are only *s without changing the semantics of the program. This rule is known as **wire introduction (WireI)** and is shown in the left above.

Wire Duplication. We can also duplicate wires and eliminate such duplications, known as **wire duplication introduction (WireDupI)** and **wire duplication elimination (WireDupE)**, shown on the left and right below, respectively.

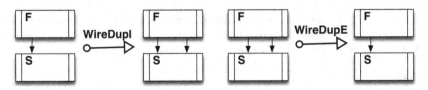

In these cases we must show that the wires are indeed proper duplications, i.e. initially the wires are the same, the same values are always written and consumed.

5.2 A Note on Preconditions

We have informally discussed some of the preconditions of applying the rules, however there are additional complications in the presence of asynchronous wires (the use of *) due to the concurrent nature of the box scheduling. To illustrate, consider a box with matches

```
1.  (x,y) -> ... |
2.  (*,y) -> ... | ...
```

In a configuration where the match at line 1 always succeeds, introduction of an identity box on the first input wire may result in the value on this wire arriving a step later, which may cause match 2 to succeed instead. This can have global impact on correctness. The * pattern is not used for any examples in the following section, so we have ignored this potentially complicated issue.

6   Reasoning about Hume Programs with the Box Calculus

In this section we will illustrate use of the box calculus. Sections 6.1 and 6.2 use the calculus for the transformations informally shown in Section 4.6, while Section 6.3 shows how to parallelise the fold function for multi-core applications. This examples uses many of the properties we proved about fold in Section 3.9.

6.1   Decomposing NAND into AND and NOT

Consider again the NAND box from Section 4.6:

```
box NAND
in (x::BIT,y::BIT)
out (z::BIT)
match
  (0,0) -> 1 |
  (0,1) -> 1 |
  (1,0) -> 1 |
  (1,1) -> 0;
```

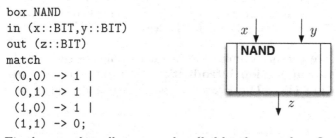

Firstly note that all cases are handled by the matches. Our first transformation step composes all matches into one match (with a **case** expression) by applying the **MCompI** rule. This creates the following box:

```
box NAND
in (x::BIT,y::BIT)
```

```
out (z::BIT)
match
   (x,y) -> case (x,y) of
                   (0,0) -> 1 |
                   (0,1) -> 1 |
                   (1,0) -> 1 |
                   (1,1) -> 0;
```

Next we fold the case expression into a function using the **EFoldI** rule, which creates the new function[8]:

```
nand (x,y) =  case (x,y) of
                   (0,0) -> 1 |
                   (0,1) -> 1 |
                   (1,0) -> 1 |
                   (1,1) -> 0;
```

and the new box:

```
box NAND
in (x::BIT,y::BIT)
out (z::BIT)
match
   (x,y) -> nand (x,y);
```

Using BMF style reasoning, similar to **MCompE** at the expression layer, the case expression can be replaced by pattern matching:

```
nand (0,0) = 1;
nand (0,1) = 1;
nand (1,0) = 1;
nand (1,1) = 0;
```

Logical AND can be represented by the following function:

```
and (0,0) = 0;
and (0,1) = 0;
and (1,0) = 0;
and (1,1) = 1;
```

and logical NOT by the following function:

```
not 0 = 1;
not 1 = 0;
```

Next, we can see that NAND is the same as AND followed by NOT

---

[8] Strict calculus use is unlikely to come up with names that "makes sense", so many steps are followed by a renaming application. However, to ease the reading we are using more descriptive names directly.

Theorem 10.
$$nand(x, y) = not(and(x, y))$$

Proof. This equality can easily be proven by drawing up the truth table:

x	y	nand (x,y)	and(x,y)	not(and(x,y))
0	0	1	0	1
0	1	1	0	1
1	0	1	0	1
1	1	0	1	0

With Theorem 10 we can apply the **ESubst** rule to replace nand (x,y) by not(and(x,y)) in the NAND box:

```
box NAND
in (x::BIT,y::BIT)
out (z::BIT)
match
  (x,y) -> not(and (x,y));
```

not(and(x,y)) is the same as (not o and) (x,y), thus we can apply the **VCompE** rule to decompose this box into two sequential boxes. We then rename the boxes (by rule **Rename**) to AND and NOT, and input and output wires (using **RenameWire**), which creates the following configuration:

```
box AND
in (x::BIT,y::BIT)
out (z::BIT)
match
  (x,y) -> and (x,y) ;

box NOT
in (x::BIT)
out (y::BIT)
match
  x -> not x;
```

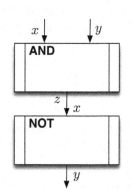

```
wire AND(...) (NOT.x);
wire NOT (AND.z) (...);
```

Next we unfold the definition of the not function into a case expression using BMF style reasoning

```
not x = case x of 0 -> 1 | 1 -> 0;
```

and show that it is identical to the original (pattern matching) version. We then unfold this function in the NOT box using the **EFoldE** rule:

```
box NOT
in (x::BIT)
```

```
out (x'::BIT)
match
   x -> case x of 0 -> 1 | 1 -> 0;
```

and split the `case` expression up into several matches using the **MCompE** rule:

```
box NOT
in (x::BIT)
out (x'::BIT)
match
  0 -> 1 |
  1 -> 0;
```

The exact same strategy can be applied to the AND box, giving:

```
box AND
in (x::BIT,y::BIT)
out (z::BIT)
match
    (0,0) -> 0 |
    (0,1) -> 0 |
    (1,0) -> 0 |
    (1,1) -> 1;
```

which completes the transformation.

6.2   Decomposing IMPLIES into NOT and OR

We will now apply the box calculus to the transformation of IMPLIES into NOT followed by OR as illustrated in Section 4.6. We start with the IMPLIES box:

```
box IMPLIES
in (x::BIT,y::BIT)
out (z::BIT)
match
  (0,0) -> 1 |
  (0,1) -> 1 |
  (1,0) -> 0 |
  (1,1) -> 1;
```

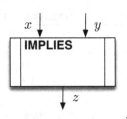

First we apply the **MCompI** rule to turn the matches into a `case` expression. We then apply the **EFoldI** rule to separate this `case` expression into a function we call `implies` and unfolds the `case` expression in the function using BMF reasoning. As a result the IMPLIES box is replaced by the following box:

```
box IMPLIES
in (x::BIT,y::BIT)
out (z::BIT)
match
    (x,y) -> implies (x,y);
```

which uses the function:

```
implies (0,0) = 1;
implies (0,1) = 1;
implies (1,0) = 0;
implies (1,1) = 1;
```

Next, we define OR in the expression layer as a function:

```
or (0,0) = 0;
or (0,1) = 1;
or (1,0) = 1;
or (1,1) = 1;
```

and introduce the following auxiliary function:

```
negatefirst (0,0) = (1,0);
negatefirst (0,1) = (1,1);
negatefirst (1,0) = (0,0);
negatefirst (1,1) = (0,1);
```

We then show that

Theorem 11.

$$implies(x, y) = or(negatefirst(x, y))$$

Proof. This can be shown by a truth table:

x	y	implies (x,y)	negatefirst(x,y)	or(negatefirst(x,y))
0	0	1	(1,0)	1
0	1	1	(1,1)	1
1	0	0	(0,0)	0
1	1	1	(0,1)	1

By applying Theorem 11 we can replace implies with or(negatefirst(x,y)) in the IMPLIES box using the **ESubst** rule:

```
box IMPLIES
in (x::BIT,y::BIT)
out (z::BIT)
match
    (x,y) -> or (negatefirst (x,y));
```

We then apply sequential decomposition (**VCompE**):

```
box NEGATEFIRST
in (x::BIT,y::BIT)
out (x'::BIT,y'::BIT)
match
   (x,y) -> negatefirst (x,y);
```

```
box OR
in (x::BIT,y::BIT)
out (z::BIT)
match
   (x,y) -> or (x,y);
```

```
wire NEGATEFIRST (..) (OR.x, OR.y);
wire OR (NEGATEFIRST.x', NEGATEFIRST.y') (..);
```

Next, we apply BMF reasoning to replace the patterns in the **or** function with a **case** expression. We then unfold this function in the OR box by applying the **EFoldE** rule. Then we move the **case** expression into the match with the **MCompE** rule, creating the following new OR box:

```
box OR
in (x::BIT,y::BIT)
out (z::BIT)
match
   (0,0) -> 0 |
   (0,1) -> 1 |
   (1,0) -> 1 |
   (1,1) -> 1;
```

We now want to transform the NEGATEFIRST box. Firstly, we observe that the first argument is always negated. We then observe that the second argument is left unchanged. Thus, we have the following fact:

Theorem 12.
$$negatefirst\ (x,y) = (not\ x,y)$$

Proof. This can be easily shown by a truth table.

Using Theorem 12 we apply **ESub** to the NEGATEFIRST box, which gives us the following box:

```
box NEGATEFIRST
in (x::BIT,y::BIT)
out (x'::BIT,y'::BIT)
match
   (x,y) -> (not x,y);
```

We then observe that the box has one match with two arguments, and the expression can be decomposed such that the first argument in the expression only uses the first input, and the second only uses the second input. This means that we can horizontally decompose the box into two parallel boxes using the **HCompE** rule. We then rename the boxes accordingly (using the **Rename** rule), creating the following box configuration:

```
box NOT
in (x::BIT)
out (y::BIT)
match
    x -> not x;

box Id
in (x::BIT)
out (y::BIT)
match
    y -> y;

box OR ...
```

```
wire NOT (..) (OR.x);
wire Id (..) (OR.y);
wire OR (NOT.y,Id.y) (..);
```

Next we unfold the definition of the not function into a case expression using BMF style reasoning and show that it is identical to the original (pattern matching) version. We then unfold this function in the NOT box using the **EFoldE** rule, before we move the case expression into the match by **MCompE** creating the new NOT box:

```
box NOT
in (x::BIT)
out (y::BIT)
match
    0 -> 1 |
    1 -> 0;
```

Finally, we observe that, as the name implies, the Id box behaves as an identity box and can therefore be eliminated by the **IdE** rule. We then have the following box configuration:

```
box NOT
in (x::BIT)
out (y::BIT)
match
    0 -> 1 |
    1 -> 0;

box OR
in (x::BIT,y::BIT)
out (z::BIT)
match
    (0,0) -> 0 |
    (0,1) -> 1 |
    (1,0) -> 1 |
    (1,1) -> 1;
```

```
wire NOT (..) (OR.x);
wire OR (NOT.y,..) (..);
```

which completes the transformation.

6.3   Parallelising Fold

Our final application of the box calculus relates to the very timely problem of parallelising programs, for example to explore multi-core architectures. We will address the problem of parallelising the fold combinator which we described previously. We make the same assumptions about the function being folded as in Section 3.9 and we utilise several of the theorems proved there.

Two-Box Fold. First we will address the problem of splitting one fold into two parallel applications, and after that generalise to N boxes. Obviously, there is a cost of parallelisation, thus this would only make sense when the function f :: a -> b -> b which we fold over performs some heavy and time-consuming computations over a list xs and we want to fold the result of each computation. Assuming an initial value r::b, we start with the following box:

```
box foldbox
in (i :: [a])
out (o ::  b)
match
    xs -> fold f r xs;
```

Henceforth we will not give such Hume code for boxes and separate diagrams, but integrate the matches into the diagram. In this notation the foldbox looks as follows:

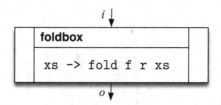

Firstly, we define some abbreviations to make the code more readable :

```
append' (xs,ys) = append xs ys;
left xs = take ((Length xs) div 2) xs;
right xs = drop (Length xs) div 2) xs;
split2 xs = (left xs, right xs);
```

With these definition it follows from Theorem 7 that:

$$\text{fold } f \ r \ xs = \text{fold } f \ r \ (\text{append'}(\text{left } xs, \text{right } xs))$$

Then, from Theorem 9 we have that:

$$\text{fold } f \ r \ (\text{append'}(\text{left } xs, \text{right } xs)) =$$

$$f \ (\text{fold } f \ r \ \text{left } xs) \ (\text{fold } f \ e \ \text{right } xs)$$

Thus, by transitivity of $=$ we know that

$$\text{fold } f \ r \ xs = f \ (\text{fold } f \ r \ (\text{left } xs)) \ (\text{fold } f \ e \ (\text{right } xs)) \qquad (1)$$

Further from the definition of uncurry we know that

$$f \ x \ y = (\text{uncurry } f) \ (x, y)$$

from before. Using this (1) becomes by BMF:

$$\text{fold } f \ r \ xs = (\text{uncurry } f) \ (\text{fold } f \ r \ (\text{left } xs), \text{fold } f \ e \ (\text{right } xs))$$

Using this fact, we apply the **ESub** rule creating the following new match for foldbox:

```
xs -> (uncurry f) (fold f r (left xs), fold f e (right xs))
```

This is sequential application of two function, which we lift to the box level by the **VCompE** rule, together with some box renaming[9]:

---

[9] Note that a single wire label means that this name is used for both the output of the first box (applyfold_box) and input of the second box (combine_box).

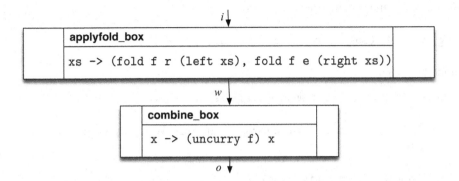

We know that the output wire of the `applyfold_box` is a pair which can be split by the **TupleE** rule. After this split the match of `combine_box` becomes:

`(a,b) -> (uncurry f) (a,b)`

Next, we curry this function, which by the **ESub** rule gives us the match:

`(a,b) -> (curry(uncurry f)) a b`

From Theorem 4 we have that:

$$\text{curry(uncurry } f) = f$$

Using this theorem we apply the **ESub** rule to get the following new configuration:

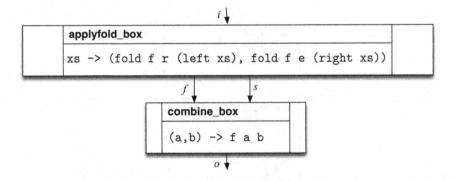

We have now completed the transformation of `combine_box`. Next we start transforming `applyfold_box`. First we apply **EFoldI** to fold the expression into a new function h:

`h xs  = (fold f r (left xs), fold f e (right xs));`

and the box match becomes:

`xs ->  h xs`

Next, we define a new function

```
g (a,b) = (fold f r a, fold f e b);
```

and show that

$$\text{h } xs = \text{g (left } xs, \text{right } xs)$$

which hold by unfolding both function definitions. We apply **ESub** to create a new match:

```
xs -> g (left xs, right xs)
```

We know that:

$$(\text{left } xs, \text{right } xs) = \text{split2 } xs$$

by the definition of `split2`. Using this we apply the **ESub** rule creating the following new match:

```
xs -> g (split2 xs)
```

Again, this is sequential composition of two function, which we can lift to the box level by rule **VCompE**. By making some suitable renaming we obtain the following box configuration:

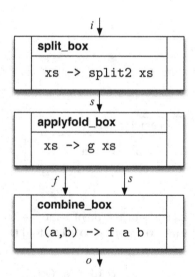

As above, the wire between the two new boxes is a pair which we can split by the **TupleE** rule:

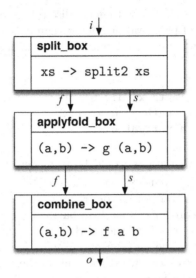

The transformation of the split_box box is now completed. and we start on applyfold_box. First, we unfold the g function by rule **EFoldE** creating the new match:

```
(a,b) -> (fold f r a, fold f e b)
```

Next we observe that the first element of the expression only uses the first pattern, while the second element only uses the second pattern, hence we can apply the horizontal box decomposition, that is rule **HCompE**, creating the following final box configuration

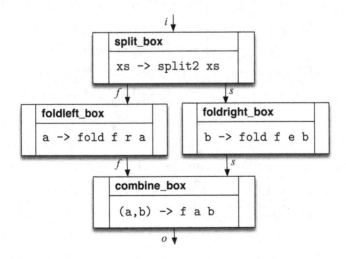

which completes the transformation.

N-Box Fold. We now outline how to generalise this into N cores. We assume that N is fixed for ease of presentation (but we can also abstract over N). First we generalise `left`, `right` and `split2` with an additional argument n specifying the size of the chunks:

```
left n x = take ((length x) div n) x;
right n x = drop ((length x) div n) x;
splitN n x = (left n x,right n x);
```

Note that the previous definitions would be equivalent to setting n to 2. The idea is that we we want to split a given list x into $\frac{\text{length } x}{N}$ chunks and apply (a slight adaption of) the transformation from above $N - 1$ times, so that each chunk is executed on a core with equal load balancing.

The difference for each transformation is that we use the more general version `splitN`. Firstly, we apply the transformation with N given as argument, i.e. `splitN N`. The first output wire will then contain the first $\frac{1}{N}$ parts of the list and this will be sent to the first core. The remaining $\frac{N-1}{N}$ parts of the list are sent down the second wire. Since we have used one core (the first wire), we have $N - 1$ cores left. Thus, we reapply this transformation to the second wire with `splitN (N-1)` to get a chunk equal to to the first wire. This transformation is recursively applied $N - 1$ times, which will create an "arrow-headed" shape

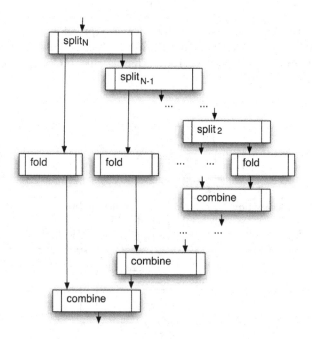

where we need to flatten the "top" and "bottom", creating the following shaped box configuration:

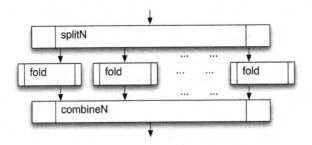

The top can be flatten by a sequence of the transformations discussed next, which shows how two boxes at the ath $(2 < a \leq N)$ step can be combined (after unfolding splitN):

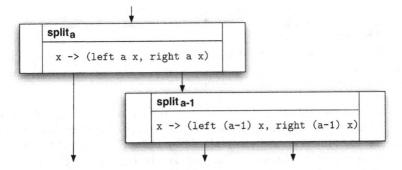

First we apply **IdI** to introduce an identity box on the first output wire:

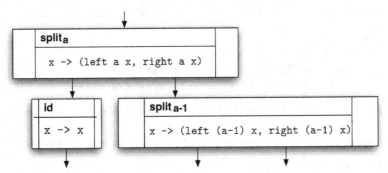

Then we horizontally merge this box with the second box by the **HCompI** rule which creates the following configuration:

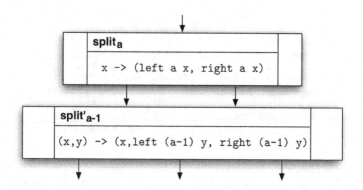

We can then vertically compose these two boxes with **VCompI**, creating

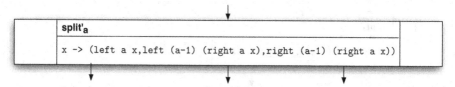

Notice that the result of the transformation is to make a copy of the last element e of the tuple in the expression of the box, so `(...,e)` becomes `(...,e,e)`. If we are at level k, then the first e is replaced by `left (N-k) e` and the second e is replaced by `right (N-k) e` – so the tuple is now `(...,left (N-k) e,right (N-k) e)`.

Reverting to our transformation. If we assume that $a > 3$, the result of incorporating the "split box" at the next level down, is the following match:

```
x -> (left a x,
        left (a-1) (right a x),
          left (a-2) (right (a-1) (right a x)),
            right (a-2) (right (a-1) (right a x)))
```

Note that we start at the top of the "arrow-head" diagram when combining boxes.

When merging the results, the match of each box looks as follows:

```
(x,y) -> f x y
```

Two such boxes can be combined with exactly the same approach of introducing an identity box (**IdI**), followed by horizontal (**HCompI**) and then vertical composition **VCompI**, giving a new box with the match

```
(x1,x2,x3) -> f x1 (f x2 x3)
```

Since we assume that f is associative this can be rewritten to:

```
(x1,x2,x3) -> f (f x1 x2) x3
```

Applying the associative rewrite to the next box it becomes

```
(x1,x2,x3,x4) -> f (f (f x1 x2) x3) x4
```

and so on. At the end the box will have the following match schema:

```
(x1,x2,x3,x4,...,xn) -> f (...(f (f x1 x2) x3) x4 ...) xn
```

This is the result of applying the fold function!

Theorem 13.
$$f \; x \; y = fold \; f \; x \; [y]$$

Proof. Firstly, remember that $[y]$ is shorthand for $(y : [])$. The proof follows from two unfoldings of the definition of fold:

$$\text{fold } f \; x \; (y : []) \rightarrow \text{fold } f \; (f \; x \; y) \; [] \rightarrow f \; x \; y$$

Next we prove the following property about fold:

Theorem 14.

$$f \; (fold \; f \; x \; ys) \; z = fold \; f \; x \; (ys + \!\!+ [z])$$

Proof. By structural induction on ys:

Base case: $\quad f$ (fold f x []) $z =$ fold f x ([]$+\!\!+[z]$)	
fold f x ([]$+\!\!+[z]$)	$\rightarrow$ (++)
fold f x $[z]$	$\rightarrow$ (fold def (twice))
f x z	$\rightarrow$ (fold def)
f (fold f x []) z	
Recursion case: f (fold f x $(y : ys)$) $z =$	
fold f x $((y : ys)+\!\!+[z])$	
Assumption: $\quad f$ (fold f x ys) $z =$ fold f x $(ys+\!\!+[z])$	[induction hyp.]
fold f x $((y : ys)+\!\!+[z])$	$\rightarrow$ (++)
fold f x $(y : (ys+\!\!+[z]))$	$\rightarrow$ (fold)
fold f $(f \; x \; y)$ $(ys+\!\!+[z])$	$\rightarrow$ (induction hyp.)
f (fold f $(f \; x \; y)$ ys) z	$\rightarrow$ (fold)
f (fold f x $(y : ys)$) z	

By first applying Theorem 13 to the innermost f application, and then reapplying Theorem 14 until we are left with a large fold expression we end up with the following property:

```
f (...(f (f x1 x2) x3) x4 ...) xn = fold f x1 [x2,...,xn]
```

With this we apply **ESub** to get the following match:

```
(x1,x2,x3,x4,...,xn) -> fold f x1 [x2,...,xn]
```

This completes the following transformation:

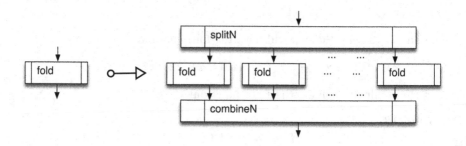

7 Conclusion

We have surveyed the Hume programming language and shown how the explicit separation of coordination and computation aids formal reasoning about programs. In particular, we have introduced the box calculus for reasoning about coordination and shown how, in conjunction with extant reasoning systems for computation, it is possible to construct robust proofs of substantial program constructs for parallelism through systematic transformation.

We envisage two important avenues for future activity. First of all, effective box calculus deployment clearly requires a graphical tool-set to support, and ultimately automate, scalable program transformation. Secondly, there are excellent opportunities in complementing the box calculus with resource analysis to enable resource directed program development in a "costing by construction" style. Here again, this should be supported by an integrated tool-set which can flexibly account for different resource modalities such as time, space and power consumption.

Acknowledgements. We would like to thank our collaborators Kevin Hammond of the University of St Andrews, Hume's co-designer, Andrew Ireland of Heriot-Watt University, who helped develop the box calculus, and the anonymous reviewer for very constructive feedback.

Hume Resources

The Hume home page is:

http://www-fp.cs.st-andrews.ac.uk/hume/index.shtml.

Hume tools and documentation may also be found at:

http://www.macs.hw.ac.uk/~greg/hume/.

The Hume Report is at:

http://www.macs.hw.ac.uk/~greg/hume/hume11.pdf

and the Hume Manual is at:

http://www.macs.hw.ac.uk/~greg/hume/manual.pdf

References

[BD77]   Burstall, R.M., Darlington, J.: A transformation system for developing recursive programs. Journal of the Association for Computing Machinery 24(1), 44–67 (1977)

[BdM97]   Bird, R., de Moor, O.: Algebra of Programming. Prentice-Hall (1997)

[Bir87]   Bird, R.S.: An introduction to the theory of lists. In: Broy, M. (ed.) Logic of Programming and Calculi of Discrete Design, pp. 3–42. Springer, Heidelberg (1987)

[BLOMP97]   Breitinger, S., Loogen, R., Ortega Mallen, Y., Pena, R.: The Eden Coordination Model for Distributed Memory Systems. In: Proceedings of the 1997 Workshop on High-Level Programming Models and Supportive Environments (HIPS 1997), pp. 120–124. IEEE Computer Society, Washington, DC (1997)

[Bur69]   Burstall, R.: Proving properties of programs by structural induction. Computer Journal 12(1), 41–48 (1969)

[Chu36]   Church, A.: An unsolvable problem of elementary number theory. American Journal of Mathematics 58, 345–363 (1936)

[CJP07]   Chapman, B., Jost, G., van der Pas, R.: Using OpenMP: Portable Shared Memory Parallel Programming (Scientific and Engineering Computation). MIT (2007)

[Dij75]   Dijkstra, E.W.: Guarded commands, non-determinacy and derivation of programs. Commuications of the ACM 18(8), 453–457 (1975)

[eAB+99]   Peyton Jones, S.L. (ed.), Augustsson, L., Boutel, B., Burton, F.W., Fasel, J.H., Gordon, A.D., Hammond, K., Hughes, R.J.M., Hudak, P., Johnsson, T., Jones, M.P., Peterson, J.C., Reid, A., Wadler, P.L.: Report on the Non-Strict Functional Language, Haskell (Haskell98). Technical report, Yale University (1999)

[GM08]   Grov, G., Michaelson, G.: Towards a Box Calculus for Hierarchical Hume. In: Morazan, M. (ed.) Trends in Functional Programming, vol. 8, pp. 71–88. Intellect (2008)

[GM11]   Grov, G., Michaelson, G.: Hume box calculus: robust system development through software transformation. In: Higher Order Symbolic Computing (July 2011), doi:10.1007/s10990-011-9067-y

[Gro09]   Grov, G.: Reasoning about correctness properties of a coordination language. PhD thesis, Heriot-Watt University (2009)

[Hal60]   Halmos, P.R.: Naive Set theory. Van Nostrand (1960)

[HM03]   Hammond, K., Michaelson, G.: Hume: A Domain-Specific Language for Real-Time Embedded Systems. In: Pfenning, F., Macko, M. (eds.) GPCE 2003. LNCS, vol. 2830, pp. 37–56. Springer, Heidelberg (2003)

[Hoa69]   Hoare, C.A.R.: An axiomatic basis for computer programming. Communications of the ACM 12, 576–583 (1969)

[Hoa78]   Hoare, C.A.R.: Communicating Sequential Processes. Communications of the ACM 21(8), 666–677 (1978)

[Hod77]   Hodges, W.: Logic. Pelican (1977)

[Inm88]   Inmos: Occam Reference Manual. Prentice-Hall (1988)

[Kne63]   Kneebone, G.: Mathematical Logic and the Foundations of Mathematics. Van Nostrand (1963)

[McC62]   McCarthy, J.: A basis for a mathematical theory of computation. Technical Report Memo 31. MIT (1962)

[MF94]   MPI-Forum: MPI: A message passing intrface standard. International
           Journal of Supercomputer Application 8(3-4), 165–414 (1994)
[Mil82]   Milner, R.: A Calculus of Communicating Systems. Springer (1982)
[Mil99]   Milner, R.: Communicating and mobile systems - the Pi-calculus.
           Cambridge University Press (1999)
[MTHM97]   Milner, R., Tofte, M., Harper, R., MacQueen, D.: The Definition of
           Standard ML (Revised). MIT Press (1997)
[Nid62]   Nidditch, P.H.: Propositional Calculus. Routledge and Kegan Paul
           (1962)
[Pet67]   Peter, R.: Recursive Functions. Academic Press (1967)
[Qui64]   Quine, W.V.: Word and Object. MIT (1964)
[Weg68]   Wegner, P.: Programming Languages, Information Structures, and
           Machine Organization. McGraw-Hill (1968)

Parallel and Concurrent Programming in Haskell

Simon Marlow

Microsoft Research Ltd., Cambridge, U.K.
simonmar@microsoft.com

Abstract. Haskell provides a rich set of abstractions for parallel and concurrent programming. This tutorial covers the basic concepts involved in writing parallel and concurrent programs in Haskell, and takes a deliberately practical approach: most of the examples are real Haskell programs that you can compile, run, measure, modify and experiment with. We cover parallel programming with the Eval monad, Evaluation Strategies, and the Par monad. On the concurrent side, we cover threads, MVars, asynchronous exceptions, Software Transactional Memory, the Foreign Function Interface, and briefly look at the construction of high-speed network servers in Haskell.

1 Introduction

While most programming languages nowadays provide some form of concurrent or parallel programming facilities, very few provide as wide a range as Haskell. The Haskell language is fertile ground on which to build abstractions, and concurrency and parallelism are no exception here. In the world of concurrency and parallelism, there is good reason to believe that no *one size fits all* programming model for concurrency and parallelism exists, and so prematurely committing to one particular paradigm is likely to tilt the language towards favouring certain kinds of problem. Hence in Haskell we focus on providing a wide range of abstractions and libraries, so that for any given problem it should be possible to find a tool that suits the task at hand.

In this tutorial I will introduce the main programming models available for concurrent and parallel programming in Haskell. The tutorial is woefully incomplete — there is simply too much ground to cover, but it is my hope that future revisions of this document will expand its coverage. In the meantime it should serve as an introduction to the fundamental concepts through the use of practical examples, together with pointers to further reading for those who wish to find out more.

This tutorial takes a deliberately practical approach: most of the examples are real Haskell programs that you can compile, run, measure, modify and experiment with. For information on how to obtain the code samples, see Section 1.1. There is also a set of accompanying exercises.

In order to follow this tutorial you should have a basic knowledge of Haskell, including programming with monads.

V. Zsók, Z. Horváth, and R. Plasmeijer (Eds.): CEFP 2011, LNCS 7241, pp. 339–401, 2012.
© Springer-Verlag Berlin Heidelberg 2012

Briefly, the topics covered in this tutorial are as follows:

- Parallel programming with the `Eval` monad (Section 2.1)
- Evaluation Strategies (Section 2.2)
- Dataflow parallelism with the `Par` monad (Section 2.3)
- Basic Concurrent Haskell (Section 3)
- Asynchronous exceptions (Section 3.3)
- Software Transactional Memory (Section 3.4)
- Concurrency and the Foreign Function Interface (Section 3.5)
- High-speed concurrent servers (Section 3.6)

One useful aspect of this tutorial as compared to previous tutorials covering similar ground ([12; 13]) is that I have been able to take into account recent changes to the APIs. In particular, the `Eval` monad has replaced `par` and `pseq` (thankfully), and in asynchronous exceptions `mask` has replaced the old `block` and `unblock`.

1.1   Tools and Resources

To try out Parallel and Concurrent Haskell, and to run the sample programs that accompany this article, you will need to install the Haskell Platform[1]. The Haskell Platform includes the GHC compiler and all the important libraries, including the parallel and concurrent libraries we shall be using. This version of the tutorial was tested with the Haskell Platform version 2011.2.0.1, and we expect to update this tutorial as necessary to cover future changes in the platform.

Section 2.3 requires the `monad-par` package, which is not currently part of the Haskell Platform. To install it, use the `cabal` command:

```
$ cabal install monad-par
```

(The examples in this tutorial were tested with `monad-par` version 0.1.0.3).

Additionally, we recommend installing ThreadScope[2]. ThreadScope is a tool for visualising the execution of Haskell programs, and is particularly useful for gaining insight into the behaviour of parallel and concurrent Haskell code. On some systems (mainly Linux) ThreadScope can be installed with a simple

```
$ cabal install threadscope
```

but for other systems refer to the ThreadScope documentation at the aforementioned URL.

While reading the article we recommend you have the following documentation to hand:

- The GHC User's Guide[3],

---

[1] http://hackage.haskell.org/platform/

[2] http://www.haskell.org/haskellwiki/ThreadScope

[3] http://www.haskell.org/ghc/docs/latest/html/users_guide/

– The Haskell Platform library documentation, which can be found on the main Haskell Platform site[4]. Any types or functions that we use in this article that are not explicitly described can be found documented there.

It should be noted that none of the APIs described in this tutorial are *standard* in the sense of being part of the Haskell specification. That may change in the future.

Sample Code. The repository containing the source for both this document and the code samples can be found at `https://github.com/simonmar/par-tutorial` . The current version can be downloaded from `http://community.haskell.org/~simonmar/par-tutorial-1.2.zip`.

1.2   Terminology: Parallelism and Concurrency

In many fields, the words *parallel* and *concurrent* are synonyms; not so in programming, where they are used to describe fundamentally different concepts.

A *parallel* program is one that uses a multiplicity of computational hardware (e.g. multiple processor cores) in order to perform computation more quickly. Different parts of the computation are delegated to different processors that execute at the same time (in *parallel*), so that results may be delivered earlier than if the computation had been performed sequentially.

In contrast, *concurrency* is a program-structuring technique in which there are multiple *threads of control*. Notionally the threads of control execute "at the same time"; that is, the user sees their effects interleaved. Whether they actually execute at the same time or not is an implementation detail; a concurrent program can execute on a single processor through interleaved execution, or on multiple physical processors.

While parallel programming is concerned only with efficiency, concurrent programming is concerned with structuring a program that needs to interact with multiple independent external agents (for example the user, a database server, and some external clients). Concurrency allows such programs to be *modular*; the thread that interacts with the user is distinct from the thread that talks to the database. In the absence of concurrency, such programs have to be written with event loops and callbacks—indeed, event loops and callbacks are often used even when concurrency is available, because in many languages concurrency is either too expensive, or too difficult, to use.

The notion of "threads of control" does not make sense in a purely functional program, because there are no effects to observe, and the evaluation order is irrelevant. So concurrency is a structuring technique for effectful code; in Haskell, that means code in the IO monad.

A related distinction is between *deterministic* and *nondeterministic* programming models. A deterministic programming model is one in which each program can give only one result, whereas a nondeterministic programming model admits programs that may have different results, depending on some aspect of the

---

[4] `http://hackage.haskell.org/platform/`

execution. Concurrent programming models are necessarily nondeterministic, because they must interact with external agents that cause events at unpredictable times. Nondeterminism has some notable drawbacks, however: programs become significantly harder to test and reason about.

For parallel programming we would like to use deterministic programming models if at all possible. Since the goal is just to arrive at the answer more quickly, we would rather not make our program harder to debug in the process. Deterministic parallel programming is the best of both worlds: testing, debugging and reasoning can be performed on the sequential program, but the program runs faster when processors are added. Indeed, most computer processors themselves implement deterministic parallelism in the form of pipelining and multiple execution units.

While it is possible to do parallel programming using concurrency, that is often a poor choice, because concurrency sacrifices determinism. In Haskell, the parallel programming models are deterministic. However, it is important to note that deterministic programming models are not sufficient to express all kinds of parallel algorithms; there are algorithms that depend on internal nondeterminism, particularly problems that involve searching a solution space. In Haskell, this class of algorithms is expressible only using concurrency.

Finally, it is entirely reasonable to want to mix parallelism and concurrency in the same program. Most interactive programs will need to use concurrency to maintain a responsive user interface while the compute intensive tasks are being performed.

2   Parallel Haskell

Parallel Haskell is all about making Haskell programs run *faster* by dividing the work to be done between multiple processors. Now that processor manufacturers have largely given up trying to squeeze more performance out of individual processors and have refocussed their attention on providing us with more processors instead, the biggest gains in performance are to be had by using parallel techniques in our programs so as to make use of these extra cores.

We might wonder whether the compiler could automatically parallelise programs for us. After all, it should be easier to do this in a pure functional language where the only dependencies between computations are data dependencies, and those are mostly perspicuous and thus readily analysed. In contrast, when effects are unrestricted, analysis of dependencies tends to be much harder, leading to greater approximation and a large degree of false dependencies. However, even in a language with only data dependencies, automatic parallelisation still suffers from an age-old problem: managing parallel tasks requires some bookkeeping relative to sequential execution and thus has an inherent overhead, so the size of the parallel tasks must be large enough to overcome the overhead. Analysing costs at compile time is hard, so one approach is to use runtime profiling to find tasks that are costly enough and can also be run in parallel, and feed this information back into the compiler. Even this, however, has not been terribly successful in practice [1].

Fully automatic parallelisation is still a pipe dream. However, the parallel programming models provided by Haskell do succeed in eliminating some mundane or error-prone aspects traditionally associated with parallel programming:

– Parallel programming in Haskell is *deterministic*: the parallel program always produces the same answer, regardless how many processors are used to run it, so parallel programs can be debugged without actually running them in parallel.
– Parallel Haskell programs do not explicitly deal with *synchronisation* or *communication*. Synchronisation is the act of waiting for other tasks to complete, perhaps due to data dependencies. Communication involves the transmission of results between tasks running on different processors. Synchronisation is handled automatically by the GHC runtime system and/or the parallelism libraries. Communication is implicit in GHC since all tasks share the same heap, and can share objects without restriction. In this setting, although there is no explicit communication at the program level or even the runtime level, at the hardware level communication re-emerges as the transmission of data between the caches of the different cores. Excessive communication can cause contention for the main memory bus, and such overheads can be difficult to diagnose.

Parallel Haskell does require the programmer to think about **Partitioning**. The programmer's job is to subdivide the work into tasks that can execute in parallel. Ideally, we want to have enough tasks that we can keep all the processors busy for the entire runtime. However, our efforts may be thwarted:

– **Granularity**. If we make our tasks too small, then the overhead of managing the tasks outweighs any benefit we might get from running them in parallel. So granularity should be large enough to dwarf the overheads, but not too large, because then we risk not having enough work to keep all the processors busy, especially towards the end of the execution when there are fewer tasks left.
– **Data dependencies** between tasks enforce sequentialisation. GHC's two parallel programming models take different approaches to data dependencies: in *Strategies* (Section 2.2), data dependencies are entirely implicit, whereas in the *Par monad* (Section 2.3), they are explicit. This makes programming with Strategies somewhat more concise, at the expense of the possibility that hidden dependencies could cause sequentialisation at runtime.

In this tutorial we will describe two parallel programming models provided by GHC. The first, *Evaluation Strategies* [8] (Strategies for short), is well-established and there are many good examples of using Strategies to write parallel Haskell programs. The second is a dataflow programming model based around a `Par` monad [5]. This is a newer programming model in which it is possible to express parallel coordination more explicitly than with Strategies, though at the expense of some of the conciseness and modularity of Strategies.

2.1   Basic parallelism: The Eval Monad

In this section we will demonstrate how to use the basic parallelism abstractions in Haskell to perform some computations in parallel. As a running example that you can actually test yourself, we use a Sudoku solver[5]. The Sudoku solver is very fast, and can solve all 49,000 of the known puzzles with 17 clues[6] in about 2 minutes.

We start with some ordinary sequential code to solve a set of Sudoku problems read from a file:

```
import Sudoku
import Control.Exception
import System.Environment

main :: IO ()
main = do
    [f] <- getArgs
    grids <- fmap lines $ readFile f
    mapM_ (evaluate . solve) grids
```

The module `Sudoku` provides us with a function `solve` with type

```
solve :: String -> Maybe Grid
```

where the `String` represents a single Sudoku problem, and `Grid` is a representation of the solution. The function returns `Nothing` if the problem has no solution. For the purposes of this example we are not interested in the solution itself, so our `main` function simply calls `evaluate . solve` on each line of the file (the file will contain one Sudoku problem per line). The `evaluate` function comes from `Control.Exception` and has type

```
evaluate :: a -> IO a
```

It evaluates its argument to *weak-head normal form*. Weak-head normal form just means that the expression is evaluated as far as the first constructor; for example, if the expression is a list, then `evaluate` would perform enough evaluation to determine whether the list is empty (`[]`) or non-empty (`_:_`), but it would not evaluate the head or tail of the list. The `evaluate` function returns its result in the `IO` monad, so it is useful for forcing evaluation at a particular time.

Compile the program as follows:

```
$ ghc -O2 sudoku1.hs -rtsopts
[1 of 2] Compiling Sudoku          ( Sudoku.hs, Sudoku.o )
[2 of 2] Compiling Main            ( sudoku1.hs, sudoku1.o )
Linking sudoku1 ...
```

and run it on 1000 sample problems:

---

[5] The Sudoku solver code can be found in the module `Sudoku.hs` in the samples that accompany this tutorial.

[6] http://mapleta.maths.uwa.edu.au/~gordon/sudokumin.php

```
$ ./sudoku1 sudoku17.1000.txt +RTS -s
./sudoku1 sudoku17.1000.txt +RTS -s
  2,392,127,440 bytes allocated in the heap
     36,829,592 bytes copied during GC
        191,168 bytes maximum residency (11 sample(s))
         82,256 bytes maximum slop
              2 MB total memory in use


Generation 0:  4570 collections, 0 parallel, 0.14s, 0.13s elapsed
Generation 1:    11 collections, 0 parallel, 0.00s, 0.00s elapsed


Parallel GC work balance: -nan (0 / 0, ideal 1)

                      MUT time (elapsed)       GC time  (elapsed)
Task  0 (worker) :     0.00s  (  0.00s)        0.00s  (  0.00s)
Task  1 (worker) :     0.00s  (  2.92s)        0.00s  (  0.00s)
Task  2 (bound)  :     2.92s  (  2.92s)        0.14s  (  0.14s)


SPARKS: 0 (0 converted, 0 pruned)


INIT   time    0.00s  (  0.00s elapsed)
MUT    time    2.92s  (  2.92s elapsed)
GC     time    0.14s  (  0.14s elapsed)
EXIT   time    0.00s  (  0.00s elapsed)
Total  time    3.06s  (  3.06s elapsed)


%GC time       4.6%  (4.6% elapsed)


Alloc rate     818,892,766 bytes per MUT second


Productivity  95.4% of total user, 95.3% of total elapsed
```

The argument +RTS -s instructs the GHC runtime system to emit the statistics
you see above. These are particularly helpful as a first step in analysing parallel
performance. The output is explained in detail in the GHC User's Guide, but
for our purposes we are interested in one particular metric: Total time. This
figure is given in two forms: the first is the total CPU time used by the program,
and the second figure is the *elapsed*, or wall-clock, time. Since we are running on
a single processor, these times are identical (sometimes the elapsed time might
be slightly larger due to other activity on the system).

This program should parallelise quite easily; after all, each problem can be
solved completely independently of the others. First, we will need some basic functionality for expressing parallelism, which is provided by the module
Control.Parallel.Strategies:

```
data Eval a
instance Monad Eval

runEval :: Eval a -> a
```

```
rpar :: a -> Eval a
rseq :: a -> Eval a
```

Parallel coordination will be performed in a monad, namely the Eval monad. The reason for this is that parallel programming fundamentally involves *ordering* things: start evaluating a in parallel, *and then* evaluate b. Monads are good for expressing ordering relationships in a compositional way.

The Eval monad provides a runEval operation that lets us extract the value from Eval. Note that runEval is completely pure - there's no need to be in the IO monad here.

The Eval monad comes with two basic operations, rpar and rseq. The rpar combinator is used for creating parallelism; it says "my argument could be evaluated in parallel", while rseq is used for forcing sequential evaluation: it says "evaluate my argument now" (to weak-head normal form). These two operations are typicaly used together - for example, to evaluate A and B in parallel, we could apply rpar on A, followed by rseq on B.

Returning to our Sudoku example, let us add some parallelism to make use of two processors. We have a list of problems to solve, so it should suffice to divide the list in two and solve the problems in each half of the list in parallel. Here is some code to do just that[7]:

```
1    let (as,bs) = splitAt (length grids 'div' 2) grids

3    evaluate $ runEval $ do
4        a <- rpar (deep (map solve as))
5        b <- rpar (deep (map solve bs))
6        rseq a
7        rseq b
8        return ()
```

line 1 divides the list into two equal (or nearly-equal) sub-lists, as and bs. The next part needs more explanation:

3 We are going to evaluate an application of runEval

4 Create a parallel task to compute the solutions to the problems in the sub-list as. The expression map solve as represents the solutions; however, just evaluating this expression to weak-head normal form will not actually compute any of the solutions, since it will only evaluate as far as the first (:) cell of the list. We need to fully evaluate the whole list, including the elements. This is why we added an application of the deep function, which is defined as follows:

```
deep :: NFData a => a -> a
deep a = deepseq a a
```

deep evaluates the entire structure of its argument (reducing it to *normal form*), before returning the argument itself. It is defined in terms of the function deepseq, which is available from the Control.DeepSeq module.

---

[7] Full code in sample sudoku2.hs

Not evaluating deeply enough is a common mistake when using the rpar monad, so it is a good idea to get into the habit of thinking, for each rpar, "how much of this structure do I want to evaluate in the parallel task?" (indeed, it is such a common problem that in the Par monad to be introduced later, we went so far as to make deepseq the default behaviour).

5 Create a parallel task to compute the solutions to bs, exactly as for as.

6-7 Using rseq, we wait for both parallel tasks to complete.

8 Finally, return (for this example we aren't interested in the results themselves, only in the act of computing them).

In order to use parallelism with GHC, we have to add the -threaded option, like so:

```
$ ghc -O2 sudoku2.hs -rtsopts -threaded
[2 of 2] Compiling Main              ( sudoku2.hs, sudoku2.o )
Linking sudoku2 ...
```

Now, we can run the program using 2 processors:

```
$ ./sudoku2 sudoku17.1000.txt +RTS -N2 -s
./sudoku2 sudoku17.1000.txt +RTS -N2 -s
  2,400,125,664 bytes allocated in the heap
     48,845,008 bytes copied during GC
      2,617,120 bytes maximum residency (7 sample(s))
        313,496 bytes maximum slop
              9 MB total memory in use


Gen  0: 2975 collections, 2974 parallel, 1.04s, 0.15s elapsed
Gen  1:    7 collections,    7 parallel, 0.05s, 0.02s elapsed


Parallel GC work balance: 1.52 (6087267 / 3999565, ideal 2)


                    MUT time (elapsed)       GC time  (elapsed)
Task  0 (worker) :    1.27s  (  1.80s)       0.69s  (  0.10s)
Task  1 (worker) :    0.00s  (  1.80s)       0.00s  (  0.00s)
Task  2 (bound)  :    0.88s  (  1.80s)       0.39s  (  0.07s)
Task  3 (worker) :    0.05s  (  1.80s)       0.00s  (  0.00s)


SPARKS: 2 (1 converted, 0 pruned)


INIT  time    0.00s  (  0.00s elapsed)
MUT   time    2.21s  (  1.80s elapsed)
GC    time    1.08s  (  0.17s elapsed)
EXIT  time    0.00s  (  0.00s elapsed)
Total time    3.29s  (  1.97s elapsed)


%GC time     32.9%  (8.8% elapsed)


Alloc rate    1,087,049,866 bytes per MUT second


Productivity  67.0% of total user, 111.9% of total elapsed
```

Note that the `Total time` now shows a marked difference between the CPU time (3.29s) and the elapsed time (1.97s). Previously the elapsed time was 3.06s, so we can calculate the *speedup* on 2 processors as 3.06/1.97 = 1.55. Speedups are always calculated as a ratio of wall-clock times. The CPU time is a helpful metric for telling us how busy our processors are, but as you can see here, the CPU time when running on multiple processors is often greater than the wall-clock time for a single processor, so it would be misleading to calculate the speedup as the ratio of CPU time to wall-clock time (1.67 here).

Why is the speedup only 1.55, and not 2? In general there could be a host of reasons for this, not all of which are under the control of the Haskell programmer. However, in this case the problem is partly of our doing, and we can diagnose it using the ThreadScope tool. To profile the program using ThreadScope we need to first recompile it with the `-eventlog` flag, run it with `+RTS -ls`, and then invoke ThreadScope on the generated `sudoku2.eventlog` file:

```
$ rm sudoku2; ghc -O2 sudoku2.hs -threaded -rtsopts -eventlog
[2 of 2] Compiling Main         ( sudoku2.hs, sudoku2.o )
Linking sudoku2 ...
$ ./sudoku2 sudoku17.1000.txt +RTS -N2 -ls
$ threadscope sudoku2.eventlog
```

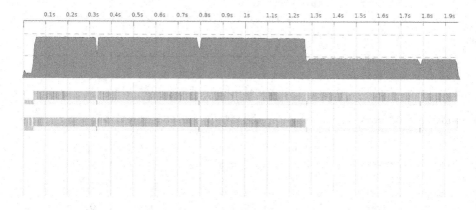

Fig. 1. Sudoku2 ThreadScope profile

The ThreadScope profile is shown in Figure 1; this graph was generated by selecting "export to PNG" from ThreadScope, so it includes the timeline graph only, and not the rest of the ThreadScope GUI. The x axis of the graph is time, and there are three horizontal bars showing how the program executed over time. The topmost bar is known as the "activity" profile, and it shows how many processors were executing Haskell code (as opposed to being idle or garbage collecting) at a given point in time. Underneath the activity profile there is one bar per processor, showing what that processor was doing at each point in the execution. Each bar has two parts:: the upper, thicker bar is green when that processor is executing Haskell code, and the lower, narrower bar is orange or green when that processor is performing garbage collection.[8]

As we can see from the graph, there is a period at the end of the run where just one processor is executing, and the other one is idle (except for participating in regular garbage collections, which is necessary for GHC's parallel garbage collector). This indicates that our two parallel tasks are uneven: one takes much longer to execute than the other, and so we are not making full use of our 2 processors, which results in less than perfect speedup.

Why should the workloads be uneven? After all, we divided the list in two, and we know the sample input has an even number of problems. The reason for the unevenness is that each problem does not take the same amount of time to solve, it all depends on the searching strategy used by the Sudoku solver[9]. This illustrates an important distinction between two partitioning strategies:

- **Static Partitioning**, which is the technique we used to partition the Sudoku problems here, consists of dividing the work according to some pre-defined policy (here, dividing the list equally in two).
- **Dynamic Partitioning** instead tries to distribute the work more evenly, by dividing the work into smaller tasks and only assigning tasks to processors when they are idle.

The GHC runtime system supports automatic distribution of the parallel tasks; all we have to do to achieve dynamic partitioning is divide the problem into small enough tasks and the runtime will do the rest for us.

The argument to **rpar** is called a *spark*. The runtime collects sparks in a pool and uses this as a source of work to do when there are spare processors available, using a technique called *work stealing* [7]. Sparks may be evaluated at some point in the future, or they might not — it all depends on whether there is spare processor capacity available. Sparks are very cheap to create (**rpar** essentially just adds a reference to the expression to an array).

So, let's try using dynamic partitioning with the Sudoku problem. First we define an abstraction that will let us apply a function to a list in parallel, **parMap**:

```
1  parMap :: (a -> b) -> [a] -> Eval [b]
2  parMap f [] = return []
3  parMap f (a:as) = do
4    b <- rpar (f a)
5    bs <- parMap f as
6    return (b:bs)
```

This is rather like a monadic version of **map**, except that we have used **rpar** to lift the application of the function **f** to the element **a** into the **Eval** monad. Hence, **parMap** runs down the whole list, eagerly creating sparks for the application of

---

[8] The distinction between orange and green during GC has to do with the kind of GC activity being performed, and need not concern us here.

[9] In fact, we ordered the problems in the sample input so as to clearly demonstrate the problem.

f to each element, and finally returns the new list. When `parMap` returns, it will
have created one spark for each element of the list.

We still need to evaluate the result list itself, and that is straightforward with
`deep`:

```
evaluate $ deep $ runEval $ parMap solve grids
```

Running this new version[10] yields more speedup:

```
Total time    3.55s  ( 1.79s elapsed)
```

which we can calculate is equivalent to a speedup of $3.06/1.79 = 1.7$, approaching
the ideal speedup of 2. Furthermore, the GHC runtime system tells us how many
sparks were created:

```
SPARKS: 1000 (1000 converted, 0 pruned)
```

we created exactly 1000 sparks, and they were all *converted* (that is, turned into
real parallelism at runtime). Sparks that are *pruned* have been removed from
the spark pool by the runtime system, either because they were found to be
already evaluated, or because they were found to be not referenced by the rest
of the program, and so are deemed to be not useful. We will discuss the latter
requirement in more detail in Section 2.2.

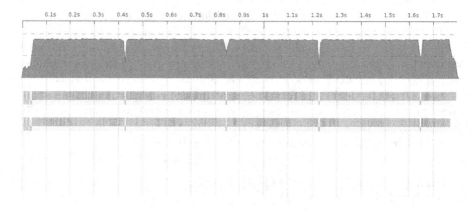

Fig. 2. Sudoku3 ThreadScope profile

The ThreadScope profile looks much better (Figure 2). Furthermore, now
that the runtime is managing the work distribution for us, the program will
automatically scale to more processors. On an 8 processor machine, for example:

```
Total time    4.46s  ( 0.59s elapsed)
```

which equates to a speedup of 5.2 over the sequential version.

---

[10] Code sample `sudoku3.hs`

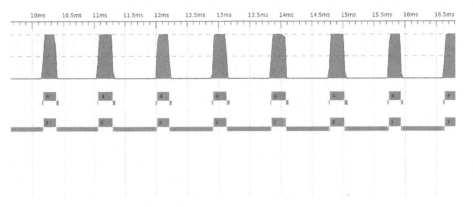

Fig. 3. Sudoku3 (zoomed) ThreadScope profile

If we look closely at the 2-processor profile there appears to be a short section near the beginning where not much work is happening. In fact, zooming in on this section in ThreadScope (Figure 3) reveals that both processors are working, but most of the activity is garbage collection, and only one processor is performing most of the garbage collection work. In fact, what we are seeing here is the program reading the input file (lazily) and dividing it into lines, driven by the demand of `parMap` which traverses the whole list of lines.

Since reading the file and dividing it into lines is a sequential activity anyway, we could force it to happen all at once before we start the main computation, by adding

```
evaluate (length grids)
```

(see code sample `sudoku4.hs`). This makes no difference to the overall runtime, but it divides the execution into sequential and parallel parts, as we can see in ThreadScope (Figure 4).

Now, we can read off the portion of the runtime that is sequential: 33ms. When we have a sequential portion of our program, this affects the maximum parallel speedup that is achievable, which we can calculate using Amdahl's law. Amdahl's law gives the maximum achievable speedup as the ratio

$$\frac{1}{(1 - P) + \frac{P}{N}}$$

where P is the portion of the runtime that can be parallelised, and N is the number of processors available. In our case, P is $(3.06 - 0.033)/3.06 = 0.9892$, and the maximum speedup is hence 1.98. The sequential fraction here is too small to make a significant impact on the theoretical maximum speedup with 2 processors, but when we have more processors, say 64, it becomes much more important: $1/((1 - 0.989) + 0.989/64) = 38.1$. So no matter what we do, this tiny sequential part of our program will limit the maximum speedup we can obtain with 64 processors to 38.1. In fact, even with 1024 cores we could only achieve

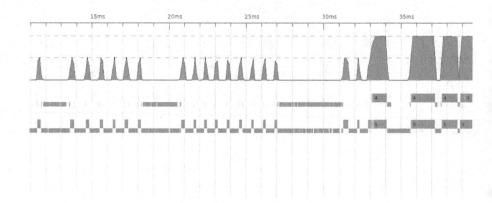

Fig. 4. Sudoku4 ThreadScope profile

around 84 speedup, and it is impossible to achieve a speedup of 91 no matter how many cores we have. Amdahl's law tells us that not only does parallel speedup become harder to achieve the more processors we add, in practice most programs have a theoretical maximum amount of parallelism.

2.2   Evaluation Strategies

Evaluation Strategies [14; 8] is an abstraction layer built on top of the Eval monad that allows larger parallel specifications to be built in a compositional way. Furthermore Strategies allow parallel coordination to be described in a modular way, separating parallelism from the algorithm to be parallelised.

A Strategy is merely a function in the Eval monad that takes a value of type a and returns the same value:

```
type Strategy a = a -> Eval a
```

Strategies are identity functions; that is, the value returned by a Strategy is observably equivalent to the value it was passed. Unfortunately the library cannot statically guarantee this property for user-defined Strategy functions, but it holds for the Strategy functions and combinators provided by the module Control.Parallel.Strategies.

We have already seen some simple Strategies, rpar and rseq, although we can now give their types in terms of Strategy:

```
rseq :: Strategy a
rpar :: Strategy a
```

There are two further members of this family:

```
r0 :: Strategy a
r0 x = return x

rdeepseq :: NFData a => Strategy a
rdeepseq x = rseq (deep x)
```

r0 is the `Strategy` that evaluates nothing, and `rdeepseq` is the `Strategy` that evaluates the entire structure of its argument, which can be defined in terms of `deep` that we saw earlier. Note that `rseq` is necessary here: replacing `rseq` with `return` would not perform the evaluation immediately, but would defer it until the value returned by `rdeepseq` is demanded (which might be never).

We have some simple ways to build Strategies, but how is a Strategy actually *used*? A `Strategy` is just a function yielding a computation in the `Eval` monad, so we could use `runEval`. For example, applying the strategy s to a value x would be simply `runEval (s x)`. This is such a common pattern that the Strategies library gives it a name, `using`:

```
using :: a -> Strategy a -> a
x 'using' s = runEval (s x)
```

`using` takes a value of type a, a Strategy for a, and applies the Strategy to the value. The identity property for `Strategy` gives us that

```
x 'using' s == x
```

which is a significant benefit of Strategies: every occurrence of `'using' s` can be deleted without affecting the semantics. Strictly speaking there are two caveats to this property. Firstly, as mentioned earlier, user-defined `Strategy` functions might not satisfy the identity property. Secondly, the expression x `'using'` s might be less defined than x, because it evaluates more structure of x than the context does. So deleting `'using' s` might have the effect of making the program terminate with a result when it would previously throw an exception or fail to terminate. Making programs more defined is generally considered to be a somewhat benign change in semantics (indeed, GHC's optimiser can also make programs more defined under certain conditions), but nevertheless it is a change in semantics.

A Strategy for Evaluating a List in Parallel. In Section 2.1 we defined a function `parMap` that would map a function over a list in parallel. We can think of `parMap` as a composition of two parts:

- The algorithm: `map`
- The parallelism: evaluating the elements of a list in parallel

and indeed with Strategies we can express it exactly this way:

```
parMap f xs = map f xs 'using' parList rseq
```

The benefits of this approach are two-fold: not only does it separate the algorithm from the parallelism, but it also *reuses* `map`, rather than re-implementing a parallel version.

The `parList` function is a Strategy on lists, defined as follows:

```
parList :: Strategy a -> Strategy [a]
parList strat []     = return []
parList strat (x:xs) = do
```

```
x'  <- rpar (x 'using' strat)
xs' <- parList strat xs
return (x':xs')
```

(in fact, parList is already provided by Control.Parallel.Strategies so you don't have to define it yourself, but we are using its implementation here as an illustration).

The parList function is a *parameterised* Strategy, that is, it takes as an argument a Strategy on values of type a, and returns a Strategy for lists of a. This illustrates another important aspect of Strategies: they are compositional, in the sense that we can build larger strategies by composing smaller reusable components. Here, parList describes a family of Strategies on lists that evaluate the list elements in parallel.

On line 4, parList calls rpar to create a spark to evaluate the current element of the list. Note that the spark evaluates (x 'using' strat): that is, it applies the argument Strategy strat to the list element x.

As parList traverses the list sparking list elements, it remembers each value returned by rpar (bound to x'), and constructs a new list from these values. Why? After all, this seems to be a lot of trouble to go to, because it means that parList is no longer *tail-recursive* — the recursive call to parList is not the last operation in the do on its right-hand side, and so parList will require stack space linear in the length of the input list.

Couldn't we write a tail-recursive version instead? For example:

```
parList :: Strategy a -> Strategy [a]
parList strat xs = do go xs; return xs
  where go [] = return ()
        go (x:xs) = do
          rpar (x 'using' strat)
          go xs
```

This typechecks, after all, and seems to call rpar on each list element as required.

The difference is subtle but important, and is best understood via a diagram (Figure 5). At the top of the diagram we have the input list xs: a linked list of cells, each of which points to a list element (x1, x2, and so forth). At the bottom of the diagram is the *spark pool*, the runtime system data structure that stores references to sparks in the heap. The other structures in the diagram are built by parList (the first version). Each strat box represents (x 'using' strat) for an element x of the original list, and xs' is the linked list of cells in the output list. The spark pool contains pointers to each of the strat boxes; these are the pointers created by the rpar calls.

Now, the spark pool only retains references to objects that are required by the program. If the runtime finds that the spark pool contains a reference to an object that the program will never use, then the reference is dropped, and any potential parallelism it represented is lost. This behaviour is a deliberate policy; if it weren't this way, then the spark pool could retain data indefinitely, causing a space leak (details can be found in Marlow et al. [8]).

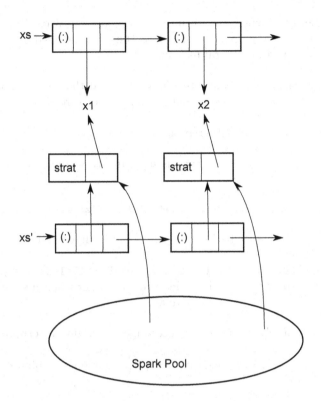

Fig. 5. parList heap structures

This is the reason for the list xs'. Suppose we did not build the new list xs', as in the tail-recursive version of parList above. Then, the only reference to each strat box in the heap would be from the spark pool, and hence the runtime would automatically sweep all those references from the spark pool, discarding the parallelism. Hence we build a new list xs', so that the program can retain references to the sparks for as long as it needs to.

This automatic discarding of unreferenced sparks has another benefit: suppose that under some circumstances the program does not need the entire list. If the program simply forgets the unused remainder of the list, the runtime system will clean up the unreferenced sparks from the spark pool, and will not waste any further parallel processing resources on evaluating those sparks. The extra parallelism in this case is termed *speculative*, because it is not necessarily required, and the runtime will automatically discard speculative tasks that it can prove will never be required - a useful property!

While the runtime system's discarding of unreferenced sparks is certainly useful in some cases, it can be tricky to work with, because there is no language-level support for catching mistakes. Fortunately the runtime system will tell us if it garbage collects unreferenced sparks; for example:

```
SPARKS: 144 (0 converted, 144 pruned)
```

A large number of sparks being "pruned" is a good indication that sparks are being removed from the spark pool before they can be used for parallelism. Sparks can be pruned for several reasons:

- The spark was a *dud*: it was already evaluated at the point it was sparked.
- The spark *fizzled*: it was evaluated by some other thread before it could be evaluated in parallel.
- The spark was garbage collected, as described above.

In fact, GHC from version 7.2.1 onwards separates these different classifications in its output from +RTS -s:

```
SPARKS: 144 (0 converted, 0 dud, 144 GC'd, 0 fizzled)
```

Unless you are using speculation, then a non-zero figure for GC'd sparks is probably a bad sign.

All of the combinators in the library `Control.Parallel.Strategies` behave correctly with respect to retaining references to sparks when necessary. So the rules of thumb for not tripping up here are:

- Use `using` to apply strategies: it encourages the right pattern, in which the program uses the results of applying the Strategy.
- When writing your own `Eval`-monad code, remember to bind the result of `rpar`, and use its result.

Using Parlist: The K-Means Problem. The `parList` Strategy covers a wide range of uses for parallelism in typical Haskell programs; in many cases, a single `parList` is all that is needed to expose sufficient parallelism.

Returning to our Sudoku solver from Section 2.1 for a moment, instead of our own hand-written `parMap`, we could have used `parList`:

```
evaluate $ deep $ map solve grids 'using' parList rseq
```

Let's look at a slightly more involved example. In the K-Means problem, the goal is to partition a set of data points into clusters. Finding an optimal solution to the problem is NP-hard, but there exist several heuristic techniques that do not guarantee to find an optimal solution, but work well in practice. For example, given the data points shown in Figure 6, the algorithm should discover the clusters indicated by the circles. Here we have only shown the locations of the clusters, partitioning the points is achieved by simply finding the closest cluster to each point.

The most well-known heuristic technique is Lloyd's algorithm, which finds a solution by iteratively improving an initial guess, as follows:

1. Pick an initial set of clusters by randomly assigning each point in the data set to a cluster.
2. Find the centroid of each cluster (the average of all the points in the cluster).

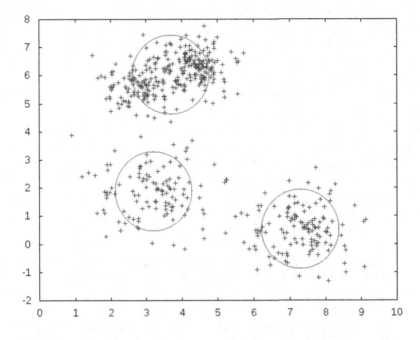

Fig. 6. The K-Means problem

3. Assign each point to the cluster to which it is closest, this gives a new set of clusters.
4. Repeat steps 2–3 until the set of clusters stabilises.

Of course the algorithm works in any number of dimensions, but we will use 2 for ease of visualisation.

A complete Haskell implementation can be found in the directory **kmeans** in the sample code; Figure 7 shows the core of the algorithm.

A data point is represented by the type **Vector**, which is just a pair of **Doubles**. Clusters are represented by the type **Cluster**, which contains its number, the count of points assigned to this cluster, the sum of the **Vectors** in the cluster, and its centre. Everything about the cluster except its number is derivable from the set of points in the cluster; this is expressed by the function **makeCluster**. Essentially **Cluster** caches various information about a cluster, and the reason we need to cache these specific items will become clear shortly.

The function **assign** implements step 3 of the algorithm, assigning points to clusters. The **accumArray** function is particularly useful for this kind of bucket-sorting task. The function **makeNewClusters** implements step 2 of the algorithm, and finally **step** combines **assign** and **makeNewClusters** to implement one complete iteration.

```
 1   data Vector = Vector Double Double

 3   addVector :: Vector -> Vector -> Vector
 4   addVector (Vector a b) (Vector c d) = Vector (a+c) (b+d)

 6   data Cluster = Cluster
 7                   {
 8                       clId    :: !Int,
 9                       clCount :: !Int,
10                       clSum   :: !Vector,
11                       clCent  :: !Vector
12                   }

14   sqDistance :: Vector -> Vector -> Double
15   sqDistance (Vector x1 y1) (Vector x2 y2)
16       = ((x1-x2)^2) + ((y1-y2)^2)

18   makeCluster :: Int -> [Vector] -> Cluster
19   makeCluster clid vecs
20       = Cluster { clId = clid,
21                   clCount = count,
22                   clSum = vecsum,
23                   clCent = centre }
24     where
25       vecsum@(Vector a b) = foldl' addVector (Vector 0 0) vecs
26       centre = Vector (a / fromIntegral count)
27                       (b / fromIntegral count)
28       count = fromIntegral (length vecs)

30   -- assign each vector to the nearest cluster centre
31   assign :: Int -> [Cluster] -> [Vector] -> Array Int [Vector]
32   assign nclusters clusters points =
33     accumArray (flip (:)) [] (0, nclusters-1)
34         [ (clId (nearest p), p) | p <- points ]
35     where
36       nearest p = fst $ minimumBy (compare 'on' snd)
37                           [ (c, sqDistance (clCent c) p)
38                           | c <- clusters ]

40   -- compute clusters from the assignment
41   makeNewClusters :: Array Int [Vector] -> [Cluster]
42   makeNewClusters arr =
43     filter ((>0) . clCount) $
44         [ makeCluster i ps | (i,ps) <- assocs arr ]

46   step :: Int -> [Cluster] -> [Vector] -> [Cluster]
47   step nclusters clusters points =
48     makeNewClusters (assign nclusters clusters points)
```

Fig. 7. Haskell code for K-Means

To complete the algorithm we need a driver to repeatedly apply the `step` function until convergence. The function `kmeans_seq`, in Figure 8, implements this.

How can this algorithm be parallelised? One place that looks straightforward to parallelise is the `assign` function, since it is essentially just a `map` over the points. However, that doesn't get us very far: we cannot parallelise `accumArray` directly, so we would have to do multiple `accumArrays` and combine the results, and combining elements would mean an extra list append. The `makeNewClusters` operation parallelises easily, but only in so far as each `makeCluster` is independent of the others; typically the number of clusters is much smaller than the

```
kmeans_seq :: Int -> [Vector] -> [Cluster] -> IO [Cluster]
kmeans_seq nclusters points clusters = do
  let
      loop :: Int -> [Cluster] -> IO [Cluster]
      loop n clusters | n > tooMany = return clusters
      loop n clusters = do
        hPrintf stderr "iteration %d\n" n
        hPutStr stderr (unlines (map show clusters))
        let clusters' = step nclusters clusters points
        if clusters' == clusters
          then return clusters
          else loop (n+1) clusters'
  --
  loop 0 clusters
```

Fig. 8. Haskell code for kmeans_seq

number of points (e.g. a few clusters to a few hundred thousand points), so we don't gain much scalability by parallelising makeNewClusters.

We would like a way to parallelise the problem at a higher level. That is, we would like to divide the set of points into chunks, and process each chunk in parallel, somehow combining the results. In order to do this, we need a combine function, such that

```
points == as ++ bs
  ==>
step n cs points == step n cs as 'combine' step n cs bs
```

Fortunately defining combine is not difficult. A cluster is a set of points, from which we can compute a centroid. The intermediate values in this calcuation are the sum and the count of the data points. So a combined cluster can be computed from two independent sub-clusters by taking the sum of these two intermediate values, and re-computing the centroid from them. Since addition is associative and commutative, we can compute sub-clusters in any way we wish and then combine them in this way.

Our Haskell code for combining two clusters is as follows:

```
combineClusters c1 c2 =
  Cluster {clId = clId c1,
           clCount = count,
           clSum = vecsum,
           clCent = Vector (a / fromIntegral count)
                           (b / fromIntegral count)}
  where count = clCount c1 + clCount c2
        vecsum@(Vector a b) = addVector (clSum c1) (clSum c2
)
```

In general, however, we will be processing N chunks of the data space independently, each of which returns a set of clusters. So we need to reduce the N sets of sets of clusters to a single set. This is done with another `accumArray`:

```
reduce :: Int -> [[Cluster]] -> [Cluster]
reduce nclusters css =
  concatMap combine $ elems $
    accumArray (flip (:)) [] (0,nclusters)
      [ (clId c, c) | c <- concat css]
  where
    combine [] = []
    combine (c:cs) = [foldr combineClusters c cs]
```

Now, the parallel K-Means implementation can be expressed as an application of `parList` to invoke `step` on each chunk, followed by a call to `reduce` to combine the results from the chunks:

```
1   kmeans_par :: Int -> Int -> [Vector] -> [Cluster]
2              -> IO [Cluster]
3   kmeans_par chunks nclusters points clusters = do
4     let chunks = split chunks points
5     let
6         loop :: Int -> [Cluster] -> IO [Cluster]
7         loop n clusters | n > tooMany = return clusters
8         loop n clusters = do
9           hPrintf stderr "iteration %d\n" n
10          hPutStr stderr (unlines (map show clusters))
11          let
12              new_clusterss =
13                  map (step nclusters clusters) chunks
14                    `using` parList rdeepseq

16              clusters' = reduce nclusters new_clusterss

18          if clusters' == clusters
19            then return clusters
20            else loop (n+1) clusters'
21          --
22    loop 0 clusters
```

the only difference from the sequential implementation is at lines 11–14, where we map `step` over the chunks applying the `parList` strategy, and then call `reduce`.

Note that there's no reason the number of chunks has to be related to the number of processors; as we saw earlier, it is better to produce plenty of sparks and let the runtime schedule them automatically, since this should enable the program to scale over a wide range of processors.

Figure 9 shows the speedups obtained by this implementation for a randomly-generated data set consisting of 4 clusters with a total of approximately 170000 points in 2-D space. The Haskell `normaldistribution` package was used to generate the data, in order to generate realistically clustered points[11]. For this benchmark we used 1000 for the `chunk` parameter to `kmeans_par`.

The results show the algorithm scaling reasonably well up to 6 cores, with a drop in performance at 8 cores. We leave it as an exercise for the reader to analyse the performance and improve it further!

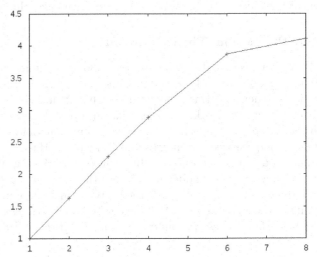

Fig. 9. Scaling of parallel K-Means

Further Reading. We have barely scratched the surface of the possibilities with the `Eval` monad and Strategies here. Topics that we have not covered include:

- Sequential strategies, which allow greater control over the specification of *evaluation degree* than is provided by `rseq` and `rdeepseq`. See the documentation for the `Control.Seq` module [12].
- Clustering, which allows greater control over granularity.
- `parBuffer`: a combinator for parallelising lazy streams.

To learn more, we recommend the following resources:

- The documentation for the `Control.Parallel.Strategies` module [13].
- Marlow et al. [8], which explains the motivation behind the design and implementation of `Eval` and Strategies.

---

[11] The program used to generate the data is provided as `kmeans/GenSamples.hs` in the sample code distribution, and the sample data we used for this benchmark is provided in the files `kmeans/points.bin` and `kmeans/clusters` (the `GenSamples` program will overwrite these files, so be careful if you run it!)

[12] `http://hackage.haskell.org/packages/archive/parallel/3.1.0.1/doc/html/Control-Seq.html`

[13] `http://hackage.haskell.org/packages/archive/parallel/3.1.0.1/doc/html/Control-Parallel-Strategies.html`

- Peyton Jones and Singh [13], an earlier tutorial covering basic parallelism in Haskell (beware: this dates from before the introduction of the Eval monad).
- Trinder et al. [14], which has a wide range of examples. However beware: this paper is based on the earlier version of Strategies, and some of the examples may no longer work due to the new GC behaviour on sparks; also some of the names of functions and types in the library have since changed.

2.3   Dataflow Parallelism: The Par Monad

Sometimes there is a need to be *more explicit* about dependencies and task boundaries than it is possible to be with Eval and Strategies. In these cases the usual recourse is to Concurrent Haskell, where we can fork threads and be explicit about which thread does the work. However, that approach throws out the baby with the bathwater: determinism is lost. The programming model we introduce in this section fills the gap between Strategies and Concurrent Haskell: it is explicit about dependencies and task boundaries, but without sacrificing determinism. Furthermore the programming model has some other interesting benefits: for example, it is implemented entirely as a Haskell library and the implementation is readily modified to accommodate alternative scheduling strategies.

As usual, the interface is based around a monad, this time called Par:

```
newtype Par a
instance Functor Par
instance Applicative Par
instance Monad Par

runPar :: Par a -> a
```

As with the Eval monad, the Par monad returns a pure result. However, use runPar with care: internally it is much more expensive than runEval, because (at least in the current implementation) it will fire up a new scheduler instance consisting of one worker thread per processor. Generally speaking the program should be using runPar to schedule large-sale parallel tasks.

The purpose of Par is to introduce parallelism, so we need a way to create parallel tasks:

```
fork :: Par () -> Par ()
```

fork does exactly what you would expect: the computation passed as the argument to fork (the "child") is executed concurrently with the current computation (the "parent").

Of course, fork on its own isn't very useful; we need a way to communicate results from the child of fork to the parent, or in general between two parallel Par computations. Communication is provided by the IVar type[14] and its operations:

```
data IVar a   -- instance Eq
```

---

[14] IVar is so-called because it is an implementation of I-Structures, a concept from the Parallel Haskell variant pH.

```
new :: Par (IVar a)
put :: NFData a => IVar a -> a -> Par ()
get :: IVar a -> Par a
```

new creates a new IVar, which is initially empty; put fills an IVar with a value, and get retrieves the value of an IVar (waiting until a value has been put if necessary). Multiple puts to the same IVar result in an error.

The IVar type is a relative of the MVar type that we shall see later in the context of Concurrent Haskell (Section 3.2), the main difference being that an IVar can only be written once. An IVar is also like a *future* or *promise*, concepts that may be familiar from other parallel or concurrent languages.

Together, fork and IVars allow the construction of *dataflow* networks. The nodes of the network are created by fork, and edges connect a put with each get on that IVar. For example, suppose we have the following four functions:

```
f :: In -> A
g :: A -> B
h :: A -> C
j :: (B,C) -> Out
```

Composing these functions forms the following dataflow graph:

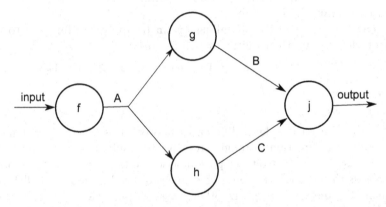

There are no sequential dependencies between g and h, so they could run in parallel. In order to take advantage of the parallelism here, all we need to do is express the graph in the Par monad:

```
do
    [ia,ib,ic] <- replicateM 4 new

    fork $ do x <- get input
              put ia (f x)

    fork $ do a <- get ia
              put ib (g a)

    fork $ do a <- get ia
              put ic (h a)
```

```
fork $ do b <- get ib
          c <- get ic
          put output (j b c)
```

For each edge in the graph we make an IVar (here ia, ib and so on). For each node in the graph we call fork, and the code for each node calls get on each input, and put on each output of the node. The order of the fork calls is irrelevant — the Par monad will execute the graph, resolving the dependencies at runtime.

While the Par monad is particularly suited to expressing dataflow networks, it can also express other common patterns too. For example, we can build an equivalent of the parMap combinator that we saw earlier in Section 2.1. First, we build a simple abstraction for a parallel computation that returns a result:

```
spawn :: NFData a => Par a -> Par (IVar a)
spawn p = do
  i <- new
  fork (do x <- p; put i x)
  return i
```

The spawn function forks a computation in parallel, and returns an IVar that can be used to wait for the result.

Now, parallel map consists of calling spawn to apply the function to each element of the list, and then waiting for all the results:

```
parMapM :: NFData b => (a -> Par b) -> [a] -> Par [b]
parMapM f as = do
  ibs <- mapM (spawn . f) as
  mapM get ibs
```

Note that there are a couple of differences between this and the Eval monad parMap. First, the function argument returns its result in the Par monad; of course it is easy to lift an arbitrary pure function to this type, but the monadic version allows the computation on each element to produce more parallel tasks, or augment the dataflow graph in other ways. Second, parMapM waits for all the results. Depending on the context, this may or may not be the most useful behaviour, but of course it is easy to define the other version if necessary.

A Parallel Type Inferencer. In this section we will parallelise a type inference engine using the Par monad. Type inference is a natural fit for the dataflow model, because we can consider each binding to be a node in the graph, and the edges of the graph carry inferred types from bindings to usage sites in the program.

For example, consider the following set of bindings that we want to infer types for:

```
f = ...
g = ... f ...
h = ... f ...
j = ... g ... h ...
```

This pattern gives rise to a dataflow graph with exactly the shape of the example 4-node graph in the previous section: after we have inferred a type for f, we can use that type to infer types for g and h (in parallel), and once we have the types for g and h we can infer a type for j.

Building a dataflow graph for the type inference problem allows the maximum amount of parallelism to be extracted from the type inference process. The actual amount of parallelism present depends on the structure of the input program, however.

The parallel type inferencer can be found in the directory **parinfer** of the code samples, and is derived from a (rather ancient) type inference engine written by Phil Wadler. The types from the inference engine that we will need to work with are as follows:

```
 1  type VarId = String  -- variables

 3  data Env --  environment for the type inferencer

 5  -- build environments
 6  makeEnv :: [(VarId,Type)] -> Env

 8  data MonoType -- monomorphic types
 9  data PolyType -- polymorphic types

11  -- Terms in the input program
12  data Term = Let VarId Term Term | ...
```

The input to this type inferencer is a single **Term** which may contain **let** bindings, and so to parallelise it we will strip off the outer **let** bindings and typecheck them in parallel. The inner term will be typechecked using the ordinary sequential inference engine. We could have a more general parallel type inference algorithm by always typechecking a **let** binding in parallel with the body, rather than just for the outer **lets**, but that would require threading the **Par** monad through the type inference engine, so for this simple example we are only parallelising inference for the outer bindings.

We need two functions from the inference engine. First, a way to infer a polymorphic type for the right-hand side of a binding:

```
inferTopRhs :: Env -> Term -> PolyType
```

and secondly, a way to run the inference engine on an arbitrary term:

```
inferTopTerm :: Env -> Term -> MonoType
```

The basic idea is that while the sequential inference engine uses an **Env** that maps **VarId**s to **PolyType**s, the parallel part of the inference engine will use an environment that maps **VarId**s to **IVar PolyType**, so that we can **fork** the inference engine for a given binding, and then wait for its result later[15]. The environment for the parallel type inferencer is called TopEnv:

```
type TopEnv = Map VarId (IVar PolyType)
```

All that remains is to write the top-level loop. We will write a function inferTop with the following type:

```
inferTop :: TopEnv -> Term -> Par MonoType
```

There are two cases to consider. First, when we are looking at a let binding:

```
1   inferTop topenv (Let x u v) = do
2       vu <- new

4       fork $ do
5           let fu = Set.toList (freeVars u)
6           tfu <- mapM (get . fromJust . flip Map.lookup topenv
                ) fu
7           let aa = makeEnv (zip fu tfu)
8           put vu (inferTopRhs aa u)

10      inferTop (Map.insert x vu topenv) v
```

On line 2 we create a new IVar vu to hold the type of x. Lines 4–8 implement the typechecking for the binding:

4 We fork here, so that the binding is typechecked in parallel,

5 Find the IVars corresponding to the free variables of the right-hand side

6 Call get for each of these, thus waiting for the typechecking of the binding corresponding to each free variable

7 Make a new Env with the types we obtained on line 6

8 Call the type inferencer for the right-hand side, and put the result in the IVar vu.

The main computation continues (line 10) by typechecking the body of the let in an environment in which the bound variable x is mapped to the IVar vu.

The other case of inferTop handles all other expression constructs:

```
1   inferTop topenv t = do
2       let (vs,ivs) = unzip (Map.toList topenv)
3       tvs <- mapM get ivs
4       let aa = makeEnv (zip vs tvs)
5       return (inferTopTerm aa t)
```

This case is straightforward: just call get to obtain the inferred type for each binding in the TopEnv, construct an Env, and call the sequential inferencer on the term t.

---

[15] We are ignoring the possibility of type errors here; in a real implementation the IVar would probably contain an Either type representing either the inferred type or an error.

This parallel implementation works quite nicely. For example, we have constructed a synthetic input for the type checker, a fragment of which is given below (the full version is in the file `code/parinfer/example.in`). The expression defines two sequences of bindings which can be inferred in parallel. The first sequence is the set of bindings for x (each successive binding for x shadows the previous), and the second sequence is the set of bindings for y. Each binding for x depends on the previous one, and similarly for the y bindings, but the x bindings are completely independent of the y bindings. This means that our parallel typechecking algorithm should automatically infer types for the x bindings in parallel with the inference of the y bindings, giving a maximum speedup of 2.

```
let id = \x.x in
    let x = \f.f id id in
    let x = \f . f x x in
    let x = \f . f x x in
    let x = \f . f x x in
    ...
    let x = let f = \g . g x in \x . x in
    let y = \f.f id id in
    let y = \f . f y y in
    let y = \f . f y y in
    let y = \f . f y y in
    ...
    let y = let f = \g . g y in \x . x in
    \f. let g = \a. a x y in f
```

When we type check this expression with one processor, we obtain the following result:

```
$ ./infer <./example.in +RTS -s
...
Total time     1.13s  (  1.12s elapsed)
```

and with two processors:

```
$ ./infer <./example.in +RTS -s -N2
,..
Total time     1.19s  (  0.60s elapsed)
```

representing a speedup of 1.87.

The Par Monad Compared to Strategies. We have presented two different parallel programming models, each with advantages and disadvantages. Below we summarise the trade-offs so that you can make an informed decision for a given task as to which is likely to be the best choice:

– Using Strategies and the `Eval` monad requires some understanding of the workings of lazy evaluation. Newcomers often find this hard, and diagnosing problems can be difficult. This is part of the motivation for the Par monad: it makes all dependencies explicit, effectively replacing lazy evaluation with explicit put/get on IVars. While this is certainly more verbose, it is less fragile and easier to work with.

Programming with rpar requires being careful about retaining references to sparks to avoid them being garbage collected; this can be subtle and hard to get right in some cases. The Par monad has no such requirements, although it does not support speculative parallelism in the sense that rpar does: speculative paralelism in the Par monad is always executed.

– Strategies allow a separation between algorithm and parallelism, which allows more reuse in some cases.
– The Par monad requires threading the monad throughout a computation which is to be parallelised. For example, to parallelise the type inference of all let bindings in the example above would have required threading the Par monad through the inference engine (or adding Par to the existing monad stack), which might be impractical. Par is good for localised parallelism, whereas Strategies can be more easily used in cases that require parallelism in multiple parts of the program.
– The Par monad has more overhead than the Eval monad, although there is no requirement to rebuild data structures as in Eval. At the present time, Eval tends to perform better at finer granularities, due to the direct runtime system support for sparks. At larger granularities, Par and Eval perform approximately the same.
– The Par monad is implemented entirely in a Haskell library (the monad-par package), and is thus readily modified should you need to.

3   Concurrent Haskell

Concurrent Haskell [11] is an extension to Haskell 2010 [9] adding support for explicitly threaded concurrent programming. The basic interface remains largely unchanged in its current implementation, although a number of embellishments have since been added, which we will cover in later sections:

– Asynchronous exceptions [3] were added as a means for asynchronous cancellation of threads,
– Software Transactional Memory was added [2], allowing safe composition of concurrent abstractions, and making it possible to safely build larger concurrent systems.
– The behaviour of Concurrent Haskell in the presence of calls to and from foreign languages was specified [6]

3.1   Forking Threads

The basic requirement of concurrency is to be able to fork a new thread of control. In Concurrent Haskell this is achieved with the forkIO operation:

```
forkIO :: IO () -> IO ThreadId
```

`forkIO` takes a computation of type `IO ()` as its argument; that is, a computation in the `IO` monad that eventually delivers a value of type `()`. The computation passed to `forkIO` is executed in a new *thread* that runs concurrently with the other threads in the system. If the thread has effects, those effects will be interleaved in an indeterminate fashion with the effects from other threads.

To illustrate the interleaving of effects, let's try a simple example in which two threads are created, once which continually prints the letter A and the other printing B[16]:

```
1  import Control.Concurrent
2  import Control.Monad
3  import System.IO
4
5  main = do
6    hSetBuffering stdout NoBuffering
7    forkIO (forever (putChar 'A'))
8    forkIO (forever (putChar 'B'))
9    threadDelay (10^6)
```

Line 6 puts the output `Handle` into non-buffered mode, so that we can see the interleaving more clearly. Lines 7 and 8 create the two threads, and line 9 tells the main thread to wait for one second (`10^6` microseconds) and then exit.

When run, this program produces output something like this:

```
AAAAAAAAAABABABABABABABABABABABABABABABABABABABABABABAB
ABABABABABABABABABABABABABABABABABABABABABABABABABABABAB
ABABABABABABABABABABABABABABABABABABABABABABABABABABABAB
ABABABABABABABABABABABABABABABABABABABABABABABABABABABAB
```

Note that the interleaving is non-deterministic: sometimes we get strings of a single letter, but often the output switches regularly between the two threads. Why does it switch so regularly, and why does each thread only get a chance to output a single letter before switching? The threads in this example are contending for a single resource: the `stdout` Handle, so scheduling is affected by how contention for this resource is handled. In the case of GHC a Handle is protected by a lock implemented as an `MVar` (described in the next section). We shall see shortly how the implementation of `MVars` causes the ABABABA behaviour.

We emphasised earlier that concurrency is a program structuring technique, or an abstraction. Abstractions are practical when they are efficient, and this is where GHC's implementation of threads comes into its own. Threads are extremely lightweight in GHC: a thread typically costs less than a hundred bytes plus the space for its stack, so the runtime can support literally millions of them, limited only by the available memory. Unlike OS threads, the memory used by Haskell threads is movable, so the garbage collector can pack threads together tightly in memory and eliminate fragmentation. Threads can also expand and

---

[16] This is sample `fork.hs`

shrink on demand, according to the stack demands of the program. When using multiple processors, the GHC runtime system automatically migrates threads between cores in order to balance the load.

User-space threading is not unique to Haskell, indeed many other languages, including early Java implementations, have had support for user-space threads (sometimes called "green threads"). It is often thought that user-space threading hinders interoperability with foreign code and libraries that are using OS threads, and this is one reason that OS threads tend to be preferred. However, with some careful design it is possible to overcome these difficulties too, as we shall see in Section 3.5.

3.2 Communication: MVars

The lowest-level communication abstraction in Concurrent Haskell is the `MVar`, whose interface is given below:

```
data MVar a   -- abstract

newEmptyMVar :: IO (MVar a)
newMVar      :: a -> IO (MVar a)
takeMVar     :: MVar a -> IO a
putMVar      :: MVar a -> a -> IO ()
```

An `MVar` can be thought of as a box that is either empty or full. The operation `newEmptyMVar` creates a new empty box, and `newMVar` creates a new full box containing the value passed as its argument. The `putMVar` operation puts a value into the box, but blocks (waits) if the box is already full. Symmetrically, the `takeMVar` operation removes the value from a full box but blocks if the box is empty.

MVars generalise several simple concurrency abstractions:

- `MVar ()` is a *lock*; `takeMVar` acquires the lock and `putMVar` releases it.[17] An `MVar` used in this way can protect shared mutable state or critical sections.
- An `MVar` is a one-place channel, which can be used for asynchronous communication between two threads. In Section 3.2 we show how to build unbounded buffered channels from `MVar`s.
- An `MVar` is a useful container for shared mutable state. For example, a common design pattern in Concurrent Haskell when several threads need read and write access to some state, is to represent the state value as an ordinary immutable Haskell data structure stored in an `MVar`. Modifying the state consists of taking the current value with `takeMVar` (which implicitly acquires a lock), and then placing a new value back in the `MVar` with `putMVar` (which implicitly releases the lock again).

We can also use `MVar`s to do some simple asynchronous I/O. Suppose we want to download some web pages concurrently and wait for them all to download before continuing. We are given the following function to download a web page:

---

[17] It works perfectly well the other way around too, just be sure to be consistent about the policy.

```
getURL :: String -> IO String
```

Let's use this to download two URLs concurrently:

```
do
    m1 <- newEmptyMVar
    m2 <- newEmptyMVar

    forkIO $ do
        r <- getURL "http://www.wikipedia.org/wiki/Shovel"
        putMVar m1 r

    forkIO $ do
        r <- getURL "http://www.wikipedia.org/wiki/Spade"
        putMVar m2 r

    r1 <- takeMVar m1
    r2 <- takeMVar m2
    return (r1,r2)
```

Lines 2–3 create two new empty MVars to hold the results. Lines 5–7 fork a new thread to download the first URL; when the download is complete the result is placed in the MVar m1, and lines 9–11 do the same for the second URL, placing the result in m2. In the main thread, line 13 waits for the result from m1, and line 14 waits for the result from m2 (we could do these in either order), and finally both results are returned.

This code is rather verbose. We could shorten it by using various existing higher-order combinators from the Haskell library, but a better approach would be to extract the common pattern as a new abstraction: we want a way to perform an action *asynchronously*, and later wait for its result. So let's define an interface that does that, using forkIO and MVars:

```
newtype Async a = Async (MVar a)

async :: IO a -> IO (Async a)
async io = do
    m <- newEmptyMVar
    forkIO $ do r <- io; putMVar m r
    return (Async m)

wait :: Async a -> IO a
wait (Async m) = readMVar m
```

Line 1 defines a datatype Async that represents an asynchronous action that has been started. Its implementation is just an MVar that will contain the result; creating a new type here might seem like overkill, but later on we will extend the Async type to support more operations, such as cancellation. The wait operation uses readMVar, defined thus[18]:

---

[18] readMVar is a standard operation provided by the Control.Concurrent module.

```
readMVar :: MVar a -> IO a
readMVar m = do
  a <- takeMVar m
  putMVar m a
  return a
```

that is, it puts back the value into the `MVar` after reading it, the point being that we might want to call `wait` multiple times, or from different threads.

Now, we can use the `Async` interface to clean up our web-page downloading example:

```
1  do
2      a1 <- async $ getURL "http://www.wikipedia.org/wiki/
       Shovel"
3      a2 <- async $ getURL "http://www.wikipedia.org/wiki/
       Spade"
4      r1 <- wait a1
5      r2 <- wait a2
6      return (r1,r2)
```

Much nicer! To demonstrate this working, we can make a small wrapper that downloads a URL and reports how much data was downloaded and how long it took[19]:

```
sites = ["http://www.google.com",
         "http://www.bing.com",
         ... ]

main = mapM (async.http) sites >>= mapM wait
  where
    http url = do
      (page, time) <- timeit $ getURL url
      printf "downloaded: %s (%d bytes, %.2fs)\n"
             url (B.length page) time
```

which results in something like this:

```
downloaded: http://www.google.com (14524 bytes, 0.17s)
downloaded: http://www.bing.com (24740 bytes, 0.18s)
downloaded: http://www.wikipedia.com/wiki/Spade (62586 bytes, 0.60s)
downloaded: http://www.wikipedia.com/wiki/Shovel (68897 bytes, 0.60s)
downloaded: http://www.yahoo.com (153065 bytes, 1.11s)
```

Channels. One of the strengths of `MVars` is that they are a useful building block out of which larger abstractions can be constructed. Here we will use `MVars` to construct a unbounded buffered channel, supporting the following basic interface:

```
data Chan a

newChan   :: IO (Chan a)
readChan  :: Chan a -> IO a
writeChan :: Chan a -> a -> IO ()
```

---

[19] The full code can be found in the sample `geturls.hs`

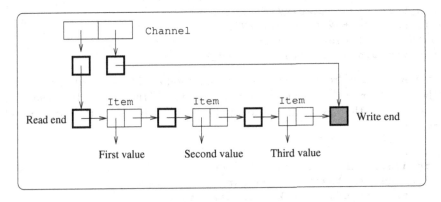

Fig. 10. Structure of the buffered channel implementation

This channel implementation first appeared in Peyton Jones et al. [11] (although the names were slightly different), and is available in the Haskell module Control.Concurrent.Chan. The structure of the implementation is represented diagrammatically in Figure 3.2, where each bold box represents an MVar and the lighter boxes are ordinary Haskell data structures. The current contents of the channel are represented as a Stream, defined like this:

```
type Stream a = MVar (Item a)
data Item a    = Item a (Stream a)
```

The end of the stream is represented by an empty MVar, which we call the "hole", because it will be filled in when a new element is added. The channel itself is a pair of MVars, one pointing to the first element of the Stream (the read position), and the other pointing to the empty MVar at the end (the write position):

```
data Chan a
= Chan (MVar (Stream a))
       (MVar (Stream a))
```

To construct a new channel we must first create an empty Stream, which is just a single empty MVar, and then the Chan constructor with MVars for the read and write ends, both pointing to the empty Stream:

```
newChan :: IO (Chan a)
newChan = do
    hole    <- newEmptyMVar
    readVar  <- newMVar hole
    writeVar <- newMVar hole
    return (Chan readVar writeVar)
```

To add a new element to the channel we must make an Item with a new hole, fill in the current hole to point to the new item, and adjust the write-end of the Chan to point to the new hole:

```
writeChan :: Chan a -> a -> IO ()
writeChan (Chan _ writeVar) val = do
```

```
new_hole <- newEmptyMVar
old_hole <- takeMVar writeVar
putMVar writeVar new_hole
putMVar old_hole (Item val new_hole)
```

To remove a value from the channel, we must follow the read end of the Chan to the first MVar of the stream, take that MVar to get the Item, adjust the read end to point to the next MVar in the stream, and finally return the value stored in the Item:

```
1  readChan :: Chan a -> IO a
2  readChan (Chan readVar _) = do
3    stream <- takeMVar readVar
4    Item val new <- takeMVar stream
5    putMVar readVar new
6    return val
```

Consider what happens if the channel is empty. The first takeMVar (line 3) will succeed, but the second takeMVar (line 4) will find an empty hole, and so will block. When another thread calls writeChan, it will fill the hole, allowing the first thread to complete its takeMVar, update the read end (line 5) and finally return.

If multiple threads concurrently call readChan, the first one will successfully call takeMVar on the read end, but the subsequent threads will all block at this point until the first thread completes the operation and updates the read end. If multiple threads call writeChan, a similar thing happens: the write end of the Chan is the synchronisation point, only allowing one thread at a time to add an item to the channel. However, the read and write ends being separate MVars allows concurrent readChan and writeChan operations to proceed without interference.

This implementation allows a nice generalisation to *multicast* channels without changing the underlying structure. The idea is to add one more operation:

```
dupChan :: Chan a -> IO (Chan a)
```

which creates a duplicate Chan with the following semantics:

- The new Chan begins empty,
- Subsequent writes to either Chan are read from both; that is, reading an item from one Chan does not remove it from the other.

The implementation is straightforward:

```
dupChan :: Chan a -> IO (Chan a)
dupChan (Chan _ writeVar) = do
  hole       <- takeMVar writeVar
  putMVar writeVar hole
  newReadVar <- newMVar hole
  return (Chan newReadVar writeVar)
```

Both channels share a single write-end, but they have independent read-ends. The read end of the new channel is initialised to point to the hole at the end of the current contents.

Sadly, this implementation of dupChan does not work! Can you see the problem? The definition of dupChan itself is not at fault, but combined with the definition of readChan given earlier it does not implement the required semantics. The problem is that readChan does not replace the contents of a hole after having read it, so if readChan is called to read values from both the channel returned by dupChan and the original channel, the second call will block. The fix is to change a takeMVar to readMVar in the implementation of readChan:

```
readChan :: Chan a -> IO a
readChan (Chan readVar _) = do
  stream <- takeMVar readVar
  Item val new <- readMVar stream  -- modified
  putMVar readVar new
  return val
```

Line 4 returns the Item back to the Stream, where it can be read by any duplicate channels created by dupChan.

Before we leave the topic of channels, consider one more extension to the interface that was described as an "easy extension" and left as an exercise by Peyton Jones et al. [11]:

```
unGetChan :: Chan a -> a -> IO ()
```

the operation unGetChan pushes a value back on the read end of the channel. Leaving aside for a moment the fact that the interface does not allow the atomic combination of readChan and unGetChan (which would appear to be an important use case), let us consider how to implement unGetChan. The straightforward implementation is as follows:

```
unGetChan :: Chan a -> a -> IO ()
unGetChan (Chan readVar _) val = do
  new_read_end <- newEmptyMVar
  read_end <- takeMVar readVar
  putMVar new_read_end (Item val read_end)
  putMVar readVar new_read_end
```

we create a new hole to place at the front of the Stream (line 3), take the current read end (line 4) giving us the current front of the stream, place a new Item in the new hole (line 5), and finally replace the read end with a pointer to our new item.

Simple testing will confirm that the implementation works. However, consider what happens when the channel is empty, there is already a blocked readChan, and another thread calls unGetChan. The desired semantics is that unGetChan succeeds, and readChan should return with the new element. What actually happens in this case is deadlock: the thread blocked in readChan will be holding the read-end MVar, and so unGetChan will also block (line 4) trying to take the read end. As far as we know, there is no implementation of unGetChan that has the desired semantics.

The lesson here is that programming larger structures with MVar can be much trickier than it appears. As we shall see shortly, life gets even more difficult when we consider exceptions. Fortunately there is a solution, that we will describe in Section 3.4.

Despite the difficulties with scaling MVars up to larger abstractions, MVars do have some nice properties, as we shall see in the next section.

Fairness. Fairness is a well-studied and highly technical subject, which we do not attempt to review here. Nevertheless, we wish to highlight one particularly important guarantee provided by MVars with respect to fairness:

> No thread can be blocked indefinitely on an MVar unless another thread holds that MVar indefinitely.

In other words, if a thread T is blocked in takeMVar, and there are regular putMVar operations on the same MVar, then it is guaranteed that at some point thread T's takeMVar will return. In GHC this guarantee is implemented by keeping blocked threads in a FIFO queue attached to the MVar, so eventually every thread in the queue will get to complete its operation as long as there are other threads performing regular putMVar operations (an equivalent guarantee applies to threads blocked in putMVar when there are regular takeMVars). Note that it is not enough to merely *wake up* the blocked thread, because another thread might run first and take (respectively put) the MVar, causing the newly woken thread to go to the back of the queue again, which would invalidate the fairness guarantee. The implementation must therefore atomically wake up the blocked thread *and* perform the blocked operation, which is exactly what GHC does.

Fairness in practice Recall our example from Section 3.1, where we had two threads, one printing As and the other printing Bs, and the output was often perfect alternation between the two: ABABABABABABABAB. This is an example of the fairness guarantee in practice. The stdout handle is represented by an MVar, so when both threads attempt to call takeMVar to operate on the handle, one of them wins and the other becomes blocked. When the winning thread completes its operation and calls putMVar, the scheduler wakes up the blocked thread *and* completes its blocked takeMVar, so the original winning thread will immediately block when it tries to re-acquire the handle. Hence this leads to perfect alternation between the two threads. The only way that the alternation pattern can be broken is if one thread is pre-empted while it is not holding the MVar; indeed this does happen from time to time, as we see the occasional long string of a single letter in the output.

A consequence of the fairness implementation is that, when multiple threads are blocked, *we only need to wake up a single thread.* This single wakeup property is a particularly important performance characteristic when a large number of threads are contending for a single MVar. As we shall see later, it is the fairness guarantee together with the single-wakeup property which means that MVars are not completely subsumed by Software Transactional Memory.

3.3   Cancellation: Asynchronous Exceptions

In an interactive application, it is often important for one thread to be able to *interrupt* the execution of another thread when some particular condition occurs. Some examples of this kind of behaviour in practice include:

- In a web browser, the thread downloading the web page and the thread rendering the page need to be interrupted when the user presses the "stop" button.
- A server application typically wants to give a client a set amount of time to issue a request before closing its connection, so as to avoid dormant connections using up resources.
- An application in which a compute-intensive thread is working (say, rendering a visualisation of some data), and the input data changes due to some user input.

The crucial design decision in supporting cancellation is whether the intended victim should have to poll for the cancellation condition, or whether the thread is immediately cancelled in some way. This is a tradeoff:

1. If the thread has to poll, there is a danger that the programmer may forget to poll regularly enough, and the thread will become unresponsive, perhaps permanently so. Unresponsive threads lead to hangs and deadlocks, which are particularly unpleasant from a user's perspective.
2. If cancellation happens asynchronously, critical sections that modify state need to be protected from cancellation, otherwise cancellation may occur mid-update leaving some data in an inconsistent state.

In fact, the choice is really between doing only (1), or doing both (1) and (2), because if (2) is the default, protecting a critical section amounts to switching to polling behaviour for the duration of the critical section.

In most imperative languages it is unthinkable for (2) to be the default, because so much code is state-modifying. Haskell has a distinct advantage in this area, however: most code is purely functional, so it can be safely aborted or suspended, and later resumed, without affecting correctness. Moreover our hand is forced: purely functional code cannot by definition poll for the cancellation condition, so it must be cancellable by default.

Therefore, fully-asynchronous cancellation is the only sensible default in Haskell, and the design problem reduces to deciding how cancellation appears to code in the IO monad.

It makes sense for cancellation to behave like an exception, since exceptions are already a fact of life in the IO monad, and the usual idioms for writing IO monad code include exception handlers to release resources and clean up in the event of an error. For example, to perform an operation that requires a temporary file, we would use the **bracket** combinator to ensure that the temporary file is always removed, even if the operation raises an exception:

```
bracket (newTempFile "temp")
        (\file -> removeFile file)
        (\file -> ...)
```

where bracket is defined thus:

```
bracket :: IO a -> (a -> IO b) -> (a -> IO c) -> IO c
bracket before after during = do
  a <- before
  c <- during a 'onException' after a
  after a
  return c
```

and onException executes its first argument, and if an exception is thrown, executes its second argument before re-throwing the exception.

```
onException :: IO a -> IO b -> IO a
```

We want exception handlers to run in the event of cancellation, so cancellation should be an exception. However, there's a fundamental difference between the kind of exception thrown by openFile when the file does not exist, for example, and an exception that may arise *at any time* because the user pressed the "stop" button. We call the latter kind an *asynchronous* exception, for obvious reasons. (We do not review the Haskell support for *synchronous* exceptions here; for that see the Haskell 2010 report [9] and the documentation for the Control.Exception module).

To initiate an asynchronous exception, Haskell provides the throwTo primitive which throws an exception from one thread to another [3]:

```
throwTo :: Exception e => ThreadId -> e -> IO ()
```

the Exception constraint requires that the exception value being thrown is an instance of the Exception class, which implements a simple hierarchy [4]. The ThreadId is a value previously returned by forkIO, and may refer to a thread in any state: running, blocked, or finished (in the latter case, throwTo is a no-op).

To illustrate the use of throwTo, we now elaborate the earlier example in which we downloaded several web pages concurrently, to allow the user to hit 'q' at any time to stop the downloads.

First, we will extend our Async mini-API to allow cancellation. We add one operation:

```
cancel :: Async a -> IO ()
```

which cancels an existing Async. If the operation has already completed, cancel has no effect. The wait operation cannot just return the result of the Async any more, since it may have been cancelled. Therefore, we extend wait to return Either SomeException a, containing either the exception raised during the operation, or its result:

```
wait :: Async a -> IO (Either SomeException a)
```

(SomeException is the root of the exception hierarchy in Haskell.) In order to implement the new interface, we need to extend the Async type to include the

ThreadId of the child thread, and the MVar holding the result must now hold
Either SomeException a.

```
data Async a = Async ThreadId (MVar (Either SomeException a))
```

Given this, the implementation of cancel just throws an exception to the thread:

```
cancel :: Async a -> IO ()
cancel (Async t var) = throwTo t ThreadKilled
```

(ThreadKilled is an exception provided by the Haskell exception library and is
typically used for cancelling threads in this way.) The implementation of wait
is trivial. The remaining piece of the implementation is the async operation,
which must now include an exception handler to catch the exception and store
it in the MVar:

```
async :: IO a -> IO (Async a)
async io = do
  m <- newEmptyMVar
  t <- forkIO $ (do r <- io; putMVar m (Right r))
               `catch` \e -> putMVar m (Left e)
  return (Async t m)
```

Now, we can change the main function of the example to support cancelling the
downloads:

```
1  main = do
2    as <- mapM (async.http) sites

4    forkIO $ do
5      hSetBuffering stdin NoBuffering
6      forever $ do
7        c <- getChar
8        when (c == 'q') $ mapM_ cancel as

10   rs <- mapM wait as
11   printf "%d/%d finished\n" (length (rights rs)) (length
       rs)
```

Line 2 starts the downloads as before. Lines 4–8 fork a new thread that repeatedly
reads characters from the standard input, and if a q is found, calls cancel on
all the Asyncs. Line 10 waits for all the results (complete or cancelled), and line
11 emits a summary with a count of how many of the operations completed
without being cancelled. If we run the sample[20] and hit 'q' fast enough, we see
something like this:

```
downloaded: http://www.google.com (14538 bytes, 0.17s)
downloaded: http://www.bing.com (24740 bytes, 0.22s)
q2/5 finished
```

---

[20] Full code is in the sample geturlscancel.hs

Note that this works even though the program is sitting atop a large and complicated HTTP library that provides no direct support for either cancellation or asynchronous I/O. Haskell's support for cancellation is modular in this respect: most library code needs to do nothing to support it, although there are some simple and unintrusive rules that need to be followed when dealing with state, as we shall see in the next section.

Masking Asynchronous Exceptions. As we mentioned earlier, the danger with fully asynchronous exceptions is that one might fire while we are in the middle of updating some shared state, leaving the data in an inconsistent state, and with a high probability leading to mayhem later.

Hence, we certainly need a way to control the delivery of asynchronous exceptions during critical sections. But we must tread carefully: it would be easy to provide the programmer with a way to turn off asynchronous exception delivery temporarily, but such a facility is in fact not what we really need.

Consider the following problem: a thread wishes to call `takeMVar`, perform an operation depending on the value of the `MVar`, and finally put the result of the operation in the `MVar`. The code must be responsive to asynchronous exceptions, but it should be safe: if an asynchronous exception arrives after the `takeMVar`, but before the final `putMVar`, the `MVar` should not be left empty, instead the original value should be replaced.

If we code up this problem using the facilities we already seen so far, we might end up with something like this:

```
1  problem m f = do
2    a <- takeMVar m
3    r <- f a 'catch' \e -> do putMVar m a; throw e
4    putMVar m r
```

There are at least two points where, if an asynchronous exception strikes, the invariant will be violated. If an exception strikes between lines 2 and 3, or between lines 3 and 4, the `MVar` will be left empty. In fact, there is no way to shuffle around the exception handlers to ensure the `MVar` is always left full. To fix this problem, Haskell provides the `mask` combinator[21]:

```
mask :: ((IO a -> IO a) -> IO b) -> IO b
```

The type looks a bit confusing, but it isn't really[22]. The `mask` operation defers the delivery of asynchronous exceptions for the duration of its argument, and is used like this:

```
1  problem m f = mask $ \restore -> do
2    a <- takeMVar m
3    r <- restore (f a) 'catch' \e -> do putMVar m a; throw e
4    putMVar m r
```

---

[21] Historical note: the original presentation of asynchronous exceptions used a pair of combinators `block` and `unblock` here, but `mask` was introduced in GHC 7.0.1 to replace them as it has a more modular behaviour.

[22] For simplicity here we are using a slightly less general version of `mask` than the real one in the `Control.Exception` library.

mask is applied to a *function*, that takes as its argument a function restore, that can be used to restore the delivery of asynchronous exceptions to its present state. If we imagine shading the entire argument to mask except for the expression (f a), asynchronous exceptions cannot be raised in the shaded portions. This solves the problem that we had previously, since now an exception can only be raised while (f a) is working, and we have an exception handler to catch any exceptions in that case. But a new problem has been introduced: takeMVar might block for a long time, but it is inside the mask and so the thread will be unresponsive for that time. Furthermore there's no good reason to mask exceptions during takeMVar; it would be safe for exceptions to be raised right up until the point where takeMVar returns. Hence, this is exactly the behaviour that Haskell defines for takeMVar: we designate a small number of operations, including takeMVar, as *interruptible*. Interruptible operations may receive asynchronous exceptions even inside mask.

What justifies this choice? Think of mask as "switching to polling mode" for asynchronous exceptions. Inside a mask, asynchronous exceptions are no longer asynchronous, but they can still be raised by certain operations. In other words, asynchronous exceptions become *synchronous* inside mask.

All operations which may block indefinitely[23] are designated as interruptible. This turns out to be the ideal behaviour in many situations, as in problem above.

In fact, we can provide higher level combinators to insulate programmers from the need to use mask directly. For example, the function problem above is generally useful when working with MVars, and is provided under the name modifyMVar_ in the Control.Concurrent.MVar library.

Asynchronous-Exception Safety. All that is necessary for most code to be safe in the presence of asynchronous exceptions is to use operations like modifyMVar_ instead of takeMVar and putMVar directly. For example, consider the buffered channels that we defined earlier. As defined, the operations are not asynchronous-exception-safe; for example, writeChan was defined like this:

```
1  writeChan :: Chan a -> a -> IO ()
2  writeChan (Chan _ writeVar) val = do
3    new_hole <- newEmptyMVar
4    old_hole <- takeMVar writeVar
5    putMVar writeVar new_hole
6    putMVar old_hole (Item val new_hole)
```

there are several windows here where if an asynchronous exception occurs, an MVar will be left empty, and subsequent users of the Chan will deadlock. To make it safe, we use modifyMVar_:

```
1  writeChan (Chan _ writeVar) val = do
2    new_hole <- newEmptyMVar
3    modifyMVar_ writeVar $ \old_hole -> do
4      putMVar old_hole (Item val new_hole)
5      return new_hole
```

---

[23] Except foreign calls, for technical reasons.

We saw a use of the `bracket` function earlier; in fact, `bracket` is defined with mask in order to make it asynchronous-exception-safe:

```
1  bracket before after during =
2    mask $ \restore -> do
3      a <- before
4      r <- restore (during a) 'catch' \e -> after a; throw e
5      _ <- after a
6      return r
```

Timeouts. A good illustration of programming with asynchronous exceptions is to write a function that can impose a time limit on a given action. We want to provide the timeout wrapper as a combinator of the following type:

```
timeout :: Integer -> IO a -> IO (Maybe a)
```

where `timeout` t m has the following behaviour:

1. `timeout` t m behaves exactly like `fmap Just` m if m returns a result or raises an exception (including an asynchronous exception), within t microseconds.
2. otherwise, m is sent an asynchronous exception of the form `Timeout` u. `Timeout` is a new datatype that we define, and u is a unique value of type `Unique`, distinguishing this particular instance of `timeout` from any other. The call to `timeout` then returns `Nothing`.

The implementation is not expected to implement real-time semantics, so in practice the timeout will only be approximately t microseconds. Note that (1) requires that m is executed in the context of the current thread, since m could call `myThreadId`, for example. Also, another thread throwing an exception to the current thread with `throwTo` will expect to interrupt m.

The code for `timeout` is shown in Listing 1.1; this implementation was taken from the library `System.Timeout` (with some cosmetic changes for presentation here). The implementation is tricky to get right. The basic idea is to fork a new thread that will wait for t microseconds and then call `throwTo` to throw the `Timeout` exception back to the original thread; that much seems straightforward enough. However, we must ensure that this thread cannot throw its `Timeout` exception after the call to `timeout` has returned, otherwise the `Timeout` exception will leak out of the call, so `timeout` must kill the thread before returning.

Here is how the implementation works, line by line:

1–2 Handle the easy cases, where the timeout is negative or zero.
5 find the `ThreadId` of the current thread
6–7 make a new `Timeout` exception, by generating a unique value with `newUnique`
8-14 `handleJust` is an exception handler, with the following type:

```
handleJust :: Exception e
           => (e -> Maybe b) -> (b -> IO a) -> IO a
           -> IO a
```

Listing 1.1. Implementation of `timeout`

```
1  timeout n m
2    | n < 0     = fmap Just m
3    | n == 0    = return Nothing
4    | otherwise = do
5        pid <- myThreadId
6        u <- newUnique
7        let ex = Timeout u
8        handleJust
9          (\e -> if e == ex then Just () else Nothing)
10         (\_ -> return Nothing)
11         (bracket (forkIO $ do threadDelay n
12                               throwTo pid ex)
13                  (\t -> throwTo t ThreadKilled)
14                  (\_ -> fmap Just m))
```

Its first argument (line 9) selects which exceptions to catch: in this case, just the `Timeout` exception we defined on line 7. The second argument (line 10) is the exception handler, which in this case just returns `Nothing`, since timeout occurred.

Lines 11–14 are the computation to run in the exception handler. `bracket` (Section 3.3) is used here in order to fork the child thread, and ensure that it is killed before returning.

11-12 fork the child thread. In the child thread we wait for n microseconds with `threadDelay`, and then throw the `Timeout` exception to the parent thread with `throwTo`.

13 always kill the child thread before returning.

14 the body of `bracket`: run the computation `m` passed in as the second argument to `timeout`, and wrap the result in `Just`.

The reader is encouraged to verify that the implementation works by thinking through the two cases: either `m` completes and returns `Just x` at line 14, or, the child thread throws its exception while `m` is still working.

There is one tricky case to consider: what happens if *both* the child thread and the parent thread try to call `throwTo` at the same time (lines 12 and 13 respectively)? Who wins?

The answer depends on the semantics of `throwTo`. In order for this implementation of `timeout` to work properly, it must not be possible for the call to `bracket` at line 11 to return while the `Timeout` exception can still be thrown, otherwise the exception can leak. Hence, the call to `throwTo` that kills the child thread at line 13 must be synchronous: once this call returns, the child thread cannot throw its exception any more. Indeed, this guarantee is provided by the semantics of `throwTo`: a call to `throwTo` only returns after the exception has been raised in the target thread[24]. Hence, `throwTo` may block if the child thread is currently masking

---
[24] Note: a different semantics was originally described in Marlow et al. [3].

asynchronous exceptions with mask, and because throwTo may block, it is therefore *interruptible* and may itself receive asynchronous exceptions.

Returning to our "who wins" question above, the answer is "exactly one of
them", and that is precisely what we require to ensure the correct behaviour of
timeout.

Asynchronous Exceptions: Reflections. Abstractions like timeout are certainly difficult to get right, but fortunately they only have to be written once.
We find that in practice dealing with asynchronous exceptions is fairly straightforward, following a few simple rules:

- Use bracket when acquiring resources that need to be released again.
- Rather than takeMVar and putMVar, use modifyMVar_ (and friends) which
  have built-in asynchronous exception safety.
- If state handling starts getting complicated with multiple layers of exception
  handlers, then there are two approaches to simplifying things:
  - Switching to polling mode with mask can help manage complexity. The
    GHC I/O library, for example, runs entirely inside mask. Note that inside
    mask it is important to remember that asynchronous exceptions can still
    arise out of interruptible operations; the documentation contains a list
    of operations that are guaranteed *not* to be interruptible.
  - Using Software Transactional Memory (STM) instead of MVars or other
    state representations can sweep away all the complexity in one go. We
    will describe STM in Section 3.4.

The rules are usually not onerous: remember this only applies to code in the IO
monad, so the vast swathes of purely-functional library code available for Haskell
is all safe by construction. We find that most IO monad code is straightforward
to make safe, and if things get complicated falling back to either mask or STM
is a satisfactory solution.

In exchange for following the rules, however, Haskell's approach to asynchronous exceptions confers many benefits.

- Many exceptional conditions map naturally onto asynchronous exceptions.
  For example, stack overflow and user interrupt (e.g. control-C at the console)
  are mapped to asynchronous exceptions in Haskell. Hence, control-C not only
  aborts the program but does so cleanly, running all the exception handlers.
  Haskell programmers have to do nothing to enable this behaviour.
- Constructs like timeout always work, even with third-party library code.
- Threads never just die in Haskell, it is guaranteed that a thread always gets
  a chance to clean up and run its exception handlers.

3.4   Software Transactional Memory

Software Transactional Memory (STM) is a technique for simplifying concurrent
programming by allowing multiple state-changing operations to be grouped together and performed as a single atomic operation. Strictly speaking, "Software

Listing 1.2. The interface provided by `Control.Concurrent.STM`

```
1  data STM a -- abstract
2  instance Monad STM -- amongst other things

4  atomically :: STM a -> IO a

6  data TVar a -- abstract
7  newTVar   :: a -> STM (TVar a)
8  readTVar  :: TVar a -> STM a
9  writeTVar :: TVar a -> a -> STM ()

11 retry     :: STM a
12 orElse    :: STM a -> STM a -> STM a

14 throwSTM  :: Exception e => e -> STM a
15 catchSTM  :: Exception e => STM a -> (e -> STM a) -> STM a
```

Transactional Memory" is an implementation technique, whereas the language construct we are interested in is "atomic blocks". Unfortunately the former term has stuck, and so the language-level facility is called STM.

STM solves a number of problems that arise with conventional concurrency abstractions, that we describe here through a series of examples. For reference throughout the following section, the types and operations of the STM interface are collected in Listing 1.2.

Imagine the following scenario: a window manager that manages multiple desktops. The user may move windows from one desktop to another, while at the same time, a program may request that its own window moves from its current desktop to another desktop. The window manager uses multiple threads: one to listen for input from the user, one for each existing window to listen for requests from those programs, and one thread that renders the display to the user.

How should the program represent the state of the display? One option is to put it all in a single `MVar`:

```
type Display = MVar (Map Desktop (Set Window))
```

and this would work, but the `MVar` is a single point of contention. For example, the rendering thread, which only needs to look at the currently displayed desktop, could be blocked by a window on another desktop moving itself.

So perhaps we can try to allow more concurrency by having a separate `MVar` for each desktop:

```
type Display = Map Desktop (MVar (Set Window))
```

unfortunately this approach quickly runs into problems. Consider an operation to move a window from one desktop to another:

```
moveWindow :: Display -> Window -> Desktop -> Desktop -> IO
   ()
moveWindow disp win a b = do
  wa <- takeMVar ma
  wb <- takeMVar mb
  putMVar ma (Set.delete win wa)
  putMVar mb (Set.insert win wb)
 where
  ma = fromJust (Map.lookup disp a)
  mb = fromJust (Map.lookup disp b)
```

Note that we must take both MVars before we can put the results: otherwise another thread could potentially observe the display in a state in which the window we are moving does not exist. But this raises a problem: what if there is concurrent call to moveWindow trying to move a window in the opposite direction? Both calls would succeed at the first takeMVar, but block on the second, and the result is a deadlock. This is an instance of the classic Dining Philosophers problem.

One solution is to impose an ordering on the MVars, and require that all agents take MVars in the correct order and release them in the opposite order. That is inconvenient and error-prone though, and furthermore we have to extend our ordering to any other state that we might need to access concurrently. Large systems with many locks (e.g. Operating Systems) are often plagued by this problem, and managing the complexity requires building elaborate infrastructure to detect ordering violations.

Transactional memory provides a way to avoid this deadlock problem without imposing a requirement for ordering on the programmer. To solve the problem using STM, we replace MVar with TVar:

```
type Display = Map Desktop (TVar (Set Window))
```

TVar stands for "transactional variable", and it is a mutable variable that can only be read or written within a transaction. To implement moveWindow, we simply perform the necessary operations on TVars in the STM monad, and wrap the whole sequence in atomically:

```
moveWindow :: Display -> Window -> Desktop -> Desktop -> IO
   ()
moveWindow disp win a b = atomically $ do
  wa <- readTVar ma
  wb <- readTVar mb
  writeTVar ma (Set.delete win wa)
  writeTVar mb (Set.insert win wb)
 where
  ma = fromJust (Map.lookup a disp)
  mb = fromJust (Map.lookup b disp)
```

The code is almost identical to the MVar version, but the behaviour is quite different: the sequence of operations inside atomically happens indivisibly as far as the rest of the program is concerned. No other thread can observe an intermediate state; the operation has either completed, or it has not started yet. What's more, there is no requirement that we read both TVars before we write them, this would be fine too:

```
moveWindow :: Display -> Window -> Desktop -> Desktop -> IO
           ()
moveWindow disp win a b = atomically $ do
  wa <- readTVar ma
  writeTVar ma (Set.delete win wa)
  wb <- readTVar mb
  writeTVar mb (Set.insert win wb)
 where
  ma = fromJust (Map.lookup disp a)
  mb = fromJust (Map.lookup disp b)
```

So STM is far less error-prone here. The approach also scales to any number of TVars, so we could easily write an operation that moves the windows from all other desktops to the current desktop, for example.

Now suppose that we want to swap two windows, moving window W from desktop A to B, and simultaneously V from B to A. With the MVar representation we would have to write a special-purpose operation to do this, because it has to take the MVars for A and B (in the right order), and then put both MVars back with the new contents. With STM, however, we can express this much more neatly as a composition. First we need to expose a version of moveWindow without the atomically wrapper:

```
moveWindowSTM :: Display -> Window -> Desktop -> Desktop
                 -> STM ()
moveWindowSTM disp win a b = do ...
```

and then we can define swapWindows by composing two moveWindowSTM calls:

```
swapWindows :: Display
            -> Window -> Desktop
            -> Window -> Desktop
            -> IO ()
swapWindows disp w a v b = atomically $ do
  moveWindowSTM disp w a b
  moveWindowSTM disp v b a
```

This demonstrates the *composability* of STM operations: any operation of type STM a can be composed with others to form a larger atomic transaction. For this reason, STM operations are usually provided without the atomically wrapper, so that clients can compose them as necessary, before finally wrapping the entire operation in atomically.

So far we have covered the basic facilities of STM, and shown that STM can be used to make atomicity scale in a composable way. STM confers a qualitative improvement in expressibility and robustness when writing concurrent programs. The benefits of STM in Haskell go further, however: in the following sections we show how STM can be used to make blocking abstractions compose, and how STM can be used to manage complexity in the presence of failure and interruption.

Blocking. An important part of concurrent programming is dealing with *blocking*; when we need to wait for some condition to be true, or to acquire a particular resource. STM provides an ingenious way to do this, with a single operation:

```
retry :: STM a
```

the meaning of `retry` is simply "run the current transaction again". That seems bizarre - why would we want to run the current transaction again? Well, for one thing, the contents of some `TVars` that we have read may have been changed by another thread, so re-running the transaction may yield different results. Indeed, there's no point re-running the transaction *unless* it is possible that something different might happen, and the runtime system knows this, so `retry` waits until a `TVar` that was read in the current transaction has been written to, and then triggers a re-run of the current transaction. Until that happens, the current thread is blocked.

As a concrete example, we can use `retry` to implement the rendering thread in our window-manager example. The behaviour we want is this:

- One desktop is designated as having the *focus*. The focussed desktop is the one displayed by the rendering thread.
- The user may request that the focus be changed at any time.
- Windows may move around and appear or disappear of their own accord, and the rendering thread must update its display accordingly.

We are supplied with a function `render` which handles the business of rendering windows on the display. It should be called whenever the window layout changes[25]:

```
render :: Set Window -> IO ()
```

The currently focussed desktop is a piece of state that is shared by the rendering thread and some other thread that handles user input. Therefore we represent that by a `TVar`:

```
type UserFocus = TVar Desktop
```

Next, we define an auxiliary function `getWindows` that takes the `Display` and the `UserFocus`, and returns the set of windows to render, in the `STM` monad. The implementation is straightforward: read the current focus, and look up the contents of the appropriate desktop in the `Display`:

```
getWindows :: Display -> UserFocus -> STM (Set Window)
getWindows disp focus = do
  desktop <- readTVar focus
  readTVar (fromJust (Map.lookup desktop disp))
```

---

[25] We are assuming that the actual window contents are rendered via some separate means, e.g. compositing

Finally, we can implement the rendering thread. The general plan is to repeatedly read the current state with `getWindows` and call `render` to render it, but use `retry` to avoid calling `render` when nothing has changed. Here is the code:

```
1   renderThread :: Display -> UserFocus -> IO ()
2   renderThread disp focus = do
3     wins <- atomically $ getWindows disp focus
4     loop wins
5     where
6     loop wins = do
7       render wins
8       next <- atomically $ do
9               wins' <- getWindows disp focus
10              if (wins == wins')
11                 then retry
12                 else return wins'
13     loop next
```

First we read the current set of windows to display (line 3) and use this as the initial value for the `loop` (line 4). Lines 6-13 implement the loop. Each iteration calls `render` to display the current state (line 7), and then enters a transaction to read the next state. Inside the transaction we read the current state (line 9), and compare it to the state we just rendered (line 10); if the states are the same, there is no need to do anything, so we call `retry`. If the states are different, then we return the new state, and the loop iterates with the new state (line 13).

The effect of the `retry` is precisely what we need: it waits until the value read by `getWindows` could possibly be different, because another thread has successfully completed a transaction that writes to one of the `TVars` that is read by `getWindows`. That encompasses both changes to the `focus` (because the user switched to a different desktop), and changes to the contents of the current desktop (because a window moved, appeared, or disappeared). Furthermore, changes to other desktops can take place without the rendering thread being woken up.

If it weren't for STM's `retry` operation, we would have to implement this complex logic ourselves, including implementing the signals between threads that modify the state and the rendering thread. This is anti-modular, because operations that modify the state have to know about the observers that need to act on changes. Furthermore, it gives rise to a common source of concurrency bugs: *lost wakeups*. If we forgot to signal the rendering thread, then the display would not be updated. In this case the effects are somewhat benign, but in a more complex scenario lost wakeups often lead to deadlocks, because the woken thread was supposed to complete some operation on which other threads are waiting.

Implementing Channels with STM. As a second concrete example, we shall implement the `Chan` type from Section 3.2 using STM. We shall see that using STM to implement `Chan` is rather less tricky than using `MVars`, and furthermore

Listing 1.3. Implementation of TChan

```
1  data TChan a = TChan (TVar (TVarList a))
2                      (TVar (TVarList a))

4  type TVarList a = TVar (TList a)
5  data TList a = TNil | TCons a (TVarList a)

7  newTChan :: STM (TChan a)
8  newTChan = do
9    hole <- newTVar TNil
10   read <- newTVar hole
11   write <- newTVar hole
12   return (TChan read write)

14 readTChan :: TChan a -> STM a
15 readTChan (TChan readVar _) = do
16   listhead <- readTVar readVar
17   head <- readTVar listhead
18   case head of
19     TNil -> retry
20     TCons val tail -> do
21       writeTVar readVar tail
22       return val

24 writeTChan :: TChan a -> a -> STM ()
25 writeTChan (TChan _ writeVar) a = do
26   new_listend <- newTVar TNil
27   listend <- readTVar writeVar
28   writeTVar writeVar new_listend
29   writeTVar listend (TCons a new_listend)
```

we are able to add some more complex operations that were hard or impossible using MVars.

The STM version of Chan is called TChan[26], and the interface we wish to implement is as follows:

```
data TChan a

newTChan    :: STM (TChan a)
writeTChan  :: TChan a -> a -> STM ()
readTChan   :: TChan a -> STM a
```

that is, exactly the same as Chan, except that we renamed Chan to TChan. The full code for the implementation is given in Listing 1.3. The implementation is similar in structure to the MVar version in Section 3.2, so we do not describe it line by line, however we shall point out a few important details:

---

[26] The implementation is available in the module Control.Concurrent.STM.TChan from the stm package.

- All the operations are in the STM monad, so to use them they need to be wrapped in atomically (but they can also be composed, more about that later).
- Blocking in readTChan is implemented by the call to retry (line 19).
- Nowhere did we have to worry about what happens when a read executes concurrently with a write, because all the operations are atomic.

Something worth noting, although this is not a direct result of STM, is that the straightforward implementation of dupChan does not suffer from the problem that we had in Section 3.2, because readTChan does not remove elements from the list.

We now describe three distinct benefits of the STM implementation compared to using MVars.

More operations are possible. In Section 3.2 we mentioned the unGetChan operation, which could not be implemented with the desired semantics using MVars. Here is its implementation with STM:

```
unGetTChan :: TChan a -> a -> STM ()
unGetTChan (TChan read _write) a = do
  listhead <- readTVar read
  newhead <- newTVar (TCons a listhead)
  writeTVar read newhead
```

The obvious implementation does the right thing here. Other operations that were not possible with MVars are straightforward with STM. For example, it was not possible to define an operation for testing whether a Chan is empty without suffering from the same problem as with unGetChan, but we can define this operation straightforwardly on TChan:

```
isEmptyTChan :: TChan a -> STM Bool
isEmptyTChan (TChan read _write) = do
  listhead <- readTVar read
  head <- readTVar listhead
  case head of
    TNil -> return True
    TCons _ _ -> return False
```

Composition of blocking operations. Suppose we wish to implement an operation readEitherTChan that can read an element from either of two channels. If both channels are empty it blocks; if one channel is non-empty it reads the value from that channel, and if both channels are non-empty it is allowed to choose which channel to read from. Its type is

```
readEitherTChan :: TChan a -> TChan b -> STM (Either a b)
```

We cannot implement this function with the operations introduced so far, but STM provides one more crucial operation that allows blocking transactions to be composed. The operation is orElse:

```
orElse :: STM a -> STM a -> STM a
```

The operation orElse a b has the following behaviour:

- First a is executed. If a returns a result, then that result is immediately returned by the orElse call.
- If a instead called retry, then a's *effects are discarded*, and b is executed instead.

We can use orElse to compose blocking operations atomically. Returning to our example, readEitherTChan could be implemented as follows:

```
readEitherTChan :: TChan a -> TChan b -> STM (Either a b)
readEitherTChan a b =
  fmap Left (readTChan a)
    'orElse'
  fmap Right (readTChan b)
```

This is a straightforward composition of the two readTChan calls, the only complication is arranging to tag the result with either Left or Right depending on which branch succeeds.

In the MVar implementation of Chan there is no way to implement the operation readEitherChan without elaborating the representation of Chan to support the synchronisation protocol that would be required (more discussion on implementing choice with MVars can be found in Peyton Jones et al. [11]).

One thing to note is that orElse is left-biased; if both TChans are non-empty, then readEitherChan will always return an element from the first one. Whether this is problematic or not depends on the application: something to be aware of is that the left-biased nature of orElse can have implications for fairness in some situations.

Asynchronous exception safety. Up until now we have said nothing about how exceptions in STM behave. The STM monad supports exceptions much like the IO monad, with two operations:

```
throwSTM :: Exception e => e -> STM a
catchSTM :: Exception e => STM a -> (e -> STM a) -> STM a
```

throwSTM throws an exception, and catchSTM catches exceptions and invokes a handler, just like catch in the IO monad. However, exceptions in STM are different in one vital way:

- In catchSTM m h, if m raises an exception, then *all of its effects are discarded*, and then the handler h is invoked. As a degenerate case, if there is no enclosing catchSTM at all, then all of the effects of the transaction are discarded and the exception is propagated out of atomically.

This behaviour of catchSTM was introduced in a subsequent amendment of Harris et al. [2]; the original behaviour in which effects were not discarded being generally regarded as much less useful. An example helps to demonstrate the motivation:

```
readCheck :: TChan a -> STM a
readCheck chan = do
  a <- readTChan chan
  checkValue a
```

`checkValue` imposes some extra constraints on the value read from the channel. However, suppose `checkValue` raises an exception (perhaps accidentally, e.g. divide-by-zero). We would prefer it if the `readTChan` had not happened, since an element of the channel would be lost. Furthermore, we would like `readCheck` to have this behaviour regardless of whether there is an enclosing exception handler or not. Hence `catchSTM` discards the effects of its first argument in the event of an exception.

The discarding-effects behaviour is even more useful in the case of *asynchronous* exceptions. If an asynchronous exception occurs during an STM transaction, the entire transaction is aborted (unless the exception is caught and handled, but handling asynchronous exceptions in STM is not something we typically want to do). So in most cases, asynchronous exception safety in STM consists of doing *absolutely nothing at all*. There are no locks to replace, so no need for exception handlers or `bracket`, and no need to worry about which critical sections to protect with `mask`.

The implementation of `TChan` given earlier is entirely safe with respect to asynchronous exceptions as it stands, and moreover any compositions of these operations are also safe.

STM provides a nice way to write code that is automatically safe with respect to asynchronous exceptions, so it can be useful even for state that is not shared between threads. The only catch is that we have to use STM consistently for all our state, but having made that leap, asynchronous exception safety comes for free.

Performance. As with most abstractions, STM has a runtime cost. If we understand the cost model, then we can avoid writing code that hits the bad cases. So in this section we give an informal description of the implementation of STM (at least in GHC), with enough detail that the reader can understand the cost model.

An STM transaction works by accumulating a *log* of `readTVar` and `writeTVar` operations that have happened so far during the transaction. The log is used in three ways:

- By storing `writeTVar` operations in the log rather than applying them to main memory immediately, discarding the effects of a transaction is easy; we just throw away the log. Hence, aborting a transaction has a fixed small cost.
- Each `readTVar` must traverse the log to check whether the `TVar` was written by an earlier `writeTVar`. Hence, `readTVar` is an $O(n)$ operation in the length of the log.
- Because the log contains a record of all the `readTVar` operations, it can be used to discover the full set of `TVars` read during the transaction, which we need to know in order to implement `retry`.

When a transaction reaches the end, the STM implementation compares the log against the contents of memory using a two-phase locking protocol (details in Harris et al. [2]). If the current contents of memory matches the values read by readTVar, the effects of the transaction are *committed* to memory atomically, and if not, the log is discarded and the transaction runs again from the beginning. The STM implementation in GHC does not use global locks; only the TVars involved in the transaction are locked during commit, so transactions operating on disjoint sets of TVars can proceed without interference.

The general rule of thumb when using STM is never to read an unbounded number of TVars in a single transaction, because the $O(n)$ cost of readTVar then gives $O(n^2)$ for the whole transaction. Furthermore, long transactions are much more likely to fail to commit, because another transaction will probably have modified one or more of the same TVars in the meantime, so there is a high probability of re-execution.

It is possible that a future STM implementation may use a different data structure to store the log, reducing the readTVar overhead to $O(\log n)$ or better (on average), but the likelihood that a long transaction will fail to commit would still be an issue. To avoid that problem intelligent contention-management is required, which is an area of active research.

Summary. To summarise, STM provides several benefits for concurrent programming:

- **Composable atomicity**. We may construct arbitrarily large atomic operations on shared state, which can simplify the implementation of concurrent data structures with fine-grained locking.
- **Composable blocking**. We can build operations that make a choice between multiple blocking operations; something which is very difficult with MVars and other low-level concurrency abstractions.
- **Robustness in the presence of failure and cancellation**. A transaction in progress is aborted if an exception occurs, so STM makes it easy to maintain invariants on state in the presence of exceptions.

Further Reading. To find out more about STM in Haskell:

- Harris et al. [2], the original paper describing the design of Haskell's STM interface (be sure to get the revised version[27] which has the modified semantics for exceptions).
- "Beautiful Concurrency" a chapter in Wilson [15].

3.5   Concurrency and the Foreign Function Interface

Haskell has a *foreign function interface* (FFI) that allows Haskell code to call, and be called by, foreign language code (primarily C) [9]. Foreign languages also

---

[27] http://research.microsoft.com/people/simonpj/

have their own threading models — in C there is POSIX or Win32 threads, for example — so we need to specify how Concurrent Haskell interacts with the threading models of foreign code.

The details of the design can be found in Marlow et al. [6], in the following sections we summarise the behaviour the Haskell programmer can expect.

All of the following assumes that GHC's -threaded option is in use. Without -threaded, the Haskell process uses a single OS thread only, and multi-threaded foreign calls are not supported.

Threads and Foreign Out-Calls. An out-call is a call made from Haskell to a foreign language. At the present time the FFI supports only calls to C, so that's all we describe here. In the following we refer to threads in C (i.e. POSIX or Win32 threads) as "OS threads" to distinguish them from Haskell threads.

As an example, consider making the POSIX C function read() callable from Haskell:

```
foreign import ccall "read"
    c_read :: CInt        -- file descriptor
           -> Ptr Word8   -- buffer for data
           -> CSize       -- size of buffer
           -> CSSize      -- bytes read, or -1 on error
```

This declares a Haskell function c_read that can be used to call the C function read(). Full details on the syntax of foreign declarations and the relationship between C and Haskell types can be found in the Haskell report [9].

Just as Haskell threads run concurrently with each other, when a Haskell thread makes a foreign call, that foreign call runs concurrently with the other Haskell threads, and indeed with any other active foreign calls. Clearly the only way that two C calls can be running concurrently is if they are running in two separate OS threads, so that is exactly what happens: if several Haskell threads call c_read and they all block waiting for data to be read, there will be one OS thread per call blocked in read().

This has to work despite the fact that Haskell threads are not normally mapped one-to-one with OS threads; as we mentioned earlier (Section 3.1), in GHC, Haskell threads are lightweight and managed in user-space by the run-time system. So to handle concurrent foreign calls, the runtime system has to create more OS threads, and in fact it does this on demand. When a Haskell thread makes a foreign call, another OS thread is created (if necessary), and the responsibility for running the remaining Haskell threads is handed over to the new OS thread, meanwhile the current OS thread makes the foreign call.

The implication of this design is that a foreign call may be executed in *any* OS thread, and subsequent calls may even be executed in different OS threads. In most cases this isn't important, but sometimes it is: some foreign code must be called by a *particular* OS thread. There are two instances of this requirement:

– Libraries that only allow one OS thread to use their API. GUI libraries often fall into this category: not only must the library be called by only one OS thread, it must often be one *particular* thread (e.g. the main thread). The Win32 GUI APIs are an example of this.

– APIs that use internal thread-local state. The best-known example of this is OpenGL, which supports multi-threaded use, but stores state between API calls in thread-local storage. Hence, subsequent calls must be made in the same OS thread, otherwise the later call will see the wrong state.

For this reason, the concept of *bound threads* was introduced. A bound thread is a Haskell thread/OS thread pair, such that foreign calls made by the Haskell thread always take place in the associated OS thread. A bound thread is created by `forkOS`:

```
forkOS :: IO () -> IO ThreadId
```

Care should be taken when calling `forkOS`: it creates a complete new OS thread, so it can be quite expensive.

Threads and Foreign In-Calls. In-calls are calls to Haskell functions that have been exposed to foreign code using `foreign export`. For example, if we have a function `f` of type `Int -> IO Int`, we could expose it like this:

```
foreign export ccall "f" f :: Int -> IO Int
```

This would create a C function with the following signature:

```
HsInt f(HsInt);
```

here `HsInt` is the C type corresponding to Haskell's `Int` type.

In a multi-threaded program, it is entirely possible that `f` might be called by multiple OS threads concurrently. The GHC runtime system supports this (at least with `-threaded`), with the following behaviour: each call becomes a new *bound thread*. That is, a new Haskell thread is created for each call, and the Haskell thread is bound to the OS thread that made the call. Hence, any further out-calls made by the Haskell thread will take place in the same OS thread that made the original in-call. This turns out to be important for dealing with GUI callbacks: the GUI wants to run in the main OS thread only, so when it makes a callback into Haskell, we need to ensure that GUI calls made by the callback happen in the same OS thread that invoked the callback.

Further Reading

– The full specification of the Foreign Function Interface (FFI) can be found in the Haskell 2010 report [9];
– GHC's extensions to the FFI can be found in the GHC User's Guide[28];
– Functions for dealing with bound threads can be found in the documentation for the `Control.Concurrent` module.

---

[28] http://www.haskell.org/ghc/docs/latest/html/users_guide/

3.6   High-Speed Concurrent Server Applications

Server-type applications that communicate with many clients simultaneously demand both a high degree of concurrency and high performance from the I/O subsystem. A good web server should be able to handle hundreds of thousands of concurrent connections, and service tens of thousands of requests per second.

Ideally, we would like to write these kinds of applications using threads. A thread is the right abstraction: it allows the developer to focus on programming the interaction with a single client, and then to lift this interaction to multiple clients by simply forking many instances of the single-client interaction in separate threads. To illustrate this idea we will describe a simple network server[29], with the following behaviour:

- The server accepts connections from clients on port 44444.
- If a client sends an integer n, the service responds with the value of $2n$
- If a client sends the string "end", the server closes the connection.

First, we program the interaction with a single client. The function talk defined below takes a Handle for communicating with the client. The Handle is typically bound to a network socket, so data sent by the client can be read from the Handle, and data written to the Handle will be sent to the client.

```
1   talk :: Handle -> IO ()
2   talk h = do
3     hSetBuffering h LineBuffering
4     loop
5     where
6     loop = do
7       line <- hGetLine h
8       if line == "end"
9         then hPutStrLn h ("Thank you for using the " ++
10                          "Haskell doubling service.")
11        else do hPutStrLn h (show (2 * (read line ::
                    Integer)))
12                loop
```

Line 3 sets the buffering mode for the Handle to line-buffering; if we don't do that then output sent to the Handle will be buffered up by the I/O layer until there is a full block (which is more efficient for large transfers, but not useful for interactive applications). Then we enter a loop to respond to requests from the client. Each iteration of the loop reads a new line of text (line 7), and then checks whether the client sent "end". If so, we emit a polite message and return (line 8). If not, we attempt to interpret the line as an integer and to write the value obtained by doubling it. Finally we call loop again to read the next request.

Having dealt with the interaction with a single client, we can now make this into a multi-client server using concurrency. The main function for our server is as follows:

---

[29] The full code can be found in sample server.hs

```
1   main = do
2     s <- listenOn (PortNumber 44444)
3     forever $ do
4       (h,host,_) <- accept s
5       printf "new client: %s\n" host
6       forkIO (talk h 'finally' hClose h)
```

On line 2 we create a network socket to listen on port 44444, and then we enter
a loop to accept connections from clients (line 3). Line 4 accepts a new client
connection: accept blocks until a connection request from a client arrives, and
then returns a Handle for communicating with the client (here bound to h) and
some information about the client (here we bind host to the client's hostname).
Line 5 reports the new connection, and on line 6 we call forkIO to create a new
thread to handle the request. A little explanation is needed for the expression
passed to forkIO:

```
talk h 'finally' hClose h
```

talk is the single-client interaction that we defined above. The function finally
is a standard exception-handling combinator. It is rather like a specialised version
of bracket, and has the following type

```
finally :: IO a -> IO b -> IO a
```

with the behaviour that a 'finally' b behaves exactly like a, except that b
is always performed after a returns or throws an exception. Here we are using
finally to ensure that the Handle for communicating with the client is always
closed, even if talk throws an exception. If we didn't do this, the Handle would
eventually be garbage collected, but in the meantime it would consume resources
which might lead to the program failing due to lack of file descriptors. It is always
a good idea to close Handles when you're finished with them.

Having forked a thread to handle this client, the main thread then goes back
to accepting more connections. All the active client connections and the main
thread run concurrently with each other, so the fact that the server is handling multiple clients will be invisible to any individual client (unless the server
becomes overloaded).

So, making our concurrent server was simple - we did not have to change the
single-client code at all, and the code to lift it to a concurrent server was only a
handful of lines. We can verify that it works: in one window we start the server

```
$ ./server
```

in another window we start a client, and try a single request[30]:

```
$ nc localhost 44444
22
44
```

Next we leave this client running, and start another client:

---

[30] nc is the netcat program, which is useful for simple network interaction

```
$ ghc -e 'mapM_ print [1..]' | nc localhost 44444
2
4
6
...
```

this client exercises the server a bit more by sending it a continuous stream of numbers to double. For fun, try starting a few of these. Meanwhile we can switch back to our first client, and observe that it is still being serviced:

```
$ nc localhost 44444
22
44
33
66
```

finally we can end the interaction with a client by typing **end**:

```
end
Thank you for using the Haskell doubling service.
```

This was just a simple example, but the same ideas underly several high-performance web-server implementations in Haskell. Furthermore, with no additional effort at all, the same server code can make use of multiple cores simply by compiling with -threaded and running with +RTS -N.

There are two technologies that make this structure feasible in Haskell:

– GHC's very lightweight threads mean that having one thread per client is practical.
– The IO manager [10] handles outstanding blocked I/O operations using efficient operating-system primitives (e.g. the epoll call in Unix), which allows us to have many thousands of threads doing I/O simultaneously with very little overhead.

Were it not for lightweight threads and the IO manager, we would have to resort to collapsing the structure into a single event loop (or worse, multiple event loops to take advantage of multiple cores). The event loops style loses the single-client abstraction, instead all clients have to be dealt with simultaneously, which can be complicated if there are different kinds of client with different behaviours. Furthermore we have to represent the state of each client somehow, rather than just writing the straight-line code as we did in talk above. Imagine extending talk to implement a more elaborate protocol with several states — it would be reasonably straightforward with the single client abstraction, but representing each state and the transitions explicitly would quickly get complicated.

We have ignored many details that would be necessary in a real server application. The reader is encouraged to think about these and to try implementing any required changes on top of the provided sample code:

- What should happen if the user interrupts the server with a control-C? (control-C is implemented as an asynchronous exception `Interrupted` which is sent to the main thread).
- What happens in `talk` if the line does not parse as a number?
- What happens if the client cuts the connection prematurely, or the network goes down?
- Should there be a limit on the number of clients we serve simultaneously?
- Can we log the activity of the server to a file?

4   Conclusion

We hope you have found this tutorial useful! To recap, here are the main points and areas we have covered.

Haskell provides several different programming models for multiprogramming, broadly divided into two classes: *parallel* programming models where the goal is to write programs that make use of multiple processors to improve performance, and *concurrency* where the goal is to write programs that interact with multiple independent external agents.

The Parallel programming models in Haskell are *deterministic*, that is, these programming models are defined to give the same results regardless of how many processors are used to run them. There are two main approaches: `Strategies`, which relies on lazy evaluatation to achieve parallelism, and the `Par` monad which uses a more explicit dataflow-graph style for expressing parallel computations.

On the Concurrency side we introduced the basic programming model involving threads and `MVars` for communication, and then described Haskell's support for *cancellation* in the form of asynchronous exceptions. Finally we showed how Software Transactional Memory allows concurrent abstractions to be built compositionally, and makes it much easier to program with asynchronous exceptions. We also covered the use of concurrency with Haskell's Foreign Function interface, and looked briefly at how to program concurrent server applications in Haskell.

References

[1] Harris, T., Singh, S.: Feedback directed implicit parallelism. In: Proceedings of the 12th ACM SIGPLAN International Conference on Functional Programming, ICFP 2007, pp. 251–264 (2007)

[2] Harris, T., Marlow, S., Peyton-Jones, S., Herlihy, M.: Composable memory transactions. In: Proceedings of the Tenth ACM SIGPLAN Symposium on Principles and Practice of Parallel Programming, PPoPP 2005, pp. 48–60 (2005)

[3] Marlow, S., Peyton Jones, S.L., Moran, A., Reppy, J.: Asynchronous exceptions in Haskell. In: ACM Conference on Programming Languages Design and Implementation (PLDI 2001), Snowbird, Utah, pp. 274–285. ACM Press (June 2001)

[4] Marlow, S.: An extensible dynamically-typed hierarchy of exceptions. In: Proceedings of the 2006 ACM SIGPLAN Workshop on Haskell, Haskell 2006, pp. 96–106 (2006)

[5] Marlow, S., Newton, R., Peyton Jones, S.: A monad for deterministic parallelism. under submission, http://community.haskell.org/~simonmar/bib/monad-par-2011_abstract.html

[6] Marlow, S., Peyton Jones, S., Thaller, W.: Extending the Haskell foreign function interface with concurrency. In: Proceedings of the 2004 ACM SIGPLAN Workshop on Haskell, Haskell 2004, pp. 22–32 (2004)

[7] Marlow, S., Peyton Jones, S., Singh, S.: Runtime support for multicore haskell. In: ICFP 2009: Proceeding of the 14th ACM SIGPLAN International Conference on Functional Programming, Edinburgh, Scotland (August 2009)

[8] Marlow, S., Maier, P., Loidl, H.-W., Aswad, M.K., Trinder, P.: Seq no more: Better strategies for parallel haskell. In: Haskell 2010: Proceedings of the Third ACM SIGPLAN Symposium on Haskell (2010), http://community.haskell.org/~simonmar/papers/strategies.pdf

[9] Marlow, S. (ed.): The Haskell 2010 report (2010), http://www.haskell.org/onlinereport/haskell2010/

[10] O'Sullivan, B., Tibell, J.: Scalable I/O event handling for GHC. In: Proceedings of the Third ACM Haskell Symposium on Haskell, Haskell 2010, pp. 103–108 (2010)

[11] Peyton Jones, S., Gordon, A., Finne, S.: Concurrent Haskell. In: Proc. of POPL 1996, pp. 295–308. ACM Press (1996)

[12] Peyton Jones, S.: Tackling the awkward squad: monadic input/output, concurrency, exceptions, and foreign-language calls in haskell. Engineering Theories of Software Construction (2002)

[13] Peyton Jones, S., Singh, S.: A Tutorial on Parallel and Concurrent Programming in Haskell. In: Koopman, P., Plasmeijer, R., Swierstra, D. (eds.) AFP 2008. LNCS, vol. 5832, pp. 267–305. Springer, Heidelberg (2009)

[14] Trinder, P.W., Hammond, K., Loidl, H.-W., Peyton Jones, S.: Algorithm + Strategy = Parallelism 8(1), 23–60 (1998)

[15] Wilson, G. (ed.): Beautiful code. O'Reilly (2007)

Feldspar: Application and Implementation

Emil Axelsson and Mary Sheeran

CSE Dept., Chalmers University of Technology
{emax,ms}@chalmers.se

Abstract. The Feldspar project aims to develop a domain specific language for Digital Signal Processing algorithm design. From functional descriptions, imperative code (currently C) is generated. The project partners are Ericsson, Chalmers and ELTE, Budapest. The background and motivation for the project have been documented elsewhere [3]. We aim to raise the level of abstraction at which algorithm developers and implementors work, and to generate, from Feldspar descriptions, the kind of code that is currently written by hand.

These lecture notes first give a brief introduction to Feldspar and the style of programming that it encourages. Next, we document the implementation of Feldspar as a domain specific language (DSL), embedded in Haskell. The implementation is built using a library called Syntactic that was built for this purpose, but also designed to be of use to other implementors of embedded domain specific languages. We show the implementation of Feldspar in sufficient detail to give the reader an understanding of how the use of the Syntactic library enables the modular construction of an embedded DSL. For those readers who would like to apply these techniques to their own DSL embedded in Haskell, further instructions are given in section 5.

The programming examples are available in the CEFP directory of the Feldspar package, version 0.5.0.1:

http://hackage.haskell.org/package/feldspar-language-0.5.0.1

The code can be fetched by running:

> cabal unpack feldspar-language-0.5.0.1

All code is written in Haskell, and has been tested using the Glasgow Haskell Compiler (GHC), version 7.0.2, and the packages

- syntactic-0.8
- feldspar-language-0.5.0.1
- feldspar-compiler-0.5.0.1

1   Programming in Feldspar

Feldspar is domain specific language for DSP algorithm design, embedded in Haskell. It currently generates sequential C code for individual functions and it is this *Data Path* part that is presented here. The part of Feldspar that coordinates and deploys these kernels in parallel is still under development.

The aim of this part of the notes is to give the reader a brief introduction to programming algorithmic blocks in Feldspar. We first present the core language, which

V. Zsók, Z. Horváth, and R. Plasmeijer (Eds.): CEFP 2011, LNCS 7241, pp. 402–439, 2012.

is a purely functional C-like language deeply embedded in Haskell. Next, we show
how the constructs of the Vector library bring the user closer to a Haskell-like style
of programming. The Vector library is built upon the core, via a shallow embedding.
The combination of shallow and deep embedding is characteristic of the Feldspar
implementation, and has proved fruitful. It is discussed further in section 2.1. Finally, we illustrate the use of Feldspar in exploring a number of implementations of
the Fourier Transform. Our aim in designing Feldspar was to build an embedded
language that makes programming DSP algorithms as much like ordinary Haskell
programming as possible, while still permitting the generation of efficient C code.
As we shall see in the sections on implementation, the main emphasis in the design
has been on gaining modularity, and on making the language easily extensible. The
most noticeable sacrifice has been the omission of recursion in Feldspar. Feldspar
users can make use of Haskell's recursion in program definitions, but such recursion
must be completely unrolled during code generation.

1.1   The Core of Feldspar

The basis of Feldspar is a core language with some familiar primitive functions
on base types, and a small number of language constructs. A program in the
core language has type Data a, where a is the type of the value computed by the
program. Primitive constructs have types similar to their Haskell counterparts,
but with the addition of the Data constructor to the types.

For example, the Haskell functions

```
(==) :: Eq a ⇒ a → a → a
(&&) :: Bool → Bool → Bool
exp  :: Floating a ⇒ a → a
```

are matched by the Feldspar functions

```
(==) :: Eq a ⇒ Data a → Data a → Data a
(&&) :: Data Bool → Data Bool → Data Bool
exp  :: Floating a ⇒ Data a → Data a
```

The point to remember is that the type Bool, for instance, indicates a Haskell
value, while Data Bool indicates a Feldspar one.

Feldspar functions are defined using Haskell's function abstraction:

```
square :: Data WordN → Data WordN
square x = x*x
```

WordN is meant to represent an unsigned integer whose bit-width is determined
by the target platform. However, in the current implementation, WordN is implemented as a 32-bit word. We also provide the following two aliases:

```
type Length = WordN
type Index  = WordN
```

The conditional construct in Feldspar is similar to that in C. For instance, the
function f below doubles its input if it is odd.

```
f :: Data Int32 → Data Int32
f i = (testBit i 0) ? (2*i, i)
```

Applying the eval function gives

```
*Main> eval (f 3)
6
*Main> eval (f 2)
2
```

The abstract syntax tree of the function can be drawn using drawAST f:

```
*Main> drawAST f
Lambda 0
|
'- condition
   |
   +- testBit
   |  |
   |  +- var:0
   |  |
   |  '- 0
   |
   +- (*)
   |  |
   |  +- var:0
   |  |
   |  '- 2
   |
   '- var:0
```

and the result is a lambda function of one variable (numbered 0).

The generated C code (resulting from the call icompile f) is

```
================ Source ================
#include "feldspar_c99.h"
#include "feldspar_array.h"
#include <stdint.h>
#include <string.h>
#include <math.h>
#include <stdbool.h>
#include <complex.h>


/*
 * Memory information
 *
 * Local: none
 * Input: signed 32-bit integer
 * Output: signed 32-bit integer
 *
 */
```

```
void test(struct array * mem, int32_t v0, int32_t * out)
{
    if(testBit_fun_int32(v0, 0))
    {
        (* out) = (v0 << 1);
    }
    else
    {
        (* out) = v0;
    }
}
```

The additional mem parameter that appears in all generated C code is not used in the code body in this case. We will return to it in a later example. The remaining two parameters correspond to the input and output of the Feldspar function. (We will not in future show the #includes that appear in all generated C functions.)

Core Arrays. Arrays play a central role in the Digital Signal Processing domain, and so they pervade Feldspar. Core arrays come in parallel and sequential variants, but we will concentrate on the parallel version here. Core parallel arrays are created with the parallel function:

parallel :: Type a ⇒ Data Length → (Data Index → Data a) → Data [a]

The type Data [a] is the type of core arrays. The two parameters to parallel give the length of the array, and a function from indices to values.

```
arr1n :: Data WordN → Data [WordN]
arr1n n = parallel n (λi → (i+1))

*Main> eval (arr1n 6)
[1,2,3,4,5,6]

evens :: Data WordN → Data [WordN]
evens n = parallel n (*2)

*Main> eval (evens 6)
[0,2,4,6,8,10]
```

Feldspar core arrays become blocks of memory in the generated C code. Although the current version of Feldspar generates *sequential* C code for the parallel construct, the key attribute of parallel is that it is a *data parallel* construct, in that the values at different indices are independent of each other. This opens for future exploitation of parallelism, and also for optimisations based on array fusion.

The types of the remaining functions on core arrays are shown in Figure 1 These functions have the expected semantics. For example, the following function squares each element of its input array:

```
append :: Type a ⇒ Data [a] → Data [a] → Data [a]

getLength :: Type a ⇒ Data [a] → Data Length

setLength :: Type a ⇒ Data Length → Data [a] → Data [a]

getIx :: Type a ⇒ Data [a] → Data Index → Data a

setIx :: Type a ⇒ Data [a] → Data Index → Data a → Data [a]
```

Fig. 1. Functions on core arrays

```
squareEach :: Data [WordN] → Data [WordN]
squareEach as = parallel (getLength as) (λi → square (getIx as i))
```

The resulting C code is

```
/*
 * Memory information
 *
 * Local: none
 * Input: unsigned 32−bit integer array
 * Output: unsigned 32−bit integer array
 *
 */
void test(struct array * mem, struct array * v0, struct array * out)
{
    uint32_t len0;

    len0 = getLength(v0);
    for(uint32_t v1 = 0; v1 < len0; v1 += 1)
    {
        at(uint32_t,out,v1) = (at(uint32_t,v0,v1) * at(uint32_t,v0,v1));
    }
    setLength(out, len0);
}
```

The array inputs have been represented by structs of the form

```
struct array
{
    void*    buffer;   /* pointer to the buffer of elements */
    int32_t  length;   /* number of elements in the array */
    int32_t  elemSize; /* size of elements in bytes; (−1) for nested arrays */
    uint32_t bytes;    /* The number of bytes the buffer can hold */
};
```

and the at macro indexes into the actual buffer.

For completeness, we also introduce the sequential construct:

```
sequential :: (Type a, Syntax s) ⇒
              Data Length → s → (Data Index → s → (Data a,s))
              → Data [a]
```

Sequential arrays are defined by a length, an initial state and a function from index and state to a value (for that index) and a new state. For instance, the following program computes successive factorials:

```
sfac :: Data WordN → Data [WordN]
sfac n = sequential n 1 g
  where
    g ix st = (j,j)
      where j = (ix + 1) * st
```

```
*Main> eval (sfac 6)
[1,2,6,24,120,720]
```

Loops. The two important remaining constructs in the core language are the for and while loops[1]:

```
forLoop :: Syntax a ⇒ Data Length → a → (Data Index → a → a) → a
```

```
whileLoop :: Syntax a ⇒ a → (a → Data Bool) → (a → a) → a
```

The loop forLoop n i f takes a number of iterations, n, an initial state, i, and a function f from index and state to a new state. Thus, fib n computes the nth Fibonacci number.

```
fib :: Data Index → Data Index
fib n = fst $ forLoop n (1,1) $ λi (a,b) → (b,a+b)
```

This example also illustrates that it is possible, in Feldspar, to have ordinary Haskell tuples both in patterns and in expressions, due to the overloading provided by the Syntax class.

```
void test(struct array * mem, uint32_t v0, uint32_t * out)
{
    struct s_uint32_t_uint32_t_ e0;
    struct s_uint32_t_uint32_t_ v2;

    e0.member1 = 1;
    e0.member2 = 1;
    for(uint32_t v1 = 0; v1 < v0; v1 += 1)
    {
        v2.member1 = e0.member2;
        v2.member2 = (e0.member1 + e0.member2);
        e0 = v2;
    }
    (* out) = e0.member1;
}
```

In the current version of Feldspar, tuples become structs when compiled into C. In programs, such as fib, where tuples are just used to group state variables, it would make more sense to compile them into separate variables. This behavior is planned for future versions.

---

[1] There are also monadic versions of these loops, but we will not consider this extension of the language in this introduction

In similar style, the integer log base 2 function can be computed using a while loop:

```
intLog :: Data WordN → Data WordN
intLog n = fst $ whileLoop (0,n)
                (λ(_,b) → (b > 1))
                (λ(a,b) → (a+1, b 'div' 2))
```

The Feldspar user has access to the constructs of the core language, and this gives fine control over the generated C code when this is required. However, our intention is to raise the level of abstraction at which programmers work, and to do this, we must move away from the low level primitives in the core.

1.2   Above the Core: Vectors

The core constructs of Feldspar are augmented by a number of additional libraries, implemented as shallow embeddings. This eases experiments with language design, without demanding changes to the backends. Here, we illustrate this idea using the library of *Vectors*, which are *symbolic* or *virtual* arrays. Vectors are intended both to give a user experience resembling the look and feel of Haskell list programming *and* to permit the generation of decent imperative array processing code. We call vectors symbolic because they do not necessarily result in the use of allocated memory (arrays) in the generated C code. A program that uses the vector library should import it explicitly using import Feldspar.Vector.

Vectors are defined using an ordinary Haskell type:

```
— Symbolic vector
data Vector a
    = Empty
    | Indexed
        { segmentLength :: Data Length
        , segmentIndex  :: Data Index → a
        , continuation  :: Vector a
        }
```

A vector is defined, for its first *segment*, by a segment length and by a function from indices to values (as we saw in core parallel arrays). However, it also has a *continuation* vector (possibly empty) corresponding to its remaining segments. The overall length of a vector (given by the function length) is the sum of the lengths of its segments. Such segmented vectors are used in order to allow efficient vector append. Note, however, that taking the sum of a segmented array results in one for loop per segment.

```
tstLApp n = sum (squares n ++ squares (n+2))

void test(struct array * mem, uint32_t v0, uint32_t * out
{
    uint32_t len0;
    uint32_t v2;
    uint32_t v4;
```

```
len0 = (v0 + 2);
(* out) = 0;
for(uint32_t v1 = 0; v1 < v0; v1 += 1)
{
    uint32_t v5;

    v5 = (v1 + 1);
    v2 = ((* out) + (v5 * v5));
    (* out) = v2;
}
for(uint32_t v3 = 0; v3 < len0; v3 += 1)
{
    uint32_t v6;

    v6 = (v3 + 1);
    v4 = ((* out) + (v6 * v6));
    (* out) = v4;
}
}
```

We will, in the remainder of these notes, only use vectors whose continuation is Empty. Such single segment vectors are built using the indexed function.

For example, $W_n^k = e^{-2\pi i k/n}$ (also known as a twiddle factor) is a primitive n^{th} root of unity raised to the power of k. For a given n, we can place all the powers from zero to (n-1) of W_n into a vector tws as follows:

```
tw :: Data WordN → Data WordN → Data (Complex Float)
tw n k = exp (−2 * pi * iunit * i2n k / i2n n)

tws n = indexed n (tw n)
```

Here, i2n converts from an integer to a floating-point number.

In the following calls to the tws function, the reader is encouraged to examine the results for interesting patterns. How do tws 4 and tws 8 relate and why?

```
*Main> tws 2
[1.0 :+ 0.0, (−1.0) :+ 8.742278e−8]
*Main> eval (tws 4)
[1.0 :+ 0.0, (−4.371139e−8) :+ (−1.0),
(−1.0) :+ 8.742278e−8, 1.1924881e−8 :+ 1.0]
*Main> eval (tws 8)
[1.0 :+ 0.0, 0.70710677 :+ (−0.70710677),
(−4.371139e−8) :+ (−1.0), (−0.70710677) :+ (−0.70710677),
(−1.0) :+ 8.742278e−8,(−0.70710665) :+ 0.7071069,
1.1924881e−8 :+ 1.0, 0.707107 :+ 0.70710653]
```

To make a program that takes an integer as input and returns the corresponding array of twiddle factors, we simply call icompile tws. Because the output of the program is a vector, an array will indeed be manifest in memory in the resulting C code.

```
void test(struct array * mem, uint32_t v0, struct array * out)
{
    float complex v2;

    v2 = complex_fun_float((float)(v0), 0.0f);
    for(uint32_t v1 = 0; v1 < v0; v1 += 1)
    {
        at(float complex,out,v1) = cexpf((((0.0f+0.0fi)
            - ((complex_fun_float((float)(v1), 0.0f) *
            (0.0f+6.2831854820251465fi)) / v2)));
    }
    setLength(out, v0);
}
```

But if we (somewhat perversely) sum the vector, then the resulting C code does not have a corresponding array:

```
void test(struct array * mem, uint32_t v0, float complex * out)
{
    float complex v3;
    float complex v2;

    v3 = complex_fun_float((float)(v0), 0.0f);
    (* out) = (0.0f+0.0fi);
    for(uint32_t v1 = 0; v1 < v0; v1 += 1)
    {
        v2 = ((* out) + cexpf(((0.0f+0.0fi) -
            ((complex_fun_float((float)(v1), 0.0f) *
            (0.0f+6.2831854820251465fi)) / v3))));
        (* out) = v2;
    }
}
```

Mapping a function over a vector behaves as we expect:

```
squares :: Data WordN → Vector1 WordN
squares n = map square (1...n)

*Main> eval (squares 4)
[1,4,9,16]

flipBit :: Data Index → Data Index → Data Index
flipBit i k = i 'xor' (bit k)

flips :: Data WordN → Vector1 WordN → Vector1 WordN
flips k = map (λe → flipBit e k)

*Main> eval $ flips 2 (0...15)
[4,5,6,7,0,1,2,3,12,13,14,15,8,9,10,11]

*Main> eval $ flips 3 (0...15)
[8,9,10,11,12,13,14,15,0,1,2,3,4,5,6,7]
```

The function flips k flips bit number k of each element of a vector.

The type Vector1 a is shorthand for Vector (Data a). The (1... n) construction builds the vector from 1 to n. This could also have been done using the vector function and a Haskell list:

```
*Main> eval (vector [1..3::WordN])
[1,2,3]
```

Indexing into a vector is done using the infix (!) function. So, for example, the head of a vector is its zeroth element.

```
head :: Syntax a ⇒ Vector a → a
head = (!0)
```

The API of the Vector library is much inspired by Haskell's standard list-processing functions, with functions like map, zip, take, drop splitAt and zipWith.

Composing vector operations results in *fusion*: intermediate data structures are fused away in the resulting generated code. One might expect the following function to produce code with two or even three loops, but it has only one:

```
sumSqVn :: Data WordN → Data WordN
sumSqVn n = fold (+) 0 $ map square (1...n)
```

```c
void test(struct array * mem, uint32_t v0, uint32_t * out)
{
    uint32_t v2;

    (* out) = 0;
    for(uint32_t v1 = 0; v1 < v0; v1 += 1)
    {
        uint32_t v3;

        v3 = (v1 + 1);
        v2 = ((* out) + (v3 * v3));
        (* out) = v2;
    }
}
```

This code embodies one of the main aims of Feldspar. We want to write code that looks a lot like Haskell, but to generate efficient imperative code, of a quality acceptable within our domain. The key to succeeding in this is to make the language only just expressive enough for our domain! Now is the point to remember that we have no recursion in the embedded language. This pushes us towards a style of functional programming that relies heavily on familiar list functions like map, fold and zipWith, but in variants that work on vectors.

In return for limited expressiveness, the user is given very strong guarantees about fusion of intermediate vectors (and users should, in general, be programming using vectors rather than core arrays). In Feldspar, a vector may become manifest in generated code *only* in the following circumstances

1. when it is explicitly forced using the function force[2]
2. when it is the input or output of a program
3. when it is accessed by a function outside the vector library API, for example, a conditional or a for loop

These are strong guarantees, and they permit us to advocate a purely functional programming style, even when performance is important. When performance and memory use are over-riding concerns, we have the option of resorting to monads and mutable arrays (see [15]). Our hope, which we will try to confirm in an up-coming case study of part of an LTE uplink processing chain, is that some key kernels will have to be finely tuned for performance and memory use, but that the combination of such kernels will still be possible in a modular data-flow style that uses higher order functions to structure programs.

Although we have shown only the Vector library, Feldspar contains a variety of libraries implemented similarly as shallow embeddings. Examples include a clone of the Repa library [14] and libraries for building filters and stream process-ing functions. Work is also ongoing on dynamic contract checking for Feldspar, and on improving feedback to users by trying to relate points in the generated code with points in the source (a notoriously difficult problem for embedded languages).

1.3   Case Study: Programming Transforms

Discrete Fourier Transform. The discrete Fourier Transform (DFT) can be specified as

$$X_k = \Sigma_{j=0}^{n-1} x_j W_n^{jk}$$

where W_n^j is an nth root of unity raised to the power of j that we saw earlier, and encoded in the function tw n j. Using vectors and summation, it is straight-forward to translate the above specification of DFT into Feldspar.

```
dft :: Vector1 (Complex Float) → Vector1 (Complex Float)
dft xs = indexed n (λk → sum (indexed n (λj → xs!j * tw n (j*k))))
  where
    n = length xs
```

It is also clear that there are n summations, each of n elements, giving the well known $O(n^2)$ complexity of the operation.

Fast Fourier Transforms. Any algorithm that gives O(n log n) complexity in computing the same result as the DFT is known as a Fast Fourier Transform or FFT. That one can make such a reduction in complexity is due to the rich algebraic properties of the W_n^k terms – the so-called twiddle factors, and to the sharing of intermediate computations. FFT plays a central role in Digital Signal Processing, where it is one of the most used algorithmic blocks. There are many different FFT algorithms, suited to different circumstances, see reference [10] for an entertaining and informative tutorial.

---

[2] A vector can also be explicitly forced using the function desugar (see section 4.3), but this function is mostly for internal use.

Radix 2 Decimation in Frequency FFT. The best known (and simplest) FFT algorithms are those due to Cooley and Tukey [8]. In the radix two, Decimation in Frequency (DIF) algorithm, for input of length N, the even and odd-numbered parts of the output are each computed by a DFT with $N/2$ inputs. The inputs to those two half-sized DFTs can be computed by N/2 2-input DFTs. This decomposition can be used recursively, giving huge savings in the cost of implementing the algorithm.

We will visualise FFT algorithms by showing how small 2-input, 2-output DFT components are composed, and by indicating where multiplication by twiddle factors happen, see Figure 2. In this style, the structure of the radix 2 DIF FFT is visualised in figure 3.

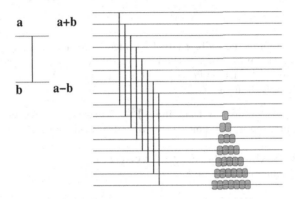

Fig. 2. Introducing the style used to visualise FFT algorithms. The vertical lines are 2-input DFT components, with inputs on the left and outputs on the right. They are drawn linking the elements of the array on which they operate. Thus, the arrangement of vertical lines to the left of the triangle indicates that DFTs are performed between array elements 0 and 8, 1 and 9 and so on. The triangle is intended to suggest multiplication by twiddle factors of increasing powers. A triangle of height n indicates multiplication by W_{2n}^0, W_{2n}^1, and so on, up to W_{2n}^{n-1}. The first of these is indicated by zero blobs, and the last by 7.

The Components of the FFT. Let us set about describing the components of the DIF algorithm in Feldspar. Consider first the butterflies, which are made of small (2-input) DFTs. To describe multiple small DFTs, each operating on pairs of values 2^k apart, we might be tempted to first construct a component that works on $2^{(k+1)}$ inputs and then to realise a combinator that allows this component to be applied repeated to sub-parts of an input array. This is how we would have described the construction in Lava (our earlier work on hardware description in Haskell [5]) and indeed the aforementioned paper contains such descriptions of FFT algorithms. Here, we choose a slightly different approach (inspired by our recent work on data-parallel GPU programming in Haskell [7]). We take the repeated application of a function on sub-parts of the input array of a given size to be the default! So, for example, we don't define vector reverse as taking a vector and returning its reverse, but rather revp k, which reverses sub-parts of its inputs, each of length 2^k.

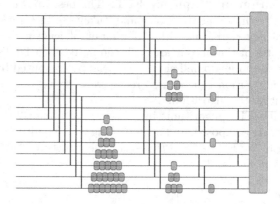

Fig. 3. An illustration of the radix 2 DIF FFT algorithm (for 16 inputs). The box on the right indicates the application of the bit reversal permutation. From left to right, the groups of 2-input DFTs (indicated by the vertical lines) correspond to bfly 3, bfly 2, bfly 1 and bfly 0 in the Feldspar code.

```
premap :: (Data Index → Data Index) → Vector a → Vector a
premap f (Indexed l ixf Empty) = indexed l (ixf ∘ f)

revp :: (Bits a) ⇒ Data Index → Vector1 a → Vector1 a
revp k  = premap ('xor' (2^k − 1))

*Main> eval (revp 3 (0...15))
[7,6,5,4,3,2,1,0,15,14,13,12,11,10,9,8]
*Main> eval (revp 2 (0...15))
[3,2,1,0,7,6,5,4,11,10,9,8,15,14,13,12]
```

We assume here that if a function like revp k is applied to an input then that input must be of length $2^{(k+j)}$, for j a natural number. (We could check this and return an appropriate error message.)

So now we would like to make (repeated) butterflies, each consisting of interleaved 2-input DFTs:

```
bfly :: Data Index → Vector1 (Complex Float)
                   → Vector1 (Complex Float)
bfly k as = indexed (length as) ixf
  where
     ixf i = (testBit i k) ? (b−a, a+b)
       where
          a = as ! i
          b = as ! (flipBit i k)
```

Each individual group of butterflies is of length 2^{k+1} For any index i into the output array, we examine bit k of the index to determine if this output is to be given by an addition or a subtraction. If the bit is high, there should be a subtraction, and as!i, which we call a, should be subtracted from its partner, b which is at a lower index because its index differs from that of a only in bit k.

Note that the bfly function is a judicious mixture of core functions (including bit manipulations) and vector operations. It is perhaps the explicit indexing into vectors that feels least Haskell-like, but it reflects the mathematics and seems also to bring brevity.

For the multiplication by twiddle factors of increasing power, which takes place only on the second half of the input array, it is again bit k of index i that decides whether or not a multiplication should happen. In calculating the twiddle factor, it is i 'mod' (2^k) that gives the required increasing powers ranging from 0 to $2^k - 1$.

```
twids0 :: Data Index → Vector1 (Complex Float)
                     → Vector1 (Complex Float)
twids0 k as = indexed (length as) ixf
  where
    ixf i = (testBit i k) ? (t*(as!i),as!i)
      where
        t = tw (2^(k+1)) (i 'mod' (2^k))
```

A First Recursive FFT. Now we are in a position to compose our first recursive FFT. Remember that the variable that is recursed over must be a Haskell level variable, known at (this first) compile time. For each sub-block of length 2^n, we perform the interleaved butterflies and then the multiplication by twiddles factors. The recursive call that corresponds to two half-size transforms is simply a call of the recursive function with a parameter that is one smaller. We must be careful to convert Haskell values to Feldspar ones (using the value function) where necessary.

```
fftr0 :: Index → Vector1 (Complex Float) → Vector1 (Complex Float)
fftr0 0 = id
fftr0 n = fftr0 n' o twids0 vn' o bfly vn'
  where
    n'  = n - 1
    vn' = value n'
```

This recursive construction demands that the bit-reversal permutation be applied to its output array if it is to produce exactly the same results as the original dft funtion that is now our specification (see [10] for further discussion of this). For blocks of length 2^k, bit reversal should reverse the k least significant bits of the binary representation of each index of the array, leaving all other bits alone.

```
*Main> eval $ bitRev 4 (0...15)
[0,8,4,12,2,10,6,14,1,9,5,13,3,11,7,15]
*Main> eval $ bitRev 3 (0...15)
[0,4,2,6,1,5,3,7,8,12,10,14,9,13,11,15]
*Main> eval $ bitRev 2 (0...15)
[0,2,1,3,4,6,5,7,8,10,9,11,12,14,13,15]
```

For completeness, we give a possible implementation, inspired by the bithacks web site, see http://graphics.stanford.edu/~seander/bithacks.html. However, we also encourage the reader to investigate ways to implement this function.

In addition, we note that such permutations of FFT inputs or outputs will sometimes in reality not be performed, but instead the block following the FFT may
adjust its access pattern to the data accordingly.

```
oneBitsN :: Data Index → Data Index
oneBitsN  k = complement (shiftLU (complement 0) k)

bitr :: Data Index → Data Index → Data Index
bitr n a = let mask = (oneBitsN n) in
    (complement mask .&. a) .|. rotateLU (reverseBits (mask .&. a)) n

bitRev :: Data Index → Vector a → Vector a
bitRev n = premap (bitr n)
```

Finally, we have a first full FFT implementation:

```
fft0 :: Index →  Vector1 (Complex Float) → Vector1 (Complex Float)
fft0 n = bitRev (value n) ∘ fftr0 n
```

We can compare to the small example simulation of an FFT written in Lava
shown in reference [5]. Doing so, we find that we have here made a different (and
we think reasonable) assumption about the order of elements of an array, so that
some calls of reverse are required if we are to mimic the calculation in the Lava
paper.

```
dt4 = zipWith (+.) (vector [1,2,3,1 :: Float]) (vector [4,−2,2,2])

*Main> eval dt4
[1.0 :+ 4.0,2.0 :+ (−2.0),3.0 :+ 2.0,1.0 :+ 2.0]

*Main> eval (reverse (fft0 2 (reverse dt4)))
[1.0 :+ 6.0,(−1.0000007) :+ (−6.0),(−3.0) :+ 2.0000002,7.0 :+ 6.0]
```

Of course, much more extensive testing should be employed, including checking
that the composition with an inverse FFT is close enough to the identity. This
is beyond the scope of thse notes.

An Iterative FFT. From the recursive description of fft0, it is not difficult to
infer a corresponding iterative description:

```
fft1 :: Data Index → Vector1 (Complex Float) → Vector1 (Complex Float)
fft1 n as = bitRev n $ forLoop n as (λk → twids0 (n−1−k) ∘ bfly (n−1−k))
```

The observant reader may wonder why we didn't just add the multiplication by
the twiddle factors directly into the definition of bfly, which would allow us to
define the entire FFT as

```
fft2 :: Data Index → Vector1 (Complex Float) → Vector1 (Complex Float)
fft2 n as = bitRev n $ forLoop n as (λk → bfly2 (n−1−k))
  where
    bfly2 k as = indexed (length as) ixf
```

```
where
  ixf i = (testBit i k) ? (t*(b-a), a+b)
    where
      a = as ! i
      b = as ! (flipBit i k)
      t = tw (2^(k+1)) (i 'mod' (2^k))
```

This is indeed quite a short and readable FFT definition. However, this kind of manual merging of components is not always desirable. There are two main reasons for this. The first is that it can be easier to replace individual components with modified versions if the components are kept separate and can be modified in isolation. (This kind of modularity is a typical benefit of working in a purely functional language.) The second is that keeping components separate allows easier experiments with new ways of combining them (and such experiments are particularly relevant in the context of FFT, which is known to have many interesting decompositions).

Playing with Twiddle Factors. We would like, eventually, to avoid unnecessary recomputation of twiddle factors. This takes two steps. First, we modify the code so that all stages compute twiddle factors that have the same subscript. Next, we force computation of an array of these twiddle factors, which later parts of the program can access, avoiding recomputation.

Let us consider the component twids0 in isolation (and later we will look at new ways of combining the resulting components). One of the important algebraic properties of the twiddle factors is the following: $W_n^k = W_{2n}^{2k}$. (You may have had an inkling of this when you examined the values of tws 2, tws 4 and tws 8 earlier.) This fact gives us the opportunity to change the twids0 program so that all twiddle factors used in an entire FFT have the same subscript (rather than having different subscripts for each different parameter k in different stages of the computation).

Defining twids1 as follows means that twids1 j k has the same behaviour as twids0 k, as long as j is strictly greater than k.

```
twids1 :: Data Index → Data Index → Vector1 (Complex Float)
                                   → Vector1 (Complex Float)
twids1 n k as = indexed (length as) ixf
  where
    ixf i = (testBit i k) ? (t * (as!i), as!i)
      where
        t = tw (2^n) ((i 'mod' (2^k)) .<<. (n-1-k) )
```

This is because we have multiplied both parameters of tw by 2^{n-1-k} (the first by relacing 2^{k+1} by 2^n and the second by shifting left by 2^{n-1-k} bits).

Forcing Computation of Twiddle Factors. Now, all stages of the 2^n-input FFT use tw (2^n) when calculating twiddle factors. We can compute the 2^{n-1} twiddle factors needed *before* starting the FFT calculation, using the force function to ensure that they get stored into an array ts. Then the call of tw (2^n) is simply replaced by ts !. This approach avoids repeated computation, which can be the downside of fusion.

```
twids2 :: Data Index → Data Index → Vector1 (Complex Float)
                                    → Vector1 (Complex Float)
twids2 n k as = indexed (length as) ixf
  where
    ts = force $ indexed (2^(n−1)) (tw (2^n))
    ixf i = (testBit i k) ? (t * (as!i), as!i)
      where
        t = ts ! ((i 'mod' (2^k)) .≪. (n−1−k))
```

The resulting FFT is then

```
fft3 :: Data Index → Vector1 (Complex Float) → Vector1 (Complex Float)
fft3 n as = bitRev n $ forLoop n as (λk → twids2 n (n−1−k) ∘ bfly (n−1−k))
```

and it gives C code that starts as follows:

```
void test(struct array * mem, uint32_t v0, struct array * v1, struct array *
out)
{
    uint32_t v13;
    float complex v14;
    uint32_t len0;
    uint32_t v24;
    uint32_t v25;
    uint32_t len2;

    v13 = (v0 − 1);
    v14 = complex_fun_float((float)((1 ≪ v0)), 0.0f);
    len0 = (1 ≪ v13);
    for(uint32_t v6 = 0; v6 < len0; v6 += 1)
    {
      at(float complex,&at(struct array,mem,0),v6) =
      cexpf((((0.0f+0.0fi) − ((complex_fun_float((float)(v6), 0.0f) *
      (0.0f+6.2831854820251465fi)) / v14)));
    }
    setLength(&at(struct array,mem,0), len0);
```

Note how one of the C arrays in the mem parameter is used to store the twiddle factors, for use by the remainder of the program. This is the role of that parameter: to provide storage for local memory in the function. Our generated functions do not themselves perform memory allocation for the storage of arrays. The necessary memory must be given to them as the first input. For the twiddlle factor array, another option would be simply to pass it as an input to the FFT function.

Radix 2 Decimation in Time FFT The final FFT that we will program in Feldspar is the Decimation in Time (DIT) radix two variant of the algorithm. One can think of it as being almost the result of running the data-flow graph that we just built for the DIF algorithm *backwards*. That is, we start with the bit reversal, then twid2 n 0, then bfly 0, then twids2 n 1 and so on. Note that we do twiddle multiplications *before* butterflies in this case.

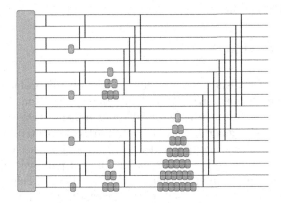

Fig. 4. An illustration of radix 2 DIT FFT algorithm (for 16 inputs). This diagram was (literally) produced from that for the DIF algorithm by flipping it vertically.

```
fft4 :: Data Index → Vector1 (Complex Float) → Vector1 (Complex Float)
fft4 n as = forLoop n (bitRev n as) (λk → bfly k ∘ twids2 n k)
```

The resulting C code is reproduced in the Appendix. It is reasonably satisfactory, but contains one annoying array copy inside the outer loop of the main FFT calculation. This copying could be avoided by using ping-ponging between two arrays, perhaps using a specially designed for loop. This would be easy to arrange, and is the approach used in the Obsidian embedded language for GPU programming [7] (although there all loops are unrolled). To get completely satisfactory performance, we would need to make an in place implementation using monads. The structure of the bflys component is well prepared for this, since each 2-input DFT has its inputs and outputs at the same indices.

The duality between the decimation in frequency (DIF) and in time (DIT) variants can be seen by examining the definitions of fft2 and fft4 and by studying the diagrams illustrating these constructions (Figures 3 and 4).

Many FFT algorithms remain to be explored. Readers wishing to experiment with Feldspar will find a wealth of interesting algorithms to program in the FFT survey in reference [10]. We should be clear that DSP algorithm designers most likely expect to be provided with fast FFT components, rather than to have to write them. However, FFT algorithms can help us to develop useful programming idioms. The development of new programming idioms is part of our current research on Feldspar. We welcome input (and code snippets) from the readers of this document.

This concludes your introduction to programming in Feldspar.

Exercise 1. Implement Batcher's bitonic sort in Feldspar [4]. See http://www.iti.fh-flensburg.de/lang/algorithmen/sortieren/bitonic/bitonicen.htm. Note that the Radix 2 DIF FFT (as shown in Figure 3) has recursive structure similar to Batcher's bitonic merger. If you ignore the blobs in that diagram, and consider the vertical lines to be 2-input, 2-output comparators, you have exactly the bitonic merger. So you may find some inspiration in the bfly and fft1 functions.

2   Implementation

The development of Feldspar has not only focused on the problem of making a language for the embedded signal processing domain. Feldspar has also served as a workbench for experimenting with different implementation techniques for embedded languages in general. This has been partly motivated by the fact that there are several partners involved in the project, and we need a very flexible design in order to make collaboration easier. In this part we will look at the general implementation techniques that have emerged out of Feldspar, and show an implementation of Feldspar based on the general techniques.

2.1   Overview

A convenient way to implement a domain-specific language (DSL) is to *embed* it within an existing language [13]. Often, the constructs of the embedded language are then represented as functions in the host language. In a *shallow* embedding, the language constructs themselves perform the interpretation of the language [12]. In a *deep* embedding, the language constructs produce an intermediate representation of the program. This representation can then be interpreted in different ways.

In general, shallow languages are more modular, allowing new constructs to be added independently of each other. In a deep implementation, each construct has to be represented in the intermediate data structure, making it much harder to extend the language. Embedded languages (both deep and shallow) can usually be interpreted directly in the host language. This is, however, rather inefficient. If performance is an issue, code generation can be employed, and this typically done using a deep embedding [11].

The design of Feldspar tries to combine the advantages of shallow and deep implementations. The goal is to have the modularity and extensibility of a shallow embedding, while retaining the advantages of a deep embedding in order to be able to generate high-performance code. A nice combination was achieved by using a deeply embedded core language and building high-level interfaces as shallow extensions on top of the core. The low-level core language is purely functional, but with a small semantic gap to machine-oriented languages, such as C. Its intention is to be a suitable interface to the code generator, while being flexible enough to support any high-level interfaces.

The architecture of Feldspar's implementation is shown in figure 5. The deeply embedded core language consists of an intermediate representation (the "Core expression" box) and a user interface ("Core language"). Additionally, the user interface consists of a number of high-level libraries with shallow implementation (their meaning is expressed in terms of the core language constructs). The most prominent high level library is the vector library (section 4.3). There are also

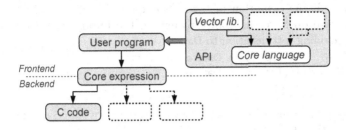

Fig. 5. Feldspar architecture

some more experimental libraries for synchronous streams, bit vectors, etc. The user's program generates a *core expression*, the internal data structure used as interface to the back ends. At the moment, there is only one back end – a code generator producing C code.

This architecture gives us certain kinds of modularity, as indicated in figure 5: high-level interfaces and back ends can be added independently of everything else. However, the core language expression type has, so far, been hard-coded in the implementation. This has made the implementation quite inflexible when it comes to changing the core language.

2.2   Early Implementations

The implementation style of the initial Feldspar versions is described in reference [2]. There, the core language expressions are defined using the data type in figure 6. Ignoring some details, this is a standard abstract syntax tree, where each constructor corresponds to a specific language construct. It is worth noting the $(:\twoheadrightarrow)$ type, which captures the notion of variable binding. For example, the second argument of Parallel is a representation of a function $\lambda i \to body$, where *body* is an expression of the element at index i.

```
data Expr a where
    Value       :: Storable a ⇒ a → Expr a
    Function    :: String → (a → b) → Expr (a → b)
    Application :: Expr (a → b) → Data a → Expr b
    Variable    :: Expr a
    IfThenElse  :: Data Bool → (a :⟶ b) → (a :⟶ b) → (Data a → Expr b)
    While       :: (a :⟶ Bool) → (a :⟶ a) → (Data a → Expr a)
    Parallel    :: Storable a ⇒ Data Int → (Int :⟶ a) → Expr [a]

data a :⟶ b = Lambda (Data a → Data b) (Data a) (Data b)

data Data a = Typeable a ⇒ Data (Ref (Expr a))
```

Fig. 6. Previous core language representation

Even though the definition in figure 6 is quite simple, it lacks the desired modularity. We do have the ability to extend the library with new high-level types by providing a translation to Data a:

```
frontEnd₁  :: MyType₁ a → Data a
frontEnd₂  :: MyType₂ a → Data a
   ...
```

(A more general translation mechanism is provided by the Syntactic class described in section 3.3.) We can also add any number of back ends:

```
backEnd₁ :: Data a → Back₁
backEnd₂ :: Data a → Back₂
   ...
```

But adding a constructor to Expr/Data requires editing the module containing their definition as well as the modules of all back ends to handle the new constructor.

Most of the constructors in the Expr type are general language constructs that are likely to be useful in other languages than Feldspar. This is especially true for variable binding, which is a tricky concept that gets reimplemented over and over again in various embedded languages. If we managed to make the language definition more modular, it should also be possible to put the most basic constructs in a library so that they can be reused in many different language implementations.

We have developed a library, Syntactic [1], that provides the extensibility and reuse described above. Section 3 introduces the Syntactic library, and section 4 gives an overview of how Feldspar is implemented using Syntactic.

3   Syntactic Library

When implementing deeply embedded DSLs in Haskell, a syntax tree is typically defined using an algebraic data type [11,2]. As an example, consider a small expression language with support for literals and addition:

```
data Expr₁ a
  where
    Lit₁  :: Num a ⇒ a → Expr₁ a
    Add₁ :: Num a ⇒ Expr₁ a → Expr₁ a → Expr₁ a
```

Expr₁ a is a generalized algebraic data type (GADT) [16] whose parameter a is used to denote the type of the value computed by the expression. It is easy to add a user friendly interface to this language by adding smart constructors and interpretation functions.

```
lit₁ :: Int → Expr₁ Int
lit₁ x = Lit₁ x

add₁ :: Expr₁ Int → Expr₁ Int → Expr₁ Int
add₁ x y = Add₁ x y
```

```
eval₁ :: Expr₁ Int → Int
eval₁ (Lit₁ x)   = x
eval₁ (Add₁ x y) = eval₁ x + eval₁ y
```

(In this case, the smart constructors only serve to hide implementation details and constraining the type, but in later implementations they will also take care of some tedious wrapping.)

The $eval_1$ function is just one possible interpretation of the expressions; we can easily extend the implementation with, say, pretty printing or any kind of program analysis. This can be done even without changing any existing code. However, adding a new construct to the language is not so easy. If we would like to extend the language with, say, multiplication, we would need to add a constructor to the $Expr_1$ type as well as adding a new case to $eval_1$ (and other interpretations). Thus, with respect to language extension, a simple GADT representation of a language is not modular. This limitation is one side of the well-known *expression problem* [18].

There are several reasons why modularity is a desired property of a language implementation. During the development phase, it makes it *easier to experiment* with new language constructs. It also allows constructs to be developed and tested independently, *simplifying collaboration*. However, there is no reason to limit the modularity to a single language implementation. For example, Lit_1 and Add_1 are conceptually generic constructs that might be useful in many different languages. In an ideal world, language implementations should be assembled from a library of generic building blocks in such a way that only the truly domain-specific constructs need to be implemented for each new language.

The purpose of the Syntactic library is to provide a basis for such modular languages. The library provides assistance for all aspects of an embedded DSL implementation:

- A generic AST representation that can be customized to form different languages.
- A set of generic constructs that can be used to build custom languages.
- A set of generic functions for interpretation and transformation.
- Generic functions and type classes for defining the user interface of the DSL.

3.1 Using Syntactic

The idea of the Syntactic library is to express all syntax trees as instances of a very general type AST^3, defined in Figure 7. Sym introduces a symbol from the domain dom, and (:$) applies such a constructor to one argument.

---

[3] The Typeable constraint on the (:$) constructor is from the standard Haskell module Data.Typeable, which, among other things, provides a type-safe cast operation. Syntactic uses type casting to perform certain syntactic transformations whose type-correctness cannot be verified by the type system. The Typeable constraint on (:$) leaks out to functions that construct abstract syntax, which explains the occurrences of Typeable constraints throughout this paper. It is possible to get rid of the constraint, at the cost of making certain AST functions more complicated.

```
data AST dom a
  where
    Sym  :: Signature a ⇒ dom a → AST dom a
    (:$) :: Typeable a  ⇒ AST dom (a :→ b) → AST dom (Full a)
                                            → AST dom b

type ASTF dom a = AST dom (Full a)

infixl 1 :$
```

Fig. 7. Type of generic abstract syntax trees

```
newtype Full a  = Full { result :: a }
newtype a :→ b = Partial (a → b)

infixr :→

class    Signature a
instance Signature (Full a)
instance Signature b ⇒ Signature (a :→ b)
```

Fig. 8. Types of symbol signatures

By instantiating the dom parameter with different types, it is possible to use AST to model a wide range of algebraic data types. Even GADTs can be modeled.

To model our previous expression language using AST, we rewrite it as follows:

```
data NumDomain₂ a
  where
    Lit₂ :: Num a ⇒ a → NumDomain₂ (Full a)
    Add₂ :: Num a ⇒ NumDomain₂ (a :→ a :→ Full a)

type Expr₂ a = ASTF NumDomain₂ a
```

The result type signatures of Lit_2 and Add_2 have a close correspondence to the Lit_1 and Add_1 constructors. In general, a constructor of type

$$C_2 :: T_2 \ (a :→ b :→ \ ... \ :→ Full \ x)$$

represents an ordinary GADT constructor of type

$$C_1 :: T_1 \ a → T_1 \ b → \ ... \ → T_1 \ x$$

Types built using $(:→)$ and Full are called *symbol signatures*, and they are defined in Figure 8.

In this encoding, the types $Expr_1$ and $Expr_2$ are completely isomorphic (up to strictness properties). The correspondence can be seen by reimplementing our smart constructors for the $Expr_2$ language:

```
lit₂ :: Int → Expr₂ Int
lit₂ a = Sym (Lit₂ a)
```

```
add₂ :: Expr₂ Int → Expr₂ Int → Expr₂ Int
add₂ x y = Sym Add₂ :$ x :$ y
```

The implementation of $eval_2$ is left as an exercise to the reader. Note that, in contrast to Add_1, the Add_2 constructor is *non-recursive*. Types based on AST normally rely on (:$) to handle all recursion.

Part of the reason for using the somewhat unnatural AST type instead of an ordinary GADT is that it directly supports definition of generic tree traversals. Generic programming using AST is not the subject of these notes, but the basic idea can be seen from a simple function returning the number of symbols in an expression:

```
size :: AST dom a → Int
size (Sym _)  = 1
size (s :$ a) = size s + size a
```

Note that this function is defined for all possible domains, which means that it can be reused in all kinds of language implementations. Such traversals are the basis of the generic interpretation and transformation functions provided by Syntactic.

3.2   Extensible Syntax

Support for generic traversals is one of the key features of the AST type. Another – equally important – feature is support for extensible syntax trees. We can note that $Expr_2$ is closed in the same way as $Expr_1$: Adding a constructor requires changing the definition of $NumDomain_2$. However, the AST type turns out to be compatible with *Data Types à la Carte* [17], which is a technique for encoding open data types in Haskell.[4]

The idea is to create symbol domains as co-products of smaller independent domains using the (:+:) type operator (provided by Syntactic). To demonstrate the idea, we split $NumDomain_2$ into two separate sub-domains and combine them into $NumDomain_3$, used to define $Expr_3$:

```
data Lit₃  a where Lit₃  :: Int → Lit₃ (Full Int)
data Add₃ a where Add₃ :: Add₃ (Int :→ Int :→ Full Int)
```

```
type NumDomain₃ = Lit₃ :+: Add₃
```

```
type Expr₃ a = ASTF NumDomain₃ a
```

The new type $Expr_3$ is again isomorphic $Expr_1$.

---

[4] The original Data Types à la Carte uses a combination of type-level fixed-points and co-products to achieve open data types. Syntactic only adopts the co-products, and uses the AST type instead of fixed-points.

Now, the trick to get extensible syntax is to not use a closed domain, such as NumDomain₃, but instead use constrained polymorphism to abstract away from the exact shape of the domain. The standard way of doing this for Data Types à la Carte is to use the inj method of the (:<:) type class (provided by Syntactic). Using inj, the smart constructors for Lit₃ and Add₃ can be defined thus:

```
lit₃ :: (Lit₃ :<: dom) ⇒ Int → ASTF dom Int
lit₃ a = Sym (inj (Lit₃ a))

add₃ :: (Add₃ :<: dom) ⇒ ASTF dom Int → ASTF dom Int → ASTF dom Int
add₃ x y = Sym (inj Add₃) :$ x :$ y
```

The definition of smart constructors can even be automated by using the function appSym (provided by Syntactic). The following definitions of lit₃ and add₃ are equivalent to the ones above:

```
lit₃ :: (Lit₃ :<: dom) ⇒ Int → ASTF dom Int
lit₃ a = appSym (Lit₃ a)

add₃ :: (Add₃ :<: dom) ⇒ ASTF dom Int → ASTF dom Int → ASTF dom Int
add₃ = appSym Add₃
```

A constraint such as (Lit₃ :<: dom) can be read as "dom contains Lit₃", which simply means that dom should be a co-product chain of the general form

```
(... :+: Lit₃ :+: ...)
```

One domain of this form is NumDomain₃, but any other domain that includes Lit₃ is also valid.

The fact that we have now achieved a modular language can be seen by noting that the definitions of Lit₃/lit₃ and Add₃/add₃ are *completely independent*, and could easily live in separate modules. Obviously, any number of additional constructs can be added in a similar way.

3.3 Syntactic Sugar

It is not very convenient to require all embedded programs to have the type AST. First of all, one might want to hide implementation details by defining a closed language:

```
type MyDomain = Lit₃ :+: Add₃

newtype Data a = Data {unData :: ASTF MyDomain a}
```

In fact this is exactly how Feldspar's Data type (see section 1) is defined (although with a different symbol domain).

Secondly, it is sometimes more convenient to use more "high-level" representations as long as these representations have a correspondence to an AST. Such high-level types are referred to as "syntactic sugar". Examples of syntactic sugar used in Feldspar are:

− The Data type
− Haskell tuples

– The Vector type (section 1.2)

One illustrating example is the fib function from section 1.1:

```
fib :: Data Index → Data Index
fib n = fst $ forLoop n (1,1) $ λi (a,b) → (b,a+b)
```

Here, the initial state is the *ordinary Haskell pair* (1,1). The body matches on the state a Haskell pair and constructs a new one as the next state. Finally, the fst function selects the first part of the state as the final result.

```
class Typeable (Internal a) ⇒ Syntactic a dom | a → dom
  where
    type Internal a
    desugar :: a → ASTF dom (Internal a)
    sugar   :: ASTF dom (Internal a) → a

instance Typeable a ⇒ Syntactic (ASTF dom a) dom
  where
    type Internal (ASTF dom a) = a
    desugar = id
    sugar   = id
```

Fig. 9. Syntactic sugar

Syntactic sugar is defined by the class in Figure 9. The desugar method converts from a high-level type to a corresponding AST representation, and sugar converts back. The associated type function Internal maps the high-level type to its internal representation. Note that this type function does not need to be injective. It is possible to have several syntactic sugar types sharing the same internal representation.

The Syntactic instance for Data looks as follows:

```
instance Typeable a ⇒ Syntactic (Data a) MyDomain
  where
    type Internal (Data a) = a
    desugar = unData
    sugar   = Data
```

In order to make a user interface based on syntactic sugar, such as Data, we simply use the function sugarSym instead of appSym that was used in section 3.1:

```
lit :: Int → Data Int
lit a = sugarSym (Lit₃ a)

add :: Data Int → Data Int → Data Int
add = sugarSym Add₃
```

As we can see, sugarSym is a highly overloaded function. But as long as it is given a sufficiently constrained type signature (that is compatible with the signature of the given symbol), it will just do "the right thing".

4   Feldspar Implementation

In this section, we give an overview of Feldspar's implementation. Although the back-end is a large part of the implementation (Figure 5), it will not be treated in this text. See reference [9] for more information about the back-end.

To make the presentation simpler and to highlight the modularity aspect, we will focus on a single language construct: parallel arrays.

4.1   Parallel Arrays

The syntactic symbols of Feldspar's array operations are defined in the Array type:

```
data Array a
  where
    Parallel :: Type a ⇒ Array (Length :→ (Index → a) :→ Full [a])
    Append   :: Type a ⇒ Array ([a] :→ [a] :→ Full [a])
    GetIx    :: Type a ⇒ Array ([a] :→ Index :→ Full a)
    SetIx    :: Type a ⇒ Array ([a] :→ Index :→ a :→ Full [a])
    ...
```

As we saw in section 1.1, we use [a] to denote an array with elements of type a. From now on, we will focus on the implementation of Parallel , and just note that the other constructs are implemented in a similar way.

After we have defined the syntactic symbol, we need to give it semantics. This is done by declaring the following instances:

```
instance Semantic Array
  where
    semantics Parallel = Sem "parallel"
        (λlen ixf → genericTake len $ map ixf [0..])
    ...
```

```
instance Render   Array where renderPart = renderPartSem
instance Eval     Array where evaluate = evaluateSem
instance EvalBind Array where evalBindSym = evalBindSymDefault
```

The Semantic instance says that Parallel has the name " parallel ", and that it is evaluated using the given lambda expression. The succeeding instances give access to functions like drawAST and eval, by deriving their behavior from the Semantic instance. This means that whenever we run something like:

```
*Main> eval $ parallel 10 (*2)
[0,2,4,6,8,10,12,14,16,18]
```

it is the function in the above semanticEval field that does the actual evaluation.

The implementation contains a number of other trivial class instances, but we will omit those from the presentation.

Now it is time to define the user interface to Parallel . This follows the exact same pattern as we saw in section 3.3:

```
parallel :: Type a ⇒ Data Length → (Data Index → Data a) → Data [a]
parallel = sugarSym Parallel
```

Note how the function (Index → a) in the signature for Parallel became a function (Data Index → Data a) in the user interface. All of this is handled by the sugarSym function.

In addition to the above simple declarations, the implementation of parallel also consists of optimization rules and code generation, which are out of the scope of these notes. However, it is important to look at what we get from those few lines of code that we have given so far. It turns out to be quite a lot:

We have defined a typed abstract syntax symbol Parallel and its corresponding user function parallel . We have derived various interpretation functions (evaluation, rendering, alpha-equivalence, etc.) by providing very minimal information about the specific nature of parallel . We even get access to various syntactic transformations (constant folding, invariant code hoisting, etc.) without adding any additional code. All of this is due to the generic nature of the Syntactic library. Note also that the implementation of parallel is completely independent of the other constructs in the language, a property due to the extensible syntax provided by Syntactic (section 3.2).

Having seen the important bits of how the core language is implemented we can now move on to see how the vector library is implemented on top of the core (recall Figure 5).

4.2   Assembling the Language

Once a number of symbol types (such as Array above) have been defined, they are assembled using the same pattern as in section 3.3,

```
newtype Data a = Data {unData :: ASTF FeldDomainAll a}
```

where FeldDomainAll is the complete symbol domain. Additionally, to make type signatures look nicer, we define the Syntax class recognized from the examples in section 1:

```
class
    ( Syntactic a FeldDomainAll
    , SyntacticN a (ASTF FeldDomainAll (Internal a))
    , Type (Internal a)
    ) ⇒
    Syntax a

instance Type a ⇒ Syntax (Data a)
```

Syntax does not have any methods; it is merely used as an alias for its super-class constraints. The most important constraint is Syntactic a FeldDomainAll, which can now be written more succinctly as Syntax a. In other words, all functions overloaded by Syntax get access to the syntactic sugar interface described in section 3.3.

The Type class is the set of all value types supported by Feldspar (for example, Bool, Int32, (Float, Index), etc.). The SyntacticN class is beyond the scope of these notes; interested readers are referred to the API documentation [1].

4.3   Vector Library

The vector library (module Feldspar.Vector) provides a type for "virtual" vectors – vectors that do not (necessarily) have any run-time representation. Vectors are defined as:

```
data Vector a
    = Empty
    | Indexed
        { segmentLength :: Data Length
        , segmentIndex  :: Data Index → a
        , continuation  :: Vector a
        }
```

This recursive type can be seen as a list of segments, where each segment is defined by a length and an index projection function. The reason for having vectors consisting of several segments is to allow efficient code generation of vector append. However, in this presentation, we are going to look at a simpler vector representation, consisting only of a single segment:[5]

```
data Vector a
    = Indexed
        { length :: Data Length
        , index  :: Data Index → a
        }
```

This is essentially a pair – at the Haskell-level – of a length and an index projection function. The meaning of a non-nested vector is given by the following function:

```
freezeVector :: Type a ⇒ Vector (Data a) → Data [a]
freezeVector vec = parallel (length vec) (index vec)
```

That is, a Vector with a given length and index projection has the same meaning as a parallel with the same length and projection function. A small example:

```
*Main> eval $ freezeVector $ Indexed 10 (*2)
[0,2,4,6,8,10,12,14,16,18]
```

With this simple representation of vectors, it becomes straightforward to define many of Haskell's standard operations on lists. Some examples are given in figure 10.

Does it work? Let us check:

```
*Main> eval $ freezeVector $ map (*2) $ Indexed 10 (*2)
[0,4,8,12,16,20,24,28,32,36]
```

---

[5] Note that for programs that do not use the (++) operation (which is the case for all but one of the examples in this document), there will only ever be a single segment, in which case the two representations are equivalent.

```
take :: Data Length → Vector a → Vector a
take n (Indexed l ixf) = Indexed (min n l) ixf

map :: (a → b) → Vector a → Vector b
map f (Indexed len ixf) = Indexed len (f ∘ ixf)

zip :: Vector a → Vector b → Vector (a,b)
zip a b = Indexed (length a 'min' length b)
                  (λi → (index a i, index b i))

zipWith :: (a → b → c) → Vector a → Vector b → Vector c
zipWith f a b = map (uncurry f) $ zip a b

fold :: Syntax a ⇒ (a → b → a) → a → Vector b → a
fold f a (Indexed len ixf) = forLoop len a (λi st → f st (ixf i))

sum :: (Num a, Syntax a) ⇒ Vector a → a
sum = fold (+) 0
```

Fig. 10. Definition of some vector operations

This is all very well, but things start to get really interesting when we note that we can actually make Vector an instance of Syntactic. A first attempt at doing this might be:

```
instance Type a ⇒ Syntactic (Vector (Data a)) FeldDomainAll
    where
        type Internal (Vector (Data a)) = [a]
        desugar = desugar ∘ freezeVector
        sugar   = thawVector ∘ sugar

thawVector :: Type a ⇒ Data [a] → Vector (Data a)
thawVector arr = Indexed (getLength arr) (getIx arr)
```

The function thawVector is the inverse of freezeVector. This works, but only for non-nested vectors. A better solution is given in figure 11. This instance works for elements of any Syntax type, which means that it even handles nested vectors.

```
instance Syntax a ⇒ Syntactic (Vector a) FeldDomainAll
    where
        type Internal (Vector a) = [Internal a]
        desugar = desugar ∘ freezeVector ∘ map (sugar ∘ desugar)
        sugar   = map (sugar ∘ desugar) ∘ thawVector ∘ sugar

instance Syntax a ⇒ Syntax (Vector a)
```

Fig. 11. Syntactic instance for Vector

Having a Syntactic instance for Vector means that they can now work seamlessly with the rest of the language. Here is an example of a function using (?)
to select between two vectors:

```
f :: Vector (Data Index) → Vector (Data Index)
f vec = length vec > 10 ? (take 10 vec, map (*3) vec)
```

Since Feldspar's eval function is also overloaded using Syntax,

```
eval :: Syntax a ⇒ a → Internal a
```

we can even evaluate vector programs directly just like any other Feldspar
program:

```
*Main> eval f [5,6,7]
[15,18,21]
```

It is important to note here that Vector is an ordinary Haskell type that is not
part of Feldspar's core language. Relating to figure 5, Vector lives in one of the
top boxes of the API, and is not part of the core language. This means that
the back ends have no way of knowing what a Vector is. The reason vectors are
still useful is that we have an automatic translation between vectors and core
expressions via the Syntactic class. This technique provides a very powerful, yet
very simple, way of extending the language with new constructs.

Vector Fusion. The fact that vectors are not part of the core language, has the
nice consequence that they are guaranteed to be removed at compile time. This
is the underlying explanation for the kind of fusion that was seen in section 1.2.
Take, for example, the scalar product function:

```
scalarProd :: (Num a, Syntax a) ⇒ Vector a → Vector a → a
scalarProd as bs = sum (zipWith (*) as bs)
```

Using the definitions of sum, zipWith, zip and map in figure 10, scalarProd can be
transformed in the following sequence of steps:

```
— Definition of zipWith and zip
scalarProd2 as bs
   = sum (
       map (uncurry (*)) (
       Indexed
           (length as 'min' length bs)
           (λi → (index as i,index bs i))
       )
   )

— Definition of map
scalarProd3 as bs
   = sum (
       Indexed
           (length as 'min' length bs)
           (λi → index as i * index bs i)
       )
```

```
— Definition of sum
scalarProd4 as bs
    = forLoop
          (length as 'min' length bs)
          0
          (λi st → st + index as i * index bs i )
```

As we can see, the end result is a single forLoop, where the multiplication and the accumulation have been fused together in the body. Note that these reductions are performed by Haskell's evaluation, which is why we can guarantee *statically* that expressions of this form will always be fused.

The only exception to this static guarantee is the function freezeVector which will compute the vector using parallel (which is not guaranteed to be fused). Functions outside of the vector API (such as forLoop) can only access vectors using desugar/sugar. Since desugar implicitly introduces freezeVector, this means that functions outside of the vector API will not be able to guarantee fusion.

We have chosen to implement vectors as an additional high-level library. It would have been possible to express all vector operations directly in the core language, and implement fusion as a syntactic transformation. However, then we would not have been able to guarantee fusion in the same way as we can now. Imagine we had this core-level implementation of reverse (available in the vector library):

```
rev :: Type a ⇒ Data [a] → Data [a]
rev arr = parallel l (λi → getIx arr (l−i−1))
    where
        l = getLength arr
```

Then we would generally not be able to tell whether it will be fused with the array arr. If arr is produced by another parallel, fusion is possible, but if arr is produced by, for example, sequential (section 1.1), fusion is not possible. This is because sequential can only produce its element in ascending order, while rev indexes in reverse order. The vector library reverse, on the other hand, will *unconditionally* fuse with its argument.

5   Discussion

We have presented Feldspar, an embedded language for DSP algorithm design. One key aspect of Feldspar is that it is purely functional, despite the fact that what we wish to do is to provide an alternative to C, which is currently used for DSP programming. We have shown how Feldspar consists of a small core at about the same abstraction level as C, and libraries built upon the core that raise the level of abstraction at which the programmer works. Thus we intend to bring the benefits of functional programming to a new audience. As a result we do not really have a novel language design to present, but rather a new setting in which functional programming with a strong emphasis on higher order functions can be used. Doing array programming in a relatively simple, purely functional language allows the Feldspar user to construct algorithmic blocks from smaller components. The purely functional setting gives a kind of modularity that is just not present in C. It is easy to explore algorithms by plugging components together in new ways. One can remove just part of an algorithm and replace it with a function with the same input-output behaviour, but perhaps different performance. The fact that Feldspar programs are compact is important here. In the first part of these notes, we tried to illustrate this aspect of Feldspar. Our hope is that this ease of algorithm exploration will be a key benefit of taking the step from C to Feldspar.

In the implementation sections, we tried to convey the most important parts of Feldspar's implementation, focusing mainly on the underlying principles (the Syntactic library), but also showing concrete details of the implementation of parallel and the vector library.

There was not enough room to go into all details of the implementation. Readers who are interested more details are encouraged to look at NanoFeldspar, a small proof-of-concept implementation of Feldspar shipped with the Syntactic package. To download NanoFeldspar, simply run:

```
> cabal unpack syntactic-0.8
> cd syntactic-0.8/Examples/NanoFeldspar
```

NanoFeldspar contains simplified versions of Feldspar's core language and the vector library. There is no back-end, but it is possible to print out the syntax tree to get an idea of what the generated code would look like. NanoFeldspar follows the modular implementation style described in section 3.2, and it should be perfectly possible to use NanoFeldspar as a basis for implementing other embedded languages.

Some additional details of the Feldspar implementation can be found in our report on adding support for mutable data structures to Feldspar [15]. This paper gives a very nice example of modular language extension using Syntactic.

An important part of Feldspar's implementation is the ability to add new libraries, such as the vector library, without changing the existing core language or the code generator. In addition to the vector library, Feldspar has (more or less experimental) libraries for synchronous streams, Repa-style arrays [14], bit vectors and fixed-point numbers, etc.

5.1   Limitations

Feldspar currently only generates pure algorithmic functions. What is missing in order to develop a complete application in Feldspar is the ability to coordinate the generated functions. This requires language support for parallelism and concurrency, memory management, real-time scheduling, etc. We are currently working on adding such support to the language.

Syntactic. Although Syntactic has worked very well for the implementation of Feldspar, we do not expect it to be suitable for all kinds of embedded languages. While the AST type can model a wide range of data types, it does not handle mutually recursive types. For example, AST is not suited to model the following pair of data types:

```
type Var = String

data Expr a where
  Var  :: Var → Expr a
  Lit  :: Num a ⇒ a → Expr a
  Add  :: Num a ⇒ Expr a → Expr a → Expr a
  Exec :: Stmt → Var → Expr a

data Stmt where
  Assign :: Var → Expr a → Stmt
  Seq    :: Stmt → Stmt → Stmt
  Loop   :: Expr Int → Stmt → Stmt
  ...
```

Here, Expr is an expression language capable of embedding imperative code using the Exec constructor. Stmt is an imperative language using the Expr type for pure expressions. In the AST type, all symbols are "first-class", which means that we cannot easily group the symbols as in the example above.

Note, however, that the above language can easily be modeled as a single data type with monadic expressions. In fact, the latest Feldspar release has support for mutable data structures with a monadic interface. Their implementation is described in [15].

It is also important to be aware that many of the reusable components provided by Syntactic (syntactic constructs, interpretations, transformations, etc.) assume that the language being implemented has a pure functional semantics. However, this is not a limitation of the AST type itself, but rather of the surrounding utility library. There is nothing preventing adding utilities for different kinds of languages if the need arises.

5.2   Related Work

Work related to Feldspar and its implementation has been covered by previous publications [3,2].

Syntactic shares common goals with a lot of related work on implementation of domain-specific languages. However, in the context of strongly typed embedded languages, Syntactic is rather unique in providing a library of reusable building blocks for language implementation. Its support for language extension is derived from Data Types à la Carte [17]. A quite different approach to extensible embedded languages is Finally Tagless [6]. Although very elegant, neither of these techniques provides libraries of reusable implementation tools.

6   Conclusion

Feldspar is a slightly strange beast: an embedded language in Haskell that tries to be as much like Haskell (or at least a simple subset of Haskell) as possible.

Once one has chosen this direction, the hard work is not in language design but in finding ways to present the user with this illusion, while generating high performance C code. We have (so far) performed only one brief test in which Ericsson engineers used Feldspar. The generated code was of satisfactory quality but what was most striking about the experiment was the realisation, by observing the reactions of our Ericsson colleagues, that it is purely functional programming, with all its familiar benefits, that we are trying to sell, and not a new language called Feldspar!

Building on the Syntactic library, Feldspar has a modular, easily extensible implementation. Much of its functionality is derived from the generic building blocks provided from Syntactic. This has been demonstrated concretely in the implementation of parallel (section 4.1):

- The implementation of parallel is independent of other language constructs.
- The implementation of parallel is covered by a few tens of lines of code, mostly in declarative form.
- A lot of details are handled by the Syntactic library: evaluation, rendering, alpha-equivalence, certain optimizations, etc. Very little extra code is needed to make these generic functions work for parallel .

Furthermore, the vector library (section 4.3) is implemented as an additional library completely separate from the core language. This design allows us to implement many of Haskell's list processing functions in just a few lines each, and still be able to generate high-performance C code from vector-based programs.

Appendix: C Code from the fft4 Function

The first page of code contains loops for computing twiddle factors and for doing bit reversal. The second page contains the two nested for loops that do the FFT calculation. (The code is split only for display purposes.)

```
/*
 * Memory information
 *
 * Local: complex float array, complex float array
 * Input: unsigned 32-bit integer, complex float array
 * Output: complex float array
 *
 */
void test(struct array * mem, uint32_t v0, struct array * v1, struct array *
out)
{
    uint32_t v19;
    uint32_t v20;
    float complex v21;
    uint32_t len0;
    uint32_t v23;
    uint32_t len1;
```

```
v19 = ~(~((4294967295 << v0)));
v20 = ~((4294967295 << v0));
v21 = complex_fun_float((float)((1 << v0)), 0.0f);
len0 = (1 << (v0 − 1));
for(uint32_t v15 = 0; v15 < len0; v15 += 1)
{
    at(float complex,&at(struct array,mem,0),v15) =
    cexpf((((0.0f+0.0fi) − ((complex_fun_float((float)(v15), 0.0f) *
        (0.0f+6.2831854820251465fi)) / v21)));
}
setLength(&at(struct array,mem,0), len0);
v23 = (v0 − 1);
len1 = getLength(v1);
for(uint32_t v11 = 0; v11 < len1; v11 += 1)
{
    at(float complex,out,v11) = at(float complex,v1,((v19 & v11) |
rotateL_fun_uint32(reverseBits_fun_uint32((v20 & v11)), v0)));
}

setLength(out, len1);
for(uint32_t v12 = 0; v12 < v0; v12 += 1)
{
    uint32_t v24;
    uint32_t v25;
    uint32_t v26;
    uint32_t len2;

    v24 = (1 << v12);
    v25 = pow_fun_uint32(2, v12);
    v26 = (v23 − v12);
    len2 = getLength(out);
    for(uint32_t v14 = 0; v14 < len2; v14 += 1)
    {
        uint32_t v27;
        uint32_t v28;
        float complex v29;
        float complex v30;

        v27 = testBit_fun_uint32(v14, v12);
        v28 = (v14 ^ v24);
        if(testBit_fun_uint32(v28, v12))
        {
            v29 = (at(float complex,&at(struct array,mem,0),
                ((v28 % v25) << v26)) * at(float complex,out,v28));
        }
        else
        {
            v29 = at(float complex,out,v28);
        }
        if(v27)
```

```
        {
            v30 = (at(float complex,&at(struct array ,mem,0),
                   ((v14 % v25) << v26)) * at(float complex,out,v14));
        }
        else
        {
            v30 = at(float complex,out,v14);
        }
        if(v27)
        {
            at(float complex,&at(struct array ,mem,1),v14) = (v29 - v30);
        }
        else
        {
            at(float complex,&at(struct array ,mem,1),v14) = (v30 + v29);
        }
    }
    setLength(&at(struct array ,mem,1), len2);
    copyArray(out, &at(struct array ,mem,1));
}
}
```

Acknowledgements. Work on Feldspar has been funded by Ericsson, the Swedish basic research funding agency (Vetenskapsrådet), the Swedish Foundation for Strategic Research (SSF), and the Hungarian National Development Agency.

Feldspar is a cooperation between Ericsson, Chalmers University and Eötvös Loránd (ELTE) University. The authors would like to thank the Feldspar team at Chalmers and ELTE for fruitful collaboration.

We acknowledge the constructive suggestions of an anonymous referee, who helped us to improve these notes.

References

1. Syntactic library, version 0.8,
   http://hackage.haskell.org/package/syntactic-0.8
2. Axelsson, E., Claessen, K., Sheeran, M., Svenningsson, J., Engdal, D., Persson, A.: The Design and Implementation of Feldspar- An Embedded Language for Digital Signal Processing. In: Hage, J., Morazán, M.T. (eds.) IFL 2010. LNCS, vol. 6647, pp. 121–136. Springer, Heidelberg (2011)
3. Axelsson, E., Claessen, K., Dévai, G., Horváth, Z., Keijzer, K., Lyckegård, B., Persson, A., Sheeran, M., Svenningsson, J., Vajda, A.: Feldspar: A Domain Specific Language for Digital Signal Processing algorithms. In: 8th ACM/IEEE International Conference on Formal Methods and Models for Codesign (MEMOCODE 2010), pp. 169–178. IEEE Computer Society (2010)
4. Batcher, K.E.: Sorting networks and their applications. In: AFIPS Spring Joint Computing Conference, pp. 307–314 (1968)

5. Bjesse, P., Claessen, K., Sheeran, M., Singh, S.: Lava: Hardware Design in Haskell. In: ICFP 1998: Proceedings of the Third ACM SIGPLAN International Conference on Functional Programming, pp. 174–184. ACM (1998)

6. Carette, J., Kiselyov, O., Shan, C.: Finally tagless, partially evaluated: Tagless staged interpreters for simpler typed languages. Journal of Functional Programming 19(05), 509–543 (2009)

7. Claessen, K., Sheeran, M., Svensson, B.J.: Expressive array constructs in an embedded GPU kernel programming language. In: Proceedings of the 7th Workshop on Declarative Aspects and Applications of Multicore Programming, DAMP 2012, pp. 21–30. ACM (2012)

8. Cooley, J.W., Tukey, J.W.: An algorithm for the machine calculation of complex Fourier series. Math. Comp. 19, 297–301 (1965)

9. Dévai, G., Tejfel, M., Gera, Z., Páli, G., Nagy, G., Horváth, Z., Axelsson, E., Sheeran, M., Vajda, A., Lyckegård, B., Persson, A.: Efficient code generation from the high-level domain-specific language Feldspar for DSPs. In: ODES-8: 8th Workshop on Optimizations for DSP and Embedded Systems (2010)

10. Duhamel, P., Vetterli, M.: Fourier Transforms: A Tutorial Review and a State of the Art. In: Madisetti, V.K., Williams, D.B. (eds.) Digital Signal Processing Handbook. CRC Press LLC (1999)

11. Elliott, C., Finne, S., de Moor, O.: Compiling embedded languages. Journal of Functional Programming 13(3), 455–481 (2003)

12. Gill, A.: Type-safe observable sharing in Haskell. In: Haskell 2009: Proceedings of the 2nd ACM SIGPLAN Symposium on Haskell, pp. 117–128. ACM (2009)

13. Hudak, P.: Modular domain specific languages and tools. In: ICSR 1998: Proceedings of the 5th International Conference on Software Reuse, pp. 134–142. IEEE Computer Society Press (1998)

14. Keller, G., Chakravarty, M.M.T., Leshchinskiy, R., Peyton Jones, S., Lippmeier, B.: Regular, shape-polymorphic, parallel arrays in Haskell. In: Proceedings of the 15th ACM SIGPLAN International Conference on Functional Programming, ICFP 2010, pp. 261–272. ACM (2010)

15. Persson, A., Axelsson, E., Svenningsson, J.: Generic Monadic Constructs for Embedded Languages. In: IFL 2011: 23rd International Symposium on Implementation and Application of Functional Languages. LNCS, vol. 7257. Springer, Heidelberg (2012)

16. Schrijvers, T., Peyton Jones, S., Sulzmann, M., Vytiniotis, D.: Complete and decidable type inference for GADTs. In: Proc. 14th ACM SIGPLAN International Conference on Functional Programming, pp. 341–352. ACM (2009)

17. Swierstra, W.: Data types à la carte. Journal of Functional Programming 18(04), 423–436 (2008)

18. Wadler, P.: The expression problem (1998), http://www.daimi.au.dk/~madst/tool/papers/expression.txt

Static Analysis of Complex Software Systems Implemented in Erlang[*]

Melinda Tóth and István Bozó

Eötvös Loránd University, Budapest, Hungary
{tothmelinda,bozoistvan}@caesar.elte.hu

Abstract. Static software analyser tools use different levels of intermediate source code representations that depend on the syntax and semantics of the language to be analysed. Most of the analyser tools use graph
representation to efficiently retrieve information. Building such graphs
for dynamically typed languages, such as Erlang, is not straightforward.
In this paper we present static analysis methods to define the Dependency Graph representation of Erlang programs. The introduced methods cover the data-, control-, behaviour-flow and dependency analyses
for sequential and parallel language constructs.

1 Introduction

Static analysis of the software products is a widely used technique to support
different phases of the software development lifecycle. These analysis techniques
can help in software development and maintenance tasks like: debugging, testing,
code comprehension, cost estimation, model visualisation of programs, coding
convention checking, or detecting possible errors. The common part of them is
the analysis of the source code without actually executing the target program.

To perform a static analysis, an intermediate representation of the source code
is required. The efficiency of the analysis highly depends on this representation.
For this reason different intermediate source code representations have to be
developed for different static analysis purposes. For instance, more detailed information is required for source code transformation and manipulation (in case
of a refactoring tool) than for extracting the model of a live code. For source
code transformation, beside the semantic information, the lexical and syntactic
information is essential. For model extraction, only the high-level entities and
the connection between them is required. Depending on the required information
for the analysis, first we need to build the basic representation from the source
code (e.g. AST). Then we extend the basic representation with the information
of higher-level of abstraction (e.g. semantic information).

In this paper we define various forms of intermediate source code representations for the programs written in Erlang [7]. The language was designed to
develop highly concurrent, distributed, fault tolerant systems with soft real-time

---

[*] Supported by TECH_08_A2-SZOMIN08.

V. Zsók, Z. Horváth, and R. Plasmeijer (Eds.): CEFP 2011, LNCS 7241, pp. 440–498, 2012.

characteristics such as telecommunication systems. The language is dynamically typed, which makes the static analysis even harder.

We introduce a Semantic Program Graph to represent lexical, syntactic and different semantic information about the source code. We also give a formal description of the language and formalise the rules for the building of Data-Flow Graph and Control-Flow Graph. The data-flow is analysed from different aspects: zeroth and first order analysis, and the concurrent data-flow through message passing. Besides the data-flow analysis, the paper covers the control dependency relations, and some examples are given to the usage.

The information derived from the presented analyses can be used in several applications. Dependency Graphs are widely used in program slicing algorithms to perform change impact analysis. We have defined the impact analysis for Erlang programs [4] to select the subset of the program containing those expressions that are potentially affected by a change on the source code. Based on the result we can determine the test cases that are affected by the change on the source code and should be rechecked.

The Dependency Graph includes the control and data dependencies among expressions. Based on these dependencies we can perform further analysis to find the parallelisable components that can be run in parallel efficiently and without high synchronisation costs. Hence we have to calculate strongly connected components on the dependency graph, and analyse the resulted components.

The presented intermediate source code representations and the result of the analyses are integrated to the source code analyser and transformer tool, RefactorErl [2,3]. We briefly introduce the semantic query language of RefactorErl, which is applicable to query the result of the presented analyses during the software development, maintenance or testing. The data-flow analysis is also used in some of the refactoring steps. To ensure safe transformation, the source code has to be analysed and allow the transformation if every precondition holds. The changes have to be propagated in the source code, so data-flow analysis is required to detect those expressions where further transformations are necessary.

The paper is structured as follows. In Section 1.1, we introduce the syntax of Erlang programs. In Section 2, we present the Semantic Program Graph to represent the Erlang programs. In Section 3, we describe the data-, behaviour- and control-flow graph building rules and further analysis based on the built graphs: data-flow reaching, concurrent data-flow analysis, control dependency analysis, program slicing. Section 4 describes the static analysis in RefactorErl and a query language to support querying the result of the presented analysis by the user. Section 5 discusses related work and Section 6 concludes the paper.

1.1   The Syntax of Erlang Programs

Our research focuses on the Erlang programs. Erlang is a dynamically typed functional programming language that was designed for building highly concurrent, fault-tolerant, distributed systems with soft-real time characteristic. In its syntax the functional style is mixed with some Prolog like elements.

In addition to the functional language constructs, the language has built in support for concurrency. The Erlang Virtual Machine handles the light-weight processes that communicate with asynchronous message passing.

We formalised the rules of our static analysis and the built graphs according to the syntax and semantics of language elements. We introduce the detailed syntax description of the language in Appendix A, and in Figure 1 we give a short overview of it.

An Erlang function (F) contains several function clauses. Each clause introduces the name of the function, the formal parameters of the function (patterns), optionally a guard expression and a sequence of expressions to be executed. The expression (E) types are detailed in Appendix A. In Figure 1 we show the syntax of the match expression $(P = E)$, the tuple constructor $(\{E, ..., E\})$ and the function call $(E(E, ..., E))$. Patterns (P) are restricted to constant values, variables and tuple and list selectors.

$V ::=$ variables (including the underscore pattern (_))
$A ::=$ atoms
$I ::=$ integers
$K ::= A \mid I \mid$ other constants (e.g. string, float, char)
$P ::= K \mid V \mid \{P, ..., P\} \mid [P, ..., P|P]$
$F ::= A(P, ..., P)$ when $E \rightarrow E, ..., E;$

$\quad \vdots$

$\quad A(P, ..., P)$ when $E \rightarrow E, ..., E.$
$E ::= K \mid V \mid \{E, ..., E\} \mid E_{List} \mid P = E \mid E(E, ..., E) \mid ...$

Fig. 1. Erlang syntax (partial)

2   Source Code Representation

Different source code analysis techniques exist, and the most common part of them is the usage of some intermediate source code representation for the analysis.

The most simple and the most current representation is the Abstract Syntax Tree (AST) of the program. The AST of a program contains the syntactic structure of the program without representing every detail about the source code. The main disadvantage of using an AST in further program analysis is the high cost of information retrieval: in most cases a whole AST traversal is needed to gather the required information about the source code. For instance, if we want to know where a function is called, you have to scan the AST of every module. Therefore, we choose a graph to represent the syntax and also the semantic information about the source code.

2.1   Semantic Program Graph

The Semantic Program Graph (SPG) is a rooted, directed, labelled and indexed graph that represents the Erlang source code in three different layers:

- *Lexical layer* – contains the token information about the source code. This layer stores information about the whitespaces and comments, and contains both the original and the preprocessed version of tokens.
- *Syntactic level* – contains the syntax tree of the source code.
- *Semantic layer* – contains extra calculated semantic information about the source code, such as module, function references, variable binding.

The SPG contains **nodes** and **directed edges** among the nodes. There are different node **classes** and edge types. The graph has a special starting node, the *root* node, the only element of the root node class. The root node is the starting point of the most of the queries on the graph. The other nodes of the SPG are the lexical (*lex*), syntactic (*file, form, clause, expr, typexp*) and semantic (*module, func, record, field, variable*) entities of the language. Every graph node has a set of **attributes** based on its class, e.g. the *function* has a *name* and an *arity* attribute. The directed edges represent the relations among the language entities. Each edge is **labelled** to represent different kinds of the certain relations between the nodes, thus we can say that the labels are the types of the edges. Each edge type points from a certain graph node class to another node class. For instance, the edge *moddef* links a *module* semantic node to a *file* syntactic node. The edges are also **indexed**, so links with the same tag and starting from the same node are maintained in their order.

We have defined the my module in Figure 2. The module contains a macro (EOL/1) and a function (f/1). The macro EOL has a string parameter and it simply appends a newline character to the end of the string. The function f has a parameter S and it calls the put_chars function from the io module with its parameter S.

```
-module(my).

-define(EOL(X), X ++ "\n").

f(S) ->
    io:put_chars(?EOL(S)).
```

Fig. 2. Example of Erlang source code

The syntax tree of the module my is shown in Figure 3. The syntax tree is built from the preprocessed source code, so all the macro applications are substituted (as {expr, 8} shows it in Figure 3).

The syntax tree is the base of the SPG. The syntactic and semantic levels of the SPG are shown in Figure 4. The oval boxes form the syntactic level of the graph (that contains the syntax tree of the program) and the hexagonal nodes and the dashed links form the semantic level of the SPG. There are semantic nodes for each defined and referred module (my, io), function (f, put_chars) and variable (S). These nodes are linked to the syntactic nodes to represent the definition or the reference to these entities (e.g. varref, varbind, moddef, fundef).

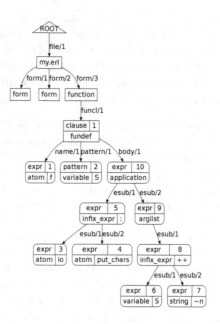

Fig. 3. Syntax tree for module my

2.2 Building the Semantic Program Graph

The first step in creating the SPG is to build the syntax tree. The syntax tree is built of the scanned token list of the program. Before building the syntax tree we have to take into account the preprocessor directives and perform the file inclusion and macro substitution. We build the syntax tree of the programs from the preprocessed tokens. However, scanners and parsers can be generated based on the grammar of the language, but the preprocessing mechanisms in most of the cases are hard coded to the system.

The necessary information for the building of the semantic level of the graph is calculated by traversing the AST. The AST (and the SPG built from the AST) can be traversed by using **path expressions**. A path expression is a sequence of graph edge labels to be followed from a starting node. For instance, if we want to find the defined functions in the system, we have to start the query from the root node, and ask first the defined modules (*module* edge) and from the modules we can ask the defined functions of the modules (*func* edge), i.e. we have to follow the *[module, func]* sequence of labels from the root node. The syntax of path expressions is described in Figure 5. The main advantage of the graph representation is that the most frequently used queries have a fixed length, and there is no need to traverse the whole graph.

The structure of the *path expressions* and the filters are written according to the Erlang EDoc type specification syntax [6] in Figure 5. The type `path()` is a sequence of `PathElem`. The `PathElem` can be a graph edge label (*Tag*) or a graph edge label with filtering options ({*Tag, Index*} or {*Tag, Filter*}).

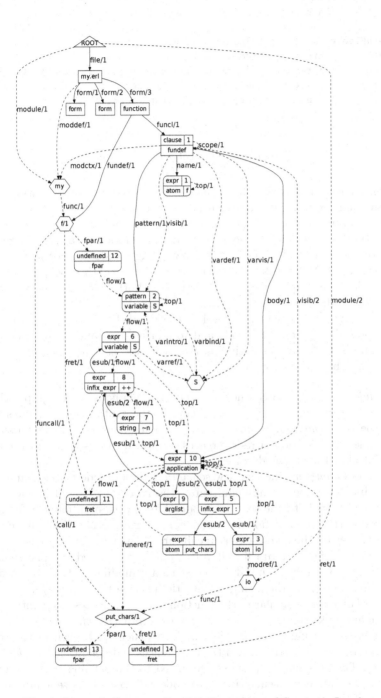

Fig. 4. Semantic Program Graph – Syntactic and Semantic Level

```
path() = [PathElem]

PathElem = Tag | {Tag, Index} | {Tag, Filter}
Tag      = atom() | {atom(), back}
Index    = integer() | {integer(), integer()} | {integer(), last}
Filter   = {Filter, 'and', Filter} | {Filter, 'or', Filter} |
           {'not', Filter} | {Attrib, Op, term()}
Attrib   = atom()
Op       = '==' | '/=' | '=<' | '>=' | '<' | '>'
```

Fig. 5. The syntax of *path expression*

The former case represents the labelled graph edges to follow during graph traversal, and the latter one makes it possible to select a subset of graph nodes during the graph traversal according to the given filtering options. It is possible to filter the result with syntactic or semantic information (`{Tag, Filter}`) and also with the indices of edges in the graph (`{Tag, Index}`). For instance, the pair `{esub, {6,8}}` denotes the sixth, seventh and eighth subexpressions of a graph node. The graph edges can be traversed both forward (`Tag = atom()`) and backward direction (`Tag = {atom(), 'back'}`).

The building of the semantic level of the graph has two phases: to gather information about the source code and to add new semantic nodes and edges to the graph. Different semantic analysers can add several kinds of semantic information about the source code:

- *Module analyser* – adds a new semantic module node to the graph when a module definition or reference is found in the syntax tree and links them to the node (*moddef, modref*). Once a module node is added for a specific module, its definition or its references are linked to this node. Each module is linked to the *root* node (*module*).
- *Function analyser* – adds a new semantic function node to the graph when the first reference or the definition of the function is found in the syntax tree and links it to the semantic node. Afterwards, each found reference is linked to the semantic function node. For instance, local calls are linked with the *funlref* labelled edge, external calls are linked with *funeref* edge, import or export references are linked with *funexp, funimp* edges. The semantic function node is also linked to the semantic module node of the defining module (*func*) and the defining syntactic function form (*fundef*).
- *Record analyser* – similar to the function analyser, creates a semantic record node and links the definition and references to it (*recref, recdef*). The analyser creates semantic record field nodes to each field given in the record definition and links them with their references and definitions (*fielddef, fieldref*). The semantic field nodes are linked to the defining semantic record node (*field*) and the semantic record node is linked to the semantic module node of the containing module (*record*).
- *Context analyser* – to help in further analysis and speed up queries on the graph, the SPG introduces some structural context edges. Every clause has

a link to its direct subexpressions (*visib*), and each compound expression has a *clause* edge to its clauses. The subexpressions are linked to their topmost super-expression with *top* edges. The clauses also have a hierarchy as the subexpressions do. Each clause is linked to its containing scope clause with a *scope* edge, and the scope clauses are linked to the containing function clause with a *functx* edge.

- *Variable analyser* – variables are analysed upon their containing scope information. Once a variable is found in the syntax tree, its scope has to be determined. The semantic variable node is linked to its scope clause with a *vardef* edge and it is linked to every clause where it is visible (*varvis*). The references and the bindings are linked to the variable node with *varref, varbind* edges.

Further semantic analysis can be performed based on the syntax tree and the listed semantic information, such as interprocedural data-flow analysis, dynamic function call analysis or control-flow analysis.

3   Source Code Analysis

Based on the syntactic and semantic information stored in the Semantic Program Graph of Erlang programs, further analyses can be applied to calculate flow or dependency information. In this section we present data-, control- and behaviour-flow analysis towards creating a Dependency Graph of Erlang programs.

When we have defined the Data-Flow, Control-Flow and Dependency Graphs, we had to consider the main features of the language. Some properties of the language make the analysis simpler (such as the limited number of data constructors and selectors, or the single assignment variables), but there are more properties that make the analysis complicated (the lack of documented evaluation strategy, the dynamic nature of the language: dynamic function calls, dynamic process starting, communication via message passing).

3.1   Data-Flow Analysis

The *Data-flow analysis* is a technique for gathering information about how a program manipulates its data and what are the possible sets of values calculated at various points in a program. Several classical data-flow analysis applications exist, such as constant-propagation analysis, liveness analysis, available expression analysis, reaching definition analysis, etc. In case of the *Reaching Definition Analysis* we are interested in each program point, which assignments may have been made and not overwritten, when execution reaches this point along some path [14], so we should statically determine which definitions may reach a certain point in the program.

Erlang is a single assignment language, so we are interested in reaching definition analysis and finding those program points which value can be a copy of a certain expression or variable. Therefore, in this section we introduce the reaching definition data-flow analysis. The analysis builds up the *Data-Flow Graph*

(DFG) of an Erlang program. The DFG contains direct data-flow information among expressions and the reaching relation defines the direct and indirect data-flow among them.

The DFG is a part of the Semantic Program Graph of RefactorErl. The analysis adds data-flow edges to the SPG based on the syntax and semantics of the language. The DFG is a directed labelled graph (DFG = (N, E)), its nodes are the Erlang expressions $(n_i \in N)$ and its edges represent the direct data-flow among them.

We can distinguish four kinds of data-flow edges:

- $\xrightarrow{f}$ (**flow edge**): $n_1 \xrightarrow{f} n_2$ represents that the result of n_2 can be a copy of the result of n_1. Their value is exactly the same, and changing the value of n_1 results in the same change of the value of n_2.
- $\xrightarrow{c_i}$ (**constructor edge**): $n_1 \xrightarrow{c_i} n_2$, represents that the result of n_2 can be a compound value that contains n_1 as the ith element.
- $\xrightarrow{s_i}$ (**selector edge**): $n_1 \xrightarrow{s_i} n_2$, represents that the result of n_2 can be the ith element of the compound data n_1.
- $\xrightarrow{d}$ (**dependency edge**): $n_1 \xrightarrow{d} n_2$, represents that the result of n_2 can directly depend on the result of n_1.

We build the DFG with a compositional syntax based on the formal data-flow rules. These rules are presented and detailed in Appendix B in Figures 24 – 26. During the data-flow analysis we traverse the syntax tree part of the SPG and try to apply one of the data-flow rules. When a syntactic element matches to a left hand side of a rule we apply the right hand side of that rule and add the given edges to the graph. This rule-based graph building method results in the *Interprocedural Data-Flow Graph* containing the direct data-flow edges. The indirect data-flow can be obtained by traversing the DFG and calculating the transitive closure of the graph. We can define this closure with the *Data-Flow Reaching* relation. We have defined the zeroth order (Section 3.2) and the first order reaching (Section 3.5).

To give the basic idea behind the rules we show some example rules in Figure 6. The *(Variable)* rule describes that the value bound to a certain variable flows to all occurrences of the same variable. Rules *(Tuple exp.)* and *(Tuple pat.)* describe the constructor and selector operations of tuples. The edge c_i denotes that the value is the ith element of the tuple, and s_i means that we select the ith element of the compound pattern. The *(Fun. call)* rule defines the data-flow from the actual parameters to the patterns of the function definition, and the flow of the result of the function back to the function application.

3.2   Zeroth Order Data-Flow Reaching

We have already defined the direct edges of the Data-Flow Graph, but we have to define the indirect data-flow relation based on this graph as well. The *Data-Flow Reaching* is defined by the $\xrightarrow{of}$ relation, where $n_1 \xrightarrow{of} n_2$ means that the value of the expression represented by n_1 in the DFG can be a copy of the value

	Expression	Direct Graph Edges
(Variable)	p binding of a variable n occurrence of a variable	$p \xrightarrow{f} n$
(Tuple exp.)	e_0: $\quad \{e_1, \ldots, e_n\}$	$e_1 \xrightarrow{c_1} e_0, \ldots, e_n \xrightarrow{c_n} e_0$
(Tuple pat.)	p_0: $\quad \{p_1, \ldots, p_n\}$	$p_0 \xrightarrow{s_1} p_1, \ldots, p_0 \xrightarrow{s_n} p_n$
(Fun. call)	e_0: $\quad$ m : $g(e_1, \ldots, e_n)$ or $\quad g(e_1, \ldots, e_n)$ m:g/n: $\quad g(p_1^1, \ldots, p_n^1)$ when $g_1 \rightarrow$ $\quad\quad e_1^1, \ldots, e_{l_1}^1;$ $\quad\quad \vdots$ $\quad g(p_1^m, \ldots, p_n^m)$ when $g_m \rightarrow$ $\quad\quad e_1^m, \ldots, e_{l_m}^m.$	$e_1 \xrightarrow{f} p_1^1, \ldots, e_1 \xrightarrow{f} p_1^m$ $\vdots$ $e_n \xrightarrow{f} p_n^1, \ldots, e_n \xrightarrow{f} p_n^m$ $e_{l_1}^1 \xrightarrow{f} e_0, \ldots, e_{l_m}^m \xrightarrow{f} e_0$

Fig. 6. Static Data-Flow Graph building rules

of n_2 – their values are equal. During defining the reaching we have to consider the followings:

- $n_1 \xrightarrow{Of} n_1$ always holds, because the value of an expression reaches itself (reflexive rule)
- If there is a flow edge $\xrightarrow{f}$ between nodes n_1 and n_2, then the value of n_1 reaches n_2 (f rule)
- A compound data structure preserves the data in its elements. When we put an element n_1 into a data structure n_2 and the compound data reaches another node n_3 and we take out the element from the compound data to n_4, then the packed value n_1 reaches n_4 (c-s rule)
- If the value of an expression n_1 reaches n_2 and the value of n_2 reaches n_3, then the value of n_1 reaches n_3, their values are equal (transitive rule)

Based on these, we can formalise the zeroth order data-flow reaching. We call it zeroth order, because it does not handle any context information, for instance about the calling context of functions.

Definition 1: Zeroth order data-flow relation The zeroth order data-flow reaching relation ($\xrightarrow{Of}$) is the minimal relation that satisfies the following rules:

$$n \xrightarrow{Of} n \qquad \text{(reflexive)}$$

$$\frac{n_1 \xrightarrow{f} n_2}{n_1 \xrightarrow{Of} n_2} \qquad \text{(f rule)}$$

$$\frac{n_1 \xrightarrow{c_i} n_2, \; n_2 \xrightarrow{Of} n_3, \; n_3 \xrightarrow{s_i} n_4}{n_1 \xrightarrow{Of} n_4} \qquad \text{(c-s rule)}$$

$$\frac{n_1 \overset{\text{Of}}{\rightsquigarrow} n_2, \; n_2 \overset{\text{Of}}{\rightsquigarrow} n_3}{n_1 \overset{\text{Of}}{\rightsquigarrow} n_3} \qquad \text{(transitive)}$$

For some application of the data-flow reaching the relevant information is the last element of a flow chain. Thus, we introduce the forward and backward compact data-flow reaching. For instance, when applying the data-flow analysis for the dynamic function call detection [8], we have to detect whether the value of a variable is unambiguously defined in the source code or it can be the result of some operation.

Definition 2: Zeroth order compact forward data-flow relation The compact forward data-flow reaching ($\overset{\text{Of}_{\text{cf}}}{\rightsquigarrow}$) is the minimal relation that satisfies the following rules:

$$\frac{n_1 \overset{\text{Of}}{\rightsquigarrow} n_2, \; \nexists n_3, \; n_3 \neq n_2 : \; n_2 \overset{\text{Of}}{\rightsquigarrow} n_3}{n_1 \overset{\text{Of}_{\text{cf}}}{\rightsquigarrow} n_2} \qquad \text{(f-compact)}$$

Definition 3: Zeroth order compact forward data-flow relation The compact backward data-flow reaching ($\overset{\text{Of}_{\text{cb}}}{\rightsquigarrow}$) is the minimal relation that satisfies the following rules:

$$\frac{n_1 \overset{\text{Of}}{\rightsquigarrow} n_2, \; \nexists n_0, \; n_0 \neq n_1 : \; n_0 \overset{\text{Of}}{\rightsquigarrow} n_1}{n_1 \overset{\text{Of}_{\text{cb}}}{\rightsquigarrow} n_2} \qquad \text{(b-compact)}$$

3.3   Zeroth Order DFG and Reaching Example

Let us consider the following Erlang module in Figure 7. The function swap/2 swaps the values of a two-tuple. The function get_1st/1 takes a tuple as an argument and swaps its values, then returns the first element of the swapped tuple. Finally, the function cons/0 calls the function get_1st/1 with the actual parameter {1,2} and returns the result of the function call.

The Data-Flow Graph of this module is shown in Figure 8. The result of the function cons/0 is the value of the variable Y. It can be traced in the graph that the constant 2 can be the value of Y: $e_{25} \overset{\text{Of}}{\rightsquigarrow} e_{32}$ (the notation e_i denotes the DFG graph node and i is the index of nodes in Figure 8). We pack the integer 2 into the tuple as its second element and pass the tuple to the argument of the function get_1st/1 that also passes that value to the parameter of swap/2. The last function unpacks the values from the tuple and packs them into a new tuple in reverse order. Thus, the second element of the tuple (the integer 2) becomes the first element. Then get_1st/1 unpacks the resulted tuple and returns the first element of the tuple, that is the integer 2. The function cons/0 binds the result of the function call to the variable Y and returns that value. Thus, the result is the integer 2.

```
-module(dataflow).

swap({A, B}) ->
    {B, A}.


get_1st(X) ->
    {E1, E2} = swap(X),
    E1.

const()->
    Y = get_1st({1,2}),
    Y.
```

Fig. 7. Example of Erlang code

Using the data-flow reaching relation we can formalise the traversal of the graph:

$$\frac{e_{22} \xrightarrow{\mathbf{f}} e_{32},\ e_{30} \xrightarrow{\mathbf{f}} e_{22},\ e_{20} \xrightarrow{\mathbf{f}} e_{30},\ p_{10} \xrightarrow{\mathbf{f}} e_{20}}{e_{22} \overset{\mathbf{Of}}{\rightsquigarrow} e_{32},\ e_{30} \overset{\mathbf{Of}}{\rightsquigarrow} e_{22},\ e_{20} \overset{\mathbf{Of}}{\rightsquigarrow} e_{30},\ p_{10} \overset{\mathbf{Of}}{\rightsquigarrow} e_{20}} \qquad \text{(f rule (4 times))}$$

$$\frac{p_{10} \overset{\mathbf{Of}}{\rightsquigarrow} e_{20},\ e_{20} \overset{\mathbf{Of}}{\rightsquigarrow} e_{30},\ e_{30} \overset{\mathbf{Of}}{\rightsquigarrow} e_{22},\ e_{22} \overset{\mathbf{Of}}{\rightsquigarrow} e_{32}}{p_{10} \overset{\mathbf{Of}}{\rightsquigarrow} e_{32}} \qquad \text{(transitive rule (3 times))}$$

$$\frac{e_{18} \xrightarrow{\mathbf{f}} e_{12},\ e_7 \xrightarrow{\mathbf{f}} e_{18}}{e_{18} \overset{\mathbf{Of}}{\rightsquigarrow} e_{12},\ e_7 \overset{\mathbf{Of}}{\rightsquigarrow} e_{18}} \qquad \text{(f rule (2 times))}$$

$$\frac{e_7 \overset{\mathbf{Of}}{\rightsquigarrow} e_{18},\ e_{18} \overset{\mathbf{Of}}{\rightsquigarrow} e_{12}}{e_7 \overset{\mathbf{Of}}{\rightsquigarrow} e_{12}} \qquad \text{(transitive rule)}$$

$$\frac{p_2 \xrightarrow{\mathbf{f}} e_6}{p_2 \overset{\mathbf{Of}}{\rightsquigarrow} e_6} \qquad \text{(f rule)}$$

$$\frac{e_{16} \xrightarrow{\mathbf{f}} p_4,\ e_9 \xrightarrow{\mathbf{f}} e_{16},\ e_{26} \xrightarrow{\mathbf{f}} e_9}{e_{16} \overset{\mathbf{Of}}{\rightsquigarrow} e_4,\ e_9 \overset{\mathbf{Of}}{\rightsquigarrow} e_{16},\ e_{26} \overset{\mathbf{Of}}{\rightsquigarrow} e_9} \qquad \text{(f rule (3 times))}$$

$$\frac{e_{29} \xrightarrow{\mathbf{f}} e_9,\ e_9 \xrightarrow{\mathbf{f}} e_{16},\ e_{16} \xrightarrow{\mathbf{f}} p_4}{e_{26} \overset{\mathbf{Of}}{\rightsquigarrow} p_4} \qquad \text{(transitive rule (2 times))}$$

$$\frac{e_6 \xrightarrow{\mathbf{c_1}} e_7,\ e_7 \overset{\mathbf{Of}}{\rightsquigarrow} e_{12},\ e_{12} \xrightarrow{\mathbf{s_1}} p_{10}}{e_6 \overset{\mathbf{Of}}{\rightsquigarrow} p_{10}} \qquad \text{(c-s rule)}$$

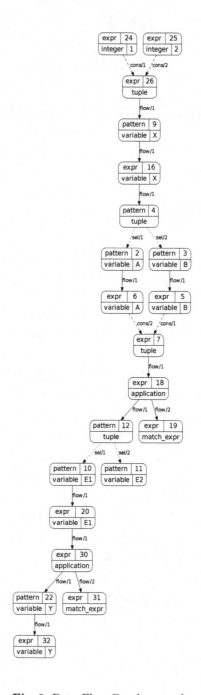

Fig. 8. Data-Flow Graph example

$$\frac{e_{25} \overset{c_2}{\to} e_{26}, \ e_{26} \overset{Of}{\rightsquigarrow} p_4, \ p_4 \overset{s_2}{\to} p_2}{e_{25} \overset{Of}{\rightsquigarrow} p_2} \qquad \text{(c-s rule)}$$

$$\frac{e_{25} \overset{Of}{\rightsquigarrow} p_2, \ p_2 \overset{Of}{\rightsquigarrow} e_6, \ e_6 \overset{Of}{\rightsquigarrow} p_{10}, \ p_{10} \overset{Of}{\rightsquigarrow} e_{32}}{e_{25} \overset{Of}{\rightsquigarrow} e_{32}} \qquad \text{(transitive rule (3 times))}$$

3.4 First Order Data-Flow Analysis

The zeroth order reaching is calculated based on the DFG. It does not consider the calling context of functions, thus the zeroth order reaching is an over-approximation (the DFG contains false positive data-flow edges). To address this problem we defined the *First order Data-Flow Reaching*. The first order analysis extends the DFG with context information about function calls to denote the entry point of the function from a given function call and the return point of the function to the same function call with the same index.

We will illustrate the calling context problem with an example and demonstrate how the first order analysis can avoid some false positive hints.

We can extend our previous example from Section 3.3 with another function, which calls the function `get_1st`. The result of the data-flow reaching changes according to the extension (Figure 9).

```
const2()->
    Z = get_1st({3,4}),
    Z.
```

In this case both the tuples {3,4} and {1,2} flow to the pattern X, and the result of the function `get_1st/1` can be either integer 2 or 4 after the swapping. The result of this function (e_{20}) flows to the applications (e_{30}, e_{41}), so these can be the values of variables Y and Z. However, it is obvious that when we call the function from `const/0`, the result is 2 and from `const2/0` the result is 4.

The problem with the zeroth order data-flow graph is that it does not store any context information about the source code. Therefore, we can refine this analysis by adding some context information about the calling context of functions and distinguish the different function call and return points.

Extended First Order Rules To achieve the first order analysis, the 0th order data-flow rules have to be extended with calling context information. Our motivating example indicates that we should distinguish the different calls to a function. Therefore, we store additional information on the entry and exit points of a function rather than considering only the flow of the parameters.

Our first order analysis introduces new data-flow relations: $\overset{call(g)}{\to}$ for entering and $\overset{ret(g)}{\to}$ for leaving the function g. The context information is added to the edge as an index: $\overset{call(g,i)}{\to}$ means the ith call of the function, and $\overset{ret(g,i)}{\to}$ means

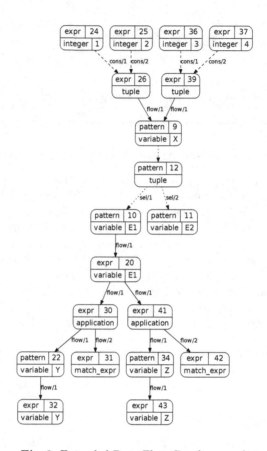

Fig. 9. Extended Data-Flow Graph example

the return point of the ith call. Figure 10 shows the compositional data-flow rule for a function call.

3.5   Extended First Order Data-Flow Relation

The presented data-flow rules describe direct flow information among Erlang expressions. Since data could flow from node n_1 to n_2, and from n_2 to n_3, we are curious whether the value of n_1 flows indirectly to n_3. The 1st order data-flow relation returns those nodes in the graph where the value of a given node can flow through a sequence of the data-flow edges.

We derive the first order data-flow relation from the zeroth order data-flow relation considering the followings:

- $\overset{0f'}{\leadsto}$ denotes the zeroth order data-flow relation calculated on the data-flow graph defined by the extended data-flow rules. The zeroth order flow relation operates on $\overset{f}{\to}$ edges, but the first order function call rule replaces the

	Expressions	Graph edges

(Fun. call)	e_0:
	    $m : g(e_1, \ldots, e_n)$
	
	$m{:}g/n$:
	    $g(p_1^1, \ldots, p_n^1)$ when $g_1 \to$
	        $e_1^1, \ldots, e_{l_1}^1$;
	      $\vdots$
	    $g(p_1^m, \ldots, p_n^m)$ when $g_m \to$
	        $e_1^m, \ldots, e_{l_m}^m$.
	
	e_0 is the ith analysed call
	to function $m : g/n$
		$e_{l_1}^1 \overset{\textbf{ret(g,i)}}{\to} e_0, \ldots, e_{l_m}^m \overset{\textbf{ret(g,i)}}{\to} e_0$,
		
		$e_1 \overset{\textbf{call(g,i)}}{\to} p_1^1, \ldots, e_1 \overset{\textbf{call(g,i)}}{\to} p_1^m$
		
		$\vdots$
		
		$e_n \overset{\textbf{call(g,i)}}{\to} p_n^1, \ldots, e_n \overset{\textbf{call(g,i)}}{\to} p_n^m$

Fig. 10. First order function call rule

corresponding $\overset{\textbf{f}}{\to}$ edges with $\overset{\textbf{call}}{\to}$ and $\overset{\textbf{ret}}{\to}$ edges. The zeroth order reaching cannot use the new edges. This results in a smaller intrafunctional $\overset{\textbf{0f}'}{\leadsto}$ relation.

- $\overset{\textbf{1f}[\mu]}{\leadsto}$ denotes the first order data-flow relation.
- In the first order relation ($\overset{\textbf{1f}[\mu]}{\leadsto}$) μ is a list of call ($\overset{\textbf{call(g,i)}}{\to}$) and return ($\overset{\textbf{ret(h,j)}}{\to}$) points. We have to record the names and the indices of the called functions, because later we have to find the corresponding exit points.
- Each node (n_i) that is reachable in the extended representation with the 0th order data-flow relation is reachable by the first order relation (0th *flow rule*).
- Similarly to the 0th order relation, if a data constructor packs ($\overset{\textbf{c}_1}{\to}$) the node n_1 into n_2 and the value of n_2 flows (with a first order flow) into the node n_3 and another data constructor unpacks ($\overset{\textbf{s}_1}{\to}$) the value into n_4, then the value of n_1 flows into n_4 (1st *c-s rule*).
- The call ($\overset{\textbf{call(g,i)}}{\to}$) and the return ($\overset{\textbf{ret(h,j)}}{\to}$) edges behave similarly as the flow $\overset{\textbf{f}}{\to}$ edges, so the data flows through them (*call rule* and *return rule*).
- The data can flow through any function call (*call concat. rule*).
- If the value of the node n_1 flows into the node n_2 through the return value of a function call and the value of n_2 flows into the node n_3 through the return value of another function call, then the value of n_1 transitively flows into the node n_3 (*return concat. rule*).
- If we enter the function through the edge $\overset{\textbf{call(g,i)}}{\to}$, then we have to leave the function through the $\overset{\textbf{ret(g,i)}}{\to}$ edge (*reduce rule*) and leaving the function body through an $\overset{\textbf{ret(g,j)}}{\to}$ ($j \neq i$) edge is not allowed (*Lemma 3*).

In Definition 4 we use the following notations:

- μ denotes a list;

- $hd(\mu)$ results the head (first) element of a list;
- $last(\mu)$ stands for the last element of a list;
- $\mu + +\rho$ denotes the concatenation of list μ and list ρ;
- μ_n denotes the nth element of list μ.

Definition 4: First order data-flow relation The data-flow relation ($\overset{1f}{\rightsquigarrow}$) is the minimal relation that satisfies the following rules:

$$\frac{n_1 \overset{\mathbf{0f'}}{\rightsquigarrow} n_2}{n_1 \overset{\mathbf{1f}[]}{\rightsquigarrow} n_2} \qquad (0^{th} \text{ flow rule})$$

$$\frac{n_1 \overset{\mathbf{c_i}}{\rightarrow} n_2, \ n_2 \overset{\mathbf{1f}[\mu]}{\rightsquigarrow} n_3, \ n_3 \overset{\mathbf{s_i}}{\rightarrow} n_4}{n_1 \overset{\mathbf{1f}[\mu]}{\rightsquigarrow} n_4} \qquad (1^{st} \text{ c-s rule})$$

$$\frac{n_1 \overset{\mathbf{call(g,i)}}{\rightarrow} n_2}{n_1 \overset{\mathbf{1f}[\mathbf{call_{(g,i)}}]}{\rightsquigarrow} n_2} \qquad (\text{call rule})$$

$$\frac{n_1 \overset{\mathbf{ret(h,j)}}{\rightarrow} n_2}{n_1 \overset{\mathbf{1f}[\mathbf{ret_{(h,j)}}]}{\rightsquigarrow} n_2} \qquad (\text{return rule})$$

$$\frac{n_1 \overset{\mathbf{1f}[\mu]}{\rightsquigarrow} n_2, \ n_2 \overset{\mathbf{1f}[\rho]}{\rightsquigarrow} n_3}{n_1 \overset{\mathbf{1f}[\mu++\rho]}{\rightsquigarrow} n_3} \quad if \ (\exists f \ \exists i : \ (hd(\rho) = call_{(g,i)})) \ or \ \rho = []$$

$$\qquad (\text{call concat. rule})$$

$$\frac{n_1 \overset{\mathbf{1f}[\mu]}{\rightsquigarrow} n_2, \ n_2 \overset{\mathbf{1f}[\mathbf{ret_{(h,j)}}|\rho]}{\rightsquigarrow} n_3}{n_1 \overset{\mathbf{1f}[\mu++[\mathbf{ret_{(h,j)}}|\rho]]}{\rightsquigarrow} n_3} \quad if \ (\exists f \ \exists i : \ (last(\mu) = ret_{(g,i)})) \ or \ \mu = []$$

$$\qquad (\text{return concat. rule})$$

$$\frac{n_1 \overset{\mathbf{1f}[\mu++[\mathbf{call_{(h,i)}}]]}{\rightsquigarrow} n_2, \ n_2 \overset{\mathbf{1f}[\mathbf{ret_{(h,i)}}]}{\rightsquigarrow} n_3}{n_1 \overset{\mathbf{1f}[\mu]}{\rightsquigarrow} n_3} \qquad (\text{reduce rule})$$

N^{th} *Order Analysis.* Based on the defined first order analysis, where we have stored the calling context in the DFG in one depth, we can generalise the second order analysis and store the calling context in two steps [19]. For example, in case of a higher order function (Figure 11), a dynamic function call in the body of the function depends on the parameter of the higher order call, thus it depends on the calling context of the higher order function. In Figure 11 we have defined the function $func/2$ that applies its first argument on its second argument: when we call this function from $call\_pear/0$ it calls the function $pear/1$, and when we call this function from $call\_apple/0$ it calls the function $apple/1$.

Based on this we can add the $\overset{call(pear,i)}{\rightarrow}$ and the $\overset{call(apple,j)}{\rightarrow}$ first order flow edges from the node of Fun(Data), and also the $\overset{ret*}{\rightarrow}$ edges. Calculating first

```
func(Fun, Data)->
    Fun(Data).
```

```
call_pear()->
    f(fun pear/1, [pear]).
```

```
call_apple()->
    f(fun apple/1, [apple]).
```

Fig. 11. Higher order functions

order reaching on the DFG from the body of *call_pear*/0 results in that both function *apple*/1 and function *pear*/1 were called and their return values were reached. A solution to that problem could be to store two depth calling context: $call((func,1);(pear,i)) \atop \rightarrow$ and $call((func,2);(apple,j)) \atop \rightarrow$.

This analysis could be generalised iteratively to an nth order flow analysis $\left(call((func_1,i_1); \dots ;(func_n,i_n)) \atop \rightarrow \right)$.

3.6   First Order DFG and Reaching Examples

The first order DFG of the previously mentioned example is shown in Figure 12. It can be traced that the integers 2 and 4 can be the result of the function get_1st/1 ($e_{25} \overset{1f[call_{(get\_1st,1)}]}{\rightsquigarrow} e_{20}$ and $e_{37} \overset{1f[call_{(get\_1st,2)}]}{\rightsquigarrow} e_{20}$), but only the integer 2 can flow to variable Y (because of the *reduce rule*).

$$\frac{e_{25} \overset{1f[call_{(get\_1st,1)}]}{\rightsquigarrow} e_{20}, \ e_{20} \overset{1f[ret_{(get\_1st,1)}]}{\rightsquigarrow} e_{32}}{e_{25} \overset{1f[]}{\rightsquigarrow} e_{32}} \quad \text{(reduce rule)}$$

3.7   Concurrent Data-Flow Analysis

Besides the function parameters there is another way to exchange data between functions (and also between different processes), that is message passing. Therefore, a naive approximation of calculating data-flow through message passing can be similar to the zeroth order data-flow through function calls. We can link each passed message to all of the receive expressions. That results a huge DFG containing lots of false flow edges. To avoid this, we should restrict the set of possible receivers of messages using context information about the message passing.

Concurrent Erlang Processes and Message Passing. The language was designed for developing concurrent and distributed applications. Spawning a processes on remote nodes is as easy as spawning it on a single node. Since Erlang uses light-weight processes and processes are spawned at the virtual machine level, the spawning and destroying of processes is quite fast. The processes are separated from operating system processes and behave in the same way on every platform. The virtual machine takes care of spawning, destroying and scheduling of processes. The processes are independent and do not share memory, as they communicate only through message passing. Message passing is asynchronous

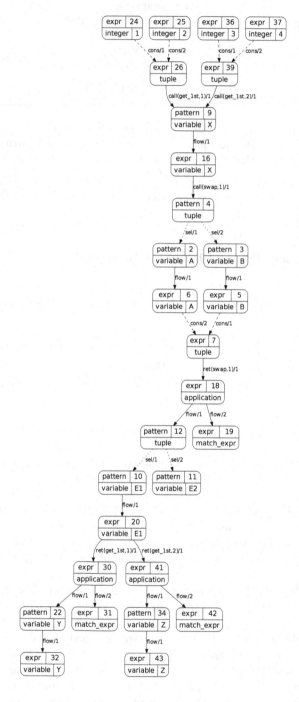

Fig. 12. First Order Data-Flow Graph example

and the messages arrive at a message queue of the process. Messages are waiting in a message queue until they are processed.

The following functions work in the same way on a local node, or even if there is a set of interconnected nodes. In this paper we will describe the message passing in case of a local node. The analysis can be extended easily to apply for distributed applications as well.

The basic language elements for concurrency are spawn, register, receive and send.

Spawning processes. With the spawn function we can create new processes. We can spawn a lambda expression, an exported function on a local node, or even on the remote Erlang node. There are some versions for this BIF (Built in Function):

spawn – The function spawn/n spawns a separate process with the given function and returns its process identifier (PID). The creating process will not be notified if the created process has terminated abnormally. The function is available with different arities: n=1,2,3,4.

spawn_link – The function spawn_link/n spawns the given function, but creates a link between the parent and the spawned process. The creating process will be notified if the created process terminates abnormally and will cause to crash the creating process if the exit is not trapped. The functions are available with different arities: n=1,2,3,4.

spawn_monitor – The function spawn_monitor/n spawns the given function and returns a tuple of a PID and a reference for the process. With this reference we can monitor the created process. The creating process will be notified if the created process terminates normally even if it crashes, but will not cause the creating process to terminate. The function is available with different arities: n=1,3.

Registering processes. With the function register/2 we can associate a local process identifier with a given name. The function will fail if there is a process registered with the same name, or the local process does not exist.

If we have several nodes connected and communicating with each other, we can also register the process globally with the function global:register_name/n (n=2,3).

If the process is registered it can be accessed by its name instead of the PID when sending it a message.

Sending messages. Since the spawned processes are independent, the only way of communication is message passing, either through the network, or only on a local node. The process can be accessed by its process identifier obtained by spawning the process, or by the given name, if it has been registered. There are some alternatives for sending messages, but we describe only the most common cases, as the other functions behave similarly.

The right-associative infix send operator ! (exclamation mark) and its function version send/2 are used most commonly. The operator takes two operands: the right operand, which is the message to be send, and the left operand, which is the destination process. As a result, the send operator returns the message. The destination can be a PID, a registered process name, or even a registered process on a remote node.

The operator ! and the `send/n` (n=1,2) send the message to the mailbox (or message queue) of the processes. To send a message to a globally registered process we can use the function `global:send/2`.

Receiving messages. The messages arrive at the mailbox of the process. We can extract messages with the `receive` expression. The receive expression looks like a case expression (or switch in other languages), except it suspends until it can extract a message form the mailbox, or the given timeout has elapsed. We can extract messages with pattern-matching and proceed with execution according to the received message.

Detecting Spawned Processes. Since the process identifiers are created dynamically or passed to the functions as parameters, statically detecting the recipient of a message is not straightforward and sometimes it is impossible to calculate. Let us consider the following Erlang function:

```
send_data(Pid) ->
    Data = do_some_computation(),
    Pid  ! {"Sending computed data", Data}.
```

In this example, if we do not have further knowledge about the function parameter `Pid`, we cannot detect where the actual message can flow. Thus we concentrate on the analysing of process identifiers and on calculating the set of functions that can be executed as processes. To solve the latter mentioned problem we have to analyse process spawning. For the sake of simplicity we describe in more detail only the function `spawn/3` hereinafter (the functions `spawn*/n` can be handled similarly):

```
Pid = spawn(ModName, FunName, ArgList)
```

The function `spawn/3` executes the given function in the new independent process and returns its unique identifier. The `spawn/3` function takes three arguments: the name of the implementing module, the name of the function to be spawned and the list of the actual parameters for this function. Thus the following triple {`ModName, FunName, length(ArgList)`} identifies the function that is spawned in a new process.

To calculate the possible values of the identifying triple we can use the sequential first order data-flow reaching defined in Section 3.4. The following sets define the possible values of the elements of the triple, where $mn \in V$ denotes the node representing the module name, $fn \in V$ denotes the node representing the function name and $arg \in V$ denotes the node representing the argument list in the Data-Flow Graph – $DFG = (V, E)$:

$$- MN = \{n \in V | n \overset{\mathbf{1f}}{\leadsto} mn, \nexists n', n' \in V, n' \neq n : n' \overset{\mathbf{1f}}{\leadsto} n\}$$

$- FN = \{n \in V | n \stackrel{1f}{\leadsto} fn, \nexists n', n' \in V, n' \neq n : n' \stackrel{1f}{\leadsto} n\}$

$- Arg = \{n \in V | n \stackrel{1f}{\leadsto} arg, \nexists n', n' \in V, n' \neq n : n' \stackrel{1f}{\leadsto} n\}$

For instance, the set MN contains those expressions which values can flow into mn, i.e. we perform static backward data-flow reaching starting from mn. When the node mn is a variable, we need only the binding of the variable and neglect its references, because only the origin of the variable holds useful information for us. We select only the source nodes from the DFG, which has zero indegree.

Ideally, the type of the elements in MN and FN are atom and the type of the elements of Arg is an n-element list expression. In this case we can unambiguously identify the spawned function. Otherwise we can use some heuristic to narrow the possible set of functions that can be executed in the spawned process which receive the sent messages (for details see Section Heuristics for process detection).

Hereinafter SF_{Pid} denotes the set of functions that could be executed by the process Pid: $SF_{Pid} = \{\{val(M), val(F), size(A)\} | M \in MN, F \in FN, A \in Arg\}$

Function val/1 returns the value of an expression instead of its node identifier in the DFG. Function size/1 returns the estimated size of a list expression. Lists have a variable length, so statically calculating the length of a list is not straightforward.

For the sake of simplicity we present the introduced sets in a simple example:

```
-module(mymod).

start(Fun, Args) ->
    Pid = spawn(?MODULE, Fun, Args).
    Pid ! start,
    Pid.

init() ->
    start(loop1, [init, []]).

process(Data) ->
    start(loop2, [proc, Data]).

loop1(State, Data) ->
    ...
loop2(Tag, Data) ->
    ...
```

The presented Erlang module mymod defines the function start/2, which spawns a process and then sends a message to the newly spawned process. The name and the parameters of the function to be executed by the process are the parameters of the function start/2, so they are not defined in the function. The first parameter of spawn/3 is given by a predefined macro application ?MODULE, the substitution of that macro is the name of the current module mymod. The function init/0 calls the function start/2 with the actual parameters loop1 and a two-element list. The function process/1 calls start/2 with the actual parameters loop2 and a two-element list. The body of the function loop*/2 is not important yet.

Using backward first order data-flow analysis we obtain the following node sets, where $\$Expr\$$ means the node representing expression $Expr$ in the data-flow ($\$Expr\$ \in V$):

- $MN = \{\$?MODULE\$\}$
- $FN = \{\$loop1\$, \$loop2\$\}$
- $Arg = \{\$[init, []]\$, \$[proc, Data]\$\}$
- $SF_{Pid} = \{\{mymod, loop1, 2\}, \{mymod, loop2, 2\}\}$

We have identified two possible functions (SF_{Pid}) that can be spawned in start/2, and these are the recipients of the message passed in expression Pid ! start.

Since we can refer to any registered processes with the associated alias, we have to analyse the calls of function register/2 too:

_True = register(Alias, PidExpr)

In this case we have to calculate the possible values of the expression Alias and to identify the function that has been spawned in a process with identifier PidExpr. To detect the possible values of these expressions, in both cases we require backward data-flow reaching:

- $AN = \{n \in V | n \overset{1f}{\rightsquigarrow} an, \nexists n', n' \in V, n' \neq n : n' \overset{1f}{\rightsquigarrow} n\}$
- $Atom_{AN} = \{n \in V \mid \exists n', n' \in AN, \exists n'', n'' \in V, n'' \overset{1f}{\rightsquigarrow} n, val(n'') = val(n), type(n') = atom, n \in MPass\}$
- $PN = \{n \in V | n \overset{1f}{\rightsquigarrow} pn, type(n) = spawn\_app\}$

In the former sets an denotes the node representing the Alias in the data-flow graph; pn represents the process identifier expression PidExpr in the data-flow graph and $MPass$ represents the elements of the message passing expression. The function type/1 returns the type on an expression; $type(n) = spawn\_app$ means that node n is an application of function spawn.

To calculate the function executed in the process referred by the given Alias we have to select the nodes representing a function call to spawn*/n. This set of nodes is denoted by PN. We have to calculate the possible functions to be executed by the processes SF_{Pid_i} for every element of PN. Since the name Alias could refer to all of these processes, SF_{Alias} will denote the union of these sets.

The main point in registering a process with an atom $atom$ alias is that the registered process can be accessed with the registered name $atom$ at different points of the program without having any information about its PID. Thus an atom used in a message passing may refer to a process spawned in another function from another module, even if there is no data-flow connection between them. Therefore, we have to identify the atoms in message passing that could refer to the same process: $Atom_{AN}$. The elements of $Atom_{AN}$ should identify the same triples as the `Alias`: $\forall A \in Atom_{AN} : SF_A = SF_{Alias}$.

Consider the modified version of the previous example, where the function `init/1` registers the spawned process with a given alias `Alias`. The function `reg_proc` calls `init/1` with the actual parameter `proc1` and then sends a message using the registered alias.

```
start(Fun, Args) ->
    Pid = spawn(?MODULE, Fun, Args).
    Pid ! start,
    Pid.

init(Alias) ->
    P = start(loop1, [init, []]),
    register(Alias, P).

loop1(State, Data) ->
    ...

reg_proc() ->
    init(proc1),
    proc1 ! some_message.
```

We can calculate that the atom `proc1` refers to the function `mymod:loop1/2` in message passing expressions:

- $AN = \{\$proc1\$\}$
  - from function call `init(proc1)`
- $Atom_{AN} = \{\$proc1\$\}$
  - from expression `proc1 ! some_msg`
- $PN = \{\$spawn(?MODULE, Fun, Args)\$\}$
- $SF_{Alias} = SF_{Pid} = \{\{mymod, loop1, 2\}\}$
- $SF_{proc1} = SF_{Alias} = \{\{mymod, loop1, 2\}\}$

Heuristics for Process Detection. Ideally the sets MN, FN and Arg contain atom nodes and list nodes with finite length, but it is not the case for industrial sized code. Therefore, we have studied some heuristics that can help to detect the possible functions to be executed in a process.

These heuristics are approximations of concurrent data-flow. The value of a variable representing the module name, the function name or the parameter list often cannot be calculated statically, therefore we want to approximate them based on the analysed source code. These heuristics are approximations of the dynamic/runtime information that is not available at compile time.

For instance, we can calculate the name of the module and the function to be spawned, but we cannot calculate the length of the parameter list. Since we have analysed the modules and functions before the message passing analysis, we can search for functions in the module without regarding the arity of the function. If we have found only one function, this must be the spawned function, otherwise there are more candidates to be spawned and we will scan each function body for the corresponding receive expressions.

These kinds of heuristics over-approximate the concurrent data-flow edges and the resulted DFG contains some false positive hints.

The used heuristics are based on the partial knowledge about the module name, function name and arity, and we extend this knowledge with information about the source code base. The used heuristics are:

1. when the name of the module (m) and the name of the function (f) are atoms – we select all functions with the name f from the module without regarding its arity n_i and we add $\{m, f, n_i\}$ to SF_*;
2. when the name of the module (m) is an atom – we select all functions from the module without regarding its name f_i and its arity n_i and we add $\{m, f_i, n_i\}$ to SF_* for each function f_i/n_i;
3. when the name of the module (m) is an atom and we can calculate the length of the parameter list (a) – we select all functions f_i from the module with the calculated arity a and we add $\{m, f_i, a\}$ to SF_*;
4. when the name of the function (f) is an atom and we can calculate the length of the parameter list (a) – we select every module (m_i) that defines a function f/n and we add $\{m_i, f, a\}$ to SF_*.

It is possible to use other heuristics (for instance, when only the arity of the function is known), but most of them result in a huge set of possible functions and thus we should generate lots of edges to the Data-Flow Graph.

Consider the following variation of our example, when the name of the function is a parameter of the function `init/2`.

```
start(Fun, Args) ->
    Pid = spawn(?MODULE, Fun, Args).
    Pid ! start,
    Pid.

init(Alias, FunName) ->
    P = start(FunName, [init, []]),
    register(Alias, P).

loop1(State, Data) ->
    ...
loop2(Tag, Data) ->
    ...
```

We can deduce that:

- $MN = \{\$?MODULE\$\}$
- $FN = \{\$FunName\$\}$
- $Arg = \{\$[init, []]\$, \$[proc, Data]\$\}$

Since the name of the function is unknown, we should use a heuristic. The name of the module is `mymod` and the arity of the function is 2, so we can use the first heuristic from the listing. We are searching for the described functions (f_i) in the module: `loop1/2` and `loop1/2`, and we add $\{\{mymod, loop1, 2\},$ $\{mymod, loop2, 2\}\}$ to SF_{Pid}.

Data-Flow through Message Passing. In the followings we concentrate on message passing expressions using the send operator (!): $e_1 \, ! \, e_2$. The left subexpression is a process identifier or an alias of a registered process stored in a variable or a simple atom. The right subexpression is the message to be sent.

The built-in function `send/2` can be analysed similarly. For the sake of simplicity we do not explain the case when the origin of the recipient of the message passing is a registered process on another node, because it is possible to extend our analysis to handle it.

To analyse a send expression we have to identify the recipient of the message, so we have to find the origin of the left-hand side subexpression e_1. We use backward data-flow reaching to find the spawn expression that returns the process identifier e_1 or to find the expression that is registered as e_1 (alias):

- $Spawn = \{n \in V | n \overset{\mathbf{1f}}{\leadsto} e_1, type(n) = spawn\_app\}$
- $Reg = \{n \in V | n \overset{\mathbf{1f}}{\leadsto} e_1, type(sup(n)) = reg\_app\}$

`sup(n)` denotes the superior expression of node n, i.e. n is a subexpression of `sup(n)`. If the spawning ($Spawn$) or registering (Reg) expressions are found, we can use the previously defined algorithm to calculate SF_{e_1}.

When e_1 is an atom or the backward reaching from e_1 returns an atom, we cannot use reaching to detect the SF_{e_1}, hence there is no data-flow connection between the used alias and the registering expression. At this point of the analysis we need the sets AN and SF_A for every register expression where $A \in Atom_{AN}$, thus it is required to calculate them in a previous stage of the analysis. In this case we have to calculate the possible atom values of $e_1 - name_1, ..., name_k -$ and select SF_{name_i} from the previously constructed sets. In this case $SF_{e_1} = \bigcup_{i=1}^{k} SF_{name_i}$.

Message passing indicates data-flow edges between the sender and the receiver expression. Therefore, after identifying the possible functions (SF_{e_1}) we have to find the possible receiver expressions. We have to collect the receiver expressions from the body of the executed function and from the body of the functions that are transitively called from the executed function:

$Rec = \{n \in V \mid type(n) = receive\_expr, \ F \in tr\_closure(SF_{e_1}), \ n \in body(F)\}$

The function `tr_closure/1` returns the transitive closure of the $\overset{\mathbf{call}}{\to}$ relation, where $f_1 \overset{\mathbf{call}}{\to} f_2$ means that function f_1 calls function f_2 and f_i is represented by the previously defined triple. The function `body/1` returns the expressions from the body of a function.

We apply the data-flow rule presented in Figure 13 for every $e' \in Rec_{e_1}$ receive expression. The sent message e_2 flows into the different patterns $(p_1, ..., p_n)$ of

	Expressions	Graph edges
(Send exp.)	e_0: $\quad e_1 \ ! \ e_2$ e': $\quad$ receive $\quad\quad p_1$ when $g_1 \to$ $\quad\quad\quad e_1^1, \ldots, e_{l_1}^1;$ $\quad\quad \vdots$ $\quad\quad p_n$ when $g_n \to$ $\quad\quad\quad e_1^n, \ldots, e_{l_n}^n$ $\quad$ after $\quad\quad e \to e_1, \ldots, e_s$ $\quad$ end	 $e_2 \xrightarrow{\mathbf{f}} e_0$ $\mathbf{e_2} \xrightarrow{\mathbf{f}} \mathbf{p_1}, \ldots, \mathbf{e_2} \xrightarrow{\mathbf{f}} \mathbf{p_n}$ $e_{l_1}^1 \xrightarrow{\mathbf{f}} e', \ldots, e_{l_n}^n \xrightarrow{\mathbf{f}} e'$ $e_s \xrightarrow{\mathbf{f}} e'$

Fig. 13. Concurrent data-flow rule

the selected receive expression, i.e. $\mathbf{e_2} \xrightarrow{\mathbf{f}} \mathbf{p_i}$. The result of the receive expression can be the value of the last expression of its clauses ($e_j^i \xrightarrow{\mathbf{f}} e'$) and the result of the send expression is the message itself ($e_2 \xrightarrow{\mathbf{f}} e_0$).

Let us consider another extension of the previous example, where we extend the body of function loop1/2 with a receive statement.

```
loop1(State, Data) ->
  receive
    start ->
      Data = initial_steps(),
      loop(started, Data);
    Msg ->
      NewData = process_msg(Msg, Data),
      loop(State, NewData);
    stop ->
      closing_steps()
  end.
```

There were two send expressions in the previous example: Pid ! start and proc1 ! some_message. In the former case we have to calculate the *Spawn* set: $Spawn = \{\$spawn(?MODULE, Fun, Args)\$\}$ and then $SF_{Pid} = \{\{mymod, loop1, 2\}\}$. There is only one receive expression in the body of the function mymod:loop1/2, so we link the sent message to its patterns: $\$start\$ \xrightarrow{\mathbf{f}} p$, where $p \in \{\$start\$, \$Msg\$, \$stop\$\}$. To analyse the latter send expression we have to calculate $SF_{proc1} = \{\{mymod, loop1, 2\}\}$, then find the receive expressions and create the link among the message and the patterns in the Data-Flow Graph: $\$some\_message\$ \xrightarrow{\mathbf{f}} p_i$.

Refining the Processes Analysis. We overestimate the concurrent data-flow edges, since the introduced static concurrent data-flow calculation algorithm does not consider the order of the sent messages or the liveness of processes. Further analyses should be performed to refine the resulted graph. The order of sent messages should be stored as context information.

It is possible to unregister the name of a process in Erlang programs, and after unregistering the process name we cannot send a message to the process by referring to its name. To detect the liveness of processes at a given point of the program we should improve our concurrent data-flow analysis and we have to use the control-flow analysis (Section 3.9) to calculate the execution paths of the program. Similarly, *exit* signals also have to be considered.

Improving the 1st Order Data-Flow Analysis. Beforehand we have introduced the process and message passing analysis for Erlang. Both sections assume that we have a data-flow reaching relation. Therefore, we split the data-flow graph building algorithm into two parts. In the first stage we calculate the sequential Data-Flow Graph based on the rules from Sections 3.1–3.4.

In the second stage we calculate the concurrent data-flow edges based on the analysis described in Sections *Detecting Spawned processes* and *Data-Flow through Message Passing*. This analysis extends the DFG with new data-flow edges, thus calculating 1st order reaching could result in a more accurate result set. Therefore, running the process analysis on the refined concurrent data-flow graph could generate new data-flow edges. It is possible to run the process analysis algorithm iteratively until it reaches its fixed point. The algorithm terminates when there is no more new message passing expression that we can analyse or we found the recipient for every message passing expression. When the analysis terminates, the resulted graph contains the possible statically calculable data-flow connections among Erlang statements. Unfortunately, with static analysis and the used heuristics we cannot avoid false hits.

Since we do not introduce new edge types for the Data-Flow Graph (only $\xrightarrow{f}$ edges are generated), the definition of the reaching relation remains the same as it was in the sequential case.

The following example demonstrates the necessity of the iterative application of the algorithm.

```
start() ->
    Pid1 = spawn(?MODULE, fun1, []),
    Pid2 = spawn(?MODULE, fun2, []).
    Pid1 ! {pid, Pid2}.

fun1() ->
    receive
        {pid, Pid} -> Pid ! some_message
    end.

fun2(Tag, Data) ->
    receive
        A -> do_sth(A)
    end.
```

The function `start/0` spawns two processes and sends the process identifier of the second process to the first process. The first process executes the function `fun1/0`, i.e. waits for a message that contains a process identifier and sends a message to the received `Pid`. The second process executes the function `fun2/0`, i.e. waits for a message and executes a function call `do_sth/1` after the message is received.

It is obvious that a backward reaching on the sequential data-flow graph does not find the origin of `Pid` in the message passing, so we cannot deduce that it refers to function `fun2/0`. However, we can perform the second stage of the data-flow analysis for the send expression `Pid1 ! {pid, Pid2}` and add a flow edge between the sent message and the receive pattern in `fun1/0`: $\{pid, Pid1\}$ $\xrightarrow{f}$ $\{pid, Pid\}$. Then by performing a backward reaching on the concurrent Data-Flow Graph we get the origin of `Pid` and we can deduce that it refers to `fun2/0`. Now, we can add the flow edge: $some\_message$ $\xrightarrow{f}$ A.

3.8   Behaviour-Flow Analysis

The behaviour-flow or Behaviour-Dependency Graph [18] describes a potential data related dependency among expressions. A data dependency relation between two graph nodes ($n_1 \leadsto n_2$) means that the behaviour of n_2 depends on the result/behaviour of n_1, so the change of node n_1 may have an impact on n_2. This kind of information is essential when we want to follow the evolution of software systems and help the developers to maintain the program. The result of this analysis can provide some information about the expressions (or functions/modules) that could be affected by a change on the source code. Based on this information the developer can decide whether the planned change on the source code is performable. The behaviour dependency relation can be computed using the data flow, data dependency and the behaviour dependency edges (described in [18]).

Definition 5. The behaviour dependency relation $\overset{b}{\leadsto}$ is defined as the minimal relation that satisfies the following rules:

$$\frac{n_1 \overset{1f}{\leadsto} n_2}{n_1 \overset{b}{\leadsto} n_2} \qquad\qquad \text{(d-rule)}$$

$$\frac{n_1 \overset{b}{\leadsto} n_2,\ n_2 \overset{b}{\to} n_3,\ n_3 \overset{b}{\leadsto} n_4}{n_1 \overset{b}{\leadsto} n_4} \qquad\qquad \text{(b-rule)}$$

Definition 6. The data and behaviour dependency relation $\leadsto$ is defined as the minimal relation that satisfies the following rules:

$$\frac{n_1 \overset{1f}{\leadsto} n_2}{n_1 \leadsto n_2} \qquad\qquad \text{(data-rule)}$$

$$\frac{n_1 \overset{\text{1f}}{\rightsquigarrow} n_2, \ n_2 \overset{\text{d}}{\rightarrow} n_3, \ n_3 \overset{\text{b}}{\rightsquigarrow} n_4}{n_1 \rightsquigarrow n_4} \qquad \text{(b-dep-rule)}$$

To informally explain these definitions we use some simple expressions examples:

```
func(...) ->
    ...
    A = 1 + 2,
    X = A,
    B = A * A,
    ...
```

Definition 5 describes that data-flow and the behaviour dependency edges ($\overset{\text{b}}{\rightarrow}$) propagate behaviour dependency among expressions (d-rule, b-rule). In our example the value of A reaches X, so when we change A that has an impact on X, changing the behaviour of A affects X too.

Definition 6 presents that data-flow reaching holds a special dependency, because those nodes from the Data-Flow Graph which could be a copy of node n_1 are affected by changing the value of n_1, so modifying n_1 could have an impact on them ($n_1 \rightsquigarrow n_2$).

Considering the expression A = 1+2 we can notice that changing the expression 1 to an atom `something_else` results that the expression `something_else+2` could not be evaluated and that it results a run-time error. Then each expression which behaviour depends on the value of 1+2 could not be evaluated. Therefore, when there is a data dependency connection between two nodes ($n_1 \overset{\text{d}}{\rightarrow} n_2 - 1 \overset{\text{d}}{\rightarrow} 1 + 2$), changing the data in n_1 may have an impact on the behaviour of n_2, and those nodes which behaviour may depend on n_2 (B = A * A), also may alter the behaviour from the same data change (b-dep-rule).

3.9   Control-Flow Analysis

The Control-Flow Graph (CFG) represents all the possible execution/evaluation paths of the program that can be chosen for every possible input. The CFG is a language dependent representation of the program as it is based on the semantics of the language.

We have defined control-flow rules for Erlang programming language based on its semantics. The language has strict evaluation, which means that before evaluating a compound expression, its subexpressions have to be evaluated. In every case the subexpressions are evaluated in left to right order. The defined control-flow rules are compositional, thus the graph can be composed from the previously computed subgraphs. We use the SPG of RefactorErl and use the same identifiers for the vertices in the CFG and we extend the set of nodes with some dummy vertices for joining branches, error nodes, etc. The rules are defined and described in more detail in Appendix C in Figures 29–32.

The notations in the figures are the followings: $e, e_i \in E$ are expressions, $g, g_j \in E$ are guard expressions, $p, p_k \in P$ are patterns and $f/n \in F$ stands for functions. The $e_0' \in E$ is a dummy node in the control flow graph, which represents an entry point of the compound expression or a joining of dummy nodes (ret) to represent the return of conditional branching expressions. The relation → represents the control-flow between the nodes. The edges that have no labels represent sequences, and edges with labels represent:

- conditional branching and pattern matching with ($\overset{\textbf{yes}}{\rightarrow}$), ($\overset{\textbf{no}}{\rightarrow}$) edges
- returning to a previous expression ($\overset{\textbf{ret}}{\rightarrow}$),
- function calls/applications with ($\overset{\textbf{call}}{\rightarrow}$),
- receive expression with ($\overset{\textbf{rec}}{\rightarrow}$),
- send expression with ($\overset{\textbf{send}}{\rightarrow}$).

The relations ($\overset{\textbf{call}}{\rightarrow}$), ($\overset{\textbf{rec}}{\rightarrow}$), ($\overset{\textbf{send}}{\rightarrow}$) represent special relations which indicate the possible dependency between the nodes of different functions (for details, see Section 3.10). In the rest of this section we describe a small example to give a general overview about the control flow in Erlang. The reader can find the listing and discussion of formal rules in Appendix C.

A Simple CFG Example The simple factorial computing function is described in Figure 14. The function gets a non negative number and returns its factorial. By definition the factorial of 0 is 1 and for larger number we can calculate the factorial by multiplying N with the factorial of N-1.

```
fact(0) -> 1;
fact(N) when N > 0 ->
    N * fact(N - 1).
```

Fig. 14. Definition of the factorial function

Figure 15 shows the CFG for this simple factorial function. The graph is built on the formal rules described in Appendix C.

The entry point of the function is the node FORM(1). The actual parameter is matched against the first formal parameter 0. If it succeeds, the $\overset{\textbf{YES}}{\rightarrow}$ edge is followed and the constant 1 value is returned, otherwise the control flows to the next pattern through the $\overset{\textbf{NO}}{\rightarrow}$ edge. As the next pattern is a variable, the pattern matching will succeed ($N \overset{\textbf{YES}}{\rightarrow} N > 0$). The next step is to evaluate the guard expression ($N > 0$). If the guard expression holds for the actual value, the body of the function is evaluated. The programming language has strict evaluation, and the subexpressions are evaluated first in left-to-right order. First the left operand of the multiplication (N) is evaluated. As it is a variable, the evaluation may proceed to the next subexpression. After that, the right operand of the multiplication is evaluated, a function application $fact(N - 1)$. As the function name may come form a compound expression that is evaluated in runtime, first the name of the function should be computed, and then the argument of the

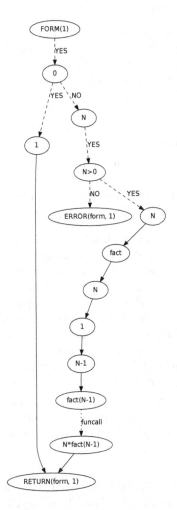

Fig. 15. The CFG for the factorial function: `fact/1` (in Figure 14)

function application (analogously to the multiplication). The step between the return of the function application and the multiplication is marked with a special edge $(fact(N-1) \overset{\text{funcall}}{\rightarrow} N*fact(n-1))$ as the evaluation of the function call may affect the return of the function (if the called function fails). This information will be used during the composition of the separately computed parts of the graph.

The graph includes a special error node `ERROR(form, 1)`, because the function is a partial function and may produce a runtime error if none of the patterns and guards match. In the current example the function fails, if it gets a negative number as an argument.

3.10   Dependency Analysis

The Dependency Graph is a labelled directed graph containing the Erlang expressions as its nodes, and data and control dependency among the expressions as its edges. We have introduced three kinds of control dependency edges, one data and one behaviour dependency edge:

- $n_1 \overset{dd}{\to} n_2$ denotes that n_2 is directly control dependent from n_1
- $n_1 \overset{resdep}{\to} n_2$ (resumption dependent) means that the node n_2 depends on the return of a given function
- $n_1 \overset{inhdep}{\to} n_2$ represent that node n_2 inherits the dependencies from n_1 based on a function call
- $n_1 \overset{datdep}{\to} n_2$ represents that n_2 is data dependent from n_1
- $n_1 \overset{behdep}{\to} n_2$ represents the behaviour dependency

To build the Dependency Graph the first step is to determine which functions are potentially involved in a dependency analysis. We select functions for the initial set and calculate the transitive closure on the call-graph of the functions. Thus we obtain a set of functions, and for these functions we build the Dependency Graph. We have to consider other types of dependencies than function calls as well, which dependencies are message passing and message receiving. When we perform impact analysis, the initial set contains the changed functions.

For the calculated set of functions we build the CFG based on the formal rules described in Appendix C. The CFG is built separately for every function, thus we obtain the intrafunctional CFG for every function. This CFG does not follow the function calls, but denotes the fact of the function call ($\overset{call}{\to}$), and this information will be used while building the Postdominator Tree (PDT) and the Control Dependency Graph (CDG). This edge is called potential control-flow edge.

Postdominator Tree. The Control Dependency Graph is defined with the help of the PostDominator Tree (PDT). A node from the CFG n_1 postdominates n_2, if every execution path from n_2 to *exit* includes n_1, where *exit* is the return node in the CFG of a function. Therefore, we extend the Control-Flow Graphs with a special node, which represents the absolute exit point of the function. We connect the return node and the possible error point of the function with this special node. We build the PDT using the extended CFG. Using the PDT and the extended CFG, we calculate the Immediate Postdominator Tree using the algorithm described in [13]. A node from the CFG n_1 *immediate postdominates* n_2, if and only if n_1 *postdominates* n_2 and $\nexists n_3$, $n_2 \neq n_3$, $n_3 \neq n_1$: n_1 postdominates n_3 and n_3 postdominates n_2.

Immediate Postdominator Tree for function $fact/1$. Figure 16 shows the Immediate Postdominator Tree of the factorial function introduced in Figure 14. The $(n_1 \to n_2)$ relation in the graph means that the node n_1 immediately postdominates the node n_2. The root of the tree is the special exit node

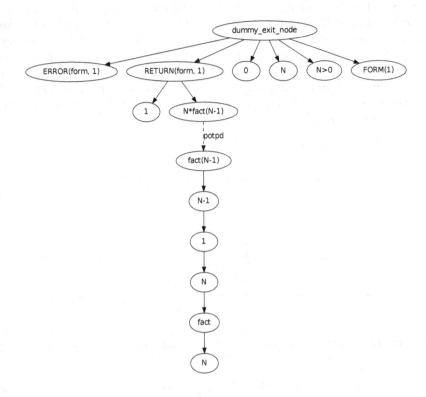

Fig. 16. The postdominator tree for the function `fact/1` (in Figure 14)

dummy_exit_node. The entry point of the CFG (FORM(1)) is postdominated by this special exit node, which means that the function may exit other than normally.

Control Dependency Graph. To determine the control dependencies among the expressions we follow the approach described in [13]. We select those edges from the CFG ($n_1 \rightarrow n_2$) that are not present in the Immediate Postdominator Tree (n_1 is not postdominated by n_2). With finding the lowest common ancestor of these nodes we can determine dependencies. The nodes on the path starting from the common ancestor ended in the node n_2 (except the starting node) are control dependent on node n_1.

We want to reduce the cost of rebuilding the Dependency Graph as much as possible. We follow a compositional approach described in [16]. We build Control-Flow Graphs, Postdominator Trees and Control Dependency Graphs separately for each function and compose the CDGs as the last step in the building of the Composed Control Dependency Graph.

Using this approach, the Control Dependency Graphs (CDG) can be maintained separately, and only the composing of the Control Dependency Graphs should be recalculated if something has changed in a subset of functions.

The next level in building the CDG for the entire program is to compose the intrafunctional CDG of the functions. The function calls, send and receive expressions should be examined at this stage. There is a potential dependency among a function application and its postdominators that comes up if there is a potential of not returning from the called function (when the execution of the called function returns abnormally). The dependency among the send and receive expressions must be also considered. These dependencies can be resolved at the composition stage of the CDGs.

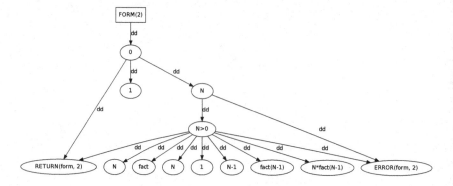

Fig. 17. The Control Dependency Graph for the function `fact/1` (in Figure 14)

Control Dependency Graph for the function fact/1 Figure 18 shows the Control Dependency Graph for the function `fact/1` in Figure 14. In this graph the potential dependencies were eliminated and were resolved as real dependencies. Let us come up with an example, how the dependencies are determined for the function `fact/1`. There is an edge $(N > 0 \overset{\textbf{YES}}{\to} N)$ in the CFG, where N does not postdominate the node N>0. The lowest common ancestor of these nodes in the Postdominator Tree is the node dummy_exit_node, thus nodes on the path from the ancestor to the node N (RETURN(form, 1), N*fact(N-1), fact(N-1), ..., fact and N) are control dependent from N>0. Now that we have the intrafunctional CDG of the factorial function, the next step is to resolve the function calls.

There is a function application in the body of the function (as it is a recursive function) to itself. The called function may fail, since it has an error node for the cases if the actual parameter does not satisfy the pattern, or guards. Two new edges are inserted to the CDG

- $(fact(N-1) \overset{\textbf{inhdep}}{\to} FORM(1))$, since the application is a recursive call, and
- $(RETURN(form, 1) \overset{\textbf{resdep}}{\to} N * fact(N-1))$, since the evaluation of the $(N * fact(N-1))$ depends on the return from the function call.

The old dependency $(fact(N > 0) \overset{\textbf{inhdep}}{\to} N * fact(N-1))$ is removed from the CDG, since the resolution of the function call has introduced a new dependency.

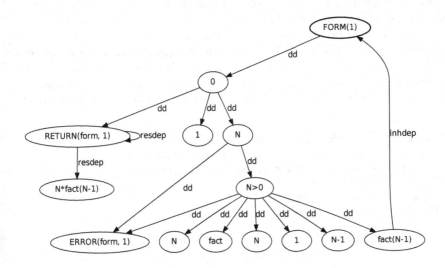

Fig. 18. The resolved Control Dependency Graph for the function `fact/1` (in Figure 14)

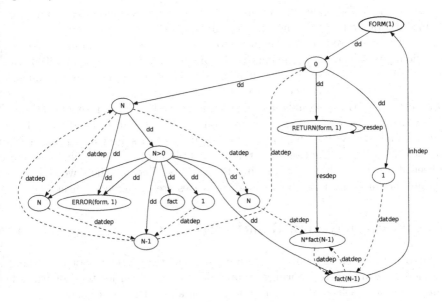

Fig. 19. The Dependency Graph for the function `fact/1` (in Figure 14)

Improving the Accuracy of the Dependency Graph. To reveal real dependencies among the statements of the program, data-flow and data dependency information is also required. The data dependency is calculated from the Data-Flow Graphs of Erlang programs described in Sections 3.1-3.7. The composed

CDG is extended with additional data dependencies, thus we obtain the Dependency Graph (DG) presented in Figure 19.

This graph can be extended with additional information like behaviour dependencies from Section 3.8. This will provide information how the behaviour of the function or the entire program is affected, if the data is changed at some statement. With these additional edges we make the DG more accurate. The draft algorithm for creating the Dependency Graph is presented in Figure 20.

```
calc_dg(SPG)->
  Functions = determine_funs(SPG)
  CFG_List  = lists:map(fun calc_cfg/1, Functions),
  CDG_List  = lists:map(fun calc_cdg/1, CFG_List),
  Comp_CDG  = compose_cdg(CDG_List),
  DCDG      = add_data_dep(CDG)
  BDCDG     = add_behav_and_data_dep(DCDG).
```

Fig. 20. Draft algorithm for creating the Dependency Graph

Usage of Dependency Graphs. The previously described flow and dependency analyses are widely used techniques in compiler optimisations and other static analysis techniques.

We use these Dependency Graphs for static forward slicing [4] of Erlang programs and for finding prallelisable program parts [17].

The slicing is a well known technique to perform static change impact analysis. For slicing we select an expression or a set of expressions and this set will be the slicing criterion. This set can be defined as a result of any change or sequence of changes in the source code. To perform slicing we traverse the Dependency Graph to select the reachable nodes, starting from the criterion set. Performing static forward slicing from these expressions the result can be used to perform impact analysis. As a result of the impact analysis, a subset of the test cases can be selected from the test suite that is possibly affected by the changes. This subset of test cases should be scheduled to run first, because there were changes in the functionalities that the selected test cases are intended to check.

4   Static Analysis in RefactorErl

RefactorErl is a static source code analyser and transformer tool for Erlang. Besides 24 available refactorings, it provides several facilities to support code comprehension tasks and to query information about the source code.

RefactorErl stores the Erlang programs in a Semantic Program Graph (Section 2.1). The lexical level of the graph stores whitespace and comment information, so it can preserve the original layout and comments of the programs during the transformations. The tool has an incremental semantic analyser framework to provide a platform to implement efficient static semantic analyses. RefactorErl stores the SPG in a database, so after a change on the source the stored Semantic Program Graph must be updated. Therefore, the incremental analysis is important, because it has a high cost to reanalyse the whole code base. After each refactoring (or manual change on the source code) only the changed parts are analysed and the necessary information is restored in their context.

The analyser framework is asynchronous and modular: each Erlang form is analysed by a separate Erlang process, and different types of analyses (module, function, variable, record, context, data-flow) are implemented in separate analysers. During the initial analysis the analysers of RefactorErl are executed in a predefined order: an Erlang process is started for every Erlang form, and each process runs the different analysers one by one sequentially. In some cases this ordering is not required (for instance, the record and variable analysers are independent). However some analysers depend on each other, such as the data-flow analyser cannot be performed without the information provided by the variable analyser or the function analyser. The order of the analysers is: context analyser, variable analyser, module analyser, function analyser, record analyser and data-flow analyser. The control-flow analyser runs after the initial loading.

Some analysers can run asynchronously on different forms without any interaction (variables are local to a function clause, so there is no communication between two variable analyser processes), but for analysers using global information synchronisation is required (to create a reference and a definition to a semantic function node must be synchronised).

The data-, control- and behaviour-flow analyses are based on the SPG of RefactorErl. The data and behaviour flow graphs are built during the initial analysis and its edges are added to the SPG. The control-flow graph is built as a separate graph, but it uses the same node identifiers, so the mapping between them is straightforward. We decided to perform the control-flow analysis after the initial loading for efficiency reason. The initial static analysis, without the control-flow analysis, takes almost twelve hours for one and a half million LOC and has 8.5 GB memory footprint. Running control-flow analysis has an extra memory and time cost. The most often used features of RefactorErl could be used without the result of control-flow analysis, so the user can only optionally run this analysis and obtain its result. Currently RefactorErl builds the Dependency Graph only when the slicing application is loaded. In this case the tool monitors the changes made by the performed refactorings on the source code and build the DG of the changed functions. Then it performs the static program slicing to detect the test cases affected by the change on the source code.

Contrarily, the result of data-flow analysis is required for several applications of the tool, therefore the DFG is a part of the semantic level of the SPG. The result of data-flow reaching is used in refactorings: the Introduce Record refactoring (transform the tuple parameter of a function to a record) calculates reaching on the selected tuple, and transform all reached expressions. The result of the data-flow reaching is available for the users through a Semantic Query Language, and can help in the maintenance task: asking the value of a certain expression (backward reaching) can help to detect and fix failures in the software.

RefactorErl introduces a user level *Semantic Query Language* for Erlang developers to ask information about the source code and to support program comprehension tasks [11,20].

The language was designed to provide help in the software development process. It uses a formalism close to the Erlang language concepts, thus a developer can easily learn and adopt it.

```
semantic_query     ::= initial_selection ['.' query_sequence]
query_sequence     ::= query ['.' query_sequence]
query              ::= selection | iteration | closure |
                       property_query
initial_selection  ::= initial_selector ['[' filter ']']
selection          ::= selector ['[' filter ']']
iteration          ::= '{' query_sequence '}' int ['[' filter ']']
closure            ::= '(' query_sequence ')' int ['[' filter ']'] |
                       '(' query_sequence ')+' ['[' filter ']']
property_query     ::= property ['[' filter ']']
```

Fig. 21. The structure of the semantic queries

The language concept were designed according to the semantic entities of the language, thus it introduces the following *entities*: module, function, variable, record, expression, macro, file. Each entity has a set of *selectors* and *properties*. A selector is a binary relation between two entity types, which selects a set of entities that meet the given requirements. A property is a function, which describes some properties of an entity type. For instance, a module has a selector *funs* to select the function defined in the module, and has a property *name* that defines the name of the module. The result of the query can be *filtered*. A semantic query is a sequence of queries starting with an *initial selector*. There are global initial selectors such as *module*, to select every module form the source code as a starting point of the query, and there are position-based initial selectors (starting with '@') to select the pointed entity in the editor: *@var, @fun, @expr*. It is also possible to iterate queries or calculate the closure of a query.

The list of usable selectors and properties for each entity type can be found in the manual of RefactorErl [2]. Here we present only a few examples of queries.

Call Chain – *@fun.(calls)+* or *@fun.(called_by)+* queries return the forward and backward call chain starting from the pointed function. It is also possible to ask the same result starting from the modules of the analysed program: *mods[name=mymod].funs[name=myfun].(calls)+*

References and Definitions – *@fun.refs, @fun.def, @record.refs*, and similar queries for each entity type return the references or the definition of a given entity. *@fun.dynrefs* returns all the dynamic references to a function.

Original Value of an Expression – *@expr.origin* results in a list of expressions which value can be flown to the pointed expression. The query

@expr.origin[type=atom] filters out the atoms from the result. In case of debugging, these queries can be useful. For instance, when we get a *badmatch* exception we can find the value of the non matching expression. This query uses the result of the defined data-flow reaching.

Following an Expression – *@expr.reach* lists all of the expressions which value can be a copy of the pointed expression based on the defined data-flow reaching.

Asking dependent nodes – *@expr.dep, @fun.dep* lists all of the expression nodes that depend on the pointed expression or function.

Considering the Erlang code from Figure 7, one can select the variable Y from the body of function **cons/0** and query *@expr.origin[type = integer]*. The result contains the integer values that can reach Y; in this example this is the integer 2.

5   Related Work

The usage of static analysis techniques was studied in several papers and books. Most of them are closely related to concrete languages or language types.

The book [14] gives a short overview of static analysis techniques and their usage to address different kinds of problems.

Dependency graphs are originally designed and used in compilers to prevent the statement execution in wrong order, i.e. the order that changes the meaning of the program [13]. This book concentrates on high level of optimisations, while our purpose was not the optimisation of Erlang programs, rather to make the information available to the developers. We have utilised some algorithms (e.g. building the postdominator tree) and ideas from this book in our analyses.

Lots of research has been done on the topic of flow analysis. These techniques are mainly used in compiler optimisations, liveness analysis, automatic parallelisation, program slicing, and so on. For instance, Olin Shiver [15] presented a general model for control-flow analysis in Scheme via abstract interpretation of a denotational semantics. The flow analysis was applied to optimisation of higher-order languages such as described in the paper [12]. In case of optimisations, data and control-flow information are calculated simultaneously, but we separate these analyses. Since RefactorErl stores the calculated information in a database, our analyses took more time than an in-memory analysis. Therefore, we decided to calculate only the data-flow information at the initial loading of files and to calculate the control-flow information upon request (e.g. when slicing has to be performed).

It is hard to compare the defined Data-Flow Graphs with flow graphs from other languages. Most of the techniques are based on solving data-flow equations. Those algorithms mainly operate on control-flow graphs, while our algorithm is based on the syntax of Erlang and operates on the extended syntax tree of Erlang programs (i.e. on the Semantic Program Graph of RefactorErl). Using the control-flow graphs they define a set of data-flow equations at the entry and exit point of the basic blocks of the programs and evaluate the flow of data between pred/succ basic blocks [14]. Contrary to this, Erlang is a single assignment language, thus the values of the variables cannot be changed. From this point of view calculating the data-flow reaching in Erlang is a less complex task.

The defined flow graphs and the Dependency Graph can be used in dependency graph based program slicing methods [9]. Most of these algorithms are using compound program or system dependency graphs, which are built from the control- and data-flow graphs of the procedures.

There are static analyser tools for Erlang such as Dialyzer [1]. The goal of this tool is to identify software discrepancies and defects, such as type mismatches, race condition defects, etc. Besides the different goals of Dialyzer and RefactorErl, there is another difference. Dialyzer analyses the Core Erlang code [5] instead of the Erlang source file. Core Erlang is an intermediate representation for Erlang programs, and it has a less complex syntax than Erlang. We decided to analyse the source code and store it in a custom semantic program graph, because RefactorErl aims to preserve the original layout of the unmodified program parts between the refactoring steps.

The refactoring tool Wrangler [10] annotates the Abstract Syntax Tree provided by the Syntax Tools library of Erlang. The Semantic Program Graph representation is more efficient in information retrieval, since instead of syntax tree traversals most of the information about the source code can be gathered by using fixed length queries.

6   Conclusions

The usage of various static analysis methods is getting widespread in different stages of the software development lifecycle. Most of the analysers work on an intermediate source code representation and the abstraction of the representation depends on the target of the static analysis. In this paper we described static semantic knowledge representation about Erlang source code in different forms.

We present a model to represent the lexical, syntactic and semantic information about the Erlang source code, the Semantic Program Graph. Besides the graph, we present a formal model for Erlang programs that is used later to describe formal data-, behaviour- and control-flow rules of Erlang programs. We can build flow graphs based on these rules from the SPG, and further analysis can be performed based on them. We have defined reaching relations on flow graphs. We have described how to build a Dependency Graph using the flow graphs, and how these graphs can be used for program slicing, or to detect parallelisable components in the source code.

The presented graphs are integrated with the RefactorErl tool, that is a static source code analyser and a refactoring tool for Erlang. We have presented a query language which is applicable to query flow and dependency information about the software for developers.

Acknowledgement. We would like to thank for the related ideas and work of the members of the RefactorErl group.

References

1. The DIALYZER: a DIscrepancy AnaLYZer for ERlang programs, http://www.it.uu.se/research/group/hipe/dialyzer
2. RefactorErl Home Page (2011), http://plc.inf.elte.hu/erlang/
3. Bozó, I., Horpácsi, D., Horváth, Z., Kitlei, R., Kőszegi, J., Tejfel, M., Tóth, M.: Refactorerl – source code analysis and refactoring in erlang. In: Proceeding of the 12th Symposium on Programming Languages and Software Tools, Tallin, Estonia (2011)
4. Bozó, I., Tóth, M.: Selecting erlang test cases using impact analysis. In: Proceedings of Symposium on Computer Languages, Implementations and Tools, Kassandra, Halkidiki, Greece (2011)
5. Carlsson, R.: An introduction to core erlang. In: Proceedings of the PLI 2001 Erlang Workshop (2001)
6. Ericsson, A.B.: EDOC – Erlang program documentation generator. Latest version, http://www.erlang.org/documentation/doc5.4.2.1/lib/edoc-0.1/doc/html/index.html
7. Ericsson, A.B.: Erlang Reference Manual, http://www.erlang.org/doc/reference_manual/part_frame.html
8. Horpácsi, D., Kőszegi, J.: Static analysis of function calls in erlang – refining the static function call graph with dynamic call information by using data-flow analysis. In: Proceedings of the Central and Eastern European Conference on Software Engineering Techniques, Debrecen, Hungary (August 2011)
9. Horwitz, S., Reps, T., Binkley, D.: Interprocedural slicing using dependence graphs. In: PhD thesis, University of Michigan, Ann Arbor, MI (1979)
10. Li, H., Thompson, S.: Tool support for refactoring functional programs. In: WRT 2008: Proceedings of the 2nd Workshop on Refactoring Tools, pp. 1–4. ACM, New York (2008)
11. Lövei, L., Hajós, L., Tóth, M.: Erlang Semantic Query Language. In: Proceedings of the 8th International Conference on Applied Informatics, ICAI 2010 (January 2010)
12. Michael Ashley, J., Kent Dybvig, R.: A practical and flexible flow analysis for higher-order languages. ACM Transactions on Programming Languages and Systems 20(4), 845–868 (1998)
13. Muchnick, S.S.: Advanced Compiler Design and Implementation. Morgan Kaufmann Publishers, Inc. (1997)
14. Nielson, F., Nielson, H.R., Hankin, C.: Principles of Program Analysis. Springer (1999) (corrected 2005)
15. Shivers, O.: Control-Flow Analysis of Higher-Order Languages. PhD thesis, Carnegie Mellon University (1991)
16. Stafford, J.: A formal, language-independent, and compositional approach to control dependence analysis. PhD thesis, University of Colorado, Boulder, Colorado, USA (2000)
17. Tóth, M., Bozó, I., Horváth, Z., Erdődi, A.: Static analysis and refactoring towards erlang multicore programming. In: Pre-proceedings of the Fourth Workshop on Programming Language Approaches to Concurrency and Communication-cEntric Software, PLACES 2011, Saarbrcken, Germany (2011)
18. Tóth, M., Bozó, I., Horváth, Z., Lövei, L., Tejfel, M., Kozsik, T.: Impact Analysis of Erlang Programs Using Behaviour Dependency Graphs. In: Horváth, Z., Plasmeijer, R., Zsók, V. (eds.) CEFP 2009. LNCS, vol. 6299, pp. 372–390. Springer, Heidelberg (2010)

19. Tóth, M., Bozó, I., Horváth, Z., Tejfel, M.: First order flow analysis for Erlang. In: 8th Joint Conference on Mathematics and Computer Science, MACS 2010 (2010)
20. Tóth, M., Bozó, I., Kőszegi, J., Horváth, Z.: Applying the Query Language to support program comprehension. Acta Electrotechnica et Informatica 11(03), 3–10 (2011) ISSN 1335-8243 (print), ISSN 1338-3957 (online)

A   The Syntax of Erlang Programs

We introduce the Erlang language in this section.

The source code of Erlang applications is organised to *modules*. Each module contains a set of *function*, *record* and *macro* definitions and some *attributes* (e.g. module declaration, exported/imported functions, specifications). We introduce the syntax of the Erlang functions in Figures 22 and 23. We do not introduce the syntax of the whole Erlang in these figures; we concentrate on those language elements that are used in the further applied complex semantic analysis such as data-flow or control-flow analyses. During the semantic analysis we consider the

$V ::=$ variables (including the underscore pattern (_))
$A ::=$ atoms
$I ::=$ integers
$K ::= A \mid I \mid$ other constants (e.g. string, float, char)
$P ::= K \mid V \mid \{P,\ldots,P\} \mid [P,\ldots,P|P]$
$F ::= A(P,\ldots,P)$ when $E \rightarrow E,\ldots,E;$

     $\vdots$

    $A(P,\ldots,P)$ when $E \rightarrow E,\ldots,E.$
$E ::= K \mid V \mid \{E,\ldots,E\} \mid E_{List} \mid$
    $P = E \mid E \circ E \mid E \: ! \: E \mid \circ E \mid (E) \mid E(E,\ldots,E) \mid$
    case E of
       P when $E \rightarrow E,\ldots,E;$

        $\vdots$

       P when $E \rightarrow E,\ldots,E$
    end $\mid$
    if
       $E \rightarrow E,\ldots,E;$
       $\ldots$
       $E \rightarrow E,\ldots,E$
    end $\mid$
    receive
       P when $E \rightarrow E,\ldots,E;$

        $\vdots$

       P when $E \rightarrow E,\ldots,E$
    after
       $E \rightarrow E,\ldots,E$
    end $\mid E_2$
$E_{List} ::= [E,\ldots,E|E] \mid [E||P\text{<-}E,\ldots,P\text{<-}E,E,\ldots,E]$

Fig. 22. Erlang syntax

Erlang programs as a set of functions. Another simplification of the presented syntax is that the *guard expressions* are represented as regular Erlang expressions, however there are only a few restricted language constructs that can be used as guards. For example, no user defined functions can be used in guards.

E_2::= try $E,\dots,E$ of
  P when E -> $E,\dots,E$;
    $\dots$
  P when E -> $E,\dots,E$
catch
  $P:P$ when E -> $E,\dots,E$;
    $\dots$
  $P:P$ when E -> $E,\dots,E$
after
  E -> $E,\dots,E$
end |
catch E |
begin
  $E,\dots,E$
end |
fun
  $(P,\dots,P)$ when E -> $E,\dots,E$;
    $\dots$
  $(P,\dots,P)$ when E -> $E,\dots,E$
end
fun E/I

Fig. 23. Erlang syntax (cont.)

In Figures 22 and 23 we use the following notations:

- V denotes the variables
- K denotes the atoms (A), integers (I) and other constants such as strings, floats, etc.
- P is a pattern that can be any constant, variable or a tuple or list of patterns
- F is a function that has one or more function clauses separated by semicolons. A function clause has a name represented by an atom and has n formal parameters $(n \in N, n \geq 0)$ represented by patterns. Optionally, the function clauses have a guard expression after the keyword **when**. The body of the function is a sequence of expressions separated by commas.
- E denotes the expressions. Several kinds of expressions are listed in Figures 22 and 23. An expression can be a constant (K), a variable (V), a tuple $(\{E, \dots, E\})$, a list (E_{List}) or can be a compound expression. A list is a sequence of elements optionally followed by the tail of the list in squared brackets and also can be a list comprehension that produces the elements of the list using some generators and filters. A tuple is an ordered list of a fixed number of elements in curly brackets.

The simplest compound expression is the pattern matching expression $(P = E)$, which binds a value to a variable. There are infix operators in Erlang $(+, -, and, or,$ etc). One of them has a special role: ! is the message passing operator in Erlang. There are also unary operators $(\circ E)$, and parenthesis expressions $((E))$.

There are different kinds of function applications in Erlang $(E(E, ..., E))$. An application can refer to a fun-expression (lambda expression) or a named function. The named functions can be called by using local or qualified function calls. The latter one refers to the called function with the implementing module name and the called function name $(Mod : Fun(Par_1, ..., Par_n))$.

There are several branching expressions in the language: case, if, receive, try expression, containing some clauses. Their clauses are similar to function clauses. The main difference is that an if clause does not contain any patterns, it only evaluates a guard, and try and receive expression have an optional after clause. Besides the try expression, a simple catch expression was introduced to handle runtime errors.

The begin-end expression is the block expression to group a sequence of expressions into a block.

Finally, like other functional languages, Erlang also introduces unnamed functions as expressions (fun-expression, lambda expression). There are explicit and implicit forms of these expressions. The explicit fun expressions are similar to function definitions and have n clauses $(n \in N, n \geq 1)$. The fun expressions begin with the keyword **fun** and are closed with the keyword **end**. The implicit fun expressions refers to named functions.

We note here that during the implementation of the Semantic Program Graph we have extended this syntax description to generate the syntax tree of Erlang modules (details in Section 2.1).

B   Data-Flow Rules

We build Data-Flow Graphs for Erlang programs using formal rules. We describe these rules in this section. We use the following notations in the data-flow rules in Figures 24–26:

- $p, p_i \in P$ are patterns,
- $e, e_i \in E$ are Erlang expressions;
- $a \xrightarrow{*} b$ $(a, b \in P \cup E, * \in \{f, c_i, s_i, d\})$ denotes that there is a $*$ type of data-flow edges between nodes a and b

Variables. Erlang binds a value to a variable in a match expression or in a pattern. This value cannot be changed during the execution of the program. Therefore, the bound value of a variable flows directly to all occurrences of that variable – *Figure 24: (Variable) rule.*

	Expression	Direct Graph Edges
(Variable)	p binding of a variable n occurrence of a variable	$p \xrightarrow{f} n$
(Match exp.)	e_0: $\quad p = e$	$e \xrightarrow{f} e_0$ $e \xrightarrow{f} p$
(Pattern)	p_0: $\quad p_1 = p_2$	$p_0 \xrightarrow{f} p_1$ $p_0 \xrightarrow{f} p_2$
(Unary op.)	e_0: $\quad \circ\ e_1$	$e_1 \xrightarrow{d} e_0$
(Infix op.)	e_0: $\quad e_1 \circ e_2$	$e_1 \xrightarrow{d} e_0$ $e_2 \xrightarrow{d} e_0$
(Parenthesis)	e_0: $\quad (e)$	$e \xrightarrow{f} e_0$
(Tuple exp.)	e_0: $\quad \{e_1, \ldots, e_n\}$	$e_1 \xrightarrow{c_1} e_0, \ldots, e_n \xrightarrow{c_n} e_0$
(Tuple pat.)	p_0: $\quad \{p_1, \ldots, p_n\}$	$p_0 \xrightarrow{s_1} p_1, \ldots, p_0 \xrightarrow{s_n} p_n$
(List exp.)	e_0: $\quad [e_1, \ldots, e_n | e_{n+1}]$	$e_1 \xrightarrow{c_e} e_0, \ldots, e_n \xrightarrow{c_e} e_0$ $e_{n+1} \xrightarrow{f} e_0$
(List gen.)	e_0: $\quad [e_1 || p \leftarrow e_2]$	$e_1 \xrightarrow{c_e} e_0,\ e_2 \xrightarrow{s_e} p$
(List pat.)	p_0: $\quad [p_1, \ldots, p_n | p_{n+1}]$	$p_0 \xrightarrow{s_e} p_1, \ldots, p_0 \xrightarrow{s_e} p_n$ $p_0 \xrightarrow{f} p_{n+1}$
(BIF 1)	e_0: $\quad \mathsf{hd}(e_1)$	$e_1 \xrightarrow{s_e} e_0$
(BIF 2)	e_0: $\quad \mathsf{tl}(e_1)$	$e_1 \xrightarrow{f} e_0$
(BIF 3)	I constant, e_0: $\quad \mathsf{element}(I, e_1)$	$e_1 \xrightarrow{s_I} e_0$

Fig. 24. Static Data-Flow Graph building rules

Match Expressions. When we bind a value to a variable in a match expression both the value of the pattern expression and the result of the match expression itself are the same as the right hand side expression – *Figure 24: (Match exp.) rule.*

Operators. There is no direct data-flow in operator expressions, because an operator does not copy the value of its argument. It evaluates some function using the value on the operands, so the result of the operator expression depends on the value of its operands – *Figure 24: (Unary op.) and (Infix op.) rules.*

Compound Expressions and Patterns. Compound expressions, such as tuples and lists, preserves the value of their elements. For instance, packing some data into a tuple, then forwarding the tuple somewhere in the program (copying its value), and then unpacking the data from the tuple result in the same data. We have to consider only the index of the elements in the compound data structure.

The rules *Figure 24: (Tuple exp.) and (Tuple pat.)* describe that we construct ($\overset{c_i}{\rightarrow}$) the tuple from its elements and we can select ($\overset{s_i}{\rightarrow}$) the elements of the tuple. The tuple constructor and selector edges are indexed by natural numbers ($i \in N$) to denote the position of the elements in the tuple, and the same index in the constructor and in the selector edges represents the same data-flow.

The rule *Figure 24: (List exp.)* describes that we construct the list from some value ($\overset{c_e}{\rightarrow}$) and optionally a list ($\overset{f}{\rightarrow}$) – so, we create it from the head elements and the tail of the list. Like construction, we can select head elements ($\overset{s_e}{\rightarrow}$) and a tail list ($\overset{f}{\rightarrow}$) from a pattern list expression – *Figure 24: (List pat.) rule*. Lists are variable sized data structures and the typical use of them makes precise index-based data-flow calculating useless, so we only distinguish the elements of the list (denoted with the index e) and the tail of the list. In general, the tail of the list contains almost every element of the list, thus we approximate this by adding the flow edge from the tail to the list.

The rule *Figure 24: (List gen.)* shows another way for constructing a list. We select an element (p) from a list (e_2) and push a new element (e_1) to the constructed list (e_0). Most of the time the head expression and the new element depends on the value of the selected element.

BIF – Built in Functions. The rules *Figure 24: (BIF 1), (BIF 2) and (BIF 3)* present the selector and constructor data-flow edges based on background knowledge about the given built in functions. The function `hd/1` selects the first element of a list, the function `tl/1` selects the tail of the list and the function `element/2` selects the Ith element of a tuple.

Branching Expressions. Conditional expressions branch the control based on pattern matching (case expression) or guard evaluation (if expression). The result of such an expression is always the result of the last expression of the branch evaluated at runtime. Since potentially any branch can be evaluated, the value of each last expression can flow to the case/if expression. Besides this, the result of the head expression of the case expression is matched to the patterns of each branch, thus it has data-flow among them – *Figure 25: (Case exp.) and (If exp.) rules.*

Function Calls. There are two different function call rules – *Figure 25: (Fun. call 1) and (Fun. call 2)*. The difference between the two rules is that in the former case we can unambiguously identify the called function and its body, but in the latter we cannot detect the called function body (because the AST of the implementing module is not available or the module or the function name is dynamic).

If the body of the called function is available in our representation, we can preform an interprocedural data-flow reaching; otherwise we can only denote the dependency from the called function and the parameters of the call (denoted by

	Expressions	Direct Graph Edges
(Case exp.)	e_0: **case** e **of** $\quad p_1$ **when** $g_1 \to e_1^1, \ldots, e_{l_1}^1;$ $\quad \vdots$ $\quad p_n$ **when** $g_n \to e_1^n, \ldots, e_{l_n}^n$ **end**	$e \xrightarrow{f} p_1, \ldots, e \xrightarrow{f} p_n$ $e_{l_1}^1 \xrightarrow{f} e_0, \ldots, e_{l_n}^n \xrightarrow{f} e_0$
(If exp.)	e_0: **if** $\quad g_1 \to e_1^1, \ldots, e_{l_1}^1;$ $\quad \vdots$ $\quad g_k \to e_1^k, \ldots, e_{l_k}^k$ **end**	$e_{l_1}^1 \xrightarrow{f} e_0, \ldots, e_{l_k}^n \xrightarrow{f} e_0$
(Fun. call 1)	e_0: $\quad$ **m** : **g**$(e_1, \ldots, e_n)$ **or** $\quad$ **g**$(e_1, \ldots, e_n)$ **m:g/n:** $\quad$ **g**$(p_1^1, \ldots, p_n^1)$ **when** $g_1 \to$ $\qquad e_1^1, \ldots, e_{l_1}^1;$ $\quad \vdots$ $\quad$ **g**$(p_1^m, \ldots, p_n^m)$ **when** $g_m \to$ $\qquad e_1^m, \ldots, e_{l_m}^m.$	$e_1 \xrightarrow{f} p_1^1, \ldots, e_1 \xrightarrow{f} p_1^m$ $\vdots$ $e_n \xrightarrow{f} p_n^1, \ldots, e_n \xrightarrow{f} p_n^m$ $e_{l_1}^1 \xrightarrow{f} e_0, \ldots, e_{l_m}^m \xrightarrow{f} e_0$
(Fun. call 2)	e_0: $\quad$ **e$_m$** : **e$_g$**$(e_1, \ldots, e_n)$ e_m or e_g not constant or $e_m : e_g/n$ not defined	$e_m \xrightarrow{d} e_0, \; e_g \xrightarrow{d} e_0$ $e_1 \xrightarrow{d} e_0, \ldots, e_n \xrightarrow{d} e_0$

Fig. 25. Static Data-Flow Graph building rules (cont.)

($\xrightarrow{d}$) edges). In the former case we can find the actual parameters of the called function and add flow edges form the formal parameters to the corresponding actual parameter of each function clause. The result of a function call is the result of the last expression of the executed function body, therefore we add flow edges from the last expressions to the function call expression.

Error Handling Expressions. The try expression rule (*Figure 26: (Try exp.)*) is similar to the case rule. The head of the try expression contains more expressions and the result of the last expression is matched to the patterns of the try, but it does not match the patterns of the catch clauses. These are evaluated when a runtime exception occurs and the exception matches them. Thus, there is no data-flow among the last expressions and the patterns of the catch clauses. The result of the try expression is the result of the evaluated clause, so the values of the last expressions (including the values of the catch clauses) flow to the try expression. The result of the after clause is simply omitted, it does not flow anywhere.

	Expressions	Direct graph Edges
(Try exp.)	e_0: try $e_1, \ldots, e_k$ of $\quad p_1$ when $g_1 \rightarrow$ $\qquad e_1^1, \ldots, e_{l_1}^1;$ $\qquad \vdots$ $\quad p_n$ when $g_n \rightarrow$ $\qquad e_1^n, \ldots, e_{l_n}^n$ catch $\quad p_{n+1}$ when $g_{n+1} \rightarrow$ $\qquad e_1^{n+1}, \ldots, e_{l_{n+1}}^{n+1};$ $\qquad \vdots$ $\quad p_m$ when $g_m \rightarrow$ $\qquad e_1^m, \ldots, e_{l_m}^m$ after $\quad e_{m+1} \rightarrow$ $\qquad e_1^{m+1}, \ldots, e_{l_{m+1}}^{m+1}$ end	$e \xrightarrow{\mathbf{f}} p_1, \ldots, e \xrightarrow{\mathbf{f}} p_n$ $e_{l_1}^1 \xrightarrow{\mathbf{f}} e_0, \ldots, e_{l_n}^n \xrightarrow{\mathbf{f}} e_0$ $e_{l_{n+1}}^{n+1} \xrightarrow{\mathbf{f}} e_0, \ldots, e_{l_m}^m \xrightarrow{\mathbf{f}} e_0$
(Catch exp.)	e_0: $\quad$ catch e	$e \xrightarrow{\mathbf{f}} e_0$
(Begin-end)	e_0: begin $\quad e_1, \ldots, e_n$ end	$e_n \xrightarrow{\mathbf{f}} e_0$
(Send exp.)	e_0: $\quad e_1 \; ! \; e_2$ e': $\quad$ receive $\quad\quad p_1$ when $g_1 \rightarrow$ $\qquad\quad e_1^1, \ldots, e_{l_1}^1;$ $\qquad\quad \vdots$ $\quad\quad p_n$ when $g_n \rightarrow$ $\qquad\quad e_1^n, \ldots, e_{l_n}^n$ $\quad$ after $\quad\quad e \rightarrow e_1, \ldots, e_s$ $\quad$ end	$e_2 \xrightarrow{\mathbf{f}} e_0$ $e_2 \xrightarrow{\mathbf{f}} p_1, \ldots, e_2 \xrightarrow{\mathbf{f}} p_n$ $e_{l_1}^1 \xrightarrow{\mathbf{f}} e', \ldots, e_{l_n}^n \xrightarrow{\mathbf{f}} e'$ $e_s \xrightarrow{\mathbf{f}} e'$

Fig. 26. Static Data-Flow Graph building rules (cont.)

The catch expression rule (*Figure 26: (Catch exp.)*) describes that the result of its body flows to the catch. In case of a runtime exception , the result of the catch is the error report of the exception.

Message Sending and Receiving. The message sending operator (!) differs from the other infix operators. Its return value is the value of its right hand side expression, so the value of the sent massage – *Figure 26: (Send exp.) rule.* The message flows to the addressed process and tries to match one of its receive expressions, so the message flows to the patterns of the corresponding receive expressions. A naive data-flow algorithm should add a flow edge to the patterns of each receive expression to represent the potential data-flow. This could result in a huge amount of edges in the graph. Instead of this, we try to calculate the corresponding receive expressions and connect them with the sent messages (for details see Section 3.7).

The receive expression is similar to other branching expressions, so its return value is the last expression of the evaluated clause. Therefore, the value of the last expression of each clause flows to the receive expression.

Implicit and Explicit Fun Expressions (Lambda Expressions). The rules of fun expressions (*Figure 27: (Fun. exp. 1) and (Fun. exp. 2)*) express similar

	Expressions	Direct Graph Edges
(Fun exp. 1)	e: $\quad\mathrm{fun}(p_1^1,\ldots,p_n^1)$ when g_1 $\rightarrow$ $\qquad e_1^1,\ldots,e_{l_1}^1$; $\qquad\vdots$ $\quad(p_1^m,\ldots,p_n^m)$ when g_m $\rightarrow$ $\qquad e_1^m,\ldots,e_{l_m}^m$ e_0: $\quad e(e_1,\ldots,e_n)$ e can be calculated by data-flow analysis	$e_1 \xrightarrow{\mathbf{f}} p_1^1,\ldots,e_1 \xrightarrow{\mathbf{f}} p_1^m$ $\vdots$ $e_n \xrightarrow{\mathbf{f}} p_n^1,\ldots,e_n \xrightarrow{\mathbf{f}} p_n^m$ $e_{l_1}^1 \xrightarrow{\mathbf{f}} e_0,\ldots,e_{l_m}^m \xrightarrow{\mathbf{f}} e_0$
(Fun exp. 2.)	$m{:}g/n$: $\quad g(p_1^1,\ldots,p_n^1)$ when g_1 $\rightarrow$ $\qquad e_1^1,\ldots,e_{l_1}^1$; $\qquad\vdots$ $\quad g(p_1^m,\ldots,p_n^m)$ when g_m $\rightarrow$ $\qquad e_1^m,\ldots,e_{l_m}^m$. e: $\quad\mathrm{fun}\ m:g/n$ or fun g/n e_0: $\quad e(e_1,\ldots,e_n)$ e can be calculated by data-flow analysis	$e_1 \xrightarrow{\mathbf{f}} p_1^1,\ldots,e_1 \xrightarrow{\mathbf{f}} p_1^m$ $\vdots$ $e_n \xrightarrow{\mathbf{f}} p_n^1,\ldots,e_n \xrightarrow{\mathbf{f}} p_n^m$ $e_{l_1}^1 \xrightarrow{\mathbf{f}} e_0,\ldots,e_{l_m}^m \xrightarrow{\mathbf{f}} e_0$
(Fun. exp 3)	e_0: $\quad e(e_1,\ldots,e_n)$ e cannot be detected by data-flow reaching or e is m:g/n or g/n by data-flow reaching but m:g/n or g/n not defined	$e \xrightarrow{\mathbf{d}} e_0$ $e_1 \xrightarrow{\mathbf{d}} e_0,\ldots,e_n \xrightarrow{\mathbf{d}} e_0$

Fig. 27. Static Data-Flow Graph building rules (cont.)

parameter value and result copying as functions and function calls, but in the most of the cases identifying them is not straightforward. The fun expressions are defined in the body of functions and they can spread among functions as data, so data-flow analysis is required to identify the definitions of fun expressions.

If it is possible to identify the definition of the explicit fun expression – *(Fun. exp 1) rule* – we link the actual parameter of the call and the corresponding formal parameter of each fun expression clause with a flow edge, and add a

	Expressions	Direct Graph Edges
(Dyn. call 1)	e_0: $\quad e_1 : e_2(e_3, \ldots, e_{n+2})$ $e_1 : e_2/n$ is m:g/n by data-flow reaching m:g/n: $\quad g(p_1^1, \ldots, p_n^1)$ when $g_1 \; \to$ $\qquad e_1^1, \ldots, e_{l_1}^1;$ $\qquad \vdots$ $\quad g(p_1^m, \ldots, p_n^m)$ when $g_m \; \to$ $\qquad e_1^m, \ldots, e_{l_m}^m.$	$e_3 \xrightarrow{\mathbf{f}} p_1^1, \ldots, e_3 \xrightarrow{\mathbf{f}} p_1^m$ $\vdots$ $e_{n+2} \xrightarrow{\mathbf{f}} p_n^1, \ldots, e_{n+2} \xrightarrow{\mathbf{f}} p_n^m$ $e_{l_1}^1 \xrightarrow{\mathbf{f}} e_0, \ldots, e_{l_m}^m \xrightarrow{\mathbf{f}} e_0$
(Dyn. call 2)	e_0: $\quad$ apply(e_1, e_2, e_3) e_1 is m, e_2 is g, e_3 is $[e_4, \ldots e_{n+3}]$ by data-flow reaching m:g/n: $\quad g(p_1^1, \ldots, p_n^1)$ when $g_1 \; \to$ $\qquad e_1^1, \ldots, e_{l_1}^1;$ $\qquad \vdots$ $\quad g(p_1^m, \ldots, p_n^m)$ when $g_m \; \to$ $\qquad e_1^m, \ldots, e_{l_m}^m.$	$e_4 \xrightarrow{\mathbf{f}} p_1^1, \ldots, e_4 \xrightarrow{\mathbf{f}} p_1^m$ $\vdots$ $e_{n+3} \xrightarrow{\mathbf{f}} p_n^1, \ldots, e_{n+3} \xrightarrow{\mathbf{f}} p_n^m$ $e_{l_1}^1 \xrightarrow{\mathbf{f}} e_0, \ldots, e_{l_m}^m \xrightarrow{\mathbf{f}} e_0$
(Dyn. call 3)	e_0: $\quad e_1 : e_2(e_3, \ldots, e_{n+2})$ $e_1, \ldots e_{n+2}$ cannot be detected by data-flow reaching	$e_1 \xrightarrow{\mathbf{d}} e_0, \ldots, e_{n+2} \xrightarrow{\mathbf{d}} e_0$
(Dyn. call 4)	e_0: $\quad$ apply(e_1, e_2, e_3) e_1, e_2, e_3 cannot be detected by data-flow reaching	$e_1 \xrightarrow{\mathbf{d}} e_0, e_2 \xrightarrow{\mathbf{d}} e_0, e_3 \xrightarrow{\mathbf{d}} e_0$

Fig. 28. Static Data-Flow Graph building rules (cont.)

flow edge from the last expression of each function body to the call representing the return value.

If data-flow reaching detects that the defining expression of the fun expression is an implicit fun expression, we have to find the definition of the referred function. Similar to the *(Fun. call 2.) rule* (Figure 26), if the AST is not available, we have to add the dependency edges to the Data-Flow Graph *(Figure 27: (Fun. exp. 3))*, otherwise we add the flow edges among the parameters and the return values *(Figure 27: (Fun. exp. 2))*.

The rule *Figure 27: (Fun. exp. 3)* describes the dependency edges when no information can be calculated about the referred function or fun expression using data-flow analysis.

Dynamic Function Calls. The rules of dynamic function calls (Figure 28) are also based on the reuse of data-flow analysis. When it is possible to detect the referred functions by data-flow analysis we link the actual parameters to the formal parameters and the return value to the function call by flow edges. The *(Dyn. call. 1)* rule describes the MFA-s (qualified function calls where the name of the module and/or the name of the function are not atoms) when the module name and the function name is statically detectable. The *(Dyn. call. 2)* rule describes that in case of an apply call the parameter list of the actual call also has to be detected. We have to calculate the arity of the function and it is also necessary to link them to the formal parameters of the referred function.

If one of the necessary information is not reachable, we only have to add the data dependency edges – *(Dyn. call. 3) and (Dyn. call. 4) rules*.

C   Control-Flow Rules

The Control-Flow Graph (CFG) represents all the possible execution/evaluation paths of the program that can be chosen for every possible input. The CFG is a language dependent representation of the program as it is based on the semantics of the language.

We have defined the control-flow rules for Erlang programming language based on its semantics. The language has strict evaluation, which means that before evaluating a compound expression its subexpressions have to be evaluated. In every case the subexpressions are evaluated in left to right order. The defined control-flow rules are compositional, thus the graph can be composed from the previously computed subgraphs. We use the SPG of RefactorErl and use the same identifiers for the vertices in the CFG. We extend the set of nodes with additional dummy vertices for joining branches, error nodes, etc. The rules are defined in Figures 29–32.

The notation in the figures are: $e, e_i \in E$ is an expression, $g, g_j \in E$ is a guard expression, $p, p_k \in P$ is a pattern and $f/n \in F$ stands for function. The $e'_0 \in E$ is a dummy node in the control flow graph, which represents the entry point of the compound expression and joining dummy nodes (ret) to represent the return value for the conditional branching expressions. The relation $\rightarrow$ represents the control-flow between the nodes. The edges that have no labels represent sequences, and edges with labels represent:

- conditional branching and pattern matching with ($\overset{\textbf{yes}}{\rightarrow}$), ($\overset{\textbf{no}}{\rightarrow}$) edges
- returning to a previous expression ($\overset{\textbf{ret}}{\rightarrow}$),
- function calls/applications with ($\overset{\textbf{call}}{\rightarrow}$),
- receive expression with ($\overset{\textbf{rec}}{\rightarrow}$),
- send expression with ($\overset{\textbf{send}}{\rightarrow}$).

The relations ($\overset{\textbf{call}}{\rightarrow}$), ($\overset{\textbf{rec}}{\rightarrow}$), ($\overset{\textbf{send}}{\rightarrow}$) represent special relations, which indicate a possible dependency between the nodes of different functions (for details, see Section 3.10). In the rest of this section we describe the formal rules for different expression and discuss the rules in more detail.

	Expressions	Control-Flow Edges
(Unary op.)	e_0: $\quad \circ\ e_1$	$e_0' \rightarrow e_1,\ e_1 \rightarrow e_0$
(Left assoc. op.)	e_0: $\quad e_1 \circ_1 e_2 \circ_2 ...$ $\quad \circ_{n-2}\ e_{n-1}\ \circ_{n-1}\ e_n$	$e_0' \rightarrow e_1,$ $e_1 \rightarrow e_2,\ e_2 \rightarrow \circ_1,\ \circ_1 \rightarrow e_3 ... e_n \rightarrow \circ_{n-1},$ $\circ_{n-1} \rightarrow e_0$
(Right assoc. op.)	e_0: $\quad e_1 \circ_1 e_2 \circ_2 \ ...$ $\quad \circ_{n-2}\ e_{n-1}\ \circ_{n-1}\ e_n$	$e_0' \rightarrow e_1,$ $e_1 \rightarrow e_2 ... e_{n-1} \rightarrow e_n,$ $e_n \rightarrow \circ_{n-1},$ $\circ_{n-1} \rightarrow \circ_{n-2}, ..., \circ_2 \rightarrow \circ_1,$ $\circ_1 \rightarrow e_0$
(Comp. infix op.)	e_0: $\quad e_1 \circ e_2$	$e_0' \rightarrow e_1,\ e_1 \rightarrow e_2,\ e_2 \rightarrow e_0$
(Andalso op.)	e_0: $\quad e_1 \circ e_2$	$e_0' \rightarrow e_1,$ $e_1 \overset{\textbf{yes}}{\rightarrow} e_2,$ $e_1 \overset{\textbf{no}}{\rightarrow} e_0,$ $e_2 \rightarrow e_0$
(Orelse op.)	e_0: $\quad e_1 \circ e_2$	$e_0' \rightarrow e_1,$ $e_1 \overset{\textbf{no}}{\rightarrow} e_2,$ $e_1 \overset{\textbf{yes}}{\rightarrow} e_0,$ $e_2 \rightarrow e_0$
(Send op.)	e_0: $\quad e_1\ !\ e_2$	$e_0' \rightarrow e_1,\ e_1 \rightarrow e_2,$ $e_2 \overset{\textbf{send}}{\rightarrow} e_0$
(Parenthesis)	e_0: $\quad (e_1)$	$e_0' \rightarrow e_1,\ e_1 \rightarrow e_0$
(Tuple exp.)	e_0: $\quad \{e_1, ..., e_n\}$	$e_0' \rightarrow e_1,$ $e_1 \rightarrow e_2,\ ...,\ e_{n-1} \rightarrow e_n,$ $e_n \rightarrow e_0$
(List exp.)	e_0: $\quad [e_1, ..., e_n | e_{n+1}]$	$e_0' \rightarrow e_1,$ $e_1 \rightarrow e_2,\ ...,\ e_n \rightarrow e_{n+1},$ $e_{n+1} \rightarrow e_0$

Fig. 29. Control-Flow Graph building rules

	Expressions	Control-Flow Edges
(List gen. 1)	e_0: $[e \| p_1 \texttt{<-} e_1, \ldots, p_n \texttt{<-} e_n]$	$e_0' \to e_1$, $e_i \to p_i,\ p_i \overset{no}{\to} e_i,\ p_i \overset{yes}{\to} e_{i+1}$, $e_i \overset{ret}{\to} e_{i-1}$, $e \to e_1$, $(i \in [1, ..., n], e_{n+1} = e)$
(List gen. 2)	e_0: $[e \| p_1 \texttt{<-} e_1, f_{(1,0)}, \ldots, f_{(1,m_1)}$ $\vdots$ $p_n \texttt{<-} e_n, f_{(n,0)}, \ldots, f_{(1,m_n)}]$	$e_0' \to e_1$, $e_i \to p_i,\ p_i \overset{no}{\to} e_i$, $e_i \overset{ret}{\to} e_{i-1}$, $p_i \overset{yes}{\to} f_{(i,0)}$, $f_{(i,j-1)} \overset{yes}{\to} f_{(i,j)},\ f_{(i,m_i)} \overset{yes}{\to} e_{i+1}$, $f_{(i,0)} \overset{no}{\to} e_i,\ f_{(i,j)} \overset{no}{\to} e_i$, $e \to e_1$, $(i \in [1, ..., n], j \in [1, ..., m_i], n, m_i \in N$ $e_{n+1} = e)$
(List gen. 3)	e_0: $[e \| f_{(0,0)}, \ldots, f_{(0,m_0)},$ $p_1 \texttt{<-} e_1, \ldots, p_n \texttt{<-} e_n]$	$e_i \to p_i,\ p_i \overset{no}{\to} e_i,\ p_i \overset{yes}{\to} e_{i+1}$, $e_i \overset{ret}{\to} e_{i-1}$, $e_0' \to f_{(0,0)}$, $f_{(0,j-1)} \overset{yes}{\to} f_{(0,j)},\ f_{(0,m_0)} \overset{yes}{\to} e_1$, $f_{(0,0)} \overset{no}{\to} e_0,\ f_{(0,j)} \overset{no}{\to} e_0$, $e \to e_1$, $(i \in [1, ..., n], j \in [1, ..., m_0], n, m_0 \in N$ $e_{n+1} = e)$

Fig. 30. Control-Flow Graph building rules (cont.)

Unary Operator. There are only a few unary operators in Erlang, like +, -, bnot, not, etc. In the case of the unary operators (*Figure 29: (Unary op.)*), first the subexpression is evaluated ($e_0' \to e_1$), then the unary operator is applied on the evaluated subexpression ($e_1 \to e_0$).

Left Associative Infix Expression. The rule in *Figure 29: (Left assoc. op.)* describes the control-flow in left associative expressions. The language is strict, the subexpressions are evaluated first from left to right order ($e_1 \to e_2$) and then the operator ($e_2 \to e_0$). The subexpressions are evaluated from left to right order.

If there is a sequence of left associative operators with the same precedence, the sequence of operators are evaluated from left to right order. First the first two subexpressions ($e_1 \to e_2$) of the first operator are evaluated and the operator is applied to these values ($e_2 \to \circ_1$), then the previous result and the result of the third subexpression ($\circ_1 \to e_3$) using the second operator ($e_3 \to \circ_3$) and so on. The left associative infix expressions are: /, *, div, rem, band, and, etc.

Right Associative Infix Expression. The rule in *Figure 29: (Right assoc. op.)* describes the control-flow in right associative expressions. The language is strict, the subexpressions are evaluated first and next the operator. The subexpressions are evaluated from left to right order.

If there is a sequence of right associative operators with the same precedence, the sequence of subexpressions is evaluated($e_1 \to e_2$, $e_2 \to e_3$, ..., $e_{n-1} \to e_n$) and then the operators are evaluated from right to left order. First the result of the last two subexpressions using the last operator is evaluated, next the previous result and the third subexpression and so on ($\circ_{n-1} \to \circ_{n-2}$, ..., $\circ_2 \to \circ_1$). The right associative operators are: ++, --, =, !, etc.

Comparative Infix Expression. The comparative infix expressions are neither left nor right associative. The rule in *Figure 29: (Comp. infix op.)* describes the control-flow of these expressions. The two subexpressions are evaluated first from left to right order, then the comparison is evaluated. There are comparison expressions like: <, >, =<, >=, etc.

Short-Circuit Expressions (Andalso, Orelse). The evaluation of the language is strict, but there are two short-circuit infix expressions. The first of them is expression **andalso** (*Figure 29: (Andalso op.)*), which evaluates its left argument first. If it evaluates to **true** the control is given to the right argument ($e_1 \overset{\text{yes}}{\to} e_2$), otherwise it returns with the result **false** and lets the right expression non-evaluated ($e_1 \overset{\text{no}}{\to} e_0$).

The second short-circuit expression is **orelse** (*Figure 29: (Orelse op.)*). It evaluates the left argument and if it evaluates to **false**, it continues with evaluating the right argument ($e_1 \overset{\text{no}}{\to} e_2$), otherwise returns with result **true** and lets the right argument non-evaluated ($e_1 \overset{\text{yes}}{\to} e_0$).

Send Operator (!). The control-flow of the send operator is described in *Figure 29: (Send op.)*. The send operator is right associative, but we describe its control-flow separately. The message sending has side effect and may affect the control-flow of other processes. By analysing the sent messages we can improve the accuracy of our analysis, thus where the send expression is detected the edge is labelled with **send** tag. The evaluation of the send expression is analogous to the right associative expressions. First the subexpressions are evaluated from left to right order, then the send expressions are evaluated from right to left order. The return value of the send expression is the sent value.

Parenthesis. With parentheses we can modify the precedence of the expressions. The control-flow rules for this expression are described in *Figure 29: (Parenthesis)*. We first evaluate the expression in the parentheses and then the parent expression gets the control.

Tuple Expression. The n-tuples are to couple coherent data with fixed size of elements, such as messages, etc. The control-flow of the n-tuples are defined in *Figure 29: (Tuple exp.)*. The elements of the tuple expression are evaluated from left to right order and then it resumes the control to the parent expression, which constructs the tuple.

List Expression. The control-flow of list expressions (*Figure 29: (List exp.)*) is similar to the **n-tuples**. The elements of the list are evaluated and then the control is passed to the parent expression.

List Comprehension. The control-flow rules for building the CFG of the list comprehension is defined in *Figure 30: (List gen. 1), (List gen. 2)* and *(List gen. 3) rules.* The list comprehension is composed of the head expression, which is an arbitrary expression, and a list of qualifiers. A qualifier is a list of either a generator or a filter expression. These three rules cover every possible list comprehension constructs and can be combined. The first rule *(List gen. 1)* describes the control-flow between the generator expressions, the second rule *(List gen. 2)* describes the control-flow among generator and filter expressions and among filter expressions, the third rule *(List gen. 3)* describes the case when the first element in a qualifier list is a filter expression.

The qualifiers are evaluated in left to right order. If the qualifier is a generator, its list expression is evaluated first (for example: $(e_0 \rightarrow e_1)$). It tries to match the values against its pattern $(e_1 \rightarrow p_1)$. If it succeeds, then continues with the next qualifier, which can be either a generator or a filter expression. If none of the values match the pattern, then it resumes the control to its preceding expression (for example the $e_1 \overset{ret}{\rightarrow} e_0$).

If the qualifier is a filter expression, it is evaluated. If it evaluates to **true** the control is resumed by the next qualifier, which can be either a generator or a filter expression. For example:

- to the next filter expression $(f_{(i,j)} \overset{yes}{\rightarrow} f_{(i,j+1)})$ or
- to the list expression of the next generator $(f_{(i,j)} \overset{yes}{\rightarrow} e_{i+1})$

If the filter expression evaluates to **false** the control is resumed to the closest generator situated to its left. For example: $f_{(i,j)} \overset{no}{\rightarrow} e_i)$.

If the end of the qualifier list is reached and even the last qualifier meets the requirements, the head expression is evaluated $((f_{(n,m_n)} \overset{yes}{\rightarrow} e)$ or $(p_n \overset{yes}{\rightarrow} e))$ and again the control is handed to the first qualifier $(e \rightarrow e_1)$.

Function. In Erlang the function may have several function clauses as the pattern matching and the guard expressions play a special role in control-flow and branching of possible execution paths. The rules for constructing the control-flow graph of the functions is described in *Figure 31:(Function)*. The actual parameters are matched against the formal parameters/patterns and guard expressions sequentially. If the pattern matches, then the guard expression is evaluated. If the guard evaluates to **true** this clause will be chosen for evaluation. If either the pattern matching fails or the guard expression evaluates to **false** the control flows to the next function clause. The expressions in the body of the function are evaluated sequentially and subexpressions are evaluated according to the rules described in this section. The return value of the function is the last evaluated expression from its body.

	Expressions	Control-Flow Edges
(Function)	f/n: $f(p_1^1,\ldots,p_n^1)$ when $g^1 \to$ $e_1^1,\ldots,e_{l_1}^1;$ $\vdots$ $f(p_1^m,\ldots,p_n^m)$ when $g^m \to$ $e_1^m,\ldots,e_{l_m}^m.$	$f/n \to p_1^1,$ $\{p_1^1,\ldots,p_n^1\} \overset{\textbf{yes}}{\to} g^1,$ $\{p_1^1,\ldots,p_n^1\} \overset{\textbf{no}}{\to} \{p_1^2,\ldots,p_n^2\},$ $\vdots$ $\{p_1^{m-1},\ldots,p_n^{m-1}\} \overset{\textbf{yes}}{\to} g^{m-1},$ $\{p_1^{m-1},\ldots,p_n^{m-1}\} \overset{\textbf{no}}{\to} \{p_1^m,\ldots,p_n^m\},$ $\{p_1^m,\ldots,p_n^m\} \overset{\textbf{yes}}{\to} g^m,$ $\{p_1^m,\ldots,p_n^m\} \overset{\textbf{no}}{\to} error,$ $g^1 \overset{\textbf{yes}}{\to} e_1^1,$ $g^1 \overset{\textbf{no}}{\to} \{p_1^2,\ldots,p_n^2\},$ $\vdots$ $g^{m-1} \overset{\textbf{yes}}{\to} e_1^{m-1},$ $g^{m-1} \overset{\textbf{no}}{\to} \{p_1^m,\ldots,p_n^m\},$ $g^m \overset{\textbf{yes}}{\to} e_1^m,$ $g^m \overset{\textbf{no}}{\to} error,$ $e_1^1 \to e_2^1, \ldots, e_{l_1-1}^1 \to e_{l_1}^1,$ $\vdots$ $e_1^m \to e_2^m, \ldots, e_{l_m-1}^m \to e_{l_m}^m,$ $e_{l_1}^1 \to ret\ f/n,$ $\vdots$ $e_{l_m}^m \to ret\ f/n,$
(Fun. call)	e_0: $e_f(e_1,\ldots,e_n)$	$e_0' \to e_f,$ $e_f \to e_1,$ $e_1 \to e_2, \ldots, e_{n-1} \to e_n,$ $e_n \overset{\textbf{call}}{\to} e_0,$

Fig. 31. Control-Flow Graph building rules (cont.)

Function Call. The rules of the control-flow in a function application is defined in *Figure 31: (Fun. call)*. First the expression that defines the module and name of the function is evaluated ($e_0' \to e_f$), then the evaluation of the actual parameters follows. The actual parameters are evaluated from left to right order (($e_1 \to e_2$), ..., ($e_{n-1} \to e_n$)). Then the evaluation should pass to the called function. Therefore, the ($e_n \overset{\text{call}}{\to} e_0$) edge indicates an interfunctional control-flow, which should be considered during the building of the control dependency graph.

	Expressions	Control-Flow Edges

(Case exp.)	e_0:
	  case e of
	    p_1 when $g_1 \to e_1^1, \ldots, e_{l_1}^1$;
	    $\vdots$
	    p_n when $g_n \to e_1^n, \ldots, e_{l_n}^n$
	  end
		$e_0' \overset{e}{\to}$, $e \to p_1$,
		$p_1 \overset{yes}{\to} g_1$, $p_1 \overset{no}{\to} p_2$,
		
		$\vdots$
		
		$p_{n_1} \overset{yes}{\to} g_{n-1}$, $p_{n-1} \overset{no}{\to} p_n$,
		$p_n \overset{yes}{\to} g_n$, $p_n \overset{no}{\to} error$,
		
		$g_1 \overset{yes}{\to} e_1^1$, $g_1 \overset{no}{\to} p_2$,
		
		$\vdots$
		
		$g_{n-1} \overset{yes}{\to} e_1^{n-1}$, $g_{n-1} \overset{no}{\to} p_n$,
		$g_n \overset{yes}{\to} e_1^n$, $g_n \overset{no}{\to} error$,
		
		$e_1^1 \to e_2^1$, $\ldots$, $e_{l_1-1}^1 \to e_{l_1}^1$,
		
		$\vdots$
		
		$e_1^n \to e_2^n$, $\ldots$, $e_{l_n-1}^n \to e_{l_n}^n$,
		
		$e_{l_1}^1 \to ret\ case$,
		
		$\vdots$
		
		$e_{l_n}^n \to ret\ case$,
		$ret\ case \to e_0$

(Receive exp.)	e_0:
	  receive
	    p_1 when $g_1 \to e_1^1, \ldots, e_{l_1}^1$;
	    $\vdots$
	    p_n when $g_n \to e_1^n, \ldots, e_{l_n}^n$
	  end
		$e_0' \overset{rec}{\to} p_1$,
		
		$\vdots$
		
		Similarly as at rule (Case exp.)
		
		$\vdots$
		
		$e_{l_1}^1 \to ret\ receive$,
		
		$\vdots$
		
		$e_{l_n}^n \to ret\ receive$,
		$ret\ receive \to e_0$

Fig. 32. Control-Flow Graph building rules (cont.)

Case Expression. The rules for building the control-flow for the case expression is described in *Figure 32: (Case exp.)*. First the head expression is evaluated, then the return value of the evaluated head expression is matched against the patterns. The control flow of the pattern matching is analogous to the one described at the *(Function)* rule. The branch of the first matching pattern and optional guard that evaluates to `true` will be evaluated. If the pattern does not match or the guard is evaluated to `false` the next pattern is examined. The return value of the case expression is the value of the last expression of the evaluated branch.

Receive Expression. The rules of control-flow of the receive expression are described in *Figure 32: (Receive exp)*. The receive expression tries to remove a message from the message queue and matches it against the patterns and guards similarly as the case expression. The execution of the process may hang until it receives an appropriate message, thus the receiving is marked with the special label rec in the control-flow.

Extending Little Languages into Big Systems*

Gábor Páli[1,2]

[1] Eötvös Loránd University, Budapest, Hungary
[2] Babeş-Bolyai University, Cluj-Napoca, Romania
pgj@elte.hu

Abstract. A classic layout for complex software applications usually involves a set of fine-tuned performance-optimized routines that are combined and controlled from a higher layer in a lightweight fashion. As the application grows, reliable operation, portability, and maintainability gets to be a real concern. However, this can be tamed by abstracting away from the platform-dependent details by modelling the components and their relation on a higher level. Using a functional programming language combined with the technique of language embedding may be an answer when implementation of such solution comes in question [1][2]. In this design, the component descriptions may be captured by an adequate embedded domain-specific language that compiles to a lower-level language but there also has to be a way for composition and therefore getting a complete working application out of them. In this paper, we propose a method for extending compiled embedded domain-specific languages into a stand-alone system with minimal effort.

1 Introduction

Nowadays it pays off to describe domain-specific algorithms, especially complex ones in a dedicated domain-specific programming language (DSL). Such languages may be expressed in terms of another language (that is called a *host* or *meta-language*) by *embedding*. It promises ease of maintainability and portability, and it is usually associated with efficient code generation. Though describing algorithms themselves is not enough to achieve that ultimate goal: one must be able to build a larger system out of them so whole applications might be constructed this way. It requires a way to express the relation between the previously captured algorithms, including some support for running them on top of an operating system or even bare hardware.

In this paper, we discuss this approach and as our contribution to the topic, we propose a simple methodology for connecting programs written in DSLs. That way we can show how to extend those little programs into larger systems with minimal added efforts (Section 2) at the expense of setting certain constraints on the language to be used (Section 5). We then construct a model from the constraints that can be used for adding execution support in view of the given

---

* Supported by KMOP-2008-1.1.2-08/1-2008-0002, Ericsson and Ericsson Software Research, POSDRU/6/1.5/S/3-2008

V. Zsók, Z. Horváth, and R. Plasmeijer (Eds.): CEFP 2011, LNCS 7241, pp. 499–516, 2012.

composition (Section 3). We believe a definite advantage of the solution is that there is no generic run-time support needed, and most of its relevant pieces can be derived and generated. Besides that it offers a comfortable and reliable way of building applications it becomes especially useful when we are talking about construction of low-level ones, e.g. operating systems (Section 4).

To motivate and investigate this approach, we are going to use three different layers of languages: the meta-language, *Haskell*, which implements a glue language *Flow*, which coordinates DSL programs with a specified interface of which *Feldspar* is an example. Haskell is a well-known contemporary functional programming language that is a popular choice for embedding languages and features a sophisticated type system to reliably support all the underlying work. Flow captures schemes referred above and provides a way to connect DSL programs into a dataflow network. Feldspar is a high-level domain-specific language for digital signal processing [3]. It is embedded in Haskell and it has a code generator for ISO C99. It targets signal processing platforms and puts emphasis on formulating vector algorithms.

To justify our choice, we note that recent works of Simon Marlow et al. [10] [11] show that expressing workflow systems in functional languages is still a hot research topic indeed. The Par monad is an extensive and generic tool to support parallel programming in a very efficient way. It does not do any I/O hence it is considered pure and therefore it can be used at many different places to describe similar (even dynamic) data-flow networks, where a scheduler can be also specified. However, it uses many tricks (like IORefs) to make it work inside Haskell and does not care about code generation. On the contrary, our proposed model tries to avoid most monadic features and rather concentrates on how to build automatically generated programs with a simpler run-time system in the background.

2   Sketching Up a Dataflow

Let us suppose we want to build a simple audio processing application from DSL programs written in Feldspar (shown on Figure 1). This application reads digitized stereo sound data from the computer's sound card, applies a given effect to it then writes the result back to the sound card, emitting the transformed sound it read previously. Since our computer possibly supports concurrent execution of programs via multi-threading, we plan to parallelize the processing by splitting the input signal by its left and right channels. Thus we get two identical lines of processing to handle the corresponding channels. We also decompose those lines into smaller steps where the spectrum of the signal is calculated first then followed by the effect, and finally it is transformed back to a waveform.

As a language focusing only on the digital signal processing elements, Feldspar clearly misses the support for every aspects of the application in question. By looking at Figure 1, we can note that while contents of each small box may be written in Feldspar, their combinations and the circle-shaped elements may not.

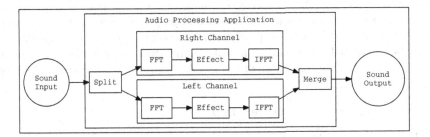

Fig. 1. An overview of a sample audio processing application

This where a glue language, **Flow** comes to the rescue. The **Flow** language builds upon combinators that help to describe data dependency graphs of computations as nodes. We are going to call such graphs *dataflows*. They always stand for a loop in an event-driven system that receives some input to produce some output as an answer. With **Flow**, our goal would be to make it easy to construct such applications from an existing set of algorithms. In the optimal case, it would even fit into a few lines of code.

```
audioproc = split --< (processing, processing) >-- merge
   where processing = fft --> effect --> ifft
```

And that is it!

2.1 Basic Flow Combinators

Let us observe the previous code snippet more closely. The whole application is named **audioproc** – it is a top-level Haskell function that also represents a **Flow** program. Each small box from Figure 1 is added as additional Haskell functions that represent a node in the dataflow graph. Note that we did a small trick here (for the sake of clarity) because the nodes are not directly Feldspar programs, they first have to be lifted (by a **liftFeld** combinator) to be part of a flow network.

```
(split,merge) = (liftFeld splitF,liftFeld mergeF)
merge = liftFeld effectF
(fft,ifft) = (liftFeld fftF, liftFeld ifftF)
```

In this application, the **liftFeld** function is used to fit Feldspar programs with signature of $\alpha \to \beta$, i.e. with programs that get an input (of type α) and produce an output (of type β). The role of lifting is to wrap the input and the output of the little programs to use that common data type for communication inside the graph. Such types are represented by a restricted set of conventional Haskell types, that we call "Flow types".

For some programs, either the input or the output type may be complex, for example a tuple, that has a special meaning in the `Flow` language. Programs producing a tuple are considered *splitters* and programs taking a tuple are considered *mergers*. This makes it possible to express an explicit (i.e. programmer-controlled) way of decomposing a piece of data into multiple parts to be processed in parallel in the later segments of the graph. Such programs may be glued by using the `--<` combinator.

```
split --< (processing, processing)
```

In this example, `split` reads the input, splits it into two, and passes each part to an instance of the audio processing line, described by `processing`, written with an ordinary Haskell pair. The results are then combined by using the `>--` combinator that denotes the opposite direction.

```
(processing, processing) >-- merge
```

Steps in `processing` are connected by the `-->` combinator. It is to describe a sequence of various computation stages, like in our example, a Fast Fourier Transform followed by an effect, and an inverse FFT. Note that even sequentially connected components may run in parallel if the communication between them is asynchronous, viz. their execution may overlap in that case.

```
processing = fft --> effect --> ifft
```

2.2   Running a Flow

One may also notice that circle-shaped nodes of Figure 1 are completely missing from the resulted code. It is because they are the implicit *source and sink nodes* for the graph. The input arrives to the application through the source node, and the output is sent to the output node. They are treated as *open nodes* of the graph. Such nodes do not have concrete programs associated in this high-level view, though they may be substituted by suitable producer and consumer functions in Haskell.

This latter becomes useful when we would like to see how a flow is working, i.e. when we want to simulate a behavior of a flow. Flow-graphs may be run and analyzed directly in a Haskell interpreter e.g. `GHCi` (for the Glasgow Haskell Compiler) by using the `simulate` and `eject` functions.

```
*Audioproc> let input = [[1..5 :: Float],[1..5]]
*Audioproc> eject (simulate audioproc input !! 31)
[[2.3,3.8,5.3,6.8,8.3],[9.8,11.3,12.8,14.3,15.8]]
```

The `simulate` function performs the computation represented by `audioproc` endlessly, since such a system never stops. Thus we pick only one of the generated states and use the `eject` function to access the output value in that step. It can be also seen that both the input and the output represent simple vectors (of size 5).

2.3 Introducing Dynamism

Now we have seen a compact example of how to create a simple data-flow graph. Though it has been quite static in its nature: the flow always behaves the same way, it only depends on the input data. Hence we may want to improve it by introducing support for more dynamism.

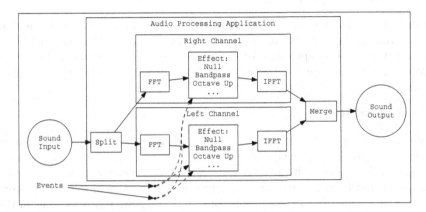

Fig. 2. An overview of the audio processing application, extended with dynamism

To motivate this, let us extend our audio processing application with a per-channel switching between multiple effects in run time (see Figure 2). This does not require too much modification, only the **effect** has to be factored out from **processing** and extended to support switching between effects. That is implemented on the level of the DSL, i.e. in Feldspar.

```
null     = ...
bandpass = ...
octaveUp = ...

fxLeftF :: Data Index -> DVector (Complex Float) -> DVector (Complex Float)
fxLeftF e input = (e == 0) ? (null, (e == 1) ? (bandpass, octaveUp))

fxRightF :: Data Index -> DVector (Complex Float) -> DVector (Complex Float)
fxRightF e input = (e == 0) ? (null, (e == 1) ? (bandpass, octaveUp))
```

The **processing** component shall then be split into **processLeft** and **processRight**, because they are going to maintain two different states, each storing an index for the currently used effect.

```
processLeft  = fft --> effectLeft  --> ifft
processRight = fft --> effectRight --> ifft

audioproc' = split --< (processLeft, processRight) >-- merge
```

Note that `effectLeft` and `effectRight` have one more argument. They have a different signature to the Feldspar programs introduced above, $\gamma \to \alpha \to \beta$. We already know that programs map input data (of type α) to output data (of type β). The additional argument (of type γ) is a configuration for the given program that may be changed while the system is running.

```
effectLeft  = liftFeld $ \(e,_) -> fxLeftF e
effectRight = liftFeld $ \(_,e) -> fxRightF e
```

where `liftFeld` now receives a shared configuration as a parameter besides the input. Similarly to the data passed between the wrapped programs, the global configuration is also expressed in the common data type because it has to be independent of the employed DSLs. For our extended application, it can be given as follows.

```
audioprocConfig = (0, 0)
```

where the corresponding elements of the Haskell pair refer to each of the initial states of the effects for the channels.

As it has been shown, by introducing a global state, i.e. a system-wide configuration, there we got a way to directly affect on the behavior of the flow network in run time by modifying the elements of that state. Note that programs in the flow cannot modify the global state in the `Flow` language, it can be only changed from outside of the graph. There can be an extended version of the previously presented `simulate` function called `simulate'` given where we can also specify the global configuration as an infinite list of states to be consumed at each step of the simulation. Elements of that list represent actual states of the configuration at given moments. With this approach, it is also possible to represent system events as changes in the global configuration.

```
*Audioproc> let input = [[1..5 :: Float],[1..5]]
*Audioproc> let config = repeat audioprocConfig
*Audioproc> eject (simulate' audioproc' input config !! 31)
[[2.3,3.8,5.3,6.8,8.3],[9.8,11.3,12.8,14.3,15.8]]
```

Let us add that dependency graphs may be represented in many other ways, `Flow` is just an example of that. As one may have noted by looking at the example, `Flow` is basically a "point-free" (tacit) language. In our opinion, this contributes to a succinct formulation of processing pipelines that may be enhanced further by adding more `Arrow`-like combinators [12], and support for loops. It is possibly straightforward to use for programmers educated in functional programming, but others may also find them intuitive. That has not yet been investigated but left to future work for now.

3   Translation to Abstract Programs

Given that the data dependency graph is described, there shall be also a way to compile it down to a less abstract platform in order to make it run on a given hardware. The intermediate representation used on that level will be called an *abstract program* for the rest of the document.

Abstract programs have two main components, *tasks* and *channels*. A task represents a run-to-completion operation to be performed on a single processing unit without interruption. This idea follows the typical hardware setup where processing units do not provide support or provide only a limited support for preemptive execution (e.g. the Cell Broadband Engine). Such units usually excel in pure computation tasks with less branching, instead.

Tasks use channels to forward data between each other. In that sense, tasks are like closed expression or *closures*: the free variables (parameters) of the encapsulated functions are bound by the values coming from the channels and the global configuration. Note that every task implicitly shares the same system-wide configuration. Channels are important for establishing asynchronicity between nodes, though they also force serialization and deserialization of data at the same time. Hence the compiler may lose the opportunity to remove intermediate data structures between nodes and it has to implement certain optimizations on passing data to avoid unnecessary copying. However, in some cases it is inevitable, and it may even result in a better overall resource utilization.

3.1 Graph Decomposition

Tasks and channels are derived from the graph by decomposition: each node paired up with its incoming and outgoing edges (as channels) is turned into a task. In Figure 3, such a decomposition is shown for the `audioproc` example. As we mentioned above, source and sink nodes (marked with grey) are not part of the original graph given by the user therefore they automatically became open nodes. For tasks, it implies that they do not have DSL programs associated thus they shall be expressed in the target language we are compiling to. However, we will have to generate wrappers for those programs too, as there must be a way for them to access the channels. This will be described later, in Section 4.

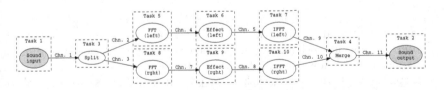

Fig. 3. Decomposing the audio processing application into tasks and channels

3.2 Execution Model

Following the decomposition of the data dependency graph into tasks and channels, the result has to be prepared for execution by multiple processing units. A naïve solution would be to launch a thread for each of the tasks (and no further processing would be needed), but it is not considered a good practice to spawn an arbitrary number of threads in general – as it may waste resources and cause longer times in context switching (if it is possible at all) for example. For better performance, it is rather recommended to not to execute more threads at a time than the number of the processing units in the hardware.

To cope with this question, the traditional thread pooling pattern is used, where a fixed number of threads is created and started to perform a number of tasks that is usually organized as a queue. Threads are considered "worker processes" or simply "workers". Workers grab tasks from the common task queue, execute them, then present the results to somewhere. Because workers may pull in new tasks when they are ready with the previous one, this scheme offers sharing the load between processing units dynamically. And due to its nature, it does not have to be specified in the program itself, instead it can be incorporated as an implicit part of the model. This approach also plays well with heterogenous computer systems, where there is a general-purpose control unit to distribute and dispatch the work to units that are heavily optimized to data processing operations.

Execution of a task involves reading from the input channels, running the encapsulated program, and finally writing the result to the output channels. Channels have to work as FIFO (First-In-First-Out) queues that may have a fixed length. Channels block writing when they are full, and they block reading when they are empty. When any of the task's (input or output) channel is blocked then the contained program itself cannot run, so its execution is skipped.

3.3   Scheduling

In order to schedule tasks for execution, *task pools* are built up for the application. A task pool is a set of tasks that can be run independently of each other, potentially in parallel. Workers are assigned to task pools as they get their jobs to be handled from there. There may be more workers per task pool, hence workers may "steal" work from each other. Since tasks are closed over their parameters, any worker may run any task, that will not change the output.

There are two primary operations for task pools that may affect on the actual performance.

- **take**. Get a task from the task pool. If the pool is empty – that is, everything from the pool has been assigned to fellow workers –, suspend execution of the given worker for a specified time and try again.
- **drop**. Put a completed task back to the pool. It shall always succeed as there must be enough place for tasks in the pool.

Note that any task may be chosen from the pool. It would be the job of a scheduler to pick a task for a worker, however, it is not required as it can be expressed with **take** and **drop**. Let **take** the first task from the pool, while **drop** concatenates the completed tasks to the end of the pool. This way we get a regular round robin scheme, see Figure 4. Obviously, it may be enhanced further to implement more sophisticated scheduling scenarios, but this is now outside of the focus of this document, and is left for future work.

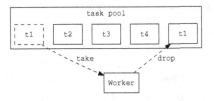

Fig. 4. Operation of a worker over a task pool

3.4 Memory Management

In addition to processor time, tasks usually require a chunk of memory for operation. A generic layout for tasks is shown in Figure 5. There we can see that tasks work with input and output buffers. The former is used for reading values from channels (there can be more), and the latter is used for storing results of the wrapped program. Size of the buffers may be derived from the size of the type of values they store. It may be then multiplied by a chunk size if multiple values travel on the channel in a single pass (thus some space has to be reserved for them in the memory).

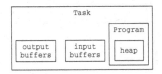

Fig. 5. Task memory layout in general

The contained program itself may also have its own memory requirements. It is called *heap* in Figure 5, which acts as a temporary storage area when the program is being run. Heap is passed to the program so it does not have use its own stack for calculations that require large amount of memory. However, an exact size for this cannot be told in advance in the data-flow layer, so the program has to provide hints.

Tasks get memory assigned when they are executed by a worker, and workers will allocate memory only on their start. That is, workers have to have enough memory allocated to be able to run *any* task in the pool they work in, since reallocating memory for each task may degrade their performance, and would also require some support for dynamic memory management. Assuming that sizes for the buffers and the program can be statically determined in compilation time, it can be given how much memory is needed for a given worker. It can be expressed by $M(\cdot)$ as follows.

$$M(w) = max \left\{ \sum_{i=0}^{n_p} S(I(p,i)) + \sum_{j=0}^{m_p} S(O(p,o)) + S(H(p)) \;\middle|\; p \in P(w) \right\}$$

where w is the worker, p is a program from a set of programs that the worker may run ($P(w)$), $S(\cdot)$ specifies size for a given entity, $H(\cdot)$ gives all program allocations (size of the program heap), $I(\cdot,\cdot)$ and $O(\cdot,\cdot)$ gives the nth input and output buffers for p, respectively.

Because of the maximum function, certain programs with high memory needs may give rise to a sub-optimal memory usage. For example, if there is only a few large-memory programs then assigned workers may allocate too much memory because they may want to run them. That is, when memory requirements are not uniformly distributed for programs, worker allocations will take the largest one that may be a waste. We do not investigate that problem in detail in this document.

4   Code Generation

Code generation depends on the target language and platform. Our approach does not restrict the choice of the target language, the only requirement is that there must be a mapping to it from the abstract program representation. For the rest of the document, we will use the C programming language as an example.

In the previous examples on `audioproc` we have not yet mentioned the types for the expressions we used. Let us now investigate the type of `audioproc'`.

```
*Audioproc> :type audioproc'
audioproc' :: Flow [Float] [Float] (Int8,Int8) C
```

As we can see here, it contains information on the following: the input and output types for the `Flow`, the type for the global configuration, and the type of the `Flow` itself, which is `C` in this case. Note that the input, output and the global configuration types are expressed in `Flow` types that are implemented for the given platform.

The "Flow type" can be imagined as a "tag" for each sub-flow that signals the target. When designing `Flow`s, it can be enforced via static typing of Haskell that only program parts (where programs can be considered trivial sub-flows) with the same target language are combined. In addition, this information is also exploited by the glue code generation as `Flow` has to have built-in support for the given target, similarly to the DSLs employed in the network. Thus the user can select only the languages that are supported for the data-flow graphs.

For each target platform, there must be at least a `compile` function implemented. It generates code for the given platform based on a file name of the constructed flow, specified as a regular Haskell `String`. It has to be invoked with an initial global configuration. For the C platform, it generates a C source code and a C header file.

```
*Audioproc> compile audioproc' audioprocConfig "audioproc"
```

4.1   Eliminating Redundancy

During the phase of code generation, it may happen easily that the same program is used at multiple places in the same flow. That is, tasks may share programs they contain. This is a consequence of the sharing properties of Haskell expressions. If this phenomenon goes unnoticed, the generated code may get bloated easily. Hence it is advised to support elimination of redundant code. A simple algorithm to resolve the problem is as follows.

- Create a look-up table for compiled code. Let this table store all the previously compiled program bodies as plain strings. Initially it is empty.
- When code generation for a program is finished then search for it in the table. The efficiency of the search may be improved by using a specialized data structure, e.g. a balanced search tree.
  - If it is found then return the position in the table and generate only a call to the given program routine. Program names can be produced in a systematic way, using a template, e.g. prog_N where N is the position in the table.
  - It it is not found then insert the generated body to the table and add the body to the generated code, and place a reference to it at the task's code generation.

When generating code for the program body, the name itself should be omitted as it may not be specific to the given program. A name is added only after the redundancy elimination algorithm has been run. Note that there could be hashes computed for program bodies. However, we should be careful with hashes as they may collide. A potential solution to amend collision of hashes is to do a full equality test on equivalence of hashes.

In summary, this method is better than the user manually naming programs in the graph. It is less prone to error (as it is automatic) and it may even spot duplicates when they are results of two different high-level code.

4.2   Interaction with User Code

Besides the considerations on how to generate code for data-flow graphs, we must discuss some of the details on how to supplement the missing parts required for getting a running binary program. The interface between automatically generated code and user-supplemented parts is the generated header file (in case of C), but it supposed that similar concept can be given for other back-ends.

The generated C header file (audioproc.h) contains the declaration for the global configuration. It can be seen that the configuration elements for audioproc is mapped to single char types in C. The order of elements in the declaration matches the order of their enumeration in the source n-tuple. Preserving the ordering is important since we want to provide a way for the user to interact with the generated source. It is the responsibility of the user to feed the network with data, consume its output and optionally change the elements of the global configuration to regulate the behavior of the flow.

```
#ifndef __AUDIOPROC_H__
#define __AUDIOPROC_H__

struct configuration {
  char cf_0;
  char cf_1;
};

extern struct configuration config;

int controller(int argc, char** argv);
void f_0(struct configuration* config, float* b0, size_t b0_insz,
  size_t* b0_ousz);
void f_1(struct configuration* config, float* b0, size_t b0_insz,
  size_t* b0_ousz);
#endif // __AUDIOPROC_H__
```

As we can see in the generated code for our example application, there has to be a function named `controller()` defined. Its purpose is manifold. It controls the life time of the system: before it is started, the necessary initialization routines are run, and after it is finished, the run-time system shuts itself down, terminating the whole program. It accesses the internals of the global configuration therefore it may change the parameters for the flow network in run time. It can be considered a `main()` function for the application.

There can be also seen some function prototypes. Those are the open nodes of the network that the user has to implement. For `audioproc`, the `f_0()` function should implement reading data (in floating-point format) from the sound card, while the `f_1()` function should implement writing data to there. These operations are not described by the `Flow` language, hence they must be added by the user.

5   Fitting a DSL to the `Flow`

As a result of the discussed topics above we have implicitly touched many requirements and constraints on domain-specific languages to be used in a `Flow` network. Let us now make them here explicit while introducing the key elements of the language interface to be implemented.

First of all, there is a common data type – the `Flow` type – employed in the graph to connect DSL programs. That type must be able to connect programs written in different little languages; thus it must be independent of them – and the languages used in the network do not know about each other, too. Hence each language has to provide a mapping for all of its specific types.

```
class FlowType (T l a) => DSLType l a where
  type T l a
  fromDSL :: l -> a -> T l a
  toDSL   :: l -> T l a -> a
```

The DSLType type class is used to describe such mapping between the types of the DSL and the Flow indexed with the given language. When running a dataflow network, the functions fromDSL and toDSL implement the conversion for the data type a for the language l. The type T l a corresponds to the Flow type for the DSL type. As it has been noted before, the Flow types are restricted Haskell types, formulated by the FlowType type class.

For example, we map the floating-point type of Feldspar to a Flow type as follows.

```
getDataRep :: Syntactic a => a -> DataRep
getDataRep = dataRep . eval

instance DSLType Feldspar (Data Float) where
    type T Feldspar (Data Float) = Float
    fromDSL _ = (getDataRep -> FloatData x) = x
    toDSL _ = value x
```

The next layer of building up a language binding is the definition of an instance for the PrimNode type class. The PrimNode class briefly summarizes all the requirements for the language. Note that besides the source (l) and the target language (t) there is also a p type variable. The p data type is used to tag the DSL program in question with the values of l and t for later processing.

```
class Backend t => PrimNode p l t where
    run     :: (DSLType l a, DSLType l b, DSLType l c) =>
        p a b c l t -> T l c -> T l a -> T l b
    -- for code generation
    compile  :: p a b c l t -> ID -> (Types t, Name, Body t)
    finalize :: p a b c l t -> Name -> Body t -> Definition t
    heapInfo :: p a b c l t -> [FwType]
```

PrimNodes may be created from programs of language l of type $\gamma \to \alpha \to \beta$ if l has an instance for the Liftable type class.

```
class Backend t => Liftable l a b c t where
    liftPN :: (DSLType l a, DSLType l b, DSLType l c) =>
        l -> ID -> (c -> a -> b) -> PrimNode (T l a) (T l b) (T l c) t
```

The liftPN function is employed inside the generic lift function where an unique identifier (ID) is assigned to each lifted program, resulting in the final type of the Flow.

```
type Flow a b c t = State ID (PrimFlow a b c t)
```

For example, this is how we got the liftFeld function used in our Feldspar application (see 2.1, 2.3).

5.1   The PrimNode Type Class

Let us take a look at the PrimNode functions. In order to be able to simulate a flow there must be way to simulate the DSL programs themselves. Therefore it is required to have a function to run them, i.e. map them to regular Haskell functions. For Feldspar, that is equivalent to using its interpreter, specified by the eval function.

For the code generation, the rest of the functions in the PrimNode type class have to be defined. The compilation of programs is divided into three phases due to the redundancy elimination and the generation of task wrapper code. First, the compile function turns a DSL program to a target-language program with a given identifier, as specified by the Backend instance of the target. Though it is even possible to combine programs expressed in multiple DSLs, the target language has to be the same for all.

```
class Backend t where
  type Types t
  type Body t
  type Definition t
```

The Backend type class groups the types used during the code generation – which may be taken as an abstract description of a simple sub-routine-oriented programming language. It consists of optional type declarations (Types t) that may be required for the routine body (Body t) then finally turned into a definition (Definition t) on the target language.

For example, the C backend is defined by the following instance.

```
instance Backend C where
  type Types       = CTypes
  type Body C      = String
  type Definition C = String
```

As it is shown above, the function body and definition are technically represented as strings in the C backend. The unusual type here is CTypes (which is not detailed further) that may be reasoned as follows. It is used to collect all the type definitions from the resulting function as multiple definitions of the same type has to eliminated somehow – otherwise it may give us incorrect C code that cannot be compiled. As a consequence, it implies checking for equivalence on type definitions. Rendering those definitions as strings then parsing them back may not result in an optimal solution, so it is more logical to ask for their abstract representation, and that is what CTypes captures here.

In the second phase, the finalize function may be invoked to put the previously translated body and its name together to a complete definition. It is because of the redundancy elimination (see 4.1). The program is first compiled without its name so the body can be checked for being redundant, and if it is not, then it is combined with its name. Note that the name may be derived from the unique identifier of the node encapsulating the program.

Finally, in the third phase, the glue code for the tasks is generated. As mentioned earlier, each task contains a DSL program, and it communicates data to other tasks in the decomposed network (see Section 3). That is, tasks still have to maintain a mapping between DSL and `Flow` types in the backend. The generic task code manages the connected channels and receives a piece of memory for the program to be run. So only a wrapper function similar to the one below has to be written for each DSL.

```
wrapper ::
  Identifier -> (CfgType,[(CID,ChanType)],[(CID,ChanType)]) ->
  Identifier -> ([FwType],[FwType],[FwType]) ->
  Definition C
```

The first set of parameters represent type information for the *outer interface*, i.e. types for the global configuration (`CfgType`), and the input and output channels (`(CID, ChanType)`), with a name for the corresponding C function (`Identifier`). Note that the outer interface is actually the same as one has to implement for the open nodes (see 4.2). The second set of parameters represent type information for the *inner interface*, i.e. types that the DSL program to be wrapped has: input, output, and heap (`FwType`), and its name in C (`Identifier`). That latter is where the `heapInfo` from `PrimNode` is utilized. The result of `heapInfo` is to tell the compiler what type of data is expected to be used during the execution of the program.

The `wrapper` function should connect these outer and inner interfaces based on its arguments. In our current implementation, it can be expressed via an abstract C program that sets up values before calling the DSL program. For example, in case of Feldspar, besides the regular input and output parameters there has to be a C `struct` passed, filled with pointers to segments of memory that the compiled Feldspar program may use while it is running.

6   Related Work

It is typical for embedded systems that the operating system is prepared to be deployed on the given hardware. Solutions based on microkernels basically provide some support for this. A prominent representative of this approach is Enea OSE [9] which is one of the most widely used real-time operating system in the industry. The primitives featured in the Enea OSE architecture is very similar to the ones we have captured in our model (processes and message passing between them), and the implementation is very sophisticated, featuring a modular, layered, fault-tolerant, distributed, event-driven, deterministic architecture with task monitoring and optimizing memory usage. Another promising attempt is ArchiDeS (Architecture, Deployment, Scheduling) [8] which is a research framework written in C++ for building large stream-processing systems on multicore processors. It supports run-time configuration of the constructed application. The key concepts for ArchiDeS are the interface ports and interface port types, containing a dedicated message handler to specify the run-time behavior for the given port. Interfaces can be assigned to single or shared component modules that are the first-class entities in the system. There is also a replaceable scheduler and a run-time system paired up with the components that supports different, large-scale multicore chips and application-specific scheduling. It features both data and pipeline parallelism, similar to our solution.

However, a drawback of these tools from our perpective is that they still have to be programmed in C/C++, i.e. though the modular design provides nice abstractions as building blocks, due to the nature of those programming languages it is hard for the compiler to figure out how to optimize the constructed applications further, like removing intermediate data structure when they are not needed or performing similar simplifications in the application. Besides that, the application code still has to be written in C or C++ which tends to be more error-prone and "noisy" compared to high-level and domain-specific languages.

On the contrary, it is a well-known technique to use domain-specific languages to generate code for operating systems. The Barrelfish operating system is the result of a research project to explore possibilities in structuring operating systems for today's and the future's hardware. Barrelfish features a development framework, named Filet-of-Fish [6], to address the aforementioned problems. In this framework, the authors have chosen a similar approach to ours: essentially, they embedded C into a functional language, which was Haskell. Filet-of-Fish gives strong static guarantees on that the generated code is valid by construction and it can be always compiled. Opposed to our approach, both Barrelfish and Filet-of-Fish solves the problem for generic operating systems, while we are focusing only on concepts that are specific to the domain.

As a related project, Ptolemy [7] studies modeling, simulation, and design of concurrent, real-time, embedded systems, focusing on assembly of concurrent components, and using well-defined models of computation that govern the interaction between the components. Ptolemy is based on the principles of object-oriented programming and it has a recent implementation in Java. Although it solves many problems (e.g. scheduling) related to the development of operating system for digital signal processing applications and even supports code generation beyond simulation, it still can be only considered a generic research on finding an appropriate modeling language for such systems, and not a way of how to provide reliable and clever compilation for the components, which is our focus. Nevertheless, results of the Ptolemy project can be re-used here to take some of the computation-related aspects of the elements to be modeled resolved.

7   Conclusion and Future Work

We have presented our proposed method for constructing larger applications from smaller programs written in domain-specific languages. As we have also seen, only the programs themselves and their data dependency relation has to be defined. The execution may be worked out procedurally as we have expressed t in terms of tasks and channels. Though the solution is not complete: one still has to feed the generated graph with input and configuration information, while consuming its output. From view-point of simulation, it is convenient as we only need to build a list out of input and configuration information. For code generation, it leaves open nodes that the user shall add in order to get a working executable. We can hopefully find a solution to resolve this, and find a solution that works well with both approaches. For the generated code, we also have implicit scheduling aided by grain of static analysis. But this is far from perfect, and it needs to be profiled and the emerging performance problems will have to be addressed. We have only given a few rule-of-thumbs for reaching an ideal performance, but it has to be researched properly in the future.

Finally we would like to thank Andor Pénzes, Gergely Dévai, and Máté Tejfel, Tamás Kozsik from the Feldspar Group, and the anonymous reviewers who contributed much to the development of this paper and the related implementation with their comments and work. This work is being supported by Ericsson Software Research, Ericsson Business Network Units and SSF (Sweden), the Hungarian National Development Agency (KMOP-2008-1.1.2), Programul Operațional Sectional Dezvoltarea Resurselor Umane 2007–2013 (POSDRU/6/1.5/S/3-2008, Romania).

References

1. Felleisen, M., Findler, B., Flatt, M., et al.: Building Little Languages With Macros, Dr. Dobb's Journal (April 2004)
2. Elliott, C., Finne, S., de Moor, O.: Compiling Embedded Languages. In: Taha, W. (ed.) SAIG 2000. LNCS, vol. 1924, pp. 9–26. Springer, Heidelberg (2000)
3. Axelsson, E., Claessen, K., Dévai, G., Horváth, Z., Keijzer, K., Lyckegård, B., Persson, A., Sheeran, M., Svenningsson, J., Vajda, A.: Feldspar: A Domain Specific Language for Digital Signal Processing algorithms. In: Eighth ACM/IEEE International Conference on Formal Methods and Models for Codesign, Grenoble, France, July 26–28 (2010)
4. Schüpbach, A., Peter, S., Baumann, A., et al.: Embracing Diversity in the Barrelfish Manycore Operating System. In: Proc. of the Workshop on Managed Many-Core Systems (MMCS 2008) (June 2008)
5. Gill, A., Launchbury, J., Peyton Jones, S.L.: A Short-Cut to Deforestation. In: Proc. Int. Conf. on Functional Programming Languages and Compiler Architecture, FPCA (1993)
6. Dagand, P.E., Baumann, A., Roscoe, T.: Filet-o-Fish: Practical and Dependable Domain-Specific Language for OS Development. ACM SIGOPS Operating Systems Review (2010)
7. Lee, E., Hylands, C., Janneck, J., et al.: Overview of the Ptolemy Project Technical Report UCB/ERL M01/11, EECS Department, University of California, Berkeley (2001)
8. Brorsson, M., Faxen, K.-F., Popov, K.: ArchiDeS: A Programming Framework for Multicore Chips. In: Swedish Workshop on Multicore Computing, MCC 2009 (2009)

9. Enea, A.B.: Enea OSE: Multicore Real-Time Operating System (2011),
   http://www.enea.com/
10. Marlow, S.: Parallel and Concurrent Programming in Haskell. In: Central European Functional Programming Summer School (CEFP), Eötvös Loránd University, Budapest, June 14–24 (2011)
11. Marlow, S., Newton, R., Peyton Jones, S.L.: A Monad for Deterministic Parallelism. In: Haskell 2011: Proc. of the 4th ACM SIGPLAN Symposium on Haskell, Tokyo, Japan. ACM (2011)
12. Paterson, R.: Arrows and Computation. In: The Fun of Programming, pp. 201–222, Palgrave (2003)

Some New Approaches in Functional Programming Based on Categories

Viliam Slodičák, Pavol Macko, and Valerie Novitzká

Faculty of Electrical Engineering and Informatics,
Technical University of Košice,
Letná 9, 04200 Košice, Slovak Republic
{viliam.slodicak,pavol.macko,valerie.novitzka}@tuke.sk

Abstract. In this paper we deal the recursion and corecursion in functional programming. We discuss about the morphisms which express the recursion or corecursion, resp. We apply the linear logic which provides a logical perspective on computational issues such as control of resources and order of evaluation. The most important feature of linear logic is that formulae are considered as actions and its truth value depends on an internal state of a dynamic system. In this paper we present an alternative way of computation based on algebras and coalgebras. The correctness of our approaches we show by Curry-Howard correspondence.

Keywords: category theory, hylomorphism, linear logic, Curry-Howard correspondence, signature.

1 Introduction

Linear logic provides a logical perspective on computational issues such as control of resources and order of evaluation. In classical logic treats the sentences that are always true or false; but in linear logic the truth value depends on an internal state of a dynamic system. We showed in [12] a new alternative way of computing factorial based on hylomorphism by using the algebras and coalgebras. Because of the checking, the correctness of the program is the most important phase of transformation into logical formulae. In this contribution we present correctness of this computing by Curry-Howard correspondence [13].

2 Basic Notions

We start our approach with the well-known notion from universal algebra: a many-typed signature (the *signature* in the following text). A signature $\Sigma = (T, \mathcal{F})$ consists of a finite set T of the basic types needed for a problem solution denoted by symbols $\sigma, \tau \ldots$ and of a finite set $\mathcal{F}$ of function symbols. Each function symbol $f \in \mathcal{F}$ is of the form $f : \sigma_1, \ldots, \sigma_n \to \tau$ for some natural n. Generally, we distinct in a signature the constructor operations which tell us how to generate data elements; the deconstructor operations, also called observers or transition functions that tell us what we can observe about data elements; and the derived operations.

V. Zsók, Z. Horváth, and R. Plasmeijer (Eds.): CEFP 2011, LNCS 7241, pp. 517–532, 2012.

2.1 Category Theory

Algebraic and coalgebraic concepts are based on category theory [1]. A category $\mathcal{C}$ is mathematical structure consisting of objects, e.g. $A, B, \ldots$ and morphisms of the form $f : A \to B$ between them. Every object has the identity morphism and morphisms are composable. Morphisms between categories are called functors, e.g. a functor $F : \mathcal{C} \to \mathcal{D}$ from a category $\mathcal{C}$ into a category $\mathcal{D}$ which preserves the structure.

2.2 Linear Logic

Girard's linear logic [4] has offered great promise, as a formalism particularly well-suited to serve at the interface between logic and computer science. This paradigm has been a cornerstone of new approach concerning connections between intuitionistic logic, functional programming and category theory [2]. We consider here intuitionistic linear logic because it is very suitable for describing of the program execution. Precisely, reduction of linear terms corresponding to proofs in intuitionistic linear logic can be regarded as a computation of programs [12]. The interpretation in linear logic is of hypotheses as resources: every hypothesis must be consumed exactly once in a proof. Its the most important feature is that formulae are considered as actions. That differs from usual logic where the governing judgment is of truth, which may be freely used as many times as necessary. Linear logic uses the causal implication: the formula $\varphi \multimap \psi$ of linear logic means that the φ is being consumed to produce the resource ψ. Thus, the formula φ after the implication does not hold. Linear logic uses two conjunctions: multiplicative $\varphi \otimes \psi$ expressing that both actions will be performed; and additive one $\varphi \& \psi$ expressing that only one of two actions will be performed and we shall decide which one. Intuitionistic linear logic uses additive disjunction $\varphi \oplus \psi$ which expresses that only one of two actions will be performed but we cannot decide which one.

3   Algebras and Coalgebras

The *rôle* of the computer program is carrying on the instructions under whose the computer system is to perform some required computations. The essential idea of the behavioral theory is to determine the relations between internal states and their observable properties. The internal states of system are often hidden. Many formal structures have been introduced to capture the state-based dynamics, e.g. automata, transition systems, Petri nets, etc. Horst Reichel firstly introduced the notion of behavior in the algebraic specifications [11]. The execution of a computer program causes a generation of some behavior that can be observed typically as a computer's input and output [5]. The observation of program behavior can be formalized by using the coalgebras. Program is considered as an element of the initial algebra arising from the used programming language. In other words it is an inductively defined set P of terms [9] which forms a suitable algebra $F(P) \to P$ where F is an endofunctor constructed over the signature. Then data type is completely determined by its constructors, algebraic operations, going into data type. Each language construct corresponds to certain dynamics captured in coalgebras. The behavior of programs is described by the final coalgebra $P \to G(P)$ where the functor G captures the kind of behavior that can be observed. Shortly, generated computer behavior amounts to the repeated evaluation of a (coinductively defined) coalgebraic structure on an algebra of terms. The state can be observed via the visible values and can be modified. In coalgebra it is realized using destructor operations pointing out of the structure.

3.1 Initial Algebras

Let F be an endofunctor from $\mathcal{C}$ to $\mathcal{C}$. An algebra with the signature F (or an F-algebra for short) is a pair (A, α) where A called the carrier is an object and the algebra structure $\alpha : FA \to A$ is a morphism in $\mathcal{C}$. For any two F-algebras (A, α) and (C, γ), a morphism $f : A \to C$ is said to be a homomorphism of F-algebras from (A, α) to (C, γ), so the following diagram at Fig. 1 commutes.

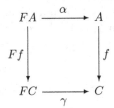

Fig. 1. Diagram of algebras

It follows from the diagram at Fig. 1 that it holds the equality $\alpha \circ f = Ff \circ \gamma$. An F-algebra is said to be an initial F-algebra if it is an initial object of the category $\mathcal{A}lg(F)$ of F-algebras. The existence of initial algebra of the endofunctor is constrained by the fact that initial algebras, when they exist, must fulfill some important properties: they are unique up to isomorphism and the initial algebra has an inverse. It follows from the first property that there exists at most one initial F-algebra. Because from the initial F-algebra exists unique homomorphism to every F-algebra, the initial F-algebra is the initial object in the category $\mathcal{A}lg$. The second property was proven by J. Lambek and it says that the initial F-algebra is the least fixed point of the endofunctor F. The initiality provides a general framework for induction and recursion. Given a functor F, the existence of the initial F-algebra $(\mu F, in_F)$ means that for any F-algebra (A, α) there exists a unique homomorphism of algebras from $(\mu F, in_F)$ into (A, α). Following [15], we denote this homomorphism by $(cata\ \alpha)_F$. This morphism is called *catamorphisms*. The morphism $(cata\ \alpha)_F : \mu F \to A$ is characterized by the universal property [15]:

$$in_F \circ f = Ff \circ \alpha \quad \Leftrightarrow \quad f = (cata\ \alpha)_F.$$

The type information is summarized in the following commutative diagram at Fig. 2.

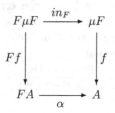

Fig. 2. Diagram of initial algebra and catamorphism

3.2   Final Coalgebras

Coalgebras are dual structures to algebras. Let F be an endofunctor from $\mathcal{C}$ to $\mathcal{C}$. A coalgebra with the signature F (an F-coalgebra for short) is a pair (U, φ), where U called the state space is an object and $\varphi : U \to FU$ called the coalgebra structure (or coalgebra dynamics) is a morphism in $\mathcal{C}$. For any two F-coalgebras (T, ψ) and (U, φ), a morphism $f : T \to U$ is said to be a homomorphism from (T, ψ) to (U, φ) between F-coalgebras, so the following diagram at Fig. 3 commutes.

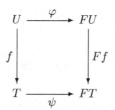

Fig. 3. Diagram of coalgebras

and it holds the equality $\varphi \circ Ff = f \circ \psi$.

The F-coalgebras and the homomorphisms between them form a category. The category $\mathcal{C}oalg(F)$ is the category whose objects are the F-coalgebras and morphisms are the homomorphisms between them. Composition and identities are inherited from $\mathcal{C}$. An F-coalgebra is said to be a final F-coalgebra if it is the final object of the category $\mathcal{C}oalg(F)$.

The existence of the final F-coalgebra $(\nu F, out_F)$ means that for any F-coalgebra (U, φ) there exists a unique homomorphism of coalgebras from (U, φ) to $(\nu F, out_F)$. This homomorphism is usually denoted by $(ana\ \varphi)_F$ and is called *anamorphism*. The anamorphism $(ana\ \varphi)_F : U \to \nu F$ is characterized by the universal property [15]:

$$f \circ out_F = \varphi \circ Ff \quad \Leftrightarrow \quad f = (ana\ \varphi)_F.$$

The type information is summarized in the following diagram at Fig. 4.

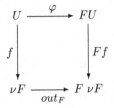

Fig. 4. Diagram of final coalgebra and anamorphism

3.3 Hylomorphism

The hylomorphism recursion pattern was firstly defined in [15]. Given an F-coalgebra $\varphi : U \to FU$ and an F-algebra $\alpha : FA \to A$, the hylomorphism denoted by $hylo(\alpha, \varphi)_F$ is the least arrow $f : U \to A$ that makes the following diagram at Fig. 5 commute.

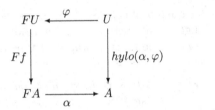

Fig. 5. Diagram of hylomorphism

The hylomorphism is defined as a composition of an anamorphism and a catamorphism [15]:

$$hylo(\alpha, \varphi)_F = (cata\ \alpha)_F \circ (ana\ \varphi)_F.$$

The hylomorphism captures general recursion by producing the complex data structure and then processing it.

4 The Computation and Logical Proof

By using the Curry-Howard correspondence [13] we are able to consider proofs as programs and execution of a program as a logical deduction in considered logical system. The first step in the design solution is constructing the type theory that we will use for a given problem. The types together with operations over them we enclose into a signature $\Sigma = (T, \mathcal{F})$.

4.1 An Alternative Method for the Factorial Calculation

Here we show an alternative method for the factorial calculation based on algebras and coalgebras. The signature consists of a finite set of the basic types:

$$T = \{int, intList, \Omega\}$$

and of a set of function symbols:

$$\mathcal{F} = \{ \; ==: intList, intList \to \Omega,$$
$$=: int, int \to \Omega,$$
$$join : int, intList \to intList,$$
$$* : int, int \to int,$$
$$pred : int \to int,$$
$$head : intList \to int,$$
$$tail : intList \to intList \; \}.$$

For our alternative method for computation the factorial we need terms, which represent catamorphism and anamorphism. The function $fact$ is based on hylomorphism; it is a composition of two functions. Listed functions are named by morphisms which they represent, namely: $cata$ and ana, resp.

Anamorphism. An anamorphism usually represents a corecursive function that starts with a single input (here int) and it returns more complex output, here a wide list ($intList$). The function ana is of type $int \to intList$. The definition of function ana is as follows:

$$ana(n) = if \; (n = 0) \; then \; ana = emptyList$$
$$elseif \; (n = 1) \; then \; ana = [1]$$
$$else \; ana = join(n, ana(pred \; n))$$

Typed term that represents the function ana has the following form:

$$n : int \vdash if \; (n = 0) \; then \; \varepsilon \; elseif \; (n = 1) \; then \; [1] \; else \; join(n, ana(pred \; n)).$$

Formula representing the function ana is:

$$(\varphi_1 \multimap \psi_1) \; \& \; (\varphi_2 \multimap \psi_2) \; \& \; ((\varphi_1^{\perp} \otimes \varphi_2^{\perp}) \multimap \psi_3)$$

where

$$\varphi_1 : (n = 0) \qquad \varphi_2 : (n = 1)$$
$$\psi_1 : ana = \varepsilon \qquad \psi_2 : ana = [1] \qquad \psi_3 : ana = join(n, ana(pred \; n))$$

Catamorphism. By applying the catamorphism in the informatics, we get a recursive function that starts with a list (here $intList$) and it returns a single numerical output (here int). The function $cata$ is of type $intList \to int$. Definition of this function:

$$cata(list) = if \; (list = emptyList) \; then \; cata = 1$$
$$else \; cata = head(list) * cata(tail(list))$$

Typed term that represents the function $cata$ has the following form:

$$l : intList \vdash if \; (list == \varepsilon) \; then \; 1 \; else \; head(list) \; * \; cata(tail(list)).$$

formula representing the function $cata(l)$ is:

$$(\theta \multimap \alpha) \& (\theta^{\perp} \multimap \beta)$$

where

$$\theta : list = emptyList \quad \alpha : cata = 1 \quad \beta : cata = head(list) * cata(tail(list)).$$

Function for Calculating the Factorial. The composition of functions ana a $cata$ creates a function $fact$ for the factorial computation. The function generates a list of natural numbers by increments from 1 to number n, and simultaneously the list is eliminated by the multiplication operation between elements of the list. The function is of type $int \to intList \to int$.
Definiton of the function $fact$:

$$fact(n) = cata(ana(n)) = if \ (ana(n) == emptyList) \ then \ fact = 1$$
$$else \ fact = n * cata(ana(predn))$$

Typed term that represents the function $cata$ has the following form:

$$n : int \vdash if \ (ana(n) == \varepsilon) \ then \ 1 \ else \ n \ * \ cata(ana(pred \ n)).$$

Formula representing the function $fact$ is:

$$((\varphi_1 \multimap \psi_1) \multimap \alpha) \ \& \ ((\varphi_2 \multimap \psi_2) \multimap \alpha) \ \& \ (((\varphi_1^{\perp} \otimes \varphi_2^{\perp}) \multimap \psi_3) \multimap \beta).$$

The Proof. A part of the logical proof of the given formula in the section 4.1 is at Fig. 6.

$$\cfrac{\cfrac{\Gamma \vdash n=0 \quad ana = \epsilon \vdash fact = 1 \quad \cfrac{\Gamma \vdash \varphi_1 \quad \psi_1 \vdash \alpha}{\Gamma, \varphi_1 \multimap \psi_1 \vdash \alpha}(\multimap_{-l})}{\Gamma \vdash ((\varphi_1 \multimap \psi_1) \multimap \alpha)}(\multimap_{-r}) \quad \cfrac{\Gamma \vdash n=1 \quad ana = [1] \vdash fact = 1 \quad \cfrac{\Gamma \vdash \varphi_2 \quad \psi_2 \vdash \alpha}{\Gamma, \varphi_2 \multimap \psi_2 \vdash \alpha}(\multimap_{-l})}{\Gamma \vdash ((\varphi_2 \multimap \psi_2) \multimap \alpha)}(\&_{-r}) \quad \cfrac{\cfrac{\Gamma \vdash n \neq 0 \ \Gamma \vdash n \neq 1}{\Gamma \vdash \varphi_1^{\perp} \otimes \varphi_2^{\perp}}(\otimes_{-r}) \quad \psi_3 \vdash \beta \quad \cdots}{\cfrac{\Gamma, (\varphi_1^{\perp} \otimes \varphi_2^{\perp}) \multimap \psi_3 \vdash \beta}{\Gamma \vdash (((\varphi_1^{\perp} \otimes \varphi_2^{\perp}) \multimap \psi_3) \multimap \beta)}(\multimap_{-r})}(\multimap_{-l})}{\Gamma \vdash ((\varphi_1 \multimap \psi_1) \multimap \alpha) \ \& \ ((\varphi_2 \multimap \psi_2) \multimap \alpha)}}{\Gamma \vdash ((\varphi_1 \multimap \psi_1) \multimap \alpha) \ \& \ ((\varphi_2 \multimap \psi_2) \multimap \alpha) \ \& \ (((\varphi_1^{\perp} \otimes \varphi_2^{\perp}) \multimap \psi_3) \multimap \beta)}(\&_{-r})$$

Fig. 6. Proof of formula expressing alternative factorial computation

When the formula is proven it means that our program is correct and it does not need any verification.

5 Implementation in *OCaml*

In this section we show the implementation of our method for the factorial calculating. We use the object-oriented functional language *OCaml* [6].

5.1   The Function *ana*

This function is defined as follows: if the argument of the function *ana* is 0 then it returns an empty list. If the argument is 1 then *ana* generates a list containing only 1 as item. Otherwise, *ana* generates a list with new element appended. The implementation of the function *ana* is:

```
let rec ana n =
match n with
| 0 -> []
| 1 -> [1]
| n -> n :: ana (n-1);;
```

5.2   The Function *cata*

This function takes as an argument a list of factors of the type *int* and returns the result of multiplicative operations over the list by multiplication of values from the input list. The result of the function is an element of the type *int* which is the result of multiplication of elements in the list. The implementation of the function *cata* is:

```
let rec cata list =
match list with
| [] -> 1
| head :: tail -> head * (cata tail);;
```

5.3   The Function *fact*

The function *fact* has been defined as composition of *cata* and *ana*; written in *OCaml* as *cata*(*ana*(*n*)). The definition of this hylomorphism function *fact* is as follows:

```
let fact n =
cata (ana n);;
```

Execution of this function with input value 4 is:

```
# fact 4;;
- : int = 24
```

We can see that our alternative method of programming based on hylomorphism provides the expected results. Because the corresponding formulae have been proven in linear logic as a formula representing one function we can say that our function is correct.

5 Basic Concepts about Action Semantics

The framework of action semantics has been initially developed at the University of Aarhus by Peter D. Mosses, in collaboration with David Watt from University of Glasgow. An action semantics is a framework for the formal description of programming languages. Its main advantage over other frameworks is pragmatic: action-semantic descriptions (ASDs) can scale up easy to real programming languages [3,7,10,14]. This is due to the inherent extensibility and modifiability of ASDs, ensuring that extensions and changes to the described language require only proportionate changes in its description. On the other hand, adding an unforeseen construct to a language may require a reformulation of the entire description in denotational or operational semantics expressed in [8].

Action semantics is fully equivalent with other semantic methods, like denotational semantics, operational semantics or axiomatic semantics. Fundamentals of action semantics are actions which are essentially dynamic computational entities. They incorporate the performance of computational behavior, using values passed to them to generate new values that reflect changes in the state of the computation. So the performance of an action directly represents the information of processing the behavior and reflects the gradual, step-wise nature of computation: each step of an action performance may access and/or change the current information. Other semantic entities used in action semantics are yielders and data. The data entities consist of mathematical values, such as integers, Boolean values, and abstract cells representing memory locations, that embody particles of information. Yielders encompass unevaluated pieces of data whose values depend on the current information incorporating the state of the computation. Yielders are occurring in actions and may access, but they are not allowed to change the current information.

A performance of an action which may be part of an enclosing action either completes (normal termination), escapes (exceptional termination), fails (abandoning an alternative) or diverges (deadlock).

The different kinds of information give rise to so called *facets* of actions which have been classified according to [7]. They are focusing on the processing of at most one kind of information at a time. The standard notation for specifying actions consists of primitive actions and action combinators. Action combinators combine existing actions, normally using infix notation, to control the order which sub-actions are performed in as well as the data flow to and from their sub-actions. Action combinators are used to define sequential, selective, iterative, and block structuring control flow as well as to manage the flow of information between actions. The standard symbols used in action notation are ordinary English words. In fact, action notation is very near to natural language:

- terms standing for actions form imperative verb phrases involving conjunctions and adverbs, e.g. check it and then escape;
- terms standing for data and yielders form noun phrases, e.g. the items of the given list.

These simple principles for choice of symbols provide a surprisingly grammatical fragment of English, allowing specifications of actions to be made fluently readable. The informal appearance and suggestive words of action notation should encourage programmers to read it. Compared to other formalisms, such as λ-notation, action notation may appear to lack conciseness.

7   Action Semantics in Functional Paradigm

Action semantics can be successfully used also for the description of functional programs. In action semantics we use generally three main actions for the description of programming languages:

- *execute* - used for executing of statements;
- *elaborate* - used with declarations;
- *evaluate* - used for evaluating expressions.

In functional paradigm we use only two main actions: *evaluate* and *elaborate*. Action *execute* is not important in functional paradigm. Typical for functional programs is that they do not deal the storage. Therefore we will not use actions of imperative facet for allocating memory locations, storing values and getting values from cells in memory in our action semantics descriptions of functional programs.

Important for functional paradigm is an evaluating of the expressions and elaborating functions. To allow referring them in the program code, they are associated to names (identifiers). These associations are called bindings. A binding can be *global*, when declared at the top level of the source code, or *local*, when declared in a *let* or *letrec* expressions that contain it. The difference between *let* and *letrec* expressions is that in the latter mutual recursion is allowed.

We provide this description of evaluation of simple expression:

elaborate⟦let I:Var = E:Expression⟧ =
    evaluate ⟦ E ⟧
        then bind I to the given value

After declaration we are able to use it anytime in our program. The value is bound to its identifier, so we can get the value of this expression simply by using *evaluate* action:

evaluate⟦ I:Var ⟧ =
    give the value bound to I

Description of function with one argument should seem like this:

elaborate⟦let I_f:Var I_{p1}:Var = E:Expression⟧ =
    evaluate⟦E⟧
        then bind I_f to the given value

In the expression E is used parameter of the function which value we can get simply with action *evaluate*:

evaluate⟦ I_{p1}:Var ⟧ =
    give the value bound to I_{p1}

7.1   The Description in Action Semantics

Let E_1 be the substitution for the function *ana*:

E_1 = match n with
    | 0 -> []
    | 1 -> [1]
    | n -> n :: *ana* (*n-1*)

We elaborate the function declaration in Action semantics as:

elaborate ⟦ let rec *ana* $n = E_1$⟧ =
    recursively bind *ana* to
      closure of
        abstraction of
          evaluate⟦E_1⟧ =
    recursively bind *ana* to
      closure of
        abstraction of
          evaluate⟦E_1⟧

and the evaluation of the action **evaluate**⟦E_1⟧ is:

evaluate⟦ match n with $| 0 -> [] | 1 -> [1] | n -> n :: ana(n-1)$ ⟧ =
evaluate ⟦n⟧
  and then
  (check the given value is equal to the number 0
    and then give the empty list
      or
  check the given value is equal to the number 1
    and then add the number 1 to the list)
      or
  check the given value is greater than the number 1
    and then add the given number to the list
      before
  add **evaluate** ⟦$ana (n-1)$⟧ to the list

The description of function *cata* in Action semantics is analogous. First we define a substitution E_2 for the *cata* function as follows:

Let E_2 = match myList with
        | [] -> 1
        | head :: tail -> head * (*cata* tail)

We also define primitive actions head and tail for the treatment the data structure list:

```
head list = give the first element of the list
```

which gives the first element of the given list, and

```
tail list =
    remove first element from the list then give the list
```

which gives the tail of the list, i.e. all elements except the first one are being returned. Now we are able to elaborate the declaration of the function *cata* and we obtain full description of it in Action semantics:

elaborate $[\![$ let rec *cata myList* $= E_2]\!] =$
   recursively bind *cata* to
     closure of
       abstraction of
        evaluate$[\![E_2]\!]$

The evaluation of the action $[\![E_2]\!]$ is defined as follows:

evaluate$[\![E_2]\!] =$
   give the value bound to *myList*
    and then
   give the *TruthValue* of (the given list is empty)
    then
   check the given *TruthValue*
     and then give the number 1
    or
   check not the given *TruthValue*
     and then
      give the multiplication of
      (head the given list
       and
      evaluate$[\![$ *cata* (tail the given list)$]\!]$)

Finally, we define the function *fact* for the computation of the factorial. The elaboration of the function *fact* declaration is:

elaborate $[\![$ let *fact n* $=$ *cata* (*ana n*)$]\!] =$
   evaluate $[\![cata\ (ana\ n)]\!]$
    then
   bind *fact n* to the given value $=$
   evaluate $[\![ana\ n]\!]$
    before
   evaluate $[\![cata$ (the given list)$]\!]$
    then
     bind *fact n* to the given value

where the actions **evaluate**$[\![ana\ n]\!]$ and **evaluate**$[\![cata\ myList]\!]$ are being evaluated in the following way:

evaluate $[\![ana\ n]\!]$
  give the value bound to
    closure of
      abstraction of
        evaluate$[\![E_1]\!]$
evaluate $[\![cata\ myList]\!]$
  give the value bound to
    closure of
      abstraction of
        evaluate$[\![E_2]\!]$

After defining all actions necessary for the description of the factorial computation we present an example for the factorial of given input value.

7.2   Example in Action Semantics

In this section we present the evaluation of factorial for the input value $n = 4$. Our alternative method of the factorial computation was defined in chapter 4.1.

evaluate $[\![\ fact\ n = cata\ (ana\ n)]\!]s\,[n \mapsto 4] =$
  give the value bound to
    evaluate $[\![cata\ (ana\ n)]\!] =$
 give the value bound to
  (**evaluate** $[\![ana\ n]\!]s\,[n \mapsto 4]$
    before
  evaluate $[\![cata\ (the\ given\ list)]\!]$)

The evaluation of the function $ana\ n$ for the input value $n = 4$ is:

evaluate$[\![ana\ x]\!]s\,[n \mapsto 4] =$
give the value bound to
  closure of
    abstraction of
      evaluate$[\![E_1]\!]s\,[n \mapsto 4] =$
give the value bound to
  closure of
    abstraction of
      give the value bound to $n\ s\,[n \mapsto 4]$
    and then
      check the given number is greater than the number 1
        and then add the given number to the list
      before
        add **evaluate** $[\![ana\ (n-1)]\!]s\,[n \mapsto 4, list \mapsto [4]]$ to the list $= \ldots$

After repeating these steps we obtain the last step of computation:

```
give the value bound to
  closure of
    abstraction of
      give the list [4, 3, 2, 1]
```

The final state is $s\,[n \mapsto 1, list \mapsto [4, 3, 2, 1]]$.

In next step, the action **evaluate** $[\![cata\ list]\!]s\,[list \mapsto [4, 3, 2, 1]]$ is being evaluated. The actions **head** and **tail** which have been defined in chapter 7.1 are being used.

$\quad$ **evaluate** $[\![cata\ list]\!]s\,[list \mapsto [4, 3, 2, 1]]$
```
  give the value bound to
    closure of
      abstraction of
        evaluate[[E₂]]=
  give the value bound to
    closure of
      abstraction of
        give the TruthValue of (list is empty)
          then
        check not the given TruthValue
          and then
            give the multiplication of
            (head list s [list ↦ [4, 3, 2, 1]]
              and evaluate [[cata (tail list)]]s [list ↦ [4, 3, 2, 1]]) = ...
```

And we again repeat those steps. Finally we obtain:
```
give the value bound to
  closure of
    abstraction of
      give the TruthValue of (list is empty)
        then
      check the given TruthValue
        and then
          give the multiplication of
          (the number 4 and the number 3
            and the number 2 and the number 1) =
give the value bound to
  closure of
    abstraction of
      give the number 24
```

The final state is $s\,[n \mapsto 24]$.

We can see that the description in action semantics seems to be very long, it is very good readable for the programmers and the results obtained by this method are correct and they correspond to real computations.

8 Conclusion

In this paper we have focused on the analysis of recursion and corecursion. We described the recursion by catamorphisms and the corecursion as a dual method of recursion by final coalgebras and anamorphisms. To define the relationship between recursion and corecursion we used algebras and coalgebras which are dual structures. The exact relation between algebra and coalgebra we defined by constructing the hylomorphism which is based on the unique coalgebra-to-algebra morphism. We presented an alternative method of how to make a computation of recursive functions by special mathematical structures - the algebras and coalgebras with the relation between them expressed by recursive coalgebras. In the last chapters we showed an unusual example for calculating the factorial of number n with our new alternative method using anamorphism, catamorphism and hylomorphism; the description of this method we presented in action semantics. Our future research will be the exact categorical formulation of those principles by using the structures for the construction of the algebras and coalgebras: monads and comonads.

Acknowledgement. This work has been supported by the Slovak Research and Development Agency under the contract No. APVV-0008-10: Modelling, simulation and implementation of GPGPU-enabled architectures of high-throughput network security tools.

References

1. Barr, M., Wells, C.: Category Theory for Computing Science. Prentice Hall International (1990) ISBN 0-13-120486-6
2. Blute, R., Scott, P.: Category theory for linear logicians. In: Erhard, T., Girard, J.-Y., Ruet, P. (eds.) Linear Logic in Computer Science. London Mathematical Society Lecture Note Series. Cambridge Univ.Press (2004)
3. Cheng, F.: Mda implementation based on patterns and action semantics. In: 2010 Third International Conference on Information and Computing, vol. 2, pp. 25–28 (2010)
4. Girard, J.: Linear logic: Its syntax and semantics. Cambridge Univ. Press (2003)
5. Jacobs, B.: Introduction to coalgebra. Towards Mathematics of States and Observations, draft (2005)
6. Leroy, X.: The objective caml system release 3.12. Tech. rep., Institut National de Recherche en Informatique et en Automatique (2008)
7. Mosses, P.D.: Theory and Practice of Action Semantics. In: Penczek, W., Szałas, A. (eds.) MFCS 1996. LNCS, vol. 1113, pp. 37–61. Springer, Heidelberg (1996)
8. Nielson, H.R., Nielson, F.: Semantics with Applications: A Formal Introduction. John Wiley & Sons, Inc. (2003)
9. Novitzká, V., Mihályi, D., Verbová, A.: Coalgebras as models of systems behaviour. In: International Conference on Applied Electrical Engineering and Informatics, Greece, Athens, pp. 31–36 (2008)
10. Planas, E., Cabot, J., Gómez, C.: Verifying Action Semantics Specifications in UML Behavioral Models. In: van Eck, P., Gordijn, J., Wieringa, R. (eds.) CAiSE 2009. LNCS, vol. 5565, pp. 125–140. Springer, Heidelberg (2009)

11. Reichel, H.: Behavioural equivalence - a unifying concept for initial and final specification methods. In: 3rd Hungarian Computer Science Conference, Akadémia kiadó, vol. 3, pp. 27–39 (1981)
12. Slodičák, V., Macko, P.: New approaches in functional programming using algebras and coalgebras. In: European Joint Conferrences on Theory and Practise of Software, ETAPS, Workshop on Generative Technologies, pp. 13–23 (2011)
13. Sørensen, M., Urzyczyn, P.: Lectures on the Curry-Howard Isomorphism. University of Copenhagen a University of Warsaw (1999)
14. Stuurman, G.: Action semantics applied to model driven engineering (November 2010)
15. Uustalu, T., Vene, V.: Primitive (co)recursion and course-of-values (co)iteration. Informatica (1999)

Author Index